PROMOTION MANAGEMENT

PROMOTION MANAGEMENT

John J. Burnett

University of Denver

Houghton Mifflin Company   Boston   Toronto

Dallas   Geneva, Illinois   Palo Alto   Princeton, New Jersey

Cover image: Courtesy of The Coca-Cola Company. © 1992 The Coca-Cola Company. "Coca-Cola", "Coke" and the Contour Bottle design are registered trademarks of The Coca-Cola Company. Front cover photography, Rodger Macuch.

Part Openers: Part opener I: p. 1, K ® is a registered trademark of Kellogg Company. All rights reserved. © 1990. Part opener II: p. 113, Ulf Skogsbergh, Ltd. Part opener III: p. 237, Jeff Burkholder/Life Images. Part opener IV: p. 566, Herman Miller's Ethospace ® Interiors. Part opener V: P. 646, Telegraph Colour Library/FPG.

Sponsoring Editor: Diane McOscar
Managing Development Editor: Patricia Ménard
Project Editor: Maria A. Morelli
Production/Design Coordinator: Martha Drury
Manufacturing Coordinator: Priscilla Bailey

Printed in the U.S.A.

Library of Congress Catalog Number: 91-72008

ISBN: 0–395–56553–7

ABCDEFGHIJ-DH-95432

Contents

PART *II* DETERMINING PROMOTIONAL OPPORTUNITIES

Contents

Preface

The Goal of This Book

For several decades managers of advertising, sales promotion, personal selling, and public relations have been separated by organization, philosophy, and budget. Yet, for the most part they are all engaged in the same activity—communicating marketing messages to customers and possible customers.

Today these four marketing communication activities find themselves in turmoil. Advertisers are angry with sales promotion for stealing their thunder and their dollars. Personal selling forces are being cut back, with surviving salespeople expected to achieve ever-higher quotas with fewer resources. Public relations has been decreased, eliminated, or integrated into other areas. Within this chaos have emerged a few still voices of reason. Their message has been concise and well-conceived. Simply, there should be an expert to manage these four marketing communication tools and produce a coordinated strategy that will help achieve the goals of all four tools, create a positive synergy, and reduce waste.

The goal of this book is to show how the four tools of promotion interact throughout the planning process. Discussing these techniques in tandem is important since they have a history of being kept separate. Likewise, demonstrating how actual companies have accomplished this integrative task has become a major part of this book. In fact, real-world examples abound in this book, not only in examples but also in the cases at the end of each chapter. Two other factors receive heavy emphasis. First, the reference point throughout the book is planning and strategy. Every concept discussed is grounded by a specific set of objectives and an ensuing strategy to reach these objectives. Second, the use of international examples and a separate international chapter acknowledges that promotion exists in a global community. It would be disadvantageous to study promotion within the confines of the American culture and assume that it works the same way in other countries.

Pedagogical Features

Several pedagogical features make this book competitive and up-to-date. Most notably, each chapter contains a Promotion in Focus box, that highlights an important issue related to the topic. Each chapter also ends with a short case that brings together the concepts discussed. The four-color inserts feature both the award-winning and superlative ad campaigns of the nineties. Finally, this is an extremely readable book. Students and industry people should find the discussions interesting, clear, and accessible.

Organization

The book is divided into five sections. Chapter 1 to 3 introduce the student to basic marketing concepts that must be understood to appreciate the role of promotion in marketing. A basic framework is provided. Chapters 4 to 6 deal with the environment in which promotion must operate, along with insights in coping with the environment. Chapters 7 to 15 present a discussion of communication theory along with the four functional areas of promotion: advertising, sales promotion, public relations, and personal selling. Chapters 13 and 14 deal specifically with media, the means used to carry mass communication messages. Chapters 16 and 17 deal with the appropriation process and performance measurement process, respectively. These are the two final factors in the management of promotion. Chapters 18 and 19 discuss two special application topics, direct marketing and international marketing and promotion. Examining promotion in these two contexts lends a great deal of credence to the forward-looking perspective offered in this book.

This book is written for junior and senior students in colleges and universities of all sizes. Although it is most suited for a course dealing with the total promotional effort, it can also be used in an advertising or marketing communication course. The book introduces students to the most modern technologies related to promotion without burdening them with technical appendices. Also, great care has been taken to be current and accurate. This book reflects the way it is actually done in the industry. Most importantly, I have tested this material in my promotion management class, and it works.

Acknowledgments

A book like this is a major undertaking. It would not have happened without the help of a great many significant others. Special thanks go to Houghton Mifflin and Patricia Menard for having faith in this book. To Maria Morelli, who was responsible for coordinating the production, thanks. There are many reviewers who endured several drafts of this manuscript. They deserve special accolades:

Robert Benson, *St. Cloud State University*
Alan Bush, *Memphis State University*

Carol Calder, *Loyola Marymount University*
Hugh Cannon, *Wayne State University*
Gary Clark, *North Harris County College—South*
Ronald Fullerton, *Southeastern Massachusetts University*
Gail Glenesk, *Western Michigan University*
Karen A. Glynn, *The University of Northern Iowa*
Marc Goldberg, *Portland State University*
Linda Golden, *University of Texas at Austin*
Geoffrey Gordon, *University of Kentucky*
Tim Hartman, *Ohio University*
Debbora Heflin-Bullock, *California Polytech University—Pomona*
Joby John, *Bentley College*
Jeff Kasmer, *California State University—Long Beach*
Herbert Katzenstein, *St. John's University*
Patricia Kennedy, *University of Nebraska—Lincoln*
Joanne Klebba, *Portland State University*
John Kuzma, *Mankato State University*
Patricia Laidler, *Massasoit Community College*
J. Daniel Lindley, *Bentley College*
Karen A. Lynn, *University of Northern Iowa*
Patricia Manninen, *North Shore Community College*
Allen S. Marber, *University of Bridgeport*
Darrel Muehling, *Washington State University*
Gary Nelson, *Central Piedmont Community College*
Charles Patti, *University of Hartford*
Stephen Ramocki, *Rhode Island College*
Gary K. Rhoads, *Idaho State University*
Ivan Ross, *University of Minnesota*
Paul Sauer, *Canisius College*
Carolyn Siegel, *Eastern Kentucky University*
Steven Soulos, *Bryant College*
Patricia Voli, *University of North Carolina at Wilmington*
Rita Wheat, *University of Southern California*
William Whitmore, *University of Missouri—Columbia*

My final and very special thanks go to my family. To my mother, Fran, I wish to express my love and appreciation. I dedicate this book to her. My children, Laura, Michael, and David, are the reasons I write books. I love them dearly. Finally, I wish to express my deepest love and gratitude to my wife, Nancy. If I achieve any success, it is because of her.

Since I am the sole author, I must take responsibility for any errors or omissions in this manuscript.

J.J.B.

PROMOTION MANAGEMENT

1

Promotion Management: An Overview

Consider This:

MARKETING TO COLLEGE STUDENTS

College students represent an attractive market for many companies. It's a big market—some twelve million people attended American colleges in 1990. And students are surprisingly affluent. The average student spends $123 of discretionary income each month, more than the average family of four.

So how do companies reach this large, rich market? Because the tastes and trends of young adults tend to change rapidly, college students are not as easy to target as are young parents or the over-70 crowd. To get college students' attention, successful marketers often use two subjects in which many students are passionately interested: sex and music.

Surveys of students' reactions to print ads show that sex sells. Three out of the students' top ten print ads in 1989—including one for Obsession—were created by Calvin Klein Industries, known for making ads so sexy that sometimes they stir up controversy.

Music is at the heart of most college entertainment. In the wake of the success of MTV, other networks have found new ways to reach audiences through combinations of music and video. Campus Network offers two programming systems, National College Television (NCTV) and Video Center Events (VCE). NCTV brings college news, educational programming, and entertainment into dorms, fraternities, and sororities on over 200 U.S. college campuses. VCE reaches a smaller audience with live concerts, Broadway shows, movies, and political debates, splitting its per-student fees with the college.

Even many students hooked on music and videos respond well to direct mail and print promotions, but the most effective advertising is word-of-mouth. Catching—and holding—students' interest is difficult, but once an item is "hot" on college campuses, its sales can skyrocket with relatively little promotion.

The one constant for marketers trying to reach a college audience is the need to keep on their toes. While surveys in the mid-1980s showed that a majority of students were focusing on power, money, and a rapid rise to the top, more recent surveys seem to indicate that ethical concerns have become more important, and greed is on the way out. Keeping up with the changing desires of the college market is important business for many companies, and it can also be excellent training for anyone interested in a career in promotion.

Sources: Marilyn Adles and Geralyn Wiener, "Student Buying Rates High Interest," *Advertising Age* (February 2, 1987): S-1. Anita M. Busch, "Me-First Mode Takes a Beating," *Advertising Age* (February 5, 1990): S-4, S-5. Anita M. Busch, "Sexier the Better, Student Body Says," *Advertising Age* (February 5, 1990): S-1. Christopher Colletti, "Youth Marketing—Special Report," *Advertising Age* (February 2, 1987): S-1, S-16. Martha Farnsworth Riche, "The Boomerang Age," *American Demographics* (May 1990): 25–30, 52.

*T*he scenario about marketing to college students points to the fact that reaching today's consumer is extremely difficult. Even market leaders such as Procter & Gamble, General Motors, IBM, and Prudential Insurance are no longer secure in their market dominance. Charging the lowest price, producing the best product, or simply being around the longest does not guarantee consumer acceptance or loyalty. Creative, informative, and interesting messages are also needed. Success requires finding out what consumers need and want and then letting them know that a product meets those needs and wants. These tasks depend on effective, coordinated communication.

Ultimately, the company that does the best job of anticipating and meeting consumers' information needs has the best chance of selling its product. For example, a personal computer that is IBM-compatible, competitively priced, warrantied, available to high-quality department and specialty stores, and supported by entertaining, informative advertisements and trade deals has a good chance of being carried by a retailer and purchased by a consumer. Planning and communicating the product's characteristics is the job of the marketer.

Marketers today must take a proactive rather than a reactive posture. They cannot wait for market and environmental changes and then scramble to save themselves. General Motors, for example, spent ten years denying that the success of Japanese automobile manufacturers was real. By the time GM responded, companies such as Toyota and Mazda had gained a significant share of the U.S. auto market. To avoid similar losses, marketers must develop a marketing program that begins with a thorough understanding of the marketplace and then sets forth clear, concise, and attainable objectives. The marketing program must also include a plan, a strategy for meeting goals, and a mechanism for assessing whether these goals have been reached.

A key part of the marketing program is promotion. In this book we aim to provide a basic understanding of the concepts associated with promotion and to provide insights into how promotional functions can be combined into a workable framework—the promotion strategy. We begin in Chapter 1 by looking more closely at what promotion is and by outlining how promotion managers can develop effective promotion strategies. Please note that although the term "promotion manager" is used throughout this book, in most companies a title such as director of marketing,

marketing vice president, or director of advertising would represent the person responsible for promotional planning.

The Meaning of Promotion

In brief, promotion is concerned with effectively communicating the results of the marketing strategy to target audiences. But in a real sense, everything the company does has promotional potential. For instance, the price of a product can communicate to a target audience in ways that advance a particular image. A company that distributes its products only through discount stores tells the consumer a great deal. Outfitting a car with a CD player and leather upholstery also sends a strong message. These three elements—price, channel of distribution, and product—combined with promotion make up the **marketing mix,** which is the set of marketing tools that the firm uses to pursue its marketing objectives in the target market.

What Is Promotion?

Since product, price, channels of distribution, and promotion all communicate to audiences, what sets promotion apart from the other elements of the marketing mix? Promotion is an active, explicit form of marketing communication. Promotion highlights the marketing elements in order to increase the odds that consumers will buy and become committed to a product. Thus, we define **promotion** as the marketing function concerned with persuasively communicating to target audiences the components of the marketing program in order to facilitate exchange between the marketer and the consumer and to help satisfy the objectives of both. Three terms in this definition require further explanation.

First, promotion is primarily concerned with *persuasive communication.* That is, promotion involves an attempt to persuade the target audience to embrace a new attitude or to engage in a new behavior. Kraft wants the consumer to believe that its cheese is the best value, compared to all other brands. Hallmark wants the purchaser to think of its cards "when you care enough to send the very best."

A second concept in our definition is that of *target audiences.* For example, the target market for Diet Coke consists of all the consumers who are diet conscious. But Diet Coke also targets its promotions to audiences (that is, people who hear or see promotion messages) both within and outside the target market. The former consists of twelve- to twenty-four-year-olds of both sexes and women aged twenty-five to forty-five. In addition, Diet Coke targets audiences outside the target market who might influence the purchase of the product, such as the Food and Drug Administration (FDA), which governs which food products are sold to the public.

Finally, promotion is goal directed. For the marketer, the objectives of promotion are to create brand awareness, to deliver information, to educate, and to advance a positive image. The ultimate goal is to sell the product or service.

Four types of activities provide the key tools to reach the goals of promotion.

- **Advertising** is any paid form of nonpersonal communication and promotion of ideas, goods, or services by an identified sponsor. Although some advertising (such as direct mail) is directed at specific individuals, most advertising messages are tailored to a group and use mass media such as radio, television, newspapers, magazines, and outdoor.

- **Personal selling** is interpersonal communication with one or more prospective purchasers for the sake of making sales. Examples include sales calls to a business by a field representative (field selling), in-store assistance of a salesclerk (retail selling), and a representative calling at homes (door-to-door selling).

- **Public relations** is a coordinated attempt to create a favorable product image in the mind of the public by supporting certain activities or programs, publishing commercially significant news in a widely circulated medium, or obtaining favorable publicity—that is, favorable presentations on radio, television, or stage that are not paid for by the sponsor.

- **Sales promotion** consists of marketing activities that add to the basic value of the product or service for a limited time and directly stimulate consumer purchasing (for example, coupons and product sampling), stimulate the distributors to carry the product and/or promote the product or service (for example, trade deals and spiffs), or stimulate the effort of the sales force (for example, contests and meetings).

These four activities are the most common active forms of marketing communication. Clearly, both proactive and reactive forms of communication are crucial. Ideally, they work together. Promotion gets the consumer to the front door of the store equipped with brand awareness, product information, a positive attitude, and an extra incentive to buy. Then the product and store attributes such as whether a fair price is being charged take over. Promotion can create positive associations that can enhance the buyer's satisfaction and thus may add to the real value of the company's offering. But even great promotion cannot save a bad product. In fact, the fastest way to kill a bad product is with a good promotion program. Such a program will quickly expose the weaknesses of the product to the people who count most.

Why Promote?

For most companies today, some promotion is essential in order to create customer awareness of a product and its characteristics. Many factors have increased the importance of promotion, but we can isolate six key factors. (See Figure 1.1.)

First, consumers today are faced with so many product choices that they often resort to less-than-optimal choices, settle on a particular "satisfactory brand," and purchase it repeatedly to reduce the effort involved in choosing another product. If you have been buying Diet Pepsi for as long as you can remember, you may not bother to think twice before buying it again, unless promotion by Diet Coke makes you do so. Thus, the target market often includes people who have established product loyalties. The marketer must promote its product in order to persuade these people to change their buying habits.

A second reason for the rising importance of promotion is the widening physical and emotional distance between producers and consumers. Once marketing intermediaries are involved, it is not enough for a producer to communicate only with the ultimate consumers or industrial users. Marketing intermediaries must also be informed about products. Wholesalers must promote products to retailers, and retailers must promote products

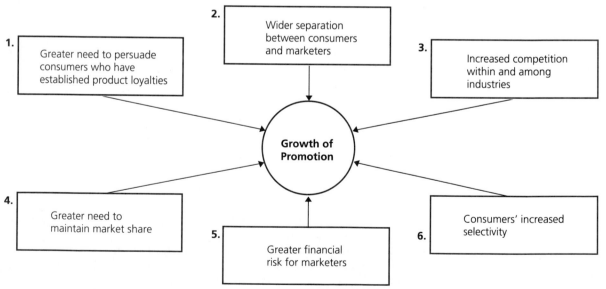

Figure 1.1

Factors contributing to the increased importance of promotion.

to consumers. Thus, a basic purpose of promotion is to facilitate the movement of products and product-related information through the marketing network.

Third, intense competition within and between industries has placed pressure on the promotional programs of individual sellers. Most colleges and universities, for example, must deal directly with other colleges and universities as well as with all other organizations that offer people educational or vocational alternatives.

Fourth, consumers are beyond the need to fulfill their basic physiological requirements and are moving toward fulfilling their desires. As they allocate their limited resources to the purchase of desires rather than basic needs, they become more selective in their choices. A good promotional program helps consumers make these choices in a more satisfying way.

Fifth, the promotional effort is usually the largest part of the total marketing expense. Managers must be certain that the high level of expenditure produces the desired results.

Finally, during times of economic decline, product planning, distribution channels, and pricing structure change little.[1] Promotion is needed in order to maintain the level of sales and profit required for a firm's survival. Redesigning messages, advertising differently and smarter, and improving sales promotion offers are some of the ways to stimulate consumer demand.

Concept Review

1. Promotion is the marketing function concerned with persuasively communicating to target audiences the various components of the marketing program in order to facilitate exchange between the marketer and the consumer and to help satisfy the objectives of both. The key tools of promotion are
   a. Advertising,
   b. Personal selling,
   c. Public relations, and
   d. Sales promotion.
2. The importance of promotion is a result of
   a. The large number of product choices,
   b. The widening physical and emotional distance between producers and consumers,
   c. Intense competition within and between industries,
   d. The movement of the consumer toward the satisfying of desires,
   e. The high cost of promotion, and
   f. The ability of promotion to help a company remain competitive during economic decline.

Strategic Planning in Marketing

The wise promotion manager knows that promotion is just one piece of the larger marketing puzzle. Effective promotion is based on astute marketing, which includes a system of information gathering and a comprehensive marketing plan that is implementable, profitable, and controllable. It involves *strategic planning,* which is defined as "the managerial process of developing and maintaining a strategic fit between the organization and its changing marketing opportunities."[2] Figure 1.2 diagrams the process of marketing planning. The complete process is complex and beyond the scope of this chapter, but we can discuss some of its key elements.

The Marketing Plan

The marketing organization is governed by the **marketing plan.** This plan is the central instrument for directing and coordinating the marketing effort. It is just one part of the **strategic plan,** which provides direction for the entire organization and is thus the broadest planning tool. It includes the mission statement, environmental assessment, company objectives, and strategies for reaching these objectives; the strategies are then implemented and evaluated. Following this same logic, the marketing plan includes the marketing strategy, which in turn includes a promotion plan.

For promotion managers, the most important part of the marketing plan is the marketing strategy. It links the overall strategic plan with specific marketing programs, including promotion. A **marketing strategy** "represents the broad principles by which the business unit expects to achieve its marketing objectives in the target market. It consists of basic decisions on total marketing expenditure, marketing mix, and marketing allocation."[3]

To illustrate these concepts, we can examine the marketing strategy followed by Healthy Choice, one of the great success stories in food marketing. Healthy Choice is a low-calorie, low-cholesterol, low-sodium frozen food line manufactured by ConAgra, Inc. Inspired by the heart attack of ConAgra chairman Mike Harper, Healthy Choice was developed to counter the cholesterol problem of men. It hoped to draw men into the market of frozen entree customers, a market formerly dominated by female buyers. However, the decision to introduce Healthy Choice was not based on the whim of the CEO. Research conducted in 1985 to 1988 showed a clear opportunity for a new growth segment. According to Stephen Hughes, vice president of new ventures at ConAgra, 29 percent of the population could not care less about what it eats. But 20 percent of Americans are restricted dieters, and a surprising 30 percent are so-called health-conscious eaters. "They're not younger, mainstream consumers who are realizing they'd better start thinking of some of these things," says

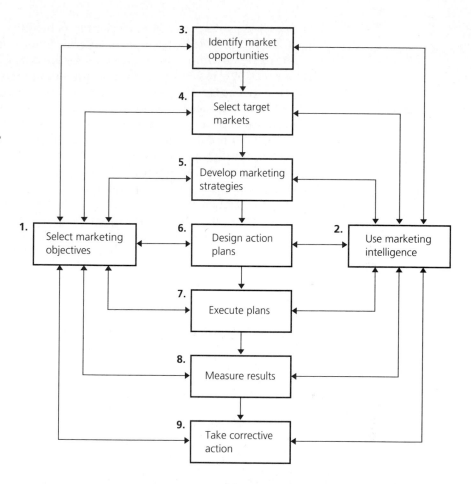

Figure 1.2

The marketing planning system is guided by marketing objectives and marketing intelligence. These two elements interact with the other elements throughout the planning process.

3. Identify market opportunities

4. Select target markets

5. Develop marketing strategies

1. Select marketing objectives

6. Design action plans

2. Use marketing intelligence

7. Execute plans

8. Measure results

9. Take corrective action

Hughes. "The number of people who know their cholesterol has gone up so fast. These people don't need restricted food every day, but once or twice a week helps them balance their portfolio."

It was also important for Healthy Choice to taste good, or it ran the risk of becoming a novelty item. "The product needed to deliver on taste to make it mainstream after trial," explains Roxann Goertz, vice president and management supervisor for Campbell-Esty-Advertising. "There were a lot of revisions." Healthy Choice is targeted at men and women thirty-five and older, although it skews forty-five and older. But its plain "home cooking" and nonexotic fare (for example, sirloin tips, Salisbury steak, turkey breast) were most popular with males.

Careful introduction and strategic positioning made the product more than a food designed to lower the risks of heart attacks. "There was a definite concern that people would perceive this product as for people with health problems. We needed to present it as healthy food for healthy people. It is a line we walked," reports Goertz. Extensive test-marketing and a public relations campaign set the stage for Healthy Choice's rapid rollout. ConAgra taste-tested its entire line of dinners in eighteen cities across the country and backed the campaign by spot advertising. Public relations agency Hill and Knowlton exhibited Healthy Choice at health conventions and conferences and sent mailings to dieticians, informing them of the new product's benefits. The agency staged a national press conference in New York, where Mike Harper talked about his heart attack and how his wife, Jose, was able to make his low-sodium diet interesting. By the time national distribution was achieved, word of mouth was rampant.

Although plagued by frozen-tight freezer space, food stores either enlarged their freezer sections or dropped poor sellers. "Accounts had heard of the item and wanted it," recalls Don Seafoss, product sales manager for Food Enterprises, a Boston food broker. "There has been a lot of consumer inquiries. Accounts had been getting phone calls about it, mentioning the chairman's heart attack." ConAgra also established the proper price points successfully at two dinners for five dollars and entrees under two dollars.

ConAgra was hoping to get 5 percent to 7 percent of the frozen-dinner market during the first year. Within seven months of its introduction, the green-boxed fourteen-item line grabbed a 25 percent share. Goertz sums up the reason for the success as follows: "Every detail was thoroughly planned. We were on-strategy at all times. Our packaging, advertising and communication defined us as a unique new product, and the retail community was very aware how health conscious the consumer has become."[4]

It is apparent that the efforts of ConAgra were successful because they followed a logical sequence of activities. Although this process will vary somewhat for each company, there is evidence that a certain sequence works best.

The specific steps in the marketing plan include the following: (1) select marketing objectives, (2) use marketing intelligence, (3) identify market opportunities, (4) select target markets, (5) develop marketing strategies, (6) design action plans, (7) execute plans, (8) measure results, and (9) take corrective action.

Selecting Marketing Objectives   Marketing objectives should state specific standards to be reached under certain operating procedures by a certain date. The objective may refer to a percentage of market share, unit sales, market saturation, traffic, or profit. For example, the Marshall Fields department store chain wishes to increase unit sales by 4 percent, profit by 9 percent, and traffic—the number of customers shopping in its stores—by 14 percent. Or ConAgra wishes to achieve 5 percent to 7 percent of the market share for Healthy Choice.

In some companies the marketing planning process generates the company's corporate objectives; in others, marketing objectives are derived directly from the company's overall corporate objectives. In most successful companies corporate objectives and marketing objectives influence each other.

Note that, in Figure 1.2, marketing objectives are outside the vertical column and are connected to all the other steps by a two-directional arrow. This suggests two things. First, marketing objectives are affected by the other planning elements. Second, these objectives directly influence all the other planning elements.

Using Marketing Intelligence   **Marketing intelligence** is any information, derived from either internal or external sources, that is useful in developing the marketing strategy. Managers use it to conduct the **situation analysis,** which is an attempt to identify and appraise all the environmental factors that affect the marketing plan. Managers may first examine the background of their own companies—their history and philosophy, products, personnel, and present methods of marketing. For example, the situation analysis might discover that the products of a men's shirt manufacturer are viewed as cheap and of poor quality because they are priced low and sold through Wal-Mart. This information has direct implications for the entire marketing plan. Managers also examine the market—customers and competitors—and then go on to appraise the economic, legal, and ethical atmosphere in which their firms operate. ConAgra, for example, spent three years researching the trends in health consciousness before they began product development.

Marketing intelligence provides information that is helpful throughout the planning process. And each stage of the process offers the opportunity for additional information gathering. Thus, in Figure 1.2, marketing intelligence, like marketing objectives, appears outside the central planning core but is connected to it by two-way arrows.

Identifying Market Opportunities   Guided by the marketing objectives and marketing intelligence, the manager must then identify and evaluate market opportunities. A **marketing opportunity** is a need or want (actual or potential) that is not being adequately satisfied. Finding the cure for AIDS is a market opportunity for hundreds of pharmaceutical and research firms.

Sometimes opportunities are identified by customers' complaints or suggestions. This was the case when hundreds of male respondents consistently told ConAgra researchers that none of the existing so-called healthy frozen entrees tasted good, and that the choices were very limited. In the case of high tech companies, opportunities are often little more than a new product looking for a problem. It took the marketing people at 3M over four years to find a profitable use for the adhesive that led to Post-it Notes.

In either case, companies must have a mechanism for collecting information, examining trends, and assessing possible opportunities.

Selecting Target Markets   A **market segment** (the topic of Chapter 2) is a group of consumers who have one or more similar characteristics. These characteristics include age, attitudes, loyalty toward a particular brand, or a similar illness, to name a few. The dog food industry, for example, segments its market by age of the dog, its weight, breed, and activity level. For most organizations there are more potential segments than one company can serve profitably. A company therefore selects market segments that can be best served from a competitive point of view. The segments selected are the **target markets.**

Developing Marketing Strategies   The manager now outlines the broad marketing strategy, or "game plan." In developing a marketing strategy, a manager faces a multitude of possible choices. Each objective can be achieved in a number of ways. For example, the objective to increase market share by 5 percent can be achieved by underpricing the product and driving down profits, by introducing a superior product, and by buying out competitors. Each marketing objective should have an associated set of alternative marketing strategies.

Selecting a particular strategy is often an arduous process requiring research, executive input, consumer feedback, and sales and financial forecasts. The marketing strategy for a new product may be very different than the one for a well-established product. Likewise, an innovative, aggressive company would employ a strategy far different from that of a conservative market follower. Ultimately, there is no one best strategy.

Designing Action Plans   Each element of the marketing strategy must now be dissected in order to develop specific action plans. Typically, at this stage marketers specify plans for each aspect of the marketing mix, that is, the product, price, channel of distribution, and promotion. Dramatic differences in marketing action programs are achieved simply by using different proportions of these mix variables. The goal is to design a marketing mix that will appeal to the target market and prove profitable, given the limitations imposed by available resources and the requirements of the marketing strategy.

The pricing component suggested for Healthy Choice, for example, must be considered in light of the initial costs to manufacture and distribute the product, how these costs will change with various levels of sales, the typical price charged for a product of this type, the price strategy employed by the retailers distributing the product, the extent to which price is an important factor used by the sales force, and so forth.

Executing Plans   Implementing the typical marketing plan requires a great number of decisions. Making sure the product reaches the warehouse at the right time, that ads are run on schedule, and that salespeople receive the right support material represent just a sample of the details that must be tracked day by day, or even minute by minute. ConAgra, for example, made the introduction of Healthy Choice even more complex when the company decided to make changes in its other product lines at the same time. Poor sellers—Banquet Foods and Armour Dinner—were cut back severely, while Armour Dinner Classics Lite underwent a complete price restructuring. These changes meant that meetings had to be scheduled with every supermarket chain in order to negotiate that the freezer space freed up by Banquet and Armour reductions would be allocated to Healthy Choice rather than to a competitor.

Poor execution has been the downfall of many excellent marketing plans. A case in point is Stouffer Foods Corporation's Right Course frozen dinner entrees. Relying heavily on its reputation for high quality, Stouffer decided to introduce an upscale, exotic set of offerings such as Chicken with Peanut Sauce and Fiesta Beef with Corn Pasta. These choices were made without any input from retailers. In addition, the advertising campaign didn't appear until four weeks after the products were introduced. Retailers therefore felt that Right Course lacked retail support.

Measuring Results   Every marketing plan must include a control component that compares actual performance with planned performance. Performance criteria include sales, market share, return on investment, and cost containment, to name a few. In most modern businesses, the computer allows access to several performance indicators that management can monitor daily or at some longer interval. Usually, an annual review is a minimum.

In addition to collecting performance data, managers should assess why these particular results have occurred. Perhaps extenuating circumstances such as a declining economy can account for lower-than-expected sales. Or the original objectives may not have been realistic in light of competitors' actions.

Taking Corrective Action   Finally, management must determine if the gap between objectives and performance is significant enough to require corrective action. Occasionally, corrective action is a necessity. For example, Procter & Gamble Co. (P&G) made a decision in 1990 to move away from the juice market and attack the juice-drink market more vigorously. Ever since P&G introduced Citrus Hill orange juice into the market in 1983, it has been a struggle to maintain a reasonable market share. In 1990 P&G's market share was 10 percent, a distant third compared with 22 percent for

Minute Maid and 20 percent for Tropicana. The division lost fourteen million dollars in 1989. P&G president Edwin Artzt decided that the company could become a much more effective competitor in the juice-drink market. In fourteen months, P&G therefore acquired Sunny Delight citrus punch, Speas Farm and Lincoln apple juices, Sunsip fruit drinks, and Hawaiian Punch.[5]

The Promotion Plan

Each of the marketing mix factors has its own plan. Product, price, and distribution are thoroughly planned for. The promotion plan is our concern here. The promotion plan is a part of the marketing plan just discussed; the difference lies in the emphasis given to the promotional elements. Whereas the marketing plan might suggest a strong emphasis on promotional messages delivered to the target market through mass media and at the point of sale, the promotion plan would specify exactly how delivery would be accomplished. The promotion plan would also account for how promotion would be indirectly influenced by the elements of product, price, and distribution. The quality of the product, the price charged, and the place where it is sold all communicate a variety of messages to the consumer that must be consistent with the promotion.

The promotion manager must be thoroughly familiar with the marketing plan and its governing strategy. Ideally, the promotion manager should contribute to the marketing plan. It does little good to develop a marketing plan that implies a promotion plan that is not affordable or is beyond the organization's expertise. In the rest of this chapter, we consider the promotion component of the marketing plan.

Concept Review

1. Promotion is one part of the marketing plan, which consists of the following stages:
   a. Selecting of marketing objectives,
   b. Using marketing intelligence,
   c. Identifying market opportunities,
   d. Selecting target markets,
   e. Developing marketing strategies,
   f. Designing action plans,
   g. Executing plans,
   h. Measuring results, and
   i. Taking corrective action (if necessary).
2. The promotion plan specifies how promotion objectives are to be achieved, along with how promotion will interact with the other marketing mix elements.

Steps in Promotion Planning

Promotion managers usually visualize promotion in the context of a campaign, which is defined as "a planned, coordinated series of promotional efforts built around a single theme or idea and designed to reach a predetermined goal."[6] In this context, the term *campaign* refers to the entire promotional effort. It is a planning tool that coordinates the delivery of the message to the various audiences. It is unified by a central idea or focal point called a theme. The theme is the central issue or idea that is carried on every promotion device.

Figure 1.3 illustrates the steps involved in creating a promotion plan.

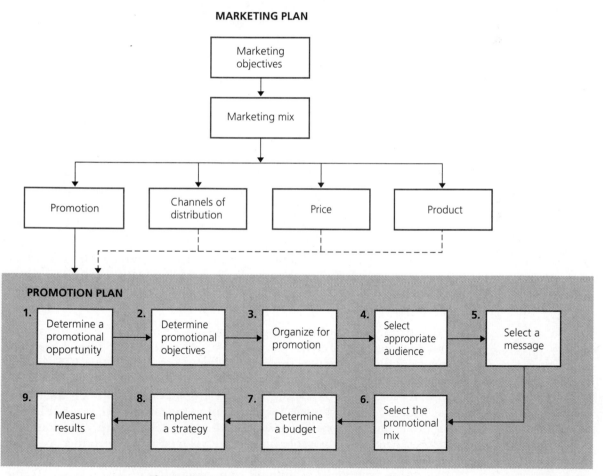

Figure 1.3

Promotion planning is derived from the marketing plan and parallels it in many ways.

The process begins with an assessment of opportunities, which in turn provides direction for determining specific promotional objectives. The **promotional strategy** details how the organization expects to achieve these objectives. In this section we briefly discuss each of these stages; subsequent chapters will add substance to this overview.

Step 1: Determining a Promotional Opportunity

Whether or not the marketing program should rely heavily on its promotional ingredient depends on the nature and extent of the promotional opportunity. Several conditions indicate a favorable opportunity for promotion:

1. *A favorable trend in demand.* It is always more effective to promote when moving with the current of customer demand rather than against it. Con Agra, for example, is following the health-oriented trend.

2. *Strong product differentiation.* If a product is very different from those offered by competitors, the task of effective promotion is eased. Toyota's Infiniti offers competitive differences that are easy to communicate.

3. *Hidden product qualities.* Hidden, or not readily obvious, product qualities—such as the taste of foods, the safety of automobiles, and the capacities of personal computers—frequently represent the competitive advantage and offer excellent promotional opportunities.

4. *Existence of emotional buying motives.* Telephone companies, Kodak, and charitable organizations such as UNICEF have all taken advantage of their inherent emotional appeals and the public's response to such themes as love, family, and human pain.

5. *Adequate funds.* If a company does not have money for promotion, there is no promotional opportunity. Small budgets suggest a predominant use of personal selling. Larger budgets permit the additional use of advertising, sales promotion, and publicity.

To identify promotional opportunities, a promotion manager should look to three general areas. One area consists of the secondary elements of communication: product, price, and channel of distribution. That is, although these elements are not part of promotion per se, they provide the basis for much of what is said through promotions. A new product, new packaging, a reduced price, and entry into a new market all provide a basis for promotional efforts. For example, Kimberly-Clark Corp., the manufacturer of Huggies disposable diapers, developed a new product for older babies. This product prompted a new promotional effort, including mass advertising, coupon distribution, and point-of-sale displays (see Figure 1.4). We discuss the promotional implications of product, price, and channels of distribution in Chapter 3.

Figure 1.4

This new product provides the basis for an entire promotional strategy.
HUGGIES and PULL-UPS are registered trademarks of Kimberly-Clark Corporation. © 1989 KCC. Reprinted with permission.

A second area in which to look for promotional opportunities is the macroenvironment, which includes demographic, social, and cultural trends; the economic environment; the ecological environment; and the technological environment. For example, the leveling of the Berlin Wall and the opening of Eastern Europe allowed hundreds of U.S. companies to both market and promote in Eastern European countries. The environment and its promotional implications are addressed in Chapter 4.

The third area is the customer. The wants and needs of consumers are constantly changing as a result both of changes in individual circumstances and in the local culture. The needs for health foods, exercise, and safe automobiles were all wants that originated with consumers, not the marketer. It is also necessary to know how consumers determined that these needs are important. Motivations, perceptions, attitudes, personality, and lifestyles all influence need determination and how consumers make choices. Chapter 5 considers all these factors associated with the individual consumer.

Step 2: Determining the Promotional Objectives

Most promotional objectives can be traced to corporate marketing objectives or to particular marketing problems. For example, when Kodak invented the disc camera, it aimed to saturate the market. This marketing objective in turn dictated promotional goals such as achieving widespread exposure of the new camera in mass media. In this case, an internal force—the development of new technology—influenced the promotional objectives. It is also possible for external factors to shape promotional objectives. When people died because someone had tampered with the contents of bottles of Extra-Strength Tylenol, defending the product became an objective of the company's advertising. Thus both internal and external forces may dictate a firm's promotional objectives.

There is a tendency to believe that the function of promotion is to advertise or to sell. But the objectives of promotion should be more specific, and they will vary. Most promotional objectives fall into five general categories:

1. *Creating awareness,* by making sure the consumer knows who the company is. This objective illustrated by the ad in Figure 1.5 for a company unfamiliar to most consumers.

2. *Creating understanding,* by providing key information useful in decision making.

3. *Creating changes in attitudes,* by dealing with issues or motives that consumers have strong feelings about. Chevron Corporation (see Figure 1.6) has attempted to change the public's negative attitude toward oil companies by showing how much the company is concerned about the environment.

4. *Creating changes in behavior,* ranging from fairly passive behavior such as calling a toll-free number to request information to buy the product. Most salespeople are assigned this objective.

5. *Creating reinforcement,* by offering tangible and intangible rewards for the consumer's favorable choices. The "Membership has its privileges" campaign for American Express does an excellent job of reinforcing card members (see Figure 1.7).

If we consider these five types of promotional objectives in conjunction with the tools of promotion, there is historical evidence that certain tools are better at achieving certain types of objectives. For example, what ad-

Figure 1.5

Movado attempts to create an awareness of its new product. Courtesy of The Movado Watch Corporation.

The Movado® Museum® Sports Edition (SE) Watch: the sportive interpretation of a classic.
A timepiece of taste, function and simplicity.

The Museum®Watch.

The Movado Museum dial is a registered trademark of The Movado Watch Corporation.
For brochure send $2 to Movado, 650 Fifth Ave., N.Y., N.Y. 10019

vertising does best is to deliver relatively simple messages to a large audience, over and over. Thus, advertising is effective at creating awareness, creating a basic understanding of the product or service, changing attitudes, and providing reinforcement. However, it may take a great deal of time and money to achieve these goals. Public relations is capable of doing many of these same things, but when compared to advertising the ability to know when an objective is achieved is quite difficult with PR. Conversely, personal selling and sales promotion are capable of delivering detailed information, including reasons to buy, to a select audience. Their emphasis is on a call to action. Consequently, personal selling and/or sales promotion are most effective when the objective is to motivate or change behavior. In later chapters we look more closely at the capabilities of each promotional tool.

Step 3: Organizing for Promotion

Unless the company is new or the use of promotion is new to the company, some sort of organization supporting promotion is already in place. Nonetheless, each time a new or revised set of promotional objectives is developed, the existing organization must be evaluated to determine whether it can achieve these objectives. Typically, modifications are minor, and the

Figure 1.6

Oil companies have been perceived as adversaries of the environment. Chevron attempts to change this negative attitude.
Courtesy of Chevron U.S.A., Inc.

existing organization is deemed capable. However, there are exceptions. For example, a company wishing to distribute product information to a national audience might discover that its current in-house advertising department is not equipped to take on this responsibility and that a large advertising agency must be hired. Similarly, if a promotion objective dictates personal contact with potential customers, a company may find that several salespeople must be added to the organization.

From this point until the end of the promotional planning process, organizational adjustments will continue. A local bank, for example, that targets the senior citizen market might decide to hire a marketing consultant knowledgeable about this group. A radio station wishing to run a sweepstakes might hire a sales promotion agency that specializes in this activity.

Figure 1.7

American Express reinforces the consumer's decision to its card with an endorsement and humor from John Cleese.

Courtesy of American Express Travel Related Services Company, Inc.

John Cleese. Cardmember since 1971.

Membership Has Its Privileges.

Don't leave home without it.
Call 1-800-THE CARD to apply.

Step 4: Selecting the Audience

Selecting the appropriate audience is undoubtedly one of the most important parts of the promotional strategy. A promotional message delivered to the wrong audience is doomed to fail. Promotional messages should be directed at the specific target for which the overall marketing program is being designed. There is a subtle difference, however, between the target market and the target audience. For example, the target market for children's toys is primarily children. Yet the target audiences might include the child, his or her parents, various government agencies concerned with product safety, and consumer groups concerned with the well-being of children. Thus, in this case, the target audience is much greater than the target market. The opposite is also possible. The target market for long distance telephone service for small businesses is all businesses spending between $150 and $1,000 per month for long distance. Yet MCI may design a win-back (former customers) sales promotion campaign targeted at Sprint customers only. The American Express ad in Figure 1.8 illustrates how well this company has targeted a specific audience within the larger target market.

For the promotion manager to properly delineate the appropriate target audience, familiarity with the product, who uses it, how it is used, and who influences its purchase and use is a necessary starting point. Consumer decision making will be discussed in Chapter 5.

Figure 1.8

This ad is directed at parents, just one section of the target market for American Express.
Courtesy of American Express Travel Related Services Company, Inc.

Step 5: Selecting the Message

Determining exactly what to say to the chosen audience is a difficult and important process. The key is the theme. For example, if you were promoting a diet soft drink, what theme would you try to convey? The Promotion in Focus segment discusses the choice made by Diet Coke. Miller Lite has retained the "tastes great—less filling" theme for nearly twenty years. Salespeople working for John Deere farm implements have touted the "quality, service, integrity" theme for over one hundred years to all their customers. The theme must tap into the most important needs and wants felt by the target audiences. It must be delivered clearly and in a timely manner.

An example of the successful use of a theme by a company's various marketing groups is the famous Marlboro campaign that began nearly forty years ago (see Figure 1.9). The "rugged cowboy" theme may work even better today when cigarette smoking is less socially acceptable, and smokers must be seen as independent and tough to continue smoking.

Step 6: Selecting the Promotional Mix

Earlier we described four common forms of promotion: advertising, personal selling, public relations, and sales promotion. The utilization of these

Promotion
in Focus

The Decisions That Made
Diet Coke A Success

Diet Coke was one of the marketing marvels of the 1980s, the soft drink of the decade. Its American production volume increased 26 percent annually for its first five years. The formula for Diet Coke's success sounds remarkably mundane: heavy promotion, a good new taste, and a brand name known around the world. Yet this seemingly simple formula required some shrewd decisions by Coca-Cola's management.

One part of Diet Coke's success—the formula for making it—continues to be a closely guarded secret known to only a few people at Coca-Cola's headquarters in Atlanta. Though the company's researchers get credit for the formula, Coke's management had the difficult job of deciding how good the new formula was. The decision to call the new drink Coke was a gamble. If Diet Coke had flopped, the failure could have tarnished Coke's image. Coca-Cola had avoided that possibility by naming its previous major diet drink Tab. But Coke executives decided that this time it was worth risking a reputation built up over almost a century.

It was no surprise that Coca-Cola decided to promote such an important product heavily. It has spent in the neighborhood of $50 million per year on Diet Coke since its introduction in 1982. But a much more crucial and difficult decision was *how* to promote it.

Clearly Coca-Cola wanted to profit from the country's ever-increasing fixation on weight and diets. But it wanted to break the public's perception that a soft drink has to lose its taste when it loses its calories. And no doubt it wanted to expand its target market.

So perhaps the most important decision in marketing Diet Coke was to sell it not on calories but on taste. "Just for the taste of it," a slogan delivered by stars like the Pointer Sisters and Whitney Houston, embodies this decision. Coca-Cola is telling people to drink Diet Coke not because they *have* to, but because they *want* to.

The success of this approach is demonstrated not just by Diet Coke's impressive gains in market share, but also by its more recent slogan: "the move is on." With this newer campaign, Coca-Cola has been positioning Diet Coke as the underdog to the giant Pepsi; the company claims that Pepsi drinkers are switching to Diet Coke. Coca-Cola executives are even predicting that Diet Coke will overtake Pepsi before the end of the decade. If it does, the company can thank the chemists who came up with the new formula—but also the managers who made the right decisions.

Source: Patricia Winters, "Diet Coke's Formula: Stress Taste, Not Calories," *Advertising Age* (January 1, 1990): 16.

Figure 1.9

This famous campaign has remained un-changed for over 35 years.
Courtesy of Glasheen Graphics.

four tools in a manner that helps achieve promotional objectives is referred to as the **promotional mix.** The various components are shown in Figure 1.10.

Determining the most effective promotional mix is difficult. In fact, for small businesses or those that have a clear need for only personal selling or sales promotion, the notion of a mix is a misnomer. Management does not know the exact extent to which advertising, personal selling, or any other promotional tool will help achieve the goals of the marketing program. Each element of the promotional mix has its particular strengths and limitations. Moreover, these inherent strengths and limitations can be increased or diminished by the capabilities of the company, the competitive situation, the other marketing elements, and so forth. The strength of NCR

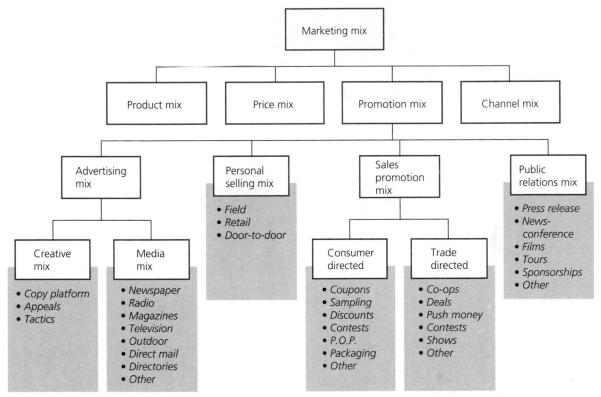

Figure 1.10
Components of the promotion mix.

Corp., for instance, lies in its field sales force. All NCR's promotional mix strategies therefore build on that strength.

Despite the advantages and disadvantages associated with each promotional tool, they can be substituted for each other to some extent. That is, in a particular situation several tools may have the potential of accomplishing the same objective. When the promotion manager recognizes a case in which two or more tools possess the same strength, the manager gains flexibility. Flexibility is especially important because of the limited budgets most promotion managers deal with.

The outcome of the promotional mix stage is a statement listing how each component of the promotional mix will be employed. The amount of detail will vary from company to company. At a minimum, percentage allocation should be assigned to each component. For example, the initial promotional mix for Ralston Purina Puppy Chow might look something like this: 40 percent mass advertising, 30 percent sales promotion, 25 percent personal selling, and 5 percent public relations. Each category would then be broken down into smaller, more specific components. The mass advertising component might be broken down further by media as follows: 30 percent network television, 25 percent print (magazines), 15 percent print (newspapers), 10 percent radio, 10 percent direct mail, 5 percent outdoor, and 5 percent specialty. Then the allocation for each of these components would be described more specifically. This process is similar regardless of the size of the business or the nature of the product, although the range of choices and level of sophistication may be lesser or greater.

Step 7: Determining a Budget

Promotional effort is expensive and is becoming more so every day. A variety of tools are used to determine a budget, none of which is foolproof. We describe budgeting techniques in Chapter 16.

Ideally, the budget should not enter the promotional planning process until after the major strategic decisions have been made. For this reason we list budget determination seventh in the planning process. In reality, however, the budget is often the starting point for the planning process, and everything else is dictated by this fixed amount. A promotion manager is told she has three million dollars to spend on promotion next year, and she plans her promotional effort accordingly.

Regardless of whether the budget has been predetermined or not, a major part of this stage is to cost out the dollar amounts to be spent on each of the promotional components identified in Step 6. How much does each network television program cost? How does this cost vary across markets, time, and ad length? What does it cost to produce and distribute 500,000 product samples? How much does it cost to have the product mentioned on a network television show? How much does a mailing list cost? The list of questions is lengthy; answering them requires people who are knowledgeable about the costs associated with all the facets of promotion. The final budget is often much greater than the amount the company intended to spend. Cuts are made. Compromises are introduced. Objectives are modified. The final set of decisions leads the promotion manager into the next stage of the process—implementation.

Step 8: Implementing the Promotional Strategy

The success of any promotional strategy is largely a function of how well it is implemented. Highly talented and experienced people greatly improve the likelihood of effective implementation. Implementation itself involves three separate stages. First, the promotion manager and his or her associates must make specific decisions about all the elements of the plan, including specific media, dates, times, sizes, talent, photographers and artists, and production schedules. Next, the promotion manager must make sure all these decisions can be implemented and that there are people as-signed to each task. Finally, the promotion manager must check to be sure that all decisions were implemented correctly.

As mentioned earlier, a **campaign** is a planning tool that coordinates the delivery of the theme to the various audiences. Many types of promotional campaigns may be conducted by a company, and several may be run con-currently. A firm may have a local, regional, or national campaign. A cam-paign may have several target audiences—consumers, resellers, and stock-holders, for example. A campaign may run for a week, a month, a year, or even longer. Three to six months is quite a common campaign length. In any event, the theme of the campaign should reflect the campaign's objec-tives and express the product's benefits, or salient attributes.

An example of a campaign that was very unusual—and therefore very risky—was the "Nature" campaign for Nissan's luxury car, Infiniti. The campaign was developed by Hill, Holiday, Connors, Cosmopoulas, Inc. and was introduced through a television ad showing little more than rocks, trees, and misty fields—but no car. This teaser ad was supported by a new distribution network; the Infiniti was not sold through the regular dealer-ships. The dealers kept the car covered for the first few days and had point-of-purchase support material on hand to reinforce the ad. When the car was finally unveiled, customers were escorted to a lounge where they lis-tened to the sounds of nature until the salesperson could personally show the car. Consumers were given various incentives for test-driving the car and additional premiums for taking it home over the weekend. Unfortu-nately, the campaign was considered a failure. After six months only forty percent of target sales were reached.[7]

A successfully operated campaign meshes the efforts of all groups con-cerned. The advertising program consists of a series of related, well-timed, carefully placed ads. The personal selling effort fits in as the salespeople explain and demonstrate the product benefits stressed in ads. The sales-people are fully informed about the advertising part of the campaign—the theme, media used, schedule of ad appearances, appeals used, and so on. The salespeople also inform the marketing intermediaries about this cam-paign and convince them to incorporate it into their marketing effort. Sales promotional devices are coordinated with the other aspects of the cam-paign. For each campaign, new display materials are prepared that reflect the ads and appeals used, in order to maximize the campaign's impact at the point of sale. Personnel responsible for physical distribution activities ensure that adequate stocks of the product are available in all outlets prior to the start of the campaign. Finally, people working in public relations are kept aware of new products, product demonstrations, new product appli-cations, and so forth. Of course it is important to provide enough lead time so that the public relations effort can be effectively incorporated into the campaign.[8]

Step 9: Measuring the Results and Taking Corrective Action If Necessary

Finally, the promotion manager must determine if the promotional effort reached the stated objectives. This activity may be carried out by the promotion manager or members of the manager's staff. The job often falls to the advertising agency, since its members have greater expertise with the measurement techniques. Three tasks must be completed in order to measure the results of promotion. First, standards for promotional effectiveness must be established. This means that the market planner must have a clear understanding of exactly what the promotion is intended to accomplish. For measurement purposes, the standards should be identified in specific and, if possible, quantitative terms. Second, actual promotional performance must be monitored. It is usually necessary to conduct experiments in which the effects of other variables are either excluded or controlled. The third step in measuring promotional efficiency is to compare performance measures against the standards. By doing so, it is theoretically possible to determine the most effective methods of promotion. Once the promotional strategy is evaluated, this information becomes part of the evaluation for the total marketing plan. The marketing manager is then able to prioritize any deficiencies and prescribe a corrective action for each.

A Final Thought

Many years ago someone coined the phrase "nothing happens until somebody sells something." This statement describes the place of promotional activities in business today. Marketing requires more than developing a good product, pricing it fairly, and making it readily available. These facets of marketing are insufficient to generate enough sales and profits for the firm to survive. Many potential buyers would never become aware of the product. Many others would not be persuaded of its merits. Competition is so intense and the marketplace so dynamic that the company must develop a comprehensive and effective program of communication and promotion. Every company is cast in the role of communicator. The only area of choice concerns how well it will be done.

Concept Review

1. To identify promotional opportunities, managers should examine the other elements of the marketing mix, the environment, and the consumer.
2. Most promotional objectives can be classified into five categories:
   a. Creating awareness,
   b. Creating understanding,
   c. Changing attitudes,

   d. Changing behavior, and
   e. Creating reinforcement.
3. After promotional opportunities have been analyzed and promotion objectives specified, promotion managers design the promotional strategy. This stage of the promotion plan requires organizing for promotion; selecting the audience, theme, and promotional mix; and determining how much to spend.
4. The process of promotion planning ends with implementation of the strategy and measurement of the results.

Case 1 *Advertising the Army*

It has not been easy recruiting young people into the military since the draft was abolished in 1973. After Vietnam, many young people mistrusted the armed forces. They saw movies and read books about the brutality of the Vietnam war, the number of innocent people killed by American bombs and bullets, and the indifference of the U.S. government to the plight of American veterans who suffered from exposure to Agent Orange. Moreover, colleges and vocational schools were becoming better marketers, competing more aggressively for high school graduates. They knew that the population of high school graduates was projected to fall to 2.3 million by 1992, down 36 percent from 1977. They understood their target market and began using clever, professional strategies to attract young people.

New People

The difficulty in attracting new recruits led the armed forces to reevaluate the kind of people they were trying to reach and the way they were reaching them. The Army's studies showed that the stereotypes of what makes a good soldier were all wrong. Intelligence is more important than Rambo-style toughness. People who do well in school, are well-adjusted socially, and come from good family backgrounds are likely to become good team players and are easier to train than their less well-adjusted peers.

New Image

So beginning in 1980, the Army set out to change its image and recruit the best young people it could find. Its "Be All That You Can Be" campaign stressed self-actualization, which had become a popular concept in the 1970s. To help back up its assertion that joining the Army was an ideal way for a young person to grow and become better educated, the Army created the Army College Fund, which enables young enlistees to save up to $25,200 while performing their military service.

The changes in recruits were dramatic. Enlistment numbers rose 64 percent from 1980 to 1986. Moreover, the quality of the recruits improved. In 1980, only 54 percent of recruits had graduated from high school, and only 25 percent were rated as being more intelligent than their average peers. Four years later, 91 percent of recruits had finished high school, and 63 percent ranked above average on intelligence tests.

However, enlistment levels began falling again in the mid-1980s as young people's values changed and the military's status was again brought into question by conflicts in the Middle East and Latin America. But the war with Iraq gave armed forces recruitment new life. For one thing, the war sparked an increase in patriotic fervor as millions of Americans vented their rage at Saddam Hussein. The military also took a four-month break from advertising during the war itself, a break that saved money and gave recruiters a chance to create a new strategy.

New Approaches

The first ads run after the war capitalized on patriotic feelings and the images of the war still fresh in people's minds. The "Count on Me" commercials emphasized that the American people could count on "confident, competent" soldiers. Another ad, "Cavalry Scout," was filmed in California before the war, but its desert scenes could have been mistaken for the Middle East. Subsequent ads stressed the intelligence of armed forces personnel and the prestige they gain from being part of an elite unit.

The Army has also been updating its personal selling strategy, emphasizing the training and economic benefits of enlisting. Recruiters traveling to high schools try to bring a Desert Storm veteran with them to demonstrate skills learned in the Army. The Army is also expanding its promotion activities to include weekend visits to Army bases, special bonuses for enlisting, and unique travel opportunities for enlistees on leave.

Case Questions

1. How well do you feel the Army has followed the processes depicted in Figures 1.2 and 1.3? Where are the gaps in its plan?

2. Is the Army ready to pick one of the two strategies? If yes, which option would be best? Why? If the Army is not ready, what should it do before making a decision?

Case Source: Steven W. Colford, "Military Launches Ads," *Advertising Age* (March 4, 1991): 1, 47. Richard Edel, "Shrinking Population Starts Recruitment War," *Advertising Age* (February 2, 1987): 5-5, 5-6. Janet Meyers, "Art Will Imitate Life in Army's Latest Ad," *Advertising Age* (October 8, 1990): 71. Janet Meyers, "No Victors: Army vs. Ayer, What Really Happened," *Advertising Age* (May 16, 1988): 24.

Summary

This introductory chapter provides important insights into the position of promotion in the contemporary marketing organization. Essentially, marketers must communicate with their audiences. Promotion is the marketing function concerned with persuasively communicating to target audiences the various components of the marketing program in order to facilitate exchange between the marketer and the consumer and to help satisfy the objectives of both.

The basis for promotion is the marketing plan. It consists of nine steps, beginning with the determination of marketing objectives and concluding with corrective action. Guided by the marketing plan, promotion initiates its own plan. This plan focuses on producing an effective message strategy using the four elements of promotion: advertising, sales promotion, public relations, and personal selling.

Discussion Questions

1. List the basic objectives of promotion. Provide some reasons why marketers should pursue promotional objectives.

2. Assume that you own a small manufacturing business that produces men's knit shirts. For your business, develop the following: two promotional objectives and a strategy for each objective.

3. Cite examples of how either advertising or another form of promotion led you to purchase a product that did not satisfy a need. Could any other form of promotion have led you to purchase it? What do you as a consumer expect from promotion?

4. Describe how the elements of the marketing strategy affect the promotion plan.

5. Assume that top management of General Equipment, Inc. has hired you to determine if a promotional opportunity exists for a fabricated part that has been developed for heavy-duty equipment. What criteria would you use as the basis of your investigation?

6. What are the four most common tools employed in promotion?

7. Discuss the definition of promotion in terms of the three specific elements mentioned.

8. Develop a promotional objective for each promotional tool.

9. "Nothing happens until somebody sells something." Comment on how promotion should respond to this adage.

10. What is a promotional campaign? Describe a well-coordinated promotional campaign in general terms.

Suggested Projects

1. Contact ten friends and interview them about the following:
    a. their understanding of marketing versus advertising,
    b. their understanding of promotion, and
    c. their understanding of the four promotional tools.
    Write a two- to three-page paper giving the results of your interviews and indicating your reaction to them.

2. Contact two local businesses and assess whether they use a promotion plan. Evaluate how their plan compares to the one outlined in this chapter. Is the plan formal, in which all the components are written down? Or is the plan informal, in which most of the information is in someone's head? How does the business owner feel about the success of the plan? Write a three-page report.

References

1. William J. Stanton, *Fundamentals of Marketing,* 7th ed. (New York: McGraw-Hill Book Co., 1984).

2. Philip Kotler, *Marketing Management: Analysis, Planning, Implementation, and Control,* 6th ed. (Englewood Cliffs, NJ: Prentice-Hall Inc., 1988): 33.

3. Kotler, 1988: 36.

4. Pamela Ellis-Simons, "One from the Heart," *Marketing and Media Decisions* (March 1990): 32–36.

5. Laurie Freedman, "P&G Shifts Strategy in Juices," *Advertising Age* (June 18, 1990): 33.

6. Stanton, 1984: 341.

7. Michael Lev, "Assessing Nissan's Zen Effort," *The New York Times* (May 14, 1990): C9.

8. Pradeep K. Korgaonkar and Danny N. Bellenger, "Correlates of Successful Advertising Campaigns: The Manager's Perspective," *Journal of Advertising Research*, 25, no. 4 (Aug./Sept. 1975): 61–71.

2 *Marketing Strategy: Segmentation and Positioning*

Consider This:

What Killed the Merkur?

When Ford's Lincoln-Mercury division decided to begin importing the Merkur XR4Ti in 1985, Ford hoped it might repeat the success of its Taurus. There was room in its product line for a small sporty car, and it hoped to capitalize on the snob appeal of the Merkur's German heritage.

The Merkur became Ford's first new nameplate since the Edsel flopped in the 1950s. Yet by the end of the decade, the Merkur was dead. The company had hoped 1990 sales would reach 100,000 units; instead, its annual sales never reached the 20,000 level predicted for 1986.

The Merkur seems to have failed because of a combination of bad marketing decisions. No one move doomed the car, but a combination of mistakes left it with neither strong advocates nor an excited group of potential buyers.

Problems started with the name. Ford had been selling the German-made car in Europe as a Sierra, but it couldn't use that name in the United States because of possible confusion with Oldsmobile's Ciera. No one knew how to pronounce Merkur, and XR4Ti just seemed like a meaningless jumble.

The car's styling also failed to win the hearts of the intended market. The design was aerodynamic and included a double-wing spoiler, but it struck many Americans as too radical, too much of a departure from the soft, sleek look that buyers had come to expect from European luxury cars.

Lincoln-Mercury dealers have been criticized for not handling the car well, hiding it behind their massive cars like Lincoln's Town Car and Mercury's Grand Marquis. Honda and other car makers have created entire new dealerships to sell their new luxury cars, but Ford wasn't willing to take that step. Lincoln-Mercury dealers assert that the company spent too little on advertising and put too high a percentage of the ad budget into print and direct-mail advertising rather than national television spots.

Although analysts may never fully agree about what went wrong with the Merkur, the various explanations seem to point to a lack of commitment on Ford's part. The Merkur's ads claimed that it would compete with cars made by BMW and Mercedes. Yet the company did not commit the resources to back up such claims, and the first shipments of Merkurs—most without leather seats, choice colors, or automatic transmissions—did not give buyers the sense that this was a classy car.

Sources: Rebecca Fannin, "Who Killed the Merkur?" *Marketing and Media Decisions* (January 1989): 66–69. Patricia Strand, "Lincoln-Mercury Fails to Build Merkur Line," *Advertising Age* (October 24, 1988): 72. James B. Treece, "A Hit in Europe, But a Miss in the States," *Business Week* (September 28, 1987): 81.

*T*he fate of the Merkur demonstrates the importance of four difficult tasks that face the promotional strategist: (1) know as much as possible about the audience, its unique behaviors, its size, and its patterns; (2) know as much as possible about the environment in which the audience members live and work; (3) know as much as possible about the product or service being offered to the audience; and (4) given an understanding of these three elements, determine the best communication strategy to reach the specified promotional objectives.

As we discussed in Chapter 1, these tasks do not occur in a vacuum; they are guided by the marketing plan and the resultant marketing strategy. However, when considering a marketing strategy, we must realize that a strategy is not a standardized, fixed path that all marketers follow. In fact, there are two general strategic approaches to the market: market aggregation and market segmentation. Selecting or emphasizing one over the other has definite consequences on the promotion manager. In this chapter we look at these two strategic approaches and how they influence promotion. We also examine the strategy of product differentiation, a means of distinguishing a product; and the end result of the process, positioning.

Strategic Options: Some Definitions

Marketers' strategic choices depend on their assessment of the market. A **market** is an aggregate of people who, as individuals or organizations, have needs for products or services and have the ability, willingness, and authority to purchase such products or services. Seldom are all the consumers in a market uniform. Usually the individuals within a market have different needs and wants and exhibit varied behaviors. Consequently, marketers must decide whether to treat their market as *homogeneous*—that is, as a single, large unit—or as *heterogeneous,* as a group of separate, smaller parts known as *segments.*

Deciding that the market is homogeneous leads to a **market aggregation strategy,** which calls for creating a single product supported by a single marketing program designed to reach as many customers as possible. When Texas Instruments Incorporated introduced the Speak 'n Spell learning aid, it followed the market aggregation approach: the company provided one version of the product supported by one marketing strategy. Market aggregation enables a company to maximize cost efficiencies in production, physical distribution, and promotion. But there are few cases in which market aggregation is truly appropriate. To speak of "the market" for deodorants, automobiles, or farm chemicals is to ignore the fact that the total market for each product consists of submarkets that differ significantly from one another.

Deciding that the market is heterogeneous leads to a **market segmentation strategy,** which divides the market into several segments, each of which tends to be homogeneous in all significant aspects, and from these segments identifies, evaluates, and selects *target markets.* A company that uses this approach aims to design products that match market demands and to develop promotional messages specifically aimed toward one or more target markets. In Chapter 1, for example, we discussed Procter & Gamble Co.'s entrance into the juice-drink market. In actuality, juice drinks have several segments, including the sports segment, the kids segment, the health-conscious segment, and so forth.

Figure 2.1 illustrates these two strategic approaches to the market. Notice that both lead to a market position, and that this position is created through the strategy of product differentiation.

Product Differentiation

As Figure 2.1 shows, product differentiation is a strategy used with both the aggregation approach and the segmentation approach. In both cases, product differentiation links the strategic approach with a third element—positioning.

It has been suggested that **product differentiation** is both a process, which consists of a series of strategic decisions, as well as a state or marketplace position in which the product offering is perceived by the consumer to differ from the competition on any physical or nonphysical product characteristic, including price.[1] As indicated, the process of product differentiation includes making both physical and nonphysical changes that affect the consumer's perception of the differences of one product versus another. The outcome of this process is a position based on how the product differentiates itself. Therefore, even though a company assumes the market is homogeneous and provides a standardized product or service, the product or service still must be differentiated from its competitors in order to offer a perceived advantage to the customer. In the case of a farm product such as a chemical fertilizer, the ingredients are regulated by the government, and farmers all use the product to satisfy the same need. The various manufacturers differentiate their fertilizer through factors such as guarantees, expert advice, and faster delivery. Promotion managers faced with the assumption on the part of marketing that the market is

Figure 2.1

Strategic options based on market assessment.

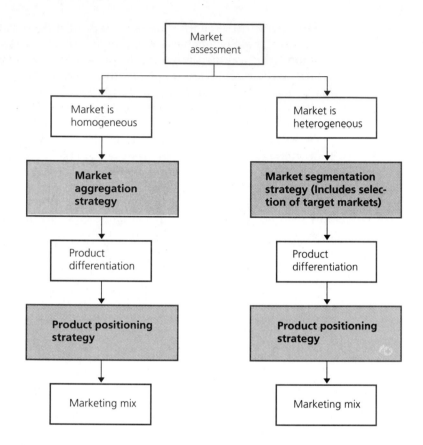

homogeneous often find themselves utilizing appeals outside the basic product, because the economies of scale advantage would be lost by modifying the actual product. These appeals are often referred to as *value-added* elements and are usually delivered as part of the personal selling effort or sales promotion.

Conversely, the Ralph Lauren Co., manufacturer of Polo clothes, assumes the market is heterogeneous and follows a segmentation approach. The company differentiates its basic products by age, gender, style, color, price, and so forth. Ralph Lauren provides very few value-added benefits (other than the prestigious reputation of the brand) since the company has done such an excellent job of customizing the product with the various segments. In general, the people who buy Polo clothes are very happy with the product and what it connotes. The promotion manager for Polo would emphasize the product and all its positive attributes. However, the real key is making sure the right people see the right messages. Thus, the media selection process is critical.

The picture that the chemical fertilizer market wants its customers to envision when they think about the company is very different from the picture that Polo wants to create in the minds of its customers. This desired picture is known as a *market position,* and the manner in which we create this position is called a *positioning strategy.*

We conclude in this chapter that product differentiation is used in conjunction with both a market aggregation strategy and a market segmentation strategy. However, although product differentiation contributes to the position of a product, a position strategy involves much more.

Product Positioning

Whether a market aggregation or a market segmentation approach is taken, the marketer must consider the product's position. A **position** is the image that the product projects in relation to images projected by competitive products and by other products marketed by the company. Stated simply, positioning is how you want the consumer to view your product. More formally, we define **product positioning** as a process that attempts to identify the salient perceptions, attitudes, and product-use habits of the consumer, assess how the marketer's product is perceived relative to these factors, and then place the product in its most advantageous light. Thus Avis positioned itself as the company that was only number two in rental cars and therefore had to "try harder."

As discussed in the previous section, product differentiation plays a role in creating a product position, but product differentiation accounts for only part of a product's position. A positioning strategy includes product differentiation factors plus how these factors are combined, how they are communicated, and who communicates them. In the case of Rolls Royce Motors, Inc., the position is created through elegant showrooms, knowledgeable salespeople, exceptional service, a minimum of print advertising in very upscale magazines, little talk of price, and a very high-priced car. K Mart Corp. maintains a very different position through a great deal of mass advertising that emphasizes low prices for name-brand merchandise. The strength of the brand presells the product; therefore very little product knowledge is required on the part of the salesperson. Self-service stores are also possible. These no-frills factors are combined in a manner that clearly reflects value.

A great many of the intangible elements representing position are delivered through the promotion strategy.

Although Figure 2.1 suggests that positioning occurs after aggregation or segmentation, the relationship between the processes is interactive once a product has been established: any change in positioning, aggregation, or segmentation will cause adjustments in the other two processes. For example, years ago Johnson & Johnson decided to expand sales of its baby shampoo to a new segment, the adult market. This decision produced a need to reposition the product through different advertising and even a slight change in the product formula. Or, a company facing excessive competition might decide to locate itself in an unoccupied position, then identify viable market segments, and finally change the product until the optimal match among strategies was found. These adjustments go on continually and can be affected by factors both under the control of the company and beyond its control.

Concept Review

1. Marketers employ three basic strategies:
   a. Market aggregation assumes that the market is homogeneous and calls for a single product supported by a single marketing strategy;
   b. Market segmentation assumes that the market is heterogeneous and results in the selection of target markets with unique marketing strategies for each; and
   c. Product positioning, a process that attempts to identify the salient perceptions, attitudes, and product-use habits of the consumer, assess how the marketer's product is perceived relative to these factors, and then place the product in its most advantageous light.
2. Product differentiation is a series of strategic decisions that results in a state or marketplace position in which the product offering is perceived by the consumer to differ from the competition on any physical or nonphysical product characteristic.

Market Segmentation

It has always been true that some brands sell well to some consumers but not in the market as a whole. These differences are not due to chance. Sound marketing practices require that managers know how market segments differ in their attitudes toward and susceptibilities to the marketing effort. From this knowledge managers can develop separate segmentation strategies—if, that is, a segmentation approach is worth the cost and effort involved.

Segmentation strategies take many forms. Often, manufacturers introduce multiple brands or other differences in the product to meet the needs of particular segments. Auto manufacturers, for example, develop different models for different market segments. But market segmentation can also be accomplished with no change in the product, through separate marketing programs, each tailor made for a particular market segment. A producer of hot cereals, for instance, can market the identical product to both the youth market and the sixty-five-plus market. In each case the promotional effort and possibly the location of the product in the store will differ.

In the extreme, a strategy of market segmentation involves the development of a different marketing program for each potential consumer. Companies that market on this basis include those that build custom yachts, specialized earth-moving equipment, and personal products such as hair pieces. For the most part, however, marketers attempt to serve not individuals but market segments. Duncan Hines cake mixes, for instance, serve the institutional market, the time-conscious market (with just-add-water mixes), and the quality-conscious market (with "supreme" mixes).

By tailoring marketing programs to pinpointed market segments, management can do a better marketing job and make more efficient use of marketing resources. First, however, managers need to identify meaningful market segments and select those segments that present marketing opportunities. In the following sections we examine first some possible bases for identifying market segments and then some steps and criteria for selecting those segments that can serve as target markets.

Segmenting Consumer Markets

There are hundreds of characteristics that can be used to separate markets into segments. As individuals, we constantly employ our own bases for categorizing people—for example, according to physical attractiveness, intelligence, and age. Marketers may not find all these categories useful, but they have successfully utilized many other bases for placing people or organizations into segments.

Perhaps the fundamental basis for segmentation is the reason for buying. Consumers who buy and use goods for their own personal or household use, constitute the **consumer market. Industrial users** are business institutions that buy products or services to use in their own businesses or to make other products. For example, a hospital may purchase accounting machines, pencils, and floor wax as part of the operation and maintenance of its business. A refrigerator manufacturer may purchase sheets of steel, wiring, and shelving as part of its final product.

Placing all markets into these two groups—consumers and industrial users—is a valuable segmenting process. But within these two categories are very real differences. We look first at the various bases for segmenting consumer markets.

Geographic Segments Probably the oldest basis for segmentation is geography. Typical geographic variables include climate, terrain, natural and legal boundaries, regions, states, countries, zip codes, and Metropolitan Statistical Areas (MSAs). Companies such as General Electric Co. begin with the broadest possible categories—domestic and foreign. Companies such as Keebler Cookies market only in the United States and divide their market into five regions: West, Southwest, Midwest, South, and Northeast. It is assumed that consumers living within these regions are homogeneous in respect to characteristics that are relevant to cookie marketing. Market segments based on location are easily identified, and large amounts of data are usually available. Many companies simply do not have the resources to expand beyond their local or regional area; thus geographic segments are meaningful to them. Several national companies also vary their advertising copy, media coverage, and product lines on a geographic basis.

Demographic Segments   By far the most common approach to segmentation identifies buyer groups according to selected demographic characteristics. Examples of demographic characteristics include age, income, sex, race, ethnicity, education, occupation, family life cycle, religion, and social class. The popularity of demographic segmentation is due primarily to the ease with which demographic traits can be identified. Also consumers' wants and purchasing patterns are strongly associated with several demographic characteristics.

Sex and age are two demographic characteristics that have proven to be particularly good bases for market segmentation. For example, children characterized as the youth group (approximately ages five to twelve) not only influence how their parents spend money but also make purchases of their own. Manufacturers of toys, records, snack foods, and video games have designed promotional efforts directed specifically at this group. More recently, senior citizens (age sixty-five and over) have grown in importance for producers of low-cost housing, cruises, hobbies, and health care. Figure 2.2 illustrates how one company has focused its marketing strategies to reach the senior market.

Another demographic trait closely associated with age and sex is the *family life cycle*. Families go through predictable behavioral patterns. For example, a young couple with one young child has far different purchasing needs than a couple in their late fifties with no children still at home. Similarly, a young unmarried couple tends to purchase different types of products than a young married couple; people in the former group are unlikely to purchase major appliances. In addition to the family life cycle, which assumes that a family goes through a traditional evolution, segmentation can also be based on *family composition*. This basis accounts for some of the important trends affecting marketers. For example, the number of singles in the United States has grown to approximately fifty-eight million; 37 percent of women and 32 percent of men eighteen and over are single.[2] Another phenomenon is young men and women who have returned to live at their parents' home. Labeled "Boomerang Kids" or "Returning Young Adults," this group is twenty-two million strong.[3] Because most of their

Figure 2.2

Ads targeted at the senior citizen market segment are becoming more common.
© *Lifeline Systems, Inc. 1992. Used by permission.*

"My dad had a heart attack last week. But he's going to be okay."

"I was so worried. But he's doing much better. In fact, he's doing so well that the hospital's going to send him home with the Lifeline service. If he needs help, he just hits the button. Mom and I can't be there every minute but, fortunately, Lifeline can."

With Lifeline, the touch of a button connects you to experienced professionals who have all of your emergency information — from neighbors' numbers to ambulance services — at their fingertips, and can summon whatever help you request.

You can rent Lifeline, for a small monthly fee, and keep it as long as you like.

Lifeline has been providing personalized emergency help, through medical facilities, for over 17 years. Today, we are among the 2500 hospitals in the United States and Canada that recommend Lifeline.

LIFELINE®
You've got a friend

To learn more, contact:

income is disposable, returning young adults are a prime market for automobiles, electronics, and vacations. They have also contributed to the plight of the "Sandwiched Generation," couples in their fifties who have both children and parents living at home. Burdened by the financial responsibility for three generations, such individuals are constantly looking for value and low prices.

Income is perhaps the most common demographic basis for segmenting a market. Income often dictates who can or cannot afford a particular product; for example, individuals earning below a certain income could not purchase a $25,000 sports car. An income of $150,000 would probably be necessary to purchase a Rolls Royce. Income tends to be a better basis for segmentation as the price tag for a product increases; it may not be quite as valuable for products such as bread, cigarettes, and motor oil.

Several other demographic characteristics influence various consumer activities. *Education* shapes product preferences as well as characteristics demanded for certain products. *Occupation* is also important. Individuals such as coal miners who perform hard physical labor may demand an entirely different set of products than teachers or bank tellers, even though their incomes are the same. *Geographic mobility* is somewhat related to occupation in that certain occupations, such as the military or corporate executives, require mobility. High geographic mobility means that a person or a family must acquire new shopping habits, seek new sources of products and services, and possibly develop new brand preferences.

Race and national origin have also been associated with product and media preferences. For example, people of Mexican descent tend to prefer radio and television over newspapers and magazines as a means of learning about products. Bilingual ads (see Figure 2.3) help coupons reach various facets of the Spanish-speaking market.

Finally, *health concerns* or *health conditions* have long served as the bases for segmenting markets. The Promotion in Focus section discusses one example. Searching for lucrative market segments, many hospitals have seized on women's health care. Women are the largest users of medical services, and in many households they determine which facility a family will use. Ads aimed at females feature maternity services and diagnostic programs for problems of most interest to women, such as osteoporosis, premenstrual syndrome, and breast cancer.

Notwithstanding its apparent advantages, demographic segmentation is often misused. A typical misuse has been to construct profiles of product users. For example, it might be said that the typical consumer of Mexican food is under thirty-five years of age, has a college education, earns more than ten thousand dollars a year, lives in a suburban fringe of a moderate-size urban community, and resides in the West. These characteristics do describe a typical consumer of Mexican food, but they also describe a lot of other consumers as well. The profile ignores an important dimension: familiarity with Mexican culture or at least a familiarity with Mexican food.

Figure 2.3
This ad for Colgate toothpaste accompanied by a coupon is targeted at Spanish-speaking consumers.
Courtesy of Colgate-Palmolive Co.

Promotion
in Focus

Changing Our Outlook on Disabilities

Experts debate how much the media—and particularly advertisements—affect how people view the world. Yet few would question that the way particular groups appear on our TV screens can influence how the majority views those groups. Recently, American television and advertisers have begun to focus on people with disabilities, with positive results for everyone.

As many as 33 million Americans are affected by a chronic limitation on their activity, and the work that about 13 million Americans of working age can do is limited because of a disability. For years, these Americans fought to be recognized and given an equal chance to succeed, and in 1990 the federal government finally granted them the civil rights that have long been available to other Americans.

While actors with disabilities have been showing up more often in movies and television shows, TV commercials have also helped to bring about this change in national attitude. A 1984 Levi's commercial focused on a man in a wheelchair, while Nissan used a woman in a wheelchair to make the point that its cars offer easy access—for everyone. McDonald's has run ads showing a couple conversing in sign language. And perhaps most striking was Nike's commercial featuring athlete Craig Blanchette, who impressed viewers with his astonishing physical prowess—before the camera revealed that he has no legs.

These ads might have some of the flavor of public service messages, but in fact they make good sense. Because there are so many Americans with disabilities, a company that can win loyalty from a segment of that group stands to profit. For instance, hearing-impaired television viewers tend to be loyal to the brands that advertise in closed-caption commercials, which now reach an audience of over 1 million.

Making commercials with physically challenged people in mind might also bring such people more into the mainstream of the American business world. Now more companies are offering services like telecommunications devices for the deaf, services that provide benefits for special customers and profits for the companies. Seeing that people with disabilities can "just do it" makes more companies realize that people once thought of as "handicapped" constitute a huge and largely untapped pool of potential employees.

Source: Judith Waldrop, "From Handicap to Advantage," *American Demographics* (April 1990): 33–35, 54.

Usage Segments　In 1964, one of the earliest departures from demographic segmentation occurred when it was proposed that consumption should be measured directly and that promotion should be aimed directly at heavy users.[4] This approach has become very popular, particularly in the beverage industry (for example, beer, soft drinks, and spirits). Research suggests that marketers can greatly enhance their marketing efforts by finding characteristics that correlate with usage rates. For example, several marketers wish to identify products that are used more often by Spanish-speaking groups. One study, conducted in the San Antonio market and sponsored by Sosa & Associates, showed that Spanish-speakers accounted for 65 percent of total sales of sugared colas. They also spend 26 percent more in the grocery store each week and 36 percent more at fast-food restaurants than other San Antonio residents.[5] This information tells cola marketers that Spanish-speaking groups are a very worthwhile market segment to pursue. Advertising in Spanish-speaking media and creating special sales promotions would be two possible tactics.

Three other bases for market segmentation have evolved from the usage-level criteria. The first is *purchase occasion*. Determining the reason why a person flies, for instance, may be the most relevant criterion for segmenting airline consumers. Four segments exist: business flier, vacation flier, emergency flier, and miscellaneous occasions flier.

The second basis is *user status*. Communication strategies must differ if they are directed, for example, at nonusers versus ex-users or one-time users versus regular users. Beer marketers typically target the heavy user, as do coffee marketers.

The third subcriterion is *loyalty*. The key category has been the brand-loyal consumer. Companies have assumed that if they can identify individuals who are loyal to their brand and the characteristics shared by these people, they have located the ideal target market. Unfortunately, there is still a great deal of uncertainty as to how to measure brand loyalty.

Psychological Segments　Psychological variables can also be a valid basis for segmentation. In a marketing context, relating psychological variables to buyer behavior is called **psychographics.** Four aspects of psychological segmentation have been directly or indirectly explored.

Attitudes　Evidence suggests that attitudes of prospective buyers toward certain products should influence the buyers' subsequent purchase or nonpurchase of the products. Thus it seems logical that if people with similar attitudes could be isolated, they would represent an important psychological segment.

Very little research has examined this hypothesis. In one study, it was concluded that a high, positive attitude and high perceptions of product quality were highly correlated with intention to buy.[6] Other evidence of how attitudes appear to affect behavior comes from observation rather than scientific research. For example, after the oil spill from the Exxon supertanker *Valdez* fouled beaches and killed wildlife in Alaska's Prince William Sound, many consumers boycotted Exxon products and twenty thousand customers cut up their credit cards and mailed them to Exxon. A similar result occurred when Nestlé Enterprises, Inc. was criticized for the marketing techniques it used to sell infant formula in Third World countries. A worldwide boycott forced Nestlé to halt these practices.[7] Conversely, Johnson & Johnson created very positive attitudes because of the way the company handled the Tylenol poisonings in 1982. These findings, although not conclusive, suggest that attitudes could serve as a viable basis for segmentation.

Personality It seems logical that consumption of particular products or brands would be related to personality. Clearly, Mazda had a personality type in mind when the company designed the Miata, as did Dr Pepper when the manufacturer suggested that people who drank the soft drink were "Peppers," that is, individuals who did their own exciting things. Yet after reviewing more than two hundred studies dealing with personality, it was concluded that the results are equivocal.[8] A few studies indicate a strong relationship between personality and aspects of consumer behavior; a few indicate no relationship; but the great majority indicate that if correlations do exist, they are so weak as to be questionable or perhaps meaningless. Yet there is still optimism that if the personality tests employed in marketing were better designed and implemented, personality could prove to be a valuable segmental base.[9]

Motives A *motive* is a reason for behavior. A buying motive is the drive that triggers purchasing activity. In theory, this is what market segmentation is all about. Measurements of demographic, personality, and attitudinal variables are really convenient measurements of less conspicuous motivational factors. People with similar [physical and] psychological characteristics are presumed to be motivated similarly. The question logically arises: Why not observe motivation directly and classify market segments accordingly?

So far, segmentation analysis based on many motivational considerations has proven to be an unsurmountable task. Current techniques of motivational research are inadequate. Because motivation research is also expensive and time consuming, it has concentrated on examining product characteristics and satisfactions. The result is *benefit segmentation*, which groups consumers according to the benefits they seek from a product. Table 2.1 is the most current version. Though it was done in 1968, it is a classic. In this case, individuals are segmented according to the benefits they seek from toothpaste. Based on this benefit, individual profiles can

Table 2.1   **Market Segments for Toothpaste**

Segment Names	Principal Benefit Sought	Demographic Strengths	Special Behavioral Characteristics	Personality Characteristics	Brands Disproportionately Favored
The Sensory Segment	Flavor, product appearance	Children	Users of spearmint-flavored toothpaste	High self-involvement	Colgate
The Sociables	Brightness of teeth	Teens, young people	Smokers	High sociability	Gleam, Ultra Brite
The Worriers	Decay prevention	Large families	Heavy users	High hypochondriasis	Crest
The Independent Segment	Price	Men	Heavy users	High autonomy	Brands on sale

Source: Adapted from Russell I. Haley, "Benefit Segmentation: A Decision-Oriented Research Tool," *Journal of Marketing* (July 1968): 33. From *Journal of Marketing*, published by the American Marketing Association. Used with permission.

be expanded to include demographics, special behavioral characteristics, personality characteristics, and brand preferences. A more current example of benefit segmentation was provided by J. D. Power and Associates, who identified six types of new-car buyers according to the benefits they sought: Gearheads, Epicures, Purists, Functionalists, Road-haters, and Negatives. As one would expect, the Functionalists want an automobile that is reliable and efficient, and they are not interested in sportiness and styling.[10]

Lifestyle   In 1988, two San Francisco entrepreneurs launched Waiters on Wheels, a home-delivery service ferrying hot meals from restaurants; it delivers two thousand meals a week, primarily to working couples.[11] This scenario illustrates a product aimed at people with a particular lifestyle. A **lifestyle** is an orientation of an individual or a group toward consumption, work, and play.

Lifestyle segmentation has become popular with marketers because of the availability of measurement devices and instruments and the intuitive categories that result from this process. As a result, producers are targeting versions of their products and promotions to various lifestyle segments. Black & Decker Corp., for example, designs special programs for the "do-it-yourselfers."[12] Lifestyle analysis tells B&D that such men are often involved firsthand in home improvements and repairs and are fascinated by electronics and computers. They also have high brand awareness and are willing to give others advice about automobiles, power tools, hand tools, tires, home building products, and home video equipment.

Lifestyle analysis begins by asking questions about the consumer's activities, interests, and opinions. If a man is an executive earning sixty thousand to eighty thousand dollars per year, with a wife and four children, he may exhibit the following lifestyle patterns: workaholic, spends little time with his family, avid hunter, watches late-night television only, has voted Republican for the last twenty years, shops by mail, and feels that a man is judged by the clothes he wears and the car he drives. In contrast, another man who has the same demographics traits exhibits very different lifestyle patterns: never brings work home, Boy Scout leader and Little League coach, family vacations together, enjoys watching television, grocery-shops for family and cooks dinner two evenings, supports Jimmy Carter and his charitable projects, and hardly ever wears a tie.

Table 2.2 outlines the components of each major lifestyle dimension. Such *AIO inventories* (activities, interests, and opinions), as they are called, reveal vast amounts of information concerning a consumer's attitudes toward product categories, brands within product categories, and user and nonuser characteristics. Lifestyle segmentation studies tend to focus on how people spend their money; their patterns of work and leisure; their major interests; and their opinions on social and political issues, institutions, and themselves. The emergence of the dual-earner middle class couple has had the greatest impact on American lifestyles. Table 2.3 shows the seven lifestyle segments within the population of dual-earning couples. For example, dual-income Young Families are jugglers. With at least one child younger than age six, at least one more of school age (six to seventeen), and two parents with jobs, it is not easy to keep all the balls in the air. It often takes the wife's earnings to put a Young Family into the middle class, and that fact explains a lot about this group's values and attitudes. Building IRAs and college funds are important goals for Young Families. They buy family-oriented leisure, educational toys, kids' furniture, bigger

Table 2.2 **Lifestyle Dimensions**

Activities	Interests	Opinions	Demographics
Work	Family	Themselves	Age
Hobbies	Home	Social issues	Education
Social events	Job	Politics	Income
Vacation	Community	Business	Occupation
Entertainment	Recreation	Economics	Family size
Club membership	Fashion	Education	Dwelling
Community	Food	Products	Geography
Shopping	Media	Future	City size
Sports	Achievements	Culture	Stage in life cycle

Source: Joseph T. Plummer, "The Concept and Application of Life-Style Segmentation," *Journal of Marketing* (January 1974): 34. Reprinted from *Journal of Marketing*, published by the American Marketing Association. Used with permission.

Table 2.3   **The Seven Lifestyles Among Dual-Earner Couples**

(Number of Couples and Income Distribution by Life-Cycle Segment)	Number (in millions)	Percent of Total	Percent Distribution of Household Income (1985 dollars)		
			< $20,000	$20,000– $40,000	$40,000 +
All dual-earner couples <age 65	26.7	100%	16%	40%	44%
Dual-earners with children in the home	17.8	67	16	40	44
Full Nesters (children aged 6–17)	6.4	24	14	43	44
Crowded Nesters (children aged 18–24)	4.9	18	8	31	61
New Parents (children <age 6)	4.0	15	24	44	32
Young Families (children <age 6 and 6–17)	2.6	10	23	47	31
Dual Earners with no children in the home	8.9	33	16	40	44
Empty Nesters (ages 50–64)	3.5	13	16	37	47
Honeymooners (<age 35)	3.4	13	20	46	35
Just A Couple (ages 35–49)	1.9	7	12	35	53

Source: American Demographics tabulation of the Census Bureau's 1986 Current Population Survey.

homes, and at least two cars. They also like stay-at-home entertainment—such as VCRs and exercise equipment—that the whole family can enjoy.[13]

Segmenting Industrial Markets

Segmentation is important to industrial as well as consumer marketers. The bases used to select segments are different from those given by consumer goods manufacturers. Industrial firms typically use one or more of three bases to segment their markets—product characteristics, organizational characteristics, and decision-making unit characteristics (see Table 2.4).[14]

Table 2.4   **Three Bases of Industrial Market Segmentation**

Product Characteristics	Organizational Characteristics	Decision-Making Unit Characteristics
End use	Industry type	Source loyalty
Size of purchase	Size of firm	Buyer characteristics
Benefits, cost, durability, etc., of product	Structure of firm	Buying center and buyer-seller exchanges

Source: Reprinted by permission of the publisher from "Industrial Market Segmentation," by Yoram Wind and Richard Cardozo, *Industrial Marketing Management* 3 (1974): 153–166. Copyright 1974 by Elsevier Science Publishing Co., Inc.

Consider first product characteristics. A seller might segment customers by *end use* (for example, steel can be used for bridge construction, automobiles, and building construction), *size of purchase* (for example, dollar value or weight), *cost,* or *durability.* This basis is difficult to implement. Different products and their components may have different names depending upon the type of industry or location. Often these statistics are not readily available. Sometimes the cost elements differ, depending upon the accounting philosophy followed. Therefore, some firms opt for an easier basis for segmentation—organizational characteristics, such as *industry type* (for example, metal mining, anthracite mining), *size* of the firm, and *structure* of the firm. Much of this information is available through the *Standard Industrial Classification* (SIC) system, which places each industrial, commercial, financial, and service organization into a unique category. Business activities are assigned a letter division, and each division is subdivided into two-digit major groups. Each major group is further divided into three-digit subgroups, and each subgroup into detailed four-digit numbers. Industrial data is available through government sources as well as private sources, such as *Sales & Marketing Management's Survey of Industrial Purchasing Power.* Unfortunately, such criteria have little to do with sales or other performance measures. A third basis for industrial segmentation consists of the decision-making unit characteristics—in other words, attributes of the people making the purchase decisions, how the decision is made, and the possible outcomes of following certain procedures. For example, in some organizations, decisions are made by one or two dominant individuals, usually the chairman of the board or president. In other organizations, all decisions are made through committees. Companies that follow the committee approach often take much longer to make decisions. In many industries, especially department store retailing, decision making has become more decentralized, allowing a division manager or even a store manager to make most purchase decisions. Of course, all of this changes when doing business in a country such as Japan, where tradition mandates a very exact, laborious process to be followed when marketing a product. Although this third basis for classification has definite advantages over the other two, gathering this information and maintaining its accuracy are very difficult.

Industrial segmentation usually yields a series of subsegments. For example, an aluminum producer might segment its market on the basis of industry (residential), end use (partially assembled, building components, mobile homes), and customer size (small, medium, large). Thus, an aluminum manufacturer such as Reynolds Aluminum might develop its product lines in respect to two major categories—manufacturing/construction and consumer—and then divide these into several subcategories (for example, manufacturing: automobile components (large and medium).

Selecting Target Markets

Segmentation can get out of hand, as Figure 2.4 illustrates. The ultimate purpose of delineating market segments is to select a target market or markets. Unless this goal is reached, it is useless to identify segments. The process of selecting a target market involves four steps.

The first step is to take segments that have been identified on the basis of product-usage levels or perceived benefits and analyze demographic, geographic, and psychological characteristics of each segment. Thus the basis for segmentation is no longer common demographic characteristics but common consumer behavior. This step usually yields four to seven segments.[15]

The second step is to collect and analyze further data about each of these segments. In particular, the number of consumers in each segment and the extent of their effective demand should be estimated.

The third step is to apply the criteria for identifying which segments present profitable marketing opportunities. Traditionally, five criteria have been employed to gauge the relative worth of a market segment:

1. *Clarity of identification*, the degree to which it is possible to identify who is inside and who is outside the segment.

2. *Actual or potential need*, a need that reflects overt demands for existing goods or services or a need that can be transformed into a perceived want through education or persuasion. The need must be large enough to justify a separate segmentation strategy.

3. *Effective demand*, created by needs plus purchasing power. A segment that needs a good but cannot buy it does not represent a promising segment. Purchasing power derived from income, savings, or credit must belong to the members of the market segment in order for it to represent a meaningful marketing opportunity.

4. *Economic accessibility*. Individuals in a market segment must be reachable and profitable. For example, members of a segment might live in the same area, shop at the same stores, or read the same magazines. Many important segments—for instance, those based on motivational characteristics—are not economically accessible.

5. *Unique reaction to marketing efforts*. There must be a reason for using different marketing approaches to the various segments. Unless different segments respond in unique ways to particular marketing inputs, using separate marketing programs for the segments will not be worthwhile.[16]

After applying these criteria it may be determined that more than one segment will qualify for consideration as the basis for marketing action, and perhaps none will qualify. At this stage, learning that a segment is not

Figure 2.4

Sometimes segmentation goes to extremes, as this cartoon suggests.
© Terry Sharbach. Reprinted with permission.

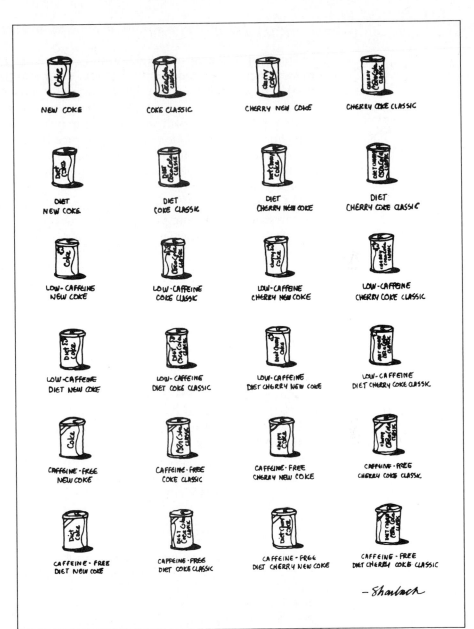

an area of potential opportunity may be as important as discovering that it is.

The final step is to select one or more segments as the target for marketing strategy. It is important to consider such additional factors as existing marketing objectives, potential profitability, perceived risk, required allocation of resources, competitive advantages and disadvantages, and potential receptivity to marketing efforts. It may be more important to select a direction that feels comfortable than to pick the one that offers the greatest mathematical potential. A target market must respond to a competitive strategy. A company should probably compete where it knows how to compete best.

Once target markets are selected, the stage is set for the development of an integrated marketing program. For example, ICI Australia is one of the country's leading agrichemical companies. Its products are sold through a network of distributors and resellers who had depended on traditional media advertising, especially radio in rural areas, to reach their prospects. It was determined that this strategy was not effective in reaching the target market: farmers using over $3,500 of chemicals annually. Instead, ICI decided to use a direct marketing approach. The company wrote to over five thousand farmers, asking them to tell ICI about themselves so that ICI could develop chemical products that would be of genuine interest in the day-to-day running of their farm business. Included with the letter was a free subscription to a magazine that ICI had developed for the benefit of the farming market. The response rate to this letter was 30 percent, a staggering result in an industry where 2 percent is the norm.[17]

Throughout this text, the segmental approach described will be illustrated. At this point, it is enough to say that segmentation strategy is the primary marketing approach used by a majority of producers. Combined with product differentiation and positioning, it is the essence of a contemporary marketing strategy.

Promoting to Target Markets

One of the primary values of segmenting is that it reduces the waste associated with trying to reach the entire market. As noted earlier, a market segment should respond favorably to some element of the marketing mix, including promotion. For example, consumers within a segment may be heavy coupon users, or they may be responsive to personal selling or technical copy, to name just a few possibilities. A marketer then has two choices. First, target markets can be selected based partially on their responsiveness to promotional techniques that the company already does well. Or marketers can identify a target market to which they are positively disposed and adjust their promotional strategy accordingly.

Having made this decision, the marketer customizes and refines the promotional mix to fit the target market as precisely as possible. This effort includes choosing the following: the message design; the media mix to deliver the message; sales promotion devices such as coupons, price discounts, contests, rebates, and so on; public relations devices such as holding open houses, sponsoring charities, and running institutional ads; and whether to have the product sold by well-trained, articulate salespeople or in self-service stores.

While discovering the proper blend may appear to be an insurmountable task, it offers a better chance of effectively communicating a message than does the shotgun approach employed by companies that assume market homogeneity. One company that has consistently matched its promotional strategy with its target market is Ralston Purina. A case in point is Cat Chow Mature, a product the company introduced in 1990. Cat Chow Mature is a "life stage" product especially formulated for mature cats. More importantly, it is targeted at the owners of mature cats, especially those who are leaving the supermarket to shop for pet foods at pet shops. It is assumed that a high-quality specialty cat food such as Cat Chow Mature would bring these people back to the supermarket. Taking into consideration the skepticism of supermarket managers about carrying a premium-priced pet food, Ralston Purina began the campaign with several trade deals to prompt the managers to provide shelf space and top locations for the new product. The next step was to locate cat lovers and send them the message along with incentives to buy. The fourteen-million-dollar introductory campaign combined a variety of media, including spots on "Wild Kingdom," direct mail coupons, samples distributed at pet shows, and magazine ads in twelve different publications read by pet lovers.[18]

Concept Review

1. Market segmentation acknowledges the heterogeneity of the marketplace and attempts to identify profitable customer groups (that is, segments) from which the marketer will select one or more target markets.
2. The bases for selecting segments of the consumer market are:
   a. Geography,
   b. Demographics (for example, age, income, race, sex, health),
   c. Usage characteristics (for example, amount, occasion, status, loyalty), and
   d. Psychological factors (for example, attitudes, personality, motives, lifestyle values).
3. Industrial markets use different bases for segmentation:
   a. Product characteristics,
   b. Organizational characteristics, and
   c. Decision-making unit characteristics.

4. Four steps are involved in selecting target markets:
    a. Convert identified segments into segments based on consumer behavior;
    b. Collect additional information about each segment;
    c. Apply the criteria of a good segment: clarity of identification, actual or potential need, effective demand, economic accessibility, and unique reaction to marketing efforts; and
    d. Select one or more segments as potential target markets.

Positioning

Suppose a home-construction company, after careful research, determines that the market can best be described as a *market-segment matrix* (see Figure 2.5). In other words, the company concludes that the three most meaningful bases for segmenting the housing market are home ownership, family size, and income, with categories within each of these as shown in Figure 2.5. Examination of the matrix reveals that the company might direct its marketing efforts to as few as one segment (for example, those who own their own home, with one or two family members, and with an income of thirty-five thousand dollars or more) or to as many as twenty-four segments. At this point, the company would have to assess the attractiveness of each segment. Then, to select segments as target markets, it would consider factors such as interest rate trends, population trends, economic conditions, building expertise, capital situation, and competition. Once the selection is complete, the company would begin the process of correctly positioning the consumer product. (Keep in mind, though, as we noted earlier, that segmentation and positioning processes interact. For example,

Figure 2.5

An example of a market segment matrix. In regard to housing, many market segments are possible, though not all are target markets.

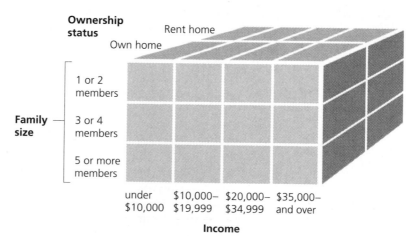

positioning may alter segmentation and bring on repositioning. Positioning does not operate in isolation.)

The importance of positioning has been cogently expressed: "Strong, accurate positioning represents the most important decision and action management has to make for the company and its marketing. . . . Everything else is execution."[19] The goal is to position a new or modified product in order to maximize profits, without cannibalizing sales and profits from the company's other products. The operational problem is to position correctly and to avoid positioning errors.

Understanding Positioning

"Product positioning is one of the most nebulous and controversial of all areas of new product development."[20] Still, there is agreement about several characteristics of positioning.

To begin with, positioning is a facilitating process that coordinates marketing functions. It helps organize certain types of information in such a way that other strategies such as segmentation and differentiation can be combined into a more effective marketing program. Ultimately, the objective is to form an integrated program with each component fulfilling its proper role in helping to position the firm in the markets management chooses to serve. Although the culmination of this effort is a particular position, a positioning strategy also serves to provide a framework.

A second area of agreement is that positioning strategy can be applied to both macro and micro levels of marketing. A positioning strategy can thus be applied to an individual consumer, as in the case of a buyer of a customized Rolls Royce, or to conventional market segments, such as the shampoo market, or to an entire country, as the U.S. government does when it markets American food exports to other nations.

Third, the position a consumer perceives for a product may be based on the product's physical characteristics or on intangible images created by the company's promotional efforts. The former is exemplified by the automobile industry's annual model changes. However, as new technologies spread ever more quickly, it becomes more difficult to maintain a competitive edge through the product's physical characteristics. Thus marketers increasingly have turned to creating intangible differences in the mind of the consumer.

Finally, to be effective, positioning must be consumer oriented. Before a product position can be determined, the marketer must identify key attitudes and perceptions of the consumer toward the key attributes of a particular product type, class, or brand, relative to competitors. Consequently, effective marketing research and effective positioning go hand in hand. Positioning is only as good as the research it is based on. This research must begin with characteristics of consumers such as their needs, perceptions, attitudes, product-use patterns, and so forth and end with how consumers react to a particular position. All of this information must also be judged in light of the marketing strategy and all of its elements. For instance, some positions are not affordable to create while others are already filled by a competitor.

Identifying Product Positions

A position may be based on

- *product features,* such as the low calorie content of Weight Watcher desserts or the on-time record of United Air Lines;
- *product benefits,* such as the ability to replace without charge broken merchandise that was purchased with an American Express card;
- *specific usage occasions,* such as "Miller Time" or the use of Gatorade after a fun workout;
- *user category,* such as the Pepsi generation (a very general category that indicates a very contemporary group) or the frequent flyer.

To identify a product's existing or desired position, we need to understand the product and the consumer. A product can be described physically in terms of its function or its sensory or physiological characteristics; socially in terms of the social uses to which it can be put; or psychologically in terms of its use in expressing human emotions, desires, or behaviors. These meanings are not inherent in the object itself but are given to it by the culture, by society, by communicators such as advertisers, and by consumers.

The process of assigning these meanings is both facilitated and distorted by the habit of **stereotyping,** which is the process of forming and applying overall impressions of categories of people, events, or things. People tend to ignore the details of the individual person, event, or situation and apply their general impression of the category. Stereotyping thus simplifies communication and comprehension. Because people constantly use stereotypes, it is critical to be able to identify the key attributes that people use when they assign objects to categories and apply stereotypes to them. Kodak, for example, has long taken advantage of the way people respond to the stereotype of a family. The Kodak ads highlight specific events such as birthdays and holidays in order to create a certain image or mood or to give an example of when to take pictures. The ad in Figure 2.6 also exemplifies the stereotype of the ideal family: mom, dad, and children sharing warm moments together, expressing love and concern.

More specifically, the strategist needs to know what attributes are important to consumers. For example, a high school senior who is trying to select a college might want to know the answers to a number of questions.

Figure 2.6

This ad utilizes the common perception many people have about family.
Courtesy of Tourisme Quebec.

How much does it cost? Do I have to live on campus? Does it have a strong reputation in my field of interest? Does it have a winning football team?

The strategist also needs to know what information consumers use to evaluate attributes and how consumers rate current brands in relation to those attributes. To assess how attributes influence brand choice, the strategist relies on laboratory or market tests. Subsequent research can then test whether the means chosen to project certain attributes are successful.

A great many methodologies have been developed to provide a way of identifying and selecting positions. They range from qualitative approaches such as **focus groups** (controlled interview situations in which eight to ten people are brought together to share ideas and answer questions about a concept or product) to sophisticated quantitative analyses such as multidimensional scaling, cluster analysis, and other multivariate approaches. These techniques are beyond the scope of this book, but we will look more closely at one method, perceptual mapping.

Perceptual mapping is a process that creates a "map" of consumers' perceptions of the similarities and differences among products or brands by applying a family of mathematical programs known as clustering and classification techniques. It is used both in developing new product positions and in repositioning existing products. The process can both identify needs that are being unfulfilled by current products, thus suggesting a position for a new product, or it can indicate changes needed to reposition an existing product to appeal to different market segments.

Figure 2.7 shows the results of a complex type of perceptual mapping called *multidimensional scaling* (MDS). Based on data provided by a sample

Figure 2.7

*Perceptual mapping is
used here to position
a new food product in
relation to existing
brands. This particular
map uses eight sepa-
rate criteria and pro-
duces size unique seg-
ments. Note that none
of the existing brands
were located in seg-
ments 6 and 4.*

Adapted from Henry As-
sael, "Evaluating New
Product Concepts and
Developing Early Predic-
tions of Trial," Market-
ing Review (May 1975):
13. Reprinted with per-
mission from American
Marketing Association/
New York.

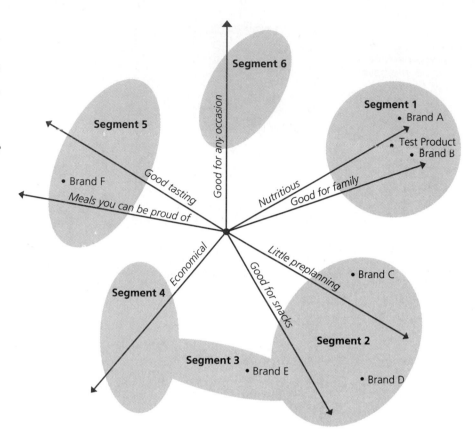

of consumers, an MDS computer program determines the relative position
of brands and concepts in a perceptual map. In this example, consumers
view the test product as similar to Brands A and B, suggesting that the test
product is in danger of positioning as a "me too" brand. In addition, consumers were asked to rate each brand by eight product benefits. The program identifies the position of each attribute by determining a vector that
provides the best fit between the attributes and the brands in the perceptual map. The vectors are shown by the eight lines in Figure 2.7. The results show, for example, that Brands A and B are most closely associated
with being nutritious and good for the family but are not associated with
being economical. Thus this analysis suggests that this perceptual position
is occupied and that it would be highly competitive and risky to enter.
Nonetheless, this is exactly where the test product finds itself.

As a final step, consumers were asked to rank their preference for each
brand and concept. Each person was positioned on the perceptual map at
a point closest to the brand preferred and farthest from the brand least

preferred. Groups of consumers who preferred similar brands were represented by circles. Six segments were identified, with the largest segment (1) preferrring the test product and Brands A and B. Based on results such as these, the marketing manager can determine strategic issues, such as where the test product is positioned relative to the competition; whether that is an advantageous position; and whether repositioning is necessary or even possible.

Product Positioning Strategies

Establishing a consensus position in the mind of the consumer is surprisingly difficult. Sears spent several years trying to position itself as a fashion leader but failed. This failure was due partly to Sears's unwillingness to follow the trends in the apparel business. Once driven by price and value, the mass-market clothing business today relies on status and style. But Sears has failed to move with the industry, as shown in the results from a fashion survey (see Figure 2.8) that indicates that less than 4 percent of U.S. women think of Sears as a fashion retailer. It is also reflected by the fact that the hottest designers—Liz Claiborne, Calvin Klein, and Adrienne Vittadini—refuse to sell their clothing to Sears, fearing it would tarnish their own fashion image.[21]

How can a company create a position for a product? Marketers have tended to follow three approaches to positioning, focusing on the consumer, on the competition, or on social accountability.

Consumer Positioning   Positioning strategies that focus on the consumer may take various forms: emphasis on the target market, the type of appeal, the usage occasions or functions, and the user category. If the emphasis is on the *target market,* the company might position a product to appeal to a specific market segment, a broad group of market segments, or anywhere on this continuum from specific to general. This choice should be based on exhaustive research, with particular emphasis on the consumers' purchasing motives.

Whatever position on the continuum is chosen, the selection brings both advantages and disadvantages. Positioning to appeal to a specific market segment provides a direct product-benefit link and guidelines for allocating resources, but it also risks alienating segments that might have a need for the product. Diet Coke, for example, clearly follows a positioning approach directed toward young adults. Older adults may be alienated by ads that portray young people drinking Diet Coke who obviously have no weight problem. A more general positioning approach might provide enough flexibility for consumers to interpret any desired benefits they care to. However, advertising vague enough to allow this flexibility may not be specific

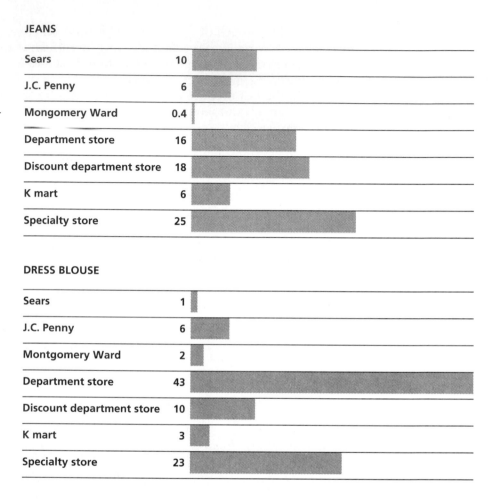

JEANS

Sears	10	
J.C. Penny	6	
Mongomery Ward	0.4	
Department store	16	
Discount department store	18	
K mart	6	
Specialty store	25	

DRESS BLOUSE

Sears	1	
J.C. Penny	6	
Montgomery Ward	2	
Department store	43	
Discount department store	10	
K mart	3	
Specialty store	23	

enough to create a clear association between a product and its benefits. Thus, in attempting to appeal to a variety of segments, it is possible to end up appealing to none.

Another approach focusing on the consumer defines the position in terms of the *type of appeal*. This form of consumer positioning creates the choice of using claims or imagery. Direct claims tend to be specific, whereas imagery tends to be general. For example, Black & Decker emphasizes particular features of its power tools that provide direct benefits. Windsong perfume attempts to create an image of the type of woman who uses the product and the benefits of using it, for example, attracting handsome, exciting men.

Positioning for specific *usage occasions or functions* reflects a third possibility. Arm and Hammer baking soda is marketed as a deodorant for refrigerators and cat litter boxes, as a supplement to laundry detergent, and as an ingredient for baking. A-1 steak sauce is now pushed as a condiment for hamburgers in addition to its earlier special positioning as a steak flavor enhancer. Figure 2.9 shows one example of usage-occasion positioning.

Positioning by *user category* represents a final consumer application. Dog food is marketed in adult and puppy varieties. Restaurants sometimes have bilingual menus as well as special menus for children or for senior citizens. Even charities position themselves differently for the heavy giver versus the moderate or light giver.

Competitive Positioning Sometimes the best positioning strategy is based on linking the product to something else familiar to the consumer. *Competitive positioning* relates claims to other brands, thus providing a clear frame of reference for the consumer. However, copying a competitor's position is not effective. Rather, a successful competitive positioning strategy must establish its own special position that is relevant to the consumer.

Figure 2.9

This ad for MIRACLE Whip shows a usage-occasion segment appeal.
MIRACLE Whip is a registered trademark of Kraft General Foods, Inc. Reproduced with permission.

Companies such as AT&T, Sprint, and MCI have all been successful in establishing a competitive positioning strategy using three different appeals: service, price, and technology, respectively.

The main danger in utilizing competitive positioning is that a distinctive position may never be established. For instance, The B. F. Goodrich Co. was forced into using a competitive positioning strategy because of the existence of Goodyear. Since so many consumers confused the two companies, Goodrich ran the "We're the one without the blimp" campaign. Still, consumer awareness of Goodyear is much higher, and many products developed by Goodrich are attributed to Goodyear. Goodyear seems to own that position. Another example is illustrated through the Alaska Airline ad (Figure 2.10), which repositions all competitors with respect to service.

Another problem with competitive positioning is that consumers may confuse the brand's position with that of competitors. A popular form of competitive positioning has been *comparative advertising* in which the competitor is either named or alluded to. Evidence shows that many comparative ads confuse the consumer, even to the point of giving the wrong company credit for sponsoring the commercial. It is worthwhile to keep in mind a timely warning: "You cannot compete head-on against a company that has a strong position. You can go around, under or over, but never head-on."[22]

Figure 2.10

Alaska Airlines does a great job of repositioning its competition.
Courtesy of Alaska Airlines, Inc.

Because of the perceived risk involved in the direct competitive position, variations have evolved that appear to retain the strengths of the competitive approach, while eliminating several weaknesses. One variation has become known as the *underdog position*, which was made famous by Avis in the 1960s. Essentially, Avis conceded the number one position to Hertz and assumed the number two position. Obviously, because Avis was the underdog, the company had to "try harder." The success of this approach is well documented.

Another variation that provided considerable success is the *ugly or unpleasant position*. An example of the unpleasant position was a campaign sponsored by Kellogg's corn flakes, called "Discover them again, for the first time." Using the idea that corn flakes are dull and cannot compete with today's fancy cereals, Kellogg's makes fun of itself but points out that its corn flakes possess better roughage benefits than all the "new" cereals. When advertisers admit a negative, the consumer is inclined to give them the position. Listerine mouthwash experienced phenomenal success in the 1970s by employing this same approach. By admitting that its product tasted bad while the competitors' products tasted good, the company was able to convince consumers of the product's increased effectiveness.

Several companies have used a strategy labeled *repositioning the competition*. In essence, companies discovered that in order to position their own brand, it was necessary to reposition their competition in the mind of the consumer. We might think of the "Just say no" campaign as following this positioning strategy because it attempts to reposition the competition (illegal drugs) in the minds of children. A classic example of an extremely successful repositioning strategy was Wendy's "Where's the beef?" campaign of the early 1980s. Clara Peller and her sidekicks visited all Wendy's competitors and comically pointed out the small beef-to-bun ratio of their burgers compared to Wendy's "single." Wendy's still owns the "quality burger" position.

Social Accountability Positioning   The role of public relations is to establish and maintain goodwill between the organization and the public. To a large extent, goodwill is the image the public has of the organization as a good or bad community citizen. Through proper positioning, an organization can be perceived as socially accountable—as a company that cares about the environment, people, the community, and social problems. Social accountability positioning helps establish this positive image.

Every marketer has become aware that the trend toward consumer and environmental protection is increasing. Issues such as AIDS, drugs, the destruction of the rain forests, the widening hole in the ozone layer, street people, and crime have all impacted on businesses. Through the use of special promotional efforts, companies have tried to project the image of good citizenship. For example, Wal-Mart has forced manufacturers to develop biodegradable products and packaging. In addition, Burger King and

McDonald's have stopped using Styrofoam containers. Phillips Petroleum Company has emphasized its research efforts in the medical area.

Selecting Positions

Research such as perceptual mapping provides the foundation for any intelligent choice of a position and a positioning strategy. By itself, however, information about existing and possible positions does not determine what to do with a product or how to do it.

There are several factors to consider when selecting the basis for a position:[23]

- The market position. Is the product a leader, a contending number two, or one of the small brands?
- The positioning used by current competitors;
- The compatibility of the desired positioning with consumers' needs, wants, and current perception of the product's positioning versus its competitors, and a given product class;
- The newness of the considered basis for positioning and its departure from the current practice in the market;
- The resources available to communicate the positioning effectively and the compatibility of the positioning with the firm's marketing strategy;
- The firm's desire for an innovative image rather than a "me too" image;
- The firm's ability to execute the chosen positioning effectively and creatively; and
- The legality of the proposed positioning.

Similar considerations should guide the selection of a positioning strategy. In particular,

- Assess the market position. One argument maintains that a competitor should never attack a leader head-on because it is too difficult to take on the leader at what it does best. Instead, the competitor should flank the leader by finding a major strength or weakness, and go around.
- Consider the current positioning of competitors and the newness of the brand. The first to fill a position will own it, unless it is not properly supported through promotion. Unless there is a distinct price differential, there is no benefit in a competitor positioning itself as a "me too" brand. Several beer producers have failed to fill the light-beer position held by Miller Brewing Co.
- Consider resources available for engaging in a lengthy, expensive positioning war. It is expensive to establish a position, and it is even more expensive to maintain it. Procter & Gamble spends several millions of

dollars each year defending its many product positions from attacks by competitors.

Positioning and Promotion

Early in the 1970s, it was argued that the rapid development of technology was ending the era in which having a unique product was sufficient to ensure success.[24] Instead, how the product was positioned in the mind of the consumer would make the real difference. Since then, many companies have indeed entered the era of positioning. Finding the critical "hot button" (or buttons) that turns on a select group of targeted customers is how Ford turned around its fortunes with the Taurus auto—and lost them again with the Merkur.

As noted earlier, positioning has increasingly come to depend not on actual physical features of a product but on intangible images created in the minds of consumers. This kind of positioning relies heavily on promotion and may be expensive and risky as an ongoing strategy. It is very difficult to maintain a fixed image because of the constant change in the needs and perceptions of the consumer. If this trend toward image creation continues, the role of promotion in positioning will also continue to grow.

Further research is needed to focus on two sets of relationships. First, what is the link between changes in the marketing strategy (product formulation, pricing, promotion, and distribution) of the firm and its competitors and changes in the firm's positioning (by segment)? Second, what is the link between changes in positioning (strategy and execution) and changes in sales, market share, and profitability?

Although all these considerations are important, the interaction between promotion and positioning is particularly critical. For example, several years ago Miller High Life made a decision to reposition itself from "the champagne of beers," a position that appeals to exclusivity, to the reward for a job well done. The new positioning was aimed at the lower-class, heavy drinker of beer. This positioning decision, however, did not necessitate a change in product, price, or method of distribution. Rather, the success of this positioning strategy was contingent totally on the effectiveness of the promotional program. A new advertising campaign was developed that created the new desired image. In conjunction with this advertising program, the Miller distributors were introduced to a set of new sales promotion strategies, including cooperative advertising, trade discounts, and point-of-purchase displays. Finally, the public relations department developed several programs that would reach the new target market.

The position strategy and the promotional mix were clearly interdependent. Not only was the promotional strategy determined by the positioning strategy, but, in turn, the positioning strategy was dependent on the capabilities and effectiveness of the promotional effort. If the advertising campaign was unable to convince the consumer of the new image, a new position might be required. In fact, this adjustment, mandated by the interaction between position and promotion, is constantly going on.

Not all positioning strategies require this level of promotional support. For example, a product such as Come-and-Get-It dog food may wish to position itself as a moderately priced dry dog food directed at the active dog. The company relies primarily on the picture on the package, sales promotion (for example, couponing), pricing, and extensive distribution to support this position. An industrial product such as a submersible water pump may expect the sales force to carry the brunt of the promotional effort, regardless of the position desired. The important point is to appreciate the relationship between the desired position and the promotional effort. Since the promotional program is dependent on the position, it is critical to specify the position clearly and in a manner that allows the delineation of the promotional strategy. Otherwise the match between the two will be inaccurate, and failure may result.

Concept Review

1. To identify a product's existing or desired position, it is important to understand both the product and the consumer. Efforts at understanding include stereotyping, assessing key product attributes through focus groups, and perceptual mapping.
2. Positioning strategies can take three forms:
   a. Consumer positioning—appeals to specific market segments,
   b. Competitive positioning—relates claims to other brands, and
   c. Social accountability positioning—creates a positive social image.
3. General guidelines for positioning:
   a. Consider the product's relative dominance in the market,
   b. Consider the position of competitors, and
   c. Consider resources.
4. Promotion is critical in relaying the selected position to the target audience.

Case 2   *Segmenting the Lawn-Mowing Public*

If you were going to buy a lawn mower, would you look for the least expensive one, find one with the best features, choose only among brand names you trust, or go back to the place you bought the last mower? Your answer places you in one of four major mower-buying categories established by a recent study of the grass-cutting public. Though information about the categories may not mean much to you, it was worth $225,000 to

Briggs & Stratton Corporation, which commissioned the survey. The company believes that if it knows why people buy lawn mowers, it can sell more lawn mower engines.

Background

It may seem odd that Briggs & Stratton would pay for a study of buying habits, since it does not sell products directly to consumers. It makes engines that supply the power to run mowers sold by companies such as Snapper, Toro, Lawn Boy, and Sears. In fact, if you own a lawn mower, it is likely to have a Briggs & Stratton engine, since the company leads the world in the manufacture of small air-cooled engines. But because Briggs & Stratton does not sell to consumers, it can use the survey information only as part of its ongoing relationship with mower manufacturers and their customers.

The Survey

The researchers contacted 120,000 households through the Market Facts Consumer Mail Panel. Those who said they had bought a lawn mower during a one-year period were mailed an extensive questionnaire that asked about brands, prices, retailers, features, and general attitudes towards lawn maintenance. The researchers focused on the attitudes of those people who purchased a walk-behind mower, and they used cluster analysis to define and name the four different buying groups.

The Results

"Outlet-oriented Conservatives" buy where they have bought before. When they need a mower, they rely on their own experience and that of their friends and relatives to help them select a brand and a store. They generally ignore the information that other groups seek and the features that motivate other buyers.

People who look for a mower on sale and focus almost solely on price were labeled "Price Fueled" by the researchers. This group pays attention to advertising and appreciates being able to buy on credit. As a group, they paid about $100 less per mower than the third group, the "Feature Fanatics." These Fanatics tend to read all they can before their purchase, buy the best brands, and pay a lot of attention to such things as the mower's quality and construction and the reputation of the retailer.

The fourth group, "Confident Brand Buyers," pays less attention to price than the other groups do, focusing instead on mower and engine names that they know and on features that will make their work easier.

Besides defining these groups, the researchers identified trends, such as an increase in the number of women buying mowers. Armed with such results, Briggs & Stratton can now take a much more knowledgeable position in its discussions with mower manufacturers. Knowing which features sell mowers to which groups, what the competition offers, and where and why people buy mowers can help the mower manufacturers appeal more successfully to the buying public. And if the manufacturers sell more mowers, Briggs & Stratton will sell more engines.

Case Questions

1. What bases were used to determine lawn mower user segments?
2. What other factors could be used to segment this consumer group? What factors might retailers of lawn mowers use to segment their market?
3. Given this information, how would you position lawn mowers? How would you promote lawn mowers?

Case Source: "Survey Defines Lawn Mower Purchasing Habits," *Quirk's Marketing Research Review* (December 1988): 26, 28–29.

Summary

This chapter examined the three strategic approaches to the marketplace— market aggregation, market segmentation, and product position. Market aggregation assumes that the marketplace is homogeneous, and a standardized marketing mix is employed. Market segmentation takes an opposite perspective. Here, the marketer views the marketplace as heterogeneous, and one or more target markets is selected. Product positioning is related to both aggregation and segmentation. It consists of selecting tangible or intangible product characteristics in order to place the product in its optimum place in the mind of the consumer. These three strategies are linked by product differentiation, which is simply changing the product, either tangibly or intangibly. The bulk of this chapter describes and analyzes market segmentation and product positioning.

The bases for segmentation include industrial vs. consumer users, geography, demographics, usage level, and psychological factors. For industrial markets, the typical bases for segmentation are product, organizational, and decision-making characteristics. Selecting a target market is the point of segmentation, and it involves four steps: (1) identify basic market segments, (2) further describe these segments, (3) apply the criteria of a good segment, and (4) select one or more target markets. Promotional efforts should be customized for each target market.

The bases for positioning are product features, product benefits, specific usage occasions, and user category. Positioning also entails several substrategies: consumer, competitive, and social accountability. Much of a company's position is created through promotional efforts.

Discussion Questions

1. Distinguish among the three strategies—product differentiation, market segmentation, and positioning.

2. What bases would you use to determine whether the toothpaste market should be grouped into a "drinker's toothpaste" segment or a "businessperson's toothpaste" segment?

3. Why is demographic segmentation alone not always a sufficient means of target market identification? Suggest a better basis.

4. Describe how an industrial market could be segmented in respect to size, geography, SICs, and decision-making process.

5. Your company markets microwavable dinners. Your research suggests that 40 percent of your customers are coupon prone. What additional information would you need to determine whether this percentage is a possible target market?

6. Select ads from four companies that depict a clear position.

7. What is perceptual mapping? How is it useful in positioning?

8. Why does the development of a promotional strategy require an understanding of positioning?

9. For what types of products is positioning likely to be an important consideration?

10. Discuss the statement "Positioning is nothing new; in fact, it is the same process as segmentation and differentiation."

Suggested Projects

1. Identify four ads that appeal to a unique market segment. Assess how well they meet the criteria for a good segment.

2. Select a product or brand that you feel has a well-established position. Suggest specific promotional decisions that would change its position for the better and for the worse.

References

1. Peter R. Dickson and James L. Ginter, "Market Segmentation, Product Differentiation, and Marketing Strategy," *Journal of Marketing*, Vol. 51, No. 2 (April 1987): 1–10.

2. "Singles Surge," *American Demographics* (January 1986): 26.

3. A. L. Otten, "Odds and Ends," *The Wall Street Journal* (September 16, 1988): 19.

4. Dick Warren Twedt, "How Important to Marketing Strategy Is the 'Heavy User'?" *Journal of Marketing* (January 1964): 71–72.

5. Pete Emgardio, Ronald Graver, Jo Ellen Davis, and Lois Therrien, "Fast Times on Avenida Madison," *Business Week* (June 6, 1988): 62–65.

6. John F. Willenborg and Robert E. Pitts, "Gasoline Prices: Their Effect on Consumer Behavior and Attitudes," *Journal of Marketing* 41 (January 1977): 24–30.

7. "Nestlé's Infant Formula: The Consequences of Spurning the Public Image," *Marketing Mistakes*, 3rd ed., Robert F. Hartley, ed. (Columbus, OH: Grid Publishing Co., 1986): 47–61.

8. Harold Kassarjian and Mary Jane Sheffit, "Personality and Consumer Behavior: An Update," in H. H. Kassarjian and T. S. Robertson, eds., *Perspectives in Consumer Behavior*, 3rd ed. (Glenview, IL: Scott, Foresman, 1981): 160–180.

9. Joseph T. Plummer, "How Personality Makes a Difference," *Journal of Advertising Research*, Vol. 24, No. 6 (December 1984–January 1985): 27–31.

10. "The Hearts of New-Car Buyers," *American Demographics* (August 1991): 14.

11. Christopher Knowlton, "Consumers: A Tougher Sell," *Fortune* (September 26, 1988): 65–74.

12. Carrie Goerne, "Survey: If You Must Know, Just Ask One of These Men," *Marketing News* (July 22, 1991): 13.

13. Bickly Townsend and Martha Farnsworth Riche, "Two Paychecks and Seven Lifestyles," *American Demographics* (August 1987): 24–29.

14. Yoram Wind and Richard Cardozo, "Industrial Market Segmentation," *Industrial Marketing Management* 3 (1974): 153–166.

15. Philip Kotler, *Marketing Management: Analysis, Planning, Implementation, and Control*, 7th ed. (Englewood Cliffs, NJ: Prentice-Hall, Inc., 1991): 278.

16. Ronald E. Frank, "Market Segmentation Research: Findings and Implications," in Frank M. Bass, Charles W. King, and Edgar A. Pessemier, eds., *The Application of the Sciences to Marketing Management* (New York: John Wiley & Sons, 1968): 39–68.

17. Tony Rambaut, "Getting Through to Business Customers," *Direct Marketing* (March 1989): 78–81.

18. Julie Liesse, "Purina's Latest Target is 'Mature' Cats," *Advertising Age* (June 18, 1990): 3.

19. Andy Marken, "Positioning Key Element for Effective Marketing," *Marketing News*, Vol. 21, No. 4 (March 3, 1987): 7.

20. Linden Davis, "Grasp Behavior Before Picking Target Markets," *Marketing News* (Chicago: American Marketing Association Publication, 1977): P 1.

21. David Snyder and Peter D. Waldstein, "Sears Clothes Woes," *Advertising Age* (July 18, 1988): 18.

22. Jack Trout and Al Ries, "The Positioning Era Cometh," *Advertising Age* 24 (April 1972): 35–38.

23. *Ibid.*

24. *Ibid.*

CHAPTER

3

Promotion and the Marketing Mix

Consider This:

Post-its—A New Product Category

Today's young people may find it hard to believe, but self-sticking note pads didn't always exist. We take the pads for granted today; they're as ubiquitous as staples and Scotch tape, another product made by Post-it's creators, 3M. But the Post-it note almost didn't make it to the public, and its history provides a number of lessons in bringing a new product to market and getting people to buy it.

Art Fry, a 3M scientist, came up with the idea for Post-its not on the job but in church, where he sang in the choir. Fry used slips of paper to keep his place in his hymnal, but they kept falling out. He recognized that the solution to his problem was an adhesive that hadn't proven sticky enough for its original application.

Although 3M is now known for its nurturing of innovative ideas, it did not respond warmly to Fry's invention in 1974. The pads seemed too expensive to replace scratch pads, and initial test marketing results were disappointing. The problem was that the pads were so new, they really weren't replacing anything, at least anything that worked better than Fry's useless slips of paper. But once 3M used all-out marketing to publicize the product in Idaho, consumer response was overwhelming.

Martin/Williams, the ad agency chosen to publicize Post-its, made a few false starts. First it tried to sell the pads as a communication breakthrough. Then it tried the line "Save time, save money." Both approaches were unsuccessful. Finally it convinced 3M that the product needed a substantial advertising budget so that it could be presented as a solution for as many different problems as possible.

This approach worked, and in fact precisely because they are so versatile, Post-its have helped make 3M one of the country's most profitable companies. People use them to carry on discussions in the company lounge, to leave messages for the mail carrier, to label moving boxes. Hundreds of Post-its were used in the creation of this very book. They are now available in 45 countries and in 300 varieties in the United States alone. Norweigians use more Post-its than the citizens of any other country, and favorite Post-it sizes and shapes vary around the world. As Post-it's ads are now printing out, the product's success proves that the simplest ideas are often the best.

Source: Cathy Madison, "13 Years Later, All the World Is Stuck on Post-Its," *Adweek* (February 19, 1990): 49.

T he success of the Post-it notes is the exception rather than the rule. Most new products fail. They fail because they were poorly researched, unfairly priced, inappropriately distributed, or simply did not meet the needs and wants of a significant number of consumers. Sometimes the results of research, price, distribution, and meeting the consumer's wants and needs are positive, but the consumer still remains uninformed or unimpressed. Thus, the promotional effort has failed. Marketing elements must all work in harmony if the product is to have its best chance for success. To help achieve this integration, the promotion manager must understand all facets of the product, tangible and intangible, as well as pricing and methods of distribution.

The intent of this chapter is to bring into focus the position of promotion within the marketing mix. We examine how aspects of the product, the price, and the place of distribution in themselves convey promotional messages, how these marketing elements affect the impact of promotion, and how they influence the selection of a promotional mix. Although no single textbook can provide a complete discussion of all the interactions that take place between promotion and other factors, it is important to begin by gaining a basic understanding of how promotion interacts with other elements of the marketing mix.

Fitting Promotion into the Mix

Of all the components of the marketing mix, promotion is the most likely to get out of hand unless all the other elements are carefully considered. Promotional strategy involves several elements and usually a number of individuals. It requires specialized, creative talent that is difficult to direct and control. Moreover, designers of promotional material are often overimpressed with the importance of their function. These factors tend to push promotional strategy away from the overall plan. Therefore, blending promotion into the rest of the marketing mix requires a strong and talented individual who has a firm understanding of the strategy as well as the marketing mix.

The best way to make sure that the promotional strategy fits with the other marketing mix elements is to assess it carefully before proceeding with the process. Three considerations are necessary.

First, the promotional strategy should be compatible with company objectives, policies, organization, and capabilities. The promotion manager, along with the marketing manager, must review promotional plans to make sure they have been kept within established constraints and are in harmony with overall corporate objectives. Recall from Chapter 1 that this process is interactive. The promotion manager is therefore aware of corporate policies and objectives at the outset of promotional planning and remains influenced by them throughout the planning process. In turn, top management may modify policies and objectives as a result of feedback from the promotional planner. This congruence between corporate objectives and promotional planning sometimes breaks down in the creative implementation. For example, in late 1990, the Volvo corporation fired its ad agency of twenty-four years, Scali, McCabe, Sloves, because the agency had rigged the Volvo car shown in a "monster truck" demonstration. This impropriety by the agency was clearly in conflict with the policies and objectives of Volvo.[1]

The match between marketing and promotion is the second consideration. Some organizational changes (that is, staffing and organizational structure) may be permitted to facilitate certain promotional tasks, but drastic reorganization of the marketing function should not be involved. In every respect, plans for promotion should be consistent with the marketing objectives and target markets specified by the marketing plan. If the objective is to create a competitive advantage or carve out a market niche, promotion will normally receive heavy emphasis. Planners must carefully scrutinize their promotional plans to make sure they are working toward that objective. They must also examine their plans in terms of the marketing target. Are the promotional efforts aimed at the precise segment the company hopes to reach? Have the sales methods and advertising media been well selected to reach these particular targets? If, for some reason, promotional plans have veered from their original marketing targets, they should be brought back on course before being incorporated into the overall plan. Land's End, direct marketer of outdoor sportswear, clearly matches its target market and its media strategy. The target market consists of males and females, twenty-four to forty-five years old, with an income over forty thousand dollars, and an interest in outdoor activities. The company promotes its products through *Sports Afield, Sports Illustrated,* and direct mailing its own catalog, its primary vehicle.

Third, managers must determine to what extent the promotional objectives and promotional strategy are compatible. Planners frequently lose sight of basic promotional objectives as they become deeply involved in the details of their plan. For Volvo, losing control of the ad agency has proven to be a painful mistake. The promotional objective—to demonstrate the safety of the Volvo—became distorted through the execution of the idea.

Concept Review It is important to understand how promotion should be integrated with the other marketing mix elements. There are three basic considerations:
1. Promotional strategy should be compatible with company objectives, policies, and capabilities.
2. There must be a match between marketing and promotion objectives.
3. Marketing and promotional objectives should be compatible.

The Product Mix

A good product is the nucleus of marketing. The term **product** refers to a bundle of attributes, both tangible and intangible, offered by the firm. It includes the elements supporting the physical product (for example, brand, package, warranty, colors) as well as its emotional components (for example, status, self-esteem, security). A product can be a single commodity or a service, a group of commodities or services, a commodity-service combination, or a combination of several commodities and services. An example of a commodity-service combination is the college or university you currently attend; the education you receive via the classroom and labs represents the commodity, which is supported by a variety of services, such as dormitories, bookstores, parking, and so forth.

The intent of the product is to meet the needs and wants of target markets. The intent of promotion is to communicate the product to those target markets. Thus, the linkage between product and promotion is vital. However, the nature of this linkage changes. That is, the role of promotion and the most effective promotional mix vary, depending on the type of product, where it is in its life cycle, and strategic components of the product itself. In this section we examine these three elements—classification, life cycle, and strategic components—and how they interact with promotion in various ways.

Product Classifications

The two most common ways to categorize products are as consumer versus industrial products and as goods products versus service products.

Consumer and Industrial Products   The traditional classification of products divides them into consumer products and industrial products. Products purchased for personal or family consumption with no intention of resale are **consumer products. Industrial products** are those purchased by an organization or an individual that will be modified for or distributed to an ultimate consumer in order to make a profit or meet some other business objective.

Sometimes this distinction is not crystal clear. For example, manufacturers purchase bathroom supplies, office supplies, and cleaning supplies just as consumers do. Similarly, consumers may purchase wholesale building supplies for a home remodeling project. Nevertheless, the two groups are consistently distinguished by size of purchase and intent to make a profit.

This classification has promotional implications. Because the decision to buy industrial products is usually made by professional purchasing agents or committees that place great importance on costs, the decision is assumed to be rational, based on factual information. Moreover, since both parties in the industrial exchange seek one another out, the matching process is much simpler. Thus, the promotional effort for industrial products often includes, in order of emphasis, (1) personal selling; (2) sales promotion, especially trade deals presented through salespeople; and (3) trade advertising that uses print media heavy on information copy. Figure 3.1, for example, shows an ad directed at credit managers who might be able to use a special financial service offered by The Dun & Bradstreet Corp.

In contrast, Figure 3.2 shows an ad for a consumer product, McDonald's McD.L.T. The ad gives little information but has considerable emotional appeal. The McDonald's Corp. spends millions of dollars on print and broadcast media and is also the fast-food leader in sales promotion (highlighted through coupons and sweepstakes) as well as public relations activities, especially in local communities.

In general, as McDonald's promotional program illustrates, promotion of consumer products responds to the physical dispersion of the market and the tendency of consumers to react favorably to emotional appeals that are light on factual content. Therefore promotion of consumer products emphasizes mass selling (through television and print advertising), sales promotion (particularly at the point of purchase), and public relations, as a type of reinforcement. Personal selling becomes relevant when the consumer product is expensive or technically or conceptually complex. The general promotional emphasis for consumer products and industrial products is summarized in Table 3.1.

Goods and Services   Another way to classify products is to label them *goods products* or *service products*. Service products are "intangible activities which provide want satisfaction when marketed to consumer and/or industrial users and which are not necessarily tied to the sale of a product or another service."[2] By this definition, insurance, repair service (but not repair parts), entertainment, housing, and education all count as service products, but "credit, delivery, and packaging services which exist only when there is a sale of an article or another service" do not. Service products are distinguished from goods products by four characteristics, each of which influences promotion:

Figure 3.1

Dun & Bradstreet's ad is a good example of an industrial product being promoted. Reprinted with permission of Dun & Bradstreet, Inc.

"Credit managers don't like to break hearts, but sometimes our sales people just ask for it. They pin their hopes on a new account, then later they ask me for a D&B. "That's too late. "I tell them, 'Customers are like sweethearts. Learn all you can before you get involved.'"

Blind dating is one thing, but new business requires that your eyes be wide open, and right from the start. Which makes that the right time to call Dun & Bradstreet.

We have up-to-date credit reports on millions of American businesses, and we'll send them to you for as little as $22 each. You'll learn how a prospect pays its bills, based on actual payment experiences. You can also get insights into the company's history and, in the majority of cases, check recent financial statements.

New business is a real commitment, so before you start wooing, make sure it's worth winning. Call D&B. The sooner the better.

Dun & Bradstreet Business Credit Services
A company of
The Dun & Bradstreet Corporation

Dun & Bradstreet
The fine art of managing risk.

1. *Intangibility.* Service products cannot be tasted, felt, seen, heard, or smelled before the purchase of the product. Thus the promotional program, especially personal selling and advertising, must describe the benefits derived from the services. This is the primary goal of service product promotion. Mass advertising can stimulate demand through the use of testimonials and other techniques that give the service product tangible features. For example, lodging companies highlight tangible representations of the product such as a check-in process or a satisfied customer.

2. *Inseparability.* Many services are created and consumed at the same time (for example, haircuts, medical care, travel). As a result, inter-

Figure 3.2

McDonald's clever promotion of a consumer product. Courtesy of McDonald's Corporation.

mediaries such as insurance brokers and travel agents often promote services. Another example of inseparability would be a sporting event such as a college football game. The excitement and satisfaction of the event are contingent upon the interaction between the players and the spectators. The enthusiasm of the home team's fans has often been cited as a primary reason for a victory.

3. *Heterogeneity.* It is virtually impossible to standardize the service product, nor is it easy to assess the quality a service purports to deliver. Heterogeneity is partly due to the intangibility of the service product. It is also a function, however, because of the tendency for service products to be labor intensive. The intangibility and the labor-intensive quality of service products are offset by attempts at creating continuity

Table 3.1 **Promotional Emphasis: Consumer Versus Industrial Products**

Promotional Emphasis On	Consumer Products	Industrial Products
Personal Selling	√	√√√
Advertising	√√√	√√
Sales Promotion	√√√	√√√
Public Relations	√√	√

and standardization. McDonald's has been very successful at doing this through its excellent training, standardized building, golden arches, slogan, and so forth. American Express Company has also produced positive results by emphasizing its "satisfied cardholder" advertising campaign using famous celebrities as representatives. Thus promotion often emphasizes evidence of past success such as films of previous vacations.

4. *Perishability.* Service products cannot be stored, and the demand level is difficult to forecast. Promotion therefore attempts to convince more consumers to use the product and to use it in a more predictable pattern. Airlines accomplish this goal by rewarding people with lower prices if they are willing to fly at certain times of the year, days of the week, or times of the day.

Two other characteristics of the promotion of services are worth noting. First, personal selling often plays a larger role with service products than with goods. Because brands are not used extensively, brand preferences and loyalties often cannot be depended upon. The salesperson is therefore depended on to build customer goodwill toward the firm. Second, many service firms, especially in the recreation-entertainment field, benefit considerably from publicity rather than spending on other promotions. Examples include sports coverage by newspapers, radio, and television; newspaper reviews of movies and plays; and travel sections in newspapers. Doctors, lawyers, accountants, and other professionals may participate in various community activities in order to get their name in front of the public. Banks and utility companies promote a community to various companies in order to attract them to the community; they assume that anything that helps the community helps them.

Product Life Cycle

A second framework that is useful in understanding the proper promotional mix for a particular product is the **product life cycle** (PLC). Products, like people, usually have a predictable pattern of development. From its birth to its death, a product exists in different stages and different competitive environments. Its adjustment to these environments determines to a great degree just how successful its life will be. The product life cycle assists the promotion planner in two ways. First, it helps determine the appropriate mix at each stage of the life cycle. Second, in providing the optimum promotion mix, the PLC also provides budgetary guidelines. Knowing that mass advertising is emphasized at a particular stage indicates to the promotion planner that a large amount of money is needed at that time.

The product life cycle is typically divided into four stages: introduction, growth, maturity, and decline (see Figure 3.3). The length of the cycle var-

Figure 3.3

*The traditional life
cycle of a product.*

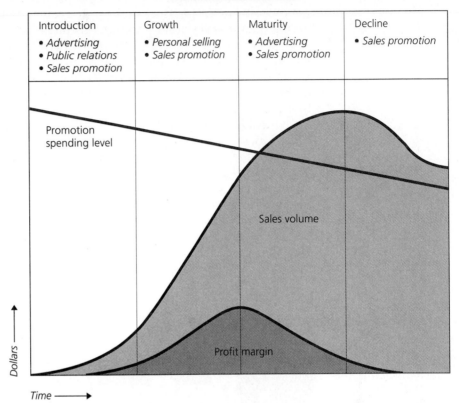

ies among products, ranging from a few weeks to several decades. The shape of the sales and profit curves may vary somewhat among products, although the basic shape and the relationship are about the same as pictured in the figure. Even the duration of each stage may be different among products, and not all products go through all stages.

Introductory Stage In this stage, a newly developed good or service is first presented to its market. In many respects, this stage is the most risky and expensive one. Operations are characterized by high costs, low sales volume, and limited distribution. The promotional program stimulates *primary* rather than *secondary demand*. That is, the type of product rather than the seller's brand is emphasized. The need to create primary demand was particularly true for Post-it notes. During the initial test market consumers viewed the product as expensive scratch paper. It was not until free samples were distributed that consumers could appreciate the value of the product.

Which promotional mix works best during the introductory stage depends partly on the product strategy. If a company launches a new product with a high price in order to recover as much gross profit per unit as possible, it must support this high price with extensive promotion. It may take an enormous amount of mass advertising and personal selling to convince the market of the product's merits at the (premium) level. Extensive promotion serves to accelerate the rate of market penetration. One example of this strategy occurred when the Gillette Sensor shaving system was introduced in 1990. The spectacular 175 million dollar promotion campaign included mass media, couponing, point-of-sale displays, product sampling, and public relations (see Figure 3.4). The product grabbed over 3 percent of the market within three months of its introduction.[3] Unfortunately, this initial success was short lived. Experts posit that the technological breakthrough suggested in the promotions was not evident, and negative word-of-mouth hurt sales.

If the product is truly an innovation, and people who want the product expect to pay a high price, then the promotional effort can be limited to informative advertising that tells the consumer where to purchase the product. This was the case with Roller-Blades. In contrast, new products that are introduced with a relatively low price require a comprehensive promotional mix to provide quick penetration of the market. Entenmann's

Figure 3.4

An extensive promotion campaign launched the Gillette Sensor shaving system.
The Gillette Company

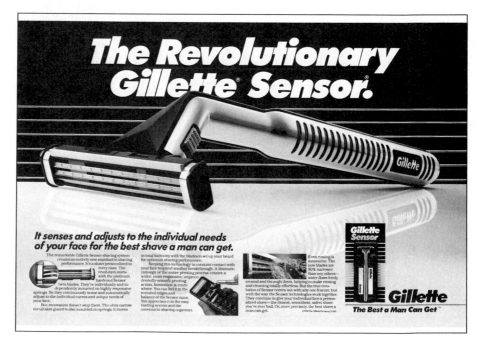

spent twenty million dollars on promotion the first year in introducing their "Good For You" line of baked goods.

Growth Stage   The second stage of the product cycle is the growth stage. By the time the good or service has reached the beginning of the growth stage, its market acceptance is assured. Success feeds upon earlier success: previous purchasers continue their purchasing, and new buyers enter in large numbers. The success of the new product attracts competitors. However, these firms require time to introduce their own versions of the product and to make inroads on the market position held by the innovator. The firm begins to add new product features and refinements to move into new parts of the market.

During this stage, companies tend to maintain their promotional expenditures at the same or a slightly higher level to meet competition and continue educating the market. The aim of advertising often shifts from building product awareness to creating brand conviction and purchase. Finally, as more competitors enter the market, the role of personal selling changes. Now the salesperson must deal with distributors more aggressively. Shelf space is bought at a premium through discounts and a variety of trade programs. As the ultimate consumer is inundated with choices, sales promotion tools such as discounts, coupons, rebates, and sampling may all become important. Premium athletic shoe marketers such as Nike, Inc. and Reebok find themselves currently in this situation.

Maturity Stage   In maturity, the company shares the market with successful and vigorous competitors. This stage is still characterized by continued sales increases, but the rate of increase continually moderates and toward the end of the period becomes almost negligible. Profits of both the manufacturer and the retailers start to decline. Marginal producers are forced to drop out of the market, and price competition becomes increasingly severe.

As these changes occur, the producer assumes a greater share of the total promotional effort as it fights to retain dealers and shelf space. Because of these changes, more of the promotional budget is allocated to trade and consumer deals. This shift to satisfying the retailer rather than the consumer occurs because the consumer has either become brand loyal, in which case promotion is unnecessary, or views the various brand choices as equivalent and is therefore affected by how the retailer promotes the brand at the point of purchase. Another strategy is to search for a new advertising appeal. For instance, the "Marlboro man" campaign was introduced when the brand had reached this stage. But, as time goes by, it is more and more difficult to identify salient product features that can be effectively featured in advertising. Essentially, all the competitors have the necessary technology to match one another, thereby creating products that are viewed as commodities by many consumers.

Decline Stage   The industry enters the decline stage with firms facing severe competition from many directions. For a single-product firm, entrance into decline may warn of eventual collapse. For the multiproduct or diversified company, this stage highlights the importance of product development. It is better to lose sales of an older product to one's own new product than to lose these sales to competitors. In addition, companies that remain in the market withdraw from selling in both small market segments and marginal trade channels. The promotional budget is reduced, advertising is cut, and the sales effort is minimal. Basic sales promotion devices are all that remain.

Sometimes marketers are able to resuscitate a dying product and engage in a *take-off strategy*. They may redesign the product, improving features, quality, or value; or they may appeal to new target markets. A company that did both was Harley Davidson Motorcycles, the manufacturer of the only motorcycle made in the United States. For over twenty years, U.S. motorcycle manufacturers have been steadily losing market share to Japanese manufacturers such as Honda and Suzuki. Harley management, determined to stay in business, redesigned its product line to compete with Japanese competitors. The company also produced television and print ads that emphasized the new designs and had a "made in America" appeal. Public relations was also successful with the placement of sympathetic stories in *Fortune* and *Business Week* and on "60 Minutes." Market share doubled within ten months after Harley made these changes.[4]

Strategic Components of the Product

For every product, regardless of where it is in its life cycle, certain strategic decisions must be made. These decisions include specifying product features and package design, branding, and establishing support services. In many organizations, these decisions are made by the product manager, who uses extensive research to carefully assess the relative importance of these product-related elements in the minds of the customer or potential customer. The equity represented by the Texaco Inc. brand name, for example, is probably more important than product features. These decisions are also made in conjunction with input from the promotion manager. This individual can tell a product manager that emphasizing a product feature that cannot be presented effectively by the sales force is probably a mistake. The result of these decisions becomes an inherent part of the product and thus part of the promotional message.

Product Features Product features of goods products include form, color, size, weight, odor, texture, and material; and reputation, image, expertise, and physical surroundings for service products. From the point of view of the consumer, product features vary in their importance and their competitiveness. In addition, the feature itself connotes unique qualities, benefits, and appeals. For example, a new car offers many features—some critical to consumers and some trivial, some better than those of competitors and some not. All automobile manufacturers offer safety features such as seat belts, reliable tires, bumpers, and safety windshields. Chrysler Corp. and several other manufacturers have taken one more step by including air bags and antilock brakes as standard equipment. Many of the new luxury cars such as Lexus and Infiniti enhance the image of the vehicle with real wood trim, computer-controlled climate systems, and carpeting.

Promotion must be based on a consideration of these features and, in particular, on two questions about them. First, what do the features communicate to the audience? Building an automobile with safety features, for example, shows the consumer that the company really cares about the consumer's well-being. All the company's promotional messages must then be compatible with that perception. Thus Chrysler ads emphasize safety features over style and power. In addition, as a type of sales promotion, Chrysler encourages insurance companies to reduce premiums for owners of Chrysler cars. Sales personnel are trained to stress safety when people enter the showroom. And the public relations department distributes brochures on driver safety.

Second, how should the features be communicated to the target audiences? Which methods of promotion are most likely to be effective depends in part on whether the product is unique. When CD recordings were a new product, for example, their promotion required visual presentation on television and in magazines, supported by a strong direct mail effort and a public relations campaign. But if a product does not have unique features, the company does not want to emphasize this fact in a national television campaign. Instead, the company might promote the product by using a well-known spokesperson and price discounting. Coca-Cola has followed this strategy with its classic brand for over a decade, using Bill Cosby as a spokesperson. Pepsi employs a similar strategy, using its own set of celebrities.

The complexity of the product also suggests specific promotional alternatives. When products are complex, emphasis is placed on promoting them through personal selling and sales promotion such as printed brochures, demonstrations, and point-of-purchase displays. Salespeople and product demonstrations allow consumers to experience the product and ask questions. In contrast, to get across simple ideas or to make consumers aware of a product whose features are easily observed, emphasis is usually placed on advertising. Similarly, advertising is commonly used for products that are familiar to consumers, because these products require only fairly simple messages.

Packaging   **Packaging** is traditionally viewed as the container that holds the product. Thus, in this context, packaging is applicable to a goods product only

Packaging serves three types of purposes: functional, informational, and promotional. *Functional features* of packaging include convenience, safety, and preassortment (that is, placing in individual or group units). Easy-open spouts, resealable openings, plastic handles, family packs, and oven-proof paperboard are all examples. *Informational aspects* of a package usually include basic information such as the names of the product and manufacturer, directions for using the product, information required by law (such as ingredients or shelf-life date), and seals or emblems (such as a USDA stamp). Kraft has also included recipes on the label of its mayonnaise for several years.

The *promotional features* of a package are worth special attention. The package itself serves as a freestanding promotional device by attracting the consumer's attention and creating awareness and a favorable image. The package is also a means of product identification. In fact, competitors often copy the package design of market leaders in order to confuse the consumer. Note the similarity between the famous Campbell Soup Company labels and those of competing store brands.

In fact, all aspects of the package have promotional implications. Functional features may form an important part of the promotional message. Makers of pain relievers boast about offering childproof-but-easy-to-open bottles, for example. Recently, L'eggs pantyhose announced that it would be replacing its plastic egg package with a small cardboard box with an ovoid peak. L'eggs is making this change to address society's increasing concern for the environment. Still, Sara Lee Corporation, the owner of L'eggs, runs the risk of alienating long-time L'eggs customers accustomed to the plastic egg. More generally, the looks and structure of the package help shape the perception of the product. Package color, for example, can affect perceptions such as taste. Red, for instance, is considered a very strong color that communicates strength. No one is likely to change the red packaging of Coca-Cola and its decades of success.

Consider a case in which a company with an established brand offered a new cracker in different packaging. Only background color distinguished the packages; some were red and others yellow. Interviewers asked comparable groups of people a number of questions about the crackers, but each group saw only one kind of package. The groups did not know they were participating in a packaging test. Except for the package, all test variables remained constant, and reactions were obtained both before and after product testing. The "after" evaluation indicated that red was more effective than yellow as a background color; those interviewed thought crackers in the red box tasted better. The crackers in both packages were identical, but, because of the packaging, consumers perceived a difference.[5]

The package itself may persuade customers to change a buying pattern without paying more per unit. *Deal packs* (multiple units of the product banded together) may attract new customers from other product types or brands, counteract the effects of new competition, or strengthen brand ties among current users. Dairy Bell yogurt changed from a single-unit package to two-cup units and increased sales 297 percent in the first week after the redesign.

Resellers are also influenced by the package. An attractive package prompts retailers to order the product and display it appropriately. Packages that take into account the retailer's special storage, handling, and shelving needs also receive favorable reactions. Replacing breakable gallon jugs of bleach with sturdy plastic containers benefited retailers as much as it did consumers. The quick reaction of Johnson & Johnson to repackage its Tylenol product after the 1982 poisonings encouraged resellers to restock the product. The Promotion in Focus section discusses another aspect of packaging that is important to resellers and consumers alike: "environment-friendly" packaging.

Colors, graphics, and typeface all contribute to the successful package that not only stands out on the shelf but also continues to appeal to customers on a functional, psychological, and aesthetic level as they use the product. By pointing out how easy the product is to use, its high status, or its great taste, scent, feel, sound, or look, the package is the only element of a marketing program that extends from point of purchase to point of use. Packaging may also play a critical role in positioning the product. A quality position must be matched with a quality package. Premium candy companies such as Godiva Chocolates carefully wrap and package each morsel of their product. Conversely, inexpensive candies made by Hershey Foods Corp. and others are packaged appropriately, given their price and where they are sold. Failure to match the product with the desired position can negate the best strategy.

In sum, packaging is an important part of the promotional strategy. It is the constant communicator. Packages that are colorful, cleverly designed, functional, and complementary to the product enhance the promotional effort. Such a package facilitates the association between the package and the brand name. Finally, the package is an effective vehicle for carrying sales promotion devices such as contests, coupons, or price discounts. For many companies that do little advertising and sales promotion, the package is a major promotional element.

Promotion in Focus

Environmentally Friendly Packaging

The American public and American companies are confused about their attitudes towards the environment. A significant segment of the public has become aware of how much trash people use and how full the landfills are, and they have demanded that companies stop making so many disposable packages and products. Towns, cities, and states have outlawed such things as styrofoam cups and plastic six-pack holders. Trying to respond to such concerns, manufacturers have come up with packaging that produces less trash. Yet often consumers reject such packages because they are less convenient. Figuring out how to use "environmental friendliness" to sell products has become a major new frontier for promotion managers.

One survey of consumers found that many are willing to pay five percent more for products that come in packages that are environmentally friendly. But it is difficult to identify "friendly" packaging and to translate such sentiments into action. For instance, most people think of cardboard as a more ecologically sound packaging material than plastic, yet waxed cardboard can't generally be recycled, while many types of plastic can.

The drive to cash in on comsumers' desires to help the environment has already led to unsubstantiated claims and a certain skepticism on the part of some consumers. Products claim to be environmentally sound for a number of reasons, some of them more convincing than others, and alert consumers must learn the difference between such things as "recycled" fibers and those made of "post-consumer waste."

The concept of environmentally friendlly packaging is in a difficult transition period, but its future looks bright. In many instances, companies have found that using less or different packaging saves them money besides producing less waste. And this new focus is creating work for eveyrone in an organization who deals with the public. Companies must become better at listening to consumers and gauging what they really want and what they're willing to sacrifice in terms of cost and convenience. At the same time, marketers must continue to improve their ways of educating the public and of coming up with ways to promote the environmental aspects of their products without being misleading. Specialists in environmental promotion are likely to be in great demand in the coming decades.

Sources: Cyndee Miller, "Use of Environment-Friendly Packaging May Take Awhile," *Marketing News* (March 19, 1990): 18. Alecia Sevasy, "Ecology and Buyer Wants Don't Jibe," *The Wall Street Journal* (August 23, 1989): B1.

Branding   A **brand** is the name, term, design, symbol, or any other feature that identifies the good, service, institution, or idea sold by a marketer. The **brand name** is that part of a brand that can be spoken, such as words, letters, or numbers. MCI is a brand name. The **brand mark,** also known as the **logo,** is that part of the brand that cannot be spoken. It can be a symbol, picture, design, distinctive lettering, or color combination. The AT&T customized globe is found on all their promotions; Figure 3.5 gives some other examples. When a brand name or brand mark is legally protected through registration with the Patent and Trademark Office of the Department of Commerce, it becomes a **trademark.** The process of developing and selecting brand names and brand marks is the **branding strategy.**

The importance of the branding strategy is evident. If a company can create a memorable brand name and then produce quality products that are associated with that name, the result is extremely powerful. For the seller, a brand name means that a product can be advertised and distinguished from substitutes. From the perspective of the buyer, the brand may imply consistent quality or satisfaction, enhance shopping efficiency, or call attention to new products. Brand names make it easier for customers to find products.

The power of a brand has been recently demonstrated by a number of companies. Eastman Kodak Co. used its name to enter the battery business, even though it does not manufacture the batteries it sells. In 1988,

Figure 3.5

Examples of logos that effectively identify their brands.
© *1992 The Coca-Cola Company. "Coca-Cola" and the Dynamic Ribbon device are trademarks of The Coca-Cola Company. HERSHEY'S is a registered trademark of Hershey Foods Corporation. Cambell's is a registered trademark of Campbell Soup Company. Kellogg's® is a registered trademark Kellogg Company. All rights reserved.*

Kodak gave its batteries the company's familiar red and yellow "trade dress" found on most of its film products. By the end of that year it had won between 5 percent and 10 percent of the five-billion-dollar worldwide market.[6] Similarly, the name of the clothing retailer, the Gap, has achieved superstar brand status. A Gap label is sewn into every garment to raise the name to the dignity of a brand in customers' consciousness.

The selection of a brand name should be made carefully and supported by solid research. The brand name is the main source of identification for the product. It is often the first thing that comes to mind when people think about a product type. All the promotional elements include the brand name, and it is permanent. Here are a few guidelines to follow in selecting a brand name.

1. The brand name should create a positive impression such as Peter Pan peanut butter. The Merkur brand name, for example, is foreign sounding to many Americans and therefore creates a negative image.

2. The brand name should be easy to distinguish from competing names and should enhance recall. It should be brief and easy to pronounce, like Head and Shoulders or Tide.

3. The brand name should be logically associated with the product, Timex and Chips Ahoy!, for example.

4. The brand name should be physically adaptable to all the ways in which it will appear, for example, on packaging, in advertising, and on other display materials. The Black & Decker Dust Buster portable vacuum is a brand name that works well on all forms of promotion. The words are easy to see and understand, and they fit both with print and broadcast media.

5. The brand name should be selected in light of the promotional strategy, which should do everything possible to reinforce the brand name. The Eveready Energizer Pink Bunny campaign is an excellent example of how a promotional strategy can support a brand name. Every ad contains the brand name and a picture of the product.

Related Services   Behind every product is a series of supporting services. For example, if you purchase a ten-speed bike at Sears, you are offered the use of Sears's credit, assembly for a small fee, delivery, an explicit warranty, a return policy, and maintenance and repair. In this world of "me too" products and high consumer expectations, the availability of support services may be the primary reason to select a particular brand. IBM, for example, is famous for a twenty-four-hour service policy and a willingness to "take care of customers, no matter what the costs."

One role of promotion is to inform consumers about support services and to provide evidence that such services are important. Sometimes, as in the case of a complex return policy or a set-up fee, a sales representative should contact the consumer and explain the service personally. In other instances, such as free delivery, the service is straightforward and can be described in the advertising copy. Unusual services can serve as the basis for a public relations campaign. For example, Sears provides a toll-free number that can be used by customers of their "crank it" battery. If the battery fails, a call to this number will send out a service vehicle to the customer at any time of the night or day. This service was highlighted in print and television ads.

Concept Review   *Product* refers to a bundle of attributes, either tangible or intangible, offered by the firm. The following elements of the product interact with promotion:
1. Product class, that is, industrial versus consumer products and goods products versus service products.
2. Life cycle of the product, that is, introductory, growth, maturity, and decline stages.
3. Strategic components, that is, product features, packaging, branding, and support services.

The Channels Mix

All products, whether goods or services, have a channel of distribution. Simply put, a **channel of distribution** is the marketing mechanism used to present, deliver, and service the product for customers. In some instances, the channel of distribution may begin with the raw materials suppliers. Automobile makers, for example, must buy steel, plastic, and rubber from raw material providers. From this perspective, the channel of distribution includes all the institutions, processes, and relationships that facilitate the achievement of a channels goal. For example, if a manufacturer utilizes direct mail to distribute products, then channel strategy revolves around the design of a system for delivering the product to the consumer, for receiving payment, and for servicing the product or allowing returns. In contrast, the channel strategy of a manufacturer of machine parts focuses on identifying wholesalers or retailers who will locate customers, sell them the product, and make sure it is delivered and serviced. Wholesalers and retailers are collectively called **resellers.**

A manufacturer must consider how the channel of distribution itself conveys a promotional message. For example, manufacturers must assess the image of a possible retail outlet. The store's image is determined by the consumer's attitude toward the retailer's advertising, services, convenience, layout, exterior appearance, location, and personnel. Consumers tend to patronize stores that fit their self-images, and successful retailers project store images to match their target customers. Therefore, Rolex watches would not expect K Mart Corp. to be able to implement its promotional strategy. Timex realizes that Nieman Marcus is unlikely to carry its watches because the promotional strategy used by Timex would detract from the image that the store tries to project.

It is critical that marketers who use resellers gain their support for the promotional strategy. To do so, the marketer should (1) design specific promotional activities that can be performed effectively and efficiently by resellers, (2) communicate this information accurately to resellers, and (3) motivate resellers to employ these promotional activities in the suggested manner.

Push and Pull Strategies

Promotional strategies may demand a little or a lot from resellers. One strategy may require that resellers do little more than stock the product; another strategy may depend on the reseller's ability to explain to consumers how a product works. Promotional strategies can be broadly classified as push or pull strategies, depending on how much is required of the reseller.

A **pull strategy** directs marketing efforts at the ultimate consumer and emphasizes large advertising expenditures. It may include additional incentives to buy through the use of coupons, rebates, free samples, or sweepstakes. These promotional efforts should create sufficient consumer demand to "pull" the product through the channels. Thus a pull strategy requires little promotional effort from the resellers. Their primary responsibilities revolve around storing, shelving, and maintaining the product.

A pull strategy seems plausible if demand for the product is high, and if it is possible to differentiate the product by its real or emotional features. Yet examples of companies that have successfully implemented a pull strategy are rare. Some markets, such as children, often respond to a pull strategy. Occasionally, a novelty product, a fad, or a one-time event can create this overt and aggressive behavior on the part of the consumer. Healthy Choice frozen dinners is an example of a product that was successfully implemented by a pull strategy.

In contrast, a **push strategy** directs marketing efforts at resellers and thus depends greatly on their personal selling abilities. The manufacturer "pushes" the product through the channels; the resellers are asked to demonstrate products, distribute sales promotion devices, and actively sell the product (see Figure 3.6).

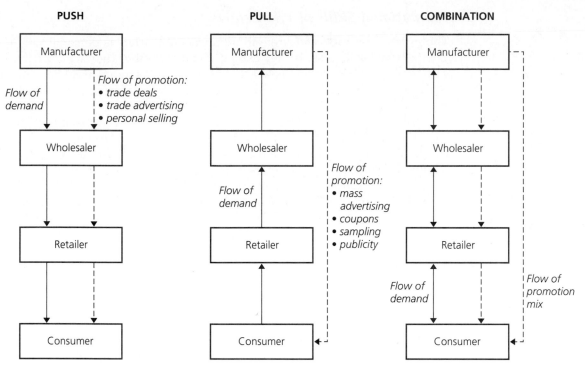

Figure 3.6
Push, pull, and combination strategies.

If the product is relatively new and many acceptable substitutes exist, then a push strategy is appropriate. Marketers of imported beers often use a push strategy to stimulate reseller support. They do not have large enough budgets to engage in mass advertising. Because much is asked of resellers, much stimulation on the part of manufacturers is required.

Most companies use various combinations of push and pull. Marketing representatives for L'eggs pantyhose call on supermarkets, discount stores, and drug stores in order to restock product, sell special promotions, offer trade deals, and fight for shelf space. The company also spends a great deal of money on a multimedia advertising campaign. A similar process is followed by 3M in promoting Post-it notes. However, since 3M sells a large percentage of the product to businesses and institutions, its push and pull strategies are far more complex than those employed by L'eggs.

Fortunately for marketers who promote through resellers, there is a high level of consistency as to which type of resellers can perform which type of promotional activity better. The promotional capabilities of wholesalers and retailers are discussed next.

Promotional Skills of Wholesalers

The primary promotional strength of most wholesalers is personal selling. The personal selling skills they exhibit dictate whether they will distribute sufficient quantities of goods to achieve success. As much as 80 percent to 90 percent of the total promotional budget in wholesaling goes toward personal selling.

Wholesalers do not often advertise. There are, however, instances when special types of advertising strategies are employed. For example, regional wholesalers are apt to use direct mail, trade papers, or catalogs. Local wholesalers may use newspapers or local radio. The copy tends to be simple and straightforward with few pictures or illustrations.

Almost all wholesalers do use sales promotion devices. The most common is the distribution of product catalogs. Since wholesalers usually carry a great many product lines, it is imperative that their salespeople have catalogs to refer to and distribute to customers. Wholesalers may also participate in trade shows by setting up booths and demonstrations.[7]

Promotional Skills of Retailers

The promotional abilities of retailers range even more widely than those of wholesalers. At one end of the continuum is a company such as Sears, Roebuck and Co., which has the capacity to match the promotional efforts of the largest manufacturers. At the other end is an individual operating a shoe repair shop who considers an entire promotional strategy to consist of good customer service and three lines in the Yellow Pages.

The role of the retailer in promoting the manufacturer's product is contingent on at least three considerations. First, what kind of store is it—convenience store, shopping store, or specialty store? Shopping and specialty stores offer greater opportunity for promotional activity, while convenience stores rely strongly on location and product variety. For convenience stores, the primary promotional technique is mass advertising. A case in point is the national advertising campaign of 7-Eleven Stores.

Second, what types of products are carried by the retailer? If the products are undifferentiated, low unit value and price are the major selling attributes, and there is little hope for a wide promotional effort.

Third, what market segment concerns the retailer? For example, if the target market is concerned with quality at any price, then retailers will employ advertising, personal selling, and elaborate point-of-purchase displays. Conversely, a price-conscious target market would prompt a low-key promotional strategy. Table 3.2 lists appropriate cost, value-added, and quality appeal for various types of retailers. The retail appeals could either be matched with those of the manufacturer, or the retailers could employ their own appeals. The latter would be particularly true in the case

Table 3.2 **Retail Type Matched with Cost, Value-added, and Quality Appeals**

Category	Cost Appeals	Value-added Appeals	Quality Appeals
Bank	Service charges; interest rates	Variety of services; easy-to-understand services	Financial stability; personal interest in customers
Building product	Low cost	Training seminars; easy to install	Easy to work with; durable
Coffee shop	Low prices; specials	Hours open; take-out items	Cleanliness; taste of food
Convenience store	Reasonable prices	Items easy to find; variety	Clean; interior
Discount store	Sales/clearances; low prices	Easy return; check cashing	Selection; well-known brands; pleasant atmosphere
Family steak house	Low prices; coupons	Salad bar; things for kids	Taste of steak; atmosphere
Furniture manufacturer (trade)	Low price; range of prices	Quick response to requests; on-time delivery	Nationally known brand name; patterns available
Furniture store	Credit policies; low prices; price ranges	Delivery; display method	Well-known brands; knowledgeable salespeople
Gas station	Low prices	Windshield cleaning equipment; speed of pumps	No alcohol in gas; octane rating
Ice cream	Low cost; specials; coupons	Container size	Taste; richness; amount of flavor; creaminess
Jewelry store	Sales; low prices; low interest rates	Personal interest in customers; fast service	Unique jewelry; custom designing
Pizza restaurant	Specials; coupons; promotions; low prices	Fast service; home delivery; take out; variety	Hot product; taste; consistent product
Psychiatric hospital	Low-cost treatment	Comfortable rooms; visitor accommodations	Experienced physicians; innovative treatment
Specialty tune-up clinic	Reasonable cost; specials	Car ready when promised; fast service	Fixed right the first time; qualified mechanics
Supermarket	Low prices	Well-stocked; check cashing	Clean; selection; specialty departments
Temporary service	Reasonable cost	Performance guarantee; follow-up	Competence of temps; understands what we need

Source: *Marketing News* (September 25, 1989): 20. Reprinted by permission.

of service products such as banks and psychiatric hospitals. For example, many psychiatric hospitals that specialize in the treatment of substance abusers use the quality appeal. Advertising usually consists of local television, newspaper, and radio ads, with the message strategy emphasizing a unique treatment, speed of recovery, and concern for the family. Such hospitals also promote to physicians and agencies that make referrals. Open houses are often part of the promotional strategy, along with the desire that hospital management maintain a high profile in the community.

Retailers can offer manufacturers personal selling, advertising, and sales promotion. For the traditional retailer, personal selling is the key to success. It is the salesperson who provides product information, handles objections, closes the sale, and takes orders.

The typical retailer is eager to advertise in local media. If the manufacturer is willing to supplement this advertising either financially or through technical expertise, all the better. The retailers' main concern is that the advertising be directed at their own customers. The media used, the copy employed, the size and frequency of ads, and so on will vary from one retailer to another. Manufacturers such as Crayola who need their product demonstrated through a medium like television will be disappointed by the newspaper approach used by supermarkets.[8]

Retailers are at their best when it comes to sales promotion, particularly display activities. Retailers have become experts in the use of both window displays and point-of-purchase displays. It is through these devices that customers compare prices and selections. In addition, displays may be the main motivator of impulse buying. Manufacturers have designed and distributed millions of dollars worth of store displays that they try to place in retail stores. Given the limited amount of space available for window, shelf, and in-store display areas, the cost of convincing retailers to use these displays may be as great as the cost of designing and producing them. Even if the space is purchased from a retailer one time, there is no assurance that this arrangement of display space will continue.

Retailers also engage in other sales promotion activities. They are willing to set up in-store demonstrations, sponsor community activities, and support cooperative efforts among retailers. These types of activities are varied, and it is difficult for manufacturers to use them effectively.

Strategies for Service-Product Channels

Service-product manufacturers also use a channel of distribution. A hospital, for example, moves the consumer (patient) through the channel, which may include an admissions stage, as assessment stage, an action stage (the treatment), a recovery stage, and a follow-up stage. Each stage requires different institutions, different expertise, methods of payment, and so forth. Hospitals also use resellers, in the form of referring physicians, ambulance services, and other medical institutions.

Promotional strategies for service-products channels have three distinctive characteristics. First, they attempt to make tangible the intangible elements in the channel. Hospitals often allow perspective patients to make a dry run, which includes introductions to personnel they will meet later. American Express Tours assigns a trip counselor to each traveler. The counselor introduces himself or herself early in the process and remains the contact person for the traveler from that point on. The traveler is also given a personal membership card. Second, since the perceived risk associated with moving through a service-products channel is high, the promoter tries to reduce the risk with additional information and incentives. A hospital can provide pamphlets describing the procedure to be performed and the step-by-step scheduling on the day of the procedure as well as an opportunity for the patient to speak with former patients who have had the procedure. By providing a free travel guide, brochures, and discount admission tickets in return for being on time, American Express Tours reduces the perceived risk in traveling to Europe for the first time. Finally, for the consumer, success in negotiating a service-product channel often depends on the capabilities of resellers. Hospitals must rely on ambulance services, pharmacies, and laboratories to service their patients. American Express Tours is at the mercy of airlines, hotels, bus drivers, and tour guides to process their customers. Therefore, the promotional plan includes incentives to motivate resellers and, possibly, explanations to customers about what can be expected from resellers.

Concept Review

1. The channel of distribution is the marketing mechanism used to present, deliver, and service the product for customers.
2. The following elements of the channel of distribution interact with promotion in a number of ways:
   a. The promotional tasks assigned to resellers, that is, push strategy versus pull strategy
   b. The type of resellers used, that is, wholesalers and retailers
   c. The promotional strategies for service products, that is, to make intangible elements tangible, reduce the perceived risk, and offer extra incentives to motivate resellers

The Price Mix

Superficially, price is easy to define. Prices allocate resources. A **price** is thus the amount the customer pays for a good or a service. However, a price has different meanings for sellers and buyers. To the seller, price is a source of revenue and the determinant of profit. To ultimate consumers, the price represents a sacrifice of purchasing power. Money spent on one product will be unavailable for other choices. Resellers who buy goods for resale view price in much the same way, as a negative element of the product. Except when they are buying prestige goods and services, people ordinarily prefer lower to higher prices.

For the promotion manager, price is a crucial consideration. All promotion must be carefully coordinated with the pricing strategy, for several reasons. First, a firm is competitive when it offers comparable satisfaction at lower prices. Most buying decisions are made by balancing expected satisfactions against the sacrifice, the price; that is, buyers weigh the price they must pay against the performance they expect to obtain. If promotion does not accurately communicate this relationship between price and performance, then the pricing strategy will fail. Furthermore, the price helps shape attitudes toward a product; for promotion to be effective, the messages sent by both the price and promotion must be consistent. Finally, promotional techniques are the primary means for delivering pricing information to consumers.

Pricing Strategies

Price is first of all a competitive weapon. Price is often the only element consumers use to differentiate one brand from another. Intelligent marketers must know when this is the case. They must also know how consumers perceive different prices, how they view the prices charged by competitors, and how they feel about price increases and reductions. For example, marketers of board games know that most of the games are bought as presents, when consumers are less sensitive to prices. Parker Brothers, a manufacturer of popular board games, has established a strong reputation in the market and a position as the price leader. Therefore, Parker charges the highest prices for its products. Competitors are forced to charge lower prices because of their weaker reputation and market position.

When a marketer decides to use price as a competitive weapon, the intent is to emphasize price as an issue by showing how the marketer's price matches or beats competitors' prices. Either a cost-based or a demand-based pricing strategy is used. The marketing strategy dictates which approach is best, and the result influences the promotion strategy. In general, a cost-based pricing strategy produces a low price relative to competition, while a demand-based pricing strategy could result in a high, moderate, or low price.

When a **cost-based pricing** strategy is used, the company competes by having lower prices than competitors. Discount stores such as K Mart and

Wal-Mart tend to use this pricing strategy. Efforts to build sales and satisfy every need of the consumer are kept to a minimum. Support services such as sales personnel, free delivery, and additional price discounts are also kept to a minimum. When a cost-based pricing strategy is used, a lower price or a better price-value relationship is the primary promotional appeal.

When a **demand-based pricing** strategy is used, the company competes by focusing on the needs and wants of consumers. Cost control is not ignored, but it is less important. The marketers of Le Menu gourmet frozen foods recognize that some consumers will pay a premium price for high-quality frozen dinner. The makers of Polo discovered that the image of a brand can dictate premium prices. When a company uses demand-based pricing, it might keep an unprofitable product in order to satisfy the consumer. Cost savings may or may not be passed on to the customer, and services are provided, either free or for a charge. In general, when a company uses demand-based pricing, promotions should encourage consumers to think of the price as much more than the figure that appears on the package. Price represents also satisfaction, status, reduced risk, increased self-esteem, value, and a host of other factors that have a positive meaning for the consumer. For example, the marketer may transform high prices into a positive feature by using them to signal high quality, as Pepperidge Farm does. This strategy is based on the assumption that price and quality have a high positive relationship in the mind of the typical consumer. In general, this assumption is valid, although there is evidence that perceived quality is determined by a number of variables, not only price. Marketers using a demand-based pricing strategy also know that the consumer is always pleased to pay significantly less than usual for a particular product. If a consumer goes into a department store expecting to pay two hundred dollars for a new suit and finds it on sale at 60 percent off, this reduction may be all the customer needs to know in order to make a purchase decision.

Charging an exceptionally low price is another demand-based pricing strategy. Ordinarily, pricing below cost is not desirable. But an aggressive marketer, especially at the retail level, may frequently charge below cost for promotional reasons. A **loss leader** is a dramatically low price offered in order to attract customers. Note that loss leaders are sold at the advertised price. In contrast, a **bait price** is intended to hook customers so that they may be switched to another, more expensive or more profitable item. Bait pricing is distinctly unethical and, in some states, illegal.

Communicating Prices

Information about pricing is probably the most important message that can be transmitted to users, purchasers, and those who influence purchases.

The package, signage, point-of-purchase materials, and coupons are all used to deliver pricing information. When price is a key promotional weapon, more than pricing information must be transmitted. A powerful, compelling message of pricing superiority must also be communicated.

Pricing information is often crucial in speeding consumer conviction. Three tactics are commonly used. First, either an ad or a salesperson may emphasize a coming event related to price. For example, a headline might read "Pre-Christmas Special—25 Percent Off on All Merchandise—Three Days Only." Or a salesperson might suggest the consumer should buy immediately because of an impending price increase.

Second, special price concessions may persuade the consumer to buy now. An advertised rebate may be all that is necessary to move the buyer to purchase the product. A salesperson may also use a negotiated price adjustment in order to close a sale.

A third technique is **price bundling,** which refers to a special price (usually lower) charged when certain products are bundled together. The bundling may include items that are difficult to sell alone. Heart surgeon Dr. Denton Cooley bundled a complete surgical procedure for fifteen thousand dollars, about 40 percent less than the national average for the same techniques priced separately.[9]

In advertising, the subject of pricing is so important that the term **price copy** has been coined to designate message content devoted principally to pricing. Most local advertising involves the transmission of pricing information. Food retailers, discount stores, furniture and appliance merchandisers, and department stores all make extensive use of promotional media to announce pricing decisions.

Concept Review

1. The price is the total value assigned to the product by customers and sellers.
2. Price can either be cost-based or demand-based.
   a. Cost-based means the company competes by having lower prices than competitors.
   b. Demand-based means the company focuses on the needs and wants of consumers.
3. Promotion is often the primary vehicle used to deliver price information.
4. Promotion should accurately reflect the price-quality relationship.
5. Three techniques are used to communicate prices:
   a. Advance advertising
   b. Special price concessions
   c. Price bundling

Case 3 *Mazda Reinvents the Sports Car*

Although you don't see many on the road any more, old British sports cars—Triumphs, MGs, Austin-Healys—still survive in the United States, sitting in garages and fields, occasionally getting tuned up for a summer drive. The companies that made these impractical, cramped two-seaters went out of business in the 1970s as fuel-efficiency, safety, and pollution control became more important to car buyers. But these cars still retain a place in the hearts of thousands of Americans who love the feel of a fast, low-slung car zipping along a winding road with the top down. It was that long-dormant market that Mazda wanted to tap with its Miata.

Background

Mazda may seem an unlikely company to replace Triumph in the hearts of sports car enthusiasts. Its last major innovation was the rotary engine, a dirty, inefficient engine introduced at just the wrong time in the early 1970s when the Arab oil embargo was making Americans more conscious about efficiency. Mazda was saved from bankruptcy by a bank bailout, but since that experience it has used most of its money and expertise to create family-oriented vehicles that sell well but don't create much excitement.

The Players

Mazda's current chairman, Kenichi Yamamoto, was a champion of the rotary engine and helped keep it alive in Mazda's expensive sports car, the RX-7. His interest in sports cars heated up in 1978, when a Mazda associate arranged for Yamamoto to drive a Triumph Spitfire. It was a glorious day, and Yamamoto had a wonderful time, experiencing the thrills that so many Americans still pine for. So when, a year later, he was visited by automotive journalist Robert Hall, he was open to Hall's suggestion that Mazda should build an updated version of the roadster. Hall, it turned out, had made the original suggestion that led to Yamamoto's eye-opening drive.

The Product

Two years later, Mazda hired Hall to work in its Irvine, California planning studio, and when Yamamoto visited, he urged Hall not to forget about the lightweight sports car. Yamamoto knew that Mazda would never make a lot of money out of a sports car, but he also thought that the company needed a product to spice up its line, to "wink at customers," as he describes it. The company didn't want to become complacent. So in 1983, Mazda embarked on a project to build a roadster.

Mazda set two planning groups—one in Tokyo besides the one in Irvine—onto the task, and in 1984 accepted the front-engine, rear-drive model that Hall and others insisted upon. A prototype was built which immediately turned heads and began winning rave reviews from automotive magazines. By building the Miata on existing assembly lines—something that American auto manufacturers are only now becoming flexible enough to do—and using computers to trim away any excess weight, Mazda managed to keep costs down and sell the car for under $14,000. The Miata's total capital budget was under two hundred million dollars, about one-tenth of the cost of many car programs.

One of Mazda's young marketers in Irvine, Rod Bymaster, came up with the name for the car which up until that point had been referred to as P729. He picked Miata, an old German word, from a dictionary of foreign terms because he liked its sound and because its definition summarized what Mazda hoped the car would represent for buyers—"high reward."

The Response

Mazda shipped its first order of three thousand Miatas—in red, white, or blue—in the summer of 1989. Because of the hype already generated by glowing reviews in the automotive press, everybody wanted the cars, and most dealers only received one or two Miatas to sell. Buyers pestered dealers and offered them bribes to be put on waiting lists, and demand ran far ahead of supply. Within six months, the first year's production of 23,000 cars had already been sold.

The car has many of the drawbacks of its ancestors—a skimpy trunk, no back seat, limited headroom. But with its convertible top and sporty feel, it offered what the old MG-lovers were looking for. And the publicity it has brought Mazda may be just what the company needs.

Case Questions

1. Employing the various elements discussed in The Product Mix section, describe the Miata. What are the strategic implications—that is, what are the strengths to build upon and the weaknesses to defend?

2. Given the product, distribution, and pricing strategies of the Miata, what would be the best way to promote this product? Would sales promotion be appropriate? What should be the role of personal selling?

Case Source: Doron P. Levin, "Hot Wheels," *New York Times Magazine* (September 30, 1990): 32–33, 72, 78.

Summary

Promotion interacts with the three other components of the marketing mix: product, channels of distribution, and pricing.

The product represents the starting point for all marketing efforts. The manufacturer, the reseller, and the customer must understand the product if the marketing effort is to succeed. The manner in which promotion and product are combined depends on the product classification, where the product is in its life cycle, and the strategic components supporting the product.

In the relationship between promotion and the channel mix, particular emphasis is placed on having a basic understanding of the promotional needs and capabilities of the two primary types of resellers, wholesalers and retailers. Push and pull promotional strategies make different demands on resellers, and the choice of strategy should take the resellers' abilities into account. Wholesalers use promotion to communicate the benefits of the manufacturer's product to retailers. They do this primarily through personal selling and sales promotion, especially trade deals. Retailers use promotion to communicate product features and store services to ultimate users. Retailers employ advertising and sales promotion, especially point of purchase and discounting.

Price has a different meaning to sellers and buyers. For sellers, it is a source of expected income and a competitive tool. For buyers, it reflects value and company image and determines the likelihood of a particular purchase. Pricing, when viewed as a competitive weapon, can be either cost-based or demand-based. Cost-based pricing emphasizes savings and value, two benefits that would be emphasized in the various promotional messages. Demand-based pricing attempts to meet the needs of the consumer, and a much broader interpretation of price is presented in the promotions. *Price copy* refers to promotions in which price is the primary emphasis.

Discussion Questions

1. Describe marketing and promotion in your own words. How does your definition of promotion relate to your definition of marketing?

2. Discuss the importance of the promotional strategy, company objectives and policies, and promotional objectives all being in harmony.

3. What is price bundling? Identify three examples of price bundling.

4. Create two messages for a window-cleaning product ad. Elaborate about the major differences between your two approaches.

5. The marketing of services is receiving more attention since consumers are spending increasing amounts of money to purchase services. How does the promotion of services differ from the promotion of goods products?

6. Outline the role of advertising and personal selling in the various stages of the product life cycle.

7. What is meant by reseller support? How can advertising, sales promotion, and personal selling be used to increase reseller support?

8. What are the primary differences between cost-based and demand-based pricing strategies? Cite examples of two promotions showing each.

9. Distinguish between a push and a pull strategy. How does the role of promotion differ in each?

10. Discuss the facets of price that would be easy to promote and those that would be difficult.

Suggested Projects

1. Select two products in your supermarket which are at opposite ends of the product life cycle. Collect any promotional material supporting each product. Itemize the various elements found in these promotions in respect to the product, channels, and price factors discussed in this chapter.

2. Interview the managers of three types of retail stores. Determine what types of promotions they use, and ask them to assess the relative success of each type. How do their assessments compare with the discussion of retailers in this chapter?

References

1. Jane Weaver, "Volvo Probing Ad Fiasco to Determine if Scali's at Fault," *Adweek* (November 12, 1990): 6, 59.

2. William J. Stanton, *Fundamentals of Marketing*, 4th ed. (New York: McGraw-Hill, 1975): 545–546.

3. Alison Fahey, "Sensor Sales Sharp," *Advertising Age* (May 7, 1990): 56.

4. Sue Woodman, "From Hats to Harley-Davidsons, Marketers Find New Uses for Old Products," *Adweek Special Report* (November 7, 1988): H.P. 42.

5. Howard Schlossberg, "Effective Packaging 'Talks' to Consumers," *Marketing News* (August 6, 1990): 6–7.

6. Brian Bagot, "Focus Pocus," *Marketing and Media Decisions* (September 1989): 73–84.

7. Martin R. Warshaw, *Effective Selling Through Wholesalers* (Ann Arbor, MI: University of Michigan Press, 1961): 48–54.

8. Dean Foust, "One Word for One Price: Success," *Business Week* (May 23, 1988): 123.

9. Mark Ivey, "Will Denton Cooley Make Medical History Again?" *Business Week* (March 27, 1989): 56–57.

II

DETERMINING PROMOTIONAL OPPORTUNITIES

4

The Sociocultural Environment

Cultures and Subcultures

Values and Consumer Behavior
Subcultures

The Demographic Environment

The Baby Boom
Senior Citizens
Mobility and Migration
Education and Occupation
The Employed Woman
Distribution of Income and Wealth
The Ethnic Surge

Social Class

Measuring Social Class
Class and Behavior

Social Groups

Reference Groups and Their Effects
The Family

Where Do We Go from Here?

Consider This:

Marketing's Green Revolution

The effects of heightened consumer consciousness about the environment go well beyond the focus on environmentally friendly packaging described in Chapter 3. Half of the consumers in one survey indicated they had decided not to purchase a particular product during the past year because of that product's effects on the environment. Conversely, innovative, environmentally friendly products and packages are winning over consumers, even though such products often cost more than standard varieties. For marketing professionals, selling to environmentally aware consumers will be one of the major challenges of the 1990s.

Because of the possibility of increasing sales by labeling a product "good for the environment," many companies have begun using such claims, sometimes without any evidence to back them up. A national forum on the subject in March 1990 drew calls from environmentalists and industry representatives alike for national regulations governing the use of terms like "biodegradable." Manufacturers want such standards because at the moment companies are in a bind about their use of environmental claims. If they do not advertise the environmental benefits of their products, they might be perceived as environmentally harmful and lose sales. However, if they make claims that they can't substantiate, they might be used for deceptive advertising and consumer fraud.

That's what happened to Mobil Corporation, marketer of Hefty trash bags. The company introduced "degradable" Hefty bags, noting on the packaging that the decomposition of the bags was "activated by exposure to the elements." Since most trash in landfills is buried and not exposed to the elements, the attorney generals in seven states decided that the "degradable" claim was misleading and took Mobil to court in 1990.

So far, the only environmental standards in the marketing field are those applied by independent certification companies and by retailers. Green Cross Certification Co. awards its Green Cross seal to products made from or packaged in the highest possible percentage of recycled material. Green Seal Inc. labels with its Green Seal products that are least harmful to the environment. On the retail level, Wal-Mart began a national trend by using special signs to indicate products that represented improvements that would "help prevent lasting environmental problems." While these developments in the free market are a start, as consumers become more sophisticated about environmental assertions, companies might turn increasingly to the government to help set the standards for marketers' environmental claims.

Sources: Christy Fisher and Judith Graham, "Wal-Mart Throws 'Green' Gauntlet," *Advertising Age* (August 21, 1989): 1. Bob Geiger, "'Green' Monster: Cry Goes Up for Uniform Ad Standards," *Advertising Age* (March 19, 1990): 2. Richard P. Wells, "Environmental Performance Will Count in the 1990s," *Marketing News* (March 19, 1990): 22.

A s our opening vignette illustrates, as the values and needs of consumers change, these changes alter how consumers view products and how they react to promotions. In order to recognize promotional opportunities, promotion managers must keep track of these changes and their impact on how consumers make decisions.

A model of consumer decision making is shown in Figure 4.1. The bottom half of the diagram, which outlines the individual decision-making process, is the topic of Chapter 5. Notice in the figure that there are two external influences on this process: (1) the firm's marketing mix, which we discussed in Chapter 3, and (2) the sociocultural environment, which is the topic of this chapter.

Consider the example of Bill Grass (formerly Grazecki), who was born in Cleveland, Ohio, in 1968. His father was a CPA, and his mother stayed home to raise Bill's four brothers and sisters. Bill went to a Catholic elementary and high school, worked after school and on Saturdays at the local Kroger supermarket, and was vice president of his senior class. He is currently a senior, majoring in advertising, at Ohio University. Since Bill is the oldest child and his father earns only forty-three thousand dollars annually, Bill is expected to contribute to the education of his brothers and sisters. Finally, Bill is in love and hopes to marry Michelle soon after he graduates.

If you are a promotion manager who hopes to influence Bill, this sketch gives you quite a lot of information about him. Yet a great deal about Bill is still unknown. What products and services does Bill purchase regularly? What media does he read or view? How does Bill decide what represents a good value? Does Bill have any disposable income? Does his modest upbringing mean he will be price conscious or coupon prone?

These questions illustrate just a few of the things that promotion managers need to know about their audiences in order to communicate their messages clearly and consistently. Whether these questions are answered through marketing research or the promotion manager's experience, the starting point should be the bigger picture—the **sociocultural environment.** It is a combination of the sociological and cultural variables that influence Bill's life.

Unlike specific questions about Bill that may require thousands of dollars to research, information about the sociocultural environment is easily available. Promotion managers can obtain this information from a wide variety of sources, including the census of the United States, trade publications,

Figure 4.1

A model of consumer decision making.

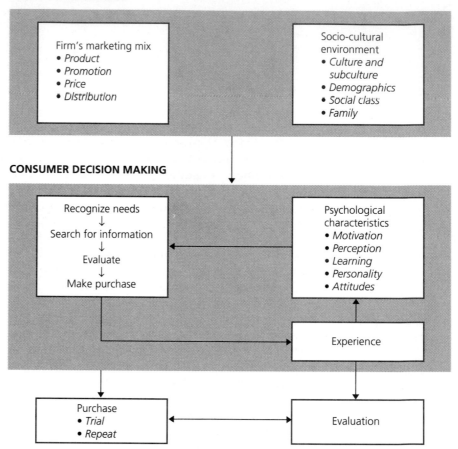

EXTERNAL INFLUENCES

Firm's marketing mix
• *Product*
• *Promotion*
• *Price*
• *Distribution*

Socio-cultural environment
• *Culture and subculture*
• *Demographics*
• *Social class*
• *Family*

CONSUMER DECISION MAKING

Recognize needs
↓
Search for information
↓
Evaluate
↓
Make purchase

Psychological characteristics
• *Motivation*
• *Perception*
• *Learning*
• *Personality*
• *Attitudes*

Experience

Purchase
• *Trial*
• *Repeat*

Evaluation

and surveys by research firms such as Louis Harris. Knowledge about patterns in the sociocultural environment also allows predictions about where we will be tomorrow based on where we were yesterday.

Several caveats are necessary before we proceed. First, the sociocultural environment changes constantly. Ongoing monitoring is therefore necessary. The tendency for a company to think that it has the behaviors and values of a group figured out is probably the first indicator that the firm has stopped paying attention. This was clearly the case with thousands of businesses that decided that the consumer no longer cared about the environment. Second, there will be exceptions to every pattern or behavior. It is important to be prepared for these exceptions but not to assume that they negate the observed pattern. Third, as target markets get larger and businesses move into other countries, finding general patterns will become more difficult because each culture must be assessed separately. This chapter will consider sociocultural factors only for American consumers. Equivalent factors for other countries will be discussed in Chapter 19.

Because the topic of the socioeconomic environment is so vast, our discussion will be restricted to those factors that have a bearing on promotional strategy. We begin the discussion with the broadest element, culture.

Cultures and Subcultures

All of us are part of a cultural fabric that affects our behavior, including our behavior as consumers. **Culture** is the sum of learned beliefs, values, and customs that regulate the behavior of members of a particular society. Through our culture, we are taught how to adjust to the environmental, biological, psychological, and historical parts of our environment.

The three components of culture—beliefs, values, and customs—are each somewhat different. A **belief** is a proposition that reflects a person's particular knowledge and assessment of something (that is, "I believe that . . ."). **Values** are general statements that guide behavior and influence beliefs and attitudes. It has been stated that the function of a value system is to help a person choose between alternatives in everyday life.[1] Values are formed at both the personal level and the cultural level. Values have both an importance and a judgment component. In family A, integrity is a very important value; in family B, it is not. In family A, integrity is equated with always standing up for one's beliefs, no matter what the consequences. In family B, integrity is equated with not cheating if there is a chance of getting caught. The formation of personal values is affected by cultural values and vice versa. Yet we retain many personal values despite contrary judgments by society. For example, the personal value of always finding humor in everything might not prove acceptable as you giggle through a professor's lecture. **Customs** are overt modes of behavior that constitute culturally approved ways of behaving in specific situations. For example, taking one's mother out for dinner and buying her presents on Mother's Day is an American custom that Hallmark and other card companies support enthusiastically. However, customs do vary from region to region and from country to country. Even families have their own set of customs. Beliefs and values are guides for behavior while customs are acceptable ways of behaving.

Values and Consumer Behavior

Marketers have a special interest in values, because values are influential in shaping behavior. Practical considerations force the marketer to be more interested in cultural values than personal values.[2] For the most part, personal values can be addressed only at the point of purchase. Marketers therefore track trends in cultural values and target their efforts toward these patterns.

Dominant cultural values are referred to as **core values;** they tend to affect and reflect the core character of a particular society. For example, if a culture does not value efficiency but does value a sense of belonging and neighborliness, few people are likely to want to use automatic teller machines. Likewise, if a culture begins to value family and personal health and relaxation over achievement and material success, this cultural trend would be of interest to many marketers.[3] As noted in the Promotion in Focus section, this change from "success to rest" is a pattern beginning to appear in our culture.

What do Americans value? To find out, Milton Rokeach originated the Rokeach Value Survey, which includes thirty-six value statements.[4] The first eighteen reflect *terminal values* (that is, end results) and are designed to measure the relative importance of personal goals. The other eighteen statements reflect *instrumental values* and measure basic approaches an individual might follow to reach the terminal values. More recently, researchers assessed the applicability of Rokeach's thirty-six items and concluded that only twenty-four apply in a marketing setting. Other researchers have proposed the simplified List of Values (LOV), which consists of nine values: (1) a sense of belonging, (2) excitement, (3) fun and enjoyment in life, (4) warm relationships, (5) self-fulfillment, (6) being well-respected, (7) a sense of accomplishment, (8) security, and (9) self-respect.[5] Still other researchers propose eleven core values and associated behaviors (see Table 4.1). The search continues for a list of core values shared by all Americans. Clearly, a catchall phrase such as the Protestant Work Ethic no longer captures American values.

Among private research firms that attempt to monitor values and look for groupings and behavioral patterns, SRI International is famous for its values and lifestyles systems (VALS), which categorize people according to their values and then identify associated consumer behaviors. VALS 1, introduced in 1978, contained nine categories. VALS 2 divides people into three basic categories: those who are principle oriented, status oriented, and action oriented. Then it estimates the resources consumers can draw upon; the result is eight subcategories (see Figure 4.2).[6]

VALS 2 differs from VALS 1 in that it does not use values and lifestyles as the basis for its segmentation scheme. Rather, VALS 2 estimates the resources consumers can draw upon, including their education, income, health, energy level, self-confidence, and degree of consumerism. Instead of asking people about their attitudes toward legalizing abortion, the new questionnaire asks them to agree or disagree to such statements as "My idea of fun at a national park would be to stay at an expensive lodge and dress up for dinner" and "I could stand to skin a dead animal."

The psychographic groups in VALS 2 are arranged in a rectangle. They

Promotion in Focus

The Reactionary 90s?

Anyone involved in selling to the public must keep abreast of changes and trends in public values and interests. One message of the 1980s was "You can have it all." In the 1990s, more people are saying, "We don't want it all." The stress of trying to be Supermom or Superdad has taken its toll, and people are realizing that managing stress by meditating on the train just isn't working. Many are rethinking whether they really need to be good at tennis as well as racquetball and questioning whether that second home is worth the overtime they have to put in to buy it. If these trends continue, companies may find that fewer executives are willing to put in 70-hour weeks just for a big year-end bonus.

Meanwhile, a generation raised during the Reagan years is coming of age. Will they follow the ways of their 60s-generation parents or fit the conservative model that was popular as they were growing up? Irma Zandl, an expert on teenage trends, insists that the 90s are "a decade of reaction." She believes today's teens want to revert to traditional gender roles: boys want to be the breadwinners and girls want to be stay-at-home mothers.

She also says that this generation has heard Reagan's call for volunteerism to take over the social work abandoned when the federal government cut off funds. Many of today's teens will get involved in recycling and other volunteer projects and enter people-serving occupations. They will not, however, follow Reagan's approach to the environment, as many of today's young people know and care more about the environment than their parents do. They also tend to be more jaded than their predecessors. "Present average teenagers with a new product," says Zandl, "and their first reaction will no longer be, 'Hey, this is cool.' It's more likely to be, 'Will this give me cancer?'" If she's right, companies wanting to sell to this new generation will need to develop new products and approaches.

Source: Judith Newman, "The 90s Teenager: Back to Basics," *Adweek* (September 11, 1989): 40, 45.

Table 4.1 **Summary of American Core Values**

Value	General Features	Relevance to Consumer Behavior
Achievement and success	Hard work is good; success flows from hard work	Acts as a justification for acquisition of goods ("You deserve it")
Activity	Keeping busy is healthy and natural	Stimulates interest in products that are time-savers and enhance leisure-time activities
Efficiency and practicality	Admiration of things that solve problems (for example, save time and effort)	Stimulates purchase of products that function well and save time
Progress	People can improve themselves; tomorrow should be better	Stimulates desire for new products that fulfill unsatisfied needs; acceptance of products that claim to be "new" or "improved"
Material comfort	"The good life"	Fosters acceptance of convenience and luxury products that make life more enjoyable
Individualism	Being one's self (for example, self-reliance, self-interest, and self-esteem)	Stimulates acceptance of customized or unique products that enable a person to "express his or her own personality"
Freedom	Freedom of choice	Fosters interest in wide product lines and differentiated products
External conformity	Uniformity of observable behavior; desire to be accepted	Stimulates interest in products that are used or owned by others in the same social group
Humanitarianism	Caring for others, particularly the underdog	Stimulates patronage of firms that compete with market leaders
Youthfulness	A state of mind that stresses being young at heart or appearing young	Stimulates acceptance of products that provide the illusion of maintaining or fostering youth
Fitness and health	Caring about one's body, including the desire to be physically fit and healthy	Stimulates acceptance of food products, activities, and equipment perceived to maintain or increase physical fitness

Source: Leon G. Schiffman and Leslie L. Kanuk, *Consumer Behavior*, 4th ed. © 1991, p. 424. Reprinted by permission of Prentice-Hall, Englewood Cliffs, New Jersey.

are stacked vertically by resources (minimal to abundant) and horizontally by self-orientation (principle, status, or action oriented). The self-orientation dimension covers three different ways of buying. Principle-oriented consumers are guided by their views of how the world is or should be; status-oriented consumers, by the actions and opinions of others; and action-oriented consumers, by a desire for social or physical activity, variety, and risk taking.

Figure 4.2

VALS 2 provides a rectangular representation of human values. Each value category is associated with a set of demographics.
Reprinted with permission © 1989, American Demographics, July 1989, p. 26.

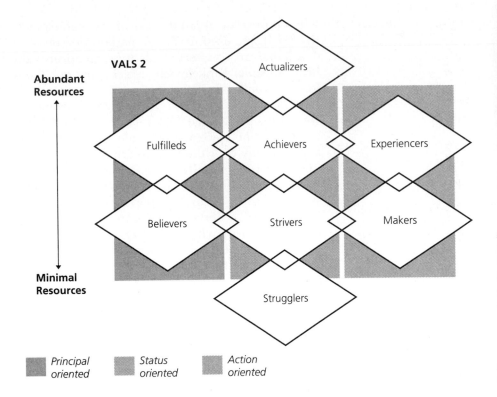

Each of these orientations has two psychographic segments, one with high and one with low resources. The two principle-oriented segments, for instance, are fulfilleds and believers. Fulfilleds are mature, responsible, well-educated professionals. Their leisure activities center on their homes, but they are well informed about what goes on in the world, and they are open to new ideas and social change. They have high incomes, but they are practical, value-oriented consumers. Believers have more modest incomes; they are conservative and predictable consumers who favor American products and established brands. Their lives are centered on family, church, community, and the nation.

An annual subscription to VALS provides businesses with a range of products and services. Businesses that do market research can include the VALS questions in their own questionnaires. SRI will analyze the data and VALS-type the respondents. Businesses can then tabulate the rest of their market research according to VALS classifications. Subscribers also have access to SRI's own consumer surveys and consulting.

The VALS 2 system is used by various companies, including Mercedes-Benz, Chevron Corporation, Eastman Kodak Co., Ogilvy & Mather, and Ketchum Communications. Chevron, for example, uses the VALS 2 classifications to categorize all its consumers into types that are then combined with information about the size of the market and geographic distribution; the results are used for target market promotions.

Another major effort to identify American values is conducted by the firm of Daniel Yankelovich, which puts out the Monitor series. It tracks forty-one cultural values, such as "antibigness," "mysticism," and "living for today," and gives the percentage of people who share the attitude as well as the percentage who are opposed to it. For example, the percentage of people who place a strong value on physical fitness and well-being has risen steadily over the years, with the main support coming from people under thirty (especially young women) and people living in the West.

Core values are slow and difficult to change. Consequently, promotion strategies must accurately portray and reflect these values. The ad for Xerox Financial Services in Figure 4.3 taps one core value, our need for financial security when we retire.

Secondary values also exist in any culture. They are less permanent and can sometimes be influenced by promotion. They serve as the basis for subcultures.

Subcultures

A natural evolution that occurs in any culture is the emergence of subcultures. Although the core values in a culture are held by virtually the entire population, secondary values are not. People who share a set of secondary values are referred to as a **subculture.** Examples include yuppies and environmentally concerned people.

Many factors can place an individual in one or several subcultures. According to one source, the most important are the following:[7]

1. *Material culture.* The way in which benefits are distributed can create various subcultures. The poor, the affluent, and the white-collar middle class all stand out as examples of subcultures that have proven important to marketers.

2. *Social institutions.* By participating in social institutions such as marriage, parenthood, a retirement community, the Army, and so on a person may become part of a subculture.

3. *Belief systems.* These include religious and political affiliation. An individual's religious beliefs and their strength can influence habits, attitudes, values, and purchase patterns. For example, traditional Amish do not use several types of products, including electricity and automobiles. A whole set of factors has also been correlated with whether a person is a Democrat, Republican, independent, or socialist.

4. *Aesthetics.* Artistic people often form a subculture of their own associated with their common interest—including art, music, dance, drama, and folklore.

Figure 4.3

This ad for Xerox Financial Services taps into one of our core values: financial security during retirement.
Courtesy of Xerox Corporation

5. *Language.* Dialects, accents, and vocabulary can quickly place a person in a particular subculture. Southerners and Northerners are two traditional categories.

   To illustrate, let us examine a subculture that has received a great deal of notoriety and investigation during the last decade—the yuppies. The term *yuppie* (young urban professional) has been popular in the United States since 1983, when columnist Bob Greene invented it. Since that time, anecdotes have suggested that the key value motivating yuppies is materialism. This value is reflected in their expensive furniture, automobiles, clothes, grooming products, and entertainment. They also prefer to live in townhouses and condominiums, drive foreign cars, and play with gadgets. They are the largest, richest, best-educated generation ever born.[8] A range of companies from Ford Motor Co. and American Express Company to Campbell Soup Company and Anheuser-Busch (Michelob) introduced advertising campaigns or designed new products to court the yuppies.

Despite the attention surrounding yuppies, some people argue that there is no such thing, in demographic terms, as a yuppie market. In order to assess whether yuppies exist, in 1986 a questionnaire was administered to more than three hundred people who fit the traditional profile of the yuppie: aged between twenty-five and forty-five; employed in white-collar professional occupations; at least some college education; earning more than thirty-thousand dollars annually; residing in an urban area.[9] Some of the findings confirmed the yuppie stereotypes, others did not. For example, the questionnaire revealed that yuppies are not more health conscious than others, but that they enjoy health clubs. Yuppies are not more mobile than the general population; they hold a less favorable attitude toward advertising. Yuppies are heavier users of convenience products and services such as fast-food restaurants, microwave ovens, and automatic teller machines. Yuppies are best characterized as having high income, optimism, leadership skills, self-confidence, and adventuresomeness. Yuppies are often associated with income management and investing; ownership of stocks, bonds, and expensive cameras; consumption of ice cream and chocolate; and a preference for Japanese cars and sports cars. This single study points to yuppies as a valid subculture that can be reached by separate promotional efforts.

Concept Review

1. A culture is the sum of learned beliefs, values, and customs that regulate the behavior of members of a particular society.
2. Values are thought to shape behavior, but attempts to identify a set of core values in the American culture have not produced any consensus.
   a. Rokeach divides values into two categories:
      (1) Terminal values, which relate to our personal goals, and
      (2) Instrumental values, which determine the means used to reach goals.
   b. Searches for general core values have been conducted by research firms such as SRI International (VALS 2) and Daniel Yankelovich (Monitor).
3. Subcultures are based on secondary values. Five factors influence the formation of subcultures:
   a. Material culture,
   b. Social institutions,
   c. Belief systems,
   d. Aesthetics, and
   e. Language.

The Demographic Environment

Imagine for a moment a strange new nation: 60 percent of the population between the ages of eighteen and twenty-five, male, unemployed and out of school, living on trust funds of twenty-five thousand dollars a year, and moving to a new home every year. A nation with this very peculiar demographic profile would certainly feature different purchasing patterns than American marketers face today. Products and services such as beer, home entertainment, sports programming, and snack foods would prosper, while dress clothes, eyeglasses, and medical care would suffer. Demographic traits such as age, sex, and income obviously mold values and behavior.

The 1990 census noted many changes in the demographic makeup of the American people. These changes were often dramatic, and the adjustments they require are far reaching.

The Baby Boom

In 1990, there were approximately 250 million people living in the United States, an increase of 23 million since 1980. The median age of the population rose from thirty in 1980 to thirty-three in 1990. But though the population as a whole is aging (for example, there are 57,000 centenarians), certain groups, such as the fifty- to fifty-nine-year-old age group and the ten- to twenty-four-year-old age group, declined (see Figure 4.4). These patterns are primarily driven by the baby boom.

The **baby boom** occurred from 1946 through 1964. In these nineteen years, 76.4 million babies were born in the United States. Today, approximately 70 million of these baby boomers are still alive. They are now between twenty-eight and forty-six years of age and make up about one-third of the total population.

Figure 4.4

This bar graph shows that the percentage of older people is increasing.
U.S. Census Bureau

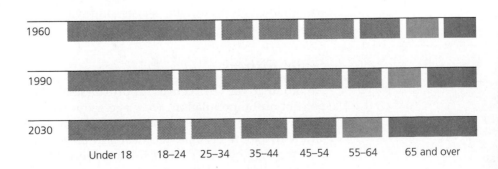

AGE DISTRIBUTION

1960

1990

2030

Under 18   18–24   25–34   35–44   45–54   55–64   65 and over

Charting the possible impacts of the baby boomers provides some interesting results. The oldest baby boomers turned forty in 1986, ushering them into midlife. What will their mature years be like? Many female baby boomers will care for or supervise the care of older parents. Eventually we can expect to see the appearance of women's elder-care collectives, with a group like the National Organization for Women perhaps coordinating this activity. Many older boomers who want to relocate when they retire are likely to go to the outskirts of a college town. This is, after all, the atmosphere in which so many of them matured, unlike their parents. Small liberal colleges will probably forge partnerships with real estate developers to build condominium townhouses in outlying areas near their academic community. With a smaller generation of college students due in coming decades, the schools will need older boomers and will make class auditing and recreational privileges part of the housing packages.[10] Early retirement will prove to be a unique event, passing from the scene by the year 2010. People will change jobs more often after age forty-five than they did in their twenties. Older boomers working part-time will alter the way businesses hire, train, and evaluate employees. Finally, *ergonomics,* the science of adapting the human-made physical environment—such as furniture— to best fit human needs, will become central to industrial design.[11] Because of their numbers and their buying power, older baby boomers will force businesses to make and build most products to fit their needs. Emphasis will be on ease of use, simplicity, and safety.

The sheer size of the baby-boom generation will also cause some serious problems. In the 90s, many baby boomers will find themselves reaching the end of their corporate climb; there will not be room for all the qualified executives in this age group to continue rising. In the long run, baby boomers will have to define success in ways other than promotion. The image of success, so much at the core of promotion in the 1980s, will have to undergo redefinition. Notice how the image of success is redefined in the ad in Figure 4.5, which points out how rewarding family sharing can be.

Table 4.2 outlines other predictions about characteristics of boomers in the 1990s. The point is that this largest group in the American population will go through predictable stages, and wise managers will be sensitive to these patterns.

Senior Citizens

According to the 1990 census, approximately 32 million Americans, or 12.5 percent of the population, were age sixty-five or over. Within this group, the fastest-growing aged groups are the oldest ones. The population aged ninety-five to ninety-nine has nearly doubled since 1980. The centenarians lead the way, however. In 1956, there were 2,000 centenarians; there were 57,000 in 1990. And the projection for the year 2000 is 168,000.[12] Because

Figure 4.5

This L.L. Bean ad does an excellent job of depicting family sharing. Courtesy of L.L. Bean, Inc.

We've been coming here since we first got married. Back then, we wouldn't even bring a tent. We'd just spread out our sleeping bags, look up at the stars and plan our future until we fell asleep. That was two children ago. Then, one night last summer, our son Jimmy got out his sleeping bag, dragged it over to the clearing, curled up and fell asleep. It was a beautiful night, so we all pulled out our bags and joined him. Just spent the night under the stars together. Reminded me of old times.

L. L. Bean.
For the outdoors inside each of us.

For 78 years, L. L. Bean has offered durable, practical products for men and women who love the outdoors. Our catalog includes active and casual apparel, footwear, equipment and accessories. All fully guaranteed and honestly priced. If you'd like a copy, please call 1-800-548-4304 anytime.

L.L.Bean
FREEPORT, MAINE

© L. L. Bean, 1990

of their physical impairments and lack of interest in products, these individuals are very difficult to target.

The importance of senior citizens to the marketer, however, is not just the tremendous growth in their numbers. Rather, the opportunities offered by seniors are found in their differences. For instance, the "young old"—those who chose early retirement and those in their 70s—are healthier and wealthier than those who formerly filled this slot. Indeed, with their paid-off houses, savings, and inflation-indexed Social Security payments, many of the young old are also doing far better than the younger generations. Promoters therefore design advertising campaigns, discounts, off-season reductions, contests, and product samples for this segment of the population.

Table 4.2 **Boomers in the 1990s**

Category	Characteristics
Parents	Nearly 90 percent of Americans will have children at some time during their lives. For a huge segment of society, that time is now.
Fathers	As the baby boomlet begins to walk, talk, and struggle with homework assignments, fathers will become more important.
The Fit	At age 40, Mark Spitz is training to swim in the 1992 Olympics. He's not alone. While most baby boomers won't try out for the Olympics, they will join him in a passionate battle against aging.
The Un-Fit	Beyond age 40, serious health problems become much more common. The number of people with chronic diseases should increase sharply with the aging of the baby boom in the 1990s.
Downscale	The pendulum of public concern is swinging back in favor of helping the poor and near-poor. We may even see a redefinition of poverty, which increases the size of the downscale segment.
Upscale	With the baby-boom generation entering its peak earning years, the number of affluent households will grow. But they won't necessarily feel rich or spend lavishly, because most Americans identify with the middle class no matter how upscale their income.
Workers	At 66 percent, the share of the population in the paid labor force is greater today than ever before in our history. Businesses can profit by helping workers balance work and home life.
Entrepreneurs	There are too many baby boomers for the few top spots in America's companies. The consequence will be new businesses started by frustrated employees, more self-employment, more moonlighting (already at a record high), more home offices, and a blurring of work and home life.
Women in charge	Over half the women who work full-time think of their work as a career rather than just a job. As career-minded baby-boom women gain in job experience, the number who control the bottom line will grow rapidly.
Housewives	Markets have fragmented, but traditional markets still exist— they've become segmented markets just like all the rest. According to recent studies, the attitudes of housewives are diverging from those of working women. These growing differences will make it easier to target the women who opt for this lifestyle.

Source: Reprinted with permission ©1990 *American Demographics* (August 1990): 2.

At the same time, nearly 20 percent of the seniors have severe physical or emotional disabilities that require full- or part-time care. For every older American in a nursing home, two others with similar needs live in the community, according to gerontologist Elaine Brody. Nearly seven million Americans provide unpaid care to older friends and family members, according to research sponsored by the American Association of Retired Persons (AARP). Three-quarters of these caregivers are women, and over half hold full- or part-time jobs. Nearly 40 percent of these caregivers also have responsibility for children. These "sandwiched" Americans have needs for a variety of services—child care, home care, home delivery—because they sacrifice so much for these senior citizens.[13]

Mobility and Migration

How often do Americans move? This is a hard question to answer, but the answer is important to many businesses. When people move, they spend money on housing, furniture, refrigerators, curtains, and many other items. Various studies have found that the "average" American moves every five, six, seven, or even eleven years. Their results vary because of differing definitions of who is moving (is it a person, family, or a homeowner?), their age (householders age forty-five to fifty-four have been in their homes a median of more than eight years, versus six months for those age twenty-five to twenty-nine), location (the median in nonmetropolitan areas of the South is ninety-seven months, compared to thirty months in large urban areas of the West), and income (many poor Americans never establish a stable residence while many rich people never move).

The most recent data suggest that typical Americans move less frequently now than in the 1950s or early 1960s. Fewer moves do not necessarily mean that people are happier with their housing. It may mean that people are stuck where they are because they cannot afford to buy a home or trade up to a better home. Furthermore, most people who do move go only a short distance—a median of about six miles.

When people do make long-distance moves, where do they go? Overall, states in the South and the West captured nearly 90 percent of the nation's growth from 1980 to 1990. The South, with eighty-seven million people in 1990, remains the country's most populated area. California gained more people than any other state—five million.[14]

High mobility and migration rates suggest problems for the promotion manager. For example, an organization such as Frito-Lay may customize its messages or promotional offers for each of their regions. People who move may become confused when they see these different messages. Likewise, direct mail promoters have found it extremely difficult to maintain accurate mailing lists.

Education and Occupation

Another change of considerable significance to marketers is our continually rising level of education. Today, over 20 percent of all adults age twenty-five and older have completed four or more years of college, compared to approximately 16 percent in 1980. In contrast, 13 percent of men and 8 percent of women age sixty-five and older have completed college. However, younger men, age twenty-five to thirty-four, are now less likely to have completed four years of college than were the baby boomers ten years ago. The high cost of education may be pushing young adults out of college and into the work force. Finally, the educational gap between men and women is narrowing. Among people age forty-five to fifty-four, the share of men with college degrees is 10 percent higher than the share of women. But among people age twenty-five to thirty-four, the difference is less than 1 percent. While the share of young men with four or more years of college has dropped since 1980, the share of young women with four or more years of college has grown.[15]

One important force behind the push for the diploma is the changing needs of the economy. Today, business is a far more sophisticated enterprise than it was not too many decades ago. Scientific management, data processing, advanced technology, and the enormous complexity of multinational and multiproduct corporate organizations have created an explosive demand for a highly skilled and well-educated work force. According to recent Bureau of Labor Statistics projections, employers who need skilled workers to perform technical jobs are likely to face shortages.

Seven out of ten new jobs in the 1990s will be white collar. However, advancing computer technology is also changing the nature of white-collar work. Many formerly fragmented tasks are being converted into jobs that require multiple skills. Computer networks that integrate diverse functions also require employees who can work as a team, more often on projects than on tasks. The shift to more complex, project-type jobs should please well-educated baby boomers, who are demanding broader responsibilities at work as they age. But because many workers, particularly younger ones, are deficient in computer literacy or even basic work skills, corporations face new pressure to educate labor.[16]

The Employed Woman

The prevalence of working women has been one of the key economic and social developments of our times. Currently, 56 percent of women are working outside the home. Among women with children under six, that figure rises to 70 percent. The overall percentage of working women will continue to increase, with 61 percent expected to be in the work force by 2000.[17]

The effects of this movement of women into the work force will continue to be far reaching. It has already changed the profile of the typical American woman. For instance, women now head 28 percent of America's 91 million households;[18] in 1987, women headed 46 percent of black households. Half of female-head householders own their own homes, 20 percent own dishwashers, 38 percent own microwave ovens, and 45 percent took a domestic trip of more than two hundred miles in the past year.[19] The demand for day care, flextime, longer leaves, service products, better clothing, and cars are all affected by the number of working women. A more complete profile of the American woman is given in Figure 4.6.

For the promotion manager, the increase in working women offers problems as well as opportunities. Reaching the working woman through mass media has become tricky. Direct marketing, telemarketing, and catalog sales have replaced traditional media. However, the concerns of the working woman are fairly homogeneous—the need for more conveniences and more time with the family. In turn, these concerns are easily turned into message appeals or promotional tactics. For example, The Prudential Insurance Co. of America ran a series of ads pointing out how women now need as much insurance as men. There was also a United Air Lines Inc. ad that showed a corporate mother dropping her daughter off at school in the morning and getting home, via United, in time to pick her up in the afternoon. Home delivery and guarantees are two sales promotion techniques that appeal to working women.

Distribution of Income and Wealth

When the topic of income is raised, two questions are often on the minds of consumers: Do we have more today than we did in the past? Are the rich getting richer and the poor getting poorer? The answer to both questions is probably yes.

The typical American family's income before taxes, as measured by the census bureau, was half again as high in 1986 as in 1960—$29,458 versus $19,500. In 1986, all types of families got richer. For women who were raising families single-handedly, the increase in income was 33 percent. Married couples with two paychecks, not surprisingly, were doing best: their incomes were up 60 percent.

While all these statistics look positive, one must be aware that income statistics are quite tricky and are often misleading. Some people argue that the census numbers tend to underestimate income, because neither capital gains nor noncash income, such as health insurance and pension funds, is included in the definition of income. Others criticize the census numbers for being too optimistic. When adjustments for inflation are included, weekly per worker income went down from $366 in 1972 to $318 in 1980 to

ARE You THE
Average
AMERICAN?

The average American is a 32-year-old woman.

The average American woman can't see over a crowd in a parade: she is only 5'4", has brown hair (69% of all Americans do). She weighs 143 pounds, and is trying to lose weight. Still, she thinks she looks younger than she is (57% of all Americans think so).

The average American wears glasses or contact lenses.

Although she hasn't been to church in the past week, the average American was born Protestant (65% of all Americans). She believes in God (94% of all Americans) and life after death (69%).

The average American owns an 8-year-old blue sedan that gets 18 miles to the gallon and costs about $3,000 a year to own and operate. The average American will drive this car almost 9,000 miles a year. Two more people will buy it before it goes to the junkyard.

By age 32, the average American is married and has a child. It will cost her more than $140,000 to raise her child to the age of 18. If it's a boy, the average American's child is named Michael. If it's a girl, Jennifer.

The average American woman wears a size 7-1/2 B shoe. Although she reports foot pain and related problems (as do 62% of all women), the average American woman wears high heels regularly (59% of all women).

The average American has lost two teeth by the age of 30. She'll lose ten by the time she's 70.

The average American woman wears a size 10 or 12 dress. In 1986, she spent $339 on clothes. She spent almost one-third of the money on blouses and sweaters, followed by dresses (16%), skirts/suits (14%), lingerie/hosiery (12%), and pants (11%). In 1985, working women with children bought an average of 37 items of clothing a year. Working women without children bought an average of 55 items.

70% of women say they wear jewelry every day, and they buy most of it themselves. The average American woman wears a size 6 ring. The median price of her engagement ring is $800.

She may not be rich, but the average American carries $104 in her purse. Also in her purse: keys (97% of all women report them in their purse), a wallet (94%), a comb (80%), checks (76%), makeup (69%), and an address book (69%).

The average American works in a technical, sales, or administrative job. She makes less than $20,000 a year. Her earnings account for only 78% of her total annual income. The rest comes from investments, government benefit programs, and self-employment.

The average American household writes 16 checks a month. As fast as the average American makes money, she spends it. She charges about $2,000 worth of goods on her ten plastic credit cards each year.

Figure 4.6

This humorous portrayal of the average American woman provides important insights for the promotion manager.
From the Almanac of the American People, by Tom and Nancy Biracree. © 1988 by Tom and Nancy Biracree. Reprinted by permission of Facts on File, Inc., New York.

$312 in 1987. Moreover, after-tax 1987 median family incomes were below those of the late 1970s. For those with little education, the situation is even bleaker. For men of all ages with only a high school diploma, the income figures were $9.90 an hour in 1973 and $8.62 an hour in 1987. Still a third group of critics contend that discretionary income is a much better measure of well-being than gross income. **Discretionary income** is "the after-tax income that is left over after expenditures that are 30 percent greater than the average for households of similar size, age and region of residence."[20] Only 29 percent of all American households have discretionary incomes. Average discretionary income increased from 1983 to 1987.

Regardless of the perspective taken toward measuring income, one fact appears clear: the improvement in living standards since the early 1970s has come less from working smarter and more from working harder.[21] One study found that Americans' leisure time declined by 3.7 percent between 1973 and 1987—from 26.2 hours a week to 16.6 hours.[22]

The distribution of wealth is the second issue of importance. By standard measures, the distribution of income and wealth has shifted toward the top since the 1950s and the 1960s. In the 1950s, 60 percent of U.S. households were middle income, 10 percent were upper income, and 30 percent were lower income. By 2000, middle-income households, will represent 30 percent, upper-income households another 30 percent, and lower-income households 40 percent.[23] The "rich," defined as the top half of 1 percent of the U.S. population, have never been richer. Even if incomes are adjusted for inflation, the number of millionaires doubled between the late seventies and the late eighties. Again, there is a glitch in these calculations.[24] If you include employees' accumulated pension rights in the calculations of wealth, the tilt toward the top turns into a slight decline.[25]

Along with this redistribution of income has come a change in the mind set of Americans. They are increasingly balancing purchasing against priorities. A few years ago, middle-income consumers could be counted on to go to a middle-priced store for most of their purchases. However, as they have become more astute shoppers, they are more likely to purchase a brand-name microwave oven from a discounter, for example, and then use the money saved to help pay for a high-end entertainment system. At the grocery store, the same consumer is likely to choose generic paper products but gourmet food.

The Ethnic Surge

Another key demographic trend that is adding its own distinct flavor to consumption patterns is the shift in the pattern of minorities. According to the 1990 census, blacks remain the largest minority group, with 12 percent of the population. Spanish-speakers represent 8 percent but have increased 44 percent since 1980 and are expected to grow even faster during the 90s. Asian and other races represent 3 percent of the total but have grown 65 percent since 1980.[26]

Spanish-speakers are an important market with distinct spending habits. Contrary to stereotypes, most Spanish-speakers are not poor. In 1988, their median family income was $21,800, versus $32,000 for all families. And they are a market for big-ticket items since family members are likely to pool their resources for major purchases such as a car. Marketers including PepsiCo., Coca-Cola, Metropolitan Life Insurance, and the Adolph Coors Co. have successfully reached the Spanish-speaking market because they have acknowledged the pivotal roles played by the Catholic church and by sports in this community. Some 70 percent of Spanish-speakers are Roman Catholic for whom the local parish is far more than just a Sunday place of worship; it is the center for social activity, charitable events, and holiday celebrations. Recognizing this fact, some thirty food and beverage companies joined together to sponsor more than one hundred celebrations and fund-raising activities in Texas and California in 1975. Similarly, because Spanish-speakers who grew up playing soccer in Mexico and South America are still passionate about the sport, the Ford Motor Co. several years ago began sponsoring amateur soccer in the United States and enlisted the world-famous soccer player Pélé as a celebrity spokesperson.[27]

Concept Review

1. The U.S. population born from 1946 through 1964 (seventy million still alive today) is called the baby boom.
2. Senior citizens represent the fastest-growing segment of the population.
3. People are moving less frequently now than twenty years ago, they are moving shorter distances, and they are moving most often to the South or West.
4. The level of education and the movement into white-collar occupations have increased.
5. Nearly 60 percent of U.S. women work outside the home, necessitating a greater demand for service products and a reformulation of the portrayal of women in promotion.
6. The numbers of affluent and poor Americans are growing the fastest.
7. Blacks remain the largest minority in the United States although the Spanish-speaking and Asian populations are growing at a much faster rate.

Social Class

So far in discussing the sociocultural environment, we have considered how consumers are influenced by very broad cultural factors and by an array of demographic traits. In addition, consumer behavior may be molded by systematic inequalities in society that create a social class system. **Social class** refers to position on a social scale based on criteria such as occupation, education, and income. These characteristics define the prestige or power of the individual and, therefore, his or her position. Members of the same social class may never meet or communicate, but they are likely to share certain values, attitudes, and behavior because of similar socioeconomic characteristics. Unlike the rigid social caste system found in India, the social class system in the United States is an *open* system, because people can move from one class to another.

Measuring Social Class

Placing people into a specific social class is an uncertain process. One of two procedures is typically followed. The first requires *objective evaluation* of individuals relative to such indicators as income, wealth, education, occupation, family, dwelling, and neighborhood. People are asked to evaluate their own standing or that of other community members in respect to these indicators. The researcher can then use these answers to create either a *single-variable index,* in which one characteristic such as occupation is used to create a hierarchy, or a *composite-variable index,* in which a number of socioeconomic factors are combined to form one overall measure of social standing. Income is not typically used as a single-variable index because it may not reflect the true wealth of the individual. That is, income does not necessarily include assets or debts.

An example of the composite measure of social class is Warner's Index of Status Characteristics (ISC). It classifies American society into six classes, as shown.

Upper-upper class (.5%). Locally prominent families with at least second- or third-generation wealth.

Lower-upper class (1.5%). Families have more recently acquired wealth but are never fully accepted by the upper-upper class.

Upper-middle class (10%). Moderately successful professional men and women, owners of medium-sized businesses, middle managers, and successful young people.

Lower-middle class (30%–35%). Small-business owners, nonmanagerial office workers, and highly paid blue-collar workers.

Upper-lower class (40%). Semiskilled production-line workers with the goals of enjoying life and living well from day to day.

Lower-lower class (15%). Unskilled workers, unassimilated ethnics, sporadically employed.[28]

A second method of measuring social class employs *subjective judgment*. People are asked to indicate where they feel they fall on the social class continuum, that is, middle class, lower class, working class, or upper class. The resulting personal perception is referred to as *class consciousness*.

Class and Behavior

To some degree, people within social classes develop and assume different patterns of behavior. Social class influences many aspects of our lives. For example, time patterns differ sharply by social class. People in the upper social class perform most daily activities an hour or so later than people in the lower class. Because of their longer, less predictable workday, people in the upper social class are likely to eat dinner out (not supper) an hour or two later, or dine out. The use of language and symbols also differs. Middle-class people use more subtle and complex forms of expression than working-class consumers. Simile and analogy are meaningful to upper-class people but often not useful to lower-class people. Perceived risk also separates the social classes. Lower-class individuals see the world as risky and perhaps dangerous. They do not feel adequate to cope with loss or adversity, they are risk averse, and they use avoidance to maintain security. Upper-class people feel risk implies both danger and opportunity; the degree of negative risk is proportional to the rate of positive return.[29]

Since social classes differ in at least some attitudes and behavior, marketers have often used social class variations in designing strategies. However, since the consumption process for many products is similar across social classes, it is not always useful to marketers to determine these variations. The applicability of using social class differences in the formulation of marketing strategies tends therefore to be product specific. For example, in respect to marketing strategies for banks, it is important to know the following variations: upper-class individuals save more money than people in the lower class. They are concerned about the liquidity of funds and the rate of return they will receive. Lower-class consumers often save only to accumulate money for a specific purchase, so they may not be concerned about the rate of interest they receive. Credit is used more by upper-class consumers, but for different reasons than people in the lower class. People in the upper class may carry half a dozen credit cards and use them often for large and small purchases, for convenience; they usually pay the entire balance each month. Lower-class consumers who have credit cards more often use their accounts as a form of installment credit to fund purchases.

A final example, and one of particular interest to promotion managers, is the differences in media habits. Lower-class consumers depend more on broadcasting for news and sports, and they are devoted to television for entertainment. The late-night television audience is largely upper social class. These viewers also watch public affairs programs and public broadcasting, prefer FM to AM radio, read the morning daily newspapers, and prefer magazines targeted at a specific social class.

Concept Review

1. In the United States, social class is determined by such criteria as occupation, education, and income.
2. According to one influential analysis, the U.S. population contains the following classes:
   a. Upper-upper,
   b. Lower-upper,
   c. Upper-middle,
   d. Lower-middle,
   e. Upper-lower, and
   f. Lower-lower.
3. Social class influences many patterns of behavior, but the applicability of using social class variations in marketing strategies depends on the product.

Social Groups

A **group** may be defined as two or more people who interact to accomplish either individual or mutual goals. Social scientists have identified, described, and classified groups in many ways. For example, people we interact with on a regular basis and whose opinion we value are considered a primary group; those we see occasionally and whose opinion is unimportant form secondary groups. Groups may also be classified as formal or informal, depending on whether they have a formal structure and well-defined roles; and as membership or symbolic groups, depending on whether a person must qualify for actual membership or simply adopts the group's values and behaviors. Groups can also be described by their meaning to their members, as friendship groups, social groups, shopping groups, or work groups. For promotion managers, however, two types of groups have special relevance: reference groups and families, which themselves serve as reference groups. These groups are the topics of this section.

Reference Groups and Their Effects

A **reference group** has been defined as any person or group that serves as a point of comparison (or reference) for an individual in the formation of general or specific values, attitudes, or behavior.[30] Although reference

groups are normally very specific, marketing finds a more general classification useful. Thus, reference groups may be thought of as contractual,
aspirational, disclaimant, and avoidance. A *contractual* reference group is
one in which a person holds membership or has regular face-to-face contact with, and of whose values, attitudes, and standards he or she ap-
proves (for example, family, friends, neighbors, coworkers). Family and
friends serve as the reference group highlighted in many promotional messages. An *aspirational* reference group is one in which a person does not
hold membership or have face-to-face contact with, but of which he or she
wants to be a member. Thus this group serves as a positive influence on
the person's attitudes or behavior. Most college students study and attend
class because they aspire to be members of the employed reference group.
A *disclaimant* group is one in which a person holds membership and does
have face-to-face contact with, but the person disapproves of the group's
values, attitudes, and behavior. The "Don't drive drunk" campaign encourages teenagers to disassociate themselves from other teenagers who
drink. Finally, an *avoidance* group is one in which a person does not hold
membership or have face-to-face contact with, and whose values, attitudes, and behavior he or she disapproves of. For example, most students
avoid contact with students who have flunked out.

Although we may belong to many groups, in a particular situation we
generally use only one group as a point of reference. Reference groups
have wide-ranging influence on individuals and thus on their behavior as
consumers. Much of this influence is exerted through norms, roles, and
opinion leaders.

Norms and Roles   Every group has **norms,** which are expectations about
what behavior is appropriate. For example, the unwritten rules about
wearing certain kinds of clothes to formal affairs, not breaking in line, and
not bursting into song on a bus all constitute norms. Norms are not universal; which norms apply depend on which groups serve as the reference
groups.

Even within a group, however, different rules apply to different people
at various times, depending on each person's role. A **role** is a prescribed
way of behaving based on the situation and a person's position in the situation. In a classroom, a teacher has one role and students, another. The
key to the role is the situation, not personality or demographic traits. Thus
a young woman reading this book may be a student, daughter, older sister,
roommate, and girlfriend. As a student, she is expected to behave in certain basic ways under certain conditions. For example, when exams are
given, she is expected to take them and not to cheat; when she talks with
an instructor, she is expected to be polite if not deferential; when she at-
tends class, she is expected to stay for the entire session and pay attention.

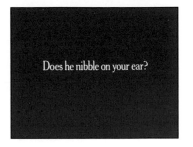

Although no one will resist these seemingly intimate headlines, Amoré's teasing small-space ads on consecutive pages are intended for the cat lover only.

©1992 Heinz Pet Products Co. Used with permission of Heinz Pet Products Co. Newport, KY USA.

The new-parent market segment will respond immediately to the cute clothing, endearing baby, and playful headline in this ad for Reebok's Weebok line.

Reprinted by permission of Reebok International, Ltd.

As a departure from traditional photography, Eaton, an industrial parts manufacturer, commissioned artist Frances Livingston to create a series of paintings, each representing one of the company's six groups of products.

Courtesy of Eaton Corporation.

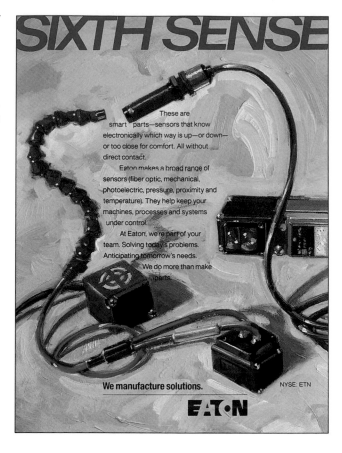

SIXTH SENSE

These are "smart" parts—sensors that know electronically which way is up—or down—or too close for comfort. All without direct contact.

Eaton makes a broad range of sensors (fiber optic, mechanical, photoelectric, pressure, proximity and temperature). They help keep your machines, processes and systems under control.

At Eaton, we're part of your team. Solving today's problems. Anticipating tomorrow's needs. We do more than make parts.

We manufacture solutions.   NYSE: ETN

E·A·T·N

CLBRTNG R 50TH BRTHDY.

The Port of Portland thanks all those who have made Portland International Airport a proud gateway of the Pacific Rim. Through your support, we now handle 200,000 flights a year, provide direct connections to over 100 cities worldwide, and offer facilities uncommon in even larger airports. From a new Airtrans cargo center to an inviting Oregon Market promenade. As PDX expands with Portland and the Northwest, we do so with a concern for efficiency, the environment, and your comfort. We've helped get you where you're going for 50 years. But you've helped get us where we are today. **PORTLAND INTERNATIONAL AIRPORT**

Portland International Airport abbreviates its headline in the style of luggage tags—humor that any traveler will instantly recognize.

Produced by Borders Perrin and Norrander, Inc. Reprinted with permission of the Port of Portland.

The 1992 Jeep Wrangler Renegade, the muscular version of the classic Jeep Wrangler, was designed to extend the life cycle of this product.

Chrysler Corporation.

No headline and stark black-and-white photography are all that is necessary in Ray Ban's ad for the ultimate, cool sunglasses—Wayfarer.

Courtesy of Bausch & Lomb, Inc. Photo: Peter Arnell. Design/ Concept: Arnell/Bickford.

The cover of this issue of *Advertising Age* points to a product category that has a very short life cycle—movies.

Reprinted with permission. Copyright 1992 by Crain Communications, Inc.

A growing fast-food restaurant chain, Taco Bell relies on price discounting as one way to maintain its competitiveness and attract new customers.

©1992 Taco Bell Corp.

When people fail to fulfill their roles, they may face punishment, ranging from a simple reprimand to removal from the role. If a student reads a novel in class, she might be rebuked; if she cheats on an exam, she might be expelled. Meeting the demands of a role is often complicated by the fact that people hold multiple roles that may call for contradictory behaviors. The resulting difficulty is called *role conflict.*

Should marketers study role membership? Substantial evidence suggests that a complement of products often goes along with a particular role. The role of cowboy, for example, suggests a certain type of clothes, tobacco, accent, beverage preference, vehicle, and places to socialize. Designing a promotional strategy to reach this group is straightforward; an ad that portrays the right kind of person dressed appropriately in the right setting is guaranteed to get the group's attention.

Over time, roles change, and marketing must be aware of these changes. Twenty-five years ago, the Halston Co. designed a campaign for their 007 Men's Cologne that followed the James Bond theme. The campaign highlighted the dominant male versus the beautiful-but-subservient female. Today, that campaign would be more likely to anger than persuade the target audience.

Conformity   Norms and roles wield great power because people tend to obey them. *Conformity* is obedience to these group rules. People may conform consciously or unconsciously, out of habit.

Several factors increase the probability that a person will conform. First, the *visibility of the situation* increases conformity. If the purchase and use of a product are public and conspicuous, the influence of the reference group will be stronger than if the product use is private and inconspicuous. Second, the more *commitment* an individual feels to a group, the more the individual will conform to the group norms. Third, the *importance* assigned to a behavior by the reference group may influence the likelihood of conformity. For example, a reference group might place great importance on what its members wear but place very little importance on the type of coffee they drink. The importance level is often difficult to gauge because products may have symbolic importance even when their functional significance is slight. A Cadillac may have little functional importance to physicians, but it may be the only automobile that can reflect the level of success required of this reference group. Finally, *lack of confidence* in a situation may increase the influence of a reference group. Research indicates that consumers tend to have limited confidence in selecting products such as color televisions, automobiles, insurance, major appliances, furniture, and clothing. When buying these products, people tend to look to a reference group for advice, example, and information.[31]

Group Communications Through Opinion Leaders   The final factor that is influenced by the reference group is the communication process. Although information is ultimately processed by an individual, in many cases one or more members of a group filter, interpret, or provide information for the group. Whether people are selecting a restaurant, a lawyer, an automobile, or a brand of cake mix, they seek the advice of knowledgeable friends or acquaintances who can provide information, give advice, or actually make the decision. The individual who provides this service is called an *opinion leader.*

For several years, identifying and influencing the opinion leader has been a major objective of marketing decision makers. This task has been complicated by the fact that opinion leaders are product specific and tend to be similar, both demographically and in personality, to those they influence. For example, an opinion leader who is knowledgeable about stock investments and a receiver of information about stock investments tend to share a variety of characteristics. However, opinion leaders are heavily involved with the mass media, particularly media that concentrate on their area of leadership. This involvement provides a partial solution to the identification problem. It is logical to assume that individuals who subscribe to one or more publications on sailing are opinion leaders on sailing. Thus, by reason of their involvement with sailing, their knowledgeability, and their subscriptions to sailing publications, they may influence others in this area.

For some product categories, there are professional opinion leaders who are easy to identify. Examples include auto mechanics, beauticians, stockbrokers, and lawn and garden experts. Perhaps the most prominent opinion leaders are physicians. Not only do they suggest medications and recommend other physicians, but they may also prescribe exercise equipment, wheelchair brands, diets, or vacation sites. Consequently, marketers of medical supplies have long concentrated marketing efforts on the opinion leader physician rather than the patient, the ultimate user of the product.

Product usage tests, pretests of advertising copy, and media preference studies are usually conducted on samples of individuals who are most likely to be opinion leaders. It is important that these people not only approve of the marketing mix but feel strongly enough about it to tell others.

The Family

The family remains one of the most influential elements in the macroenvironment. Our values, attitudes, and perceptions of life and the world are all formed by our families. The family is a key agent of **socialization,** the process by which people acquire the skills, knowledge, and attitudes necessary to function in society.

Socialization is a lifelong process, but most research has focused on the socialization of children. Although parents do not deliberately prepare children to be consumers, parental socialization shapes two types of consumer-related learning: (1) directly relevant consumer knowledge and skills, such as the ability to count, to budget, and to understand prices and contracts; (2) second-order consumer skills, such as learning to make correct decisions in specific social spheres. For example, an adolescent male learns what to do when he needs his first razor, and an adolescent female is early introduced to the process of purchasing her first bra. In fact, hobbies, car brand preferences, food choices, and travel preferences can often be traced back two generations or more.

Clearly, purchasing and consumption patterns are behaviors, reflecting attitudes and skills strongly influenced by the family unit, among other elements. These patterns depend in part on the type of family involved, the stage of the family's life cycle, and the method of decision making used by the family.

The American Family   Many statistics are reported in terms of households. A **household** is an individual or a group of people who share a common dwelling. Thus a household may consist of one person, a same-sex couple, an unmarried couple, a group living together, a married couple with or without children, or a single parent.

Most Americans, however, marry and spend the majority of their adult lives as members of a **nuclear family,** which consists of two adults of opposite sex, living in a socially approved sexual relationship with their own or adopted children. A nuclear family may be the *family of orientation*, which is the family a person is born or adopted into, or the *family of procreation*, which is the family formed by marriage. The family of orientation is the source of many of our attitudes and values. Although we carry many of these values and attitudes into the family of procreation, lifestyle and purchasing patterns usually shift drastically after marriage. The *extended family* is the nuclear family plus all other close relations—grandparents, aunts, uncles, and cousins. Since World War II, the extended family has become less important to Americans, but it remains influential in some subcultures.

Even within traditional nuclear families in the United States, one very important change has occurred: we have become a nation of small families. Lower birth rates mean fewer children per family. Of those families who have children, the mean number is 1.8, down from 3.5 in 1955. Consequently, most Americans are not likely to identify with a portrayal of a large family interacting in a television ad, and the ad might even create a negative response.

For decades, some social commentators worried that the traditional family was not only shrinking but actually becoming obsolete, in part because of increases in cohabitation and divorce. But despite increases in cohabitation during the last decade, the census bureau estimates that only about 2 percent of all households consist of unmarried people of both sexes, and most unmarried couples live together only a short time before they marry or separate. Divorce is a more significant phenomenon. The number of divorces granted each year has doubled in the last ten years, although most divorces are followed by remarriage. Census bureau demographer Paul Glick predicts of women age twenty-five to twenty-nine: "Of each 100 first marriages, 38 will end in divorce. Three-fourths, or 29, of the women from these divorces will remarry. Thirteen of these remarriages will again end in divorce."[32] Glick's figures suggest that the family is holding its own as an American institution: sixty-two of one hundred first marriages are permanent, and more than half of those who remarry form a permanent union on the second try.

The result of these remarriages is often an *aggregate*, or *blended*, *family*. Two divorced people with children remarry, bringing the children of both marriages into the new, expanded family. It is estimated that 25 percent of American children are now or soon will be members of an aggregate family.[33]

Of course, divorce may also create a household made up of just one person or a household headed by a single parent. Recent dramatic increases in the number of single-parent households have had definite marketing implications. For the single-parent family, convenience items, day-care centers, and appliances safe for young children (who cook and do other household chores unsupervised) all become important. The type of media employed to deliver advertising and the scheduling of the message should be adjusted to reach this type of family. Most single parents do not have the time to leisurely read the newspaper or a magazine; therefore, a message delivered through television or direct mail is more likely to be seen or read. However, single parents often watch television late at night after the children are in bed and the kitchen is cleaned up.

Few market segments are growing faster than *singles*—people who never married or who are divorced or widowed. According to recent studies, there are approximately fifty-eight million single adults in the United States. More specifically, 37 percent of women and 32 percent of men eighteen and older are single.[34] *Advertising Age* reported that "as a group, singles account for $330 billion in total income annually . . . 12.5% of total consumer spending, 15.5% of car sales and more than 15% of the total bill for vacations." In 1990, one in four households was headed by a person living alone (see Figure 4.7). The number of single-person households grew 26 percent in the 1980s, with those headed by men growing faster than those headed by women.[35]

A recent study attempted to determine whether the three categories of female singles (never married, divorced, widowed) differed in respect to

Figure 4.7

As shown, single-person households combined with single-parent households now represents a significant part of our society.
Reprinted with permission © 1990 American Demographics *(January 1990): 27.*

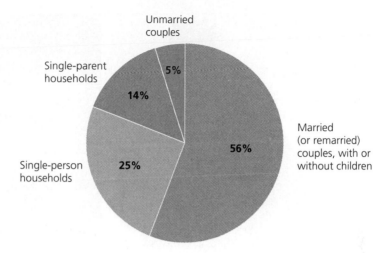

advertising-related factors. The results indicate that, compared to never-married and widowed women, divorced women are heavy users of VCRs, cable television, premium channels, conservative radio programming, and the newspaper for news and food information. The study suggests that different promotion strategies are required to reach each of these types of singles.[36] For example, widows are heavy users of coupons, FM radio, and newspapers. Never-married women can be approached in much the same way as families, using a wide range of media and appeals.[37]

Despite the growing number of singles, special media have emerged to target the traditional family unit. This group still represents nearly fifty-three million married couples, or 56 percent of all households. Moreover, more than half of these families include dual-wage earners with a relatively high discretionary income.[38] The *Family Circle Magazine* ad in Figure 4.8 illustrates this emphasis on the family.

Family Decision Making For over forty years, marketers have been studying how families make their purchasing decisions. How many members are involved in each decision? How are they involved? How does their influence work on the outcome? And what is the best way to reach each of them?

Table 4.3 shows some consumer roles played by members of a typical family. Decisions about purchases depend in part on which family member takes on which role. Studies of husband-wife decision making usually classify the decisions as being husband dominated, wife dominated, joint, or autonomic. These influences are quite fluid and depend on the specific product features under consideration. Consequently, advertisers must be

Figure 4.8

Family Circle Maga-
zine *combines a view
of traditional family
life with a hip, con-
temporary feel.*
Courtesy of Family Circle
Magazine.

sure that they are portraying the husband and wife correctly in various
decision-making scenarios.

Children play an important role in family decision making. Researchers
in one study observed the interaction between parents and children during
the purchase of breakfast foods. In 516 episodes, the most frequent scenarios were (1) the child demands a particular brand of cereal, and the
parent yields (30 percent); (2) the parent invites the child to select a brand,

Table 4.3   **Consumer Roles Within a Family**

Role	Description
Stimulator	First mentions the product or service
Filter	Regulates the flow of information about consumer goods
Influencer	Helps shape other people's evaluation of goods or services
Decider	Makes the decision to buy or consume the product
Preparer	Converts the goods to a form that can be consumed
Consumer	Uses or consumes the product
Monitor	Regulates consumption by other family members
Maintainer	Services or repairs goods
Disposer	Discards goods that are no longer wanted or needed

Source: *Why They Buy: American Consumers Inside and Out*, Robert B. Settle and Pamela L.
Alreck, copyright © 1986 John Wiley & Sons. Reprinted by permission of John Wiley &
Sons, Inc.

Table 4.4 **Earning and Spending by Family Life-Cycle (FLC) State**

Phase of Cycle	Financial Condition	Typical Purchase Patterns
Phase 1 *Young, unmarried, childless*	Both income and expenses are limited, little saving, free spending, beginning use of credit, little financial stress	Apparel, fashion goods, personal care products and services, things related to mating and dating, basic necessities and home supplies, cheap transportation, education, (shared) apartment rent
Phase 2 *Young, married, childless*	Resources adequate (two incomes), little financial burden, free spending, use of credit, little saving, little stress	Consumer durables, major appliances and furniture, audio and video home entertainment goods, air travel, restaurant meals, spectator entertainment, vacations, apparel, and personal care products
Phase 3 *Unmarried, preschool children*	Income strictly limited (unmarried new parent), cautious spending, credit not readily available, no savings, high financial stress	If home-sharing, food and housing expenses shared, dependent on FLC phase of others; if nesting, buying patterns similar to those of next phase, appliances, furniture, child-care products and services, including day care
Phase 4 *Married, preschool children*	Income limited if only one parent is working, few liquid assets, careful spending and credit, little saving, distress and discontent	Purchase and furnishing of first home, durables, especially large and small appliances, child-care products and services, life and casualty insurance, transportation and utilities
Phase 5 *Unmarried, grade school children*	Income limited, careful spending, credit used if available, little saving, high financial stress, substantial discontent	Rent or mortgage payment, economical appliances and furniture, food, clothing, education, transportation expenses for child, limited personal spending, housekeeping and/or child-care costs, low-cost recreation

Source: *Why They Buy: American Consumers Inside and Out*, Robert B. Settle and Pamela L. Alreck, copyright © 1986 John Wiley & Sons. Reprinted by permission of John Wiley & Sons, Inc.

the child does so, and the parent agrees with the selection (19 percent). Regardless of whether the parent or the child initiates the selection, the child seems to direct the brand selection for breakfast food. This dominance by children is clearly reflected in many of the cereal ads targeted at young children. The cereals are often positioned as after-school snacks and include toys and games as part of the package or offer a prize or premium.

What about other products? Do parents yield to their children's requests to purchase a particular product? Parents have been observed to yield to requests for snack foods 63 percent of the time, for toys and games 54 percent of the time, for toothpaste 39 percent, for shampoo 16 percent, for pet food 7 percent, and for Christmas gifts 43 percent.

The Family Life Cycle   Families, like individuals, move through a series of relatively distinct and well-defined stages that affect their needs and wants. Shown in Table 4.4 is a listing of the life-cycle stages and their accompanying purchase patterns. Notice the dramatic shift in the types of products from those purchased by the "young, unmarried, childless" to those purchased by the "young, married, childless."

For promotion managers, changes in the family life cycle offer opportunities to match strategies with particular life stages. A company such as Eastman Kodak Co. uses diverse ads in different media in order to match the stage of the family life cycle. The "young, unmarried, childless" individual has little money for photography and associates picture-taking with pleasurable events such as vacations. Therefore ads in such magazines as *Seventeen* and *Rolling Stone* emphasize the low cost of Kodak cameras and show young people preserving enjoyable times. The "married with preschool children" group, on the other hand, is very involved in picture-taking. Network television, direct mail, and print ads in magazines such as *Parents* portray the joy of saving the moments of childhood through photographs.

Where Do We Go from Here?

It was predicted in the 1970s that by 1990 the average workweek would be under thirty-five hours and that a major problem for Americans would be finding ways to fill the surplus hours. Instead, the time press has become even more severe, and lack of leisure time is the number-one complaint of the 90s consumer. As a result of this time press, many of the luxuries previously the prerogative of the rich are becoming the necessities of the middle class, although they tend to take a different form. For the middle class, instead of a maid, there is the franchised cleaning crew; in lieu of a nanny, there are day-care centers; in place of a cook, there are takeout meals that range from burgers to soufflés. Many of the forecasts made for the 1980s were wrong, and much of what is proposed for the 1990s will be wrong as well.

Still, the question remains—what is the best way to pitch products and services to Americans in the 1990s? According to a *Fortune* study, smart promoters will address five fundamental issues: time, quality, health, the environment, and the home.

- **Time** Any product or service that provides convenience and quality time will be valued.

- **Quality** Purchases will be based on personal judgments of value, that is, on what works best with a person's lifestyle.

- **Health** The baby boomers will fight the physical aging process as much as they can. However, the fitness craze of the eighties will lessen.

- **Environment** There will be a desire both to save and to experience the environment. A new word, *ecotourist,* describes the consumer in search of adventure.

- **Home** Thanks to technological innovations, the home will become more convenient and enjoyable. Affordable housing, home entertainment, and home security will all be very important.[39]

Concept Review

1. The reference group is any group that serves as a point of comparison for an individual in the formation of general or specific values, attitudes, or behavior. A reference group influences a person through the following:
   a. Norms,
   b. Role expectations,
   c. Conformity, and
   d. Group communications through opinion leaders.
2. The family is the most important reference group.
   a. There are various types of families, including nuclear, extended, and aggregate.
   b. Three facets of the family affect promotion:
      (1) Socialization,
      (2) Family decision making, and
      (3) The family life cycle.
3. Five key trends have been identified that influence promotion planning in the 1990s:
   a. Time and convenience
   b. Quality
   c. Health
   d. Environment
   e. Home

Case 4 *Pitching Outside Your Own Ballpark*

People tend to think of others as being like themselves. When you hear the phrase "young adults," you probably think of other college students, not of 20-year-olds in Asia or Africa who may have been farming or working in factories for half of their lives. This tendency holds true in corporate boardrooms and in advertising agencies, and because top executives and marketers are generally better off than the average American, many marketing campaigns are pitched at richer customers. As Harvard Business School professor John Quelch puts it, "The marketing community has no aspirations to address the needs of a demographic group of which it is not a member."

Obviously this attitude can greatly limit the effectiveness of a promotion. While some not-so-rich people may be motivated to buy a product because it is associated with upper-class living, many middle- and lower-class Americans feel cut off from the $200 dresses and $100 shoes they see in glossy catalogues and trendy clothing stores. Recently some companies have begun to recognize that "downscale" consumers represent a huge market that isn't being adequately addressed by most marketing campaigns.

Targeting the Working Class

This realization has led to a shift in some campaigns and products. Not surprisingly, fast-food chains have led the way; they never catered to the brie-and-chablis set anyway. McDonald's recently ran ads that emphasized the working-class background of its customers. One young man tells his date that he works in a record store and doesn't wear designer clothes, but she's still eager to go out with him. In another ad, a young daughter waits eagerly for her exhausted single-parent mother to come home and take her out to McDonald's. Burger King has followed suit by licensing the working-class characters of the hit TV series, "The Simpsons," for its own promotions.

Other companies consciously try to bridge the gap between middle-class incomes and upper-class aspirations. Gitano, for instance, uses the same kind of slick ads in classy magazines as do stylish, expensive clothing makers, but customers buy their Gitanos in discount stores like K mart and Wal-Mart. Gitano keeps prices low and sells most of its jeans in sizes much too big for the skinny models in the ads.

The Results

The potential payoffs of orienting campaigns to less wealthy consumers are illustrated by the fortunes of Birmingham Cable, in Birmingham, Alabama. The company had been using a complicated sales pitch with a glossy brochure, letter, and response form. When it simplified the mailing, emphasized the value of its service as inexpensive family entertainment, and began listing its charges on a monthly rather than a daily basis, response to the promotion more than doubled. Market research had shown that many of Birmingham Cable's potential customers earned an average of $15,000 a year and were very cost-conscious. They weren't being attracted by the same sales pitch that was winning over their richer neighbors.

These examples show that marketers can create campaigns for different classes of customers without being condescending. But many people in the field of promotion may have to make a special effort to pitch to potential consumers who are not like their friends. The old adage says "Know thyself," but in the business world, the more important aphorism is "Know thy customer."

Case Questions

1. What other sociocultural characteristics besides income could be collected in order to provide a clearer picture of the blue-collar segment?
2. Identify possible subsegments within this segment.
3. Evaluate the promotional efforts of McDonald's Corp.

Case Source: Kathleen Deveney, "Downscale Consumers, Long Neglected, Start to Get Some Respect from Marketers," *The Wall Street Journal* (May 31, 1990): B1.

Summary

Promotional strategists who plan to operate and survive in the dynamic marketing environment of the 1990s must continuously monitor and evaluate the sociocultural environment. In this chapter we discussed the primary components of the sociocultural environment.

Culture, the broadest element of the sociocultural environment, consists of three components. The first, beliefs, reflects our knowledge and assessment of something. Values, the second component, are divided into core values and secondary values. Core values predominate within a culture, while secondary values predominate at the subculture or personal level. Both types help us make choices in everyday life. The final component is customs, overt modes of behavior prescribed in a culture.

The demographic environment with important implications for promotion include the baby boom, senior citizens, migration patterns, education and occupation, the employed woman, distribution of income, and ethnic surge. Most of these elements are easily monitored and should be watched by promotion managers.

Demographic traits are often related to another key element of the sociocultural environment: social class. People in different social classes tend to follow different lifestyles, but the relevance of social class to promotion strategies depends on the product involved.

Finally, the family and other reference groups shape values, attitudes, and behavior. People tend to conform to the norms and roles established by their reference groups, and they often turn to opinion leaders within these groups for guidance. The most important reference group remains the family, which is the key agent of socialization. Consumer purchases are influenced by the type of household people live in, by their current stage in the family life cycle, and by their methods of family decision making. Changes in families and households, such as recent increases in the numbers of single-person and single-parent households, offer dramatic challenges and opportunities for promotion managers.

Discussion Questions

1. Define the sociocultural environment. What major factors should the promotion manager monitor?

2. What factors can be used to distinguish one subculture from others? What does a culture have in common with its subcultures?

3. What are core values and secondary values? Why are marketers more interested in secondary values?

4. Outline the major changes in the demographic environment during the 1980s.

5. Baby boomers were presented as one of the most important demographic elements. Identify three specific promotional strategies that would be appropriate for reaching (1) the older baby boomers and (2) the youngest baby boomers.

6. What are the marketing implications associated with the increasing growth of the senior citizen market?

7. What are the most significant trends affecting women?

8. The status of wealth and income appears to be a confusing concept. What is the basis for this confusion? What is discretionary income?

9. Gold Star is a company that manufactures dual-track video players. It wishes to design a promotional strategy targeted at the American

family. What are the key considerations Gold Star should identify before targeting this group? Is there a typical American family?

10. How do marketers go about forecasting cultural change?

Suggested Projects

1. Trace the baby-boom generation through the year 2020. Graphically show the kinds of goods and services baby boomers will need as they move toward that date.

2. Review the purchase decision-making process your family has followed during the last year. Are purchasing decisions made exclusively by one member of your family? Jointly?

References

1. Milton Rokeach, *The Nature of Human Values* (New York: Free Press, 1973): 5.

2. J. Michael Munson and Edward F. McQuarrie, "Shortening the Rokeach Value Survey for Use in Consumer Research," in *Advances in Consumer Research* Vol. 15, 1988. (Cambridge, Mass.: Association for Consumer Research): 381–386.

3. Leon G. Schiffman and Leslie Lazar Kanuk, *Consumer Behavior*, 3rd ed. (Englewood Cliffs, NJ: Prentice-Hall, Inc., 1987): 506.

4. Rokeach, 8.

5. Munson and McQuarrie, 383.

6. Martha Farnsworth Riche, "Psychographics for the 1990s," *American Demographics* (July 1989): 25–26, 30–32.

7. Philip Cateora and John M. Hess, *International Marketing,* 4th ed. (Homewood, IL: Richard D. Irwin, 1979): 90.

8. Stewart Alter, "Yuppie," *Newsweek* (December 31, 1984): 81.

9. John J. Burnett and Alan J. Bush, "Profiling the Yuppies," *Journal of Advertising Research* (April/May 1986): 27–35.

10. Lois Therrein, "Boomers at Fortysomething," *Business Week* (September 25, 1989): 142–143.

11. Walter Klores and Jerry Gerber, "20/20 Foresight: Next 30 Years for Baby-Boomers," *Advertising Age* (February 5, 1990): 27, 29.

12. "The Perils of Age," *American Demographics* (September 1989): 34.

13. Karen Buglass, "The Business of Eldercare," *American Demographics* (September 1989): 32–39.

14. Larry Long, "Americans on the Move," *American Demographics* (June 1990): 46–49.

15. Judith Waldrop and Thomas Exter, "What the 1990 Census Will Show," *American Demographics* (January 1990): 30.

16. "The Password Is 'Flexible,'" *Business Week* (September 25, 1989): 152.

17. Diane Crispell, "Women in Charge," *American Demographics* (September 1989): 27–29.

18. Betsy Sharkey, "The Chameleon Decade," *Adweek: Marketing to the Year 2000* (September 11, 1989): 16.

19. Waldrop and Exter, 29.

20. Bickly Townsend, "This Is Fun Money," *American Demographics* (October 1989): 39.

21. Sylvia Nasar, "Do We Live As Well As We Used to?" *Fortune* (September 14, 1987): 34.

22. Joe Schwartz, "Dollar Doldrums," *American Demographics* (January 1990): 9.

23. Betsy Sharkey, 15.

24. Joe Schwartz, "Income by Definition," *American Demographics* (September 1990): 64.

25. Nasar, 34.

26. William O'Hare, "In the Black," *American Demographics* (November 1989): 24–28.

27. Chester A. Sevenson, "How to Speak to Hispanics," *American Demographics* (February 1990): 40–42.

28. W. L. Warner, M. Meeker, and K. Eells, *Social Class in America: Manual of Procedure for the Measurement of Social Status* (New York: Free Press, 1968): 316–317.

29. Robert B. Settle and Pamela L. Alreck, *Why They Buy: American Consumers Inside and Out* (New York: John Wiley & Sons, 1986): 129.

30. Schiffman and Kanuk, 318.

31. D. Cartwright and A. Zonder, *Group Dynamics* (New York: Harper and Row, 1968): 139–151.

32. Martha Farnsworth Riche, "The Postmarital Society," *American Demographics* (November 1988): 22–26, 60.

33. Alvin Toffler, *The Third Wave* (New York: William Morrow, 1980): 248.

34. Thomas Exter, "Demographic Forecasts," *American Demographics* (April 1990): 55.

35. "Me-First Mode Takes a Beating," *Advertising Age* (February 5, 1990): 22.

36. Waldrop and Exter, 27.

37. Stephanie Shipp, "How Singles Spend," *American Demographics* (April 1988): 22–28.

38. Waldrop and Exter, 27.

39. Anne B. Fisher, "What Consumers Want in the 1990s," *Fortune* (January 29, 1990): 108–112.

5

Decision Making by Buyers

The Psychological Background
Motivation
Learning
Attitudes

Varieties of Decisions by Consumers

Recognizing Needs and Problems
Motivating Consumers
Dealing with Conflicting Motives

Information Search and Processing
Steps in Information Processing
Elaboration Likelihood Model

Identifying and Evaluating Alternatives
The Multiattribute Attitude Model
The Theory of Reasoned Action
Influencing Attitudes

Purchase and Postpurchase Behavior

Organizational Market Behavior
Characteristics of Organizational Buying
Stages in Organizational Buying

Consider This:

Science or Snooping?

Knowing what consumers buy and why is at the heart of marketing and indeed an important element in most business. Traditionally, market researchers have been content with gathering quantitative information and surveying shoppers in stores or through the mail. Recently, however, some marketing professionals have borrowed the tools of anthropology and taken their studies into consumers' kitchens.

These "ethnographers" may spend as much as two hours carefully dissecting and analyzing the purchases of their research "subject." If they're lucky, or smart, or happen to be in the right kitchen, they may come up with an insight that will influence a client's promotional approach.

Allison Cohen, senior vice president at Ally & Gargano, is an expert at such consumer analysis, and her research has led to a number of recent ad campaigns. Cohen's forays into people's houses led to the realization that a large number of people are closet chocaholics, keeping secret stashes of chocolate hidden in private places. The result of this work: a Swiss chocolate maker's new campaign, "The True Confessions of Chocaholics."

Perhaps the most ambitious attempt to get inside consumers' minds by studying their kitchens was undertaken by a consulting firm looking for connections between buying patterns and self-esteem. After rating an interview subject's self-esteem, the consultants noted what kinds of foods the subject bought. They concluded that high-self-esteem buyers were more likely to buy frozen chicken dinners, while low-self-esteem shoppers, who presumably lack self-control, liked portion-controlled snack items. This correlation led Sara Lee to develop a new line of snack cakes.

Many advertising agencies steer clear of such snooping, finding the invasion of privacy distasteful. And even those who support the practice would generally admit that making the leap from one buyer's kitchen to a new promotional focus requires considerable insight and intuition. But since more and more companies are pledging to please their customers, it seems certain that they will use every method possible to find out what those customers want.

Source: "You Are What You Buy," *Newsweek* (June 4, 1990): 59.

*I*n the preceding chapter, we discussed major environmental factors that influence consumers and thus promotion. But differences in sociocultural factors alone cannot explain such variations in consumer behavior as why one homemaker loves to cook and one does not, or why people prefer different brands of soft drinks even though they cannot tell one brand from another in blindfold tests. It is not enough to understand how culture, social class, and reference group influence consumers. To develop a successful promotional campaign, promotion managers also need some understanding of customers' psychological characteristics—their motives, attitudes, and personalities—and of how they make purchasing decisions. These are the topics of this chapter.

The difficulties in understanding buyer behavior are daunting. The emergence of ethnography as a market research technique suggests how difficult it is to truly understand the inner workings of the consumer. People themselves often do not understand why they buy some products rather than others, or why they lie to the researcher or to themselves. Countless variations in consumer behavior occur simply because each person is an individual with a unique personality. Nevertheless, sellers must search for some common threads so that they can appeal to many people with one promotional program.

Researchers have produced some useful generalizations about buying behavior. This chapter discusses these generalizations, particularly those that relate to promotion. Our discussion focuses on the consumer market, but we also look briefly at the behavior of the *organizational market*—specifically, producer, reseller, and government markets.

The starting point for our discussion was given in Figure 4.1, which showed a simplified, partial model of consumer decision making. In this chapter, we add substance to that model, as Figure 5.1 illustrates. We do not aim to examine the entire process of consumer decision making; we assume that readers have taken either a consumer behavior course or a basic psychology course, or both. Our emphasis is on answering this question: What does the promotional strategist need to know about consumer behavior in order to facilitate the creation of effective messages? Our discussion begins with the variables called psychological characteristics in Figure 5.1.

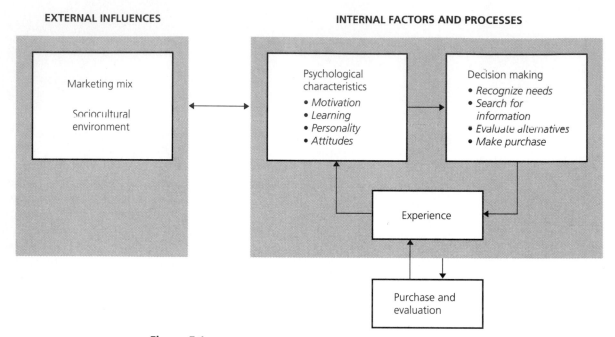

EXTERNAL INFLUENCES　　　**INTERNAL FACTORS AND PROCESSES**

Figure 5.1

This figure focuses on the specific elements that influence the consumer's decision to purchase and evaluate products and services.

The Psychological Background

Attempting to sell decorative outdoor lighting to a buyer in an industrial plant who wants lighting solely for security purposes will probably get a salesperson nowhere. If sellers do not appeal to the right motive, they will probably lose the sale. Similarly, if a company misreads its customers' beliefs, interests, attitudes, self-images, or other psychological characteristics, it risks making major mistakes. A company should learn as much as possible about the characteristics of its customers in order to learn *why* consumers buy a particular product or shop at a certain store. Furthermore, as we noted in Chapter 1, learning about these characteristics provides a way of discovering promotional opportunities. Here we provide a brief introduction to three key aspects of the psychological background for consumer behavior: motivation, learning, and attitudes. Each of these plays an important role in our later discussion of consumer decision making.

Motivation

Much of what people do can be traced to their needs. An unsatisfied need causes an inner state of tension, feelings of disequilibrium, or dissatisfaction. A **motive** is an inner drive or pressure to take action in order to eliminate tension, to satisfy a need or solve a problem, or to restore a sense of equilibrium. Unstimulated, latent needs do not motivate behavior; a need must be aroused to a certain level in order for it to serve as a motive. The sources of arousal may be internal (biological or psychological) or environmental. Hunger, for example, may be aroused by a lack of food, by thoughts about food, or by a commercial for a tasty dish.

The most widely publicized theory of human motivation was developed by Abraham Maslow. His "hierarchy of human needs" theory postulates five basic levels of human needs, which rank in order of importance from low-level (biogenic) needs to higher-level (psychogenic) needs. The theory suggests that individuals seek to satisfy lower-level needs before higher-level needs. When a lower-level need is satisfied, a new, higher-level need emerges, and so on. If a lower-level need experiences some renewed depreciation, it may temporarily become dominant again.

Promotion managers need to understand what motives stimulate what types of behavior and how these motives and behaviors are influenced by specific situations. Identifying potential motives would seem to be a first step in this task. At one time, conventional wisdom held that all motives are biologically based and innate, like hunger and thirst. But many motives are learned, primarily through socialization during early childhood. Motivations to achieve, to conform, to be powerful, to feel a sense of belonging—all reflect the effects of learning. Since each individual's personal development is unique, so are each person's motives.[1] Furthermore, even when behavior is motivated by biologically based needs, learned motivations generally guide the expression of that behavior. For example, the purchase of a particular brand of soft drink on a hot summer day may reflect both the consumer's innate need to satisfy thirst and a learned need for self-expression. Although marketers cannot control consumer thirst, they can influence the choice of soft drink.

Because of the influence of learning, the number of possible motives for consumer behavior is vast. There have been many attempts to classify these motives, but no one classification is complete or universally accepted. Probably the classification most closely associated with promotion divides motives into rational and emotional motives. **Rational motives** are supported by a systematic reasoning process that people perceive as being acceptable to their peers. A homemaker, for instance, might insist on buying foods grown without chemicals, even if they cost more than other foods, in order to enhance the family's health. Whether the arguments are valid or not is irrelevant; what matters is that the individual believes the motivation is rational. Rational motives for buying a product include lower price, greater endurance, higher quality, convenience, and better performance.

Emotional motives are characterized by feelings that may emerge without careful thought or consideration of social consequences.[2] People are often unwilling to admit emotional motives openly. Sometimes these motives—known as *latent* motives—lie below consciousness. It would be unwise to emphasize these motives in promotional messages. Motives that people are willing to acknowledge are *manifest* motives. "Be like Mike. Drink Gatorade." was the copy of a recent Gatorade ad targeted at children that used sports hero Michael Jordan. This ad plays on a manifest motive. A great many emotional motives exist, but those most often important in marketing include status, prestige, conformity, sex, loneliness, self-esteem, and the desire to be different. These motives are stimulated through such techniques as fear, anxiety, humor, and sex appeals.

Learning

Learned motives are only one example of the pervasive influence of learning on human behavior. Some forms of learning, called **cognitive learning,** involve thought and conscious awareness; problem solving is an example. Behavior is changed through **behavioral learning,** which is learning that does not require awareness or conscious effort but depends instead on an association between events.

Although several theories attempt to explain how learning takes place, there are common principles and concepts that apply to all. Learning starts with *motivation,* which is based on needs and goals. Motivation thus acts as a spur to learning, with needs and goals serving as stimuli. Suppose a consumer is motivated to begin an exercise program because he is putting on weight and feeling lethargic. A *cue*—in this case, an ad for a new health club—provides the direction the individual will follow to satisfy the goal of losing weight. The message in this ad, however, will only serve as a cue if it is consistent with the person's expectations. If he has already failed to lose weight at other health clubs, this ad will not be a useful cue. How an individual reacts to a cue constitutes his or her *response.* Learning can take place even if the response is not overt. Several cues may be processed and evaluated before an individual finally reacts to one overtly. Response is a function of one's past experiences with cues. A positive response to a beneficial experience is called *positive reinforcement;* the cue is again likely to produce a similar reaction. If the experience was unpleasant, then *negative reinforcement* has taken place, and we will not repeat the same mistake again.

Psychologists distinguish two basic types of behavioral learning: classical conditioning and instrumental conditioning. In **classical conditioning,** a response is learned as a result of the pairing of two stimuli. Assume that Bill Cosby elicits positive feelings in members of an audience. If they repeatedly see him and Coke together in a commercial, then eventually the sight of Coke alone will elicit those positive feelings. In the language of classical conditioning, Cosby and Coke are stimuli that have been paired; the positive reaction to Coke is a *conditioned response* that has been learned as a result of the pairing of the stimuli. In **instrumental conditioning,** a response is learned or strengthened because it has been associated with certain consequences. If buying Coke brings the reward of a good-tasting drink, then the act of buying Coke is *reinforced* and is more likely to occur in the future.

Attitudes

Motivation and learning both play a part in determining a third key component of the psychological background for consumer behavior: attitudes. An **attitude** is an enduring disposition, favorable or unfavorable, toward some object—an idea, a person, a thing, a situation. Thus attitudes toward brands are tendencies to evaluate brands in a consistently favorable or unfavorable way. Each attitude has three components: cognitive, affective, and behavioral. All three components must be consistent in order for a real attitude to result.

The *cognitive component* includes beliefs and knowledge about the object of the attitude. For example, an individual might believe that Shell Oil is a major manufacturer, an aggressive marketer, and is quite profitable. Each of these beliefs reflects knowledge about an attribute of the company. All one's beliefs about Shell Oil represent the cognitive component of an attitude toward the company.

If someone says "I hate Shell Oil" or "I like the gasoline from Shell Oil better than any other," the person is expressing the affective aspect of an attitude. Feelings about the object make up the *affective component* of an attitude. People typically evaluate separately each attribute of the object of the attitude; the combination of these reactions determines the overall reaction. For example, a consumer might hold separate feelings about the products of a company, its honesty, its fairness toward its workers, and so forth.

Actions taken toward the object of an attitude constitute the *behavioral component* of the attitude. Buying a product, recommending a company to friends, or requesting information are examples of behavioral components. Behavior is usually directed toward an entire object and is therefore not likely to be attribute specific. In the case of retail outlets, however, consumers may react behaviorally to specific attributes. For example, a homemaker may buy produce at one supermarket and meat at another.

How easily can attitudes be changed? The answer depends to an extent on two characteristics of the attitude: its centrality and its intensity.

Centrality depends on the degree to which an attitude is tied to values. Note that although personal values influence attitudes, the two are distinct. Values are not tied to a specific situation or object; they are standards that guide behavior and influence beliefs and attitudes. People have a large number of beliefs, a smaller number of attitudes, and even fewer values. The stronger the relationship between an attitude and a person's values, the greater the centrality of the attitude. For example, for a person who places a high value on thriftiness, social responsibility, and ecology, a favorable attitude toward recyclable containers is likely to have high centrality. If the centrality of an attitude is high, then changing it would create inconsistency between the attitude and a person's values. Not surprisingly, research suggests that the more central an attitude is, the more difficult it is to change.[3]

Intensity depends on the effective component of an attitude. The strength of feeling toward the object of an attitude constitutes the intensity of the attitude. Intense attitudes are difficult to change. Consequently, most marketing efforts are directed at creating minor changes in attitudes—from negative to neutral, from neutral to positive, or from positive to more positive. An individual who holds an intensely negative attitude toward a product or idea might best be eliminated from further marketing consideration.

Concept Review

1. The following components make up a person's psychological background.
   a. Motive is the inner drive to take action in order to eliminate tension, to satisfy a need or problem, or to restore a sense of equilibrium.
   b. Learning
      - Cognitive learning involves thought and conscious awareness.
      - Behavioral learning does not require awareness or conscious effort; it depends on an association between events.
   c. Attitude is an enduring disposition, favorable or unfavorable, toward an object, an idea, a person, a thing, or a situation.

Varieties of Decisions by Consumers

So far, we have taken a brief look at psychological characteristics that have a key influence on the decisions that a consumer makes. Our next question is, How does the consumer make decisions? What steps are involved in consumer decision making?

Figure 5.2

*Models of complex
and simple decision
making.*

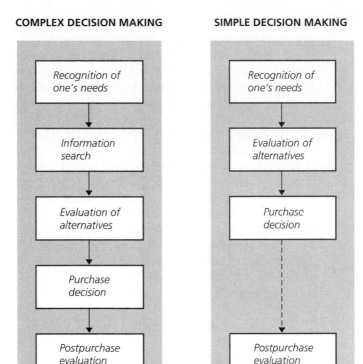

COMPLEX DECISION MAKING   **SIMPLE DECISION MAKING**

The answer depends on whether the consumer engages in simple or complex decision making. Figure 5.2 shows the differences between these two processes. Notice that whereas **complex decision making** requires a search for information and an evaluation of alternatives, simple decision making does not. In **simple decision making,** some information search and alternative evaluation may occur, but these activities are minimized. Evaluation after the purchase may or may not occur in simple decision making.

Which type of decision making occurs depends (1) on whether the decision is novel or routine and (2) on the extent of the consumer's involvement with the decision.

High-involvement decisions are those that are important to the consumer. Such decisions are closely tied to the consumer's ego and self-image. They also involve some risk to the consumer—financial risk (highly priced items), social risk (products important to the peer group), or psychological risk (the wrong decision might cause the consumer some concern and anxiety). In making these decisions, it is worth the consumer's time and energies to consider product alternatives carefully. A complex process of decision making is therefore more likely for high-involvement purchases. **Low-involvement decisions** are those that are not important to the consumer. Financial, social, and psychological risks are not nearly as great. In such cases, it may not be worth the consumer's time and effort to search for information about brands or to consider a wide range of alternatives. A low-involvement purchase therefore generally entails a limited process of decision making.[4] The purchase of a new computer is an example of high involvement, while the purchase of a pizza is a low-involvement decision.

When a consumer has bought a product many times in the past, the decision making is likely to be simple, regardless of whether it is a high- or a low-involvement decision. Suppose a consumer initially bought a product after much care and involvement, was satisfied, and continued to buy the product. The customer's careful consideration of the product has produced **brand loyalty,** which is the result of involvement with the product decision. Once a consumer is brand loyal, a simple decision-making process is all that is required for subsequent purchases. The consumer now buys the product through **habit,** which means making a decision without the use of additional information or the evaluation of alternative choices. This is a simple but high-involvement decision.

Habitual buying may also reflect low-involvement, simple decision making. If a consumer is not highly involved in the initial decision to buy a product and makes no commitment to the product but simply responds to the positive reinforcement it provides, the person may develop a type of brand loyalty called **inertia.** The consumer thus buys the product passively.

Even when a consumer buys a brand for the first time, if it is an inexpensive, unexciting product that is purchased regularly, the consumer is likely to exert very little thought or effort in choosing the product; this is a simple, low-involvement decision process. The purchase of a package of ball-point pens falls into this category. Now consider the case of a consumer deciding whether to buy for the first time an expensive, personal, or emotion-laden product such as a car or medical care. It is fairly safe to assume that the consumer will expend a great deal of effort on the process; this is a complex, high-involvement decision process.

In the rest of this chapter, we examine complex decisions to buy a new product and discuss each of the steps outlined in Figure 5.2. Thus we turn next to a consideration of how consumers recognize needs.

Concept Review

1. The decision-making process involved in buying a product may be characterized by its complexity, novelty, and consumer involvement.
2. Unlike complex decision making, simple decision making does not re-

quire information search, alternative evaluation, or postpurchase evaluation.
3. High-involvement decisions occur when a product has high relevance, emotional appeal, or risk.
4. Habitual purchases may reflect high- or low-involvement simple decision making.

Recognizing Needs and Problems

Earlier we discussed the difference between latent needs, which do not stimulate behavior, and unmet needs, which do motivate behavior. Another way of distinguishing between latent and unmet needs is to view the former as nonproblems and the latter as problems. For example, a recent college graduate may have a latent need for a new car to replace a 1986 pickup but takes no action. Within six months, the pickup requires a new battery and a brake job, and the garage has just called with a repair estimate for $374. The latent need has now been converted into an unmet need, or a problem to be solved. Essentially, consumers view themselves as problem solvers, not need satisfiers. It is this "problem" perspective that is used in marketing, and it offers important insights for the promotion manager as well.

Every day, people face a myriad of consumption problems. Some are routine, such as filling the car with gasoline or buying milk. Other problems occur infrequently, such as searching for a good life insurance policy or a fiftieth-anniversary gift. Whether the problem is routine or infrequent, the process of buying starts when an unsatisfied need creates tension and thus motivation. As discussed earlier, the motive may be aroused by internal sources or by external sources such as an ad. Whether people recognize a need often depends on the type of information received and how it is perceived.

Even if people recognize a need, whether they act to resolve the problem depends on two factors: (1) the magnitude of the discrepancy between what they have and what they need and (2) the importance of the problem. Every person has his or her own personal hierarchy of needs. This hierarchy varies from person to person, as well as across time and situations. For some people, having a cup of coffee the first thing every morning is a need with a very high priority. A consumer may want a new Mercedes and own a ten-year-old VW. Despite the large discrepancy between the current possession and the need, if the problem is relatively unimportant compared with other problems, the consumer is not likely to be motivated to buy the Mercedes. For buying to proceed, people must be motivated both to acknowledge the need and to do something about it.

Furthermore, the problem must be defined in such a way that the consumer can initiate action to bring about a solution. In many cases, problem recognition and problem definition occur simultaneously, as happens when a person runs out of toothpaste. But consider a more complicated problem that is involved with status and image—how we want others to see us. A consumer may know that she is not satisfied with her appearance; because she may not be able to define the problem more precisely, she might not do anything about the situation. Consumers do not usually begin to solve a problem until it is adequately defined. As we discuss in the following sections, promotion may help consumers both to recognize a need and to define it in a way that makes a particular purchase likely.

Motivating Consumers

Marketers become involved in the need-recognition stage in two ways. First, if they know what problems consumers are facing, they may develop a marketing mix to solve them. Marketers begin by measuring problem recognition using a variety of market research techniques, including surveys, focus groups, observations, and the collecting of consumer suggestions or complaints. Promotion managers in particular find this research useful as a basis for selecting primary appeals for ads or for deciding whether to employ coupons, sweepstakes, and so forth.

Second, marketers themselves may activate problem recognition. The ad in Figure 5.3, for example, points out a problem many of us would like to solve.

Marketers can also shape the definition of the need or problem. If a consumer needs a new coat, does he define the problem as a need for inexpensive covering, for a way to stay warm on the coldest days, for a garment that will last several years, for a warm covering that will not attract odd looks from his peers, or for an article of clothing that will express his personal sense of style? A salesperson or an ad may shape his answers.

The potential influence of promotion on need definition is great in part because people usually experience several motives at a time. And people usually act because of a mixture of rational and emotional motives. That is, when a consumer buys a product, the person is probably influenced by rational motives such as price and endurance as well as by emotional motives such as a desire for prestige. Commercials, point-of-purchase displays, and sales presentations often appeal to both types of motives. In fact, when a product inherently appeals to one type of motive, promoters may find it effective to stress the other type. For example, because automobiles and clothing inherently appeal to emotional motives such as self-esteem, it is wise to include appeals to rational motives when promoting these products. But because the inherent appeal of a lawn mower is prob-

Figure 5.3

As in the case with this ad for cosmetic surgery, marketers must activate recognition of a problem. © North Memorial Medical Center.

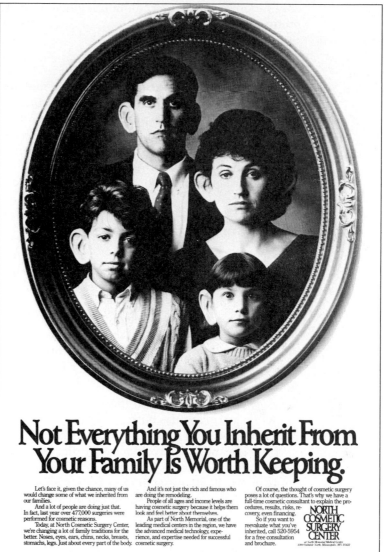

Not Everything You Inherit From Your Family Is Worth Keeping.

Let's face it, given the chance, many of us would change some of what we inherited from our families.

And a lot of people are doing just that. In fact, last year over 477,000 surgeries were performed for cosmetic reasons.

Today, at North Cosmetic Surgery Center, we're changing a lot of family traditions for the better. Noses, eyes, ears, chins, necks, breasts, stomachs, legs. Just about every part of the body.

And it's not just the rich and famous who are doing the remodeling.

People of all ages and income levels are having cosmetic surgery because it helps them look and feel better about themselves.

As part of North Memorial, one of the leading medical centers in the region, we have the advanced medical technology, experience, and expertise needed for successful cosmetic surgery.

Of course, the thought of cosmetic surgery poses a lot of questions. That's why we have a full-time cosmetic consultant to explain the procedures, results, risks, recovery, even financing.

So if you want to reevaluate what you've inherited, call 520-5954 for a free consultation and brochure.

NORTH COSMETIC SURGERY CENTER
at North Memorial Medical Center
3300 Oakdale North, Minneapolis, MN 55422

ably rational, effective promotion is likely to include appeals to emotional motives.

Dealing with Conflicting Motives

People often experience not just multiple motives but conflicting motives. Suppose Bill Jones has decided that his existing three-bedroom home is too small now that his wife is pregnant with their third child. At the same time, Bill has decided that his unhappiness with his present job is prompting him to consider changing careers. He faces conflict between his desire for a new home and his need to change careers.

Until people resolve motivational conflicts like Bill's, the buying process for a product stops. Promotion can help consumers resolve their conflicts in a way that moves them to buy a particular product. Three types of motivational conflict are relevant to promotion:[5]

1. *Approach-approach motivational conflict.* When consumers face a choice between two attractive options, they have an approach-approach conflict. The more equal the options, the greater the conflict. For example, a consumer who has recently received a large inheritance may be torn between taking a European vacation or buying a new sports car. Both personal and commercial sources (friends and salespeople) may influence people who face this type of conflict. A well-designed ad placed in the appropriate medium may be all that is necessary to push the respondent toward a particular alternative.

2. *Approach-avoidance motivational conflict.* This type of conflict occurs when an option has both positive and negative consequences. If a consumer loves doughnuts but is worried about weight gain, the person faces an approach-avoidance conflict when trying to decide whether to buy them. Low-calorie varieties of desserts, diet soft drinks, and light beer are all attempts to offer consumers a solution to this type of conflict. Because approach-avoidance conflicts are difficult to resolve, anxiety often remains after the purchasing decision is made.

3. *Avoidance-avoidance motivational conflict.* Sometimes consumers face two undesirable options. If the family refrigerator fails, the consumer may not want to spend money on a new one, but neither can the household go without a refrigerator. Rent-to-buy programs, credit, and installment plans help consumers resolve this kind of conflict. The decision to buy life insurance provides another example of an avoidance-avoidance conflict. People may want to provide financial security for their family, but they may be unhappy about spending money on something that does not provide an immediate benefit. Life insurance companies try to alleviate this conflict by emphasizing the investment aspects of insurance.

Concept Review

1. The buying process begins with recognition of an unsatisfied need.
2. Consumers must be motivated both to acknowledge and to resolve a need in order for the buying process to proceed.
3. In any situation, people are likely to be motivated by a mixture of rational and emotional motives and by conflicting motives.
4. Marketing may influence consumers in the need-recognition stage by stimulating problem recognition, by helping them to define problems and deal with conflicting motives in a way that leads to purchase of the product, or by developing a marketing mix that meets consumers' needs.

Information Search and Processing

When a problem has been recognized, a state of tension occurs that causes the consumer to search for information that will help in decision making. The information search is the second step in complex decision making and involves mental as well as physical activity. The search takes time, energy, and money and can often require giving up more desirable activities.[6] The benefits of the information search, however, often outweigh the costs. Engaging in a thorough information search may ultimately mean saving money, receiving better quality, or reducing risk.

The consumer becomes involved in two types of information search: internal and external. In an internal search, the consumer attempts to resolve problems by recalling previously stored information. For example, people who suffer from allergies can easily recall what they did last year for relief. They may even remember the location of the drugstore where they last purchased allergy medication. When problems cannot be resolved through an internal search, people search externally for additional information. The external sources may include family, friends, professionals, government or corporate publications, ads, sales personnel, or displays.

The sources that a person uses may depend on the importance of the decision, past experience, confidence in particular sources, and psychological makeup. Some consumers find it too troublesome to search for information and are willing to rely on the information provided by a salesclerk for a minor purchase. But when these same people buy a new car, they may go through a very elaborate search that includes writing for information, comparing government reports, driving from dealership to dealership, and talking with people who are considered knowledgeable about the product.

When the search actually occurs, what do people do with the information? How do they spot, understand, and recall information? In other words, how do they process information? This broad topic is important for understanding communication in general as well as buying behavior in particular, and it has received a great deal of study. Understanding the process people go through when they receive information, including promotional messages, has direct benefits for the promotion manager.

Steps in Information Processing

Assessing how a person processes information is not an easy task. Often observation has served as the bases. Yet, there are many theories as to how this process takes place. Figure 5.4 shows one widely accepted outline of the information-processing sequence. It includes five steps.

Exposure   Information processing starts with the **exposure** of consumers to some source of stimulation such as watching television, going to the supermarket, or driving past a particular billboard. In order to start the process, marketers must attract consumers to the stimulus or put it squarely in the path of people in the target market. Thus promotion messages contain celebrity endorsements or coupons to attract consumers, and they appear in a media mix marketers feel consumers will be exposed to. As a specific example, Nike, Inc. uses Michael Jordan in commercials to endorse its Air Jordans in order to attract consumers; the company then runs the commercial twelve times during the NBA Game of the Week to ensure that consumers will hear the message.

Attention   Exposure alone does little unless people pay attention to the stimulus. At any moment, people are bombarded by all sorts of stimuli, but they have a limited capacity to process this input. They must devote mental resources to stimuli in order to process them; in other words, they must pay **attention.** If attention is not given, no further information processing occurs, and the message will be lost.

Attention is selective. We have neither the cognitive capability nor the interest to pay attention to all the messages we are exposed to. Some stimuli are more attention-getting than others. For example, bright colors and movement both attract attention. Contrast (that is, size of the stimulus relative to its background) and intensity (for example, loudness, brightness) also prompt attention.[7] Personal attributes also influence which stimuli will attract attention. People are likely to pay attention to a message when it provides information that is relevant to problems that evoke high involve-

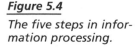

Figure 5.4

The five steps in information processing.

ment and that they are motivated to resolve.[8] People also tend to pay attention to messages that are perceived to be consistent with their attitudes and ignore those perceived not to be in agreement.[9] Several attention-enhancing advertising methods have been identified. For example, ads that are positioned first in a series of ads are more likely to gain attention, as are humorous ads and those that use a sexual appeal.[10] The positioning of a print ad on a newspaper page is more likely to receive attention if it is placed in the center of the reader's optical field. Buying a full-page ad eliminates this positioning problem. The ad in Figure 5.5 does an excellent job of providing stimuli that will attract one segment of the advertiser's target audience.

Figure 5.5

This ad uses humor to gain the reader's attention.

Courtesy of Hershey Foods Corporation. The conical configuration, the attached plume device, and the words HERSHEY'S and HERSHEY'S KISSES are registered trademarks of Hershey Foods Corporation and are used with permission.

Perception   Step three in the information-processing sequence is perception. It involves classifying the incoming signals into meaningful categories, forming patterns, and assigning names or images to them. **Perception** is the assignment of meaning to stimuli received through the senses.

Perceptions are shaped by (1) the physical characteristics of the stimuli, (2) the context, and (3) the individual perceiving the stimuli. The senses transmit signals about the shape, color, sound, and feel of stimuli, but each individual perceives those stimuli within a particular context shaped by the person's own frame of reference. Thus a person's past learning, attitudes, personality, self-image, and current motivations and emotions shape what is perceived. Some stimuli are perceived totally, some partially, some accurately, some inaccurately. In any event, the result of the perceptual process is a highly personalized mental representation of sensory stimuli, a representation that differs from person to person.

The actual process of human perception has been well researched. In general, perception is thought to be a three-stage process: selection, organization, and interpretation of stimuli. Although we are not always conscious of it, we exercise a great deal of selectivity in determining which stimuli we will perceive. It would be impossible for us to perceive all the stimuli in a typical supermarket, for instance. Which stimuli we select depends on our previous experience with the stimuli and our motives at that time. The more experience or familiarity we have with a setting or situation, the more selective we are. A student enters a classroom with a set of expectations about what he or she will see, hear, and smell on entering the room. Given everything is as expected, the student will perceive only those things selected as relevant (for example, an available seat near the door). If expectations can be changed dramatically, it is possible to influence the selection process. This is called creating *contrast*, which is what Infiniti did when the company produced a television ad that did not show the car. Motivation, as discussed earlier, is a somewhat similar phenomenon. People tend to perceive things they need or want; the stronger the need, the greater the motivation to perceive stimuli that will satisfy their need or want and to ignore stimuli that will not.

We do not perceive stimuli from the environment as separate and discrete sensations; rather, we tend to organize them into groups and perceive them as unified wholes. This tendency to organize and integrate stimuli into a group to which we judge they belong greatly simplifies our lives. We organize stimuli according to the figure and ground relationship, grouping, and closure. The figure and ground relationship refers to the idea of contrast mentioned earlier. A darker color on a lighter color and a louder sound compared to a softer sound are examples of contrast. The element *in figure* is more clearly perceived because it appears to be dominant; by contrast, *ground* appears to be subordinate and therefore less important. For some people, classical music will always be ground, while for others it will be in figure. This example suggests that we learn which stimuli are perceived as in figure and ground. Advertisers try to make sure that the element they want noted is seen as figure and not as ground.

There is evidence that we automatically group stimuli in a manner that forms a unified picture or impression. We tend to *group* stimuli in order to facilitate memory and recall. Telephone numbers, social security numbers, and addresses are common examples of grouping. Soft drink companies are famous in their attempts to group their products with a positive experience.

We all like to know how an unfinished story, movie, or even joke turns out. This desire reflects our need for *closure*, organizing perceptions so that they paint a complete picture. Even when a message is incomplete, we tend to consciously or subconsciously complete it. Coke told consumers it was "IT," hoping people would interpret "IT" in a positive way. Pepsi uses "Uh-huh" in a similar way.

Finally, an individual interprets stimuli according to a set of prescribed criteria. Although this interpretation can be affected by many factors, there are a few general factors that appear to always operate. Clarity of the stimulus is critical; stimuli that are ambiguous or fuzzy run the risk of being misperceived. A person's past experience also influences interpretation. Prejudice, either racial or some other type, is simply taking certain stimuli and generalizing from our experience, whether accurate or inaccurate. Our motives and interests also influence interpretation. We tend to interpret clearly when we are interested in the topic.

Comprehension is part of the perceptual process, but it goes beyond labeling and identification to produce a more thorough evaluation of the perceived stimuli. Our first exposure to a red bicycle simply provides the perceptual reaction: "This is a red bike." A split second later we add to that assessment through comprehension: "Red bikes are best" or "Red bikes are ugly." In general, people comprehend messages in a way that makes them consistent with pre-existing attitudes and opinions. People who believe that American-made automobiles are best therefore tend to discount or distort perceptions that challenge this view.

Retention Storage of information for later reference, or **retention,** is the fourth step of the information-processing sequence. Actually, the role of memory in the sequence is twofold. First, memory holds information while it is being processed throughout the sequence. For example, in order for a stimulus to be perceived at all, it must first be held for an extremely brief time in what psychologists call *sensory memory*. Second, memory stores information for future, long-term use.

Memory itself is a process, involving several stages. First is *encoding:* before a person can remember anything, it must be put into a form the memory system can use. If a person reads a paragraph, for example, she might encode the general meaning of the passage, the image of the printed words, or the sound of the words. Once encoded, information can be stored in memory.

Information can be encoded and stored automatically, without conscious effort. But *rehearsal*, the mental repetition of material, is often necessary to ensure that these processes occur. Rote repetition is sometimes sufficient, but it is not as effective as *elaborative rehearsal*, which involves thinking about the information and relating it to other, already stored information. A person might remember a name if he simply repeats it to himself, but he is more likely to remember it if he also thinks about the name and associates it with something else.

Whenever possible, promotional messages are couched in a way that encourages elaborative rehearsal.[11] Many Kodak ads, for instance, are intended to trigger a stream of pleasant thoughts about milestones in one's life. Black & Decker shows a man having a difficult time assembling a desk in the first part of their television ad and then shows how a Black & Decker portable screwdriver can make the task easier. Thus the ad encourages the neophyte carpenter to think about past negative experiences with building and then offers the Black & Decker product as a solution to these difficulties.

Retrieval and Application   The process by which information is recovered from the memory storehouse is called **retrieval.** Combined with **application,** retrieval represents the final stage in information processing. If the consumer can retrieve relevant information about a product, brand, or store, he or she will apply it to solve a problem or meet a need.

Research findings suggest that the most effective way for marketers to facilitate retrieval of product information is to provide information about the product's benefits and attributes and then ensure a strong connection between them. This association between attributes and benefits is clearly illustrated in the cereal industry, which presents the key attribute of high fiber as a means of achieving the benefit of cancer prevention. Auto companies that include air bags as standard safety equipment provide a similar connection between the attribute and the benefit—in this case, prevention of serious injury in a car crash.

Elaboration Likelihood Model

Variations in how each step is carried out in the information-processing sequence also occur. Especially influential is the degree of elaboration. **Elaborate processing,** also called **central processing,** involves active manipulation of information. A person engaged in elaborate processing pays close attention to a message and thinks about it; he or she develops thoughts in support of or counter to the information received. In contrast,

nonelaborate, or **peripheral, processing** involves passive manipulation of information. It is demonstrated by most airline passengers while a flight attendant reads preflight safety procedures. This description of the degree of involvement closely parallels the low-involvement, high-involvement theory discussed earlier, and the same logic applies.

A very useful way has been developed of understanding why variations in elaboration occur and how they influence communication.[12] It is known as the **elaboration likelihood model,** or **ELM.** According to ELM, elaboration varies with involvement. ELM suggests a continuum from elaborate (central) processing under high-involvement conditions to nonelaborate (peripheral) processing when involvement is low. The more relevant the message to a consumer's needs, the greater the likelihood that the consumer will elaborate on the message. Thus a man watching a commercial that discusses the danger of heart disease is more likely to elaborate on the message if he knows someone who has had a heart attack. He is likely to interject his own thoughts, such as "I really should get a checkup" or "I really should watch my diet."

Furthermore, according to ELM, when elaboration is high, the quality of the central message has the greatest impact. Thus when consumers are highly involved, persuasion is likely to depend on the cognitive content of a message. For example, it was found that involved consumers are likely to retain and organize advertising messages if those messages help them to choose a brand.[13] As a result, promotion managers must be cognizant of accurate wording and valid portrayal of the problem when designing messages for high-involvement situations.

In contrast, when involvement is low, consumers are merely passive recipients of information; in other words, elaboration is minimal. Consumers then devote little attention to the message and do not bother to think about it. According to ELM, the best way to influence passive consumers is through stimuli that are peripheral to the message—for example, through the use of color, background music, or a celebrity spokesperson in an ad. Uninvolved consumers view advertising more for form than content. They are likely to notice elements of the ads, such as music, characters, or scenery, without linking these elements to the brand. The humor used in the very serious message shown in Figure 5.6 illustrates an attempt to use peripheral elements to influence consumers.

A general assumption of ELM is that a tradeoff exists between central and peripheral processing. As scrutiny of an argument increases, central cues become more important determinants of persuasion and peripheral cues become less important. In general, research supports this idea.[14] However, other tests of this tradeoff assumption are still needed. There appear to be valid criticisms of the ELM model. For example, research[15] has shown that a "peripheral cue" can sometimes influence attitudes of high-involvement subjects. In response, it has been suggested[16] that, under

Figure 5.6

This ad demonstrates a key element of ELM approach to information processing. The peripheral elements of a serious message are presented humorously. Courtesy of the American Cancer Society.

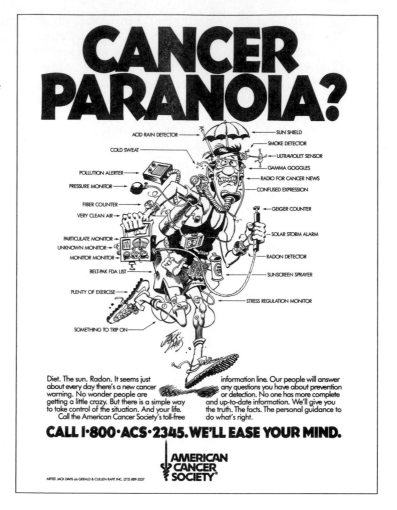

some conditions, features associated with the source may be relevant to the advertised message and may therefore serve as a central cue. Some researchers caution that the distinction between central and peripheral processing depends on whether message-relevant thinking occurs, not on whether consumers focus on verbal or nonverbal cues per se. This approach contradicts the assumption held by many researchers that "central" cues are verbal and "peripheral" cues are nonverbal. Instead, many nonverbal aspects of an advertised message (for example, the attractiveness of a source in an ad for a beauty product) may be highly message relevant and thus serve as central cues.

In summary, there are several exceptions to ELM yet unexplained or unaccounted for. Still, the model offers promotion managers some practical guidelines in strategy development. Most notably, creating relevance in the promotional message is probably the most important factor in effective communication.

Concept Review

1. The information search may involve internal and external sources of information.
2. The search is just part of information processing, which involves six steps:
   a. Exposure,
   b. Attention,
   c. Perception,
   d. Comprehension,
   e. Retention, and
   f. Retrieval and application.
3. The elaboration likelihood model (ELM) suggests that high involvement increases the likelihood of elaborate processing and that the quality of the central message is the key element in persuading the highly involved consumer. In contrast, when involvement is low, peripheral elements may be most persuasive.

Identifying and Evaluating Alternatives

Once a need is recognized and defined and the information search is completed, alternatives are identified and evaluated. How people search for alternatives depends in part on such factors as (1) the cost in time and money, (2) how much information they already have, (3) the perceived risk associated with a wrong decision, and (4) their predispositions about making choices. That is, some people find the process of looking at alternatives to be difficult and disturbing. As a result, they tend to keep the number of alternatives to a minimum, even if they do not have enough information to determine that they are looking at their best options. Other people feel compelled to collect a long list of alternatives, a tendency that can slow down decision making.

Once people know their alternatives, how do they evaluate and choose among them? In particular, how do people choose among brands of a product? Current descriptions of this process emphasize the role of attitudes.

The Multiattribute Attitude Model

A great deal of marketing strategy is based on the idea that the cognitive, affective, and behavioral components of an attitude tend to be consistent.

Thus, if it is possible to change what people believe about Shell Oil, their feelings and their actions may eventually change as well.[17] This relationship among the three components of an attitude seems to be situation or even product specific.[18] For example, attitudes tend to predict behavior better in high-involvement decisions. Thus, if someone has a strong attitude about wearing stylish clothes, then it is possible to predict that the person will restrict purchases to a particular set of brands. In an early study, consumers were interviewed in three different time periods regarding their attitudes toward the consumption of nineteen brands in seven product categories. There was a clear relationship between attitudes and behavior: 58 percent of those who rated a brand as excellent actually used the brand.[19] In a more recent study of mass transit, beliefs about bus travel correlated positively with behavior.[20]

Furthermore, we do not react to products in isolation. The situation, or our attitude toward the situation, plays an important role in how well attitudes predict behavior. For example, assume that a consumer likes beer but does not like Budweiser. In a social setting where only Budweiser is being served, this person might drink Bud rather than not drinking at all. A situational factor important to promotion managers is the consumer's attitude toward a type of promotion or promotion strategy. For example, many consumers hold extremely negative attitudes toward doctors or lawyers who advertise. Advertisers who use sexual innuendo risk the wrath of consumers who hold strong negative attitudes toward such appeals.

Despite limitations on the predictive power of attitudes, attitudes can help us understand how choices are made. However, we need to carefully assess the validity of the attitude-behavior relationship for each situation and product. And we need to understand how to measure attitudes.

Attitudes toward most objects are based on evaluations of and reactions to the various characteristics, or attributes, associated with the object. A number of methods have been developed to predict individuals' overall attitudes toward an object from a knowledge of their reactions to specific attributes of the object. Most marketing applications use a version of this approach known as the multiattribute model.[21]

According to the **multiattribute attitude model,** a person's overall attitude toward a brand can be measured by determining (1) the consumer's evaluation of individual attributes of the brand, (2) the consumer's ideal for those attributes, and (3) the importance the consumer assigns to those attributes. More specifically, most versions of this model hold that an individual's attitude toward a particular brand is based on the sum of how much that brand's performance on each attribute of the product differs from the consumer's ideal performance for that attribute, weighted by the importance of that attribute to the consumer. This definition may be formulated in the following way:

$$A_b = \sum_{1=i}^{n} W_i \,[I_i - X_{ib}]$$

in which:

A_b = the consumer's attitude toward a particular object

W_i = the importance the consumer attaches to attribute i

I_i = the consumer's ideal performance on attribute i

X_{ib} = the consumer's belief about object b's performance on attribute i

n = number of attributes considered

As an example, suppose that a consumer perceives Crest toothpaste to have the following levels of performance on four attributes:

	1 2 3 4 5 6 7	
Low Price	_ I _ _ X _ _	High Price
Good Taste	_ _ _ I X _ _ _	Poor Taste
High Cavity Prevention	I X _ _ _ _ _ _	Low Cavity Prevention
Good Breath Freshener	_ I _ _ _ X _	Poor Breath Freshener

In this example, the consumer believes (that is, the Xs) that Crest is fairly high priced, has a fair taste, is a better-than-average cavity preventer, and is a poor breath freshener. The ideal toothpaste (that is, the Is) would be low priced, taste good, prevent cavities, and be a good breath freshener. For each attribute, the consumer assigns an importance weight.

Attribute	Importance
Price	10
Taste	20
Cavity Prevention	50
Breath Freshening	20
	100 Points

Cavity prevention is easily the most important attribute, followed by flavor, breath freshening, and price. By taking for each attribute the difference between the ideal and the actual score times the weight, the attitude score for this consumer toward Crest toothpaste would be as follows:

$$A_{\text{Crest}} = (10)(2 - 5) + (20)(3 - 4) + (50)(1 - 3) + (20)(2 - 6)$$
$$= (10)(3) + (20)(1) + 50(2) + (20)(4)$$
$$= 30 + 20 + 100 + 80$$
$$= 230$$

Determining whether this attitude score of 230 is good or bad can only be ascertained by computing an attitude index with 0 as the strongest favorable attitude (that is, perceived scores and ideal are identical) and the other end of the index reflecting the maximum possible difference between desired and perceived beliefs. In this example, the maximum possible difference is 530. Therefore, an attitude score of 230 suggests a somewhat favorable attitude toward Crest, since it is on the favorable half of the index. It is also important to compare this attitude score with the scores for competing brands. The comparison might show Crest in a more favorable light, or it might show this score to be relatively bad.

The Theory of Reasoned Action

The multiattribute model provides a way of measuring attitudes, but as an explanation of how consumers evaluate and choose brands it is incomplete. A fuller explanation is provided by the theory of reasoned action, which is outlined in Figure 5.7.

Like the basic multiattribute model, the theory of reasoned action incorporates a cognitive component, an affective component, and a conative or behavioral component. However, according to the **theory of reasoned action,** the best predictor of behavior is intention to act. An intention, in turn, depends on (1) the attitude toward behavior and (2) the subjective norm. The *attitude toward behavior* is an overall favorable or unfavorable evaluation toward the act of purchasing a product or service. It can be directly measured as affect. The *subjective norm* reflects both the consumer's beliefs about what relevant others (such as family, friends, coworkers) would think of the contemplated action and the consumer's motivation to comply with their opinion. For example, Figure 5.8 shows an attempt by Southwestern Bell to activate a subjective norm by appealing to the value a typical mother places on pleasing her children. Applying the logic of reasoned action to another scenario, suppose a student were interested in purchasing a new CD player. In order to predict behavior, a marketer would first have to assess the consumer's attitude toward purchasing a CD player. Is the person knowledgeable about such products? Can the individual ask the right questions? Will the consumer respond to these questions emotionally? Second, the marketer would have to identify the relevant others (parents and roommate, for example) and the consumer's beliefs as to how each would respond to the purchase of the CD player. Finally, the marketer would have to understand the person's motivation to comply

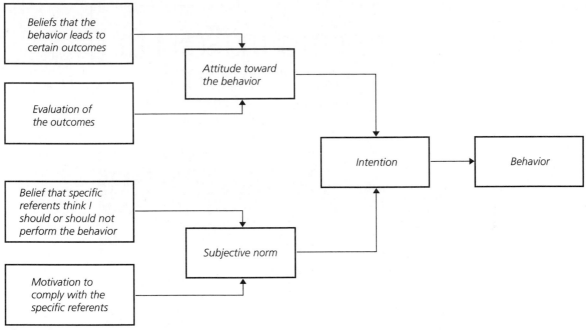

Figure 5.7

The theory of reasoned action.
Icek Ajzen/Martin Fishbein, Understanding Attitudes and Predicting Social Behavior,
©1980, p. 84. Adapted by permission of Prentice-Hall, New Jersey.

with parents and/or roommate. Using this information, the marketer could understand the person's intention and thus predict behavior.

The theory of reasoned action has empirical support and is considered a valid planning tool for promotion managers.[22] It also helps clarify the consumer's decision-making process. By pointing out that the consumer's attitude toward the behavior may be more important than attitude toward the object, the theory suggests important message variables. Likewise, the consideration of subjective norms may serve as the primary appeal for a particular promotion device.

Influencing Attitudes

Given the hypothesis that attitudes influence buying behavior, how can a company bring its products and consumers' attitudes into a consistent state, that is, into a situation where consumers evaluate a given product or brand as satisfying their need? Marketers have two choices: either they can change consumers' attitudes to be consistent with their product, or they can change the product to match attitudes. It is easier to change the product than to change consumers' attitudes. Nevertheless, attitudes can

Figure 5.8

Southwestern Bell's attempt to activate a subjective norm. Courtesy of Southwestern Bell Corporation.

Bottom of the seventh.
Two on. Two out.
And Vicki Graham
hits a home run.

There's only one thing Vicki loves more than her work. Her family. So this afternoon, only one meeting could have been more important than the one with her client. The one with her son.

But Vicki's got connections. She has cellular phone service from Southwestern Bell. So from the third base line of her son's game, she can still be in touch with her office.

Which is how we like to think of all of our products and services. From portable phones to pagers. From cordless phones and cellular phone service, to fax machines and Yellow Pages. As tools that give you the freedom to get a little more from your everyday life.

Which could simply mean being able to do your job from anywhere. Or stay in touch from the middle of nowhere.

Or, as in the case of Vicki Graham, being able to have your head in one place. And your heart in another.

Southwestern Bell Corporation

The one to call on.

sometimes be modified. Modifying attitudes may be the only reasonable choice, as when a firm is introducing a truly new product or an unusual new use for an existing one.

Marketers should face the fact that it is extremely difficult to change consumers' attitudes. If there is to be a change, it is most likely to occur when people are open minded in their beliefs or when an existing attitude is of weak intensity, that is, when there is little information to support the attitude or very little ego involvement on the individuals' part. The stronger a person's brand loyalty is to a certain product, for example, the more difficult it is to change that attitude.

Highly persuasive communication is ordinarily needed if a seller is to

Figure 5.9

This ad attempts to change the market's attitudes toward the product by providing the consumer with new information.
Reprinted with permission of The Quaker Oats Company.

have any hope of changing a buyer's attitude. The communication should attempt to change one or more of the three dimensions related to an attitude. For instance, the use of coupons, free samples, or cents-off sales might induce buyers to change their action patterns to try a new brand. Even then, buyers must be open minded and willing to let their present brand preferences be challenged. Figure 5.9 shows one attempt to change attitudes by providing new information.

Concept Review

1. Identification and evaluation of alternatives takes place once a need is recognized and defined.
    a. People employ attitudes as the basis for evaluating alternatives.

According to the multiattribute attitude model, a person's overall attitude toward a brand can be measured by determining
- the consumer's evaluation of individual attributes;
- the consumer's ideal for those attributes;
- the importance the consumer assigns to those attributes.
   b. The theory of reasoned action takes attitudes one step further by suggesting that the least predictor of behavior is the intent to act.

Purchase and Postpurchase Behavior

After searching and evaluating, at some point consumers have to decide whether they are going to buy or not. Anything marketers can do to simplify the decision making will be attractive to buyers because most people find it hard to make a decision. Perhaps marketers can suggest in their advertising the best size of a product for a particular use or the right wine to drink with a particular food. Sometimes several decision situations can be combined and marketed as one package. For example, travel agents often package travel tours, combining air fare, ground transportation, and hotels.

To do a better marketing job at this stage of the buying process, a seller needs to know answers to many questions about consumers' shopping behavior. For instance, how much effort is the consumer willing to spend in shopping for the product? What factors influence where a consumer will shop? Do stores each have an image? If so, is the image important to a shopper when selecting a store? What are the differentiating characteristics, if any, of impulse buyers? Promotion managers can play a very important role at the purchase stage. Providing basic product, price, and location information through advertising, personal selling, and public relations is an obvious starting point. Sales promotion, in particular, is critical at this stage. Product sampling, coupons, rebates, and premiums are a few of the sales promotion devices used to encourage the customer to purchase. For many purchase decisions, the salesperson is the key. This is particularly true for industrial products and retail sales. In recent years, direct marketers have played a prominent role in reshaping the purchasing process of millions of consumers. Because of time constraints and the risks associated with traditional purchasing mechanisms, direct marketers have responded with better products, improved service, and reduced risks through warranties and guarantees. These benefits are highlighted in promotional messages produced by direct marketers.

A consumer's feelings and evaluations after the sale are also significant to a marketer because they can influence repeat sales and what the consumer tells others about the product or brand. Keeping the customer satisfied is what marketing is all about. As noted in the Promotion in Focus section, this is easier said than done.

Consumers typically experience some postpurchase anxiety after all but routine and inexpensive purchases. This anxiety reflects a phenomenon called **cognitive dissonance.** According to this theory, people strive for consistency among their cognitions (knowledge, attitudes, beliefs, values).[23] When there are inconsistencies, dissonance exists, which people will try to eliminate. In some cases, the consumer makes the decision already aware of dissonant elements. In other instances, dissonance is aroused by disturbing information received after the purchase.

To avoid or eliminate dissonance, consumers may avoid negative information. They may change their behavior, their opinions, or their attitudes. They may seek information or opinions that support their purchase. Sometimes the consumer's attempt to reduce dissonance can produce dire consequences for the marketer. For example, in the process of convincing oneself that the purchase of a new GE microwave oven was a good decision, the consumer seeks additional information from friends. Unfortunately, the consumer's best friend says she had a terrible experience with her GE microwave oven.

The marketer may take specific steps to reduce postpurchase dissonance. Advertising that stresses the many positive attributes or confirms the popularity of the product can be helpful. Providing personalized reinforcement has proven effective with big-ticket items such as automobiles and major appliances. Salespeople in these areas may send cards or publicity materials or may even make personal calls in order to reassure customers about their purchase.

Concept Review

1. Purchase and postpurchase behavior represent the last two stages in the consumer decision-making process.
2. The marketer needs to know the answers to many questions about why and how the actual purchase process takes place.
3. Likewise, the reduction of consumer dissatisfaction after purchase (cognitive dissonance) is an important marketing goal.

Organizational Market Behavior

Those who supply goods and services to consumer markets are themselves in need of goods and services to run their businesses. These organizations—producers, resellers, and governments—make up vast organizational markets that buy a large variety of products, including equipment, raw material, labor, and other services. Some organizations sell exclusively to other organizations and never come in contact with consumer buyers.

Promotion in Focus

The Goal—Customer Satisfaction

Ask the average American businessperson what the goal of his or her business is and you're likely to hear "customer satisfaction." Although there are still plenty of unsatisfied customers around, a great number of companies have embraced the idea that satisfying customers is their main objective. How did this idea gain such importance in American organizations, and what does it really mean?

Many experts say that customer satisfaction has always been part of the foundation of American business; it seems like a new idea now only because complacent companies lost sight of it. Customer satisfaction became such a popular buzz word in the 1980s because of changes in the business world that have given customers more options. A company that has little competition doesn't have to worry much about customer satisfaction. But in the global marketplace, with companies from around the world competing for customers, few companies can afford to be complacent. The deregulation of a number of industries added to the competition, and Americans learned to expect satisfaction from products made in Europe and Japan. Now perhaps more than at any time in history, a dissatisfied customer has somewhere to turn.

Now that customer satisfaction has achieved such importance in American business, researchers are devising ways of measuring such satisfaction, and everyone seems to have a different idea of how to define it and improve it. Business people are learning to listen better to their customers, to communicate with them in their own language, and to understand what their perceptions of quality are. Most consultants agree that pursuing customer satisfaction must be an on-going process, not something that can be accomplished once and then forgotten about. And it must involve the whole organization, not just the marketing arm.

Some consultants caution that customer satisfaction is expensive, time consuming, and difficult.

Just as "quality" has come to be applied to every aspect of an organization's operations, not just the finished product, "customer satisfaction" is likely to take on new meanings. Companies are finding that changing their operations and distribution can please customers as much as can changing their product. In many organizations, real commitment to customer satisfaction requires major changes in organizational culture. So we may be witnessing the start of a customer satisfaction revolution.

Source: Howard Schlossberg, "Customer Satisfaction Serves and Preserves," *Marketing News* (May 28, 1990): 8.

Despite the importance of organizational markets, far less research has been conducted on factors that influence their behavior than on factors that influence consumers. However, we can identify characteristics that distinguish organizational buying from consumer buying and typical steps in the organizational buying process.

Characteristics of Organizational Buying

Many elements of the sociocultural environment discussed in the previous chapter influence organizational as well as consumer buying, but some additional forces are salient only in the organizational setting. In particular, each organization has its own business philosophy that guides its actions in resolving conflicts, handling uncertainty and risk, searching for solutions, and adapting to change. For example, Peabody Coal, which is part of a declining industry, relies on a conservative purchase strategy in an attempt to maintain the status quo.

Five characteristics mark the organizational buying process.[24]

1. In organizations, many individuals are involved in making buying decisions.

2. The organizational buyer is motivated by both rational and emotional factors in choosing products and services. Although the use of rational and quantitative criteria dominate in most organizational decisions, the decision makers are people, subject to many of the same emotional criteria used in personal purchases.

3. Organizational buying decisions frequently involve a range of complex technical dimensions. A purchasing agent for Volvo Automobiles, for example, must consider a number of technical factors before ordering a radio to go into the 240 DL model. The electronic system, the acoustics of the interior, and the shape of the dashboard are a few of these considerations.

4. The organizational decision process frequently spans a considerable time, creating a significant lag between the marketer's initial contact with the customer and the purchasing decision. Since many new factors can enter the picture during this lag time, the marketer's ability to monitor and adjust to these changes is critical.

5. Organizations cannot be grouped into precise categories. Each organization has a characteristic way of functioning and a personality.

The first item in this list of characteristics has important implications. Unlike the consumer buying process, organizational buying involves decision making by groups and enforced rules for making decisions. These two characteristics greatly complicate the task of understanding the buying process. For example, to predict the buying behavior of an organization with certainty, it is important to know who will take part in the buying process, what criteria each member uses in evaluating prospective suppliers, and what influence each member has. It is also necessary to understand something not only about the psychology of the individuals involved but also how they work as a group.

Who makes the decision to buy depends in part on the situation. Three types of buying situations have been distinguished:[25] the straight rebuy, the modified rebuy, and the new task. The *straight rebuy* is the simplest situation: The company reorders a good or service without any modifications. The transaction tends to be routine and may be handled totally by the purchasing department. With the *modified rebuy*, the buyer is seeking to modify product specifications, prices, and so on. The purchaser is interested in negotiation, and several participants may take part in the buying decision. A company faces a *new task* when it considers buying a product for the first time. The number of participants and the amount of information sought tend to increase with the cost and risks associated with the transaction. This situation represents the best opportunity for the marketer.

Stages in Organizational Buying

The organizational buying process is shown to contain eight stages, or key phases, which are below.[26]

1. Problem recognition
2. General need description
3. Product specification
4. Suppliers' search
5. Proposal solicitation
6. Supplier selection
7. Order-routine specification
8. Performance review

Although these stages parallel those of the consumer buying process, there are important differences that have a direct bearing on the promotional strategy. The complete process only occurs in the case of a new task. Even in this situation, however, the process is far more formal for the industrial buying process than for the consumer buying process. Most of the information an industrial buyer receives is delivered through direct contacts such as sales representatives or information packets. It is unlikely that an industrial buyer would use the information provided though a trade ad as the sole basis for making a decision. In modified rebuy and straight rebuy situations, the role of promotion is even more limited, because the emphasis is on product specifications and performance.

Problem recognition The process begins when someone in the organization recognizes a problem or need that can be met by acquiring a good or service. Problem recognition can occur as a result of internal or external stimuli. External stimuli can be a presentation by a salesperson, an ad, or information picked up at a trade show.

General need description Having recognized that a need exists, the buyer must add further refinement to its description. Working with engineers, users, purchasing agents, and others, the buyer identifies and prioritizes important product characteristics. Table 5.2 lists several sources of information used by organizational buyers. Note how many are part of promotion. Clearly, the salesperson serves as the primary information source for many industrial customers. Armed with extensive product knowledge, this individual is capable of addressing virtually all the product-related concerns of a typical customer. To a lesser extent, trade advertising provides valuable information to smaller or isolated customers. Noteworthy is the extensive use of direct marketing techniques (for example, toll-free numbers and information cards) in conjunction with many trade ads. Finally, public relations plays a significant role through the placement of stories in various trade journals.

Product specification Technical specifications come next. This is usually the responsibility of the engineering department. Engineers design several alternatives, depending on the priority list established earlier.

Supplier's search The buyer now tries to identify the most appropriate vendor. The buyer can examine trade directories, do a computer search, or phone other companies for recommendations. Marketers can participate in this stage by contacting possible opinion leaders and soliciting support or by contacting the buyer directly. Personal selling plays a major role at this stage.

Proposal solicitation Qualified suppliers are next invited to submit proposals. Some suppliers will send only a catalog or a sales representative. Proposal development is a complex task that requires extensive research and skilled writing and presentation. In extreme cases, such proposals are comparable to complete promotional strategies found in the consumer sector.

Supplier selection At this stage, the various proposals are screened and a choice is made. A significant part of this evaluation is evaluating the vendor. One study indicated that purchasing managers felt that the

Table 5.1 **Industrial Buyer Information Sources**

Information Source	Description
Salespeople	Sales personnel representing manufacturers or distributors of the product in question.
Technical sources	Engineering types of personnel internal or external to the subject's firm.
Personnel in buyer's firm	Peer group references (for example, other purchasing agents in the subject's firm).
Purchasing agents in other companies	Peer group references external to the buyer's firm.
Trade association	Cooperatives voluntarily joined by business competitors designed to assist its members and industry in dealing with mutual problems (for example, National Association of Purchasing Management).
Advertising in trade journals	Commercial messages placed by the manufacturer or distributor of the product in question.
Articles in trade journals	Messages relating to the product in question but not under the control of the manufacturer or distributor.
Vendor files	Information pertaining to the values of various sources of supply as developed and maintained by the buyer's firm.
Trade registers	Buyer guides providing listings of suppliers and other marketing information (for example, *Thomas' Register*).
Product literature	Specific product and vendor information supplied by the manufacturing or distributing firm.

Source: H. Lee Matthews, James Robeson, and Peter J. Banbic, "Achieving Seller Accept-ability in Industrial Markets: Development of the Communication Mix," in *Consumer and Industrial Buying Behavior,* eds. Arch Woodside, Jagdish N. Sheth, and Peter D. Bennett (New York: Elsevier-North Holland, 1977): 223. Reprinted by permission.

vendor was often more important than the proposal. Purchasing man-agers listed the three most important characteristics of the vendor as: delivery capability, consistent quality, and fair price.[27] Another study found that the relative importance of different attributes varies with the type of buying situation.[28] For example, for routine-order products, de-livery reliability, price, and supplier reputation are highly important. These factors can serve as appeals in sales presentations and in trade ads.

Order-routine specification   The buyer now writes the final order with the chosen supplier, listing the technical specifications, the quantity needed, the warranty, and so on.

Performance review   In this final stage, the buyer reviews the supplier's performance. This may be a very simple or a very complex process.

**Concept
Review**

1. Characteristics of organizational buying
    a. Multiple-decision making
    b. Rational and emotional decision factors
    c. Complexity
    d. Lengthy time frame
    e. Diverse classification of organization types
2. The following steps are typical in organizational buying
    a. Problem recognition
    b. General need description
    c. Product specification
    d. Suppliers' search
    e. Proposal solicitation
    f. Supplier selection
    g. Order-routine specification
    h. Performance review

Case 5 *Gillette Goes High Tech*

Background

In 1977, John Francis was one of about forty engineers, metallurgists, and physicists who spent most of their time thinking about nothing but shaving at Gillette Co.'s research facility in Reading, England. Francis built a prototype of a new razor that was actually a combination of two good ideas. One was to make a thinner razor blade, something the company had been working on so that it could make its cartridges easier to clean. The other was to make razor blades "float" across the face, cutting beard but not skin. Francis first wanted to mount the blades on rubber tubes, perhaps filled with a compressible fluid. But he eventually put the blades onto springs. He thought the new razor worked pretty well, and he passed the prototype on to his boss. Thus began the most expensive product development in Gillette's history, which resulted in the razor now called the Sensor.

Understanding the Market

A great deal of the money spent on Gillette's Sensor went to consumer research. Gillette has learned the hard way that many of the assumptions about shaving that were valid in the 1960s are no longer valid today. Shaving used to be a male rite of passage; little boys once watched their fathers shave and dreamed of the day when they too could shave, most probably using the same shaving equipment as Dad.

Research conducted by Gillette in 1973 showed that shaving was no longer viewed with respect. Instead, young men considered shaving a bother, an activity to be done as quickly and painlessly as possible. Shaving products no longer commanded much brand loyalty. When asked to evaluate shaving equipment, young men talked mostly about shaving effectiveness and price.

For most of its history, Gillette has focused on effectiveness. The double-edged safety blade of the 1950s was followed by several improvements, including Teflon-coated blades, the Trac I, Atra, and Trac II. Competitors, such as Bic and Schick, followed a mixed strategy. Bic introduced a disposable razor, an idea soon copied by other companies. But disposables are less profitable than shaving systems, so Gillette continued to try to create the most effective razor.

One of the difficulties of developing a high-tech razor is that the market tends to change quickly, and therefore the window of opportunity for a new product is limited. Creating a radical new product requires extensive research, but that research usually must be done quickly and secretively.

Tests with early Sensor prototypes showed that the blades could not get close enough to the stubble to provide a clean shave. Engineers developed firmer springs that sat on cantilevered plastic. New tests showed that the springs lost their bounce over time, so engineers turned to a different resin, Noryl, that kept its bounce. In 1983, 500 men tested Sensor prototypes and preferred it to Gillette's existing razors.

In 1985, Gillette introduced the Sensor into twenty-five test cities throughout the United States. Because of the need for tight security when testing new shaving products, the cities selected were quite small and isolated. In addition to testing the technical components, the company tried out various prices and names and used focus groups and surveys. After six months of such tests, the company's Safety Razor Division persuaded Gillette's board to spend ten million dollars developing manufacturing equipment for the Sensor.

Was the consumer research worthwhile? Analysts thought the company might have spent too much on developing the Sensor. They estimated that the new razor needed to boost Gillette's market share four percentage points in the United States and Europe just to pay for its advertizing budget.

Gillette introduced the Sensor razor with commercials during the 1990 Super Bowl. Although the company planned a $50 million media blitz, it canceled some of its ads because it could not keep up with product demand. But it overcame its supply problems, and by the third quarter of 1990, Sensor had grabbed a nine percent share of the wet-shave market. Retailers were delighted. Not only were people buying every Sensor retailers could get to their shelves, they were also coming in for replacement blades, proving that they liked the product. Thirteen years and millions of Gillette's dollars later, John Francis's ideas paid off.

Case Questions

1. What types of consumer motives is Gillette trying to target in the Sensor?
2. Discuss the buying process an adult male goes through in purchasing a razor.
3. Identify places where promotion would fit into this decision process.

Case Sources: "At Gillette, Disposable Is a Dirty Word," *Business Week* (May 29, 1989): 54–55. Keith Hammonds, "It's One Sharp Ad Campaign, But Where's the Blade?" *Business Week* (March 5, 1990): 30. "How a $4 Razor Ends Up Costing 100 Million," *Business Week* (January 29, 1990): 62–63. Alison Fahey, "Sensor Sales Sharp," *Advertising Age* (May 7, 1990): 56.

Summary

This chapter looks at how individuals and organizations make decisions, along with the promotional implications of the process. Consumer decision making is influenced by the sociocultural environment, the marketing mix, and individual characteristics such as motivation and attitudes. The novelty of the purchase and the consumer's involvement influence whether the decision-making process is complex or simple. Complex decision making involves five steps: need recognition, information search, evaluation of alternatives, purchase, and postpurchase. Simple decision making does not require information search or evaluation. The behavior is based on habit.

Most of the chapter deals with complex decision making. Three psychological concepts are inherent in such decision making. Motivation is an inner drive or pressure to take action in order to eliminate tension. Learning is a process of taking in information, processing it along with existing information, and producing new knowledge. An attitude is an enduring favorable or unfavorable disposition toward some object. These three psychological concepts influence the various stages of complex decision making. The process begins with need recognition. A need becomes a problem requiring resolution only after we are motivated to do so. Information search and processing are mental and physical activities. Again, internal motivation is necessary for these activities to occur. There is a model of information processing that has proven useful to marketers. It includes five steps: exposure, attention, perception, retention, and retrieval and application. The elaboration likelihood model (ELM) attempts to explain how this process takes place. It suggests that we engage in central processing when the issue is high involvement and peripheral processing when the issue is low involvement. Identifying and evaluating alternatives is the third step in complex decision making. Attitudes appear to play a central role in making choices. The multiattribute attitude model suggests that the way we evaluate the attributes of the product or brand is reflective of our attitude. The theory of reasoned action extends the multiattribute model by suggesting that "intention to act" is a better predictor of behavior than attributes. Purchase and postpurchase behavior are the last stages in the decision-making process.

The chapter concludes with a discussion of organizational market behavior. In general, this type of decision tends to be less emotional and employs more information. Other characteristics distinguishing consumer decision making from organizational decision making were discussed. The eight steps of the organizational buying process ended the chapter.

Discussion Questions

1. Based on your understanding of motives, develop some general guidelines or directives for practicing promotion.

2. How can promoters influence a person's motivation to take action? How can they facilitate learning?

3. Define an attitude. Discuss the components of an attitude. What are the implications for promotion? Use the multiattribute perspective to measure your attitude toward two different brands of jeans.

4. Present a diagram of the consumer decision process. What is the role of each form of promotion in each stage of this process?

5. Distinguish between high-involvement and low-involvement decision making.

6. How is the elaboration likelihood model useful to the promotion manager?

7. Discuss the key assumptions of the theory of reasoned action. Think of an example in your own life that illustrates how it works.

8. What are the differences between the consumer decision-making process and the organizational decision-making process?

9. Assume that you are training a salesperson to sell industrial products. Although this salesperson has a strong track record, she has been selling consumer products. What would you emphasize during training?

10. Discuss several reasons why marketers continue to have a hard time understanding, predicting, and explaining consumer behavior.

Suggested Projects

1. Locate an individual who has purchased a new automobile during the last year. Using the five-step decision-making process, ask this person to indicate how he or she accomplished each step.

2. Contact ten students. Ask them to list the three primary motives they considered when selecting which university to attend. Ask them whether they would still use these same motives. Have them indicate any replacements. Write a paper addressing the value of motives in understanding decision making.

References

1. C. N. Coffer and M. H. Appley, *Motivation: Theory Research* (New York: John Wiley & Sons, 1964).

2. K. Levien, *A Dynamic Theory of Personality* (New York: McGraw-Hill, 1935): 88–91.

3. Robert B. Zojonic and Hazel Markus, "Affective and Cognitive Factors in Preferences," *Journal of Consumer Research* 9 (September 1982): 123–131.

4. Henry Assael, *Consumer Behavior and Marketing Action*, 3rd ed. (Boston: Kent Publishing, 1987): 84.

5. W. J. McGuire, "Psychological Motives and Communication Gratification," in *The Uses of Mass Communication: Current Perspectives on Gratification Research*, eds. J. G. Blumler and C. Katz (Beverly Hills, CA: Sage Publications, 1974): 167–196.

6. R. Kelly, "The Search Component of the Consumer Decision Process—A Theoretic Examination," in *Marketing and the New Science of Planning*, ed. C. King (Chicago: American Marketing Association, 1968): 273.

7. James Bettman, *An Information Processing Theory of Consumer Choice* (Reading, MA: Addison-Wesley, 1979).

8. Richard E. Petty, John T. Cacioppo, and David Schumann, "Central and Peripheral Routes to Advertising Effectiveness: The Moderating Role of Involvement," *Journal of Consumer Research* 10 (September 1983): 135–146.

9. F. H. Nothman, "The Influence of Response Conditions on Recognition Thresholds for Taboo Words," *Journal of Abnormal and Social Psychology* 65 (1962): 154–161.

10. Peter H. Webb and Michael L. Ray, "Effects of TV Clutter," *Journal of Advertising Research* 19 (June 1979): 7–12. Thomas J. Madden and Marc G. Weinberger, "The Effects of Humor on Attention in Magazine Advertising," *Journal of Advertising* 11, No. 3 (1982): 8–14.
    Michael A. Belch, Barbara E. Holgerson, George E. Belch, and Jerry Koppman, "Psychophysiological and Cognitive Responses to Sex in Advertising," in *Advances in Consumer Research*, Vol. 9, ed. Andrew Mitchell (Pittsburgh: Association for Consumer Research, 1982): 424–27.

11. A. A. Mitchell, "An Information Processing View of Consumer Behavior," in *Research Frontiers in Marketing: Dialogues and Directions*, ed. S. C. Jain (American Marketing Association, 1978): 188–197.

12. Richard E. Petty and John T. Cacioppo, "Issue Involvement Can Increase or Decrease Persuasion by Enhancing Message Relevant Cognitive Responses," *Journal of Personality and Social Psychology* 37 (October 1979): 1915–1926.

13. Meryl Gardner, Andrew Mitchell, and J. Edward Russo, "Strategy-Induced Low Involvement with Advertising," paper presented at the first Consumer Involvement Conference, New York University, June 1982.

14. Richard Petty and John T. Cacioppo, "Issue Involvement as a Moderator of the Effects on Attitude Advertising Content and Context," in *Advances in Consumer Research*, ed. K. B. Monroe, Vol. 8 (Ann Arbor, MI: Association for Consumer Research, 1981): 20–24. Richard E. Petty and John T. Cacioppo, *Attitudes and Persuasion: Classic and Contemporary Approaches* (Dubuque, IA: William Brown Co., 1983).

15. Lynn R. Kahle and Pamela M. Homer, "Physical Attractiveness of the Celebrity Endorser: A Social Adaptation Perspective," *Journal of Consumer Research* 11 (March 1985): 954–961. Richard E. Petty and John T. Cacioppo, *Communication and Persuasion: Central and Peripheral Routes to Attitude Change* (New York: Springer-Verlag, 1986).

16. *Ibid.*

17. Zajonic and Markus.

18. D. G. Regan and R. H. Fazio, "On the Consistency Between Attitudes and Behavior: Look to the Method of Attitude Formation," *Journal of Experimental Psychology*, Vol. 13 (1977): 28–45.

19. Alvin A. Achenbaum, "Knowledge Is a Thing Called Measurement," *Attitude Research at Sea*, Lee Adler and Irving Crespi, eds., (New York: American Marketing Association, 1966): 111–126.

20. David J. Reibstein, Christopher H. Lovelock, and Ricardo de P. Dobson, "The Direction of Causality Between Perceptions, Affect, and Behavior: An Application to Travel Behavior," *Journal of Consumer Research* 6 (March 1980): 370–376.

21. William L. Wilkie and Edgar A. Pessemeir, "Issues in Marketing Use of Multiattribute Attitude Models," *Journal of Marketing* (November 1973): 428–441.

22. Terence A. Shimp and Alican Kavas, "The Theory of Reasoned Action Applied to Coupon Usage," *Journal of Consumer Research* 11 (December 1984): 795–809. Barbara Loken, "The Theory of Reasoned Action: Examination of the Sufficiency Assumption for a Television Viewing Behavior," *Advances in Consumer Research*, Richard P. Bagazzi and Alice M. Tybout, (Ann Arbor, MI: Association for Consumer Research, 1983): 100–105.

23. L. Festinger, *A Theory of Cognitive Dissonance* (Stanford, CA: Stanford University Press, 1957).

24. Michael D. Hutt and Thomas W. Speh, *Industrial Marketing Management* (Chicago: Dryden Press, 1981): 15–16.

25. Patrick J. Robinson, Charles W. Fares, and Yoram Wind, *Industrial Buying and Creative Marketing* (Boston: Allyn & Bacon, 1967): 7.

26. *Ibid*, 14.

27. William A. Dempsey, "Vendor Selection and the Buying Process," *Industrial Marketing Management* 7 (1978): 257–267.

28. Donald R. Lehmann and John O'Shaughnessy, "Difference in Attribute Importance for Different Industrial Products," *Journal of Marketing* (April 1974): 36–42.

6

The Legal Environment

Consider This:

Volvo and the Question of Deceptive Advertising

Since a Supreme Court decision twenty years ago, advertisers have known that it is illegal to use any form of deception in making demonstration ads. In the 1960s, Campbell Soup Company put marbles in its soup to make the food float to the top, and Colgate shaved a piece of Plexiglas, claiming it was sandpaper. But anyone in the advertising business knows about the furor those cases caused, and most advertisers steer clear of anything that hints of deception.

That's why the 1990 revelations about a Volvo ad came as such a shock. Since it entered the American market in the 1950s, Volvo has touted the safety and structural strength of its cars. Its ads have highlighted Volvos' structural prowess in a number of ways, and in 1990, Volvo's ad agency, Scali, McCabe, Sloves, New York, thought it had an amusing new way to get the message across. In a benefit for an arthritis foundation in Vermont, a "monster truck" had rolled over a lineup of cars, leaving only the Volvo relatively unscathed. The agency decided to film a similar event in Austin, Texas.

The resulting commercial showed a monster truck named Bear Foot pounding its way over a number of cars, crushing all except the Volvo. The ad seemed like a success until the attorney general's office in the state of Texas investigated a tip that the cars had been tampered with.

It turned out that the car-crushing event had been stacked in Volvo's favor. The roof supports of most of the cars in the lineup had been cut, making the cars easier to crush. And the Volvo had been reinforced with extra steel framework so it would withstand Bear Foot's weight.

In the flurry of allegations and legal proceedings that followed the disclosure, it wasn't clear who had authorized the illegal tampering. The agency said it knew nothing about it, but it resigned its $40 million contract with Volvo anyway. Volvo also claimed ignorance about the tampering, but it withdrew the commercials, apologized in print ads, and paid a fine to Texas.

Despite these legal settlements, the effects of the deception are not likely to die soon. Volvo's previously sterling reputation has been tarnished. Around the country, advertising agencies and their clients worry that the scandal will make viewers even more skeptical about demonstration ads and make advertisers' jobs more difficult. The deception made for better ad footage, but its costs were astronomical.

Sources: Kim Foltz, "Scali Quits Volvo Account, Citing Faked Commercials," *New York Times*, November 14, 1990, D1; Barbara Holsomback, "Who Called the Volvo Shots?," *Adweek*, November 26, 1990, 1–2; Raymond Serafin and Gary Levin, "Ad Industry Suffers Crushing Blow," *Advertising Age*, November 12, 1990, 1; Raymond Serafin and Gary Levin, "Four More Volvo Ads Scrutinized," *Advertising Age*, November 26, 1990, 4.

T here is no way that Volvo of North America or Scali, McCabe, Sloves can justify the deceptive acts each is accused of. Each claims the other is responsible. Unfortunately, such incidents have not only a direct bearing on the owners and potential owners of Volvos but also discredit the attempts of other promoters who communicate accurately and fairly with consumers and businesses. Public demands for more socially responsible business practices appear to be increasing. These demands have often led to statutes and public policy statements that significantly influence marketing decision makers, particularly in their decisions about promotion.

The intent of this chapter is threefold: (1) to provide an overview of legislation that affects promotion, (2) to consider the legal implications unique to the promotional subcategories, and (3) to examine the attempts at self-regulation by the promotion industry. Because of the vast body of law, no attempt will be made to discuss any of the laws in detail. Rather, the material related here should give the reader a greater appreciation for the tremendously complex legal environment in which promotional strategists must work.

The Antitrust and Consumer Movements: A Brief History

In the early days of the United States, small, dispersed organizations served relatively small, local markets. With improvements in transportation and communication, however, nonlocal markets became more accessible. A newly developed organization form—the corporation—not only pursued the new markets but also began integrating horizontally and vertically in order to realize the benefits of economies of scale and to take advantage of a tax break that was available to vertically integrated firms. This process of accumulating power through internal and external expansion continued throughout the nineteenth century until most economic and political power was controlled by an alarmingly small number of individuals.

Accumulation of power was also facilitated by the prevailing social doctrine of the 1800s. Specifically, laissez-faire ideology suggested that business be controlled only by market forces and the survival be realized by the economically fittest. To survive, companies aimed to expand, eliminate competitive pressures, and improve production processes. Some developed trusts and holding companies and thus achieved monopolization of entire industries, organized pools to divide markets without competing, offered rebates to secure customers, discriminated in price to favored customers, and engaged in horizontal and vertical price fixing. Widespread practice of such abuses placed free enterprise in serious jeopardy.[1]

Consumers faced other abuses, some of which even threatened their lives. Nowhere was this more evident than in the food industry, where deplorable processing and storage standards led to thousands of deaths annually. This situation was graphically portrayed in Upton Sinclair's 1906 novel about the meat-packing industry, *The Jungle.*

The first attempts to deal with consumer abuses often came not from the federal government but from the states. In the case of loose regulations for food processing and storage, for example, the state of New Jersey passed the "Seven Sisters" laws that regulated questionable food-processing activities practiced by a family-owned food business. Today, too, state laws and regulators protect businesses and consumers from unscrupulous practices. Because of the diversity of state laws, however, an extensive examination of how state and local governments influence promotion is beyond the scope of this text. Instead, we focus on some key points in the history of federal regulation of the marketplace. Some of these laws are listed in Table 6.1.

The Sherman and Clayton Acts

During the latter part of the nineteenth century, people began to understand the dangers of monopolies and conspiracies to eliminate competition. The first attack on monopolies was directed at railroads and resulted in passage of the Interstate Commerce Act of 1887. Then, in 1890, the government moved to eliminate other monopolies by enacting the **Sherman Antitrust Act,** which eventually became one of the most significant weapons for attacking countercompetitive business activities.

The Sherman Act required that businesses function independently rather than in concert with competing businesses. The act's proponents wanted to maintain free competition by eliminating unfair accumulations of power. Thus the act prohibited "every contract, combination, or conspiracy, in restraint of trade or commerce, among the several states, or with foreign nations" (Section 1) and "monopolies or attempts to monopolize" (Section 2). In 1911, however, the courts reinterpreted the act to refer only to restraints that are "unreasonably restrictive of competition." With the adoption of this *rule of reason* concept, it became the courts' role to interpret the reasonableness of restraints in order to ascertain their legality.

Table 6.1   **An Overview of Important Federal Laws Designed to Protect Businesses and Consumers**

Laws Protecting Consumers

Federal Food and Drug Act (1939)
Flammable Fabrics Act (1953)
Fair Packaging & Labeling Act (1966)
Truth in Lending Act (1968)
Fair Credit Reporting Act (1971)
Consumer Product Safety Act (1972)
Fair Credit Billing Act (1975)
Magnuson-Moss Warranty Act (1975)
Equal Credit Opportunity Act (1975)
Fair Debt Collection Practice Act (1978)

Laws Regulating Competition

Robinson-Patman Act (1936)
Miller-Tydings Resale Price Maintenance Act (1937)

Laws Maintaining a Competitive Environment

Sherman and Clayton Acts (1890; 1914)
Federal Trade Commission Act (1914)
Wheeler-Lea Amendment (1938)

Within two decades after passage of the Sherman Antitrust Act, it became evident that the law had some major deficiencies. First, it lacked a specific definition of the legality of business practices. Second, reasonable restraints had to exist before the Sherman Act could be applied. To remedy these problems, Congress passed the Clayton Act in 1914. Under the Sherman Act, practices were legal unless the government could specifically identify that competition had been adversely affected. Under the **Clayton Act,** practices could be declared illegal if they had the *probable* effect of substantially lessening competition or creating a monopoly. Specifically, the Clayton Act prohibited practices "where the effect of the practice may be to substantially lessen competition or tend to create a monopoly in any line of commerce." Other specific provisions prohibited practices such as price discrimination, exclusive dealer arrangements (limiting buyers' sources of supply), and tying contracts, or forcing sales of some products with others.

The Clayton Act remained unchanged until the 1930s, a decade that brought the rapid rise of supermarket chain stores. Since these giant stores purchased in large quantities, they could influence sellers to offer them special prices and services that were not available to smaller, independent food stores. These practices placed independent grocers at a competitive disadvantage. In order to restrict discriminatory practices between sellers and large-scale buyers, Congress passed the **Robinson-Patman Act** (1936) as an amendment to Section 2 of the Clayton Act. The Robinson-Patman Act imposed the following prohibitions:

- It is illegal to discriminate in prices between purchasers of commodities of like grade and quality where the effect of the discrimination may be to lessen competition substantially or to create a monopoly. But the seller can justify a price differential if (1) it costs the seller less to transact with a particular buyer or (2) the price change is based on changes in market conditions or deterioration of merchandise.

- A seller may offer a price differential if it is made in good faith to meet the equally low price of a competitor.

- Brokerage discounts can be given only to third-party brokers who are independent of both buyer and seller.

- Services, facilities, and promotional allowances (that is, cooperative advertising) cannot be offered to a buyer unless the assistance is offered to all competing buyers on proportionally equal terms.

- It is unlawful for a person to induce as well as receive a discrimination in price.

Enforcement of the Robinson-Patman Act was one job of an important federal agency that had been established earlier by the Federal Trade Commission Act.

The Federal Trade Commission Act

As a reaction to the development of trusts, continued problems with the Sherman Act, and demands by businesses for protection from the anticompetitive activities of other businesses, in 1914, President Wilson re-emphasized the need for unambiguous antitrust legislation. After considerable debate in Congress, it became evident that a specific definition of illegal business activities was futile; there would be numerous exceptions to any definition, and new, unidentified, illicit activities would undoubtedly appear after passage of such a law. Congress therefore agreed on a flexible law that declared unfair methods of competition to be illegal and established the **Federal Trade Commission (FTC)** as an investigative and regulatory agency.

The FTC was originally established to monitor and take legal action against business practices that were unfair (for example, price fixing) and that had a harmful impact on competitors. Concurrent with passage of the act, however, came the rapid expansion and concentration of markets and improvements in transportation and communication. Quick to take advantage of these opportunities, nationally oriented marketers proliferated and began campaigns to encourage and coerce consumers into purchasing their newly developed brands. This situation ultimately resulted in widespread quackery, the promotion of half-truths and false claims, and the perpetuation of the concept of *caveat emptor* ("let the buyer beware"). It was soon apparent that the common law and the FTC Act were not enough to control these deceptive and devious practices. In 1922, a Supreme Court ruling placed deceptive advertising within the scope of the FTC's authority, giving the agency the right to regulate unfair methods of competition such as false labeling and advertising. Unfortunately, the situation worsened as a result of the Supreme Court's ruling in *FTC v. Raladam Company*, which indicated that the FTC was powerless to control false and deceptive advertising unless competition was also injured by the deceptive promotion.

The **Wheeler-Lea Amendment** of 1938 reversed the FTC's weak position by giving the agency authority to control both "unfair methods of competition" and "deceptive acts and practices." Section 12 of the amended act specifically made it unlawful "for any person, partnership, or corporation to disseminate, or cause to be disseminated, any false advertisement . . . for the purpose of inducing . . . directly or indirectly, the purchase of food, drugs, devices, or cosmetics."[2] Thus the FTC's role was established—to protect both businesses and consumers from business activities that are unfair, deceptive, or anticompetitive. The FTC also provided true consumer protection for the very first time.

Consumer Protection Statutes

Both because of the insensitivity of some businesses to the needs of consumers and their exploitation of consumers, Congress enacted a series of laws designed to protect consumers. The first of these laws—the Food, Drug, and Cosmetic Act—was passed in 1906 and amended in 1938 to protect consumers from the adulteration of food and the misbranding of food, drugs, cosmetics, and therapeutic devices. Some companies also found it profitable to substitute an inexpensive product for an expensive one without notifying consumers of the switch. To protect consumers by requiring accurate identification of various products, Congress enacted the Wool Products Labeling Act (1939), the Fur Products Labeling Act (1951), and the Textile Fiber Products Identification Act (1958). In the 1960s and 1970s, other consumer inequities were identified and resolved through a Congressional *consumer right to know/consumer protection* mandate. Following is a summary of the laws that resulted:

■   Fair Packaging and Labeling Act (1966): Prevented deceptive labeling of consumer products and facilitated price comparisons.

Marketers Have Mixed Reactions to New Label Laws

With the nation's attention focused on health, fitness, and diets, our attitudes towards food labels have changed. People want to know what's in the foods they eat and whether particular foods are going to clog their arteries or prolong their lives. Responding to this demand, food makers have come up with some new products, and marketers have found ways to make both new and old sound healthier. Where once it seemed that every package was "giant," now it seems that every food is "light" (or "lite").

Responding to food makers' claims, a number of states began to pass laws requiring that food makers have proof for any claims and regulating the use of words like "light." Some went even further, taking companies to court over what they said were unsubstantiated advertising claims. Food makers began envisioning a nightmare in which every state required different labeling information and different definitions for key marketing terms.

Therefore, when Congress passed a law in 1990 mandating federal standards for labeling and nutritional claims, many food companies and their marketers were pleased. At least now they would have to respond to only one standard. The new Food and Drug Administration guidelines defined terms like "low fat" (3 grams of fat or less per serving of 100 grams or more), "light" (one-third fewer calories than would be found in a comparable product), and "low calorie" (fewer than 40 calories per serving of 100 grams or more). The FDA also changed the requirements for how labels listed nutrients and ingredients. In keeping with current health concerns, the FDA now requires food labelers to disclose how much fat, cholesterol, calcium, and fiber a food contains, but dropped requirements for listing three B-vitamins that are plentiful in most American diets.

As companies began reading the fine print of the new regulations, their enthusiasm began to wane. Large food companies foresaw spending tens of millions of dollars to change all their labels. Makers of bread and crackers complained about the new definition of low-fat, marketers worried about label clutter, and everyone groaned about the expense of having virtually every food item analyzed for nutrition and fat content. Most food companies agree that they prefer to have one standard, but that standard is going to cause major adjustments in the food industry.

Sources: "An End To Label Hype?" *Consumer Reports*, January 1992, 32–33; John Carey, "Snap, Crackle, Stop," *Business Week*, September 25, 1989, 42–43; Richard Gibson, "Food Industry Finds Label Plan Hard to Swallow," *The Wall Street Journal*, January 13, 1992, B1, B2.

- Truth in Lending Act (1968): Required creditors to disclose credit terms so that consumers could make informed decisions.
- Fair Credit Reporting Act (1971): Gave consumers the right to inspect credit reports and to correct mistakes made in them.
- Consumer Product Safety Act (1972): Monitored and regulated matters related to product safety; established safety rules; banned and recalled products; gave jurisdiction to administer the Flammable Fabrics Act, the Federal Hazardous Substances Act, the Poison Prevention Packaging Act, and the Refrigerator Safety Act.
- Fair Credit Billing Act (1975): Helped credit customers correct mistakes made on their billing statements.
- Magnuson-Moss Warranty Act (1975): Required disclosure of warranty terms in easily understood language.
- Equal Credit Opportunity Act (1975): Prohibited discrimination in any aspect of the credit transaction because of sex, marital status, race, national origin, religion, age, or receipt of public assistance.
- Fair Debt Collection Practice Act (1978): Made it illegal to harass or abuse any person, make false statements, or use unfair methods when collecting a debt.

Despite this long list of legislation, the issue of food labeling is still unresolved. As discussed in Promotion in Focus, this issue has a significant impact on food promoters.

Concept Review

1. The Sherman Antitrust Act of 1890 attempted to eliminate monopolies by prohibiting "every contract, combination, or conspiracy, in restraint of trade or commerce, among the several states, or with foreign nations."
2. The Clayton Act of 1914 attempted to rectify limitations found in the Sherman Act, by prohibiting practices "where the effect of the practice may be to substantially lessen competition or tend to create a monopoly in any line of commerce." It also prohibited price discrimination, exclusive dealer arrangements, and tying contracts.
3. The Robinson-Patman Act (1936) was an amendment to the Clayton Act. Among its provisions, it prohibited the initiation or reception of price discrimination practices.
4. The Federal Trade Commission Act of 1914 established the Federal Trade Commission. The Wheeler-Lea Amendment of 1938 brought deceptive advertising under the control of the FTC.

Regulatory Agencies Today

The regulatory agency of greatest importance to promotion is the FTC. In the following sections, we examine its current organization and authority. In addition, we take a brief look at other groups that shape the promotional environment today.

The Federal Trade Commission

The FTC today has extremely broad authority to regulate numerous activities of American business. It controls unfair competitive practices and also acts as a consumer protection agency. Specifically, it has been given authority to regulate credit, labeling, packaging, warranties, and advertising.

Organization of the FTC Figure 6.1 outlines the organization of the FTC. It is directed by five commissioners who are appointed by the President of the United States for a term of seven years. One commissioner is designated by the President as chairperson and is given managerial responsibilities for the FTC's operations. Other staff members of the FTC, such as executive director and chief administrative law judge, are appointed by the chairperson and confirmed by the commissioners.

A formal FTC proceeding is similar to a court trial, except that it tends to be interrupted for substantial periods and to take much longer. An administrative law judge presides and FTC staff attorneys represent the commission; the accused parties (known as respondents) are entitled to representation by their lawyers. If the administrative law judge decides the case in favor of the FTC, he or she issues an order requiring the respondents to cease and desist their unlawful practices. The order can be appealed to the full five-member commission. If affirmed there, a further review is available in a federal court of appeals; some cases are appealed all the way to the U.S. Supreme Court.

Changing Powers of the FTC The Wheeler-Lea Amendment of 1938 allowed the FTC the following responsibilities:

- Initiate investigation against companies without waiting for formal complaints.

- Regulate acts and practices that deceive consumers (not just businesses).

- Issue **cease and desist orders.** The "cease and desist" order requires that the advertiser stop the specified advertising pratice within thirty days and prohibits the advertiser from engaging in the practice.

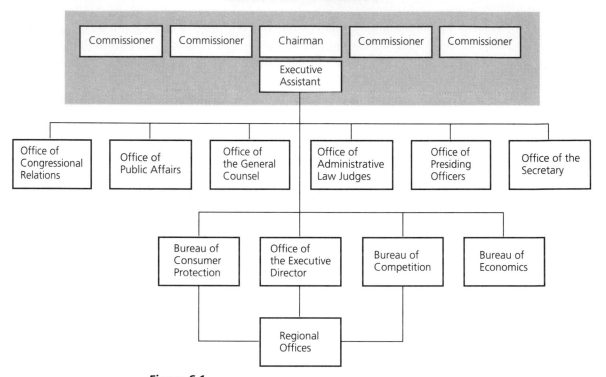

FEDERAL TRADE COMMISSION

Figure 6.1

Organizational chart of the Federal Trade Commission.
1986–1987 U.S. Government Manual.

- Fine companies for not complying with cease and desist orders. Companies were required to appeal these orders within sixty days.

During the 1970s, the Alaska Pipeline Act (1973) and the Federal Trade Commission Improvement Act (1975) strengthened the rule-making and regulatory powers of the FTC as well as its consumer orientation. After enactment of these laws, the FTC had the power to do the following:

- Obtain injunctions against unfair or deceptive acts or practices.

- Use an expanded concept of trade regulation rules (that is, industry-wide rules that define unfair practices before they occur) and define specific practices that are unfair or deceptive.

- Impose a ten-thousand-dollar fine per violation on people or companies that violate either (1) a trade regulation rule or (2) a cease and desist order previously given to the offender *or* to any other firm in the industry. In other words, a cease and desist order given to one firm is applicable to all firms in the industry. Each day of noncompliance with the order represents a separate violation. Firms must therefore carefully monitor legal developments in their industries.

- Rescind or reform contracts in order to obtain restitution for deceived customers.

- Refund money or return property obtained through deceptive or unfair acts or practice.

- Order payment of damages; the FTC does not, however, have the authority to impose punitive damages.

- Order public notification of a violation or unfair practice. For example, Warner-Lambert had falsely represented that Listerine would cure or prevent colds. A corrective message was necessary in order to change consumers' perception that the mouthwash was a cold preventative. In 1975, the FTC therefore required Warner-Lambert to include the statement "Listerine will not help prevent colds or sore throats or lessen their severity" in all Listerine ads until ten million dollars had been spent on such advertising.[3]

In addition, the FTC Improvement Act of 1975 allowed the agency to fund the participation of consumer groups and other interest groups in rule-making proceedings.[4] The most publicized and controversial action during this period was a 1977 proposal to ban or place severe restrictions on all television advertising addressed to children.

But public viewpoints were changing. In a grassroots ground swell against overregulation, editorials lampooned the FTC as the "National Nanny." FTC maternalism was fought by the advertising community. The mood of Congress also changed.

In 1978 and 1979, Congress left the FTC without a budget, voted it only contingency funds, and set restrictions on its operation. In 1980, Congress passed the FTC Improvement Act, stripping the commission of a number of its powers and prerogatives. Most importantly, the commission could no longer promulgate industrywide trade rules about unfairness.

The diminished power of the FTC has encouraged both self-regulation (which we discuss later in this chapter) and an increase in private litigation between advertisers. The Lanham Act, applied in the past mainly to trademark disputes, has been used as the basis for this private litigation. Section 43(a) of this act reads:

> Any person who shall use in connection with any goods or services . . . any false descriptions or representations . . . and shall cause such goods or services to enter into [interstate] commerce . . . shall be liable to a civil action by any person . . . likely to be damaged.[5]

Figure 6.2

This ad acknowledges the increase in legal responsibilities associated with advertising.
Courtesy of Kinney & Lange.

Advertisers have persuaded federal courts to apply this section to advertising disputes, thus allowing advertisers to sue competitors for violations other than product disparagement or trade libel. The promotional opportunity created by this increased litigation has not gone unrecognized, as Figure 6.2 illustrates.

Other Regulatory Groups

Besides the changing direction of the FTC, the 1980s brought another major development. Through the National Association of Attorneys General, the attorneys general of the states began working together to regulate advertising at the state level. For example, in 1990, thirty-four attorneys general issued a fifteen-page document asking the FDA to uphold the current federal law that prohibits the use of disease-related health claims such as cereal manufacturers suggesting that their cereal reduces the risk of cancer. The states also outlined recommendations for rules that are more stringent than the policy the FDA proposed for health claims in 1987. Individual attorneys general have also been active in bringing suits in their respective states. For example, Robert Abrams, New York Attorney General, forced Coca-Cola to change the artificial sweetener labeling on Diet Coke. Campbell Soup Company has had to change some ad claims for its soups, and Kraft has had to modify ads for Cheez Whiz.

Although it is not a regulatory agency, the U.S. Postal Service also controls advertising, both directly and indirectly. Its direct control stems from its right to control advertising that depends on use of the mails—specifically, direct-mail advertising and mail-order advertising. If the Postal Service judges an ad to be fraudulent, it may take the offender to court. It may also conduct an administrative proceeding. If it finds that a violation has been committed, the local postmaster is directed to stamp "Fraudulent" on all mail addressed to the offending party and to return the mail to the sender.

The Postal Service also retains indirect control since it has jurisdiction over advertising carried in any publication that goes through the mails. Its power is based on the fact that the Postal Service can grant, and revoke, second-class mailing privileges. These privileges amount to a government subsidy in favor of periodicals that have a "public character," that is, that contain news, literature, scientific information, or the like, and have a legitimate list of subscribers. The Postal Service can also revoke these privileges as punishment for a periodical carrying a misleading ad.

Finally, the **Federal Communications Commission (FCC)** exercises power over some advertising. Created by the Communications Act of 1934, the FCC regulates radio and television stations and networks. It is concerned with eliminating messages that are deceptive or in poor taste. The commission has sometimes informally brought what it considers objectionable advertising to the attention of a station. The FCC has the power to revoke or refuse to renew a station's license. In most cases, the FCC refers problems concerning advertising to the FTC.

Concept Review

1. The Federal Trade Commission is headed by five commissioners appointed for a term of seven years; it regulates credit, labeling, packaging, warranties, and advertising.
   a. The Wheeler-Lea Amendment of 1938 increased the capabilities of the FTC.
   b. The Alaska Pipeline Act (1973) and the Federal Trade Commission Improvement Act (1975) strengthened the rule-making and regulatory powers of the FTC and made it more consumer oriented.

c. The second FTC Improvement Act of 1980 limited the powers of the FTC.
2. The National Association of Attorneys General regulates advertising at the state level.
3. The U.S. Postal Service controls advertising by monitoring materials sent through the mails.
4. The Federal Communications Commission regulates radio and television stations and networks.

Promotion and the Law

Thus far we have been discussing federal laws related to marketing with little concern for the impact these laws have on promotion. Although it could be argued that all these laws affect promotion tangentially, there are several areas of direct impact.

Deceptive Acts and Practices

The primary focus of the FTC in promotional matters has been on practices that have the capacity to deceive and that are therefore impermissible. These include the following activities:

- False representations of approval or sponsorships (that is, false endorsements or testimonials). In a 1991 case against the Diamond Mortgage Corporation of Illinois and A. J. Obie Associates, the FTC declared that a celebrity's statements in ads may be considered endorsements when they have the capacity to lead reasonable consumers to believe that the endorsements reflect the celebrity's opinions, findings, or beliefs.

- Implications that the product possesses certain qualities. In 1990, the FTC administrative law judge ruled that the claim that Kraft Singles contain more calcium than most imitation cheese slices is false.

- Deceptive pricing ("free" goods and "bait" advertising). In 1990, Amy Travel was found to have engaged in telemarketing fraud in the sale of vacation passports and vouchers. Scripts through which the products were sold created the misleading impression that the cost of the vacation passport equaled the price of the entire vacation package.

- Deception by not disclosing important aspects of the product. In 1971, ITT-Continental, maker of Profile Bread, was found guilty of giving false information about the product.

- Ambiguous statements (each statement may be true, but taken as a whole, the message has the capacity to deceive). In 1984, the FTC charged International Harvester Corp. with "deception, likely to mislead," because of certain wording in their ad.

The general criteria that the FTC used to gauge deception changed dramatically in 1983. Prior to that time, the FTC had the power to judge deception and unfairness merely by looking at the advertising and making a judgment. An ad was deceptive if it had the capacity to deceive either through multiple meanings, combining facts so as to deceive, or being misread in a deceptive way. At the end of 1983, the commission's majority statement suggested that deception must have three essential elements:[6]

1. There must be a representation, omission, or practice that is likely to mislead the consumer.

2. The deception must be considered from the perspective of a consumer acting reasonably in the circumstances.

3. The representation, omission, or practice must be a "material" one. The basic question is whether the act or practice is likely to affect the consumer's conduct or decision with regard to a product or service. If so, the practice is material, and consumer injury is likely because consumers probably would have chosen differently without the influence of the deception.

This new interpretation makes deception a much more difficult violation to prove. The commission now has to prove that deception was intended and that "reasonable consumers" were misled. The authority of the FTC has thus been lessened. Although the early policies on advertising substantiation, unfairness, and affirmative disclosure are still on the books, both advertisers and legislators are confused about ultimate interpretations.

There are a few areas, however, in which legal precedent is fairly clear cut. These will be discussed next.

Unreasonable Basis for Making a Claim   Before an affirmative advertising claim can be made about product performance, the advertiser must have a reasonable basis for making the claim. If prior proof of the validity of the claim is unavailable, the ad is illegal even if the claim is true and the product performs as advertised.

Scientific studies to assess product performance and substantiate claims are not required. The FTC has suggested that in order to determine the reasonableness of a claim, a case-by-case analysis of the following factors must be conducted:

■ Type and specificity of claim made

■ Type of product

■ Possible consequences of the false claim

■ Degree of reliance by consumers on the claim

■ Type and accessibility of evidence adequate to form a reasonable basis for making the particular claim.[7]

Misleading Demonstrations   A demonstration of a product or product performance on television must not mislead viewers. There are instances—for
example, in the case of food products—when additives or substitutes can
be legally employed, because the hot lights, film quality, and other aspects
of the medium do not provide an accurate portrayal of the product. The
issue is whether the demonstration shows the product in a normal way or
setting without falsely upgrading the consumer's perception of the product. Demonstrations are usually evaluated by the FTC on a case-by-case
basis.

Reinforcement of False Beliefs   In addition to focusing on deception
through false claims and statements and misleading images, the FTC has
recently given attention to ads that create or reinforce false beliefs. What
is critical is how members of the audience perceive the ad and how it affects their opinions and beliefs about the advertised product or service.
Deception exists when consumer perception of the truthfulness of a claim
is inconsistent with its actual truthfulness.

Some observers argue that the FTC's first step in identifying deception
should be to test consumer perception of and belief in advertisers' claims.
In other words, does the consumer believe in a claim, and is it relevant to
brand selection? If the answer is yes and the claim cannot be adequately
substantiated by the advertiser, then the ad is deceptive. However, the
FTC has not yet developed a program of using consumer input to identify
deception.

Unfair Comparison Advertising   In narrow terms, **comparison advertising**
involves the comparison of two or more specifically named or recognizably
presented brands of the same generic product or service class in terms of
one or more specific product or service attributes. One of the more widely
publicized comparison ads were the Pepsi Challenge, in which people
were asked to blind-taste Coke and Pepsi and indicate which they preferred. Depending on the criteria employed, this type of ad represents
from 3 percent to 20 percent of all ads.[8]

Although the effect of comparison ads on market share, advertiser image, and competitor image is still uncertain, comparison ads do provide
consumers with biased information on the relative importance of two or
more brands, and disparage competitive brands either by implication or by
direct criticism. These inherent characteristics of comparison advertising
have served as the basis for most public policy decisions. The FTC has
restated its advocacy of the consumer's right to know by supporting comparison advertising as a method of disseminating information with which
consumers can make decisions. On the other hand, concern with the negative implications of competitive disparagement and unfair utilization of
comparative approaches has been reflected in recent FTC decisions, trademark law, state law, common law, and self-regulation.[9]

A recent case demonstrating the dangers of unfair comparisons involved Sterling Automobiles and BMW. Sterling Automobiles ran an ad showing a vandalized BMW, implying that the BMW was not sufficiently protected from theft. BMW sought immediate court relief and argued that, in showing a stripped BMW, the car was being shown in a false light; the product had been "trash-canned." It was also argued that the advertising was deceptive and an unfair trade practice: although the BMW was equipped with antitheft devices, the ad made it appear unprotected. Soon after, Sterling withdrew its ads.

Guidelines developed by self-policing organizations and television networks primarily emphasize the necessity of fair and accurate reporting of significant comparisons. As firms deviate from this fairness standard, the FTC treats the practice as an unfair method of competition.

Bait Advertising   **Bait advertising** is an alluring but insincere offer to sell a product or service that the advertiser does not really intend or want to sell. In one case, Sears, Roebuck and Co. allegedly advertised home appliances with no intention of attempting to sell the advertised items. When customers entered the store on the strength of the attractive bait ad, salespeople not only made no attempt to sell the advertised item but attempted to persuade customers to purchase higher-priced alternatives. Sears was finally ordered to maintain an inventory that is reasonably adequate to meet demand for the sale items and to display a copy of the ad conspicuously in the home appliances department.

The FTC is clear about its attitude toward bait-and-switch tactics. It maintains that the ad that does not represent a bona fide offer to sell the advertised product should not be released. Also, ads should not misrepresent the actual price, quality, or salability of the product in such a manner that, on disclosure of the facts, the purchase may be switched from the advertised product to another, more desirable product.[10] It is also illegal to discourage customers from purchasing the advertised merchandise. Activities that indicate to the FTC that bait-and-switch tactics have occurred include the following:

- Refusing to demonstrate or sell the product as advertised.
- Disparaging any aspect of the advertised product or services that accompany the product (that is, credit, service, and so forth).
- Failing to maintain an inventory that is reasonably adequate to meet demand.
- Refusing to take orders for the advertised merchandise to be delivered within a reasonable period of time.
- Showing a defective product.
- Using compensation methods that discourage salespeople from selling the advertised product.

False Endorsements and Testimonials   An **endorsement** or **testimonial** is any advertising message that consumers perceive as reflecting the opinions, beliefs, or experiences of an individual, group, or institution. Although any individual can endorse a product or service, some advertisers utilize the services of motion picture celebrities, television stars, or sports personalities.

Since consumers may rely on these endorsements when making purchase decisions, it is important that the endorser use the product and be qualified to make expert judgments. When an expert endorses a product, the endorsement must be supported by an actual exercise of his or her expertise in evaluating product features or characteristics. The expert must examine the product as extensively as would another person with similar credentials in order to support conclusions about the product or service. If endorsers compare competing brands, then they must also evaluate the selected brands. Finally, if an organization makes an endorsement, the organization must employ selection procedures that will ensure that the endorsement fairly reflects the collective judgment of the organization. If, on the other hand, one can reasonably ascertain that a message does not reflect the opinion of the announcer, the message is not an endorsement.

A public opinion poll or market survey is the equivalent of a testimonial on a mass scale, and its results must be used with care. In addition, reference to a poll or survey in advertising copy assumes that proper sampling techniques were used and that the sample was of meaningful size.

"Free" Bargains   Normally, special promotions or bargains are presented as two-for-one sales, cents-off sales, multiple purchase discounts, or special offerings. Regardless of the language utilized to describe the special deals, they generally suggest to the consumer that something is being offered free of charge or at a discount. The FTC's attitude toward such discounting programs is reflected in an industry guide concerning the use of the word *free* as well as in the Fair Packaging and Labeling Act.

When used as a promotional tool, the FTC states that the word *free* means that the consumer pays nothing for the item; if receipt of the item is tied to the purchase of another, physically identical item, the tying item must be offered at a price that does not exceed regular price. The FTC considers the *regular* price to be the lowest price at which the item was sold during the thirty-day period immediately prior to commencement of the special bargain. If the bargain is an introductory offer and no regular price has been established, such a "buy one, get one free" sale is probably not appropriate.

FTC Remedies for Deception

Prior to the 1970s, the FTC's primary weapons against deceptive practices were the cease and desist order and minimal fines for violation of orders.

However, as the consumer movement gained momentum and researchers learned more about the lasting impact of ads on consumer beliefs and perceptions, FTC action to expand the breadth of alternative remedies was significantly accelerated.[11]

Corrective Advertising   The idea of employing corrective advertising was introduced to the FTC by a group of law students at George Washington University in 1969. Although the FTC successfully negotiated several consent agreements requiring corrective advertising, doubt surrounding the court's attitude toward this new FTC weapon was not dispelled until 1975 in the *Warner-Lambert v. FTC* case that was discussed earlier. One significant result of this case was that the FTC was given the right to apply retrospective remedies as well as to attempt to restrict future deceptions (see Table 6.2). A second significant result was that the contention that corrective advertising requirements violate the advertiser's First Amendment rights was dispelled.

An issue that was not resolved, however, involves the length of time a deceptive ad must appear before corrective advertising is needed to dispel its residual effects. How long must an ad appear before consumer attitudes are affected? At what point is competition injured? How long does it take to affect purchase intentions? In the case of Listerine, research results showed that the corrective ad had significant impact on the target belief (prevention of colds and sore throats) but no impact on related beliefs such as Listerine's germ-killing ability. Moreover, seven out of eight consumers could not recall the corrective message the day after having seen it. Finally, at the end of the corrective campaign, 42 percent of Listerine users still believed that Listerine was still being promoted as effective against colds and sore throats. Five criteria are suggested for corrective advertising:[12]

1.   The remedy must be prospective rather than retrospective in nature (that is, it should clear up potential future deceptions).

2.   The remedy must be nonpunitive in nature (for example, it should not hurt sales).

3.   The remedy must bear a reasonable relation to the violation in question (that is, it is limited to the violation only).

4.   The remedy should not infringe on the First Amendment rights of the firm (that is, the rights to free speech and to remain silent).

5.   The remedy should be in the least burdensome form necessary to achieve an effective order (that is, it should minimize disruptions and other side effects).

A typical order requires that 25 percent of a product's annual advertising expenditures be devoted to corrective ads, approved in advance by the FTC, stating that the previous claims were subject to misinterpretation and giving the facts. For example, "Profile bread is not effective for weight

Table 6.2 **Early Corrective Advertising Cases**

Company	Product	Claim	Order Type	Disclosure Features
Amstar Corp. (1973)	Domino sugar	Sugar benefits	Consent	25% of ad costs
Beauty-Rama Carpet Center (1973)	Retailer	Prices	Consent	Firm used "bait and switch"
Boise Tire Co. (1973)	Uniroyal tires	Tire ratings	Consent	One ad
ITT Continental Baking (1971)	Profile bread	Caloric content	Consent	25% of one year's ads
Lens Craft Research (1974)	Contact lenses	Medical claims	Consent	Four weeks
Matsushita Electric of Hawaii (1971)	Panasonic TV sets	Hazard ratings	Consent	One ad
National Carpet (1973)	Retailer	Prices	Consent	Firm used "bait and switch"
Ocean Spray Cranberries (1972)	Cranberry drink	Food energy claim	Consent	One of every four ads
Payless Drug Co. (1973)	Motorcycle helmets	Safety	Consent	Equal number to original ads
Rhode Island Carpets (1974)	Retailer	Prices	Consent	Firm used "bait and switch"
RJR Foods Inc. (1973)	Hawaiian punch	Juice content	Consent	Every ad until effects are shown
Shangri La Industries (1972)	Swimming pools	Availability and terms	Consent	25% of one year's ads
STP Corp. (1976)	Oil additive	Effectiveness	Consent	One ad, fourteen media
Sugar Information (1974)	Sugar	Sugar benefits	Consent	One ad, seven media
Warner-Lambert (1975)	Listerine	Effectiveness claim	Litigated	Correction in $10 million of ads
Wasems Inc. (1974)	Wasems vitamins	Vitamin benefits	Consent	One ad, seven insertions
Yamaha International (1974)	Yamaha motorcycle	Motorcycle safety	Consent	Corrective letter

Source: William L. Wilkie, Dennis L. McNeill, and Michael B. Mazis, "Marketing's Scarlet Letter: The Theory and Practice of Corrective Advertising," *Journal of Marketing* 48, No. 2 (Spring 1984): 14. Reprinted from *Journal of Marketing* published by the American Marketing Association. Used with permission.

reduction." The complexity of the issue is evident and suggests that researchers and the FTC must conduct more conclusive studies to help policy makers determine future directions for corrective advertising.

Substantiation of Advertising Claims   Until 1971, firms could, without substantial fear of FTC intervention, advertise various performance, safety, efficacy, quality, and comparative price claims that had no factual basis. In that year, responding to consumer demands for accurate information, the FTC adopted a resolution that requires firms to submit on demand documentation to substantiate advertising and product uniqueness claims. Information the FTC collects from advertisers to support claims is subsequently presented to the public for inspection and comment.

When the FTC issues a complaint against a company, it is the company's responsibility to show that there is a reasonable basis for the product claims it has made. Although the FTC has not delineated any specific guidelines or research procedures for establishing a "reasonable basis" for advertising or uniqueness claims, it has indicated that scientific, objective, and acceptable research procedures should be utilized. Tests should also be extensive and well documented.

Since its adoption in 1971, the advertising substantiation program has become extensive. Supporting data have been requested for air conditioners, acne preparations, automobiles, shampoos, hearing aids, pet foods, and detergents, to name a few products. A widely reported substantiation case occurred in 1977 when General Electric Co. agreed to a Federal Trade Commission consent settlement. The case stemmed from the company's statement that its television sets required less servicing than competing sets. The agreement, published by the commission for public comment, enjoined General Electric from claiming superiority over a competing product unless the nature of the superiority was specified or was discernible to the consumer.

Affirmative Disclosure   In order to help consumers make objective, informed decisions, the FTC has instituted a program that requires that some advertisers "disclose positive information about their product as well as information about the product that would help the consumers avoid being harmed or dissatisfied." Early FTC affirmative disclosure decisions were primarily directed at the food and drug industry to require disclosure of possible side effects or dangers and to provide package fill information. More recent action has been directed toward land deals, computer schools, hair replacement centers, and tobacco companies. The affirmative disclosure order that has had the most widespread and significant impact was directed at the cigarette industry. All ads must display the surgeon general's warning of potential health hazards of smoking.

Cooling-off Period   The FTC has frequently accompanied affirmative disclosure orders with a *cooling-off* directive. For example, Hair Replacement Centers of Boston was directed to give customers three days in which to cancel contracts. The cooling-off rule requires sellers to print the following statement on contracts for the sales of consumer goods and services:

> You, the buyer, may cancel this transaction at any time prior to midnight of the third business day after the date of this transaction. See

the attached notice of cancellation form for an explanation of this right.

The cooling-off rule applies only to sales made at locations other than the seller's place of business. It does not apply to telephone or mail transactions, the sale of insurance or securities, sales made at a retail facility where goods are displayed, or maintenance service at the buyer's home.

Consumer Redress   The Magnuson-Moss Warranty–FTC Improvement Act authorizes the FTC to obtain consumer redress when an individual or firm engages in an act or practice "which a reasonable man would have known under the circumstances was dishonest or fraudulent." The forms of relief that can be granted to consumers include rescission or reformation of contracts, refund of money or return of property, payment of damages, and public notification.

Public Relations and the Law

Although most of the legal issues related to promotion concern advertising, some laws affect public relations as well. The most common areas of concern in public relations law are defamation, privacy, copyright, and contract negotiations.

Defamation   **Defamation** can be construed as anything that tends to damage a reputation. To be actionable, defamation must be communicated in some form to a third party and the person defamed must be identified, though not necessarily by name. If the person can be recognized from a description such as "the bald-headed, bearded guy who always sits in the corner of the lunchroom," that would be sufficient identification.

Usually defamation is divided into slander and libel; *slander* is classified as *oral* defamation and *libel* as *written* defamation. However, this distinction has become clouded with the inclusion of radio and television. Is it libel or slander when a commentator makes a remark considered defamatory? If there is any trend, it is toward considering such utterances as libel, no matter what the source.

Public relations practitioners may be involved in libel actions in two ways. One of the practitioner's clients might be libeled, or, more likely, the practitioner could be accused of libel in a news release, speech, or other communication.

Privacy   Rights of privacy are somewhat vague. The circulation of a story that was of public interest, that involved a public figure, that was already a matter of public record, or that had some social value would not normally be considered an invasion of privacy. Of particular concern in recent years is the violation of our privacy rights through databases. Over the past couple of decades, computers have collected a vast store of data on average people. Few people realize that this information is largely unprotected by rules, laws, or codes of ethics. Instead, it can be pored over, analyzed, sold, and perhaps paired with other data to draw an intimate profile based on a person's daily habits. Privacy rights basically protect people from four types of violations:

1. **Intrusion:** Actual invasion of a person's seclusion, solitude, or private affairs.
2. **Disclosure:** Revelation of embarrassing private facts about a person.
3. **False light:** Publicity that places a person in a false light in the public eye.
4. **Appropriation:** Use of a person's name or likeness without that person's permission. To avoid the charge of appropriation, public relations must obtain permission for the use of a person's name, likeness, or statement. A photographer cannot, for example, photograph a group of shoppers walking through a city's downtown area and later use that picture with a caption suggesting the shoppers are headed for a particular bank.

Copyright   The essence of the copyright laws is to request permission for any substantial reprinting. To obtain a copyright for a work, all that is needed is to publish it with a copyright notice. No filing is necessary. The copyright claim is lost, however, if the work is published without the copyright notice. On January 1, 1978, the copyright law received its first major revision since 1909. In general, the revision extends the length of copyright protection and makes wholesale copying much more difficult. The advent of duplicating machines had much to do with these changes.

The period of copyright protection is segmented: works created after January 1, 1979, and works neither copyrighted nor in the public domain before January 1, 1978, are eligible for copyright for the period of the author's life plus fifty years. Works "made for hire," and thus likely to be copyrighted by corporations, are eligible for copyright for a period of seventy-five years from the year of first publication, or one hundred years from the date of creation, whichever expires first. Works originally copyrighted within twenty-eight years prior to January 1, 1978, will be eligible for a renewal period of forty-seven years when the original protection expires.

The key phrase in copyright law is **fair use.** This term seeks to define conditions under which material may be reproduced or included in other works. The definition is relative, however, and each case that goes to court is decided on its own merits. For example, the definition of fair use may depend on whether the reprinted material is used for profit, the nature of the copyrighted work, the amount and substantiality of the portion excerpted, and the effect the use may have on the market for the original work.

The basic idea behind all copyright provisions is that people's work is their own and they are entitled to appropriate compensation for its use. This concept applies not only to written materials but to artwork, photography, trademarks, and other tangible results of creativity.

Contract Negotiations   Ordinarily, contracts are drawn up with the help of an attorney, but certain documents become so familiar that the users forget they are dealing with actual contracts. When a public relations practitioner gives a printer a brochure to print, both people are entering into a contract. Contract negotiations may be equally informal with many public relations suppliers—photographers, artists, free-lance writers, models, typographers, and film producers. Standard forms should be used for these transactions, and they should be re-evaluated from time to time.

Personal Selling and the Law

Both the salesperson and the sales manager must be aware of several legal considerations. Laws regarding commercial bribery are probably the most significant. **Commercial bribery** is the act of influencing or attempting to influence the actions of an employee, such as a purchasing agent or buyer, by giving the employee a gift without knowledge of the employer.

It is important to note that the attempt to bribe is itself a crime. There is no general federal statute against commercial bribery, but it is considered an unfair method of competition under the FTC Act. Commercial bribery is generally controlled by state law. State laws also make it illegal to bribe government officials, and federal laws prohibit attempts to bribe federal employees and employees of federal contractors.

A good rule for avoiding commercial bribery charges is to provide only limited entertainment. Most sales managers do not consider lunch, dinner, tickets to a sporting event, or other traditional gifts to be unethical. But cash and elaborate entertainment such as vacations are usually considered beyond the bounds of propriety.

Price fixing is the illegal act of setting prices in concert with competitors. Agreements to allocate markets among suppliers are also illegal. Price fixing occurs most often in concentrated industries where several major competitors exist. Often, the price fixers are sales managers. Jail sentences as well as fines are increasingly being meted out.

There are a variety of other legal considerations in selling. The FTC Act forbids unfair methods of competition; it is therefore illegal to interfere with competitors or disparage a competitor's products or services. *Tying arrangements*, in which a seller forces a buyer to purchase one product to obtain the right to purchase another, are illegal under the Clayton and

Sherman acts. It is also illegal to arrange for *reciprocal dealing,* the "I'll buy from you if you'll buy from me" type of deal.

Sales Promotion and the Law

Most of the laws related to sales promotion deal with incentives. For example, a 1969 FTC statement regarding in-pack coupons (1) requires full disclosure on the product package of all terms of the offer on enclosed coupons, (2) bars unreasonably short expiration dates on the coupons, and (3) requires disclosure if the coupon is good only for a price reduction on the next purchase of the same item or on a purchase of a different product. Another ruling by the FTC, in 1972, dealt with products such as soaps and detergents; it states that cents-off as well as introductory and related offers must reflect a true reduction of the initial price. This initial price must stay intact for thirty days after the product is introduced. In 1972, the FTC also ruled that a recipient has no obligation to return or to pay for unsolicited merchandise received in the mail.

A great deal of confusion surrounds the legal distinctions among contests, lotteries, and sweepstakes. A **contest** requires some act of skill that necessitates a judge or judges to make a relative comparison. A **lottery** involves a payment or other legal consideration in exchange for a chance to win a prize. All three elements—chance, consideration, and prize— must be present, or the promotion is not a lottery. A prize lawfully may be awarded by chance if there is absolutely no charge or obligation of any kind. So-called **sweepstakes,** with coupons distributed free to all consumers, fall into this category.

Warranties represent another sales promotion device that the government has scrutinized. A law on warranties for consumer products that went into effect in 1975 requires a designation of whether the warranty is full or limited. A full warranty must include a statement of the time period during which it will remain operative. A limited warranty must set forth clearly what limitations are included. In 1985, the FTC published guides for the advertising of warranties. It is clear that any copywriter using the term *warranty,* or its equivalent, must be certain that the use of the term fits the advertiser's policies.

Concept Review

1. The FTC evaluates acts and practices that have the capacity to deceive. Since 1983, when the FTC issued a position paper on deceptive acts and practices, deception is a difficult violation to prove.
2. The FTC does have clear prohibitions regarding deception based on the following:
   a. Unreasonable basis for making a claim,
   b. Misleading demonstrations,

     c.   Reinforcement of false beliefs,

     d.   Unfair comparison advertising,

     e.   Bait advertising,

     f.   False endorsements and testimonials, and

     g.   "Free" bargains.

3. The FTC offers several remedies for deception:

     a.   Corrective advertising,

     b.   Substantiation of advertising claims,

     c.   Affirmative disclosure,

     d.   Cooling-off period, and

     e.   Consumer redress.

4. Several legal issues also affect public relations

     a.   Defamation

     b.   Privacy

     c.   Copyright protection

     d.   Contract negotiation

5. The salesperson and the sales manager need to be aware of the legal ramifications of commercial bribery and price fixing.

6. Sales promotion devices such as contests, lotteries, and sweepstakes each have distinct legal definitions.

Self-Regulation of Promotion

One reason for the heavy regulation of marketing at both the federal and state levels is the long-standing assumption that marketing involves illegal and unethical activities. Promotion has unfortunately caught the brunt of this criticism. The American Association of Advertising Agencies even developed ads to counter some of the criticism (see Figure 6.3). Whether fair or not, the criticism has spawned innumerable laws, and the typical promotion manager constantly faces decisions that may have legal consequences. Consequently, professionals working in promotion have developed stringent guidelines and codes of ethical conduct so that promotion managers and their companies can avoid violations of federal and state laws.

The Promotion Clearance Process

It would be a mistake, however, to assume that promotion managers look to outside agencies to keep them out of trouble. Most companies, agencies, and media have an elaborate network for reviewing promotional efforts. Although this review process tends to differ from company to company, it

Figure 6.3

There are many negative perceptions about advertising, some of which are effectively challenged in this ad.
© *American Association of Advertising Agencies.*

DESPITE WHAT SOME PEOPLE THINK, ADVERTISING CAN'T MAKE YOU BUY SOMETHING YOU DON'T NEED.

Some people would have you believe that you are putty in the hands of every advertiser in the country.

They think that when advertising is put under your nose, your mind turns to oatmeal.

It's mass hypnosis. Subliminal seduction. Brain washing. Mind control. It's advertising.

And you are a pushover for it.

It explains why your kitchen cupboard is full of food you never eat.

Why your garage is full of cars you never drive.

Why your house is full of books you don't read, TV's you don't watch, beds you don't use, and clothes you don't wear.

You don't have a choice. You are forced to buy.

That's why this message is a cleverly disguised advertisement to get you to buy land in the tropics.

Got you again, didn't we? Send in your money.

ADVERTISING
ANOTHER WORD FOR FREEDOM OF CHOICE.
American Association of Advertising Agencies

typically starts with the creative team and ends with the medium that carries the promotion. At each step in the process, the promotional piece is critiqued from a number of different perspectives to make sure it meets all reasonable standards of ethics and taste as well as legal requirements. Lawyers may review the piece at several different stages. The agency often has a set of standards against which it measures all work. These standards may be reproduced as scaled items, with each item evaluated and scored by a number of key people within the agency as well as by the client. Ads that receive scores below a certain level are rejected. This process may take several days, weeks, or even months.

Virtually every major medium has guidelines for acceptable promotions. *Reader's Digest*, for example, has a long list of unacceptable product categories as well as message appeals. The three major television networks probably have the toughest standards. Ads that might air on cable or Fox may not be seen on NBC, CBS, or ABC. Even if ABC finally accepts an edited version of a questionable ad, the network may allow it to be shown only after 9 P.M.

Promotion managers have determined that a vigorous internal review process is beneficial. The risks of allowing an unethical or illegal promotion to be seen or heard by the public are simply too great.

Self-Regulation by Professional Groups

To date there are very few, if any, universal standards by which to judge promotional activities. Promotion managers do not agree among themselves as to what is legal or ethical, and critics apply their own ethical standards. Despite the lack of consensus, uncertainty about what is permissible has decreased during the last two decades. Most of this change comes as a result of the activities of independent organizations that impose regulation through public pressure, and codes developed by groups within the promotion industry that are attempting self-regulation. These codes are usually area specific and deal with topics such as testimonials, personal selling techniques, or couponing.

The National Advertising Review Council (NARC)   Perhaps the most ambitious example of self-regulation occurred in 1971, when the American Advertising Federation, the American Association of Advertising Agencies, the Association of National Advertisers, and the Council of Better Business Bureaus established the **National Advertising Review Council (NARC)** to implement a program of self-regulation. As an intermediary between consumers and the federal government, the NARC is charged with maintaining high standards of honesty and accuracy in national advertising.

The NARC has been successful in monitoring false and misleading advertising and in setting a state-by-state precedent for self-regulation. In its first year of operation, the NARC got eighty-four advertisers to withdraw or modify ads. More recently, the NARC was successful in getting Sprint Long Distance to modify three ads, Topps Co. (a manufacturer of baseball cards) to drop a print ad, American Airlines, Inc. to change the wording in a print ad for its Los Angeles to Hong Kong route, and Glidden Paints to drop an unsubstantiated claim about durability.[13]

Complaints regarding the truth and accuracy of ads may be initially submitted by consumers, consumer groups, industrial organizations, or advertising firms to the NARC's investigative staff, the **National Advertising**

Division (NAD). After a complaint is filed, the NAD evaluates the legitimacy of the complaint and, if it is justified, attempts to resolve the problem. If the advertiser or advertising agency is unwilling to change or withdraw the ad, the complaint is appealed to the **National Advertising Review Board (NARB).** This regulatory group consists of thirty members representing national advertisers, ten members representing advertising agencies, and ten members representing public or nonindustry fields. Upon receipt of the appeal, the chairman of the NARB appoints a five-person panel from the membership to resolve the issue. After reviewing both the NAD's findings and the advertiser's counterarguments, the NARB panel arrives at a decision that is communicated to the top executive level of the offending firm. If, after exhausting all appropriate remedies, the advertiser still is unwilling to accept the NARB's decision, the federal government is informed of the violation.

The NAD and the Children's Advertising Review Unit   The NAD has a special Children's Advertising Review Unit and has published guidelines and a bibliography on children and advertising. This unit was established in 1974 in response to the special problems of advertising that is directed to children. Its purpose is to promote truthful, accurate advertising that is sensitive to the special nature of its audience. The areas it primarily investigates include (1) how products are presented to children, (2) the amount of information provided, and (3) the amount of overt pressure to buy.

The NAB and Other Media Groups   The media have attempted to regulate advertising by screening and rejecting ads that violate their standards of truth and good taste. *Modern Maturity* magazine, for example, refuses to carry ads that demean senior citizens in any way. *Reader's Digest* does not accept tobacco or liquor ads. Each medium has discretion to accept or reject a particular ad. The **National Association of Broadcasters (NAB)** has separate codes of conduct for radio and television that specify products that cannot be advertised and give guidelines that should be followed in presenting ads or offering contests, premiums, and offers.

Many of the initial guidelines changed as a result of a civil antitrust suit filed against the NAB in 1979. The suit charged that NAB rules that regulated television advertising were anticompetitive and in restraint of trade. In 1982, a consent decree signed by all parties basically eliminated the NAB code. There are now no formal standards concerning the following:[14]

- The number of commercial minutes per hour
- The number of commercials per hour
- The number of consecutive commercials at each commercial interruption

- The number of products that can be promoted at each commercial interruption
- The purchase of network time for liquor ads
- The actual consumption of beer or wine on television.

Although the NAB codes are no longer in force, many broadcasters, including the major television networks, have adopted significant portions of the codes in their own standards. Each of the three networks has a Standard and Practices Division, which carefully reviews all ads submitted for possible broadcast.

Other Agents of Self-Regulation   Self-regulation has also been supported by the Better Business Bureau, local advertising review boards, advertising agencies, advertising media, and public relations firms. The **Better Business Bureau (BBB)** has been one of the most effective agencies for monitoring and publicizing unfair and deceptive practices. Supported by local businesses, the BBB investigates complaints, attempts to persuade offenders to stop unfair practices, and, if necessary, employs legal restrictions on aspects of advertising.

Since advertising agencies can also be liable for the false and misleading ads of their clients, they—like many advertisers—have instituted internal programs of self-regulation by monitoring copy, demanding substantiation of claims from clients, and extensively utilizing legal counsel.

Despite all these safeguards, something definitely went wrong with the execution of the Volvo campaign discussed earlier. Did Scali, McCabe, Sloves engage in deception intentionally? Was the deception decided on independently by one or two individuals? Did it occur because of pressure placed on the agency to produce a blockbuster television campaign? Regardless, the consequences have been dire. A major agency may go out of business, and a prominent automobile manufacturer may never again regain its credibility.

The Public Relations Society of America drafted a Code of Professional Standards in 1954 that it revised and strengthened in 1977. The code covers the practitioner's relationships with clients, the media, and the public. It stresses honesty and fair dealings with all segments of society, including competitors.[15]

Self-Regulation by the Promotion Manager

It should be clear by now that a promotion manager working for a major corporation could spend all his or her time screening ads, contests, coupon programs, and personal selling approaches in order to judge their legality and morality. Instead, promotion managers establish policies and mechanisms to review promotional programs efficiently and effectively. There is no standard procedure for setting up policies and reviewing mechanisms, but there are some general rules of thumb. First, the promotion manager must be thoroughly familiar with the level of risk that the company is willing to take in its promotional efforts. This risk-taking philosophy should be stated by top management and interpreted by the chief marketing officer. The philosophy is often reflected in past promotions but may change because of new leadership or new pressures. Promotion managers must determine whether they want to work for an organization that communicates in a manner that may conflict with their own values.

Second—assuming the promotion manager understands the communication philosophy of the organization and is willing to comply—he or she should be sure that all employees and contract people understand the philosophy as well. A policy statement, specific explanations, and examples should be developed for copywriters, artists, television production crews, special events directors, and sales managers, among others.

Finally, the promotion manager must establish a mechanism to make sure that the promotion strategy is implemented in accordance with the stated communication philosophy. This mechanism might be very elaborate and include multiple screenings of every outgoing message. At a minimum, every message should be reviewed by the company's legal staff. Several large corporations use outside consultants as well.

Although self-regulation is clearly not the most glamorous part of a promotion manager's job, doing it correctly is critical. Even slight mistakes may produce consequences as serious as those faced by Volvo and its agency.

Promotion's Responsibility to Society

In Chapter 4, we discussed the role of values in cultures and subcultures. Essentially, values are guidelines for making judgments. Honesty, hard work, and love of family are values common to many cultures. When individuals or institutions appear to violate key values, the violations become *societal issues*. That is, the violations represent behavior that part of society wishes to change.

Several societal issues have been associated with promotion. These are not activities that are illegal per se, but the organization that ignores them is likely to lose goodwill or business. The promotion manager must be aware of these societal issues and be prepared to adapt his or her strategy. These issues differ from one culture to another as well as from one subculture to another. A message that seems unremarkable in a large city may become an issue in a small town. The dual role of promotion is (1) to benefit the marketers by delivering unique messages to the consumer that make the product or service more competitive and (2) to benefit the consumer by providing relevant and accurate information to enhance the probability of making an optimal decision. Achieving the first without achieving the second is likely to mean that the promotional effort will ultimately fail. We will discuss those societal issues that interest most consumers in the United States.

Manipulation   The primary criticism of promotion is that it manipulates people so that they purchase products and services that they neither need nor want. This criticism raises an extremely difficult issue. On the one hand, there do appear to be gullible people who believe everything they hear or read. There are also people who buy everything they see, regardless of whether they can afford it. Some people—including children, the senile, or the poorly educated—may not have the intellectual or physical capabilities to judge good from bad or real from unreal. Other individuals may simply have a personality quirk that makes them more susceptible to certain irrational behaviors. The extent to which promotion stimulates these behaviors is impossible to determine. Many other factors, both internal and external, influence irrational behavior. On the other hand, no amount of promotion is going to make most people do something they do not want to do. Freedom of choice is a right that promotion cannot negate.

However, it is the responsibility of the promotion manager to be sensitive to audiences that are easily confused or influenced. We have already addressed the great care that is taken when promoting to children. Similar protection is available for senior citizens and the disadvantaged. Finally, intelligent, relevant, and honest promotional messages do not manipulate; rather, they facilitate wise decision making.

Privacy   One basic human right is privacy—the right to be left alone. Critics argue that promotion violates our personal privacy. Ads confront us on parking meters, grocery store shopping carts, movie screens, rented video cassettes, and television monitors at airports. Ads are sent to fax machines, and few nights go by without a household's receiving at least one telephone sales call, usually during dinner. Parents are upset with Channel One, a network that force-feeds commercials to students under the guise of a news program.

The criticism of privacy violation appears valid. Promotion strategists must find less offensive ways of reaching consumers than bombarding them wherever they go. Doing a better job of identifying consumers who are truly interested in the product is part of the solution. Providing a mechanism for consumers to initiate the communication process—by calling a toll-free number, for example—is also helpful.

Puffery   Consumers do not like to be lied to. But do they mind puffery? **Puffery** is advertising or other sales representations which praise the item to be sold with subjective opinions, superlatives, or exaggerations, vaguely and generally, stating no specific facts.[16] Statements such as "Nestlé makes the very best chocolate" and "When you say Budweiser you've said it all" are mild forms of puffery.

Regulatory agencies deal with deceptive promotional messages but have no jurisdiction over those that exaggerate. Critics argue that promotional messages should contain useful information, not puffery. Defenders suggest that reasonable people know that puffery just shows enthusiasm for a product, and that consumers understand this aspect of selling. Clearly, puffery is risky. Defining puffery and determining whether to encourage, tolerate, or avoid it require personal evaluation by the promotion manager.

Offensive Products and Appeals   We have come a long way since the 1950s, when an advertising executive coined the term *B.O.* (body odor) for use in a print ad for a deodorant, because consumers would be offended by the word *sweat*. Nevertheless, consumers may still be offended or irritated by certain types of appeals and by promotions for certain products.

Recent controversial appeals include Mel Tilles stuttering a message for Fina gasoline, Reebok showing a person who is not wearing the sponsor's shoes apparently being killed after a bungee jump, and Frito-Lay showing the consequences of using another bean dip. The use of sexual appeals is also offensive to many consumers. Calvin Klein, Budweiser Beer, Johnny Walker, and L'Oréal are a few of the companies that have been accused of using overt sex appeals.

In some cases, the product itself is the problem. Any promotional appeal for condoms, bras, laxatives, feminine-hygiene products, and adult diapers embarrasses some consumers, especially if they are not alone when they are exposed to the promotion. Promotion managers tend to ignore these protests, assuming that they represent only small pockets of discontent. However, there are significant, organized protests against the promotion of alcohol and tobacco. As this book goes to press, legislation is pending that would regulate the ways in which tobacco and alcohol products can be promoted.[17] One industry report indicates that as many as 165 magazines would fold without tobacco advertising.[18]

Promotion managers who use controversial appeals and promote controversial products argue that their messages are appropriate for the target audience. But managers must be sensitive to the fact that people outside the target audience also receive these messages. When people feel that promoters have gone too far, they are likely to put pressure on promoters to change their messages and on resellers to stop carrying the products.

Stereotyping   The portrayal of people, not products, has also become a social issue. Promotions are accused of being discriminatory by presenting stereotypes in their promotions. *Stereotyping* ignores differences among individuals and presents a group in an unvarying pattern. Stereotypes of women are one prominent target of criticism. Recent studies have shown that females are more scantily dressed than their male counterparts in the same ad.[19] Ads often depict women as sexualized bodies, with their status based on how they look.[20] The two most prominent images of women presented in ad campaigns, those of the "innocent virgin" and of the "dark lady," pit innocence and romance against knowledge and sexuality.[21] Although there is still concern about sexual stereotyping, more promoters are recognizing the diversity of women's roles.

Racial and ethnic groups also complain of stereotyping in promotion. Minorities may be the basis of a joke or, alternatively, consigned to the background. Other critics complain that minorities are underrepresented in advertisements.

Another group frequently stereotyped is senior citizens. Critics often object to the use of older people in roles that portray them as slow, senile, and full of afflictions. Such portrayals are definitely on the decline.

Concept Review

1. Promoters engage in self-regulation in order to prevent violations of state and federal laws.
   a. The National Advertising Review Board monitors false and misleading advertising.
   b. The Better Business Bureau monitors and publicizes unfair and deceptive practices.
   c. The various media have their own standards for accepting possible ads.
2. Each promotion manager must establish a mechanism for monitoring promotional efforts.
3. Promotion managers must also be responsive to societal issues, especially the following:
   a. Privacy
   b. Manipulation
   c. Puffery
   d. Offensive products and appeals
   e. Stereotyping

Case 6   *Will Power's Surveys Lose Their Punch?*

Consumers shopping for a car are in a difficult position, especially if they are interested in new models. Dealers, of course, sing the praises of their brands, but other than such things as EPA miles-per-gallon ratings, consumers have very few objective yardsticks by which to measure one manufacturer's cars against another. Many eagerly await *Consumer Reports* yearly car-buying guide, which includes the magazine's ratings of new cars and its subscribers' ratings of cars they own. But although salespeople may be eager to tell prospective customers about the magazine's ratings, *Consumer Reports* refuses to let manufactures use its ratings in advertisements.

The Surveys

So to provide consumers with objective evidence of their products' quality, car manufacturers turn to J. D. Power & Associates. Power publishes four major surveys each year, based on information collected from some 30,000 car owners. Consumers' satisfaction with the buying process is reflected in the Sales Satisfaction Survey. The Initial Quality Survey measures how owners feel after they've had their car three months, the Customer Satisfaction Survey rates customers' assessments of car quality and dealer service a year after purchase, and the Vehicle Dependability Index indicates how owners feel after five years.

Only Good News

Consumer advocates generally approve of the way that Power gathers its information, but some criticize what the company does once it has compiled its surveys. Car manufacturers pay hundreds of thousands of dollars for the surveys; they are, in effect, Power's clients. Until 1986, Power released all its findings, positive and negative. But the manufacturers—Power's clients—complained that a poor rating from Power could hurt car sales, so now Power makes public only positive ratings. The surveys also rate entire car lines—all Buicks, for instance—rather than individual models, which makes it more difficult for consumers to know how good a particular model is likely to be.

The Bad News

What threatens Power's credibility is the proliferation of ads that use the results of Power's surveys. As many as a dozen different cars may be promoted with Power's rankings at one time. These ads aren't lying; they're just using isolated pieces of the surveys. The major surveys include twenty or more categories, so it is relatively easy for a manufacturer to say that its product was rated "highest in its class" or "tops among American cars in its class," even though the car in question may in fact have done poorly in the overall ratings or when compared to imported models. The Chevrolet Lumina, for instance, was advertised as "the most trouble-free car in its class," according to Power's Initial Quality Survey. What the ad didn't say was that the Lumina had actually scored below average in the Survey; it's just that the other cars in the "midsize specialty class" did even worse.

J. D. Power himself, who started his company in 1971, recognizes the risks of his name being overused. In 1986, he began reviewing—for a hefty fee—all ads that referred to his company's surveys. Policing ads for their validity is a good step, critics say, but it alone won't stop the devaluing of Power's survey results. It seems that car buyers may still have to do their own research just to find out what the Power survey results mean.

Case Questions

1. What are the possible legal and/or social problems faced by auto makers who use the J. D. Power survey data?

2. What are some of the long-term risks the promotion manager takes in using data provided by J. D. Power?

Sources: Kim Foltz, "J. D. Power's Big Problem: Popularity," *The New York Times*, August 17, 1990, C-5; Barry Meier, "A Car Is Rated Most Trouble-Free, But How Good Is That?," *The New York Times*, October 13, 1990, 16.

Summary

Promotion is the most legislated element of marketing. Because of its visibility, the consumer, competitors, and legislators are constantly aware of what promotion is doing. In this chapter, laws and institutions that impinge on promotion were discussed. Federal laws that are particularly relevant to promotional strategists include the Sherman Act, the Clayton Act, the Robinson-Patman Act, and the Federal Trade Commission Act. The Sherman Act dealt with restraint of trade and made all such activities, including monopolies or attempts to monopolize, illegal. The Clayton Act modified the Sherman Act by declaring illegal all practices that have a probable effect of substantially lessening competition or creating a monopoly. The Robinson-Patman Act dealt primarily with price discrimination and price allowances. The Federal Trade Commission Act established the

Federal Trade Commission, a regulatory agency that controls much of what promotion does.

The primary focus of the FTC is on deceptive acts and practices. In 1983, the FTC adopted three criteria that make deception difficult to prove. However, the definition of what constitutes deception is fairly clear in the case of several practices: unreasonable basis for making a claim, misleading demonstrations, reinforcement of false beliefs, unfair comparison ads, bait advertising, false endorsements and testimonials, and "free" bargains. The FTC requires several possible remedies for promoters engaged in deceptive practices: corrective advertising, substantiation of advertising claims, affirmative disclosure, cooling-off period, and consumer redress.

Other legal issues affect each area of promotion. Legal issues relevant to public relations include defamation, violation of privacy, copyright violation, and contractual obligations. In personal selling, key legal concerns include commercial bribery, price fixing, and other unfair methods of competition. In conducting sales promotions, managers must pay particular attention to laws and regulations regarding incentives and warranties as well as to legal distinctions among contests, lotteries, and sweepstakes.

Promoters have come to realize that it is better to monitor and modify their activities prior to government intervention. The National Advertising Review Board is the primary self-regulatory agency reviewing all advertising. The Better Business Bureau, the National Association of Broadcasters, other media groups, and individual promotion managers all play key roles in self-regulation.

The chapter concludes with a discussion of social issues influencing promotion. Four such issues were considered: privacy, puffery, offensive products and appeals, and stereotyping.

Discussion Questions

1. Provide an overview of the most important pieces of government legislation affecting promotional strategies and tactics.

2. Outline the responsibilities of the Federal Trade Commission as they relate to promotion.

3. What criteria does the FTC use to gauge deception in advertising? What are the Federal Trade Commission's remedies for deceptive advertising?

4. "Corrective advertising has proven harmful to most advertisers forced to engage in the process." Discuss your agreement or disagreement.

5. Assume that you are a judge. What factors would you use to determine whether or not a retailer was indeed practicing bait-and-switch advertising?

6. What is being done to develop ethical codes for the self-regulation of promotion?

7. Why does the development of a promotional strategy or program require an understanding of the legal environment?

8. What advice would you give to a person who is developing a claim for use in an advertised message?

9. What is stereotyping? Is stereotyping always bad? How can the promotion manager avoid it?

10. "In general, federal legislation became more probusiness during the 1980s." Comment on this statement.

Suggested Projects

1. Contact your regional FTC office. Ask a representative to send you examples of three advertising-related cases that have been evaluated during the last year. What criteria were considered? What was the final judgment?

2. Collect three print ads that demonstrate obvious sexual appeals. Ask five students to indicate their response to these ads. Ask five older adults. Analyze the responses in a three-page report.

References

1. Yale Brozen, "Antitrust Out of Hand," *The Conference Board Record* (March 1974): 14–19.

2. Federal Trade Commission v. Raladam Company, 283 U.S. 643 (1931).

3. Warner-Lambert Company v. Federal Trade Commission, 562 F.2d 749 (1977).

4. Robert E. Wilkes and James B. Wilcox, "Recent FTC Actions: Implications for the Advertising Strategist," *Journal of Marketing* 38 (January 1974): 55–56.

5. Ray O. Werner, "Legal Developments in Marketing," *Journal of Marketing* (July 1991): 66.

6. "Letter to Congress Explaining FTC's New Deception Policy," *Advertising Compliance Service* (Westport, CT: Meckler Publishing, November 21, 1983).

7. *Ibid.*

8.   M. D. Bernacchi, "Substantive Advertising Standards: Discretion and Misinformation by the FTC," *Journal of Advertising* 5 (Spring 1976): 26.

9.   John F. Cady, "Advertising Restrictions and Retail Prices," *Journal of Advertising Research* 16 (October 1976): 29.

10. Gary J. Ford and John E. Calfee, "Recent Developments in FTC Policy on Deception," *Journal of Marketing* 50 (July 1986): 82–103.

11. William L. Wilkie, Dennis L. McNeill, and Michael B. Mazis, "Marketing's Scarlet Letter: The Theory and Practice of Corrective Advertising," *Journal of Marketing* 48, No. 2 (Spring 1984): 25–26.

12. *Ibid*. Used with permission.

13. Janice Kelly, "Sprint Splits in Double-Header with NAD," *Advertising Age* (October 22, 1990): 55.

14. William H. Bolen, *Advertising* (New York: John Wiley & Sons, 1984): 59.

15. *Code of Professional Standards for the Practice of Public Relations*, Public Relations Society of America, April 29, 1977.

16. "The Image of Advertising," *Editor and Publisher* (February 9, 1985): 18.

17. Mark Landler, "Consumers Are Getting Mad, Mad, Mad, Mad at Mad Ave," *Business Week* (April 30, 1990): 70–73.

18. Scott Donaton, "Publishers Bracing for Smoke-Free Pages," *Advertising Age* (March 12, 1990): 3.

19. Nancy A. Reese, Thomas W. Whipple, and Alice E. Courtney, "Is Industrial Advertising Sexist?" *Industrial Marketing Management* (1987): 231–239.

20. Jane Root, *Pictures of Women* (London: Pandora Press, 1984): 27.

21. Diane Barthel, *Putting on Appearances* (Philadelphia: Temple University Press, 1986): 6.

PART

III

THE PROMOTIONAL MIX

7

Marketing Communication

Consider This:

Selling From Beyond the Grave

In an era when many people complain that America no longer has any heros, marketers often build advertisements around famous people of the past. IBM used a Charlie Chaplin look-alike to sell personal computers. Nike used long segments of music written by the late 1960s hero, John Lennon, to sell shoes. With new technology that allows filmmakers to take an image from the past and superimpose it on a scene from the present, advertisers have been able to bring people like Humphrey Bogart and Louis Armstrong back to "life," joining living celebrities to pitch various products.

The dead person who seems to "live on" most successfully in the United States is Elvis Presley. Stories about Presley-sightings and pictures of the "living" Presley continue to dominate the tabloids, and books and songs constantly invoke Presley's memory and images of Graceland, his Nashville home. It should come as no surprise, therefore, to find Presley's presence showing up in ads for his wife Priscilla's perfume.

The perfume is called Moments, and the ad's not-so-subtle approach is to get viewers to identify with and long for the kind of moments that Priscilla presumably had with Elvis. Priscilla talks about her moments with unidentified men, pondering such decisions as whether to kiss a man, and saying things like "A single moment can change your life." The ghost of Elvis seems to hover in the background of all four of the ad's moments, perhaps encouraging viewers to think that if they wear Moments, Elvis will appear on their doorstep.

Media critics complained about the ad, saying that Elvis's memory had been summoned "disingenuously." Priscilla Presley's supporters might hope that she could sell a product on her own, without having to call up the specter of her dead husband. But as many observers have noted, Elvis has been a much more powerful and less ambiguous force dead than he was for the last decade of his life. Elvis's myth is easier for advertisers to control than was Elvis's life. And that may be why the trend to use dead people in ads will continue—the dead aren't going to do anything tomorrow to undermine the ad they starred in yesterday.

Source: Barbara Lippert, "Priscilla Sells an Elvis Souvenir Disguised as Perfume," *Adweek* (July 2, 1990): 13.

*A*re the elaborate efforts behind the Presley ads necessary? The answer seems to be yes. The premise of this book is that even a marketer with the best product and the lowest price is unlikely to be successful unless there is effective communication with target audiences. With thousands of marketers delivering their stories at the same time, the messages combine to produce a roaring noise that may irritate and confuse listeners. Promotion is the way a marketer blends all communication efforts to create a harmony that is understood and believed by the audience. It should address the needs and wants of the audience. If all goes well, promotion brings listeners to prefer the sponsor's brand, idea, or service to the alternatives.

Promotion begins with a basic understanding of human communication and, more specifically, of communication that attempts to persuade. This chapter describes how communication takes place and which components of the process can be manipulated in order to enhance persuasiveness. It builds on our discussion in Chapter 5 about consumer behavior. Understanding people is a prerequisite for effective persuasive communication. We begin, however, by taking an overview of the context in which promotion occurs. That context is known as marketing communication.

Basic Features of Marketing Communication

The role of marketing communication is to support the marketing plan and help key audiences understand and believe in the marketer's advantage over the competition. As Figure 7.1 illustrates, marketing communication has an external and an internal flow.

The *external flow* is directed at past, present, and potential customers; at resellers, both wholesalers and retailers; at other companies; and at various audiences, such as government agencies, private agencies, and experts in the field. A large, multinational company such as Polaroid, for example, maintains an elaborate network of external communications. It communicates with past customers through advertising and direct mail; with current customers through advertising, warranties, product updates, and material on how to use its products; and with potential customers through advertising, point-of-purchase displays, salespeople, and so on. Through direct mail and its sales force, Polaroid also communicates information

Figure 7.1

The flow of marketing communication.

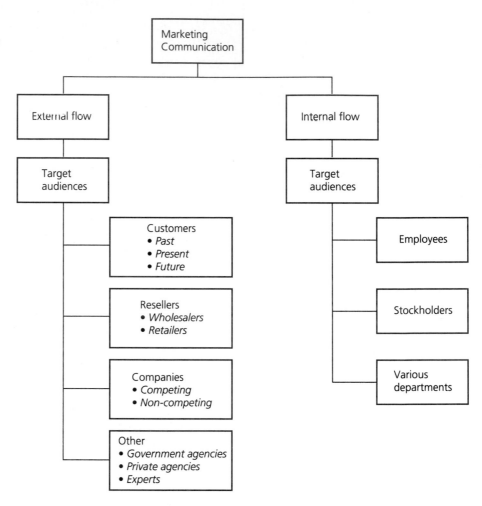

about its products, pricing, and promotion to resellers. It exchanges similar information with competitors and with companies that sell complementary products such as photo albums. Finally, Polaroid keeps government agencies (such as the Federal Trade Commission) and consumer interest groups (for example, photography clubs) informed about its efforts.

The *internal flow* of marketing communication involves employees in general, specific departments of the organization, and stockholders. Employees often need to know what marketing is doing, especially when the organization is introducing new products or deleting old ones, changing prices, or distributing the product in new outlets or markets. By influencing how employees perceive their organization, marketing communication can help shape their morale and performance. If employees feel they are working for an innovative market leader that produces highly regarded ads, for example, they are likely to work harder, stay with the company longer, and become positive opinion leaders in public. Marketing must communicate with other areas of the firm as well. Research and engineering departments, for example, share product information with marketing, and vice versa. Through sales forecasts, marketing determines the day-to-day level of production. Stockholders also need to be informed about marketing activities. If they are going to buy stock and recommend the company to other buyers, they must be convinced that marketing decisions are in their best interest.

Marketing must also communicate with members of the firm in different locations. Making sure that employees in different cities and regions receive the same messages and understand them in a similar way is critical for the cohesion of the organization as well as for the coordinated implementation of the business strategy. Of course, this task becomes even more difficult when a company must communicate internationally. On an international level, the flow of vital intrafirm information can easily be distorted by factors such as cultural differences and physical distance.

Whether the flow is internal or external, effective communication means reaching the right people with the right information through the right sources at the right time. It requires an integrated strategy, which should:[1]

1. Assess the relative importance that members of the audience place on specific categories of information. Do they want objective information, replete with facts and comparisons? Or do they desire emotional appeals, which prompt them to act? What do they already know?

2. Select communication vehicles that are most effective in delivering information. Which vehicles does the audience use regularly? Which are trusted most? Does the audience turn to different vehicles for some purposes, such as an expensive purchase?

3. Gauge where the communicator stands in relation to competing sources. Is the audience committed to a particular source, such as friends or *Consumer Reports*? Is the audience open to new sources? What are they?

4. Provide guidelines to determine what mix of communication techniques to use and how best to allocate funds. These guidelines should be based on the communication objectives, available resources, and so forth.

Implementing a strategy requires a thorough understanding of the needs and wants of the various audiences, a working knowledge of the available communication techniques and how they blend together, and an awareness of competing communicators, including other companies, friends, the government, the news media, and so forth. In short, a great deal of data must be gathered before the marketer can implement a communication strategy.

The promotion strategy is part of this overall communication effort by marketing. Promotion is concerned with communication intended to persuade. Thus, promotional activity is basically an exercise in communication. If executives understand communication, they should be able to better manage a promotional program. In the rest of this chapter, we discuss basic ideas about how people communicate and present some keys to effective communication.

Concept Review

1. The role of marketing communication is to support the marketing plan by helping key audiences understand and believe in the marketer's advantage over the competition.
2. An integrated communication strategy should assess the relative importance of information to consumers; select which vehicles can deliver this communication best; gauge the level of communication competition; and provide guidelines for the communication mix.

The Human Communication System

The study of communication has a long and varied tradition in Western culture. The scholars of classical Greece and Rome studied communication (or rhetoric) intensively; since that time, the process of how one person communicates with others has been a topic of fascination.

What is meant by communication? The word *communication* is derived from the Latin *communis,* meaning "common." To communicate is to use symbols to share some idea, attitude, or information so that meaning is held in common. Scholars through the ages have tried to formulate more precise definitions. Dance and Larson examined 126 definitions of communication and concluded, "Although there are several points of difference in many definitions of communication, upon at least one aspect the vast majority of scholars seem to be in relative agreement. Most students view communication as a process."[2] In other words, communication has a beginning, middle, and ending and is guided by the communication objectives of the participants. Beyond this point of agreement, two definitional perspectives are popular today.

The first perspective assumes that for something to be communication, the person producing the message must intend to influence someone's behavior through a symbolic message. Critics of this perspective argue that this view ignores apparently subconscious attempts to communicate feelings or fears. Those who favor the intentional approach answer that intent can be either conscious or unconscious. Thus, an ad for Perrier water communicates directly through the words and music contained in the ad. The ad also communicates at the unconscious level through the use of certain types of actors, their outfits, and the location of the commercial.

According to the second perspective, communication does not require an intent to influence. Rather, this perspective holds that everything we do or say and every event around us is communication if someone perceives meaning in it. This means that if someone assigns meaning to a behavior or an event, then communication has occurred, whether or not anyone engaged in an intentional act. Thus, simply for another person to perceive meaning in a stimulus makes a behavior communication.

Both of these perspectives contain some truth. In this text, we encompass both points of view by defining human **communication** as a process in which two or more persons attempt to consciously or unconsciously influence each other through the use of symbols.

The Process of Communication

Figure 7.2 illustrates the basic elements of the process of human communication. Note, however, that these elements are all closely related. In fact, even something as complex as communication within a large factory can be viewed as a single entity, with components and interrelationships within it. If one element is changed, each of the others is altered. In other words, speakers, messages, and listeners together form a *system*.[3] Still, in order to understand the system, we need to discuss each component separately.

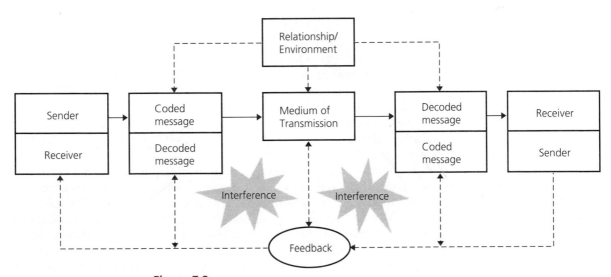

Figure 7.2

A model of human communication.

First, consider the **communicators,** a component of every communication system. In the traditional communication model, the two communicators are referred to as the sender (encoder) and the receiver (decoder). The **source,** or **initiator,** of the communication process can be an individual, a group, or an institution that wishes to transmit a message to the **receiver,** which may be another individual, group, or institution. The sender accomplishes the transmission of the message by selecting and combining a set of symbols in order to convey some meaning to the receiver. The greater the similarity or overlap between the sender and receiver, the more likely that communication will be effective and the less likely that miscommunication will take place. Therefore, if the overlap is not natural, it behooves the sender to learn as much about the receiver as possible. Successful salespeople, for example, are adept at qualifying a prospective customer.

This process of transforming thoughts into a sequence of symbols is called *encoding*. When encoding, the source should consider the characteristics of the receiver. The symbols used should be familiar to the receiver and viewed positively. Just as important, the message must be delivered through a medium that the receiver uses and at an opportune time. Delivering the same message through two different media can produce very different results. Possible media may be classified as either personal or nonpersonal.

Although the receiver does not initiate the communication process, the receiver is just as much a communicator as the sender. The receiver communicates with the sender through **feedback.** The same set of symbols available to the sender is available for feedback. When the receiver provides feedback to the sender, they have reversed roles: the receiver is now the sender. Sometimes feedback is explicit and entails words, pictures, or overt signs or gestures. On other occasions, feedback is implicit and could entail subtle glances or even "no response." The latter is certainly the case with mass communication, especially advertising, where feedback is implicit and delayed. When feedback is implicit and delayed, it is difficult to gauge whether the sender has effectively communicated. The nature of the feedback is determined by how well the receiver **decodes,** or interprets, the message delivered by the sender.

Several factors affect decoding. The nature of the relationship between the sender and receiver is one such factor. A note to a family member, for example, would be far less formal than a letter to a potential customer. Likewise, the environment in which the communication takes place can influence communication. The environment can be internal or external. The *internal environment* includes the inherent characteristics of the communicators, such as their experiences, attitudes, values, and biases. The *external environment* consists of factors outside the communicators—the weather, time of day, competing messages, and so on. Whenever the relationship between the communicators or environmental factors distort the communication process, the distortion is called **interference** (noise).[4]

Types of Communication Systems

Several types of communication systems exist. They vary in complexity, level of contact between communicators, time lag of feedback, and communicators' ability to adjust to feedback. (See Figure 7.3.)

Interpersonal Communication Systems   The basic level of communication systems is called interpersonal communication. An *interpersonal communication system* may consist of as few as two people or two major subsystems; the upper level of complexity for interpersonal communication is limited only by the ability of all participants to interact with each other face to face and to have the opportunity to affect each other. When the system consists of just two people or major subsystems, it is called a *dyad*. As the system becomes more complex and more subsystems are added, the *small group* emerges. The upper limit of the small group is usually between fifteen to twenty people. If more people are involved, the group must impose artificial regulations on itself, such as parliamentary procedure.

Interpersonal communication is also affected by mediating delivery. That is, a salesperson talking face to face to a customer is engaging in direct communication. That same salesperson delivering the same message via telephone, letter, or fax is mediating the communication process by using technology. To a certain extent, using such technology limits the advantages of interpersonal communication.

Personal selling occurs within the interpersonal framework. This close contact between communicators allows some important advantages. The salesperson is able to customize the sales message to suit the audience, receives immediate feedback, and can adjust the message accordingly. The message itself can be complex, since explanation is possible. Unfortunately,

Figure 7.3

Types of communication systems and their characteristics.

	Characteristics			
Types	Complexity	Contact	Time lag	Adjustment
Interpersonal	Low	High	Short	High
Organizational	Moderate	Moderate	Moderate	Moderate
Public	High	Low	Long	Moderate
Mass	High	Low	Long	Low

communicating interpersonally also brings disadvantages. It is very time consuming, and some members of the target audience will be missed. That is, some interested consumers are not going to be reached by the salesperson because they are inaccessible or because there simply is not enough time to call on all customers. Salespeople working for Eli Lilly and Company, for example, attempt to call on 50 percent of their customers once each month, 25 percent once each six months, and contact 25 percent by letter or telephone two or three times annually.

Organizational Communication Systems　In a bank, factory, retail store, or government, communication is much more complex than in an interpersonal system. Each has an *organizational communication system,* which is composed of a large collection of subsystems all organized around common goals. The subsystems all exist as separate entities yet interrelate with each other. Consequently, both a formal and an informal network of communication is often required. For example, members of a marketing channel of distribution employ an organizational communication system. The promoter must communicate special prices, coop packages, price rebates, or other deals to resellers.

Communicating in an organizational system is difficult because feedback is often delayed and partial. Channel members, for example, are receiving messages from a number of marketers simultaneously, and they may be unwilling to communicate their honest assessments. Moreover, messages tend to be standardized, thus losing the personalization gained through interpersonal communication.

To communicate effectively in an organizational system, managers must learn as much as possible about the organizations with which they communicate. Furthermore, their messages should include common benefits desired by the majority of these organizations.

Public Communication Systems　A *public communication system* usually involves communication from one person to a large group of people, as occurs when a person gives a speech to an audience. Although everyone affects everyone else to some degree in every communication system, in public communication, the speaker does most of the talking and has the primary effect on the people who are listening. The feedback available to the speaker is less obvious, more subtle, than the feedback provided in interpersonal and organizational systems. The speaker needs considerable sensitivity to detect this feedback, which is frequently nonverbal and includes facial expressions or bodily postures assumed by listeners.

Certain types of personal selling use public communication. Party selling such as Amway is an example.

Mass Communication Systems　Compared with public communication, *mass communication* offers even less opportunity for people to interact freely with one another or to affect one another mutually. Although there is feed-back in mass communication (through such means as letters, phone calls, and coupons), the distinguishing characteristic of this system is that all feedback is delayed. In such a system, the originator of the mass message cannot possibly receive feedback from all the people who receive the message. Promotion managers must therefore establish a formal feedback system that constantly monitors the feelings, attitudes, and behaviors of audience members. They should never assume that because they hear nothing from the audience that everything is fine. The necessity for a formal feedback system may change with the emergence of technology such as the two-way video.

Persuasive Communication

People communicate in an endless number of ways, almost constantly. In promotion, however, one specific type of communication is primary: persuasion. Even if an individual ad or sales promotion piece is intended to reach an intermediate objective, such as to deliver information, remind, or build awareness, the explicit goal of the entire promotional strategy is to persuade. In the case of advertising and public relations, persuasion may take a longer time and require several intermediate steps. With personal selling and sales promotion, the road to persuasion is much shorter. When one person's achievement of a goal is blocked by the goal-seeking behavior of others, persuasion can be used to convince those others to redefine their goals or alter their means of achieving them. Thus persuasion attempts to reduce the estrangement between parties while still changing behavior; it aims for mutually satisfying results.[5]

In promotion, the objectives of persuasive communication are derived from the marketing objectives, which, in turn, are based on company objectives. To ensure that all of the components of the promotion mix work toward these overall objectives, each component is guided by a set of communication objectives. Some of these objectives may be very subtle, but together, they should all work to create a change in behavior. Thus the objectives of promotion tend to be sequential, beginning with the creation of name or brand awareness, next providing meaningful information, then changing attitudes and perceptions, and ultimately creating conviction and behavioral change. All these objectives lead toward a change in behavior, the primary indicator that persuasion has taken place.

Effective persuasion requires sensitivity to the logic of others. The persuader must locate some common ground with the audience. Thus the persuader must understand the thought processes of others. How do people process information? How do they make decisions? How does persuasion take place? We discussed theories that attempt to answer these questions in previous chapters. In the rest of this chapter, we look at the variables that can alter the outcome of a particular persuasive effort. These variables can be placed in one of three categories: source factors, message factors, and audience factors.

Concept Review

1. In a human communication system, two or more parties are simultaneously sender and receiver. Besides these communicators, the process involves the encoding and decoding of messages, a medium of transmission, relationships, feedback, environment, and interference.
2. There are four types of communication systems—interpersonal, organizational, public, and mass—which differ in type of contact and ability to adjust to feedback.
3. The effectiveness of persuasive communications depends on characteristics of the source, the message, and the audience.

Characteristics of the Source

The source of a message is the speaker, communicator, or endorser—the person whose message is directed at the audience. To be more precise, we can distinguish three types of sources. The *sponsor source* is the manufacturer who pays for the message and is usually identified somewhere in the message itself. The *reseller source* is either a wholesaler or retailer that associates its name with the message. The *message presenter* is the person who delivers the actual message. Thus, one newspaper ad promoting AT&T telephone equipment contains the AT&T name (the sponsor source), the name of a local discount store carrying the product (the reseller source), and a picture of Cliff Robertson (the message presenter). But research on persuasive communications does not distinguish among these types of sources, so we will simply refer to all three as the source.

What makes one source more effective in persuasive communications than another? In 1983, Chrysler introduced a series of ads using a source that had rarely been used in the past. The ads featured the CEO of the company, Lee Iacocca. Iacocca proved to be an extremely effective source. Chrysler Corp., plagued by poor products and ineffective management, was on the verge of bankruptcy, and few industry experts felt it would last the year. Thanks to Iacocca's personal plea, the situation improved; the American public began to empathize with Chrysler. Why? Iacocca apparently had high levels of three characteristics that contribute to persuasiveness: credibility, attractiveness, and power.

Credibility

The extent to which the receiver perceives the source to be truthful or believable is called source **credibility.** Highly credible sources tend to create an immediate change in attitude. Highly credible groups (such as the American Medical Association) are even more effective sources than highly credible individuals.[6]

Credibility depends on two related factors. The first is the expertise attributed to the source. Characteristics such as intelligence, knowledge, maturity, and professional or social status all lend an air of expertise to an individual or group. The second factor determining credibility is the objectivity attributed to the source—in other words, the receiver's assessment of how willing the source is to discuss the subject honestly. For example, Michael Jordan and Bo Jackson are highly credible sources for athletic shoes, while former Surgeon General C. Everett Koop was a highly credible source in a public service announcement advising people to stop smoking. Objectivity seems to be less important than knowledge or expertise, however, perhaps because most people do not expect the sponsor of a message to be objective. Obviously, Michael Jordan is being said to promote Air Jordans.

Despite the importance of expertise in determining credibility, the source should not be too perfect and should exhibit human flaws. Why? Perhaps the perfect source is too obviously a fabrication, or perhaps perfection detracts from a second determinant of persuasiveness: source attractiveness.

Attractiveness

The greater the perceived attractiveness of the source, the more persuasive the message.[7] Ed McMahon, who acts as a spokesperson for Budweiser Beer, Publishers Clearing House, and a variety of products sponsoring "The Tonight Show," for example, is an attractive source to many audiences. However, it is not just because he is handsome or wears expensive clothes, although these characteristics certainly can be part of the attractiveness equation. Source attractiveness is the extent to which the receiver identifies with the source. It results from similarity, familiarity, or likability. For the people who have been watching Ed for twenty-five years, he represents all these components.

Research suggests that the more receivers feel that a source is similar to themselves, or how they would like to think of themselves, the more likely they are to be persuaded. This similarity can be exhibited through ideologies, attitudes, and behaviors. Political candidates are experts at saying the right things to various audiences in order to make themselves appear similar to each audience.

The second source of attractiveness, familiarity, is normally created through past association. People have been seeing Bill Cosby for many years. He appears in concerts, on records, on television, and at charity fund raisers. Children especially relate to him, because he is funny and

one of the most patient, loving, and unusual fathers ever to appear on television. For Jell-O and its pudding and gelatin desserts, Bill Cosby is the ideal spokesperson. By association, Jell-O is fun too. It is not surprising that this well-established familiarity with Cosby has made him one of the most attractive sources in promotion history.

In fact, the American public has had a love affair with the entire Huxtable family. Figure 7.4 shows one source whose likability has made her an attractive source. The more we like a source, the more attractive that source is to us. Liking, however, is hard to measure and tends to be a transitory feeling that changes quickly.

Power

In addition to credibility and attractiveness, power can make a source attractive. **Power** depends on the receiver's perception that the source has the ability to administer rewards or punishments. It has three components: perceived control, perceived concern, and perceived scrutiny.[8] For example, salespeople gain perceived control over prospective customers through their knowledge of the product or access to important benefits not available to the customer directly. Many public relations efforts try to create the idea that the sponsoring company feels concern for members of the audience. IBM asks us to have a positive attitude toward the company because it is concerned with preserving the arts in America. Government agencies, banks, employment agencies, and other organizations attain power through their perceived ability to scrutinize our lives. A letter from the Internal Revenue Service is quickly opened and carefully read.

Word-of-Mouth: An Indirect Source

Most individuals seek information from a variety of sources outside the sponsoring organization. These external sources may be formally set up to distribute information (for example, the Small Business Administration), may provide information in line with their expertise (for example, doctors, investment analysts, and auto mechanics), or they may be individuals whose opinion is trusted on a particular topic (such as family, friends, neighbors, or coworkers). The last two sources provide what is commonly called word-of-mouth information.[9] Unlike the producer, reseller, or spokesperson, **word-of-mouth** sources do not benefit from the acceptance of the message and are not under the control of the sponsor.

Gordon Weaver, executive vice president of Paramount Pictures, claims, "Word of mouth is the most important marketing element that exists."[10] Its importance is well documented. Promoters must therefore attempt to influence those who may create word of mouth.

Mazda certainly followed this prescription when it introduced the Miata in 1989. It did not leave word of mouth to chance. Instead, the public relations people at Mazda made sure that positive stories about the car appeared in key publications such as *Business Week, Motor World,* and *The New York Times.* Mazda dealers had brochures about the Miata on hand for customers before the car arrived. The result? The car was back-ordered, and individuals were offering as much as forty-five thousand dollars for this sixteen-thousand-dollar sports car.

The impact of negative word of mouth has also been well documented. The scandal associated with Shearson Lehman Brothers, and the conviction of top strategist Ivan Boesky for insider trading, had a devastating effect on that organization. Negative word of mouth in the form of rumors was particularly harmful to a firm like Shearson, where trust is mandatory. Within days of Boesky's conviction, most of Shearson's regional offices were closed and hundreds of employees were fired.

Not all problems generate negative word of mouth. When is it likely? Albert Hirschman[11] proposed a model that suggests some answers. According to Hirschman, a dissatisfied customer may make one of three responses: (1) *exit:* voluntary termination of the relationship, (2) *voice:* any attempt to change rather than escape from an objectionable state of affairs, by directing dissatisfaction at management or anyone willing to listen, and (3) *loyal:* the customer continues with the dissatisfying product or seller and suffers in silence, confident that things will soon get better.

The response a customer selects depends on characteristics of both the individual and the industry. The key individual characteristics are (1) the perceived probability that complaining would help, (2) the worthwhileness (costs benefits) of complaining, and (3) the sophistication of the consumer, such as his or her awareness of a mechanism for making a complaint. The industry characteristics are essentially structural. Is the industry concentrated, highly competitive, or a loose monopoly? Negative word of mouth is most likely in concentrated industries and least likely in loose monopolies.[12] For example, there is a great deal of negative word of mouth in the automobile industry but very little in the nursery plant industry, where three or four growers control the entire output of house plants sold in the United States. Hirschman's model has been empirically tested and appears to accurately portray the likelihood of negative word of mouth.

Concept Review

1. ·The source of a message is the speaker, communicator, or endorser. The persuasiveness of the source is affected by three characteristics:
    a. Credibility—the extent to which the receiver perceives the message source to be truthful or believable—depends on the perceived expertise and objectivity of the source.
    b. Attractiveness—the extent to which the receiver identifies with the source—is determined by similarity, familiarity, and liking.
    c. Power of the source is determined by perceived control, perceived concern, and perceived scrutiny.
2. Word of mouth—messages distributed by individuals not under the control of the sponsor—is a powerful indirect source of information.

Message Variables

The specific elements used to communicate an idea and the way these elements are organized constitute the **message variables.** The role of the promotion manager is to take the information provided by marketing and translate it into a message format that is most effective. Message variables are divided into two categories: structure and content.

Message Structure

The overall context and readability of the message provide its structure. Aspects of message structure include whether it is verbal or nonverbal, its readability, the order of the ideas, repetition, and the presence or absence of counterarguments.

Verbals vs. Nonverbals   When we think about delivering a message, we think about using words, or verbals. Verbals can be powerful. They can make us laugh, cry, or feel terrified. Classic ads are often recalled in terms of specific verbals. Clara Peller asked, "Where's the beef?" Ray Charles tells potential Pepsi drinkers, "You got the right one, baby! Uh huh!" Still, nonverbals also play an important role in effective communication. Is a picture worth a thousand words? According to a study conducted by Ogilvy and Mather, in a given message, the words create 15 percent of the impact, the tone creates 25 percent of the impact, and the nonverbals create 60 percent of the impact. In his excellent book, *Nonverbal Communication*, Stephen Weitz develops five categories of nonverbal communications:[13] (1) facial expression and visual interaction (for example, eye contact), (2) body movement and gestures (such as muscle tightening and movement toward or away), (3) paralanguage (for example, loudness, pitch, and tremor of the voice), (4) proximity behaviors (for example, appropriate distance between people for certain activities), and (5) multichannel communication (such as simultaneous interaction between various factors operating in a particular communication).

For persuasive appeals, the most effective nonverbal cues are facial and vocal behavior and timing of phrases, elements that the message designer clearly controls. More specifically, one study of several nonverbals used in a television commercial found that those communicating simplicity or singlemindedness were positively associated with persuasion. For example, nonverbals that correlated strongly with persuasibility included the characters' hands at their sides, the principal character expressing contentment, a likable spokesperson, a humorous mood, a busy setting, and a wink.[14]

There are messages that should emphasize words and others that should limit words and show pictures. Elizabeth Hirschman concludes that "for product categories [for example, financial institutions, legal services, medical organizations] which generally desire to create an impression of heightened rationality and factualness, the use of all-text or predominantly text would appear best. In contrast, when introducing new products, particularly true innovations, visual images will provide the consumer with perception of greater familiarity."[15] "New and improved" Cheer and its associated campaign (see Figure 7.5) uses a totally visual message strategy. A man wordlessly hand-washing a dirty handkerchief in cold-water Cheer and displaying the successful results tells us all the benefits we need to know.

Readability   If we concentrate on the verbal elements of a message, it is critical that the message is readable. Readable messages are understandable

to the audience and have a very good chance of being persuasive. What makes a message readable? Important factors include the arrangement of words in the core message, word frequency, and sentence length. In addition, the number of ideas used to construct the core message should be kept to a minimum, and these ideas should be restated throughout the message.[16] Ads for Miller Lite Beer used to follow this prescription. They provided two ideas—tastes great, less filling—and repeated them at least four times in every ad. Miller Lite has dropped the "tastes great, less filling" tag line and replaced it with "It's it and that's that." Although the rhythm is the same, the new tag is far less readable. Some additional guidelines for making messages readable and persuasive are listed as follows.[17]

Metaphorical expressions

Low intensity of language

Concrete words

Subordinate-category words

Rhyme

Commonly used words

No synonyms, homonyms, and negative constructions

Maximum headline length of five to eight words

A headline for Revlon Nail Enamel uses an effective metaphor in the headline: "Drop-Dead Nails." Spray 'n Wash demonstrates low-intensity language with the following tag line: "Spray 'n Wash Gets Out What America Gets Into." For several years, AT&T has used concrete words in its tagline: "AT&T, The Right Choice." Using subordinate-category words means using a simpler word in place of a more difficult one. Rather than getting into complex explanations, Pioneer Stereo tells us: "For a great sound in a space you can live with." As for rhyme, who can forget the little boy singing about his Oscar Mayer bologna. Seldane demonstrates the use of common words in a recent headline: "You've tried just about everything for your hay fever . . . now try your doctor." This headline also violates the rule of using no more than five to eight words in a headline. Finally, a classic use of a homonym was illustrated by a Bucks cigarette ad. The headline asked: "Herd of these?"

Ordering Effect   Should the primary ideas be presented at the beginning, middle, or end of the message? Research indicates that:[18]

1. When contradictory information is provided in a single message by a single source, disclaimers at the end of a message will generally be ineffective.
2. If people already feel a strong need for a product or service, supportive information should be provided first.
3. Points that are most valued by the receiver should be listed first.
4. Unfavorable information should be placed last.

In summary, the earlier the key message points are presented, the better they will be remembered.

Repetition   Repetition can take place within a message (repeating a key word or phrase), or it can be the entire message. Research suggests that repeating a message increases its believability, regardless of its content.[19] The optimum number of repetitions is still being debated. There is general agreement that one exposure is ineffective and that three may represent the maximum number, with effectiveness quickly falling off beyond three. This generalization, however, may only be true with a captive audience, because mere exposure to a message does not guarantee attention or comprehension. Therefore, the number of times an advertiser should show a national television commercial during a particular time frame is still uncertain.

In fact, repetition can even be harmful. The results of one study suggested that repetition actually reduced comprehension.[20] Excessive repetition may create *wearout*. In the case of humorous messages, wearout tends to occur much faster than with serious messages.[21] Perhaps this is one reason why the characters delivering the humor in Miller Lite ads are changed so frequently. Changing the people and the context makes a tired punchline less wearing.

Repeating a point within a single message also seems to have a positive effect on persuasion. Several studies have shown that repeating the same point in a message facilitates retention and increases believability, regardless of the presence or absence of evidence to the contrary.[22] Again, the ideal number of repetitions is uncertain, and it is possible to create wearout within the message itself.

Arguing and Counterarguing   A *one-sided message* presents an argument for the sponsor without mentioning counterarguments. Using this approach is beneficial when the audience in generally friendly, when the advertiser's position is the only one that will be presented, or when the desired result is immediate though temporary opinion change. One-sided arguments tend to reinforce the decision of the audience and do not confuse them with alternatives. McDonald's, for example, only talks about its products and benefits in its advertising.

In contrast, a *two-sided message* includes counterarguments. In general, a two-sided argument is useful with better educated audiences, who view counterarguments as being more objective and therefore more honest. Educated audiences are aware of opposing points of view and expect communicators to acknowledge and refute these views. Also, if audience members are likely to hold multiple opinions that touch on topics important to them, counterarguments improve persuasibility.[23] Coke and Pepsi have been arguing and counterarguing for several years.

Message Content

The specific words, pictures, and other devices employed in a message, along with the overall appeal, reflect the content of the message. A very general way of analyzing message content divides messages into just two categories: rational appeals and emotional appeals. A **rational appeal** tends to be factual and follows a prescribed logic. In contrast, an **emotional appeal** is directed toward the individual's feelings and is intended to create a certain mood, such as guilt, joy, anxiety, or self-pride. This distinction between rational and emotional is somewhat misleading, however, because emotions and thoughts are not things we can place in locked boxes. When someone appeals to our emotions, our cognitive processes still affect our reactions. And even nonemotional appeals may arouse strong feelings in some people.

To fashion emotional appeals, promoters can use many specific types of content. They might use eerie music to create a mood, as in the ads described at the opening of the chapter. They might use funny stories or sexy pictures. The choice of appeals is limitless. No one type of content is always persuasive; each choice brings potential risks and benefits. We discuss the primary appeals in the following sections.

Fear Appeals   Intuitively, one might expect that the more fearful the message, the more persuasive. But research does not support this assumption.

Figure 7.6

This ad successfully uses a fear appeal.
Courtesy of Geico/Earle Palmer Brown.

Another suggestion is that fear is effective up to a certain level; beyond this level, it creates negative results. Figure 7.6 does present a fear appeal that was quite successful. Note that the message not only arouses fear but also appeals to the respect and concern for human life. In general, the specific topic presented and its relevance to the audience help determine the impact of a fearful message. Its effect may depend in part on whether the fear message pertains to physical harm (such as sickness or death) or to social anxiety (such as streaked dishes or body odor).

The effectiveness of a fear appeal also depends on the audience. Demographic characteristics such as age, sex, race, and education all influence the effect.[24] Personality differences are also significant. For instance, people with high self-esteem react more favorably to high levels of fear than do people with lower self-esteem, who are more persuaded by low levels of fear. Similarly, the more vulnerable the receiver feels, the less effective a fear appeal will be, particularly if it employs high levels of fear. In conclusion, the effect of fear appeals depends on many variables, not just the level of fear aroused.

Humor   Humor can be expressed visually or verbally through puns, jokes, riddles, and so on. Investigations of the nature of humor as a communication device have produced mixed results.[25] In an early review of this topic, research concludes that humorous appeals create four positive effects:[26] they enhance source credibility, attract attention, evoke a positive mood, and increase persuasion. More recently, other research examined the use of humor in radio messages. They found that using humor increases attention paid to the commercial, reduces irritation at the commercial, improves its likability, and increases liking of the product.[27]

The use of humor brings risks, however, as the Promotion in Focus section illustrates. Not everyone finds the same things funny. Humor also can be distracting. While audiences are enjoying a humorous message, they may miss the main points of the message, including the name of the sponsor. Humor aids awareness and attention, but it may hinder recall and comprehension, need not aid persuasion, and need not increase source credibility.[28] Finally, humor wears out. Once the audience tires of the humor, they may become indifferent to the message or even irritated by it.[29] No one knows for sure how much longer people will find the Energizer bunny amusing. Undoubtedly, promoters constantly monitor ads looking for the first signs of wearout.

Despite the risks and uncertainties of using humor, it is likely to remain the favorite strategy of many advertisers. For one thing, humor creates strong memorability, a measure of success that ad agencies consider vital. A 1989 poll indicated that 88 percent of the viewers still remembered Wendy's "Where's the beef?" campaign, which stopped running in 1984. Ad executive Cliff Freeman explains advertising's love affair with humor as follows: "There's an actual physical thing that happens in the body when you laugh. You give off certain chemicals; it's a very positive thing. Therefore, the association with a product is extremely positive. . . . And if your product is good and your advertising is of that nature, it'll really begin to develop an emotional bond between the consumer and the product."[30]

Pleasant Appeals   Most people would rather feel good than feel bad. Taking advantage of this desire is the rationale behind *pleasant appeals*, which create a positive experience and a high level of liking.

A pleasant appeal can take several forms. It can use expressions of fun and entertainment, perhaps by showing people dancing, singing, or simply having a good time. Warmth is an emotion considered synonymous with liking. Homecomings, nostalgic situations, and loving relationships

Promotion in Focus

Don't Laugh At Your Customers

While it may seem easy to get laughs from friends, classmates, colleagues, even a good portion of the public, the outrage of an offended few can easily drown out the chuckles of the many.

A number of ad agencies have won awards in recent years with humorous commercials. Eveready's drumming rabbit continues to be a big hit because it pokes fun at something that almost everyone loves to hate—commercials themselves. And commercials for the Yellow Pages, like the one in which a group of cadets doing the funky chicken turns out to be listed under "Rock Drills," make their humor out of puns, plays on words not likely to offend anyone.

But FMC Corp. discovered recently that the sword of humor cuts both ways. It ran a series of ads promoting its new herbicide, Commence. Because the soybean growers that Commence wants to appeal to could already choose from so many different herbicides, FMC wanted to be sure the ads set its product apart. They did, but not exactly in the way the company intended.

The premise for the ads was that a farmer made bets with several friends about Commence's ability to kill various types of weeds. When the herbicide is successful, the losing farmers have to perform various embarrassing tasks. One eats his hat, another gets a Mohawk haircut, a third paints his $80,000 John Deere tractor bright pink.

It was these punishments that got FMC in trouble with farmers. In an era of periodic crises for American farms, farmers are trying to shake the public perception that they are foolish, slow-witted rubes, exactly the image that some farmers felt the ads were creating. FMC's mistake was making the butt of the ad's humor people with whom the target audience was likely to identify. The company quickly realized its error and stopped running the ads after a few months.

Source: Cyndee Miller, "Humor in Herbicide Ad Campaign Is Not a Big Joke to Some Farmers," *Marketing News* (February 29, 1988): 6.

all connote warmth. Babies, puppies, and kittens seem to be guarantees of created warmth. People cannot resist the Kodak ads that string together heart-warming scenes of childhood, old age, and ordinary family life. These spots are geared to gently jerk a tear or two. "They're very personal and real," says one woman. "They bring you closer to life. I always cry." People like being reminded about the bittersweet side of life.

Evidence supporting the effectiveness of pleasant appeals is strong.[31] Warm, entertaining messages are noticed more, are remembered more, increase source credibility, improve attitudes, and create feelings that are transferred to the sponsor. The Ogilvy Center for Research and Development reported a direct link between pleasant appeals and persuasiveness. After showing seventy-three prime-time commercials to 895 consumers, the center discovered that people who enjoy a commercial are twice as likely to be convinced that the advertised brand is best. "Now we can say likability enhances persuasion and that, at the very least, you don't pay any penalty if people enjoy your ad."

Subliminal Appeals   In September 1957 a public relations executive announced to the press that he had discovered a technique whereby irresistible advertising messages could be delivered to consumers without their knowledge. The words "drink Coke" and "eat popcorn" were allegedly superimposed on a movie screen at such a low light level that the audience was not consciously aware of their presence. Coke and popcorn sales purportedly soared, though no evidence was provided to support this claim. Reaction was immediate and negative. Fears were expressed that covert mind control would become widespread. Consumer protection groups and the Federal Trade Commission all took action.[32]

Subliminal persuasion is the term used to describe this alleged phenomenon. *Subliminal* means "below the threshold." In other words, those who claim that subliminal persuasion exists argue that sights or sounds too weak or too fast to be consciously perceived can still alter thoughts or behavior. Are they right?

To date, there is no persuasive documentation of subliminal persuasion. There is also no evidence that promoters use subliminal techniques. If we consider the ethical problems associated with subliminal techniques, it would be safe to conclude that advertisers and their agencies would be foolish to employ this technique, even if it works. Subliminal appeals are not part of the communication arsenal employed by the promoter and should be discounted as a valid alternative.[33]

Because the existence of true subliminal stimuli has been difficult to verify, some researchers have turned to the investigation of a quasisubliminal technique called embedding. **Embedding** buries a message, word, or picture within an ad, yet it is still visible to the naked eye. The example most often cited comes from a study by Kilbourne, Painton, and Ridley.[34] They invented embedded images for two ads. In an ad for Chivas Regal, an image of a naked woman, appearing as a reflection, was embedded in a bottle of the Scotch whiskey at a level too low to be detected easily. The ad for Marlboro Lights showed two men riding horses through rugged countryside in which an image of male genitalia was embedded in the rocks. A third of the group saw the two ads without the sexual appeals. Members of each group then evaluated the ads for credibility, attractiveness, sensuality, and the likelihood that they might buy the product. Those who saw the whiskey ad with the hidden image rated it higher on all four scales than did people who saw it without the image. The sexual image in the Marlboro ad, however, did not lead to more favorable evaluations. Note that there is no evidence that promoters use embedding.

Sex Appeals   Sex in promotion ranges from the blatancy of nudes and obvious double-entendres to devices so subtle that it takes a trained observer to recognize them. K Mart Corp. uses a fairly subtle sexual appeal when it presents actress Jaclyn Smith in advertising, at store openings, and as a public relations spokesperson.

The effectiveness of sex as a persuasive device is questionable. There is little doubt that sex is an effective attention-getting device for both men and women. Nevertheless, many people believe that the use of sexual appeals in promotion is simply not good marketing. For example, several studies have examined the ability of nudity to enhance brand recall. In every case, neutral or nonsexual scenes produced higher brand recall. Other researchers conclude that sexual appeals in the correct context produce higher attention and recall. That is, there are situations in which the use of a sexual appeal is appropriate, while in other instances, the use of a sexual appeal is included for its shock value and has nothing to do with the context. Examples of correct context are messages that provide fantasy fulfillment (such as travel), functional fulfillment (for example, fashion), or symbolic fulfillment (for example, romantic setting). In sum, sexual appeals in the correct context can produce powerful results; sex outside of this context can be disastrous.

Music   Prominent singers and musicians, background singers and instrumentalists, and jingles have all been used to deliver persuasive messages. The general consensus is that the right music can make a significant difference in the effectiveness of a particular message, but the amount of empirical evidence supporting this assumption is limited. Recent work suggests at least three potential effects of music.

First, music can influence arousal. That is, music, especially "distinctive" music, can attract consumers' attention. Certain songs and performers immediately spark the attention of different target audiences. Many youngsters believe that "I Heard It Through the Grapevine" was written especially for the California Raisin ad and have claimed the song as their own. Second, music can influence consumers' processing of the messages. Music can affect learning and persuasion by creating excitement, relaxation, empathy, news, and imagery and can enhance the perceived benefits of the message.[35] Finally, music can complement other elements in the ad, such as words, color, pictures, background, and so forth. Music can create a mood that encourages certain types of attitudes and behavior.

Concept Review

A. Aspects of the message structure that influence persuasiveness include the following:
    1. Verbal vs. Nonverbal
        a. Verbals should be emphasized when unique, meaningful messages can be delivered about the product.
        b. Some products and situations are best portrayed through nonverbals such as facial expressions, body movement, and multichannel communication.
    2. Readability
        a. Writing techniques should be clear to the audience.
    3. Ordering Effect
        a. Key ideas should be presented as soon as possible.
    4. Repetition
        a. The entire message or components of the message should be repeated.
        b. No certain number of repetitions is best.
        c. The advertiser should be concerned with wearout.
    5. Arguing and counterarguing (one-sided vs. two-sided messages)
        a. Which strategy is best depends on the audience and strength of argument.
B. Aspects of the message content include the following:
    1. Messages may present rational or emotional appeals.
    2. No particular level of fear produces the same general results.
    3. Humor attracts attention and creates a positive mood. But it brings risks of offending, wearout, and detracting attention away from the sponsor.
    4. Pleasant appeals produce positive mood and attention.
    5. Subliminal appeals are not clearly understood and are not used by promoters.
    6. Sex appeals can produce positive results if used appropriately.
    7. Music has the potential to influence arousal and message processing. It can complement other components of the ad.

Audience Factors

Are some people easier to persuade than others? We all know gullible individuals who will believe anything. Yet there is little solid evidence to support the notion that there is a general personality trait for persuasibility.

Various personal characteristics, however, can affect persuasibility. William McGuire suggests that personality factors influence persuasibility by affecting the recipient's *comprehension* of a message and *willingness* to comply with the message.[36] Self-esteem is one example. For reasons yet to be explained, people with low and high self-esteem differ in their ability to cope with simple and complex information. That is, people with low self-esteem may do better with simple information and people with high self-esteem may handle complex information better.

Gender is the lone demographic trait related to persuasion.[37] While the findings are somewhat mixed, most researchers find that women seem more persuasible than men, especially when the source is female. There is also growing evidence that males and females differ in their information-processing strategies. For example, it has been concluded that "females are more sensitive to all modalities at thresholds, with the possible exception of smell."[38] Moreover, it appears that there are gender differences in their thresholds for elaborative processing. In comparison with males, females seem to be more likely to elaborate message cues that command a somewhat limited amount of attention.

As noted in earlier chapters, there have been concerns that children and senior citizens are generally more persuadable. It has been assumed that children, in particular, are very vulnerable to the effects of persuasive communication. Children's vulnerability to persuasive communication is a vast area of research in which many important questions have been considered. Do children pay attention to advertising? Do they understand its purpose and its content? How do children process advertising messages? What is the impact of factors such as age, race, or parental education on these process effects? What is the impact of advertising on children's attitudes and behaviors? What effect does it have on the socialization process of children, that is, their learning roles as consumers?[39] Although the answers to most of these questions remain unresolved, the evidence does suggest that children of all ages are capable of distinguishing commercials from programs, but that young children (preschool age) are not able to discern the intent of commercials,[40] nor do they understand the disclaimers used in many ads. Further, advertising has a moderate impact on children's attitudes toward the advertised product, and the content of commercials does impact on children's preferences and choices, as revealed by studies in the area of food advertising to children.[41] Finally, advertising encourages children to request products from their parents, a situation that often leads to child-parent conflict. It should be noted, however, that all these influences can be tempered by parental education, family interaction, and peer integration.[42]

The stereotype about the senior citizen who is senile and believes everything he or she is told provides the basis for the assumption that seniors are easily persuaded. There is also a tendency to regard senior citizens as a homogeneous group, ignoring the distinction that is known to exist between the "young old," those under seventy-five who are still active and healthy, and the "old," those over seventy-five with infirmities of aging.[43] The majority of senior citizens are not institutionalized or living under the care of others. As to the persuasibility of seniors, the evidence to date is inconclusive. No clear link has been established between membership in senior citizen market segments and the degree to which individuals respond to the persuasive content of a message.[44]

In conclusion, persuasiveness reflects interactions among the personality and culture of members of the audience, the situation, and characteristics of the source and message. To be persuasive, a promoter should keep in mind the interests, attitudes, and values of the audience.

Concept Review

1. Audience factors that impact communication:
    a. Comprehension of a message
    b. Willingness to comply
    c. Self-esteem
    d. Gender
    e. Children
    f. Senior citizens

Case 7   *Doneghel Speaks Up*

Background

The Doneghel Furniture Company is a small, regional furniture manufacturer located eight miles west of Greensboro, North Carolina. During the last thirty-two years, the company has produced custom-made furniture for consumers living within a two-hundred-mile radius of the plant. Its major customers, however, are large furniture manufacturers that contract with Doneghel to make hardwood components of the larger pieces sold by companies such as Ethan Allen and Thomasville. Until recently, the management of Doneghel has been very satisfied with this arrangement. However, two things have occurred recently to change the future of Doneghel. First, due to the general decline of the furniture industry, several of Doneghel's manufacturer customers have reduced their orders, some by as much as 50 percent. Second, the reputation of Doneghel's custom furniture line seems to have extended beyond the immediate market. Letters from consumers from as far away as California have been requesting catalogs and general product information. Most of this interest appears to stem from positive word of mouth from satisfied customers who have moved out of the region. Doneghel does no advertising.

John Doneghel, president of the company, along with Carol Doneghel, vice president, and their two sons, Jamie and Frank, are faced with the possibility of changing the way they do business. John, Jamie, Frank, and twenty other craftspeople represent the total work force. Carol takes care of the books and pays the bills. The family loves to work with wood and to create beautiful furniture. Unfortunately, the Doneghels have little experience or interest in doing much else. Last year Doneghel's sales were $1.2 million, of which $200,000 resulted from the custom furniture business. The only element that even resembled marketing was a ten-page catalog that described the general kinds of pieces Doneghel makes and gave approximate prices. This catalog was mailed only to people who requested it.

The dilemma facing the Doneghel family is obvious. Do the Doneghels maintain the status quo and hope the market for large manufacturers improves? Or do they expand their custom furniture business and learn all they can about marketing as quickly as possible? After agonizing over this problem for several days, the decision was made to hire a consultant.

The Market

Tony Wingler is a marketing professor at a nearby university. He has conducted research for several furniture manufacturers and is thoroughly familiar with the industry. It is his recommendation that Doneghel pursue the custom furniture business. Since it would be unprofitable for the company to offer total customization, Doneghel should develop a product line that is somewhat standardized and offer two or three modifications of each piece. Wingler further indicates that the upscale consumer (that is, someone whose income is higher than seventy-five thousand dollars) should be targeted. This person would be willing to pay the higher prices charged for customized furniture. Finally, Wingler feels that distribution represents the most difficult problem facing Doneghel. Because it is unlikely that Doneghel would be able to place its furniture in stores throughout the country, direct marketing offers a better alternative. Direct mail combined with print ads in magazines such as *Southern Living* and *Town and Country* would represent the primary communication vehicles. Direct mail would also serve as a mechanism for ordering and receiving the furniture.

A meeting was set up with Wilkes Advertising to discuss the promotion strategy appropriate for Doneghel. It was determined that the primary benefits offered by Doneghel were excellent craftsmanship and the use of hardwoods. The primary limitations were twofold. First, the public could not experience the furniture firsthand. Would people buy furniture they could not touch? Second, the selection was limited to between seventy and seventy-five different pieces. Mr. Wilkes felt that combating these limitations would be difficult and that many potential customers would be lost because of them.

Case Questions

1. What are the communication problems facing Doneghel of using a direct marketing approach?
2. Suggest an initial communication strategy for Doneghel, including specific structure and content recommendations.

Summary

This chapter has explored the fundamentals of marketing communication, which is primarily persuasive communication.

There is some question as to whether true communication must be intentional or not. We define human communication as a process in which two or more people try to influence each other, consciously or unconsciously, through the use of symbols. Steps in the process occur simultaneously. The basic elements of the process include the communicators, the encoding and decoding of messages, a medium of transmission, relationships between communicators, a feedback mechanism, an internal and external environment, and factors that interfere with effective communication. Four types of communication—interpersonal, organizational, public, and mass—differ in complexity, form of contact, and ability to adjust to feedback.

Variables that influence the effectiveness of attempts to persuade fall into three groups: (1) source factors, (2) message factors, and (3) audience factors. Manipulation of the credibility, attractiveness, and power of the source can affect the ability to persuade. Message variables (that is, structure and content) show little consistency in their effect on persuasiveness;

each message-related factor must be viewed in context. The effect of audience factors is even less predictable.

Discussion Questions

1. Discuss how the communicator can be both the sender and the receiver.

2. Write a five-hundred-word essay expressing why you feel communication must be either intentional or unintentional.

3. Contrast the relative advantages and disadvantages of verbal vs. nonverbal communication. When is each most appropriate?

4. Describe the characteristics of a communication source that would appeal to (1) college students and (2) their parents.

5. "I really enjoy funny ads. I wish all ads were like that." Comment on these statements.

6. What is the result of interference in human communications? List some ways to reduce interference.

7. Contrast general communication with persuasive communication. What should be the outcome if persuasion is successful?

8. What are the advantages and disadvantages of using music in advertising?

9. Sources can be considered attractive in terms of similarity, familiarity, and liking. Give an example of each.

10. Define word-of-mouth sources of communication. Why is this source important in marketing?

Suggested Projects

1. Collect ads from magazines to locate examples of the following: high source credibility, high source attractiveness, nonverbal appeal, high fear appeal, and high humor appeal. Explain the criteria you used in each case.

2. Ask two friends to allow you to observe their conversation. Note the kinds of nonverbal cues each person uses. Quiz them afterwards as to whether they are aware they use these nonverbals.

References

1. "Communicating Differential Advantage Is Essential," *Marketing News* 25 (October 1985): 26.

2. Frank X. Dance and Carl E. Larson, *The Functions of Human Communications: A Theoretical Approach* (New York: Holt, Rinehart and Winston, 1976).

3. Werner J. Severin and James W. Tankard, Sr., *Communication Theories. Origins, Methods, Uses* (New York: Hastings House, 1979).

4. C. David Mortensen, *Communications: The Study of Human Interaction* (New York: McGraw-Hill, 1972).

5. C. Hovland, I. Janis, and H. Kelly, *Communication and Persuasion* (New Haven, CT: Yale University Press, 1953).

6. B.S. Greenberg and G.R. Miller, "The Effects of Low-Credible Sources on Message Acceptance," *Speech Monographs* 33 (1966): 127–136.

7. Jon B. Frieden, "Advertising Spokesperson Effects: An Examination of Endorser Type and Gender in Two Audiences," *Journal of Advertising Research* 24 (1984): 33–41. Denis McQuail, *Mass Communication Theory* (Beverly Hills, CA: Sage, 1984).

8. Freiden.

9. Barry L. Bayers, "Word-of-Mouth: The Indirect Effects of Marketing Efforts," *Journal of Advertising Research* 25, no. 3 (June/July 1985): 31–39. Blaine Goss, *The Psychology of Human Communication* (Prospect Heights, IL: Waveland Press, 1989).

10. Bayers.

11. Albert Hirschman, *Exit, Voice and Loyalty: Responses to Decline in Firms, Organizations and States* (Cambridge, MA: Harvard University Press, 1970). Roobina Ohanian, "The Impact of Celebrity Spokespersons' Perceived Image on Consumers' Intention to Purchase," *Journal of Advertising Research* (February/March 1991): 46–54.

12. Jagdip Singh, "Voice, Exit, and Negative Word-of-Mouth Behaviors: An Investigation Across Three Service Categories," *Journal of the Academy of Marketing Science* (Winter 1990): 1–15.

13. Stephen Weitz, *Nonverbal Communication,* 2nd ed. (New York: Oxford University Press, 1979).

14. R. Buck, "Nonverbal Behavior and the Theory of Emotion: The Facial Feedback Hypothesis," *Journal of Personality and Social Psychology* 38 (1980): 811–824. Christy Fisher, "Wal-Mart's Way: No. 1 Retailer Relies on Word-of-Mouth, Not Ads," *Advertising Age* (February 16, 1991): 3, 48.

15. Elizabeth C. Hirshman, "The Effect of Verbal and Pictorial Advertising Stimuli on Aesthetic, Utilitarian, and Familiarity Perceptions," *Journal of Advertising* 15, No. 2 (1986): 27–34.

16. James MacLachlan, "Making a Message Memorable and Persuasive," *Journal of Advertising Research* 23, no. 6 (December 1983/January 1984): 58–59. Paul M.

Herr, Frank R. Kardes, and John Kim, "Effects of Word-of-Mouth and Product-Attribute Information on Persuasion: An Accessibility-Diagnosticity Perspective," *Journal of Consumer Research* 17 (March 1991): 454–462.

17. Larry Percy, "A Review of the Effect of Specific Advertising Elements Upon Overall Communication Response," in *Current Issues and Research in Advertising*, eds. James H. Leigh and Claude R. Martin, Jr. (Ann Arbor, MI: University of Michigan, 1983): 77–118.

18. C. Hovland, *The Order of Presentation in Persuasion* (New Haven, CT: Yale University Press, 1957).

19. Michael Ray and Alan Sawyer, "Repetition in Media Models: A Laboratory Technique," *Journal of Marketing Research* 8 (1971): 20–29.

20. Betsy D. Gelb, Joe W. Hong, and George M. Zinkhan, "Communications Effects of Specific Advertising Elements: An Update," in *Current Issues and Research in Advertising*, eds. James H. Leigh and Claude R. Martin, Jr. (Ann Arbor, MI: University of Michigan, 1985): 75–98.

21. George W. Booker, "A Comparison of the Persuasive Effects of Mild Humor and Mild Fear Appeals," *Journal of Advertising* 10 (1981): 29–40.

22. Gelb, Hong, and Zenkhan. Cornelia Pechmann and David W. Stewart, "Advertising Repetition: A Critical Review of Wearin and Wearout," in *Current Issues and Research in Advertising* Vol. 11, eds. James H. Leigh and Claude R. Martin, Jr. (Ann Arbor, MI: University of Michigan Business School, Division of Research (1988): 285–329.

23. Gelb, Hong, and Zenkhan, 75–98.

24. I. L. Janis and S. Feshback, "Effects of Fear-Arousing Communications," *Journal of Abnormal and Social Psychology* 48 (1953): 1, 78–92. B. Sternthal and C. S. Craig, "Fear Appeals: Revisited and Revised," *Journal of Consumer Research* 1 (1974): 22–34. J. J. Burnett and R. E. Wilkes, "Fear Appeals to Segments Only," *Journal of Advertising Research* 20 (1980): 21–24.

25. Booker, 29–40.

26. B. Sternthal and C. S. Craig, "Humor in Advertising," *Journal of Marketing* 37 (1973): 12–18.

27. Donald L. Duncan and James Nelson, "Humorous Advertising in Radio," *Journal of Advertising Research* 25, No. 4 (October/November 1985): 84–87.

28. Thomas J. Madden and Marc G. Weinberger, "The Effects of Humor on Attention in Magazine Advertising," *Journal of Advertising* 11, No. 3 (1982): 8–14.

29. William B. Beggs, Jr., "Humor in Advertising," *Link* (November/December 1989): 12–15.

30. *Ibid.*

31. Gelb, Hong, and Zenkhan, 75–98. Herbert Fried, "Humor Is Our Best Tool," *Advertising Age* (April 8, 1991): 26.

32. Timothy E. Moore, "Subliminal Delusions," *Psychology Today* (July 1985): 10–11. David M. Zeitlin and Richard A. Westwood, "Measuring Emotion

Response to Advertising," *Journal of Advertising Research* 26 (October/November 1986): 34–44.

33. Joel Salgert, "Why Marketing Should Quit Giving Subliminal Advertising the Benefit of the Doubt," *Psychology and Marketing* 4 (Summer 1987): 107–120. Nicholas E. Synodinos, "Subliminal Stimulation: What Does the Public Think About It?" *Current Issues and Research in Advertising,* Vol. 11, eds. James H. Leigh and Claude R. Martin, Jr. (Ann Arbor, MI: University of Michigan Business School, Division of Research, 1988): 157–88.

34. William E. Kilbourne, Scott Painton, and Danny Ridley, "The Effect of Sexual Embedding on Responses to Magazine Advertisements," *Journal of Advertising* 14, No. 2 (1985): 48–56.

35. W. J. McGuire, "Resistance to Persuasion Confirmed by Active and Passive Prior to Refutation of the Same and Alternative Counter Arguments," *Journal of Abnormal and Social Psychology* 63 (1961): 326–332.

36. J. Nunally and H. Bolerex, "Variables Concerning the Willingness to Receive Communications on Mental Health," *Journal of Personality* 27 (1959): 38–46.

37. Joan Meyers-Levy and Brian Sternthal, "Gender Differences in the Use of Message Cues and Judgments," *Journal of Marketing Research* 28 (February 1991): 84–96.

38. Diane McGuinness and Karl H. Pribram, "The Origins of Sensory Bias in the Development of Gender Differences in Perception and Cognition," in *Cognitive Growth and Development,* ed. Morton Bortner (New York: Bruner/Mazel Publishers): 3–56.

39. P. S. Raju and Subhash C. Lonial, "Advertising to Children: Findings and Implications," in *Current Issues and Research in Advertising,* eds. James H. Leigh and Claude R. Martin, Jr., Vol. 12 (Ann Arbor, MI: University of Michigan Business School, Division of Research, 1990): 231–274.

40. Mary Ann Stutts and Garland G. Hunnicutt, "Can Young Children Understand Disclaimers in Television Commercials?" *Journal of Advertising* 16(1) (1987): 41–46.

41. Leslie Isler, Edward T. Popper, and Scott Ward, "Children's Purchase Requests and Parental Responses: Results from a Diary Study," *Journal of Advertising Research* (4) (October/November 1987): 28–39.

42. *Ibid.*

43. Betsy Gelb, "Discovering the 65+ Consumer," *Business Horizons* (May–June 1982): 42–46.

44. Jessica M. Bailey, "The Persuadability of Elderly Consumers: A Study of Locus on Control and Responsiveness to Fear Appeals," *Current Issues and Research in Advertising,* eds. James H. Leigh and Claude R. Martin, Jr., Vol. 10 (Ann Arbor, MI: University of Michigan Business School, Division of Research, 1987): 213–247.

8 *Advertising: Its Role and Structure*

Consider This:

Furniture That People Live In

For an entire generation, Americans have spent the same percentage of their disposable income on furniture. That's not a good sign for furniture makers. And in a recession, especially a recession that hits real estate hard, furniture sales suffer. If few people are moving or buying new houses, furniture makers are not going to sell many dining room sets or sofa/love seat combinations. So in the past few years, furniture makers have been looking for ways to boost sagging sales by setting themselves apart.

One tack that a number of makers are taking is to show the furniture not in a showroom, as is the tradition, but in a place that at least looks like someone's house. Pier 1, for instance, has been running print ads showing a couple admiring their new furniture arrangement, with headlines like "How Does It Look From Where You're Sitting?" Such ads and witty headlines are intended to spark readers' imaginations and get readers to ask themselves not just "Is this a nice piece of furniture?" but "How would that look in my living room?" or "Wouldn't it be fun to be sitting where that couple is?"

Thomasville Furniture has also been shooting its print ad photos on location rather than in a studio, and it has been giving its pieces a "lived-in" look to demonstrate just how much living they can take and still look good. Using the same theme in its television commercials, Ethan Allen shows people actually living in and on its products. In one commercial, a couple is locked out of their house, and the camera follows the family dog as it moves around the Ethan Allen furniture, watching its owners' unsuccessful attempts to get back in and enjoy the furnishings.

Fiber Industries has taken this trend to a logical extreme in ads for its Fortrel fiber blend. Ads show the Fortrel sheets, not crisply tucked in as though handled by a hotel employee, but heaped on the bed and floor, as they probably are in a majority of American households.

Whether this trend towards realism will catch on in other markets is not yet clear. No doubt there are some things better left to buyers' imaginations—like what the new sofa will look like after the family pets have worked on it for a few months. But for the moment, furniture makers seem to have found a way to bring their products closer to consumers' own living rooms.

Sources: Barbara Holsomback, "Pier 1 at Home with Richards' Witty Headlines," *Adweek* (August 21, 1989): 1. Pat Sloan, "Furniture Ads Focus on Real Life," *Advertising Age* (August 13, 1990): 13.

*T*raditionally, furniture companies relied on product quality, a well-trained sales staff, and excellent service to do the job of selling their products. Advertising was just an afterthought, used primarily to keep the company's name in front of the consumer and to announce sales. Today, advertising plays a more prominent role. As the campaigns by Pier 1 and others suggest, furniture companies are attempting to reach their customers with a new message. They know that advertising that worked ten years ago may not work today. For that matter, advertising that worked today may not work tomorrow.

The only constant in advertising is that good advertising comes from good strategy. The astute promotion manager must be constantly aware of where advertising fits and its role in the overall promotional strategy. There are some large marketers (for example, Case Office Equipment) that use very little advertising and others, such as Procter & Gamble Co., that spend over one billion dollars annually on advertising. Regardless of the emphasis, the promotion manager must follow a systematic strategic process with advertising that parallels a similar process with personal selling, sales promotion, and public relations. Thus the eight-step advertising decision sequence illustrated in Figure 8.1 closely resembles the same thought process that would take place for the other three mix elements. To use this framework, however, promotion managers need to understand the field of advertising and what it can and cannot accomplish. In this chapter we therefore introduce terms unique to the field of advertising and discuss its place in the promotion mix. This discussion is equivalent to steps 1 and 2 in Figure 8.1. Armed with this information, students will be prepared to understand how all these components can be managed effectively and brought together in an advertising campaign, the topic of Chapter 9.

The Varied World of Advertising

Clyde Drexler and Michael Jordan tell thousands of Americans watching television to stay in school. A flier on their doorstep urges consumers to try the new restaurant down the street. A full-page ad in the newspaper announces that a local bank is offering reduced interest rates for home mortgages. Candace Bergen tells women to have a mammogram every

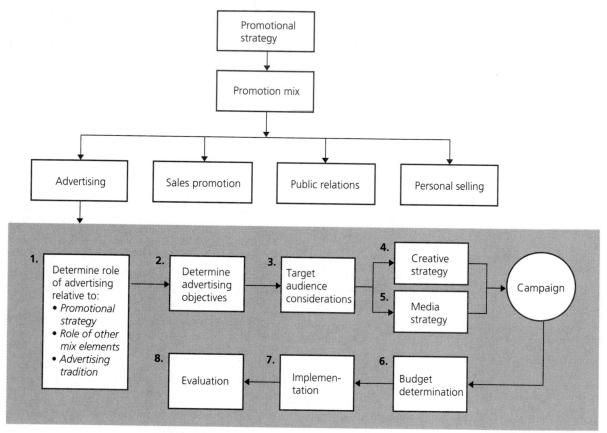

Figure 8.1

The eight-step advertising decision sequence.

year. And the U.S. Marines still "need a few good men." Varied as these messages are, they are all forms of advertising. What do they have in common, and why are such different forms used for advertising?

Defining Advertising

The definition of advertising varies with the individual's perspective. From the point of view of the consumer, advertising is a source of information or a form of entertainment. From a societal perspective, advertising provides a valuable service to society and its members. In general, advertising helps define the meaning and the role of products and institutions for the consumer, and it provides information about brands, companies, and institutions. Finally, to most business managers, advertising is an important selling tool. They believe that it facilitates the sale of products or builds the reputation of companies.

Several years ago, the American Marketing Association proposed the following definition of advertising: "Advertising is any paid form of non-personal presentation and promotion of ideas, goods, and services by an identified sponsor."[1] But a better definition is that **advertising** is the non-personal communication of marketing-related information to a target audience, usually paid for by the advertiser, and delivered through mass media in order to reach the specific objectives of the sponsor.

Four points in this definition warrant further comment. First, advertising is nonpersonal because it offers no personal interaction and is often viewed as an intrusion. Second, advertising is directed at target audiences rather than at target markets. In most cases, the target market includes the target audience plus other individuals or organizations that can influence the sale of the product. For example, the target audience for pharmaceuticals includes users, physicians, pharmacists, and the Food and Drug Administration. Third, this broad group of people can be reached best through mass media—television, radio, magazines, newspapers, and outdoor displays. Finally, advertising is intended to achieve predetermined objectives such as improved memorability, reinforcement of other promotion, change of attitudes, or product sampling.

Classifying Advertising

To examine the bewildering variety of ads, scholars have proposed several bases for classifying advertising. Understanding these classifications should help managers choose which type of advertising can best achieve their objectives.

By Audience   Perhaps the most obvious way of classifying advertising examines the intended audience. Broadly speaking, ads can thus be classified under two broad headings: those based on *geography* and those based on *market distinctions.* In the former category, there are international, national, regional, and local advertising campaigns. In the latter group, some ads are directed at the ultimate users of the product, who are referred to as the *consumer* audience. Consumer audiences can be reduced to many smaller groupings, such as wine drinkers, Spanish-Americans, and golfers. Other ads are directed to the companies or people who distribute the product; these are the *business* audience. The two most important business audiences are *dealers* and *manufacturers.*

By Advertiser   Advertising can also be classified in terms of who is doing the advertising. A manufacturer's ad is designed to build a demand for the product, regardless of where it is purchased. Retailers do not care what brand consumers buy as long as they buy it in their store. Retail advertising seeks to create a quick impact that can be easily seen. Consequently, retail advertising tends to emphasize patronage motives such as good location, breadth of product line, good service, free delivery, prices, store hours, and directions.

Advertising sponsored by an organization (for example, a college or hospital, the Red Cross, a museum, the U.S. Navy) tends to emphasize intangibles such as an idea, a value, or a promise. Consequently, the appeals are emotional, attempting to make these intangibles appear more real. Individual advertising can range from a political candidate spending millions of dollars on mass media to a student placing a classified ad for a roommate. In general, the nature of the message in individual advertising is more specific, customized for the targeted audience.

By Intention   Another way of classifying advertising looks at its intention. In product advertising, advertisers aim to inform or stimulate the market. Institutional advertising is designed to create a positive attitude toward the seller.

Product Advertising   **Product advertising** may be either direct-action or indirect-action advertising. **Direct-action advertising** is intended to produce a quick response. Ads that include a coupon with an expiration date, a toll-free number, or a sale with a deadline fall under this heading. **Indirect-action advertising** is designed to stimulate demand over a longer time. These ads inform customers that the product exists, indicate its benefits, and state where it can be purchased. Ads for the various Levi products fall under this heading.

Product advertising can also be classified as being primary or selective. *Primary advertising* aims to promote the demand for generic products. Thus ads by the American Dairy Association focus on milk and cheese; it does not matter to the association which brand is purchased. *Selective advertising* attempts to create demand for a particular brand. It typically follows primary advertising, which more or less sets the stage for selective advertising.

Product advertising can also be classified as *goods advertising* and *service advertising*. Certain inherent qualities of services shape the advertising of these products. For instance, since services tend to be intangible, advertising aims to provide tangible surrogates. Nationwide "tangibilizes" its service by providing "the Nationwide blanket of protection." Prudential Insurance Co. of America suggests that it offers consumers the stability of the Rock of Gibraltar. Because services often cannot be stored or inventoried (for example, concerts missed cannot be recreated), service advertising usually creates a sense of urgency or provides information by emphasizing the importance of being on time or noting that no rain checks are given. Because services cannot be transported, the supplier can serve only those in a limited area who can travel to the producer's location, unless there is a mechanism for delivering the tangible representation to the customer.

Thus service advertising informs the consumer of these locations or delivers the product through mass media. Amtrak tickets, for example, may be purchased by calling a toll-free number.

Institutional Advertising   Rather than selling a particular good or service, **institutional advertising** aims to establish a high level of goodwill. Institutional advertising can be further subdivided into three areas: public relations, public service, and patronage.

Public relations institutional advertising attempts to create a favorable image of the firm among employees, potential employees, stockholders, and the general public. Phillips Petroleum Company, for example, runs ads that highlight its contributions to medical technology and the environment. Public relations institutional advertising differs from *publicity*, which is the placement of stories about the company with no production or media costs. Companies choose to spend money on public relations institutional ads because they have total control over the copy and the placement. *Public service institutional advertising* urges the public to give to the United Way or to use seat belts. Also referred to as Public Service Announcements (PSAs), these ads are produced for free by the Advertising Council or by an agency, and the media do not charge for space or time. *Patronage institutional advertising* is designed to attract customers by emphasizing a patronage-buying motive rather than a product-buying motive. In other words, this kind of advertising provides reasons for patronizing a business, regardless of the products sold. For example, a retailer might inform the public of extended store hours, or a manufacturer might describe a new warranty policy.

Concept Review

1. Advertising is the nonpersonal communication of marketing-related information to a target audience, usually paid for by the advertiser, and delivered through mass media in order to reach the specific objectives of the sponsor.
2. There are a number of ways to classify advertising:
   a. By audience,
   b. By advertiser, and
   c. By intention, both product and institutional.

The History of Advertising

Emergence of Modern Advertising

Despite its early roots with the town crier and Ben Franklin, advertising as we know it really had its beginnings in the mid-1800s. The major impetus was the emergence of a literate audience. A secondary impetus was the tremendous rebuilding of the country, especially the business community, that followed the Civil War.[2] This included the technology of the Industrial Revolution, the building of the transcontinental railroad, improved highways, and better communications through the telegraph and the U.S. Postal Service. The result was movement from an agrarian to a manufacturing economy, including surplus production and the need for a mechanism to sell this extra product.

The early advertising practitioner of the 1860s was hardly an expert. He had little knowledge of copywriting or design and little interest in the product being advertised. Advertising, an unregulated industry, was notorious for its dishonesty, and those who engaged in it were sure to lose customers. Gradually, in the 1800s, written contracts were introduced, and publishers were required to provide accurate circulation figures.

The last decades of the nineteenth century brought several milestones in the development of advertising. It was in the 1880s that the first great copywriter emerged, John E. Powers. Powers' approach to advertising was simple: "Print the news of the store . . . no catchy headings, no catches, no brag, no pressure." The magazine also emerged as an advertising vehicle, thanks to E. C. Allen, who recognized the potential of magazine advertising. Through his *People's Literary Companion*, which sold for five cents, Allen made magazines affordable to the masses. J. Walter Thompson, a young advertising executive, acquired a monopoly over the field by signing the "twenty-five best American" magazines to an exclusive contract and then securing an impressive list of advertisers. Thompson is also credited with being the inventor of the modern advertising agency.

A turning point took place in 1899 when Claude C. Hopkins got together with Albert Lasker. Hopkins, considered one of the greatest copywriters, developed the *reason-why* approach to copy. He argued that a campaign should be built around a single overriding selling point presented with "dignified sensationalism." In addition, Hopkins added mail-order advertising and couponing to the tools available to advertisers. Lasker, however, was the true driving force of the duo. He made the advertising agency a professional business that included the "records of results," the counterpart of today's research department. Because of the records of results, agencies were able for the first time to tell advertisers whether objectives had been attained.

While the reason-why, hard-sell approach was the dominant style of the early 1890s, it had challengers. Theodore F. MacManus, star copywriter for General Motors, produced *impressionistic copy*, or *atmosphere advertising*. This soft-sell approach was characterized by original art, striking layouts, and elegant writing. The goal was to create a positive image of the company and its products.

During the 1920s, modern marketing research entered the world of advertising. As a result, advertising of the 1920s stressed the results of a purchase—health, happiness, love, status—rather than the object per se. The ads contained a prominent headline, sumptuous artwork, photography, and lots of color.

The Depression was not a good period for advertising, but there was one bright spot—the emergence of commercial radio. Before then, radio had carried no advertising. Writing advertising copy for radio was a new skill that required simple, conversational language, short sentences, and few pronouns.

Contemporary Advertising

Most of the growth in advertising has occurred since World War II. After the war, companies in Western Europe and the Far East once again started to compete in world markets; advertising was an essential part of this new economy. Large corporations such as IBM, General Motors Corp., and Coca-Cola Enterprises Inc. had long been active all over the world, but after 1946, many small and medium-sized companies also became international. Large advertising agencies of the United States, Western Europe, and the Far East followed the same trend, opening offices in several countries.

The decade of the 1950s was a good time for advertising. The industry was run by specialists in market research, merchandising, public relations, and sales promotion. Growth took place through mergers, consolidations, and movement into international markets. Creativity was almost non-existent. Ads were mostly "me too" messages with little copy and a great deal of mundane visualization. Probably the most successful copywriter during this period was Rosser Reeves of the Ted Bates Agency. It was Reeves who developed the USP, or Unique Selling Proposition. Essentially, Reeves argued that a marketer should discover one important attribute of the product, develop a clever way of communicating it, and repeat it over and over. It was Reeves who told candy lovers that "M&M's melt in your mouth, not in your hands" and still tells gum chewers to "double your pleasure, double your fun." Television, however, was the story of the decade. The advertising industry's total television business went from $12.3 million in 1949 to $128 million in 1951.

Creativity and the soft sell returned to advertising thanks to people such as Leo Burnett, David Ogilvy, and William Bernbach. During the period from the late 1950s through the 1960s, Burnett brought drama and warmth to advertising with characters such as the Jolly Green Giant, the Pillsbury Doughboy, and the Marlboro Man. With the Hathaway Shirt man and Colonel Whitehead, Ogilvy brought a unique intelligence and class to advertising. Bernbach combined copy, art, and humor to create the famous Volkswagen ad shown in Figure 8.2, the Avis "We try harder!" theme, and a myriad of award winners.

Figure 8.2

An example of creativity in contemporary advertising is Bernbach's famous Volkswagen ad from the 60s.

Used with the permission of Volkswagen of America, Inc.

Ugly is only skin-deep.

During the 1970s, tight economic times and the war in Vietnam inspired a return to conservatism in creativity and administration. Agencies gravitated to neutral creative strategies, emphasizing entertaining and safe, "me too" ads. Rather than hiring more copywriters and artists, they sought MBAs who understood the ins and outs of pricing, distribution, and packaging. Advertising became safe. Agencies became specialized in areas such as health care, finance, travel, and sales promotion.

This trend toward conservatism and consolidation continued in the 1980s. Media and production costs soared. Agencies responded by creating "superagencies" run by experts in management and finance. With the strong emphasis on performance and accountability, sales promotion (especially direct-response advertising) emerged as advertising's salvation. Direct-response advertising provided advertising with credibility through accountability because the results of such advertising could be measured.

Advertising today is marked by four characteristics. First, it emphasizes immediate customer response through vehicles such as direct mail, telemarketing, and overlay ads carrying coupons and toll-free numbers. Second, there is a continuation of the entertaining and "like-creating" styles made popular during the 1970s. Third, ads that feature creative and unique appeals like those made famous in the 1960s are produced by smaller agencies that are not burdened by overwhelming overhead and the conflict of client interests.[3] That is, the risky ads associated with Bill Bernbach and Leo Burnett and their large agencies are now produced by small and moderate agencies, such as Hal Riney & Associates. Finally, with the U.S. market saturated and foreign borders opened, advertising has become international. Nearly 40 percent of the billing of U.S. agencies is outside the United States. It appears that these trends will continue.

Concept Review

1. The history of advertising can be divided into two eras: the period prior to 1870, which has little resemblance to modern advertising, and the period since the 1870s, when modern advertising began.
2. The first great approach of copywriting, the hard-sell, reason-why approach, was a creation of Claude Hopkins and Albert Lasker. The second approach to copywriting, developed by Theodore MacManus, emphasized imagery and soft sell.
3. Developments in magazines, radio, and television have had a tremendous impact on advertising.

What Does Advertising Do?

Advertising is used by virtually all manufacturers and retailers today. One quantitative indication of the importance of advertising is the amount spent on it. In 1991, total advertising media expenditures in the United States were almost $132 billion—more than triple the amount spent in 1973. Worldwide spending on advertising was estimated at $180 billion in 1990. Table 8.1 lists the top fifteen brand advertisers in 1990. The leading brand was Procter & Gamble Co., spending over $2 billion.[4] Among U.S. companies that advertise in other countries, Unilever NV/PLC and Procter & Gamble Co. spent the most abroad—$1.2 billion and $932 million, respectively. Table 8.2 shows another way of measuring advertising, by sales per dollar invested in advertising. The patterns vary by type of industry and time of year, but in general, companies are spending more on advertising. In fact, advertising expenditures have been rising faster than the gross national product, national income, or any other measure of business activity.

The Functions of Advertising

Many business people advertise because they expect an ad to create a sale directly. In the case of direct-action advertising, which uses techniques such as toll-free numbers, coupons, and "bingo cards," this view is reasonable. (We discuss direct-action advertising further in Chapter 18.)

Table 8.1   **Top Fifteen Brand Advertisers in 1990**

Rank '90	'89	Advertiser	Ad Spending in 1990
1	2	Procter & Gamble Co.	$2,284.5
2	1	Philip Morris Cos.	2,210.2
3	3	Sears, Roebuck & Co.	1,507.1
4	4	General Motors Corp.	1,502.8
5	5	Grand Metropolitan	882.6
6	6	PepsiCo	849.1
7	17	AT&T Co.	796.5
8	7	McDonald's Corp.	764.1
9	18	K Mart Corp.	693.2
10	16	Time Warner	676.9
11	8	Eastman Kodak Co.	664.8
12	20	Johnson & Johnson	653.7
13	9	RJR Nabisco	636.1
14	11	Nestlé SA	635.9
15	15	Warner-Lambert Co.	630.8

Reprinted with permission from *Advertising Age* (September 25, 1991): 1. Copyright ©, Crain Communications Inc. 1989.

Table 8.2   **Sales Per $1 Invested in Advertising**

Advertiser	For 100 leaders in 3rd quarter, 1988 and 1987		
	1988	1987	$ chg
Airlines	$120.87	$124.68	−3.1%
Automotive	114.06	142.62	−20.0%
Chemicals	184.10	202.50	−9.1%
Entertainment	35.50	38.89	−8.7%
Food	25.52	25.20	1.3%
Miscellaneous	170.69	197.06	−13.4%
Office equipment	315.67	251.51	25.5%
Pharmaceuticals	22.03	20.34	8.3%
Photography	46.55	46.91	−0.8%
Restaurants	22.30	25.70	−13.2%
Retail	128.78	116.54	10.5%
Soaps & cleaners	19.41	16.59	17.0%
Soft drinks	17.54	17.76	−1.2%
Telephone	151.36	183.01	−17.3%

Table 8.2 **Sales Per $1 Invested in Advertising (cont.)**

| Advertiser | For 100 leaders in 3rd quarter, 1988 and 1987 | | |
	1988	1987	$ chg
Tobacco	91.61	96.87	−5.4%
Toiletries	11.07	14.38	−23.0%
Toys	15.43	17.18	−10.2%
Wine, beer & liquor	18.03	20.23	−10.9%

| Advertiser | In 2nd quarter, 1988 and 1987 | | |
	1988	1987	$ chg
Airlines	$ 82.08	$ 77.28	6.2%
Automotive	113.66	110.62	2.7%
Chemicals	153.26	137.90	11.1%
Entertainment	40.91	44.09	−7.2%
Food	26.29	24.73	6.3%
Miscellaneous	176.90	148.73	18.9%
Office equipment	326.23	204.38	59.6%
Pharmaceuticals	19.09	18.35	4.1%
Photography	35.32	27.54	28.2%
Restaurants	25.83	23.54	9.7%
Retail	124.75	113.87	9.6%
Soaps & cleaners	20.44	20.88	−2.1%
Soft drinks	19.20	17.58	9.3%
Telephone	165.41	159.56	3.7%
Tobacco	90.23	74.79	20.6%
Toiletries	9.29	12.07	−23.1%
Toys	9.86	10.47	−5.9%
Wine, beer & liquor	21.47	19.93	7.8%

Most advertising today remains indirect, and expecting an ad to lead directly to a sale is unrealistic. However, the fact that most advertising is designed to facilitate sales rather than to accomplish a complete selling process does not necessarily diminish the significance of actual sales as a measure of advertising effect. This fact also leads to two basic assumptions about advertising. First, it is logical to assume that the effects of most ads are psychological in nature, that is, that advertising can change only mental states and predispose the audience toward purchase of what is advertised. Second, it is logical to conclude that advertising is essentially a form of communication. As such, its primary responsibility is to deliver relevant information to a specific target audience.

The promotion manager wants the answers to several questions before a decision is made whether or not to use advertising. If we refer back to step 1 in Figure 8.1, there are a host of questions that relate to identifying tasks that advertising can do as well or better than other promotional mix elements. There are also questions about the proper mixing of advertising with the other promotional elements. The ability of advertising to interface with the other marketing mix elements is another basic assessment to be made by the promotion manager.

Finally, there is the issue of past advertising. How much advertising has the company done previously? Was it successful? Does the company have a great deal of equity invested in a particular style, spokesperson, or tag line? Can it build on past advertising?

The answers to these questions will of course vary across companies, situations, and time. However, there are guidelines that prove useful in understanding the strategic applications of advertising. Although there are several perspectives as to the general functions performed by advertising, the hierarchy of effects model provides an understandable portrayal that parallels the consumer decision-making process discussed in Chapter 5.

A Hierarchy of Effects Model   Combining the findings of research on communication and on consumer behavior, many researchers view the function of advertising in terms of a **hierarchy of effects model.** This model proposes that ads can move consumers closer to buying a product step by step—from being unaware of a product to buying it. An ad is effective if it moves the consumer a step further along in this process. This is the function of advertising.

Various researchers have proposed different versions of a hierarchy of effects model. One version that has stood the test of time well was developed by Lavidge and Steiner (see Figure 8.3).[5] They propose that people go through seven steps to reach the threshold of purchase:

1.   Unawareness of the good or service,

2.   Awareness of the product,

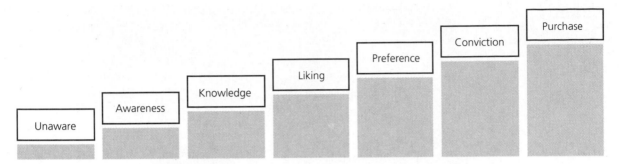

Figure 8.3

The hierarchy of effects model developed by Lavidge and Steiner.
Used with the permission of Journal of Marketing.

3.   Knowledge of what the product offers,

4.   Liking for, or a favorable attitude toward, the product,

5.   A preference for one brand over others,

6.   A desire to buy the product and a conviction that buying it would be wise, and

7.   Purchase.

   Ads are effective if they move people up a step in this hierarchy of effects. For example, Chrysler Corp., Bristol-Myers Squibb Company, and others use music and spokespeople to create a nostalgic mood in order to attract attention. The Partnership for a Drug-Free America and the Advertising Council claim that their "Just say no!" campaign changes the attitudes of children toward drugs. The ad for Hyatt Corp. in Figure 8.4 aims to create conviction and encourage purchase; it is run at the beginning of the ski season and includes a toll-free number to facilitate purchase.

   The steps in the hierarchy of effects are not necessarily equidistant from each other, and consumers can move up several steps simultaneously. The consumer's commitment influences his or her path through the steps; more committed purchasers take longer to go through the process. In its simplest form, the model assumes that all consumers start from scratch. In reality, however, some consumers have a negative attitude, which must be changed before they can move up the seven steps.

   Traditional hierarchy of effects models like the Lavidge-Steiner version have been criticized for implying that ads generate a single response pattern, regardless of the product or service being advertised. In fact, as we discussed in Chapter 5, the degree of involvement influences how a person responds to information and makes decisions. Research suggests that traditional hierarchy of effects models do not apply when the consumer has

low involvement with a purchase. In these instances, the consumer's lack of interest in the product may mean that the decision process simply begins with attention and goes directly to purchase.

One researcher proposes[6] that three sets of factors influence the relationship between the consumers' involvement level and the elements of the hierarchical process they utilize:

- Characteristics of the person receiving the advertising message (such as the individual's value system and unique experiences),
- Physical characteristics of the stimulus (such as the type of media and content of the ad),

Figure 8.5

An ad that serves the function of precipitation.
Courtesy of The Häagen-Dazs Company, Inc.

I was talking to my boyfriend as I unwrapped my Häagen-Dazs® Vanilla Almond Bar. Slowly his voice started to drift away. Completely consumed, I carefully lifted the thick Belgian chocolate off. Then I immersed myself in the creamy center. Of all the wonderful things I can say about Häagen-Dazs, I can't say it's great for conversation.

Häagen-Dazs

Täaste the Passion.™

© Häagen-Dazs Company, Inc.   Also available at Häagen-Dazs shops.

■   The situation (such as where the person is in the purchase cycle for the product).

Sheth Model   A broader framework for understanding what advertising can do is provided by Sheth.[7] He describes four basic, sequential functions of advertising: precipitation, persuasion, reinforcement, and reminder.

An ad that serves the *precipitation* function stimulates needs and wants and creates general awareness. Figure 8.5 shows an ad that serves this function by moving the consumer to a point at which purchase is a distinct possibility. The descriptive copy and up-close photography spurs the consumer to accept this new product as something worth noting.

Ads that serve the *persuasion* function move the consumer to the point of purchase. This process may take minutes, hours, days, months, or even years, but it is the ultimate goal of all advertising. An ad may persuade by appealing to emotions such as love or fear or to rational motives such as savings or quality. In its Mr. Goodwrench ads, General Motors Corp. tries to persuade the consumer to choose Mr. Goodwrench by pointing out that it offers a fast-or-free guarantee (see Figure 8.6).

By making people feel good about their previous decisions to buy a product, advertising serves a *reinforcement* function. Automobile ads therefore report the results of consumer research to show that consumers "ranked Honda number one in satisfaction," "reported that BMW had the best re-

Figure 8.6

In its Mr. Goodwrench ad, General Motors attempts to persuade the consumer to use its services by offering a fast-or-free guarantee.
Courtesy of General Motors Corp.

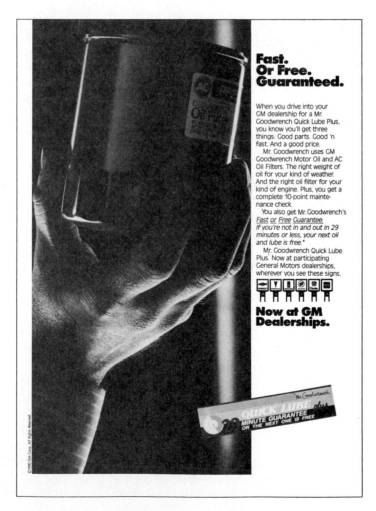

sale value," and so forth. The use of testimonials is another advertising technique designed to reinforce.

Reminder ads are intended to keep the advertiser's name fresh in the minds of the target audience. Through repetition and minimal context, ads such as the one for Pepsi-Cola products (see Figure 8.7) provide top-of-the-mind awareness.

Advertising and Value-Added   It is common knowledge that consumers perceive brands as more and more similar. Trying to establish brand loyalty in an era when this behavior is rapidly eroding has proven to be one of the major challenges facing marketers. Experts agree that advertising is still

Figure 8.7

A reminder ad such as this one provides top-of-the-mind awareness.
Provided courtesy of Pepsi-Cola Company. Pepsi, Diet Pepsi, and Mountain Dew are registered trademarks of PepsiCo, Inc.

the most effective method of nurturing a brand's image over the long haul. Thus, a function of advertising is to increase the perceived value of a brand through advertising. Such ads have the capability of endowing a brand with a symbolic meaning that makes it more valuable in the consumer's eyes.

According to this reasoning, a consumer will choose a brand of baby powder when it conveys an image of nurturing parent, select a brand of cola when it is tied to a positive group identification, buy a brand of running shoe for its ability to communicate fitness, or purchase an expensive automobile because it communicates affluence.

Advocates of this value-added capability of advertising suggest that brand erosion is partially due to cuts in advertising support. For example, Mars Inc. surpassed Hershey Foods Corp. as the nation's largest chocolate maker because it spent more to advertise M&M's and its other brands than Hershey did. "Brands can take short-term cuts in ad spending," says Roy J. Bostack, chairman of D'Arcy Masius Benton & Bowles. "But there's a time bomb waiting to go off."[8]

Marketers have an interest in maintaining strong brand franchises because they can then price their products at a premium. In doing so, America's consumer marketers have been able to generate much higher profits.

Not everyone agrees with the value-added abilities of advertising. One critic notes that "Advertising can actually add value only in one specific situation: where consumers' egos are highly involved and they are buying the product primarily for its symbolic value—and then only provided it really is a worthwhile product. The Polo logo and the Rolex name may add value to shirts and watches, but each is attached to a well-designed, well-made product. Opportunities for such value-added advertising, however, are limited."[9]

This position appears overly limited, given the many examples in which advertising has provided the added value. In the gasoline and telecommunications industries, where products are somewhat homogeneous, advertising has been primarily responsible for establishing a brand image. Shell Oil, Texaco Inc., and AT&T are outstanding examples. As for the requirement of an exceptional product, it has already been acknowledged that good advertising cannot save a bad product.

Advertising and the Other Mix Components

The adversarial relationship between advertising and the other promotional mix components has been noted for several decades. Because of its high profile, advertising traditionally received all the attention from the top management as well as from those outside the organization. As a result, personal selling, sales promotion, and public relations took a bitter back seat to advertising. As this situation is gradually changing, advertising is learning by necessity to work with and facilitate the work of the other three promotional elements.

This change has not necessarily been by choice. Marketers' demand for greater accountability has led to a de-emphasis on image-building advertising, where sales are not always the immediate result. Not so with price discounts or coupons, which give sales a quick, easily measured boost. Companies now spend 70 percent of their marketing budgets on sales promotion, leaving just 30 percent for advertising. The tie-in between advertising and sales promotion has been very successful. Advertising has served as a vehicle for delivering sales promotions such as coupons, samples, and discounts. Advertising has also served as a communication device for supporting sales promotion offers such as sweepstakes and special events. The highly praised ads starring Ray Charles and his bluesy rendition of "You got the right one, baby! Uh huh" represents one of the best brand-image campaigns of 1991. The commercials also invited viewers to send in videos featuring their own rendition of the jingle. A few were chosen for use in future Diet Pepsi commercials, and those viewers will win cash prizes. Pepsi also had their summer "Chill Out" campaign, a slickly produced series of ads that offered discounts, cash prizes, and 130 new cars.

A similar relationship exists between advertising and public relations (PR). In addition to *public relations advertising,* which carries public relations messages through paid-for media, advertising also carries a variety of PR messages. For example, an event such as a marathon or a parade is announced through advertising. New product introductions often require public relations and advertising to work together. When Campbell Soup Company recently reintroduced its Campbell Kids campaign, appearances by the kids in various supermarkets (organized by the PR department) was announced through local newspaper ads.

The most difficult relationship to establish has been between advertising and the sales force. Although advertising has the capability to simplify the job of the salesperson in a variety of ways, it has been difficult to convince salespeople of this fact. When the relationship is harmonious, the sales force often provides ideas for advertising appeals and copy. In turn, these ads help presell the products and services, giving the salesperson a distinct competitive advantage. The prospective customer is familiar with the brand name and its key benefits, and some level of trust has been established. This kind of customer preparation saves the salesperson time and energy, reduces anxiety, and increases the likelihood of a successful sale.

Advertising and Profitability

It has already been noted that a link between a specific ad and a particular sale is difficult, if not impossible, to establish. However, the general relationship between spending money on advertising and profitability does appear verifiable. In 1985, the Strategic Planning Institute (SPI) published a study that analyzed the contribution of advertising for marketers in the business-to-business sector. The success of this study led the Ogilvy Center to propose joint sponsorship with the institute of a similar investigation of consumer businesses. Through the use of the PIMS (Profit Impact of Market Strategy) data, the researchers were able to relate advertising expenditures to sales and to profits for over seven hundred consumer businesses. Their findings are summarized as follows: (1) businesses with higher relative advertising-to-sales ratios earn a higher return on investment, and (2) relative advertising expenditures and market share are related.[10]

Studies by the American Business Press examined the relationship between advertising and sales in 143 companies during the severe 1974–75 economic downturn. Companies that did not cut advertising during either year had the highest growth in sales and net income during the two study years and the following two years. The studies also proved that companies that cut advertising during both years had the lowest sales and net income increases during the two study years and the following two years.[11] A study by McGraw-Hill of both the 1974–75 and 1981–82 recessions confirmed the long-range advantage of keeping a strong advertising presence. It found that companies that cut advertising in 1981–82 increased sales by only 19 percent between 1980 and 1985, while companies that had continued to advertise in 1981–82 enjoyed a 275 percent sales increase.[12]

The Limits of Advertising

Managers need to keep in mind both the powers and the limitations of advertising. Some advertising is more effective than others, and advertising seems to work better with certain types of products. Certain consumers will not buy in spite of extensive advertising, and some will buy without any advertising. Not all institutional reputations are enhanced by advertising. Many other marketing forces may affect product and institutional success. And the effect of specific ads may vary widely from consumer to consumer and from time to time.

Advertising is just a part of the total marketing effort required for success. Marketers must make a quality product that performs its function well, and this product must be priced fairly and competitively. The product must be available to consumers in locations where they expect to find it. Finally, the product must be sold through an aggressive promotional strategy that may include all the elements of promotion or just one.

In the final analysis, advertising is only valuable to businesses if it can create easy consumer identification of the advertised brand or institution.

With this identification, however, comes a serious risk. Although advertising helps consumers identify the brand they wish to buy, it also helps them make a positive identification of those brands or institutions they wish to avoid because of bad reports or bad experiences. The continued advertising of a particular brand or institution over several years is an implied warranty to the consumer that the product has met the test and is being used. The measure of success for any product is repeat purchase. The greater the consumer's satisfaction and the more repeat purchases, the bigger the economic base from which continuing advertising expenditures can be generated.

Concept Review

1. A hierarchy of effects model proposes that ads can move consumers closer to buying a product step by step—from being unaware, to knowledge, to liking, to preference, to desire/conviction, to purchase.
2. The basic functions of advertising are the following:
   a. Precipitation: to create awareness and stimulate needs and wants,
   b. Persuasion: to encourage action and create commitment,
   c. Reinforcement: to support customers' past decisions, and
   d. Reminder: to create habit.
3. Advertising's ability to add value to the brand suggests that ads have the capability of endowing a brand with a symbolic meaning that makes it more valuable in the consumer's eyes.
4. Advertising has the capability to complement the other promotional mix elements:
   a. It delivers sales promotions directly and supports them indirectly,
   b. Advertising often carries public relations messages and announces public relations activities, and
   c. Advertising presells the salesperson's product.
5. There is sufficient evidence to suggest that advertising does increase sales and profitability.

Organizing for Advertising

Advertising is big business, in terms of both dollars and complexity. During the last two decades, advertising has adopted a formal managerial approach. Still, within the industry, there is a wide variety of approaches. At one extreme, a single individual may create, approve, and place ads in the media. The person who writes and places a small business ad in a newspaper is an example. At the other extreme, an advertiser may retain a full-service agency to create and place advertising. Within the agency, specialized groups plan and execute the advertising programs. The greater the advertising appropriation, the more likely the work will be done by a full-service advertising agency and specialists employed by the agency or company.

The Players and Their Roles

Whether an advertiser uses an agency or does the advertising in-house or chooses some combination of the two, several basic functions must be performed. As noted in Figure 8.8, there are four principal players: the advertiser (subject of the ad), the advertising agency, media specialists, and service providers.

First, consider the advertiser. Individuals who are in charge of the advertiser's effort have a variety of responsibilities, some of which they accomplish themselves and some of which they may delegate to an advertising agency. They must do the following:

■ Decide what products, institutions, or ideas are to be advertised,

■ Decide whether to prepare advertising programs themselves or turn the work over to an advertising agency,

■ Engage and give direction to the advertising agency if an agency is used,

■ Develop their own advertising work or approve the advertising programs brought to them by the advertising agency,

■ Pay the advertising bill,

■ Determine the extent to which the ads helped, and

■ Reach the stated objectives.

Figure 8.8

The four key players in advertising.

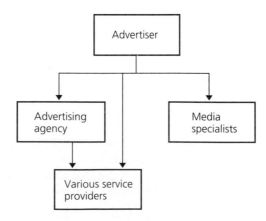

The second player, the advertising agency, typically creates and produces advertising materials and places them in the media. To do this, the agency must be familiar with the advertiser—its products, problems, opportunities, and peculiarities. More will be said about agencies later in this chapter.

Media specialists, the third group of players, facilitate the advertising process. Media specialists vary in the kind of expertise they possess and the level of service they provide. For example, a local television station is a media specialist of one kind of medium—television. Local media institutions such as newspapers, television and radio stations, are particularly useful to small advertisers that cannot afford the services of an advertising agency. These media institutions can provide technical expertise, consumer information, scheduling advice, and assistance in ad design. Thus a restaurant can bypass an agency and go directly to the local newspaper or television station in order to get all the help necessary for a fraction of the cost. Another option available to advertisers as well as to agencies is the media-buying company. It operates as a wholesaler, or broker, of media by buying large blocks of time or space at a wholesale rate and then selling them to clients at prices below those charged by the media. This institution is relatively new. Media brokers do not assist in creative areas. Since it only buys media, it can coexist with a client's conventional agency. In fact, because of the high cost and risk of acquiring media for clients, many agencies have gladly given up that part of the business. Because media buying and planning have become very complicated, there has been an emergence of media specialists and media agencies. Media specialists have often had years of agency experience and have started their own media agencies in order to satisfy the demand of advertisers. These agencies offer media planning, buying, analysis, and postevaluation services. Ford Motor Co., for example, has traditional ad agencies to do all the creative work and separate media agencies to do all the media-related work. Some media agencies receive a negotiated fee; others split the savings they realize with the advertiser. In some cases, a media agency can save an advertiser millions of dollars through careful planning and shrewd negotiations.

Finally, there are the service providers, a wide variety of suppliers of production, research, and other services that are critical to the success of the advertising enterprise. Sometimes the advertiser contracts for such services directly; sometimes the agency contracts for them on behalf of the advertiser.

The net result is that most national and regional advertising and some local advertising reflect the collective efforts of several individuals and institutions. Rather than attempt to discuss all of these institutions, we will present the two most prominent ones: the company advertising department and the advertising agency.

The Company Advertising Department

The organizational structure of an advertising department depends heavily on the size and complexity of the business. In an advertising department with fewer than ten employees, everyone usually reports to one individual who supervises the entire process. In larger companies, two structures tend to emerge. In one type (found at Black & Decker Corp.), each division has a marketing operation with its own ad manager and staff. In the second type (as at Procter & Gamble Co.), brand managers are responsible for the success of specific products. Knowing the nature of the advertising strategy better than anyone else, the product manager identifies the skills necessary to implement the advertising strategy. The ad manager then selects the specific specialist who will be assigned to the campaign. Although the Black & Decker arrangement is more efficient and individuals become acquainted with each other's capabilities, the Procter & Gamble approach ensures that the best people for a particular campaign are used.

Regardless of size, advertising departments have similar responsibilities: the formulation and supervision of an overall advertising program. Advertising managers tend to be held responsible for everything classified as advertising and sales promotion, even if it is designed by an outside advertising agency.

The Advertising Agency

An advertising agency is an independent organization that specializes in providing one or more advertising-related services to companies. The relationship continues from year to year until one side or the other decides, for whatever reason, to end it. For the most part, these relationships tend to last for several years. In the United States, there are more than ten thousand agencies, which vary tremendously in size, services provided, skills, profitability, and the kinds of clients served. Table 8.3 lists some of the most successful agencies.

Even relatively small agencies may qualify as full-service agencies. A **full-service agency** tends to have five functional areas:

1. *Creative:* This area includes designing, recommending, and creating ads, and/or managing their production.
2. *Media:* This area includes analyzing the target markets, developing media strategies, and purchasing the specified media units.
3. *Financial:* Maintaining proper records in order to pay individual media whose facilities have been used.
4. *Support services:* This area may include marketing research, sales promotion, retail advertising, direct mail, and talent.

Procter & Gamble demonstrates how one company is responding to our culture's increasing concern for protection of the environment.

Robert Haller.

OshKosh B'Gosh taps into the common experiences of most parents with young children.

OshKosh B'Gosh, Inc.

Fireflies

The Tooth Fairy

Training Wheels

Owies

Night Lights

Knock-Knock Jokes

Bubble Gum

Goodnight Kisses

Kids

OshKosh B'Gosh

As genuine as ever.

Is it any wonder the prisons are full?

In the mid 1950's, researchers at the University of Pennsylvania began conducting what has become a landmark study.

Its purpose: to determine the effect violent toys have on our children.

What they found was rather disturbing. The researchers stated that violent toys cause children to become more violent. That they actually may, in fact, teach children to become violent.

At Dakin, we've always tried to produce toys that teach children some other things.

Toys that, rather than teach a child how to maim, would teach a child how to love.

That, rather than teach a child how to hurt, would teach a child how to care for something.

Toys that, rather than being designed to be played with in only one way, would challenge the child's imagination to use them in a variety of ways. From playing house. To playing veterinarian. To playing Mr. Big Shot Hollywood movie director.

Naturally, researchers and child psychologists have had something to say about toys like the Dakin stuffed animal you see on the left: That they can play a very important role in helping children develop into secure, well-adjusted individuals.

You see, as parents ourselves, we at Dakin don't design toys solely on the basis of whether or not they'll make money.

We design them on the basis of whether we'd want our children playing with them.

DAKIN

Gifts you can feel good about.

Dakin uses an opportunity to influence buyers in this juxtaposition of violent toys and a cuddly stuffed animal.

There's convention and then there's CAROLYN JEFFERSON.

What do we mean? Well, how many people do you know who spend their Monday nights bowling with friends in formal evening wear? Not too many, we'd wager. But then, Carolyn's an original.

Yet, when we asked her why she bought her Saturn SC, she reeled off some pretty mainstream responses. Like how well her car handles the mountain roads at Lake Tahoe. How easy it is to take care of. How she's gotten used to the driver's seat lumbar support she didn't even know she needed.

For the most part, it all seemed to be reasonable enough. But according to Carolyn, the real reason she bought her coupe was for its front-end styling. She loves it. And as if the front end wasn't enough, she loves the way the rear end looks, too.

Now, a lot of people probably wouldn't admit they bought a car just because of the way it looks. Say, about as many as would tell you they're getting into bowling. But the folks who designed the coupe appreciate Carolyn's frankness. Not to mention her 152 average.

A DIFFERENT KIND OF COMPANY. A DIFFERENT KIND OF CAR.

If you'd like to know more about Saturn, and our new sedans and coupe, please call us at 1-800-522-5000.

In line with its motto "A Different Kind of Company. A Different Kind of Car.", Saturn depicts the not-so-typical personalities of its typical customers.

Courtesy of Saturn Corporation. Photography: Mark Seliger.

Product benefits:

Too fast.
Doesn't blend in.
People will talk.

PORSCHE

Porsche seems to be reading the minds of those who covet ownership of this sleek, elusive automobile.

Porsche and the Porsche crest are registered trademarks of Dr. Ing. h.c. F Porsche AG.

Attempts to customize its message might be one reason why Pepsi is a leading soft drink among the Spanish-American population.

PEPSI and PEPSI-COLA are registered trademarks of PepsiCo, Inc. Reproduced with permission of PepsiCo, Inc. 1992, Purchase, New York. Photograph by Marlene W. Garcia.

Subaru draws attention to its practicality by making a humorous jab at expensive luxury cars.

Client: Subaru of America. Advertising Agency: Wieden & Kennedy.

The Subaru Legacy

Weld a peace sign to the hood and make believe you're driving a Mercedes that gets really great gas mileage.

With its SmartRing option, GTE capitalizes on a common problem in households with teenagers.

Courtesy of GTE Corporation. Advertising Agency: DDB Needham Worldwide, Inc.

Table 8.3 **Advertising Age's Top 10 Agencies of 1989**

Top 10 Agencies Worldwide			Top 10 Agencies by U.S. Gross Income		
Rank	Agency	Worldwide Gross Income	Rank	Agency	U.S. Gross Income
1	Dentsu Inc.	$1,316.4	1	Young & Rubicam	409.5
2	Saatchi & Saatchi Advertising Worldwide	890.0	2	Saatchi & Saatchi Advertising Worldwide	395.2
3	Young & Rubicam	865.4	3	BBDO Worldwide	373.6
4	Backer Spielvogel Bates Worldwide	759.8	4	Backer Spielvogel Bates Worldwide	310.7
5	McCann-Erickson Worldwide	715.5	5	Ogilvy & Mather Worldwide	305.1
6	Ogilvy & Mather Worldwide	699.7	6	DDB Needham Worldwide	302.9
7	BBDO Worldwide	656.6	7	Leo Burnett Co.	288.8
8	J. Walter Thompson Co.	626.4	8	Foote, Cone & Belding Communications	280.5
9	Lintas: Worldwide	593.3	9	J. Walter Thompson Co.	266.5
10	Hakuhodo Inc.	585.5	10	Grey Advertising	240.7

Reprinted with permission from *"Advertising Age's* Top 10 Agencies of 1989," *Advertising Age* (March 26, 1990): 5–1. Copyright ©, Crain Communications, Inc., 1990.

5. *Account management:* The account manager or account executive (AE) is responsible for client-agency relationships. This individual interprets the client's strategy to the people in the agency working on the account and interprets the efforts of the agency to the client.

In a typical agency, most of the staff works in the creative area, followed by the account management area.

Advertising agencies earn their money through media commissions, production add-ons, and fees. The commission system is the best known of these techniques. It operates as follows: (a) the television station or magazine bills the client for the actual amount plus 15 percent, (b) the agency passes this invoice onto the client and collects the total amount, (c) the agency reimburses the medium the total amount minus 15 percent. Thus, if ABC billed Campbell Soup Co. $1 million for three prime time TV spots, the agency would receive $150,000 (15% × $1,000,000) and ABC would receive $850,000.[13]

Under a fee arrangement, the agency and advertiser agree on the agency's compensation without reference to the 15 percent commission. The agency simply estimates how many hours of work will be required to complete the ad, multiplies this figure by an hourly rate, and adds on any costs for materials, outside production, and so forth. The fee system is generally used when agencies have been undercompensated because clients have demanded excessive service or when clients believe that the agency is overcompensated by the 15 percent commission.

Agencies can also earn money through production add-ons. When agencies subcontract for services for their clients, they charge their clients for the service plus a markup of from 15 percent to 20 percent; 17.65 percent is the norm. This markup is the agency's attempt to earn the equivalent of its traditional media commission on noncomissionable purchases of photography, typography, engraving, printing, and so forth.

A **boutique agency** is a specialty shop that deals in a few services. Most concentrate on the creative services—art and copy. Since they tend to specialize, they keep their costs down and can charge lower fees. Owners of boutiques claim that they are restoring the basic purpose of the ad agency—creating ads.

One of the biggest changes taking place in advertising agencies is the introduction of high technology. Most decisions in the modern agency are facilitated by the computer. Agencies use computers to store their own data, to merge it with other data, and to retrieve data about markets and products directly from the client's computer. Often the entire media department is totally on-line. Massive media buys that took hours to complete ten years ago can now be completed in seconds. Even creative departments are using computers (see Promotion in Focus).

Concept Review

1. There are a number of ways to organize for advertising. The following are considered:
   a. The advertiser
   b. The advertising agency
   c. Media specialists
   d. Service providers
2. The company advertising department is part of the advertiser's business organization.
   a. One type of advertising department has responsibility for creating and placing ads.
   b. A second type of department supervises the advertising process and coordinates the efforts of agencies, media planners, and so forth.
3. An advertising agency is an independent organization that specializes in providing one or more advertising-related services to companies.
   a. Full-service agencies include five functional areas: creative, media, financial support services, and account management.
   b. Limited-service agencies (boutiques) specialize in creative or media services.

Promotion in Focus

Creating by Computer

Computers have become as indispensable to advertising agencies as they are to other businesses. In a 1990 survey conducted by *Adweek* magazine, 97 percent of the agencies polled had bought or leased computers, using them at the rate of one for every two employees. All of the agencies with computers were using them for word processing, and most also relied on computers to create spreadsheets, analyze income, and keep records of billings. Over half of the agencies were gathering information with computers, and in about one-third of the agencies, people were communicating through electronic mail.

The last bastion of pencil-and-paper work in most advertising agencies is the art department, and even the creative artists are beginning to lose their fear of computers. As one agency creative director puts it, "If you treat [the computer] as competition . . . you feel hestitation. But if you treat it as a tool, it's on your side."

More art departments are seeing that computers are on their side as the software becomes more user-friendly and the tools themselves become better adapted to the artists' needs. One big step for many artists was the perfection of scanners which can "read" anything on the page—a pencil drawing, for instance, or a photograph—and transfer it into the computer. Once in the computer, the drawing can be altered, enlarged, manipulated, or integrated with other art or copy.

The most advanced agencies do everything on the computer, producing camera-ready ads. Many of the ads they create would be impossible or prohibitively expensive to produce any other way.

The Volkswagen ad in figure 8.9 is the result of a mixture of action photography and computer graphics manipulation. The creative team began by developing the scene as they wanted it on the computer. The actual car was then photographed on a blue turntable. The final result blends graphics and real photographs in a seamless way so that the VW logo, the driver, and the roadway dissolve into each other and the real car stands out against a surreal background.

The ad allows VW to distance itself from its Beetle image without losing its well-known logo. It could, perhaps, have been created without a computer, but it would have taken much more time. As even art departments are learning, computers don't necessarily make people more creative, but by radically speeding the process through which idea becomes ad, they give creative people more time to think.

Sources: Betsy Sharkey, "The Art Department Timidly Turns to Computer Science," *Adweek* (February 29, 1988): 25. "Special Report: Computers in Advertising," *Adweek* (August 6, 1990): 25. Jon Berry, "Playing for Keeps," *Adweek* (August 6, 1990): 24.

Figure 8.9
This ad integrates live-action photography with graphics through use of a computer.
Used with permission of Volkswagen of America, Inc.

Case 8 *Diet Coke Changes the Battlefield*

Traditionally, it was easy to keep straight the competitors in the soft drink wars. Coke competed against Pepsi, Tab against Diet Pepsi, Sprite against Mountain Dew, and on down the line. But when Coca-Cola introduced diet Coke in 1982, it aimed high. It wasn't going to be content with just outselling Diet Pepsi; the company wanted diet Coke to be the number two soft drink of any kind, and by 1989, company executives were predicting that their dream would soon come true. Diet Coke's promotional strategy demonstrates how a big company goes about changing the rules of a major competition.

Taste, Not Calories

Coca-Cola began by redefining the purpose of a diet cola. They didn't invite people to drink diet Coke in order to lose weight or keep a trim figure; they told people to drink it "Just for the taste of it." Coke's taste emphasis was particularly effective because diet Coke was a new entry into the market rather than a reformulation. Diet Pepsi has been around for decades, undergoing a number of reformulations, including one necessitated when cyclamates were banned. If Diet Pepsi had begun a taste-oriented campaign, skeptical viewers might have responded "that's not what you said last year."

The taste campaign also provided the groundwork for diet Coke's assault on Pepsi. Because diet Coke was being sold on taste, not on its lack of calories, it made sense for it to compete against every other drink that people selected primarily for taste.

Men *and* Women

Diet Coke quickly overtook Diet Pepsi, and by 1989, it was favored over Pepsi by the group that traditionally has bought the majority of diet drinks: women. So one of the major thrusts of the diet Coke ad campaign has been to convince men that they don't have to be weight-conscious to drink diet Coke. Already, men buy more than a third of all diet soft drinks, and that percentage has been rising sharply. To make sure that men who move away from sugar switch to diet Coke, Coca-Cola has recruited macho heros like Wayne Gretsky and Don Johnson, and it has been advertising diet Coke in sports magazines specifically aimed at men: *Sports Illustrated*, *Sport*, and *Inside Sports*.

The War Rages On

Coca-Cola's assault on Pepsi has often been direct and aggressive. During the 1989 Super Bowl, as part of its "the move is on" campaign, Coke ran ads claiming that one-quarter of the 2 million families that had stopped drinking Pepsi in 1988 had switched to diet Coke. Pepsi responded with ads claiming that 90 percent of those people eventually switched back to Pepsi, and Coke ended up revising its ads. Pepsi also used its commercials to make fun of how Coke came up with its numbers. And while Coke had exclusive rights to the Super Bowl, Pepsi reduced the effects of this monopoly somewhat by having Diet Pepsi sponsor a pre-game show starring NFL players.

Diet Pepsi issued its own taste challenge in 1989, using Mike Tyson to claim that Diet Pepsi's taste was better than diet Coke's. Coca-Cola counterpunched, citing research that proved Pepsi wrong, and Pepsi eventually stopped running the ads. To make up for damage done to its image, Coke used some imaginative promotions like giving a coupon for diet Coke to everyone buying Pepsi at particular supermarkets. Again, Coke seems to have gained by defining the battle as diet Coke against Pepsi, rather than as diet versus diet.

Coca-Cola has been promoting diet Coke heavily, during some quarters spending more on its diet drink than on its flagship, Coke Classic. It has used innovative techniques like "roadblocks," running the same commercial at the same time on different channels. And it hasn't neglected cable; diet Coke spots have shown up on MTV, ESPN, and TBS. Keep your eye on the latest market share ratings to see whether diet Coke is reaching its goal, but also watch the latest ads to see if Coca-Cola is still managing to define the battlefield.

Case Questions

1. What functional role did advertising play in introducing Diet Coke? How has this function changed?

2. How would you assess the relative contribution of advertising to the success of Diet Coke?

3. What risks does Diet Coke take by moving away from its original theme?

Case Sources: Rebecca Fannin, "Diet Coke: #2 by 1992?" *Marketing and Media Decisions* (September 1989): 63–69. Patricia Winters, "Diet Coke's Formula: Stress Taste, Not Calories," *Advertising Age* (January 1, 1990): 16.

Summary

This chapter introduces the basic concepts associated with advertising. It begins by defining advertising from three perspectives: that of the consumer, society, and the advertiser. A comprehensive definition is that advertising is the nonpersonal communication of marketing-related information to a target audience, usually paid for by the advertiser, and delivered through mass media in order to reach the specific objectives of the sponsor. Advertising can be classified by audience (for example, geographical size/location, consumer, dealers, manufacturers), by advertiser (such as national and local), and by intention (that is, product and institutional).

The chapter also includes a discussion of the effects and functions of advertising. The hierarchy of effects model was offered as one portrayal of how advertising can move the consumer from unawareness to the product to purchase.

Four sequential functions of advertising are to precipitate, to persuade, to reinforce, and to remind. A different type of advertising might be required to achieve each function.

Four players are relevant to the implementation of advertising: the advertiser, the advertising agency, media specialists, and production specialists. The responsibilities of each are discussed.

Discussion Questions

1. What is wrong with using your own experience with advertising to judge the effectiveness of a particular ad?

2. How is the consumer's definition of advertising different from that of a business person's?

3. Give some examples of situations in which primary demand product advertising might be fruitful. When would selective demand product advertising be useful?

4. Distinguish between product and institutional advertising.

5. In a brief paragraph, describe the evolution of modern advertising.

6. Assume that you have been charged with organizing an in-house advertising department for a growing consumer products company. The first task is to hire an advertising manager who will have ultimate responsibility. What responsibilities should be mentioned in the job description for this position?

7. In what ways is a media-buying service different from a full-service advertising agency? How is each compensated for the service that it performs?

8. "Every ad should generate sales." Comment on this statement.

9. Outline the basic functions of advertising.

Suggested Projects

1. Collect two ads for each function of advertising. Evaluate their effectiveness in accomplishing these four tasks.

2. Interview an advertising agency account executive. Determine how advertising objectives are established and assess what factors he or she feels impede reaching these objectives.

3. Write a short essay entitled "Is advertising worth the money?"

References

1. Ralph S. Alexander and the Committee on Definitions, *Marketing Definitions* (Chicago: American Marketing Association, 1963): 9.

2. James P. Wood, *The Story of Advertising* (New York: The Ronald Press Co., 1958).

3. Stephen Fox, *The Mirror Makers* (New York: Vintage Books, 1985).

4. "100 Leading National Advertisers," *Advertising Age* (September 25, 1991): 1.

5. Robert C. Lavidge and Gary A. Steiner, "A Model for Predictive Measurement of Advertising Effectiveness," *Journal of Marketing* 25 (October 1961): 59–62.

6. Judith Lynne Zaichkowsky, "Measuring the Involvement Construct," *Journal of Consumer Research* (December 1985): 341–352.

7. Jadish N. Sheth, "Measurement of Advertising Effectiveness: Some Theoretical Considerations," *Journal of Advertising* 3, no. 1 (1974): 8–11.

8. Mark Landler, "What Happened to Advertising?" *Business Week* (September 23, 1991): 72.

9. Lawrence H. Wortzel, "Value-Added Ads: The Problem, Not the Solution," *Advertising Age* (November 6, 1989): 37.

10. "Does Advertising Pay? The Impact of Advertising Expenditures on Profits for Consumer Business," *The Strategic Planning Institute and the Ogilvy Center for Research and Development* (San Francisco, 1986).

11. *How Advertising in Recession Periods Affects Sales* (New York: American Business Press, Inc., 1979).

12. McGraw-Hill Research Report No. 5262.1, Laboratory of Advertising Performance (New York: McGraw-Hill, 1985).

13. Frederic R. Gamble, *What Advertising Agencies Are—What They Do and How They Do It*, 4th ed. (New York: American Association of Advertising Agencies, 1963): 4.

9 *Planning an Advertising Campaign*

The Campaign Process

Elements in an Advertising Campaign

Setting Objectives

Types of Advertising Objectives
Objectives for Campaigns
Establishing Meaningful Objectives

Designing the Creative Strategy

Creativity and the Manager
Desired Effects
Creative Strategies
Basic Appeals
Basic Tactics
The Creative Mix

Consider This:

The Creation of a Great Commercial

Football fans watching the 1984 Superbowl may have missed the most historic moment of that telecast, because it occurred not on the field but during a commercial break, when many viewers headed for their refrigerators. During a 60-second spot, Apple Computer aired its "1984" commercial introducing Macintosh computers. It was a tremendous gamble: the commercial was bold and unusual, and Apple paid half a million dollars for the air time. Yet it succeeded in a number of ways. Apple sold almost 50 percent more Macintoshes in the first 100 days than it had projected. The commercial created such a stir that portions of it were replayed on news and entertainment shows. And at the end of the decade, *Advertising Age* magazine declared the commercial to be "TV commercial of the decade."

Most people get their conceptions of what goes on in an ad agency from shows like *thirtysomething*, whose two male ad-agency stars come up with bursts of inspiration while doodling or shooting baskets with miniature balls in their offices. While most commercials require more sweat than inspiration, "1984" did in fact spring from a few such creative moments.

The process began when Apple's cofounder, Steven Jobs, gave his marketing director a newspaper clipping about the marketing of the movie *Star Wars*. The film's producer, George Lucas, had done such good advance work with marketing and promotion companies to create a big stir when the film opened that it appeared to be an instant hit.

Jobs wanted the same kind of "event marketing" for the Macintosh.

The commercial itself grew out of a half-hour brainstorming session among three top members of Apple's ad agency. The central idea was to create a world straight out of George Orwell's novel *1984*, in which a Big Brother government watches and regulates every move a citizen makes. Apple wanted viewers to connect industry giant IBM with Big Brother and to greet the introduction of the Macintosh with the same enthusiasm they felt when the rebellious woman in the commercial raced through the audience of clones and smashed the TV screen projecting Big Brother's face.

Everyone in the ad agency and Apple liked the idea, and Apple put up the money to give the commercial feature-film quality production. Because the company planned to introduce the Macintosh at its shareholders' meeting on January 24, the January 22nd Superbowl seemed the perfect event during which to show the commercial. Ironically, the commercial almost didn't run. Apple's board of directors, concerned about the cost of air time and the company's image, told the marketing department to shelve the idea. But Apple couldn't find anyone to buy its air time, so the show went on. And Macintosh quickly became the only real alternative to IBM personal computers and their clones.

Source: Cleveland Horton, "Apple's Bold '1984' Scores on All Fronts," *Advertising Age* (January 1, 1990): 12, 38.

*A*fter hearing the story of the "1984" ad, students might begin to wonder whether success depends more on luck than on strategy. Luck did have a lot to do with the fact that the ad appeared on the air. But the ad itself reflected excellent planning and execution. It had the power to counteract the underlying inertia found in all consumers. Viewers became interested and excited about this new and affordable technology. The day after the Super Bowl, Apple's switchboard was deluged with thousands of phone calls asking about the product and where it could be purchased. Other consumers went directly to retail outlets looking for the home computer. A few purchased the product sight unseen.

Admittedly, this enthusiastic response to a single ad is rare. In most instances, it takes time and many ads before the consumer responds to the advertising message as intended. Managers therefore need to think of promotion as a process that presents multiple exposures, multiple tactics, and multiple messages. Thinking of advertising as a process led by objectives and strategies rather than as a one-shot proposition is the idea of a campaign. Apple, for example, produced hundreds of other ads during the last decade. All of them use a constant underlying theme—the "power" provided to the consumer by Apple and Macintosh products.

The objective of this chapter is to introduce students to the campaign process. It shows how everything we have discussed thus far can be utilized in a way that produces a consistent and creative series of ads that accomplish objectives. More importantly, the campaign process provides a framework for integrating all the other promotional elements into one coordinated whole. Even though the concept of a campaign is most commonly used in the context of advertising, the promotion manager must view the entire promotional effort as a campaign. What we discuss in this chapter will therefore have applicability to the chapters that follow as well.

The Campaign Process

By taking the campaign approach to advertising, the planner increases the likelihood that the advertising efforts will mesh with the other marketing communication activities being used by the company. An **advertising campaign** includes a series of ads, placed in various media, that are designed to meet objectives and are based on an analysis of marketing and communication situations.[1] The advertising campaign is not created in a vacuum. It is guided explicitly by the promotion and advertising plans and implicitly by the corporate and marketing plans. The campaign encapsulates all these elements and reflects them in a set of ads that are centered around long-term objectives. That is, campaigns are normally a commitment to a creative strategy that will last at least one year. Companies that create one ad at a time and constantly change the core message are not involved in a campaign process.

In Chapter 8, we discussed the primary elements that influence the advertising planning process (see Figure 8.1, stage 1). In this chapter, we consider the next three stages shown in Figure 8.1. The remaining stages (that is, media strategy, budget determination, implementation, and evaluation) will be discussed in later chapters and will also be considered as they apply to all four promotional mix elements, since the techniques have comparable application.

Elements in an Advertising Campaign

An advertising campaign is a complex set of interlocking activities that must be integrated. There is a logical sequence in which these activities should be handled in order to create continuity. This sequence is not fixed, however, and there are many instances when the order is modified. These elements are also considered simultaneously by the promotion manager. For example, research is conducted in light of the research needs of sales promotion, public relations, and personal selling. Likewise, advertising objectives cannot be developed separately from the objectives for sales promotion, advertising, and personal selling. Therefore, as we discuss elements in an advertising context, be aware that the same considerations are being made within the other three mix areas. Moreover, a decision made in one area may completely change the strategic decisions made in the other three.

The following nine elements are generally considered important in developing an advertising campaign:

- Conduct appropriate research,
- Set advertising objectives,
- Define target markets,
- Determine the advertising appropriation,
- Design the ad,
- Pretest the advertising campaign,
- Develop the media plan,
- Select sales promotions to support the advertising effort, and
- Evaluate the campaign.

Conduct Appropriate Research The advertising campaign usually begins with and is supported by research. Although research can never substitute for careful analysis or creative solutions, sound research can provide insights into difficult advertising problems. A framework for determining the types of research needed is illustrated in Table 9.1.[2] The table suggests, for example, that concept testing research would be useful in selecting an appropriate theme for an advertising campaign. A concept test employs a focus group format: eight to ten people are gathered in a room and asked to assess whether they understand and like a proposed concept such as "saving money," "personal safety," and so forth. Likewise, copy research techniques evaluate every element of the message. More will be said about this kind of research in a later chapter.

Four research areas are particularly valuable:

1. *Consumer research.* The consumer should be described demographically and psychographically in order to answer the following kinds of questions: Who buys the product? What do they buy? When do they buy? How frequently do they buy? How do they use the product?

2. *Product research.* This research should consist of a review of the product in terms of its uses, packaging, quality, price, unit of sale, brand image, distribution, positioning, and product life cycle.

3. *Target market analysis.* This involves finding those variables that indicate who and where the best prospects are in respect to demographic characteristics, geographic location, sociopsychological groupings, or degree of product usage. It also includes an assessment of the accessibility of the target market. In the case of direct-action advertising, for

Table 9.1 **Advertising Campaign Questions and Answers**

To Make This Decision	One Must Choose a	Using
What to say	Theme, copy platform	Concept tests, positioning studies
To whom	Target audience	Market segmentation studies
How to say it	Copy, commercial execution	Copy research, commercial test
How often	Frequency of exposure	Studies of repetition
Where	Media plan	Media research modes
How much to spend	Budget level	Sales analysis, marketing models

Source: Charles Ramond, *Advertising Research: The State of the Art* (New York: Association of National Advertisers, 1976): 3–4. Reprinted with permission of the Association of National Advertisers, Inc.

instance, the availability of an extensive and accurate database is critical if messages are going to reach the target market.

4. *Competitive situation.* This involves keeping up with the activities of competitors in respect to market share, how they have advertised, the amount they spend in each medium, and at what times they have advertised.

Set Advertising Objectives   Every advertising campaign should have a clear and precise written statement of objectives. David Aaker and John Myers have identified three functions of advertising objectives.[3] First, they serve as a communication device. That is, advertising objectives are a practical method of informing all levels of management about which tasks have been assigned to advertising. A second function of advertising objectives is to serve as the basis for decision making. Objectives can be used as a measure of the anticipated results of an advertising campaign. Management can then evaluate the potential of various advertising approaches. Finally, advertising objectives serve as criteria for evaluating results. By providing a goal, the objectives of the campaign can then be used as the measure of the results of the program.

To select specific advertising objectives, promotion managers need to consider the overall corporate and marketing goals as well as the possible effects of advertising, which we discussed in Chapter 8. Since there may be many separate ads, each with its own objectives, within a campaign, the process of setting objectives can get very complicated. We discuss it in more detail later in this chapter.

Define Target Markets   The research conducted at the beginning of the planning process combined with the direction provided through the corporate objectives should prove useful in deciding which target markets to emphasize. As pointed out in Chapter 2, target markets can be segmented along a number of lines—by demographics, psychographics, and product usage, for example. It is necessary to know the relative importance of each target market as well as how it can best be reached by the promotional campaign.

Obviously, how the target markets are defined has a substantial influence on other campaign decisions, most notably on the message and media strategies. To illustrate, if a cafeteria chain decides to offer a special menu for senior citizens, the creative approach would probably emphasize price and nutrition, and people of the same age group would be shown in the commercials.

The paradox of advertising is that although the objective is to reach the masses with the message, the most effective sales message is still the personal one delivered to an individual. To get a fix on a precise target, it is necessary to dig deeper than demographics and look into life style and behavioral information. Though targeting may eliminate potential prospects, it helps the creative staff write messages to real audiences and thereby communicate effectively.

Determine the Advertising Appropriation The budget governs all proposed expenditures by placing upper limits on what can be spent. There is still much disagreement about how budgets should be determined and how a proper allocation should be developed.[4] These issues are discussed in detail in Chapter 16.

Decisions about advertising appropriations usually involve top management. In fact, in many cases, these decisions are taken out of the hands of the advertising planner. Purely financial decisions by top management often stop campaigns that appear to offer excellent potential. In the case of the "1984" Apple commercial, cost considerations led the board of directors first to reject and then to approve airing of the commercial. Regardless of who makes the final decision, the advertising planner should attempt to provide as much input into budgeting and allocation decisions as possible.

Design the Ad The process of actually creating the ad is complex. Essentially, this effort can be divided into two elements: creative strategy and creative tactics. The **creative strategy** concerns what to say to the audience. It flows from the advertising objectives and should outline the impressions the campaign intends to convey to the target audience. For example, Kraft Miracle Whip Salad Dressing occupies such a dominant position in its market that a major part of its marketing strategy is to devise ways to increase product usage. As a result, individual ads emphasize new uses for the product, particularly during the holidays. **Creative tactics** outline the means for carrying out the creative strategy. For Kraft, the tactics include the sponsorship of two Kraft Music Hall television specials, including twelve separate spots with voice-over by long-time announcer Ed Herlihey. Each ad emphasizes the tradition of Kraft Salad Dressing, product quality, and delicious recipes using the product as an important ingredient.

Pretest the Advertising Campaign With rapidly rising media costs, overwhelming numbers of advertising messages, and more and more advertising voices seeking to be heard, advertisers cannot afford to wonder if their campaign message is heard and understood. Most authorities agree that advertising should be pretested, preferably at the strategic stage before execution. Why? "To avoid costly mistakes, to predict the relative strength of alternative strategies and tactics, and to increase the efficiency of advertising generally."[5] Advertising pretesting is also done "to select the best appeals, advertisements, and campaigns so that advertising communications can be measured."[6]

Some authorities argue against pretesting. Critics suggest that pretesting is useless unless there is an indication that the advertising is considered untruthful, misleading, in bad taste, insulting to the intelligence, or in some other way repels rather than attracts. There are also serious doubts about the validity of tests designed to predict success for advertising strategies and executions. Also, practicing professionals contend that their expertise and experience enable them to develop and executive successful campaigns and that it is wrong to ask uninformed consumers to evaluate advertising about which they may have little knowledge or interest. Finally, advertising is often created under enormous time constraints. Waiting for pretest results is a luxury not available to many advertisers.

In the final analysis, the basic advantage of campaign pretesting is to gain some measure of assurance in the creative product for a rather modest investment. The cost-benefit ratio seems favorable when compared to the media investment. For example, a media investment of five million dollars may require a pretesting investment of fifty thousand dollars. It seems much wiser to invest creative research funds before using the material rather than to conduct lengthy posttests to determine if the advertising was successful. Indeed, if sufficient pretest information could be gathered, the need to posttest extensively would be lessened.

Once the decision to pretest has been made, the next decision is whether to test strategies or executions. A strategy includes factors such as whether the ads and media work together, whether the timing is correct, and whether the consumers' responses to the ad campaign are as expected. Unfortunately, most research methodologies concentrate on methods of evaluating executions rather than on strategy. Yet the strategy is basic; if it is incorrect, no execution can save it. Therefore, it is the strategy that should first be pretested, not the execution. Market tests, focus groups, surveys, and computer simulation tests are a few of the techniques used to pretest strategy.

In the end, the advertising campaign planner must appreciate that good pretest results simply mean that the likelihood of success is good, not guaranteed. The methods used in pretesting will be detailed in Chapter 17.

Develop the Media Plan   The media plan is just as important as the creative plan and is developed simultaneously with it. It is even possible that the promotion manager has already decided that a certain medium must be used, and the creative effort is designed accordingly. Because the world of media planning is extremely complex, the ability of a media planner to select a media mix that blends perfectly with the creative effort is both an art and a science. Fortunately for the planner, the computer is now able to perform media-related tasks in seconds that formerly took hours. In addition, the information available about consumer media habits and behavior has made media targeting far more exact and less wasteful. Still, the choices appear endless, and the costs are enormous. Even large marketers such as the Clorox Company, maker of Clorox Bleach, have found it difficult to find the right media plan to reach the elusive working woman. Traditional daytime television and women's magazines have given way to specialty magazines and direct mail. Choosing the media plan has become a major undertaking. It will be further examined in Chapters 13 and 14.

Select Sales Promotions to Support the Advertising Effort In most cases, advertising and sales promotion interact closely. That is, good advertising tends to enhance the effectiveness of good sales promotion, and vice versa. Sales promotion is a complement to advertising rather than subservient to it, although in many instances they compete for funds.

Other than the obvious differences in technique, the major differences between advertising and sales promotion are expectation and accountability. Recall from Chapter 1 that the intent of sales promotion is to provide an incentive to buy through the addition of extra value. Thus, sales promotion is tied to immediate sales. An increase in sales promotion should result in an increase in sales. In contrast, advertising tends to have several intermediate objectives leading to sales. Accomplishing these objectives takes time. Moreover, an entire campaign may seek simply to create brand awareness and have no sales expectations. Advertising relies heavily on the other mix elements, especially personal selling and sales promotion, to close the sale. The proper blending of advertising with sales promotion has proven to be very effective. A print ad containing a coupon, for example, has shown to increase recall scores eightfold as compared to the same ad without the coupon. More will be said about sales promotion in the next two chapters.

Evaluate the Campaign Evaluation is the final and, in some respects, most important step in developing an advertising campaign. Many companies overlook this step, which is indeed unfortunate. Evaluation allows for changes that may ensure the success of the total program. Campaign evaluation is concerned with questions of effectiveness: Does the campaign work? Does it do what needs to be done? What were the results? It is also concerned with questions of taste and judgment: Is the campaign fair and accurate? Does it mislead?

Two problems make evaluation particularly difficult. First, there is the disjointed nature of the advertising effort. Despite the best efforts of the creative director and account executive, copywriters and art directors often work independently. Thus, while some individuals may feel that the campaign was a huge success, others may consider it a disaster. A second problem is that there is little agreement on what should be measured, sales or communication effects. While it is true that advertisers understand that advertising does not necessarily lead directly to sales, the expectation is still there. Pepsi-Cola experienced tremendous success with ad campaigns featuring Michael Jackson, Lionel Ritchie, and Ray Charles; on the other hand, ad campaigns that featured Madonna were a disaster. With the former campaigns, recall, awareness, attitudes, and sales increased; with the latter, only letters of protest increased.

Nevertheless, evaluation must take place. Essentially, two types of evaluations may be made: ongoing evaluation while the campaign is running, and evaluation at the end of the campaign. The former allows the advertiser to make adjustments before the problems become too severe. Maxwell House Coffee decided on an ongoing evaluation when the company discovered that consumers were afraid that the new coffee was a potential health risk. Using the information collected, Maxwell House was able to quickly develop print and broadcast ads that carefully explained the controversial issues. Had Maxwell House been concerned only with evaluating sales rather than communication effectiveness, it would have been too late to solve the problem.

Postevaluation allows the advertiser to make major adjustments so that mistakes will not be repeated. Cadillac Motors, for example, went through a period where its campaigns were changed every six months. Postevaluation indicated that the target audience was having a difficult time determining the primary idea in Cadillac ads. Specific techniques used to measure campaign performance will be discussed in Chapter 17.

Concept Review

1. The advertising campaign consists of making sound strategic decisions that can be carried out by designing a series of ads and commercials and placing them in various media.
2. Steps in the advertising campaign:
   a. Conduct appropriate research on the consumer, the product, the target market, and the competitive situation,
   b. Set advertising objectives,
   c. Define target markets,
   d. Determine the advertising appropriation,
   e. Design the ad,
   f. Pretest the advertising campaign,
   g. Develop the media plan,
   h. Select sales promotions to support the advertising effort, and
   i. Evaluate the campaign.

Setting Objectives

Although promotion managers realize that setting objectives is a key part of planning a campaign, there is still a great deal of confusion about what objectives are appropriate for advertising. While the motel chain Red Roof Inn wants occupancy rates to increase dramatically because of its six-million-dollar investment in mass advertising, its agency knows that it will take time to create the awareness and trust necessary to foster sales. Ultimately, the measure of success for any advertising is its ability to increase sales and market share for the advertiser. Sponsors naturally want every dollar they spend to trigger increased sales; but as discussed in Chapter 8, an ad does not usually lead directly to a sale. In this section, we take a closer look at the types of objectives appropriate for ads and advertising campaigns and at how to set useful objectives.

Types of Advertising Objectives

The possible effects of advertising provide a starting point for selecting an appropriate objective. Recall from Chapter 8 that ads may provide reinforcement or reminders as well as set into motion the hierarchy of effects from awareness, to knowledge, to liking, to preference, to desire and conviction, to purchase. Notice that this hierarchy moves from an intangible effect (awareness) to a tangible effect (behavior). It suggests two classes of objectives: *sales objectives* and *communication objectives.*

In an advertiser's dream world, every ad would trigger new sales immediately and directly. Sales objectives are attractive, but except in the case of direct-action advertising, they are usually inappropriate for an ad, for three reasons. First, as we discussed in Chapter 8, sales are affected by many factors besides advertising. Second, the lag time between when a person is exposed to an ad and when that ad contributes to an actual sale could be quite long. An ad for a Sears washer and dryer may appear in *Reader's Digest* in February but not spur sales until July, when one is thumbing through the February issue because the family's washer just broke. Third, using sales objectives may push the consumer past the preliminary steps suggested in the hierarchy model discussed earlier. Retailers, for example, wonder why people shop at their stores only when their newspaper ads feature price discounts. Shoppers may know the address but not the name of the store, and they clearly have no commitment. Rushing advertising too quickly toward sales has dangerous repercussions.

These problems with sales objectives suggest that the objective set for an ad should be a communication objective—such as creating awareness, providing information and knowledge, and modifying attitudes and intentions. For example, Paramount Pictures might have determined that one ad for *Godfather, Part III* should create a specified level of awareness and knowledge: 60 percent to 70 percent of the target audience should know that *Godfather, Part III* was opening at theaters on December 25, 1990.

Communication objectives also present two important problems. First, measuring communication effects is complicated. (We examine this problem in Chapter 17.) Second, even if the communication objective is met, it may not lead toward the ultimate goal of the consumer's purchase of the sponsor's brand. There are several reasons for this disappointing outcome. For instance, it is possible that the communication tactic that was very successful at creating brand awareness or recall did not lead to sales because the well-remembered tactic was offensive. This is often the case with ads utilizing sexual innuendo or stereotyping. There is also the possibility that the media strategy is faulty, and the wrong people are viewing the ad. Thus the ad wins creative awards and is loved by the public because of its entertainment value, but sales are not affected. A third scenario is that the ad is being pitched to a market in which brand loyalty is high, as is true for the bar soap market. It is unlikely that a print ad for Dove Soap is going to impact sales without the inclusion of a coupon.

Objectives for Campaigns

Planners should set objectives for a campaign as well as for each ad in each medium used. In designing the campaign objectives, the logic of the hierarchy of effects model described in Chapter 8 is basic. That is, the components of a campaign should build on each other and create a positive synergy, thereby improving the chances that the consumer will select the advertiser's brand. Advertisers refer to this sequence as movement from *awareness advertising* to *direct-action advertising*—in other words, from communication objectives to sales objectives.

Consider the campaign run by AT&T when it introduced a universal credit card. Because the universal card represented a new product category in a new market, AT&T had to start from scratch. It began with awareness ads followed by other ads intended to accomplish different objectives. Telemarketing and direct-mail marketing were used to make final sales.

In contrast, when Procter & Gamble Co. introduced new Tide in 1990, it concentrated on direct-action advertising. Because Procter & Gamble has a powerful brand name and because the product did not represent a new category, P&G did not need to spend resources on awareness advertising. The introductory print campaign included coupons so that consumers could purchase the product right away at a reduced price. This ad campaign was coordinated with a massive sampling program.

There is no rule that all advertising must follow a specific set of guidelines in order to accomplish certain objectives. One ad can be repeated after a year's interval to accomplish very different goals, because a variety of factors have changed over the ensuing year. The consumer's needs or wants, the reputation of the brand and product, or the economic environment may have altered. Consequently, advertisers must constantly monitor and modify their objectives and advertising.

Establishing Meaningful Objectives

Regardless of whether objectives are applied to advertising, manufacturing, or personnel, several basic factors must be considered in order to produce meaningful objectives: priority, timing, structure, and minimum criteria.

Priority of Objectives   Managers are always confronted with alternative objectives that must be evaluated and ranked. At a given time, the accomplishment of one objective is relatively more important than others. Priorities must be established in order to allocate resources rationally. In the case of advertising, the budget often dictates which objectives receive priority. It is unfortunate, but objectives that are most affordable to reach often receive priority. For example, creating general brand awareness is usually more affordable than creating high recall of specific message components. Sales-related objectives tend to be ranked higher by the advertiser, while communication-related objectives are ranked higher by agencies. This difference in ranking objectives serves as a source of conflict between the two parties and is often the reason why agencies are fired.[7]

Timing of Objectives   Many organizations develop different plans for different periods of time. Their activities are guided by objectives with varying durations; it is traditional to speak of short run, intermediate, and long run. *Short-run objectives* extend for a period of less than a year; *intermediate objectives* cover one to five years; and *long-run objectives* extend beyond five years. These three time frames in turn should provide a sequencing or building-up of objectives. That is, accomplishing all the short-run objectives should facilitate accomplishing all the intermediate objectives, which should lead to reaching long-run goals. Strategically, the process should begin with the long-run goals and work toward short-run goals. For example, suppose a dishwasher manufacturer such as Whirlpool wants to produce the following long-run results: to clearly position Whirlpool dishwasher as the best value in the market in the minds of consumers with the following characteristics: age twenty-three to thirty, married, children, a combined income of thirty-five thousand dollars and over. Intermediate advertising objectives are twofold: to increase store visits by 50 percent and to improve attitude scores by 30 percent. Short-run advertising objectives revolve around improved accuracy measures of message content and awareness scores. Through the use of this three-tiered time perspective, management is then in a position to know the effectiveness of each year's activities in terms of achieving not only short-run but also long-run objectives.

Admittedly, the culture in advertising emphasizes short-run objectives.

This is partly due to the demand made by advertisers for their agencies to produce positive results as quickly as possible. Consequently, even campaigns tend to last no more than one year. This short-term emphasis is counter to the long-term orientation of strategic planning. Critics cite the short-run orientation of advertising as a reason for the minimal success of many campaigns.[8]

Structure of Objectives   Every organization, including advertising departments and advertising agencies, has a specific organizational structure. Furthermore, each element within a structure has specific tasks, and consequently its own set of objectives. For example, a typical advertising agency consists of production, copywriting, media, and account executives. Separate but complementary objectives should be assigned to each area. But the existence of multiple objectives in the firm creates problems. Achieving the objectives of one unit may jeopardize achieving the objectives of another. A copywriter may want to create high memorability through the use of a celebrity, while the account executive thinks a very conservative image should be the goal of the campaign.

The problem of multiple objectives can be understood by recognizing a second aspect of the structure of objectives. Many diverse groups have potentially conflicting interests in the firm's operation. Stockholders, employees, customers, suppliers, creditors, and governmental agencies are all concerned with the operation of the firm. The process of objective setting must recognize the relative importance of these groups, and plans must incorporate and integrate their interests. Determining the exact form and relative weight to be given to any particular interest group is precisely management's responsibility. Delineation of campaign objectives must take into account all these factions.

Minimum Criteria   A number of criteria must be considered in the development of objectives. The minimum criteria can be reduced to one overall statement:

> Objectives must be stated in terms that are understood and acceptable to those who produce the effort to achieve them.

Implied in this statement are several secondary considerations.

First, objectives should be developed with the input of all the parties who are expected to achieve them. This does not necessarily mean that top management meets separately with each relevant employee, but it does imply a feedback mechanism that allows all relevant people, both inside and outside the organization, to provide input.

This input helps to ensure that two other criteria are met. First, there should be agreement that the objectives are realistic. Second, the objectives should include all relevant information. In addition, internal consistency is created, since everyone was involved in the development of objectives. All parties interpret the objectives in the same way.

Understanding of objectives is enhanced through precise wording. A campaign objective should specify who is to be affected, by what, how, when, and exactly what the result should be. For example, objectives for an ad campaign for Campbell's Chunky Soups might specify the following:

■ *Who is to be affected?* Caucasian men, age thirty-five to fifty-five, blue-collar occupations, with incomes of under forty thousand dollars

■ *By what?* An appeal to the virtue of obtaining the hearty taste of home-made soup by buying a premium-price canned soup

■ *How?* Through a greater understanding of the product's benefits

■ *When?* During the next three months

■ *Result?* Sales increase of 20 percent from this group

It is helpful to assign numerical values to as many components as possible. Therefore, the objectives might further specify:

■ that the advertiser wants to reach 40 percent of the target audience through the campaign;

■ that the attitude score of the benefits of Chunky Soup versus home-made soup should reach 3.5 on a 6-point attitude scale after the individual has seen the ads;

■ that sales after the campaign should show an increase of 12 percent over sales before the campaign;

■ and that the three-month period would not start until four days after the start of the campaign.

Quantifying objectives allows the manager to measure more accurately whether objectives have been attained. It also allows comparison with other strategic alternatives employed by the organization.

Finally, objectives should be written and distributed to all parties responsible for their attainment.

Concept Review

1. Advertising objectives may be classified into two categories: sales objectives and communication objectives.
2. Except in the case of direct-action advertising, sales objectives are usually inappropriate for advertising. Using communication objectives, however, brings the risk that even if the objective is reached, the ad may not contribute to the ultimate goal of increasing sales or market share.

3. Objectives must be stated in terms that are understandable and ac-
    ceptable to those who must meet them. To achieve this,
    a. All affected parties should be able to contribute to the determina-
        tion of objectives.
    b. The objective should specify who is to be affected, by what, how,
        and when.
    c. Numerical values should be assigned to as many components of
        the objective as possible.
4. In order for objectives to be meaningful, they must:
    a. Be prioritized.
    b. Be assigned a time duration.
    c. Be structured.
    d. Be considered within minimum criteria.

Designing the Creative Strategy

Objectives provide direction for the creative effort. The actual translation
is contained in the **copy platform,** a document that outlines the creative
strategy. Not all agencies use a document like this, and some call their
planning document by a different name, such as workplan or blueprint.
The first elements in a copy platform are the basic decision areas already
discussed—objectives and target audience. Other elements might include
a statement of the advertising problem, the product position, the psychological appeal, the creative approach, and the selling premise. Formats
vary from agency to agency. The copy platform used by Karsh & Hagan
Advertising is the following set of questions:

What is the problem/opportunity?

What net effect do we want from advertising?

Who are we trying to reach?

What is the doubt in the mind of our prospect?

What or who is the competition?

What is our key persuasion?

How do we support the above?

How will we measure effectiveness?

Are there any obligatory elements to consider?

The copy platform can be very long but is usually short, a mere outline, in
fact. Brevity is desirable. If the plan is very long, it is more difficult to use
on a day-to-day basis. It can also be subject to more misinterpretation.

Who is actually responsible for the copy platform and its ensuing implementation depends on how advertisers organize the advertising function

and whether or not they utilize an agency. More than likely, senior advertising managers within the advertiser's company or managers of the advertising agency are responsible for the completion of this task. It may take weeks or months to work out. In most agencies, the responsibility falls to the senior account person in conjunction with the senior creative person assigned to the account.

Creativity and the Manager

Most ads are the result of much sweat, tears, and persistence. As our description of Apple's "1984" ad also suggested, effective ads require creativity too. First, the promotion manager needs to become as creative as possible in order to find new ways of looking at problems and concepts. Second, the promotion manager needs to hire people who are creative or have the motivation to become creative. Hiring such individuals requires some understanding of creativity.

No one really knows why one person can create one successful ad after another, and why someone else meets with repeated failure. A creative individual can be identified as one who:

- Possesses conceptual fluency (that is, who can produce a large number of ideas quickly),
- Is original,
- Separates source from content in evaluating information,
- Suspends judgment and avoids early commitment,
- Is less authoritative,
- Accepts personal impulses,
- Is capable of independent judgments, and
- Possesses a rich, bizarre fantasy life.[9]

Other researchers say that only one identifiable trait distinguishes the highly creative person: the ability to associate. That is, given a particular problem, this person can immediately begin to associate "hundreds and thousands and millions of symbols that may lead to an ideal solution."[10] The creative person clearly has more ability to associate data into problem-solving advertising communication.[11]

The creative process is not necessarily systematic, but it appears to contain common components. Alex Osborn,[12] who established the Creative Education Foundation, suggests that the creative process involves the following steps:

- *Orientation:* pointing up the problem,
- *Preparation:* gathering pertinent data,
- *Analysis:* breaking down the relevant material,

- *Ideation:* piling up alternative ideas,
- *Incubation:* putting the problem aside to invite spontaneous ideas at some later, unguarded time,
- *Synthesis:* putting the pieces together, and
- *Evaluation:* judging the resulting ideas.

The two most important steps in producing creative results are ideation—which can be facilitated through study, gathering information, talking with people, and so forth—and incubation. Incubation in particular appears to be a creative trait that can be developed. Retaining key information, either mentally or through an informal card catalog, allows an individual to call back important bits of information. Memory techniques and simple organization techniques are useful. Putting things in storage in a computer is also helpful.

Desired Effects

Figure 9.1 outlines the elements of the creative strategy, which begins with desired effects. The objectives established by the campaign strategy suggest which effects should be sought in ads. Few ads can produce the entire sequence described by the hierarchy of effects, nor should they. In Table 9.2, for example, possible advertising objectives are placed in three categories: perception, education, and persuasion. The objectives in the upper left-hand corner represent communication objectives; the objectives become increasingly tangible and behavior oriented as we move toward the lower right-hand corner. For example, a positive disposition is the intended effect of the ad in Figure 9.2. Figure 9.3, an ad for Jordan Marsh, is intended to increase traffic by providing information about product features, particularly price.

A campaign that appears to have moved over time from perceptual objectives to persuasion objectives is John Hancock's "real life, real answers" campaign started in 1984. "Single," the very first spot in 1985, showed an older brother counseling his younger sibling, an up-and-coming yuppie, on the need to invest. He was shocked that his brother was making adult money and still did not have any "stuff." Other ads followed, both broad-

Figure 9.1

An outline of the elements of creative strategy.

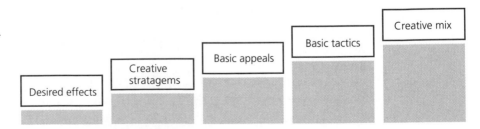

Table 9.2   **Framework for Advertising Objectives**

Perception	Education	Persuasion

Attention
    Create awareness
    of product,
    brand, ad
Interest
    Create concern,
    excitement
Memory
    Recognize ad,
    image, slogan,
    logo, copy points,
    position
    Recognize brand,
    product
    Recall ad, image,
    slogan, logo,
    copy points,
    position
    Recall brand
	Learning
	    Register claim,
	    features, selling
	    premise
	    Associate product
	    with logo, slogan,
	    theme, key visual,
	    jingle, life style,
	    image, mood
	    Establish position
	    Reposition
	    Comprehend selling
	    premise, viewpoint
	    Differentiate
	    features, claims
		Emotion
		    Register response
		    to appeal
		Attitudes
		    Register positive
		    disposition
		    Evaluate features,
		    claims, views
		    positively
		    Create preference
		    for brand
		Argument
		    Accept claim
		    Reason, promise
		    Correct false
		    impression
		    Challenge position,
		    claim, viewpoint
		    Counter facts
		Behavior
		    Increase traffic
		    Stimulate inquiries,
		    trial, purchases,
		    repurchases

Source: Sandra E. Moriarity, *Creative Advertising: Theory and Practice,* 2nd ed., © 1991, p. 59. Reprinted by permission of Prentice-Hall, Englewood Cliffs, New Jersey.

cast and print, that reaffirmed the "real life, real answers" theme through testimonials and life-threatening situations. These ads were able to create awareness through a sound idea presented both visually and verbally. The ads were not gimmicky, and they were placed in media that ensured that the right people were reached.

The ads also created a high level of interest through the clear presentation of a relevant problem—our own economic survival. The Hancock ads did not soft-sell this problem. They emphasized over and over again that these problems are serious and that not solving them has disastrous consequences on both us and our loved ones.

The 90s corollary to these early ads suggests that Hancock now feels persuasion objectives are attainable. "Lifeboat," one of four spots introduced in 1991, shows what happens when the balloon bursts. A woman is standing in her den, rifling through some cartons next to a computer and a file cabinet. When her young daughter asks what she is doing, the woman answers, "Where Mommy works, people are losing their jobs."

Figure 9.2

The intended effect of this ad is a positive disposition.
Courtesy of St. John's Church. Created by Scott Carlton and Ritch Goldstein.

The child says that her friend's dad lost his job and they "had to move." The woman says, "Well, this is your home, sweetie. And nothing's going to make us move. That's why Mommy is starting her own business." She asks if the little girl is scared. "No, are you?" the child replies, starting a round robin of laughing no's.

Hancock's highly successful campaign also demonstrates two effects that enhance the attainment of objectives: familiarity and learning. Though the campaign is several years old, the theme has remained consistent, as has the portrayal of the key ideas. The campaign surrounds us; we empathize with the characters, we anticipate their responses, and we know the name of the sponsor within the first few seconds of the commercial. This familiarity has several side benefits. Most notably, it creates a high attention

Figure 9.3

By featuring product descriptions and price information, this ad intends to increase consumer traffic. Courtesy of Jordan Marsh.

level, greater trust, more involvement, interest, and memorability. John Hancock has been able to stay with this campaign for so long because the initial strategic benefit, "real life, real answers," was carefully researched so that it would grow in relevance.

The John Hancock campaign also facilitated learning by breaking down one of life's most complicated topics into small chunks. With each ad, we learned a little more about insurance, until research told Hancock management that we "understood." The next series of ads then took us to a higher level of knowledge, and so forth. Most importantly, the ads have never let us get bored, nor have their creators ever forgotten that personal relevance is all that really matters.

Strategically, the John Hancock campaign shows what advertising is about. Driven by sound research, realistic objectives, and an intelligent creative strategy impeccably implemented, John Hancock serves as a model for all advertisers.

Creative Strategies

A campaign and its individual ads should be guided by an overall creative approach that is found consistently in all messages. The *creative strategy* follows on the message itself—what is said and how it is said.

There are five basic strategies employed in advertising:[13]

1. *Information*. A straightforward statement of fact using news announcements and assertions. Information must be relevant to the audience and should be unique. The information strategy is used to introduce new products and describe technical products and, in highly competitive situations, to announce results of tests and trials. The print ad sponsored by the Magazine Professionals Association (MPA), for example, highlights the interest of the magazine industry in conservation.

2. *Argument*. Essentially a rational appeal that uses logic to develop a reason why, benefit, or position. Because the audience must follow through the logic, this strategy requires a moderate level both of interest and of information-processing skills. This strategy is most effective in highly competitive situations in which products have distinct technological differences. An example of an argument strategy is shown in the print ad for U.S. Sports, which attempts to position the product as much higher in quality than competing brands, but lower in price. See Figure 9.4.

3. *Image*. Uses the process of association to establish identification of the brand or identification with a lifestyle. The emphasis is on psychological associations rather than logical ones. The goal is to develop a "reputation platform" for the brand or company that will be indirect and last for a long time. Companies that have achieved substantial market leadership use this strategy to maintain a positive, self-enhancing image.

4. *Emotion*. Tries to excite feelings such as love, anger, hate, fear, sorrow, or humor. An emotional appeal is useful for differentiating products and for presenting those that elicit a low level of involvement or commitment. The Spray 'n Wash spot evokes poignancy with visuals and a voice-over stating: "In a world no bigger than the sandbox . . . it's Spray 'n Wash that has gotten out the food, grease and grass the little ones get into. . . . And that has given more mothers the quiet strength to send them back out into the world to do it all over again."

Figure 9.4

An example of an argument strategy.
Courtesy of U.S. Sports.
Pagano Schenck and Kay
Advertising.

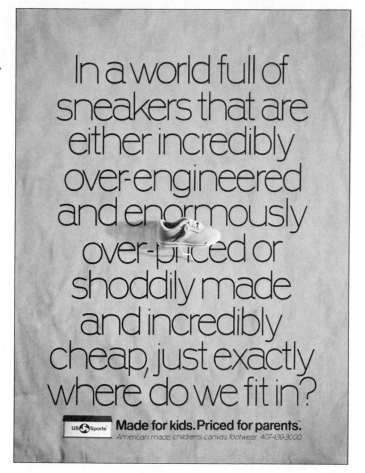

5. *Entertainment*. Grabs and holds attention by presenting amusing and interesting messages. A device that can break through the clutter, captivate, and mesmerize, entertainment is used primarily with parity products (those among which there is little differentiation) and frequently purchased, low-involvement, low-loyalty, and relatively inexpensive products. Entertainment strategies are seen as rewards to the viewer for paying attention. Newspaper ads, especially those for hardware stores, are not known to be entertaining. The exception is the ad for Elliot's True Value. See Figure 9.5.

These five strategies are not mutually exclusive. For most ads, two or more strategies are combined, although one tends to dominate.

Figure 9.5

An entertaining ad is an effective way to attract consumers to mundane products.
Courtesy of Elliot's True Value Hardware.

If you're
going to
nail it,
screw it,
drill it,
clamp it,
saw it,
cut it,
sand it,
strip it,
hinge it,
mount it,
shelve it,
join it,
hang it,
roof it,
screen it,
thread it,
plumb it,
light it,
wire it,
varnish it,
paint it,
stain it,
plane it,
file it,
finish it,
grind it,
buff it,
wash it,
polish it,
glue it,
glaze it,
caulk it,
weld it,
plant it,
hoe it,
mow it,
edge it,
trim it,
or clip it,
here's where
to buy it.

Maple and Motor in Dallas,
(214)634-9900. And now open
in Grapevine, Main St. and
Northwest Hwy., (817)424-1424.

Elliott's
Hardware made easy.

Basic Appeals

Once the general strategy has been selected, the next step is to identify the basic appeal, the central message to be used in the ad. This appeal should arouse an innate or latent desire and thus should speak to a human need that can be met by the advertised product.

The number of possible human needs is vast, but eight are basic: (1) food and drink, (2) comfort, (3) freedom from fear and danger, (4) feeling superior, (5) companionship of the opposite sex, (6) welfare of loved ones, (7) social approval, and (8) living longer.[14] Maslow proposed that human motives can be classified into several types: physiological, safety, love and affection, self-esteem, and self-actualization. As we noted in Chapter 5, however, no one list of basic needs or categories of needs is universally accepted.

No rules can specify which appeal to use in order to arouse a certain need. To a great extent, the effectiveness of an appeal depends on the product and the situation. The most common appeals used in advertising are listed below. Three significant appeals—projected savings, self-enhancement, and fear—are discussed in detail.

Projected savings

Self-enhancement

Fear

Unique product feature

Relative competitive advantage

Perceived price advantage

Major change or breakthrough

Popularity

Free samples

Projected Savings   An opportunity to save time, money, or energy is always appealing to consumers. In ads that use this appeal, price is never an issue. Rather, the ads claim that regardless of the price of the product, the savings generated through its use will be substantial. A case in point is the campaign of Owen-Corning Fiberglass, manufacturers of insulation. The total thrust of the campaign is the money consumers will save in fuel costs through proper home insulation with the company's product. Economy automobiles have also used this appeal to emphasize the importance of saving on gasoline costs by reporting miles per gallon.

Self-Enhancement   Helping us feel better about ourselves is an appeal we find difficult to reject. Many personal care and image products—for example, deodorants, perfumes, clothes, automobiles, and jewelry—are promoted through this type of appeal. Ads normally suggest that the products deliver value not because of their utilitarian features or benefits but because of their ability to add a personal dimension to users. Since products in this category use a great deal of mass advertising, it is not surprising that self-enhancement ads appear to dominate the airwaves. Even the U.S. Army tells people "You can be all you want to be!" (see Figure 9.6). There is still controversy over whether these emotional appeals are fair to the consumer, or whether they will continue to be effective in light of the recent popularity of more rational appeals.

Figure 9.6

*Self-enhancement is
the appeal used in this
ad.*

Army photographs cour-
tesy U. S. Government,
as represented by the
Secretary of the Army.

Creating Fear   In a fear appeal, an ad presents a threatening situation that
is resolved through the use of the product or service. A fear message deals
with social or physical harm, as illustrated by the stop smoking campaign
that shows the physical harm smoking can do. Social anxiety appeal is
often used by deodorant companies or dishwashing detergent producers
who suggest the personal embarrassment that will result from perspiring
uncontrollably or having spotted dishes. Recall from Chapter 7 that many
variables shape the effect of fear- and anxiety-provoking messages. We all
appear to have personal fear thresholds.

Advertisers tend to shy away from fear appeals because they worry that
these appeals will leave a negative impression on the consumer. However,
no empirical evidence supports this concern.

Basic Tactics

After selecting a strategy and an appeal, it is clear what an ad should say to its audience, but the appeal must still be transformed into an actual ad. The number of tactics available is vast, and more than one tactic can successfully initiate the same appeal.

Product Comparison Comparing characteristics, performance, reputation, or other characteristics of two or more products is an increasingly popular tactic. Sometimes the comparison is made without mentioning brand names. For example, the sponsoring product may be compared to unnamed "leading competitors" or "brand X." But sometimes names are given, as in the case of the Pontiac ad (see Figure 9.7) in which the competition is compared. It is also possible to make comparisons through the use of testimonials. For several years, Robert Young told consumers how he had tasted all the other brands of coffee but felt Instant Sanka was best. A final way to devise a comparison ad is by combining it with the demonstration technique. Showing two products being used side by side with the sponsor's product always winning is still a common tactic. Duracell uses this tactic, comparing itself with Eveready to show us that the toy with the Duracell battery "keeps going, and going, and going." Oldsmobile Cutlass compares its gas mileage to those of several competitors by comically showing how the driver of the competitor's vehicle ran out of gas. The FTC demands that these comparisons be actual tests and that all variables be similar except the products shown.

Statement of Fact Very few ads state important facts about the product. Ads for industrial products, however, generally use a straightforward, unemotional discussion of salient facts about the product. Most trade journals carry a majority of ads of this type. The traditional assumption is that these ads will be read by purchasing managers and other corporate managers who make their decisions based on concise, hard data.

Although some consumer ads also emphasize facts, there is a need to embellish factual ads with provocative headlines or intriguing pictures because of the tremendous competition for consumers' minds. Once the consumers' attention has been gained, it is hoped that they will continue to read about the product. As consumers become more discriminating in terms of product features, quality, and price, this type of format should grow in popularity. Factual ads must be well researched so that the information is both important to the target consumer and understandable.

Association An interesting advertising technique is the use of association. This tactic suggests an effect or an experience of product use through

Figure 9.7
The use of product comparisons is becoming an increasingly popular tactic.
Courtesy of General Motors Corporation.

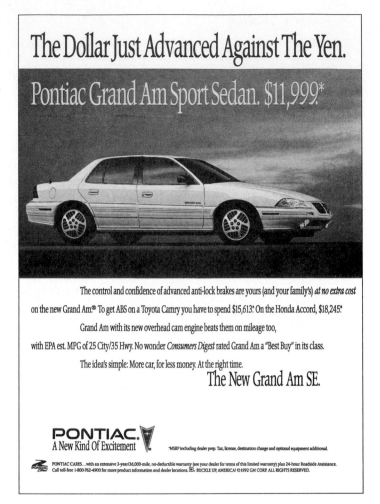

an association of the product with a person or an atmosphere that is neither directly nor literally related to the product. The use of Cher as a spokesperson for President and First Lady Fitness Centers is an example. Cher suggests that by joining this health club the consumer can develop a body like hers. Another example is the Pearle Vision ads that use Chicago Bears middle linebacker, Mike Singletary, who represents the intelligent pro football player to many consumers. Association is used a great deal in ads for highly personal products such as perfumes and colognes in which a sensuous woman suggests that using the product will bring the consumer looks, glamour, and romance.

The product must be believable in the setting. For example, using deodorant rather than perfume as a basis for a more exciting social life may be viewed as contrived. A successful association is quickly copied by competitors. This not only dilutes the original idea but also shortens its life span. To illustrate, Calvin Klein originated the abstract association approach for his line of clothing by showing naked people. After this approach was shown to be successful, both Jordache Enterprises, Inc. and Bugle Boy employed the same type of association.

Demonstration   The product may be demonstrated in actual use, or it may be shown in some sort of staged demonstration designed to highlight or emphasize a particular competitive strength. For many years, John Cameron Swayze demonstrated how a Timex watch could be strapped to everything from an outboard motor to an ice skater and "still keep on ticking." BMW shows the exact handling of its automobiles on rain-slick highways. The key consideration is whether the attribute being demonstrated is relevant to the consumer. Sometimes a performance characteristic is innovative and impressive, but only to a person trained in engineering or some other technical discipline. In other instances, the feature may be so innovative and spectacular that the consumer does not believe it.

Humor   Advertisers tend to use humor as their primary tactic when they wish to attract attention to the product in a pointed way. However, as noted in Chapter 7, humorous messages are not without problems. Coming up with an ad that is considered funny by everyone in the target audience is very difficult, and humor tends to wear out quickly. Since humorous messages can take many forms, including jokes and anecdotes, we are not always sure which type of humor is working or failing. Finally, humor can overwhelm the selling message and draw attention to itself and away from the product advertised. There are many ads that consumers enjoy, but they cannot name the company sponsoring the commercial. This problem is discussed in the Promotion in Focus section.

Perhaps the main consideration in designing a humorous ad is good taste. The ad should not ridicule the product, the users, or the nonusers of the product.

Hyperbole   Closely akin to the use of humor is the use of hyperbole as an advertising tactic. Hyperbole is exaggeration. It may amuse us, but its primary purpose is to present some fact about the product in a form that is larger than life. It is not necessary that we are amused; it is only important that we get the point of the exaggeration. An example is the dancing raisins ad sponsored by the California Raisin Advisory Board that repositioned raisins as a fun product rather than as a dull one.

Spokesperson   With this technique, a person—either a well-known celebrity or someone unknown to the consumer—presents the basic advertising

Promotion in Focus

Great Ad, But . . .

By now, every American television viewer knows the battery ads with the pink bunny. For the first 15 seconds or so, the ad appears to be pitching some other product in a dull, cliched way. Then the bunny interrupts, beating its drum across the commercial's set while embarrassed actors look on. Perhaps because the commercial pokes fun at commercials themselves, it has been a hit both with viewers and with critics. But before you read the next paragraph, think fast: Whose batteries does the bunny advertise?

If you said Duracell's, you're wrong, but you're in good company. Two out of five people who chose the commercial as the best on television thought that Duracell created the ads, when actually they're pitching Energizer batteries made by Duracell's rival, Eveready. Respondents to the 1990 survey ranked Energizer's ads the second best on television, but because so many of the people who liked the bunny ads thought Duracell made them, Duracell too broke into the top 10 for the first time. In fact, A. C. Nielsen reports that during the first months of the bunny campaign, Eveready actually lost market share to Duracell, an assertion that Eveready disputes, citing its own figures.

Spokespeople for Eveready and its ad agency, Chiat/Day/Mojo, say the confusion may have arisen because the bunny was originally conceived as a parody of Duracell's own bunny. Ad executives also admit that people don't spend much time thinking about batteries until they actually need them, so they're likely to ignore the brand name. The agency is trying to overcome the problem by featuring the Energizer brand more prominently in the commercials and by using the bunny in store displays where it is clearly linked to Energizer batteries.

The bunny campaign isn't the first one that has confused viewers and led to unintended results. When James Garner and Mariette Hartley advertised Polaroid cameras, many people were sure they were pitching Kodak. And viewers thought that an Anheuser-Busch parody of a Miller Lite commercial was the real thing. Clearly it doesn't always pay for the Number-Two product in a category to link itself to Number One. People may remember only the top name. More generally, Eveready's bunny problem demonstrates how difficult it is to mount a successful promotional campaign. The bunny commercials are among the most acclaimed and memorable of all time—yet apparently they aren't fulfilling their fundamental purpose of selling batteries.

Sources: Joanne Lypmain, "Too Many Think the Bunny Is Duracell's not Eveready's," *Wall Street Journal* (July 31, 1990): B1. Julie Liesse, "Duracell Ups Lead over Energizer," *Advertising Age* (April 16, 1990): 4.

message. This tactic is often combined with some other tactic such as product comparison, demonstration, or hyperbole.

Using a spokesperson brings two main risks. First, the spokesperson may dominate the presentation to the detriment of the product. The Quaker Oats campaign featuring Wilford Brimley is an example. Listeners are so enthralled with Brimley's down-to-earth, convincing message that they forget to notice the name of the sponsor. Second, the private life of the spokesperson may reduce his or her advertising credibility. Anita Bryant, a long-term spokesperson for the Florida orange juice industry, was removed from this job after controversial incidents in her private life. Companies must constantly monitor their ads to check for these and other problems.

Nevertheless, the tactic of using a spokesperson has proven to be very successful. American Express Company relied heavily on a series of celebrities to deliver a common message: "Do you know me?" Clothing retailer, The Gap, has used several customers, including Michael Keaton and Whitney Houston, in its print ads. Budweiser Beer has employed Ed McMahon as spokesperson for several years.

Testimonial   In a testimonial, as in the spokesperson tactic, an individual delivers the advertising message. The difference is that in a testimonial the assertions made are based on the person's own experience with the product. Thus Michael Jordan tells us how he has been a Wheaties eater all his life and feels it is a superior product. Many legal requirements must be met before this tactic can be used. Another problem is selecting a person who can deliver the message professionally and credibly. Credibility was quickly lost when the public learned that Cybill Shepherd, spokesperson for the Beef Council, was a vegetarian.

Still Life   A tactic that is just the opposite of the testimonial technique is the still life. With this tactic, a product that can stand alone and needs neither a great deal of copy nor an impressive spokesperson is visually highlighted either because it photographs well or is impressive in some other way. Jewelry, sports cars, flowers, and food can all serve as the emphasis in an ad.

Borrowed Interest   Sometimes the focal point of the ad has high inherent interest but no direct relation to the advertised product. The soft drink industry has used this tactic extensively. For example, Coke and Pepsi both have employed homecoming and family reunion themes in several ads. Seeing a young man walking up a country road and surprising his parents with his arrival has little to do with the soft drink but provides a more interesting and attention-getting format than the product might by itself.

Sex Using sex as a tactic has always been popular. What has changed is the definition and implementation of this tactic. The use of sex can range from very subtle humor to nudity; the latter is quite common in South America and parts of Europe. The tactic can include risqué language, implicit promiscuity, overt touching, and so on. While this tactic can be appealing to members of the target audience, it can also prove offensive to others who are exposed to the message through the mass media. It is therefore often detrimental to a company's image. In a recent nationwide study of four thousand people, DDB Needham Worldwide found that 84 percent of the females and 72 percent of the males surveyed said television commercials placed too much emphasis on sex.[15] Nevertheless, for the right audience, the use of sex is an effective attention-getting device.

Figure 9.8

Samsonite successfully combines the verbal and the visual in its ad for a new product. Courtesy of Samsonite.

The Creative Mix

The final consideration in designing the creative strategy is the **creative mix**—the manner in which visual and verbal elements are combined in an ad. Although there are no precise rules to follow in delineating the mix, a few general guidelines have proven to be helpful:

1. *Product facts.* When facts about the product are important in accomplishing the advertising objective, the verbal aspects become more important. When we consider purchasing a technical product, such as an automobile, power tools, or stereo equipment, there are certain basic facts that we consider important. We see what the product looks like in the ad's visual elements, but we probably make our primary decision based on its verbal elements. Honda has been extremely successful in filling the consumer's mind with positive facts about its product line. These facts serve as an important basis for word-of-mouth communication.

2. *Product appearance.* Where the appearance of a product is important in the ultimate purchase, the visual aspect is best emphasized. An example is designer jeans. It is not the workmanship, fabric, or zipper quality that is important; all that matters is what the product looks like.

3. *Product newness.* The newer the product, the more likely that verbal elements will be more effective. People naturally have questions about the product: What does it look like? How does it operate? People may not verbalize these questions, but they are there all the same and usually demand verbal answers. As the ad campaign goes on and consumers become familiar with the answers, the creative people are more likely to emphasize the visual aspects, feeling that it is no longer necessary to repeat the factual information. Samsonite Corp. has done an excellent job of blending the visual with the verbal in the ad for its new product (see Figure 9.8).

4. *Emotional associations.* The more important it is to make emotional associations with the product, the more likely the visual aspects will be emphasized. Emotional appeals are often difficult to put into words, and the visual approach offers a richer and wider range of association. Products such as perfume, furs, certain foods, and vacations are usually presented in a visual manner.

5. *Narration.* The more important narration is in making the point of an ad, the more important words will be to develop interest in the characters, the situation, and the outcome. Mazda produced a series of television ads narrating the benefits of its four-wheel minivan by showing humorous situations in which kids who expect to lose a competition wind up winning it, because the weather prevented the other team from getting to the event.

6. *Action.* Words are more effective than pictures in ads that suggest a certain action be taken by the consumer. Mail-order advertising, for example, often includes a great amount of copy. This copy is partly to provide answers to questions consumers have the opportunity to ask in person and partly to outline the action.

Concept Review

1. Objectives provide direction for the creative effort. The copy platform outlines the creative strategy.
2. Creativity is a difficult chara͟ːristic to define clearly, and many approaches have been proposed.
    a. The two most important steps in producing creative results are ideation and incubation.
3. There are five basic creative strategies employed in advertising.
    a. Information
    b. Argument
    c. Image
    d. Emotion
    e. Entertainment
4. Once the general strategy has been selected, the next step is to identify the basic appeal.
5. Basic tactics are chosen to implement the intended strategy and appeal.
6. Finally, the manner in which visual and verbal elements are combined (the creative mix) is determined.

Case 9 *Remaking a Big Image With a Little Humility*

People responsible for creating and selling a company's image are often asked to do big jobs: boost sales, improve morale, change public perceptions, ensure that customers return. But few such jobs can be more daunting than the task of recreating the image of General Motors.

General Motors is not just the world's largest automobile maker and one of its largest companies, it has long stood as a symbol of what's good—and bad—about American industry in general. When the economy was booming and before imports posed a serious threat, GM was viewed as stable, rock-solid, its Chevrolets and Buicks as strong and dependable as the country itself. But the size and weighty tradition that made GM so stable started to look like a curse when oil crises and Japanese imports began to undermine the dominance of American car manufacturers. Critics said that GM was too big, too slow-moving, too addicted to power and size to see that the future would belong to the efficient. Sticking by its gas-guzzlers, GM added arrogance to its image, preferring to pressure Washington to lower fuel-efficiency standards rather than dedicate its considerable resources to build efficient cars.

But by the late 1980s, even those GM executives accused of being out of touch realized that the company needed major change. Red ink was filling the company's account books, America's desire for Japanese cars showed no signs of waning, and GM had not produced a new best-selling model to rival Ford's Taurus or Chrysler's Caravan.

So in May 1990, GM launched a huge image campaign: "Putting Quality on the Road." An important aspect of the new campaign was an attempt to shed the arrogant image and establish credibility by confessing past mistakes. Some of the campaign's print ads admitted that the company's cars still have more defects than some Japanese models. The company hopes that its honesty will make buyers pay attention to other ads which list surveys showing how much GM's quality has improved and how some GM vehicles are now ranked highly in their class.

Along with the print ads came commercials showing that GM's cars are built well and keep going. Chevys start in arctic cold and Oldsmobiles survive desert heat. The commercials convey the attitude that General Motors is trying to prove its cars to the buying public, as would a small car maker, rather than rely on glitz and reputation.

According to GM, consumers see only a small part of the entire campaign. GM is trying to enlist everyone, including present workers and retirees, to sell cars. It gives out wallet cards listing important selling points. It awards plaques to suppliers whose parts meet quality standards. It publishes newsletters stressing the campaign's theme.

Although 1990 was not a banner year for GM quality—the new 4-door Blazer was particularly harshly criticized—the first few months of the new campaign seemed to indicate that it was working. Before the campaign began, 47 percent of people surveyed said that GM built high-quality vehicles and 52 percent said they would consider buying a GM car or truck. Three months later, 56 percent of people who had seen the new campaign thought highly of GM quality, and the same number said they would consider buying a GM vehicle. Those numbers may not seem huge, but in an industry where a single percentage point of market share can mean hundreds of millions of dollars profit, these initial figures must be taken as an indication that GM may finally have found the secret to shedding its too-big-to-win image.

Case Questions

1. Evaluate the impact of the products sold by General Motors on its advertising campaign.

2. Do you agree with the creative approach selected by GM? Suggest other possibilities.

3. What are the difficulties in achieving an objective such as image change?

Case Source: Joseph B. White, "GM's New Ad Campaign Puts a Shine on Its Image—But Not Yet a Deep One," *Wall Street Journal* (October 8, 1990): B1, B7.

Summary

This chapter described the elements that make up the advertising campaign. Key factors that influence the typical advertising campaign are the corporate strategy and marketing plan, the product, the consumer, the competition, the advertiser, the advertising agency, the advertising production people, and the various media.

Planning the campaign involves nine steps: (1) conducting appropriate research, (2) setting advertising objectives, (3) defining target markets, (4) determining the advertising appropriation, (5) designing the ad, (6) pretesting the advertising campaign, (7) developing the media plan, (8) selecting sales promotions, and (9) evaluating the campaign.

A great deal of attention was given to the process of setting advertising objectives. Objectives were discussed as either communication-related or sales-related. Problems associated with objective-setting as well as factors influencing the process were considered.

The process of designing an ad was covered, beginning with the selection of desired effects, creative strategy, and basic appeals. Appeals that are frequently used include savings, self-enhancement and fear through nonuse. Tactics and a creative mix must also be determined. The most common creative tactics are product comparison, statement of fact, association, demonstration, humor, hyperbole, spokesperson, testimonial, still life, borrowed interest, and sex.

Discussion Questions

1. Why do many advertising professionals regard advertising campaign formulation as a complicated task?

2. Assume that you are working on the campaign for a new Wish-Bone Cheddar and Bacon Dressing. What research would have to be done to support this campaign?

3. Discuss the various elements in setting objectives. How do campaign objectives differ from individual ad objectives?

4. Explain the difference between creative strategies, creative appeals, creative tactics, and creative mix.

5. Develop a rudimentary copy platform for Old Spice shaving cream.

6. List and describe the various types of appeals. What criteria can you use to select the most effective appeal?

7. In what circumstances should you stress the visual elements of the creative mix?

8. When should the verbal elements of the creative mix receive emphasis?

9. You are a creative director for Crestview Linens. A television ad is being considered that shows a blackened screen; all you hear are the voices of a man and a woman discussing the positive qualities of Crestview Sheets. At the end of the ad, you hear giggles and bodies moving. What are the risks associated with this tactic?

10. Describe the difference between an ad that employs a spokesperson and one that uses the testimonial format. What are the problems associated with each?

Suggested Projects

1. Select a print ad for either a perfume or an automobile. Analyze it in respect to creative appeals, tactics, and mix.

2. Document the evolution of a print campaign for a brand.

References

1. S. Watson Dunn and Arnold M. Barban, *Advertising: Its Role in Modern Marketing*, 7th ed. (New York: The Dryden Press, 1989): 232.

2. Charles Ramond, *Advertising Research: The State of the Art* (New York: Association of National Advertisers, 1976): 3–4.

3. David A. Aaker and John G. Myers, *Advertising Management: Practical Perspectives*, 3rd ed. (Englewood Cliffs, NJ: Prentice-Hall, Inc., 1987): 85.

4. M. A. McNiven, *How Much to Spend for Advertising* (New York: Association of Advertisers, 1969).

5. C. H. Sandage and Vernon Fryburger, *Advertising Theory and Practice*, 9th ed. (Homewood, IL: Richard D. Irwin, 1975): 545.

6. Richard E. Stanley, *Promotion* (Englewood Cliffs, NJ: Prentice-Hall, Inc., 1977): 122.

7. Judann Dagnoli, "Recession's Bleak Legacy," *Advertising Age* (July 29, 1991): 1.

8. Jim Kirk, "Older Beers Battle Newer Suds," *Adweek* (September 2, 1991): 20–21.

9. Gary Steiner, *The Creative Organization* (Chicago: University of Chicago Press, 1965): 17–19.

10. Hanley Norins, *The Complete Copywriter* (New York: McGraw-Hill, 1966): 93.

11. L. N. Reid and H. J. Rotfeld, "Toward an Associative Model of Advertising Creativity," *Journal of Advertising* (Fall 1976): 19.

12. Alex Osborn, *Applied Imagination* (New York: Charles Scribner & Sons, 1953): 125.

13. Sandra E. Moriarty, *Creative Advertising: Theory and Practice*, 2nd ed. (Englewood Cliffs, NJ: Prentice-Hall, Inc. 1991): 91.

14. Melvin Hattwick, *How to Use Psychology for Better Advertising* (Englewood Cliffs, NJ: Prentice-Hall, Inc., 1980).

15. Cyndee Miller, "We've Been Cosbyized," *Marketing News* (April 16, 1990): 1–2.

10 *Sales Promotion to Consumers*

Sales Promotion: An Overview

Sales Promotion and the Promotional Mix
The Growth of Sales Promotion
Drawbacks of Sales Promotion

Planning a Sales Promotion

Assessing the Environment
Developing Objectives
Selecting Appropriate Strategies

Techniques of Consumer Promotions

Price Deals
Contests and Sweepstakes
Event Sponsorship
Premium Offers
Continuity Programs
Consumer Sampling

Managing Consumer Sales Promotions

Consider This:

Miller's New Pitch

Coming up with a new beer promotion must be difficult, especially if your client is a giant like Miller Brewing Company. Miller has come out with new products like Miller Lite and Genuine Draft, it sponsors sporting events and concerts, it shows plenty of beautiful women and guys having fun in its commercials. So what can an agency like William A. Robinson Inc. offer Miller to perk up its sales and perhaps inch closer to rival Anheuser-Busch?

Robinson's answer? Play Ball! Miller likes to pitch its products, especially its light beer, as part of an active, fun-loving lifestyle. Miller people, one can assume, play a lot of softball in the summer, and after the game, along with a few Millers, they probably consume a fair amount of pizza. So Robinson put the three interests together and, with help from Pizza Hut, came up with the "Pizza Hut 3rd Base Club" promotion.

Through in-store offers and a direct mailing—paid for by Pizza Hut—Miller distributed 120,000 "season passes" to Chicago-area softball players. With the pass and the purchase of a medium pizza, players can get up to four more pizzas for about half price. Teams also get a pitcher with the Miller Lite and 3rd Base Club logos.

According to William A. Robinson, the promotion worked for both partners. Pizza Hut liked the idea well enough that it was willing to absorb the cost of the pizza discounts as well as of the mailings. The promotion increased its business in the late evening, after the games finished, traditionally a slow time for pizza sales. For its part, Miller gained an advantage with a big account, Pizza Hut, a major victory in the intense competition between beer makers. One effect of the promotion was that Miller Lite knocked its Bud Lite rival out of a number of Pizza Huts. Most Pizza Huts carry beers made by both companies, but not competing brands from each maker, so winning the battle of the lights is crucial. Miller was so pleased it was considering making its pitch in different leagues.

Source: Scott Hume, "Miller Gets on Base," *Advertising Age* (July 2, 1990): 23.

T he typical college student is a big user of sales promotion. College students buy clothes on sale, use coupons for fast food and dry cleaning, and, as we have seen, members of a softball team are likely to eat a Pizza Hut pizza and drink a Miller beer on occasion. The student is only one number away from winning the latest McDonald's game, and small samples of various products are scattered around the kitchen and bath.

The goal of this chapter is to introduce the second element of the promotion mix—sales promotion. The chapter outlines a framework for planning sales promotions and examines specific techniques of sales promotion targeted at consumers. Chapter 11 will discuss sales promotion targeted at salespeople and resellers.

Sales Promotion: An Overview

Thirty years ago, sales promotion was viewed as everything that is left over after one accounts for advertising, personal selling, and public relations. In the ensuing years, definitions were developed by looking at what sales promotion agencies (a recent institution) did. For example, one definition held that "sales promotion includes those activities which enhance and support mass selling and personal selling and which help compete and/or coordinate the entire promotional mix and make the marketing mix more effective."[1] This definition positions sales promotion as an ancillary element of the promotional strategy, less important than advertising and personal selling. This perspective is no longer valid. Today, sales promotion and advertising are equivalent and complementary promotional strategies. Although there are important differences, important similarities remain as well.

A better definition comes from the American Marketing Association: "Sales promotion is media and nonmedia marketing pressure applied for a predetermined, limited period of time in order to stimulate trial, increase consumer demand, or improve product quality."[2] Unfortunately, this definition does not capture all the elements of modern sales promotion. We noted a serviceable definition of sales promotion in Chapter 1: it is a marketing activity that adds to the basic value of the product for a limited time and directly stimulates consumer purchasing, seller effectiveness, or the effort of the sales force.

Three points provide the key to understanding sales promotion. First, sales promotion is just as important as advertising and requires the same careful planning and strategy development as other areas of marketing. Second, sales promotion may be targeted at three audiences: consumers, resellers, and the sales force. Finally, sales promotion is a competitive weapon that provides an extra incentive for the target audience to buy or support one brand rather than another. It is this extra motivation to purchase or continue support that distinguishes sales promotion from the other three promotional mix tactics. Unplanned purchases, for example, can be directly traced back to one or more sales promotion offers. Sales promotion is based on the premise that each brand or service has an established perceived price or value, and that sales promotion changes this accepted price-value relationship by increasing the value, lowering the price, or both.

Sales Promotion and the Promotional Mix

The differences between sales promotion and other components of the promotion or marketing mix are important in understanding both the basic role of sales promotion and how to use it effectively. Table 10.1 lists key differences among sales promotion and advertising, public relations, and personal selling. In brief, sales promotion tends to operate on a short time frame, employs a more rational appeal, provides tangible, or real, value, is intended to create an immediate sale, and makes a high contribution to profitability. Table 10.1 reflects a synthesis of the research and options on sales promotion to date. There are, of course, exceptions to many of these labels. One could argue, for example, that a sales promotion technique such as a sweepstakes might use a very emotional appeal, while a business-to-business ad might prove quite rational. In general, however, the labels noted have proven accurate. "Contribution to profitability" may also be confusing. It is simply the ratio between what is spent on a promotional mix compared to the direct profitability generated by that expenditure. Again, there are exceptions.

Table 10.1   A Comparison of Sales Promotion with Other Promotion Mix Elements

	Advertising	Sales Promotion	Public Relations	Personal Selling
Time frame	long term	short term	long term	short/long term
Primary appeal	emotional	rational	emotional	rational
Primary objective	image/brand position	sale	goodwill	sale/relationship
Contribution to profitability	moderate	high	low	high

These distinctions among the elements of the promotional mix become somewhat blurred because sales promotion is often used jointly with other promotional techniques. For example, sales promotion offers (for example, coupons, rebates, contests) are often delivered through a direct-action ad. Price deals may be presented by members of the sales force, and a public relations department may have partial responsibility for managing a contest. The synergy provided when sales promotion is combined with these other promotion elements is its real strength.

The Growth of Sales Promotion

Sales promotion has grown substantially in recent years. Donnelley Marketing estimates that spending on sales promotion hit $135 billion in 1989.[4] This amount is greater than the amount spent on media billing. More promotion dollars are being spent on sales promotion than on advertising (roughly 65 percent versus 35 percent). Sales promotion is growing at a 9 percent annual rate while the growth rate for advertising is approximately 6 percent. Much of this growth in sales promotion reflects the continuing popularity of couponing, which is used by over 93 percent of all the companies surveyed.

There are several reasons for this dramatic growth in sales promotion. The stimulation has come from both consumers and business.

Consumer Acceptance of Sales Promotion   There are inherent reasons why consumers should be amenable to sales promotion. Sales promotion offers consumers the opportunity to get more than they thought possible. From the consumer's perspective, sales promotion also reduces the risk associated with buying. Product sampling, for example, allows consumers to try the product without buying it. Furthermore, many people are reluctant decision makers who need some incentive to make choices. Sales promotion gives them the extra nudge they need in order to become active customers. An extra discount or a rebate may mean the consumer is now ready to buy that new Miata.

Finally, sales promotion offers have become an integral part of the buying process, and consumers have learned to expect them. According to a recent survey of five hundred shoppers sponsored by the Promotion Marketing Association of America,

- 98 percent used at least one coupon on a purchase in the previous six months, 54 percent used rebates, 26 percent used sweepstakes, and 17 percent used premiums;
- Eight of ten people surveyed said they regularly check newspaper ads for coupons, and nearly half said they also look for the other three types of promotional offers;

- 70 percent said they bought a new product because of a coupon offer, 40 percent because of a premium offer, 20 percent because of a sweepstakes offer, and 38 percent because of a rebate;

- 75 percent said they switched to another brand because of a coupon offer, 50 percent switched because of a rebate, 40 percent switched because of a premium, and 20 percent switched because of a sweepstakes offer. (Products particularly susceptible to brand switching were batteries, coffee, personal appliances, shampoo, and toothpaste.)[5]

Business Acceptance of Sales Promotion　For the most part, the evolution of sales promotion has been stimulated by business, especially big business. The needs and wants of the product manager serve as the initial impetus. Product managers find it extremely difficult to differentiate their product in a real way from that of competitors, because each buyer has so many choices among brands and among different types of products that provide the same sort of satisfaction. A product manager faced with the challenge of differentiating his or her brand usually develops sales promotion techniques. When these techniques prove to be effective, they attract the attention and support of top management.

Top managers have also played a more direct role in encouraging the recent growth of sales promotion. Heads of companies today focus more and more on short-term results. They want to get sales tomorrow, not next quarter or next year. Sales promotion can provide an immediate boost in sales. Manufacturers have learned to pump new life, albeit short lived, into ailing brands by dropping coupons in the mail. This technique may erode brand loyalty since competitors offer coupons as well, but it does speed up the move to economies of scale in production. Simply stated, the concept of economies of scale means that the greater the number of units produced, the lower the price per unit. Sales promotion has the potential to drive the cost of a product down to a point where the savings more than cover the profit margins lost through the sales promotion costs. More importantly, sales promotion may also eliminate competitors unable to achieve these same savings.

New technology, especially the computer, has also created greater acceptance of sales promotion by managers wanting to measure results. For example, scanning equipment in retail stores enables manufacturers to get rapid feedback on the results of promotions. Redemption rates for coupons or figures on sales volume can be obtained within days. Changes in sales promotion can then be made as needed.

The use of sales promotion has also been stimulated by several factors that have made advertising more difficult. For example, industry groups and regulators have made it more difficult for advertisers to clearly set their products apart by requiring that their claims be substantiated in ever-greater detail. Another problem is the high cost of mass media advertising. Rates for network television are escalating while the networks' share of prime time audiences has dropped to under 70 percent. As a result, advertisers are exploring new media forms, especially sales promotion.

The growing power of retailers has also spurred the use of sales promotion. Historically, the manufacturer was the most powerful member of the channel of distribution. Mass marketers used national advertising to talk directly to consumers, creating consumer "pull" that left stores with little choice but to stock the heavily advertised brands. As retailers have consolidated and gained access to sophisticated information by using computers and bar codes on packages, however, the balance of power is shifting in their favor. Retailers now want custom-designed programs that will help them complete and increase sales in their market area. Sales promotion is an effective and satisfying answer to this demand for account-specific marketing programs. Retailers, who typically work on very small profit margins, need the increased sales volume provided through sales promotion. They also benefit from the immediate feedback from sales promotion that limits the tendency to stay with an unsuccessful program too long. For example, PepsiCo., Inc. developed a sales promotion program for a Winn-Dixie store in Nashville—one product, in one category, in one city, for one retail chain.

Sales promotion is no longer the exclusive property of the fast food and package goods manufacturers. It now knows no boundaries. In financial services, Frankel & Co. provided "Visa Cards with our compliments" to clients; in the computer industry, Apple's small-business campaign included a free video and CD; and, among airlines, the concierge service offered by the Trump Shuttle was quite successful. However, sales promotion is far from perfect.

Drawbacks of Sales Promotion

While sales promotion is an effective strategy for creating immediate, short-term, positive results, it is not a cure for a bad product, bad advertising, or an inferior sales force. Although a consumer may use a coupon for the first purchase of a product, for example, the product itself must take over after that.

Unfortunately, sales promotion activities may bring several negative consequences, chiefly clutter from increased competitive promotions. Because new approaches are quickly copied by competitors, promotions try to be more creative, shout louder, or deliver ever-increasing discounts to get the attention of consumers and the trade.

Furthermore, consumers and resellers have learned how to take advantage of the sales promotion game. Most notably, consumers now wait to buy certain items, knowing that eventually they will be reduced in price. Resellers learned this strategy long ago and have become experts at negotiating deals and knowing how to manipulate competitors against one another.

As we discuss specific sales promotion techniques, we will examine other problems with their use. The most severe criticism leveled at sales promotion, however, is that it diminishes the value of the brand. It takes years to build positive equity in a brand. Brand equity is the positive trust, faith, and credibility associated with a particular brand. It is the reputation of the brand and the most precious facet of a product. Critics say that the move from product strategies to pricing strategies and from brand-building advertising to trade promotions and couponing has produced a consumer who views all products as commodities. "Saving a dollar becomes far more important to consumers than Grade A ingredients," notes Herbert Baum, president of Campbell USA.[6]

Despite its limitations, sales promotion is a viable promotion strategy. It has the ability to stimulate the consumer to action, an outcome that is difficult for advertising or public relations to achieve. When properly combined with the other marketing techniques, it produces important results. Its success, however, is contingent on how well sales promotion is planned.

Concept Review

1. Sales promotion is a marketing activity that adds to the basic value of the product for a limited time and directly stimulates consumer purchasing, seller effectiveness, or the efforts of the sales force.

2. Unlike the other elements of the promotional mix, sales promotion tends to operate on a short time frame, employs a more rational appeal, provides tangible value, is intended to create an immediate sale, and makes a high contribution to profitability.

3. Consumers have accepted sales promotion because
   a. They desire more value,
   b. Sales promotions reduce risk,
   c. Promotions stimulate decision making, and
   d. Promotions have become an expected part of the buying process.

4. Business has accepted sales promotion because
   a. It provides additional product differentiation through value-added components not offered by competitors,
   b. It offers short-term results, which top management has come to emphasize,
   c. Improved technology allows tracking of sales promotion,
   d. The effectiveness of advertising relative to sales promotion has dropped, and
   e. Retailers have gained in power.

Planning a Sales Promotion

Sales promotion should be included in a company's strategic promotional planning, along with advertising, personal selling, and public relations. But many sales promotion tools are short-run, tactical devices. Coupons, premiums, and contests, for example, are designed to produce immediate responses. Thus, managing sales promotion over the long run is particularly difficult.

The process of planning sales promotion techniques should begin with an assessment of the environment, followed by the establishment of goals and the selection of strategies. A separate budget should be set up for sales promotion, and management should evaluate the performance of sales promotions. Sales promotion is fortunate to have scanner technology, which does an excellent job of evaluating results. Budgeting and evaluation are examined in Chapters 16 and 17, but in this section we discuss the other steps in sales promotion planning.

Assessing the Environment

Many factors both inside and outside the organization determine whether sales promotion is warranted and, if so, which techniques would be effective. Some companies, such as Mercedes-Benz, have an internal policy that prohibits use of sales promotion devices. Entire professions, such as health care, feel it is denigrating to use sales promotion. Conversely, J. M. Smucker Co., maker of jams and jellies, found itself in a flat-growth market in which the consumer was inundated with competitors' price discounts and coupons. Research indicated that two distinct market segments existed: the "flavor segment" (which included all ages and all family sizes, especially higher-income households) and the "volume segment" (which included larger households of all incomes, with school-age children). Smucker developed two separate sales promotion campaigns. To appeal to the flavor segment, the company offered a holiday cookbook and rear-pack recipes (that is, several recipes attached to the back of the package) using Smucker variety flavors. The cookbook was distributed through take-one order blanks at the point of sale. For the volume segment, Smucker did a tie-in with the Disney movie *The Fox and the Hound*. The tie-in included a point-of-sale display highlighting the movie and offering a free with mail-in beverage mug featuring one of the movie characters, with purchase of a Smucker product. Both programs were a result of a careful assessment of their environment, and both were highly successful.

Developing Objectives

Following the environmental assessment is the development of specific objectives. The sales promotion statement of objectives requires a three-tiered format.

First, unique objectives apply to each of the target markets. Sales promotion is intended to *motivate* the sales force, *stimulate* the consumer, and *gain the cooperation* of resellers. That is, there are separate sales promotion objectives for the sales force, which must be motivated to sell harder, emphasize a certain brand, or use a certain set of selling tools. Resellers must also be willing to buy into the company's marketing strategy, which begins with stocking the product, setting up displays, accepting coupons, and so forth.

Second, sales promotion has a series of strategic objectives that tend to be either proactive or reactive. Of the proactive, long-range objectives, four are most common: (1) to create additional revenue or market share, (2) to enlarge the target market, (3) to create a positive experience with the product, and (4) to enhance product value and brand equity. American Express did an excellent job accomplishing the last objective. On its thirtieth anniversary, the company mailed a handsome, specially developed and printed coffee-table book entitled *Theater in America* to a group of its best customers. The letter that accompanied the book simply said, "Thank you for being one of our best customers over the years." There was no sales pitch, no discount offer, and not even a suggestion to go out and use the card or the services. The number of companies that employ long-range objectives are few in number. As a result, the true potential of sales promotion has not been realized by many promotion planners.

Reactive objectives are responses to a negative or short-term situation. Examples of reactive objectives are (1) to match competition, (2) to move inventory, (3) to generate cash, and (4) to go out of business. Because negative situations may emerge with little warning, management is often unable to anticipate and plan. The resulting objectives often produce deleterious aftershocks. Because companies are trying to make the best out of a bad situation, sales promotion is viewed as a technique of last resort.

A third set of sales promotion objectives is tied directly to the specific sales promotion technique employed. They range from very subtle, hard-to-measure results such as increasing product value to direct, easy-to-measure results such as product purchase. For example, it's very difficult to determine how much the distribution of premiums contributes to customers' perceived value of the product. Several techniques have multiple objectives or objectives that must be accomplished sequentially. As we discuss specific sales promotion techniques in this chapter and the next, we will also describe their objectives.

Selecting Appropriate Strategies

The most difficult step in sales promotion management is to decide which sales promotion tools to use, how to combine them, and how to deliver them to the three target audiences. The choices are vast, and the combinations appear endless. Each tool has its own advantages and disadvantages, which may change when it is used with another technique or delivered through a different medium. Having a thorough understanding of the various sales promotion techniques is a necessary starting point. Some of the factors that influence the choice of sales promotion tools are as follows:

1. *The organization's promotional objectives.* If a company desires to create a dramatic positive change in the consumer's attitudes, sales promotion techniques such as premiums and samples that provide implicit, longer-term benefits are appropriate.

2. *The target market for the sales promotion.* The target market for the Radisson Hotel chain is the frequent business traveler. Extra services, frequent usage discounts, and sampling are sales promotion techniques that have worked in this market.

3. *The nature of the product, its competitive position, and its stage in the life cycle.* Gold'n Plump gourmet chicken parts is a new product with a great number of larger competitors. Couponing and product sampling may be the only way to get consumers to try this new product.

4. *The cost of the tool.* Product sampling is an extremely expensive sales promotion technique, especially if special packaging or labeling is required. Price discounting requires only inexpensive signage and re-marking the product.

5. *The current economic conditions.* When the economy is down, consumers tend to be motivated by tangible savings such as discounts, rebates, and coupons. Rewards such as premiums work better in a strong economy.

Combining various sales promotion tools is also part of the strategy. Sales promotion planners should consider three questions in particular when mixing sales promotions.

First, how will these tools be perceived by the three target audiences? For example, grocery retailers expect manufacturers to offer consumer coupons, displays, and price reductions; marketers unwilling to offer all three will not get shelf space. But a salesperson who has emphasized a "high price for high quality" appeal will be discredited if the company starts a discounting strategy. And consumers expect to find products that are highly promoted with discounts and coupons in certain types of stores— for example, supermarkets rather than gourmet shops.

Second, how should the various sales promotion tools be combined physically? Will they be designed as separate promotional devices? Or will they be designed as an **overlay,** that is, combined with other tools and delivered through the same vehicle (see Figure 10.1)? Will the tool be combined with a product of another noncompeting marketer? This is a **tie-in** and allows the marketer to take advantage of the brand strength of another

company. Kingsford Charcoal has done a tie-in with Armour Hot Dogs for several years—buy a bag of charcoal and a package of hot dogs and save one dollar.

Third, can or should sales promotion be integrated with other elements of the promotional strategy? A coupon is often part of an existing advertising campaign and has the capability of stimulating recall of an old campaign. The ad for Titralac Antacid demonstrates how an ad is combined with a free mail-in certificate.

A final decision in selecting the strategy—besides choosing the tools and the ways of combining them—is choosing the type of media to use in delivering the promotion. Coupons are typically delivered through print media such as newspapers, magazines, and direct mail or through freestanding inserts (FSIs). An FSI is a separate set of pages carrying coupons that is inserted in newspapers. Contests and sweepstakes are often more exciting if they are announced on television rather than in print. Product sampling can be done through some magazines, although many magazines are not equipped to carry samples. More will be said about media in Chapters 13 and 14.

Concept Review
The sales promotion planning process includes the following steps:
1. Assess the environment
2. Develop objectives
3. Select appropriate strategies
    a. Select sales promotion tools
    b. Decide how to combine tools
    c. Decide how to deliver the sales promotions

Techniques of Consumer Promotions

Consumer sales promotions are directed at the ultimate users of the product. Typically, the subjects of these promotions are products used by individuals, especially the products in the local supermarket. The same techniques are also used to promote products sold by one business to another, such as computer systems, communication networks, automobile fleets, cleaning supplies, and machinery. In contrast, **trade sales promotions** are targeted at resellers, that is, wholesalers and retailers, that carry the marketer's product. In this chapter, we examine sales promotions directed at consumers. Chapter 11 discusses sales promotions directed at the sales force and the trade.

The primary strengths of consumer sales promotions are variety, flexibility, and motivation to action. Many techniques can be combined to meet almost any objective of the sales promotion planner. Any target market can be reached through some type of sales promotion. This flexibility means that sales promotion can be employed by all kinds of businesses, small and large, those selling goods or services, those that are for profit or nonprofit. Finally, sales promotion causes people to act in a predictable manner. The following sections describe some of the key techniques in the arsenal of varied consumer-oriented sales promotions.

Price Deals

A consumer **price deal** saves the customer money when he or she purchases the product. The price deal is designed to encourage trial use of a new product or line extension, to induce new users to try a mature product, or to persuade existing customers to continue to purchase, increase their purchases, accelerate their use, or purchase multiple units of an existing brand. Price deals work best when price is the primary criterion considered by the consumer and when brand loyalty is low. When brand loyalty is high, deals are unlikely to overcome the consumer's perception that his or her preferred brand offers advantages. There are four principal types of consumer price deals: price discounts, price pack deals, refunds (rebates), and coupons.

Price Discounts   Customers learn about **price discounts,** or **cents-off deals,** either at the point of sale or through advertising. At the point of sale, the price reduction might be listed on the package or on signs near the product or in storefront windows. Advertising that notifies consumers of upcoming discounts includes fliers, newspaper and television ads, and so forth. Price discounts are particularly prevalent in the food industry, where local supermarkets run weekly specials.

The manufacturer, the retailer, or the distributor may initiate the price discount. The manufacturer may "preprice" the product and then convince the retailer to cooperate on this temporary discount. Extra incentives may be offered in order to gain the retailer's cooperation. To be effective, national price reduction strategies require the support of all distributors. The many packages you have seen in the supermarket on which the manufacturer's price is covered by the retailer's price serve witness to the power of retailers. Retailers may initiate price discounts for a number of reasons. For example, they might reduce the price of a particularly popular item in order to increase store traffic. They may have overbought a particular item and need to eliminate it from their inventory. Or severe discounting may be the only way to sell the product either as the result of severe discounting by competitors or simply because the product is not selling and must be moved off the shelves.

Determining how much of a discount to offer is difficult. Experts recommend at least 15 percent to 20 percent off the regular price, but the exact amount may differ across product categories. Pretesting various amounts is necessary.

For existing customers, discounts are perceived as a reward and may cause them to buy in larger quantities. But price discounts by themselves usually will not induce people to buy a product for the first time. Other information must be provided through mass media or product sampling.

The primary advantages of price discounts are ease of implementation and flexibility. Such changes are quickly made—just a few strokes with a marker and the retailer can respond to the price discounts made by competitors. In department stores, where scanner tags are now the norm, clipping old tags and replacing them with new ones can be done quickly. In addition, the increased volume produced by a discount may generate more profitability than the higher original price, because of economies of scale; in other words, the marginal cost is lower for each additional unit sold.[7] Yet another advantage of price discounts is the attention they arouse and their effect on decisions at the point of purchase. Experts estimate that anywhere from 30 percent to 60 percent of purchase decisions are unplanned. A price discount may play a major role in prompting people to buy when they did not expect to.

The disadvantages of price discounts are substantial, as the Promotion in Focus section illustrates. First, competitors can easily combat the discounts. Thus there is always the danger of triggering a price war in which no one benefits. Second, discounting causes constant short-term brand switching, which makes sales forecasting, product planning, and the measurement of objectives very hard. Third, the effectiveness of price discounts depends on making the offer very visible. If the consumer cannot see the new price, the program will fail. Finally, many consumers perceive a strong relationship between price and quality. Therefore a reduction in price may make them suspicious about the quality of the item and they may reject the product.[8] As noted earlier, price discounting has been identified as a primary reason for the erosion of brand equity. Once the consumer doubts the price-quality relationship for a particular brand, trust in that brand diminishes.

Price Pack Deals A price pack deal may take the form of a bonus pack or a banded pack. When a **bonus pack** is offered, an additional quantity of the product is free when a standard size of the product is purchased at the regular price. This technique is commonly used in marketing cleaning products, food, and health and beauty aids. Examples include Ivory Dishwashing Liquid offering an extra three ounces, Chiclets offering two extra pieces of gum, and Prell Shampoo providing 30 percent more—for the same price as the regular-size package. A bonus pack rewards present users but has little appeal to users of competitive brands. Often this technique is used as a way of introducing a new large size. It is also a way to "load" customers up with the product.

Although the bonus pack can serve as the basis for a new promotional campaign, it has problems. The expense of designing and manufacturing the new packages can be high. Transporting the product and handling and shelving it at the retail level may be difficult. The manufacturer must have a good relationship with the retailer since these packs require more handling and shelf space than regular sizes.

When two or more units of a product are sold at a reduced price compared to the regular single-unit price, a **banded pack** offer is being made. Sometimes the products are physically banded together, as is the case with

Promotion
in Focus

The Lessons of the Soft Drink
Price Wars

The Cola Wars were one of the long-running business stories of the 1980s. Coke came out with new products, Pepsi paid stars like Michael Jackson millions to promote its products, and both ran ads that sniped at the other's products as well as promoting their own.

While slugging it out on TV screens, the two soft drink giants were also competing at the checkout line. They offered so many discounts and specials on their products that some customers began to think that 2-liter cola bottles always sell for 99 cents. The price wars were on, and consumers loved it.

Towards the end of the decade, however, the price competition began letting up, and analysts began to make sense of its effects. Bottlers were delighted when prices began inching up. Besides giving them a few cents more profit per bottle, the higher prices may mean that customers choose their soft drinks based on actual preference rather than price. Bottlers complained that during the price wars, many consumers lost their brand loyalty and just bought whatever was cheapest.

As was to be expected, the higher prices led consumers to make fewer purchases. While soft drink consumption grew at a 5 percent annual rate in the mid-1980s, that growth slowed in 1989, when prices began going back up. To try to attract more customers without lowering prices again, soft drink makers turned to different kinds of promotions, like Coke's 1990 MagiCan and 1991 music giveaway campaigns.

The effect of the end of the "wars" on smaller soft-drink companies wasn't immediately clear. A slowing of the overall soft drink market doesn't help anyone, but a general price increase gives all bottlers more room to maneuver. And some smaller soft drink makers hoped that bottlers would begin producing more alternatives to the big two as a way to increase their volume even while demand for Coke and Pepsi was flat.

Don't be surprised if you continue to see discounted soft drinks at your supermarket. Prices vary by region, and both Coke and Pepsi control only about half of their bottlers, so no one can simply order a nationwide price increase. For the future, it seems likely that the soft drink wars will continue to provide observers with insight into how the promotional mix and the laws of supply and demand operate.

Sources: Direct Excerpts from Patricia Winters, "Soft-Drink Price Wars Lose Fizz," *Advertising Age* (October 16, 1989): 38. "Coke Targets Youth Market with CD, Tape Promotion," *Marketing News* (April 29, 1991): 5.

toothbrush-and-toothpaste offers. In most cases, the products are simply offered in a two-for, three-for, or ten-for format. Or a smaller size of the product may be attached to the regular size.

The banded pack offers essentially the same advantages and disadvantages as the bonus pack. There is some evidence that if the deal is attractive enough, nonusers might be attracted to load up on the promoted product. But the offer of a banded pack must comply with FTC guidelines on deceptive pricing. According to these guidelines, when the offer refers to a "previous suggested price," the reduced price must be based on the average price charged for the product during the prior six months. This stipulation prevents businesses from raising the price just prior to the sale.

Refunds and Rebates A **refund** promotion is an offer by a marketer to give back a certain amount of money when the product is purchased alone or in combination with other products. Refunds are used to increase the quantity or frequency of purchase, to encourage customers to load up, to dampen competition by temporarily taking consumers out of the market, to stimulate purchase of postponable goods (for example, major appliances), and to create on-shelf excitement or encourage special displays. **Rebate,** a term made popular by the automobile industry, means the same thing as refund. Unlike price discounts, there is evidence that consumers look at refunds and rebates as a reward for purchase. This after-the-fact experience appears to build brand loyalty rather than diminish it.[9]

The key to a successful refund is to make it as uncomplicated and unrestricting as possible. Possible formats include a cash rebate plus a low-value coupon for the same product or other company product, a high-value coupon alone, or a coupon good toward the brand purchased plus several other brands in the manufacturer's line. Maxell Corp. developed an interesting combination by offering customers who bought two or more videocassettes either a five-dollar rebate on their cable bill or a free thirteen-week subscription to *TV Guide.*

An interesting aspect of refunds is *slippage:* some customers who respond to the refund offer by purchasing the product do not send for the refund. The rate of slippage varies with the value of the refund, the number of required proofs of purchase, and the method of advertising. The higher the slippage, the lower the cost to the marketer. A 1987 study, conducted by Jolson, Wiener and Rosecky, found the slippage rate to be 30 percent, ranging from 26 percent for "heavy" rebate users to 33 percent for "light" rebate users. Among the reasons people cited for not sending for the refund were that they forgot, they lost the forms, it was too costly in time and postage, and it would take too long to receive the refund.[10]

Although refunds tend to enhance brand loyalty, in that they provide a reward for continued purchase, and have a relatively low cost, particularly in light of high slippage, they bring distinct drawbacks. Most notably, a refund is a direct discount on the product. If it is not large enough to gain significant sales, it can seriously hurt profitability. Furthermore, refunds are often used by customers who would have purchased the brand anyhow. Finally, sales generated through refunds may not show up for a long time, because it takes a while for consumers to purchase the product and then return the refund card. To overcome this delay problem, some companies mail checklike refund certificates directly to consumers before purchase, so they can cash in the "check" when purchasing the product.

One company that represents a variety of marketers and is very much in favor of rebates is Donnelley Marketing, owner of the Carol Wright coupon program. Through a direct mailing (see Figure 10.2), they invite consumers to dial a 900 number to order rebates ranging from ten dollars to fifty dollars on product categories such as automotive supplies, consumer electronics, home office equipment, and kitchen appliances. Each call costs three dollars. Callers select a category of merchandise and hear rebate offers for brands in that category. The consumer is mailed personalized rebate certificates, which can then be mailed, along with proof of purchase, to the marketer.[11]

Coupons   In 1859, Grape-Nuts cereal created a new promotional technique by offering a 1-cent coupon. **Coupons** are legal certificates offered by manufacturers and retailers that grant specified savings on selected products when presented for redemption at the point of purchase. Manufacturers bear the cost of advertising and distributing their coupons, redeeming their face values, and paying retailers a handling fee. Retailers who offer double or triple the amount of the coupon bear the extra cost themselves. Retailers who offer their own coupons incur the total cost, including paying the face value of the coupon. Retail coupons are equivalent to a cents-off deal.

Coupons have an obvious attraction to consumers who are sensitive to

Figure 10.2

Carol Wright enables customers to order rebates by phone.
Courtesy of Donnelley Marketing, Inc.

price. They may also bring less tangible benefits. According to a study conducted by D'Arcy Masius Benton & Bowles, the typical coupon shopper is a middle-aged married working white woman who has a household income of twenty-nine thousand dollars and knocks six dollars off her weekly seventy-four-dollar grocery bill by using coupons. Among coupon clippers' greatest satisfactions is the belief that they are somehow beating the system. Others say using coupons relieves the boredom of shopping by creating a gamelike situation.[12]

Research has shown that the tendency to use coupons rises if consumers (1) need to tighten their budgets, (2) like to experiment with new products, or (3) often use products that are purchased at regular intervals throughout the year, such as breakfast cereals, coffee, and plastic garbage bags.[13] According to Donnelley Marketing, Spanish-speaking Americans form the market segment that is the highest user of coupons.[14] Customers least likely to use coupons are shoppers with strong brand loyalty or those who feel that the cost of clipping coupons is greater than the savings.[15]

Coupon Distribution   Manufacturers distribute their coupons in several ways. They may deliver them directly—by mail or dropped door to door or delivered to a central location such as a shopping mall. They may distribute them through the media—in magazines, newspapers, Sunday supplements, or freestanding inserts (FSI) in newspapers. They may insert a coupon into a package or attach it to or print it on the package. Coupons may also be distributed by a retailer, who uses them to generate store traffic or to tie in with a manufacturer's promotional tactic. Retailer-sponsored coupons are typically distributed through print advertising or at the point of sale. Occasionally, specialty retailers (for example, ice cream, electronics, restaurants) or newly opened retailers will distribute coupons door to door or through direct mail.

Recently, coupon distribution has been affected by two trends. The first is a shift away from distributing coupons in the media to delivering coupons in stores. This shift is the result of the increasing cost of media, including the insert fee charged for FSI, and the proliferation of coupons. Newspapers charge an insert fee to the advertiser for placing the FSI in the newspaper. This fee is in lieu of the space charge newspapers would receive if the ad were placed in the actual newspaper. A second trend is the growth of electronic coupons. The UPC bar-coded scanner automatically records a purchase and gives coupons redeemable on the next purchase. In a program sponsored by Catalina Marketing, for example, consumers earn instant coupons and accumulate frequent-shopper points toward prizes such as color televisions and luggage. And a joint venture of P&G, Donnelley Marketing, and Checkrobot Inc. is testing a system called VISSON; it includes a color monitor on the counter that displays a video praising the customers' savings.[16]

Coupon Costs   In 1990, the number of coupons distributed grew to 280 billion, a 5 percent increase from 1989. The increase from 1985 to 1986 had been 18 percent. Meanwhile, face values rose; between 1984 and 1988, the percentage of coupons with a face value of thirty cents or more doubled. The average face value of coupons redeemed in 1989 was forty-four cents.[17] Thus, even though growth in the number of coupons distributed has slowed, rising face values have increased the cost of sponsoring coupons.

In fact, the face value of a coupon is just part of its cost. Traditionally, retailers receive a handling fee of eight cents per coupon. (This fee may be changed by agreement with the retailers or their trade organizations.) In addition, the clearing-house or other organization that gathers the coupons, reimburses the retailer, and bills the manufacturer also makes a charge. Large companies, such as Donnelley Marketing, as well as small regional companies provide this coupon-clearing function. Although the cost varies tremendously, the rule of thumb is to include about four cents per coupon for this service.

Distributing the coupons also takes money. For example, the newspaper ad space may cost one thousand dollars, plus three hundred dollars for production of the ad. In contrast, the cost charged by the newspaper for inserting a freestanding insert is approximately seven dollars per thousand. Actually producing FSI-distributed coupons might cost as much as one hundred fifty dollars per thousand.

The next step in forecasting coupon costs is to estimate the redemption rate for the newspaper ad. If the newspaper's circulation is two hundred thousand, and a fairly typical 3 percent redemption rate is assumed, then approximately six thousand coupons will be redeemed ($200,000 \times 0.03$). The cost of the coupons so far is

6,000 coupons at a face value of 50 cents	$3000.00
8 cents per coupon to dealer for handling	480.00
4 cents per coupon for clearing-house costs	240.00
space in newspaper	1000.00
production cost	300.00
	$6020.00

In this case, the cost per coupon redeemed is not the fifty-cent face value but over one dollar each.

Misredemption   We should add one more cost: misredemption. *Misredemption* is paying the holder of the coupon the face value even though the product was not purchased. If misredemption is approximately 10 percent, only 5,400 coupons are actually being redeemed for the product (100% − 10% = 90% × 6000 = 5400). Misredemption increases the cost per coupon to $1.11.

Misredemption often occurs when a coupon is mistakenly redeemed even though the appropriate product was not purchased, usually because the check-out clerk is not careful. Better clerk training is an effective cure. The Food Marketing Institute, in *Guidelines of Hard-to-Handle Coupons,* also suggests some specific do's and don'ts, including a recommended size for coupons—6 inches long, with tolerance to 3 inches, by 2 1/2 inches in width, with tolerance to 2 1/16 inches.[18]

Misredemption can also be intentional. A store employee may knowingly redeem a coupon for a product not purchased, or a forged coupon may be redeemed for a product that has no coupon program. Many manufacturers attempt to curtail intentional misredemption by checking product inventory and invoices against coupons submitted. It is estimated that 10 percent to 15 percent of all coupons redeemed are misredeemed.[19]

Are Coupons Effective? Are coupons worth their high cost? For the manufacturer, coupons help meet a variety of objectives. An excellent study of couponing found that coupons have the ability to attract new triers, attract brand switchers, increase category consumption, maintain or enhance repeat purchase rates, defend market share, gain in-store promotional support, motivate the sales force, reinforce or enhance print media advertising, and gain trial for another product.[20] Considering both conceptual and empirical support, the best established roles for couponing are for attracting new triers and brand switchers.

When manufacturers use coupons, they can control when the offer is run; thus couponing allows optimum coordination with other promotional activities. Furthermore, non–price-sensitive consumers continue to pay the full price for the product.

Any manager contemplating the use of coupons, however, must weigh their advantages against their cost, including the cost of misredemption and fraud, a very expensive problem and one that is difficult to control. A second problem is coupon clutter, which may account in part for declining redemption rates. Although 98 percent of households save coupons, a recent tally found that they had redeemed only 3.5 percent of them.

To cut through coupon clutter, manufacturers have devised several ways to differentiate their coupons. One is to combine coupons with other offers such as contests. The "buy one, get one free" offer is sometimes used as part of a coupon. Other innovations include the *cross-ruff coupon,* which is a coupon on one product that is packaged with or printed on the package of another, usually complementary product. Diet Coke cans recently carried one-dollar-off and three-dollar-off coupons for regional amusement parks. An offshoot of the cross-ruff coupons are those printed on the back of a sales receipt, often for nearby businesses. *Self-destruct coupons* are printed in an overlap fashion; using one destroys the other. The fact that the redemption rate has not increased suggests that these techniques are not very effective. This lack of increase is particularly discouraging in light of the high costs associated with couponing.

Contests and Sweepstakes

Historically, there has been a great deal of confusion about the two terms contests and sweepstakes. Stated simply, a *contest* requires the entrant, in order to be deemed a winner, to perform some task (for example, draw a picture, write a poem) that is then judged. This is referred to as a contest of skill. A *sweepstake* is a random drawing, which may or may not require a consideration such as buying a ticket or purchasing a product. Sweepstakes are sometimes called chance contests. A contest requires a judging process; a sweepstake does not. The use of sweepstakes has grown dramatically in recent decades, thanks largely to changes in the legal distinctions that determine what is or is not a lottery. Before these changes, being associated with a lottery carried negative stereotypes of gamblers or organized crime. A *lottery* is a promotion that involves the awarding of a prize on the basis of chance with a consideration required for entry. In a sales promotion, the consideration is the box top or other purchase token asked for by the advertiser. For many years, advertisers employed contests, thus eliminating the element of chance and removing the lottery stigma. The familiar "twenty-five words or less" contest and many other similar devices were common. However, liberalization of legal interpretations, including the ability to ask for a sales receipt as proof of purchase, made sweepstakes feasible.

In addition to legal changes, concern for costs encouraged a switch to sweepstakes. Judging and processing contests are expensive procedures. Administering a contest costs about $350 per thousand entries. But the cost of processing a sweepstakes has recently ranged from just $2.75 to $3.75 per thousand. In addition, the level of participation in contests is very low. As a result, contests have largely yielded to sweepstakes.

Today, contests require participants to compete for a prize or prizes based on some sort of skill or ability. Sweepstakes require only that participants submit their names for a drawing or another type of chance selection. Although the figures are sketchy, it is estimated that $87 million was spent on contests and sweepstakes in 1977, and $175 million in 1989. Fewer than 20 percent of all households have ever entered a contest or sweepstakes.

There are many criticisms leveled at the use of contests and sweepstakes. Most notably, designing an effective contest or sweepstake is costly, and selecting appropriate prizes is particularly difficult. The prize must be attractive to the consumer, yet it must not overshadow the product. The relative attractiveness of cash, merchandise, or travel as a prize often depends on the particular market segment targeted. The media strategy employed to communicate the contest may also be complex and costly. Retailers may resent their participation. Also, critics suggest that contests generate more ill will than goodwill. Losers may become opinion leaders against the company. Another criticism is that great care must be taken to meet the letter of the law in designing contests. For example, all prizes must be awarded. There is also the possibility that a sweepstake may be used deceptively to sell real estate, water softeners, and aluminum siding. Time-share developers require winners to go through a tour and a hard sell by a salesperson in order to collect prizes.

A final criticism concerns the effectiveness of contests. It is difficult to know what level of sales increase is generated by the contest or sweepstake. More importantly, determining whether these customers are new or existing purchasers and whether they will remain customers are important yet unanswered questions. Contests and sweepstakes are not very effective in developing trial users or attracting new ones. This fact is borne out by a recent tie-in promotion among McDonald's Corp.; Holiday Inns, Inc.; Coca-Cola Enterprises, Inc.; Disneyland; and Sears, Roebuck and Co. using a Scrabble game format. To quote one executive, "From an awareness standpoint, it was extremely successful. But we were hoping it would generate more instant traffic than it did. There was a lot of disappointment among the dealers."[21]

The arguments in favor of contests are also convincing. The primary argument is that contests and sweepstakes generate mass interest and excitement—entries may number in the millions—as well as real enthusiasm among customers and employees. The Bud Bowl sweepstakes, run during the NFL play-offs and the Super Bowl, has continued to create positive results since its inception in 1988. Contests also provide something new for the company to advertise. Contest copy is generally easy to write because it is supported by lots of background enthusiasm and excitement. Contests appeal to the consumer's desire to play, to compete, to win, and to get a prize. The impact tends to be positive.

A good contest has the ability to gain a high degree of consumer involvement, revive lagging sales, help obtain on-floor displays, furnish merchandising excitement for dealers and salespeople, give vitality and a theme to advertising, add interest to an ad, and create enthusiasm for a low-interest product.

Event Sponsorship

According to events consulting expert International Events Group (IEG), companies spend over two billion dollars annually associating their products with everything from jazz festivals to golf tournaments to stock car races. In fact, companies like RJR Nabisco, Inc. and Anheuser-Busch have separate divisions or departments that handle nothing but special events.

One of the world's largest agencies, Saatchi & Saatchi DFS Compton, has a group called HMG Sports that manages sports events, including the Olympics, a ski tour for Sanka and Post Cereals, a bass-fishing contest for Hardee's, and a worldwide yacht-racing event for Beefeater's Gin.[22] Event management is often part of the responsibility of public relations and will be discussed again in Chapter 12.

There are several good reasons why so many marketers have jumped on the special events bandwagon. First, events tend to attract a homogeneous audience that is very appreciative of the sponsors of the events. Therefore, if a product fits with the event, the impact of the sales promotion dollars will be quite high. Lalique Crystal should not sponsor a tractor pull but Marlboro should. Second, events sponsorship may build support from trade and from employees. Those employees who manage the event may receive recognition and even awards. Few things are more appealing to the president of Kemper Insurance than presenting a $300,000 check to the winner of the Kemper Open on national television. Finally, compared to producing a series of ads, event management is simple. Many elements of events are now prepackaged. An organization such as MCI Communications Corp. can use the same group of people to manage many events. It can use booths, displays, premiums, and ads repeatedly by simply changing names, places, and dates.

Event sponsorship does have two pitfalls. The first is a poor match between the event and the company. For example, through trial and error, cigarette manufacturers Philip Morris Tobacco and RJR Nabisco, Inc. learned to sponsor sports events that do not require particularly high degrees of physical fitness. They would not consider sponsoring running, track and field, or gymnastics competitions. Second, many uncontrollable factors can influence an event. Poor planning, poor weather, an unpopular winner, or bad losers can all destroy an event. Philip Morris has sponsored the Virginia Slims' World Championship professional tennis series for women since 1970. In 1990, pickets outside the tournament protested the cigarette company's involvement, and an attempt was made to replace the sponsor.

Premium Offers

A **premium** is a tangible reward received for performing a particular act, usually purchasing a product. The premium may be free; if not, the amount the consumer pays for it is well below market price. Getting an extra amount of a product is a premium, as is receiving the prize in a Cracker Jack box, a free glass with a purchase of detergent, or a free atlas with the purchase of Allstate Insurance. The premium industry generated over fifteen billion dollars in revenue in 1989, with an annual growth rate of nearly 83 percent. Consumer premiums represent approximately 45 percent of this total and trade premiums 55 percent.[23]

Companies usually choose premiums that tie in with their product or that appeal to their most obvious customers. Quaker Oats Co. recently gave away a package of aluminum foil with its Aunt Jemima pancake mix. Liggett & Myers offered pantyhose to Eve cigarette buyers. The many varieties of premiums fall into two general categories: direct premiums and mail premiums.

Direct Premiums Incentives that are given free with the purchase at the time of the purchase are called **direct premiums.** There is no confusion about money, mailing, clipping, chance, packaging, saving things, or tearing off box tops. Best of all, there is no waiting.

Four basic variations qualify as direct premiums. First, the truly direct premium provides an incentive given separately at the time of a product purchase. For example, when a man goes to the counter to pay for his new suit, he finds it comes with a direct premium—a hanging storage bag. Second, *in-packs* are inserted into the package at the factory. Planters Nuts, for example, included a nut dish inside its fancy nuts package. Third, *on-packs* are another form of factory pack that rides outside the package, firmly affixed to it by a plastic band, sleeve, or other device. A free toothbrush attached to Gleem toothpaste is an example. Fourth, *container premiums* reverse the idea of the in-pack, putting the product inside the premium. Maker's Mark, a high-quality bourbon maker, sells fancy decanters of its liquor at Christmas.

Other versions of the direct premium are traffic builders, door-openers, and referral premiums. The *traffic-builder* premium is an incentive (for example, the gift of a small kitchen utensil) to bring a prospect to a place of business. A *door-opener* premium is aimed at consumers in their homes or businesspeople in their offices. In the direct-selling field, door-opening favors are a staple device. Their use is a subtle foot in the door during house-to-house canvassing and sometimes a clincher when telephoning for an appointment. Door-openers serve similar purposes in many other industries. For example, a copier manufacturer offers a silver dollar to an executive who agrees to an office demonstration. The final category of premiums is based on *referrals* provided by the purchaser. Sellers get sales leads from satisfied customers and reward them with a premium for their assistance. For example, Massachusetts Mutual Life Insurance provides leather-bound address books for such leads.

Mail Premiums Unlike direct premiums, **mail premiums** require the customer to take some action in order to receive the premium through the mail. The *self-liquidator* is the primary type of mail premium. It was invented during the Depression of the 1930s, a time of enforced thrift.[24] Savings measured in pennies were important to the average consumer. And since promotion budgets were often tight, the idea of giving a premium that did not cost the advertiser anything was most attractive. The self-liquidator was the answer. It was called self-liquidating because the price the consumer paid for the premium was identical to the cost incurred by the advertiser (that is, the premium liquidated itself).

A self-liquidating premium is offered in return for one or more proofs of purchase and the payment of a charge that covers the cost of the item, handling, mailing, packaging, and taxes (if any). The premium represents a bargain, since the consumer cannot buy this item in the market at the same amount. Figure 10.3 gives an example. Self-liquidating premiums can be offered cooperatively by two companies. The major disadvantage of self-liquidating premiums to the consumer is the delay in receiving the premium.

The food industry is by far the largest single user of the self-liquidator; other heavy users of mail-in promotions are detergents and cleansers, toiletries, and beer, ale, and soft drinks. The self-liquidator uses extensive supermarket displays. Star-Kist Foods offered the consumer three choices for obtaining a Morris the cat T-shirt. The consumer could get the T-shirt free for thirty cat food labels, pay $2.75 plus ten labels, or pay $5 with no labels.

There are two other types of mail-in premiums. The first is the *coupon-plan* or *continuity-coupon* premium. The customer saves coupons or special labels attached to the product. Usually a catalog describes the prizes and the redemption process. *Free in-the-mail* premiums require the consumer to

Figure 10.3

An ad with a self-liquidating premium. Courtesy of Kellogg Company.

mail a request and proof of purchase to the advertiser. The merchandise need not be related to the advertised product. An example is U.S. Sprint's Caller's Plus program in which premiums are tied in with the amount of long-distance billing.

Using Premiums   Premiums may be used to attract customers to a particular store, to buy a particular product, or to stimulate the purchase of larger amounts of a product. Do premiums work? The objective of a premium is to make up the cost of a premium by increasing sales. In the fall of 1989, Kal, Inc., a Los Angeles–based vitamin maker, attached dinosaur-shaped pencil toppers to bottles of Dinosaurs children's vitamins. "We sold a year's worth in two and a half months," says director of marketing Gary Nelson.[25] Critics argue that premiums encourage buyers to keep switching brands and that poorly designed premiums can cause problems. Taco Bell hastily recalled three hundred thousand plastic sports bottles autographed by cyclist Greg LeMond after a report that a child had dismantled the bottle top and tried to swallow the mouthpiece.

In sum, marketers view premiums as a way of rewarding customers without cutting price. Premiums are considered a true value-added item and are replacing refunds and couponing. Premiums also often play a big role in frequent-shoppers or continuity programs that reward customers for repeat purchases.

Continuity Programs

The intent of a **continuity program** is to hold a brand user for a long time by offering ongoing incentives. Self-liquidating premiums are one-shot deals; continuity programs require consumers to keep saving something before they get the premium. Trading stamps, made popular in the 1950s and 1960s by companies such as S&H and Gold Bond, are an example. The customer usually got one stamp for every dime spent in a participating store. The stamp company provided a store where stamps could be redeemed for merchandise and a catalog that listed the number of books of stamps required for each item.

Today, airlines' frequent-flyer clubs and hotels' frequent-traveler plans as well as the Sears Discover credit program are examples of modern continuity programs. Most common when competing brands have reached parity, continuity programs provide differentiation. They are also effective in combating a new and threatening competitor by offering long-standing customers a reward for their loyalty. Maintaining brand loyalty through a continuous reward program is what a continuity program is all about. Retail-driven frequent-shopper plans concentrate on core customers to build store loyalty; manufacturer-sponsored programs generally encourage product loading and repeat purchase from any store.

The success of a continuity program depends on a thorough understanding of loyal customers and their motivation. What does the consumer value? How does the consumer make trade-offs? There is also a need to evaluate the benefits of maintaining loyalty versus the costs. There is a big difference between trying to motivate purchase of a six-hundred-dollar plane trip versus that of a forty-nine-cent can of soup. The reward for consistently flying Air West, for example, is an upgrade on one or more free flights. However, the costs may be high as well—inconvenient flying times, connecting flights, and so on. Consistently buying Campbell Soup in order to receive one free can of soup requires little effort from the consumer, and minimal rewards.

✈ *Consumer Sampling*

One of the keys to success for many marketers is getting the product into the hands of the consumer. In some cases, particularly if the product is new or is not a market leader, an effective strategy is **consumer sampling**—giving the product to the consumer either free or for a small fee. R. J. Reynolds Tobacco Co. recently did an extensive sampling of its More Lights 100s cigarettes. On the back of each pack was a coupon that read: If you are twenty-one years of age or older, clip this coupon from this two-sided, four-color insert and redeem it for a free pack of More Lights 100s cigarettes. Because of the extremely high costs of this technique, great care must be taken in employing it.

Some Basic Guidelines   The first rule of sampling is to use this technique only when the product virtually sells itself. That is, the product must possess benefits or features that are easily discerned by the consumer. Second, it is important to give the consumer enough of the product to accurately judge its quality. The use of trial sizes of the product dictate how much product they will receive.

Should the product be provided free or should a nominal charge be imposed? Giving the product away guarantees that the target market is sampled but does not ensure that the product will actually be used. Many samples are small, and the consumer easily discards them or puts them away for future use. In addition, some consumers view products that cost nothing as being worth nothing. The nominal fee helps defray the costs of this promotional technique. But any charge, no matter how small, works against the basic idea of sampling and may defeat the sampling operation. Pretesting sampling alternatives will help resolve this dilemma.

Products that are sampled tend to be low in price and have high turnover (for example, gum, detergents, deodorants). But more expensive products such as perfume, wines, and gourmet foods may also be sampled selectively with certain target markets. For example, Stonyfield Farms yogurt was taste-sampled in the grocery store. The consumer was also given a coupon toward the purchase of the product. Even service products can be effectively sampled. For example, health clubs have attracted members by offering free visits to the club to a select group of people.

Distribution Techniques There are several ways of distributing samples to consumers. The most popular is through the mail. However, the tremendous increase in postage costs, combined with packaging and bundling requirements, makes this method increasingly less attractive. An alternative is to use organizations that specialize in door-to-door distribution. For example, the commercial firm Welcome Wagon provides a hired hostess to call on newcomers to the community. After welcoming them and answering their questions, she leaves product samples or coupons good for samples from noncompeting manufacturers or retailers.

Door-to-door distribution is particularly attractive when the items are bulky or reputable distribution organizations exist. It permits selective sampling—certain neighborhoods, dwellings, and even people can be selected. Also, the product may simply be hung on the doorknob or delivered face to face.

Samples may also be distributed in conjunction with advertising. An ad may include a coupon that the consumer can mail in for the product, or an address may be mentioned in the body of an ad. A product can also be sampled directly through prime media using scratch-n-sniff cards and foil pouches. However, there are risks. Ken L Ration recently came under the scrutiny of *Consumer Reports* when the magazine reported that a scratch-n-sniff card promoting a new bacon-flavored dog food could not be smelled by dogs, just their owners. Using the media to distribute samples is costly. The cost of distributing samples through advertising may be high because of the cost of advertising space and the low response rate.

Products can also be sampled directly through the retailer, who simply sets up a display unit near the product or hires a person to give the product to consumers as they pass by. This technique helps build goodwill for the retailer and is effective in reaching the right consumers. On the other hand, retailers often resent the inconvenience and require high payments in order to cooperate. This technique might also create conflict with other brands sold by the retailer.

The final form of distribution deals with specialty types of sampling. For instance, several companies specialize in packing samples together and delivering the package to a homogeneous consumer group such as newlyweds, new parents, students, or tourists. Such packages may be delivered at hospitals, hotels, or student centers. Because many long-term product decisions are made when people are seventeen to nineteen years old, incoming college freshmen are often given packages of products or coupons. Selecting the appropriate products is critical.

An Evaluation   Numerous arguments support the view that sampling is a viable sales promotion device. Most notably, sampling appears to help marketers solve the increasingly difficult problem of getting consumers to notice their products, particularly a new one, when "speed of trial" is often the most important ingredient in the brand's success. This was certainly true when Nintendo was introduced. Over three thousand toy stores across the United States had display areas provided by Nintendo where kids could sample the product. However, sampling is also effective when an improved or superior brand enters an established category. (If the brand is not superior, sample triers will revert to their previous brand.) Sampling is also beneficial when mass advertising cannot demonstrate the product's benefits. Sometimes a product must be experienced in order to be appreciated (see Figure 10.4), as is particularly true for very technical products, services, and emotion-laden products. Samples can also be distributed in conjunction with other elements of the promotional mix, greatly improving the impact of the overall strategy. Pharmaceutical sales representatives, for example, use product sampling with physicians as an ongoing strategy. The job of the salesperson is made easier when the product is actually in the hands of the consumer. As a matter of fact, sampling may be the primary reason why a retailer selects one manufacturer's product over another. Finally, consumers like samples, especially when there is no risk.

The criticisms of sampling are also real. Sampling costs may be excessive when the overall results are considered. Measuring sampling effectiveness

Figure 10.4

Product sampling is one of the most effective ways products can break into the market. Courtesy of Green Mountain Coffee, Inc.

Create the
Ultimate Cup Of Coffee

Start with our Green Mountain Coffee Roasters Coffee. It's *freshly roasted* in small batches *just hours* (not weeks or months!) before we rush it to you. The difference in flavor is *extraordinary*. We guarantee it!

Call 1-800-223-6768 for a FREE $5 GIFT CERTIFICATE and a brochure of 50 delicious gourmet coffees or mail the coupon below.

G·R·E·E·N
MOUNTAIN
Coffee
33 Coffee Lane
Waterbury, VT 05676
1-800-223-6768

☐ Yes, please rush my FREE $5 certificate and catalog of all 50 gourmet coffees.

Name _____

Address _____

City _____

State _____ Zip _____

is difficult. Perhaps the most serious criticism is that marketers may be unable to determine precisely whether the product is appropriate for sampling. A sample will convince the consumer to go out and purchase the product only if the product is unique or of exceptional quality. Finally, sampling may create a negative image. For many people, sample products are synonymous with junk mail and are resented.

In summary, when sampling is used as part of a coordinated promotional campaign to introduce a new product or to expand the trial of a current one, the effect on initial trial and subsequent repurchase can be strong enough to defray sampling expense.

Concept Review

Consumer sales promotions are directed at the ultimate users of the product.

1. A price deal is a temporary reduction of price. It may be offered through the following:
   a. Price discounts or cents-off deals,
   b. Pack deals, either bonus packs or branded packs,
   c. Refunds and rebates, and
   d. Coupons, legal certificates offered by manufacturers and retailers that grant specified savings upon purchase.
2. Contests, sweepstakes, and lotteries can require skill, random chance, or a consideration in order to create excitement.
3. Event sponsorship allows marketers to create support among a homogeneous market segment.
4. Premium offers provide a tangible reward for purchasing the product.
5. Continuity programs tie the consumer to the company by offering ongoing incentives.
6. Consumer sampling offers trial sizes of a product either free or for a small price.

Managing Consumer Sales Promotions

In our discussion of specific sales promotion techniques, we have seen that they have many pitfalls. Promotion clutter and the tendency of promotions to diminish the value of the brand are two general drawbacks. Repeated use of price-related techniques may reduce the perceived value of the product. More specifically, consumer couponing is now so pervasive that some consumers will not buy the product unless it is couponed. Continued use of price-related sales promotions such as coupons may reduce the lowest acceptable price consumers will consider. Price-sensitive users may switch to another low-priced brand when the price reduction is not available. Furthermore, some sales promotion techniques may simply cause consumers to "forward buy"; thus the producers have merely "borrowed" future sales. Finally, some sales promotion techniques lend themselves to abuse. Misredemption of coupons in some form is likely. Theft of premiums may be a problem if the premiums are easily removed from a pack. Contests and sweepstakes are sometimes prematurely won by consumers who figure out a solution to the games.

In fact, as Figure 10.5 shows, the use of some of these sales promotion

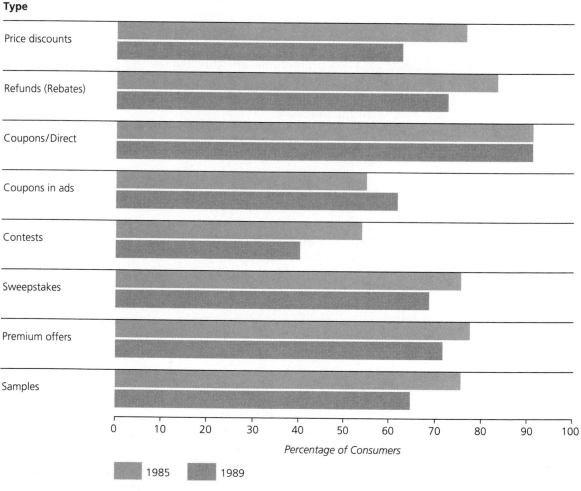

Figure 10.5

Comparison of consumers' response to sales promotion techniques in 1985 and 1989.

Used with the permission of Donnelley Marketing Twelfth Annual Survey of Promotional Practices for 1985, 1987, 1988, 1989.

techniques is declining. Nevertheless, 74 percent of companies in one recent survey used money-back offers, and 73 percent used premiums. In 1990, consumers saved almost $4.6 billion by redeeming coupons.[26]

Consumer-oriented sales promotions serve several specific objectives:

- to prompt trial by new users,
- to introduce new or improved products,
- to stimulate repeated use of the product,
- to encourage more frequent purchase or multiple purchases,
- to counter competitors' activities,
- to encourage trade-up in size or cost,
- to keep customers by providing an implied reward,
- to reinforce advertising or personal selling, and
- to stimulate trade support.

As we have seen, some techniques are better suited to meeting certain of these objectives than are others. Table 10.2 summarizes appropriate objectives for specific techniques.

Table 10.2 **Some Sales Promotion Techniques**

Technique	Objectives	Method of Distribution
A. Some consumer price deals		
Price discounts	Stimulate incremental and trial purchases, increase purchases per transaction	Point of purchase, mass media, cents-off label, bonus pack
Refunds (Rebates)	Stimulate trial purchases, encourage multiple purchases	Sales force, direct mail, mass media, in-pack or on-pack
Coupons	Stimulate trial purchases, increase frequency of purchases, encourage multiple purchases, motivate resellers, encourage consumer trade-up	Sales force, direct mail, newspapers, magazines, FSIs, in-pack or on-pack
B. Contests and Sweepstakes	Encourage multiple purchases, enhance brand image, create enthusiasm	Sales force, mass media, direct mail
C. Premium offers	Add value, encourage multiple purchases, stimulate trial purchases	Self-liquidator, in-pack or on-pack, point of purchase, proof of purchase
D. Continuity programs	Maintain consumer loyalty	Sales force, mass media, direct mail
E. Samples	Stimulate trial purchases, encourage consumer trade-up	In-pack or on-pack, direct mail, magazines, point of purchase

Planning consumer promotions so that techniques match objectives is the responsibility of the advertising campaign planner, the advertising department, and the advertising or sales promotion agency or staff sales promotion experts. Then sales promotion specialists either inside or outside the organization implement the plans.

Viewing consumer sales promotion as a strategic element of the promotion mix is quite recent. For many years, the term "on sale" and sales promotion were synonymous. Sales promotion was viewed as a negative alternative, implemented in a state of distress or desperation. All this has changed. Given the increased tendencies of consumers to want more value, the growth of consumer promotion is inevitable, and it requires the same careful planning and management as advertising. In later chapters on media, budgeting, and evaluation, more will be said about consumer sales promotion.

Concept Review

1. Consumer sales promotions are directed at the ultimate users of the product.
2. The objectives of consumer sales promotions include the following:
   a. To prompt trials by new users,
   b. To introduce new or improved products,
   c. To stimulate repeat use of the product,
   d. To encourage more frequent or multiple purchases,
   e. To counter competitor's activities,
   f. To encourage trade-up,
   g. To maintain present customers by providing an implied reward, and
   h. To reinforce advertising or personal selling.

Case 10   Wendy's Promotes to Kids

In 1989, Wendy's held a 10 percent share of the quick service hamburger restaurant market. Research indicated that Wendy's is perceived by consumers as the leader in product quality, menu variety, and atmosphere. However, the per unit growth in this fast food category has flattened out during the past two years. As a result, Wendy's has had to broaden its target audience to include families with children and become more promotion oriented in order to gain share from competitors.

In keeping with its image, Wendy's recently upgraded its Kids' Meal program to include better-quality premiums with good play value and began utilizing "borrowed interest" tie-ins with licensed properties to stimulate demand. Most restaurants now promote to children year round, with a major effort during the holiday season. The specific promotional objectives related to this program are as follows:

1. Increase sales and traffic versus figures from the same period during previous year,

2. Increase sales of gift certificates, which are generally redeemed in January or February,

3. Enhance Wendy's image among families with children under age twelve, and

4. Blunt the effects of competitive promotions targeted to children.

The Sales Promotion Offer

Wendy's has used virtually every type of sales promotion, concentrating on couponing, contests, and price discounts. Although these techniques appeared successful with adults, it was unlikely that they would work with children. Wendy's noted McDonald's success with tie-ins with Disney-type movies. After a thorough assessment of the pros and cons of such an arrangement, Wendy's management decided to do a tie-in with Don Bluth's movie *All Dogs Go to Heaven*, one of two major animated holiday movie releases targeted to families with children under age twelve.

The total promotional package was extensive. The primary ingredient was an exclusive offer to Wendy's customers of six high-quality PVC figurines featuring the key characters from the movie. There was an attempt to structure the promotion to maximize consumer participation and store profit by offering three ways to collect the premiums:

1. Included with each Kids' meal purchase,

2. Self-liquidated at ninety-nine cents with purchase of regular-size fries, and

3. Offered free with the purchase of five dollars' worth of gift certificates.

The promotion was to be supported with three weeks of strong network television ads beginning on November 20 with the release of the movie, plus a full array of in-store point-of-purchase material.

Franchisees were also encouraged to participate in additional promotional activities. Examples were coloring contests, costume appearances, movie theater slides, and theater tie-ins.

Wendy's feels the promotion was fairly successful. The results indicated that:

■ per store sales increased over sales during the same period in 1988,

■ Kids' Meal sales increased 100 percent during the first three weeks of the promotion, and

■ all premiums were sold through the system, leaving no costly inventory.

Case Questions

1. Was Wendy's employing offensive or defensive sales promotion techniques?

2. What were the primary risks associated with a tie-in such as Wendy's used?

3. Suggest three other types of sales promotion techniques that Wendy's might consider.

Summary

Sales promotion has become a primary part of the promotional strategy rather than a secondary element that is considered after the advertising is designed and paid for. Sales promotion is that something extra that is offered to the consumer. It may provide additional incentives to facilitate purchase.

The bulk of the chapter delineated sales promotions directed at consumers. Specific techniques include price deals (cents-off deals, price pack deals, refunds and rebates, and coupons); contests and sweepstakes; event sponsorship; premiums (direct and self-liquidating); continuity programs; and consumer sampling.

Ultimately, consumer sales promotions are short-term strategies that are not very effective in creating brand loyalty. Such tactics should be used with caution and integrated with the total marketing mix.

Discussion Questions

1. Define the term *sales promotion*. Cite some examples of how sales promotion can supplement or complement advertising and public relations.

2. What reasons can you provide for the existence of sales promotion? What is the main objective of sales promotion?

3. What do sales promotion and advertising have in common?

4. Describe the various price deals as well as the role they play in promotion. When should price deals receive emphasis?

5. Many marketers now utilize sweepstakes rather than contests. Why? Provide an example of each type of sales promotion technique.

6. Discuss the various kinds of premium offers. Under what circumstances would you select premiums over price deals?

7. Justify the following statement: "One of the keys to success for many marketers is getting the product into the hands of the consumer."

8. What is the attraction of special events? Explain.

9. Discuss the things that sales promotions can and cannot do.

10. What are the pros and cons of refunds and rebates?

Suggested Projects

1. Conduct interviews with ten consumers to get their views on price deals and coupons. Assess whether these opinions affect brand choice and retention.

2. Collect examples from magazines and newspapers of all the types of sales promotions discussed in this chapter. Determine the objectives. Assess how likely they are to reach these objectives.

References

1. John F. Luick and William L. Ziegler, *Sales Promotion and Modern Merchandising* (New York: McGraw-Hill, 1968): 11.

2. Committee on Definitions, *Marketing Definitions: A Glossary of Marketing Terms* (Chicago: American Marketing Association, 1988): 16.

3. Robert C. Blattberg and Scott A. Neslin, *Sales Promotion: Concepts, Methods, and Strategies* (Englewood Cliffs, NJ: Prentice-Hall, Inc., 1990). John A. Quelch, *Sales Promotion Management* (Englewood Cliffs, NJ: Prentice-Hall, Inc., 1989). Stan Rapp and Tom Collins, *Maxi Marketing* (New York: McGraw-Hill Book Co., 1987).

4. Russ Bowman, "Sales Promotion, Annual Report 1989: Growing Up and Out," *Marketing and Media Decisions* (July 1990): 20–21.

5. Russ Bowman, "Coupons Come of Age," *Marketing and Media Decisions* (February 1990): 74.

6. Laurie Freeman and Jennifer Lawrence, "Brand Building Gets New Life," *Advertising Age* (September 4, 1989): 3, 34.

7. Charles L. Hinkle, "The Strategy of Price Deals," *Harvard Business Review* 43 (July–August 1965): 71–79.

8. Don Schultz, "It's Time to Come Up with Strategies, Not Just Tactics," *Marketing News* (August 20, 1990): 11.

9. Louis J. Haugh, "Cash Refunds Multiply," *Advertising Age* (May 5, 1980): 48.

10. Haugh, 49.

11. Alison Fahey, "Rebate Program Rings Wright Bell," *Advertising Age* (May 21, 1990): 44.

12. Christine Stephenson, "SMU Professor Studies Psychology of Coupons," *Bryan-College Station Eagle* (April 25, 1990): 11. "Recession Feeds the Coupon Habit," *The Wall Street Journal* (February 20, 1991): B1.

13. Ira Teinowitz, "Coupons Gain Favor with U.S. Shoppers," *Advertising Age* 24 (November 14, 1988): 64.

14. "Hispanics Rank High on Coupon Redemption Scale," *Direct Marketing* (September 1988): 20–21.

15. Robert Schindler, "How Cents-Off Coupons Motivate the Consumer," from K. E. Jocz, ed., *Research on Sales Promotion: Collected Papers* (Cambridge, MA: Marketing Science Institute, 1984).

16. Jan Larson, "Farewell to Coupons," *American Demographics* (February 1990): 14–15.

17. Russ Bowman, "Coupons Come of Age."

18. *Ibid.*

19. Alison Fahey, "Coupon War Fallout," *Advertising Age* (September 4, 1989): 2.

20. Blattberg and Nelsin, 268–79.

21. Scott Hume, "Big Mac Lines Up Scrabble Players," *Advertising Age* 1 (March 13, 1989): 74.

22. Russ Bowman, "Sales Promotion: Strategic Sizzle," *Marketing and Media Decisions* (October 1989): 108.

23. *Incentive Marketing* (New York: Bell Communications, 1990).

24. Eileen Norris, "Everyone Will Grab a Chance to Win," *Advertising Age* (August 22, 1983): M10, 11.

25. Bradley Johnson, "Promo Recalls Mean New Sensitivity," *Advertising Age* (June 18, 1990): 76.

26. Russ Bowman, "Sales Promotion," *Marketing and Media Decisions* (July 1990): 20.

11

Sales Promotion to Salespeople and the Trade

Consider This:

The Dilemma of Trade Promotions

The power of retailers is increasing, and manufacturers are upset. Articles describing the present relationship between manufacturers of packaged goods and retailers use words like "hostage," "prisoner," and "addict." And no one has a quick and easy solution.

The change in power relationships has resulted from demographic and technological developments as well as from consolidation in the retail grocery business. Scanners mean that supermarkets have information on their side. The development of cable TV and the dwindling dominance of the Big 3 networks mean that manufacturers can no longer rely on big nationwide ad campaigns to sell their products. They must deal with an increasingly fragmented marketplace. Because people are ever more likely to make their purchasing decisions in the store, the importance of in-store promotions continues to grow, while brand loyalty dwindles. And the continuing consolidation of the food retailing business means that the surviving stores have more leverage. There are now only about half as many food stores as there were 25 years ago. The remaining stores are larger, but overall shelf space is increasing slowly, while a thousand new grocery-and-drug products come out each month.

All of these factors mean that if manufacturers want to sell their products, they need good retail shelf space. Increasingly, that means that manufacturers pay retailers "trade promotions," amounting to as much as $100 billion per year. Since relatively little of this money reaches the consumer in the form of price discounts, these promotions look very much like bribes. Manufacturers would love to eliminate these payoffs and use the money for other kinds of promotions, but at the moment they're caught in a bind. An individual manufacturer could simply stop paying retailers, but as long as other manufacturers continue the practice, the sole holdout would probably just lose shelf space and sales.

Ultimately, manufacturers are going to have to find a way to return to "pull marketing"—where customers' demand or "pull" dictates what stores carry—rather than the present system of "push marketing," in which customers to a large degree buy what retailers push at them. The return to pull marketing will require a resurgence of brand loyalty and the creation of clever ways to insure that both the retailer and the manufacturer benefit from a customer's preference for the manufacturer's brand. But at the moment, retailers are controlling the game, and most manufacturers are playing.

Sources: William C. Johnson, "Sales Promotion: It's Come Down to 'Push Marketing,'" *Marketing News* (February 29, 1988): 8. Keith M. Jones, "Held Hostage by the Trade?" *Advertising Age* (April 27, 1987): 18. Alvin A. Achenbaum and F. Kent Mitchel, "Pulling Away from Push Marketing," *Harvard Business Review* (May/June 1987): 38–40. Richard Edel, "Trade Price Discounts Holding Hostages," *Advertising Age* (February 6, 1986): 18, 20, 22.

W hile sales promotion directed at consumers is relatively recent, sales promotion targeted at the sales force and resellers has a long history. It is a very important competitive weapon for getting new products into stores, gaining shelf space, and motivating resellers and sales personnel. In fact, as noted in the opening vignette, among some retailers, the use of sales promotion has become so ingrained that manufacturers must offer sales promotions in order to survive. Many salespeople also expect sales promotion incentives to be offered on a regular basis.

Sales promotions targeted at the sales force and resellers are not well understood by individuals outside a particular industry, in part because of the proprietary nature of these activities. Companies do not readily share information about these programs with the outside world, nor is there a mechanism for gathering it. Because the time frame is quite short for designing and implementing these sales promotion programs, they often lack the polish and completeness found with consumer sales promotions. Still, the same planning process outlined in Chapter 10 applies not only to consumer sales promotions but also to promotions to the sales force and resellers.

Decisions regarding budgeting, using media, and measuring the effectiveness of these programs will be discussed in the chapters covering those topics. In this chapter, we provide an overview of the techniques used in sales promotions to the sales force and resellers.

Sales Force Sales Promotions

Sales promotion activities directed at the sales force are intended to motivate salespeople to increase overall sales. Short-term goals include securing new dealers, promoting sales of new or seasonal items, communicating special deals to retailers, increasing order size, and decreasing sales expense. In general, these activities build enthusiasm for the task at hand. Often, they are aimed as much at raising the morale of the sales force as at creating a sale. Enthusiastic salespeople usually work harder at supporting the marketing effort.

Diversity in the organization of the sales force complicates the task of designing a sales promotion. The sales force can be employees of the firm, a broker salesperson, or an independent sales representative. Building enthusiasm across all these possibilities is quite a challenge.

Sales promotion activities directed at the sales force are classified into two categories. The first consists of programs that prepare salespeople to do their jobs. These supportive programs include sales manuals, training programs, and sales presentations as well as films, slides, and other visual aids. The second set of activities consists of promotional efforts that motivate salespeople to work harder.

Supportive Programs

Training the sales force is usually the job of the sales manager. However, in some firms, the sales promotion staff trains and equips salespeople and designs their sales presentation. This is primarily because of the special expertise required to design such programs. Thus, depending on the company, the sales promotion staff is involved to varying degrees in the development of sales meetings and supportive materials. Such activities tend to be a minor part of a sales promotion manager's responsibility.

The Sales Meeting   One of the most common and popular ways of educating the sales force is the *sales meeting*. It can bring together a local or an international sales force, but national meetings are the norm. The meetings mix business and pleasure in varying proportions. Often local and regional meetings emphasize business, and the national meetings focus on educational and social events. Although social elements are important and can be effective motivators, training and educational elements tend to be more meaningful.

Sales meetings should be designed to meet the objectives of the participants. For relatively new salespeople, the meetings might emphasize product training and sales skills. For more experienced salespeople, the subject might be motivation. In either case, the meeting must be customized to the audience. Every detail should be settled before the meeting begins. It is important that the participants understand the extent to which each meeting is to be devoted to business rather than pleasure. The quantity and quality of sales meetings tend to be strongly affected by economic factors.

Supportive Materials   The training of a sales force also requires *supportive materials* that provide information to the salesperson or that can be used in the sales presentation. These materials include sales manuals, portfolios, and models.

The material most useful to the salesperson is usually the sales manual, because it contains both product information and elements of a sales presentation. The sales promotion staff often has a large role in designing the manual. In the case of technical companies with extensive product lines, the sales manual might be several volumes long. It usually contains product descriptions, prices, manufacturing processes, delivery times, product applications, and suggested sales techniques. The sales manual is as important to the salesperson as a playbook is to a professional football player. Because much of the information is confidential and the salesperson may make extensive notes in the manual, it is guarded closely.

Sales portfolios and *product models* are devices that are used in conjunction with the sales presentation to illustrate and highlight key points. Again, sales promotion expertise is employed to develop and design these materials. The portfolio can take many forms: for example, a flip chart, a ring binder, slides, photographs, or transparencies. If a product cannot be demonstrated effectively with a model, slides or a movie might be substituted. A prototype or scale model might work well for small equipment but look like a ridiculous toy for a three-story overhead crane.

There are also materials that the sales force receives on a somewhat regular basis. One example is the *house organ*, also known as the company newsletter, newspaper, or magazine. It relays to the personnel company programs, policies, new products, meetings, awards, and retirements. Large companies may develop special bulletins just for the sales force. These bulletins may highlight certain products, meetings, or people. An example of an in-house publication is shown in Figure 11.1. These types

Figure 11.1

An example of an in-house publication.
Courtesy of General Mills, Inc.

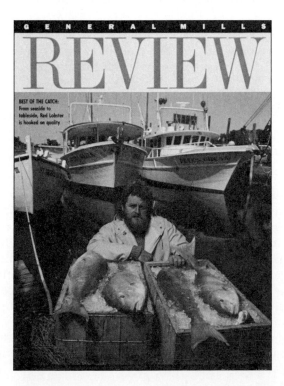

of communications can be helpful in keeping the salesperson informed and in motivating the entire sales force.

Motivational Programs

Prizes or awards to salespeople form the core of incentive programs. It is not difficult to understand why these programs are a popular tool for improving sales performance. The sales force of any company represents a more or less captive audience—the salespeople can be reached and their responses can be measured quite easily. Thus salespeople offer an ideal target for a stimulus to add profitable sales.

Developing incentive programs for the sales force is the domain of the sales promotion department. Affiliated Paper Company of Tuscaloosa, Alabama, for example, offers as its primary incentive world-class travel—ranging from a trip to Disney World, to an African safari, to a trip around the world. Although the actual design of the sales incentive programs may be the job of sales promotion experts, the strategic direction typically begins with the director of marketing. This person determines the role of personal selling in the marketing strategy, which includes how salespeople will be motivated. Motivation of the sales force per se then becomes the responsibility of the national and regional sales managers. Designing a good incentive program requires several steps.

Selecting Objectives   The first step is to determine the objectives of the incentive program. Specific objectives are as individual as the sales manager's name, but common objectives include the following:

- Introduce a product to a new distribution area,
- Reduce selling costs,
- Improve working habits,
- Offset competitive promotions, and
- Increase total sales volume.

A large mobile-home manufacturer in Kentucky combines two of these objectives—reduction of selling costs and increase in total sales. The Kingston Mobile Home Company had a national sales force consisting of sixteen men and women who called on mobile-home dealers throughout the United States. In order to reach their goal of reducing sales costs by 25 percent, salespeople were offered a cash bonus of fifteen hundred dollars. Those who reduced sales costs by 30 percent received the bonus and a Hawaiian vacation for two. Similar incentives and prizes were offered for reaching prescribed sales goals.

The overall objective of any incentive program is to get a little more sales effort from everyone in the organization. To do this, the incentives must be keyed to each participant's past performance and present potential. This personalization suggests the use of quotas as a basis for awarding incentives, and a majority of sales incentive campaigns do indeed base awards on quotas. In fact, the wisdom and equity of the quotas may determine the success of the entire program. Quotas that are too high, too low, or unfair tend to deflate rather than motivate. Management must be very careful in designing, explaining, and implementing quota programs so that actual motivation results.

Choosing Participants The second step in designing an incentive program is deciding which members of the sales force should participate. In some cases, all salespeople may be the obvious answer. But if there are several categories of salespeople, divided by product line, by type of account, or in some other manner, it may be appropriate to limit the campaign to one or two groups or to provide different goals and rules for different classes of sales personnel. American Hospital Supply, for example, rates each sales territory, and only salespeople working in like-rated territories compete against one another. Salespeople are also matched according to selling experience.

Setting the Rules The third step is to communicate to the sales force precisely what the members are expected to achieve and how they are to achieve it. This step begins by specifying the basis of awards. Three broad methods are used.

1. A fixed number of awards is given to the top producers in terms of total volume (a head-to-head contest).

2. Awards are tied to unit sales on an absolute basis, with no consideration for territory potential or previous record. The same goals and rewards are established for all the salespeople.

3. A fixed number of awards is given to those who perform best in relation to their individual quota.

An example of a company that combines these three types of programs is American Hardware Insurance Group, a commercial insurance carrier based in Minnesota. Every year there is a head-to-head competition, and the top twenty-five salespeople are awarded an annual trip—London and Hong Kong are two recent destinations. In addition, salespeople who reach a general target sales figure are given trophies and diamond rings, while those who reach personal quotas are given cash.[1]

Scheduling The fourth step involves several decisions about timing. Three choices are important: the specific break time of the promotion, the duration of the campaign, and the lead time allowed to prepare for the push.

The promotion break date is dictated by marketing decisions. For example, if the sales incentive program backs a trade or consumer promotion or if a new product is being introduced, these events will determine when the campaign begins. General Mills's Basic 4 cereal, for example, was introduced to the market in February 1991, but supermarkets were initially contacted in December 1990. The sales incentive program began on January 1, 1991, and phase one continued until April 15, 1991. The length of the incentive program is influenced by product distribution, type of salespeople, program objective, and the executives' experience or feeling about what works best for their organization. The average length is slightly more than eighteen weeks.

The other aspect of incentive scheduling is how much time is required for advance planning. In recent surveys, the average lead time has fluctuated quite a bit, between twelve and twenty weeks. During periods of economic uncertainty, this time frame is substantially reduced, because of possible reaction from competitors.

Picking the Prizes   Determining the type of awards and prize structure is the fifth step in planning an incentive program. This decision is closely related to factors such as budget, length of campaign, theme, and nature of the·salespeople. Salespeople respond differently to the same stimuli. To select effective prizes, it is important to consider salespeople as individuals, to understand characteristics such as their income level, their social and economic status, and their personal interests and tastes.

Traditionally, incentive programs offer vacation trips, merchandise, or a combination of the two as awards. Travel has become the glamour award in recent years. Planners generally consider travel awards if they are developing a relatively long-term promotion with a budget that allows them to offer trips to a fair number of winners at the top, with merchandise awards for lower qualifiers.[2] In general, top salespeople tend to be motivated internally, and incentives are the icing on the cake. Leo B. Kelly, for instance, is a senior sales executive for the business systems group of Xerox Corp. who finishes every year at least 200 percent over his quota. In his twenty years with Xerox, Kelly has been a member of the President's Club—the company's top incentive award, a four-day, first-class trip for the salesperson and spouse to a designated resort—seventeen times. "The President's Club is what we all strive for," says Kelly, "because it's how our success is measured within Xerox. I use it as a yardstick for minimum accomplishment."[3] In choosing merchandise for incentive programs, the only rules are the obvious ones of fitting types of items to the people and of matching budget allocations. To select merchandise for certain groups of salespeople or even individual salespeople, it may be useful to see what salespeople select when they are given free choice from a catalog of thousands of items.[4]

Besides merchandise and travel, two other forms of prizes are used—

cash and honor awards. Cash still remains the most popular incentive. It gives people something tangible and allows them complete freedom to customize their reward. Cash also has several drawbacks. First, it has motivational power to the same degree as the salesperson's salary or commission income but no special stimulus or recognition value. Second, the award is worth much more—up to twice as much—if the cash is put into the form of merchandise. Also, noncash awards offered to salespeople are usually in a class the recipients look on as luxuries, items they would not buy for themselves. Thus these awards are special, while the cash may not be. However, during economic down turns, cash awards may gain in appeal.

Honor awards appear to be a more positive form of reinforcement. They provide recognition in its purest form. However, if honor awards are used alone, they must be few in number in order to have real meaning. As a result, honor awards are often an ideal addition to a program that offers merchandise or travel, thereby enhancing the psychological effect of winning at small additional cost to the company.

Creating a Theme   The sixth and final step in developing a sales incentive program is selecting a theme. The theme of a sales incentive program is much the same as any other theme, except that it is sometimes a bit more outlandish. A theme provides a frame for the whole picture of the incentive program, gives unity to the promotional materials, and adds a little extra fun. Popular themes have been related to games or sports (for example, the Kentucky Derby or World Series), travel (for example, Parade to Paris, Jamaica Jamboree), the company honor club (such as NCR Corp.'s Hundred Point Club), and sales objective tie-ins (for example, sales track down, up the ladder).

Given an important objective, a realistic quota, workable rules, and attractive awards, one would think that the average salesperson would be ready to work hard. But it does not always work that way. Salespeople may know what they should do and how, they may have a clear view of their own self-interest in the program, and they may still just stand there. Salespeople have to be sold, and sold hard, at every step throughout the campaign. Their imaginations must be sparked and their enthusiasm fired up.

Concept Review

Sales force promotions are divided into two types of programs.
1. Supportive programs attempt to better prepare salespeople to do their job. Such programs include the following:
    a. Holding sales meetings,
    b. Supplying supportive materials (sales manuals, sales portfolios, and product models), and
    c. Distributing house organs.

2. Motivational programs attempt to stimulate salespeople to try harder. Steps in developing these programs are the following:
   a. Determine the objectives,
   b. Decide which members of the sales force will participate,
   c. Communicate the basis of awards,
   d. Determine the campaign's break time, duration, and lead time,
   e. Decide the type of awards and prizes, and
   f. Select a theme.

Trade Promotions

A **trade sales promotion** is directed at resellers who distribute products to ultimate consumers. The term **trade** is traditionally used to refer to wholesalers and retailers who handle or distribute the marketer's product. It is synonymous with *resellers*, the term we have used for wholesalers and retailers. To make matters more confusing, the term *dealers* is also used to represent these two groups. For clarity, we will use *trade* throughout this section.

Usually, the senior marketing officer or product manager is responsible for planning the trade promotion. Decisions about the amount of the deal and its timing are made jointly by the marketing officer, sales manager, and campaign manager. Since these deals have such direct bearing on the pricing strategy and ensuing profitability, they may have to be cleared by top management as well.

Goals of Trade Sales Promotions

The objectives of sales promotions that are aimed at the trade are different from those directed to the consumer. Trade sales promotions hope to accomplish four overall goals:

1. Develop in-store merchandising support or other trade support. Strong retail support at the store level is the key to closing the loop between the customer and the sale. Retail support can take the form of feature pricing (the special price is featured in ads or on signs), point-of-sale materials (the construction and proper placement of materials within the store), or superior store locations for the product (usually shelf space).

2. Control inventory. Sales promotions are used to increase or deplete inventory levels and to eliminate the peaks and valleys between seasonal items. Increases are desirable when introducing a product or at the start of a special promotion. Deletion is desirable at the end of a promotion, the end of a season, or when a product is being deleted.

3. Expand or improve distribution. Sales promotions can open up new areas or classes. Sales promotions are also used to distribute a new size of the product. If outlets stock the new size while maintaining the old one, the sales promotion has been most effective. Keeping and gaining shelf space is critical.

4. Motivate channel members. Sales promotions can generate excitement about the product among those responsible for selling it.

The ultimate gauge of a successful trade promotion is whether end users purchase more product as a result of improved reseller effort or superior product presentation.

Types of Trade Sales Promotions

Many promotional devices can motivate resellers to support a product. The appropriate devices depend on factors such as type of reseller, services offered, product distributed, price structure, margins, and competition. Here we examine eight prominent devices: point-of-purchase displays, contests, trade shows, sales meetings, push money, trade coupons, dealer loaders, and trade deals.

Point-of-Purchase Displays Manufacturers provide **point-of-purchase (POP) displays** free to the retailer in order to promote a particular brand or group of products. The varied forms of POP displays include special racks, display cartons, banners, signs, price cards, and mechanical product dispensers. Figure 11.2 shows the variety available. POP was an eighteen-billion-dollar industry in 1989, and it is growing at approximately 10 percent annually.

Product visibility is the basic purpose of POP displays. In an industry such as the grocery field, where a consumer spends about three-tenths of a second viewing a product, anything that gives a product greater visibility is valuable. A recent, eye-catching POP was for Jell-O Jigglers. The campaign included television, print ads, and coupons, as well as a POP that offered a set of alphabet cutouts with the purchase of Jell-O. The buyer received the cutouts right at the point of sale. Visibility is even more important when consumers make a large percentage of their choices in the store. In two recent studies, the percentage of consumer decisions made in the supermarket varied from 39 percent to 66 percent. The variation reflects differences in how consumers shop for different products. For example, almost all milk purchases are planned, but 60 percent of refrigerated dough is bought on impulse.[5] POP displays can spark the impulse to buy.

Beyond attracting attention to the product, POP displays also provide important decision information. Consumers already know some of this

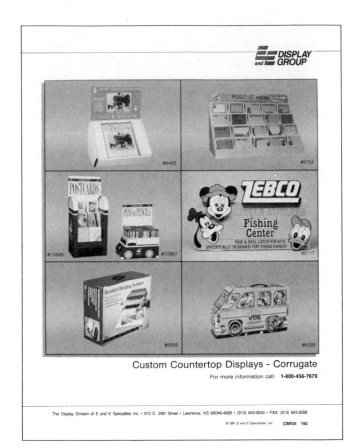

information, such as the product name, appearance of the product, and available sizes; they have seen or heard some of the information in ads before entering the store. Ads might also include additional information, such as special prices and premiums being offered. But other information will be new to consumers and might spur an unplanned purchase. Examples of these motivators are a reduced price, new model, or free sample. Since most retailing is totally or partially self-service, displays play a big role in decision making.[6]

It is one thing for manufacturers to know POP displays are good for them, but quite another to convince retailers to use them. According to a recent estimate, retailers never use as much as 50 percent of the free point-of-purchase material. Many retailers view POPs as more trouble than they are worth. They must be built and taken down (often by the retailer), they clog up store aisles, fall down, and create a general nuisance.

Probably the most effective way to ensure that a reseller will use a POP is to plan and design it with great care so that it will generate sales for the retailer. The theme of the POP should be coordinated with the theme used in ads and by salespeople. For example, Crayola Crayons used a "back to school in color" theme that was carried in several print ads, became part of the presentation used by salespeople, and was shown on the banner along the top of the POP. The display should also be well designed. It should be constructed of quality materials so that it is structurally sturdy and can be easily assembled and disassembled. Aesthetically, the display should be attractive and harmonize with the theme of the store. In addition, the display should be designed with the needs of the retailer in mind. Since shelf space is at a premium, the display should not waste it. Many of the most successful supermarket displays are end-of-the-aisle structures that take up no shelf space.

Finally, one of the most successful ways of promoting POP materials is through a professional, well-planned presentation. The presentation might be made to regional or even individual store managers. The salesperson for the bakery division of Procter & Gamble spends weeks preparing a presentation. It might include test results on the effectiveness of the display, sales forecasts, and trade deal incentives that go with the display.

Contests   For resellers as for salespeople, contests can be effective motivators. The prizes tend to be the same. Typically, a prize is awarded to the organization or person who exceeds a quota by the largest percentage.[7] For example, Cepacol Mouthwash offered supermarket managers cash prizes matched to the percentages by which they exceeded the sales quota, and a vacation to Bermuda for the manager who achieved the highest percentage. Often the program must be customized for the particular reseller group.

Great care is necessary in designing contests. The rewards may be so alluring that contestants engage in activities that are detrimental to their companies. Salesclerks may push the product of the contest company to the total exclusion of competing brands, thereby creating serious conflict among channel members. Also, the length and quality of contests need to be carefully governed. Contests are only effective if they take place periodically. Everything about the contest—its promotion, organization, and the awarding of prizes—should convey the notion that it is something special. If conducted properly, contests can provide short-term benefits and improve the relationship with resellers.

Trade Shows   Thousands of manufacturers display their wares at **trade shows,** regularly scheduled events at which manufacturers display their products and take orders.

Companies spend more than nine billion dollars annually on these shows. For many companies, all their planning efforts and much of their marketing budget and efforts are directed at the trade show. Success for the entire year may hinge on how well a company performs there.

For many businesses, trade shows provide the major opportunity to write orders for products. For others, it is a chance to demonstrate their products, provide information, answer questions, and be compared directly with their competitors. Since all the companies are attempting to provide a clear picture of their products to potential customers, information about the products is available to all competitors. Consequently, quality, features, prices, and technology can be easily compared. The Trade Show Bureau (TSB) surveyed more than nine thousand vice presidents and found that they went to trade shows for five important reasons: to gather facts for upcoming purchases, enhance their professional education, view specific exhibits, visit other industry professionals, or keep up with new product introductions.[8]

The motivational aspects of trade shows cannot be underestimated. Booths are usually staffed by the manufacturer's top salespeople who are brought into direct contact with top executives representing various middle agents. The salesperson can meet these executives, introduce the product, demonstrate it, field questions, gather information, and establish future contacts.

More importantly, the relative selling costs at a trade show are low. A McGraw-Hill study reports that more than five calls are required to close the average industrial sales lead, at a cost of $1,384 per sale. But closing a qualified trade show lead requires only .8 sales calls, for a total cost of $334.[9] Of course, trade shows are not important for all businesses.

The social aspect of trade shows is also important. The atmosphere tends to be relaxed. Free products are distributed. Parties are sponsored by most manufacturers. This social element of trade shows can get out of hand. Sales may be gained by the company that spends the most on the most outrageous party.

A well-executed campaign was developed by Wells Fargo Bank of Oakland at the San Francisco International Auto Show (see Figure 11.3). The objectives of the program were to build booth traffic and to gain interest in the firm's automobile loan service from both auto dealers and consumers. On opening night, twelve hundred auto dealers who showed up at a VIP preview party were given apothecary jars filled with saltwater taffy and coffee cups imprinted with Wells Fargo's logo. To draw traffic to the exhibit, booth visitors received a four-color, photographic auto sunshade depicting the Wells Fargo stagecoach. More than four thousand leads for auto loans were secured.[10]

Sales Meetings   Somewhat related to trade meetings, but not nearly as elaborate, are sales meetings sponsored by manufacturers or wholesalers. Whereas trade meetings are open to potential customers, sales meetings

Figure 11.3

To draw traffic to its exhibit at the San Francisco International Auto Show, Wells Fargo gave photographic auto sunshades to booth visitors.
Courtesy of Wells Fargo.

are targeted toward the company sales force and/or independent sales agents who sell the company's products or services. These meetings are usually conducted at the regional level and are directed by sales managers and their field force. Sometimes a major marketing officer from corporate headquarters directs the proceedings. The purposes of these meetings are varied. Often the meetings occur just before the buying season and are used to motivate sales agents, to explain the product or the promotional campaign, or simply to answer questions.

Besides annual or semiannual meetings, periodic meetings may be called for additional reasons, including the need to stimulate sales by means of contests or facts and figures, to discuss problems, and to announce new products. Sales training is also a major part of these meetings. However, a company must be careful whenever it takes employees away from their jobs. In many cases, special incentives must be offered just to guarantee attendance.

Push Money   An extra payment given to salespeople for meeting a specified sales goal is called **push money;** it is also known as spiffs or PM. For example, a manufacturer of refrigerators might pay a thirty-dollar bonus for sales of model A, a twenty-five-dollar bonus for model B, and a twenty-dollar bonus for model C between May 1 and September 1. At the end of that period, the salesperson would send in evidence of these sales to the manufacturer and receive a check in return. Although push money has a negative image since it hints of bribery, many manufacturers offer it.

Like most marketing techniques, push money is more effective in some situations than others. Undoubtedly, it works much better when the sales-clerk has responsibility for the sale of the product. It is most effective for products that have to be demonstrated or explained or that have a high unit cost. Push money also requires the complete cooperation of the re-tailer. If retailers feel that push money would be bad for morale or cause a disproportionate emphasis on a particular brand, they generally veto its use.

Push money can create a great deal of enthusiasm and motivation among wholesalers and retailers, but its use does raise ethical issues. For example, should salespeople push an inferior brand or one that will not solve the consumer's problem simply because they are receiving push money? Does push money put other brands carried by the retailer at an unfair competi-tive disadvantage? Despite such questions, push money continues to be used under the guidelines of the Federal Trade Commission.

Trade Coupons   In Chapter 10, we discussed manufacturer's coupons that are redeemed by the retailer who then must wait for reimbursement. Trade coupons differ from manufacturer-sponsored coupons in several respects. **Trade coupons** are offered to the local retailer as a tie-in to be carried in the retailer's ads or fliers. The manufacturer pays for the advertising and gives the retailer an allowance up front that often covers the full upper limit of redemption. The redeemed trade coupons often do not have to be returned to the manufacturer. Another difference is the time limit on re-demption. Typically, trade coupons must be redeemed within a few days; seven days is common. This time limit is intended to prompt quick trial of a new product. Retailers may add to the value of the coupons at their own expense. The consumer is not aware that these coupons are different than those distributed directly by the manufacturer.

Trade coupons are very effective if a marketer is having difficulty getting a product into a particular market. They offer the retailer an inexpensive way of promoting the store, without the difficulty of processing coupons. Trade coupons may be the only way some marketers can gain access to certain retailers.

Dealer Loaders   A **dealer loader** is a premium that is given by a manufac-turer to a retailer for buying a certain amount of product. Two types of dealer loaders are most common. The first is a *buying loader*, typically a gift given for buying a certain order size. The second is a *display loader*, in es-sence a display that is given to the retailer after it has been taken apart. For instance, General Electric Co. may have a display containing appli-ances as part of a special program. When the program is over, the retailer receives all the appliances on the display if he or she purchased the spec-ified order size.

Both buying and display loaders can be successful in the right situation. Buying loaders are most often used to get shelf space in a new retail outlet or to sell an exceptionally large amount of product. Display loaders are used in conjunction with special promotions when it is important to get the point-of-purchase display into the store. The underlying motivation for both is to move large amounts of product in a short period of time.

Trade Deals Trade deals are usually special price concessions, over and above the normal purchasing discounts, that are granted to the trade for a limited time. Trade deals incorporate a series of strategies that have one common theme—to encourage resellers to give a product special promotional attention. The attention can take the form of special displays, purchase of larger-than-usual amounts, superior store locations, or greater promotional effort. In return, retailers sometimes receive special allowances, discounts, goods, or cash.

The money spent on trade deals is substantial. In many industries, trade deals are expected and may provide the primary incentive for retail support. There are two general types of trade deals: buying allowances and advertising and display allowances.

Buying Allowances A **buying allowance** is a payment by a manufacturer to a reseller if a certain amount of product is purchased during a certain time. All the reseller must do is meet the specifications of the deal. The payment may be given in the form of a check or as a reduction in the face value of an invoice. For example, a reseller who purchases ten to fifteen cases receives a buying allowance of $6.00 off per case; a purchase of sixteen to twenty cases would result in $6.75 off per case, and so forth. In order to take advantage of a buying allowance, some retailers engage in **forward buying.** This practice is very common in grocery retailing. In essence, they buy more merchandise than they need during the deal period. They store the extra merchandise and bring it out after the sale period, selling it at regular prices. The savings gained through the buying allowance are greater than the cost of warehousing and transporting the extra merchandise.

The *count and recount* technique is one approach used as part of the buying allowance. This is the offer of a certain amount of money for each unit moved out of a wholesaler's or retailer's warehouse during a specified period. The name comes from the fact that the local sales representative takes a count of merchandise on hand at the beginning of the period and a final recount at the end of the period. Thanks to the computer, this counting process has been greatly simplified. The original count, for instance, showed 1,891 units in the retailer's warehouse; the recount was 420 units. The retailer receives an allowance of $1.60 for every unit sold over 800, or 671.

A *buy-back allowance* is another type of buying allowance. It immediately follows another type of trade deal and offers a specified amount of money for new purchases of the product based on the quantity of purchases made on the first deal. Its purpose is to motivate repurchase immediately after another trade deal on the product has depleted warehouse stock. For example, Procter & Gamble Co. might offer $1.50 off the price of a case of Head and Shoulders shampoo on a count and recount deal from July 1 to July 31, and then offer $1.00 off per case on a buy-back allowance from August 1 to August 31. The dollar amount allowed on the buy-back cannot exceed the dollar amount bought on the count and recount deal.

The *slotting allowance* has become the most controversial form of buying allowance. Slotting allowances are fees that retailers charge manufacturers for each space or slot on the shelf or in the warehouse that new products will occupy. For example, if a manufacturer introduces a new yogurt brand with fourteen items (flavors and sizes) in the line, the manufacturer will have to pay the retailer for fourteen slots. A major retailer in Los Angeles charges a slotting fee of four thousand dollars per slot for a supermarket chain. Fourteen slots times four thousand dollars equals a cost of fifty-six thousand dollars for distribution of the fourteen new yogurt items in that one chain. Distribution in five major chains in the Los Angeles market would cost $280,000.

Retailers hold that increased competition, a proliferation of new products, and small profit margins require them to ask for these fees. They argue that the monies will be spent to promote the products, redesign shelves, and reprogram computers. But grocery marketers accuse retailers of peddling the shelf space in their stores for the slotting fees. "It doesn't matter anymore how good your product is or isn't. No longer is it up to consumers whether a brand makes it or not. That decision is now made by the [grocery store] buyer," one food industry executive said.

How is the money from slotting fees used? One food industry source estimated that "70 percent of all slotting fees go directly to retailers' bottom lines. And 55 percent of all manufacturer promotional expenditures go to slotting fees," says Richard Furash, analyst with Deloitte & Touche.[11]

Are retailers ripping off marketers? The answer is not exactly. Checkout scanning, direct-profit and shelf-space management systems, and regionalization have revolutionized the way supermarkets do business. With profitability information at their fingertips, retailers are becoming less trusting and more savvy in their buying decisions. Retailers complain that marketers are not acting in their own best interest and are trying to sell products that will not necessarily benefit the retailer. They argue that national advertising (which retailers partially pay for through cooperative allowances) is not beneficial to selling products in their region, where the needs and wants of their customers differ from the norm.

Acknowledging that retailers may have some valid criticisms, marketers are slowly seeking ways to balance power more equally with the retailers. Marketers are putting together a promotional program for each store and pitching it to buyers and individual store managers. Procter & Gamble Co. recently reorganized its brand management by adding category managers to coordinate programs and prevent similar brands, such as Dash and Tide detergents, from running competing promotions at the same time. Many companies, including P&G, Quaker Oats Co., and RJR Nabisco, Inc., are working out shelf-space management and direct-product-profit programs for retailers. Miles Inc. avoided slotting allowances through a strategy based on research information; it is described in the Promotion in Focus section.

The final type of buying allowance is a *free goods allowance*. This is the offer of a certain amount of product to wholesalers or retailers at no cost if they purchase a stated amount of the same or another product of the manufacturer. The reseller is given free merchandise instead of money. A manufacturer might offer a retailer one free case of merchandise for every twenty purchased.

Advertising and Display Allowances   An **advertising allowance** is a common technique employed primarily for consumer products. The manufacturer pays the wholesaler or retailer a certain amount for advertising the manufacturer's product. The money can only be used to purchase advertising. Because policing this process may prove difficult, many manufacturers require some evidence of performance. Nevertheless, resellers may view the advertising allowance as a type of personal bonus and engage in devious behavior such as billing the manufacturer at the much higher national rate rather than at the lower local rate. (As will be discussed in the media chapters, newspapers charge national advertisers a higher rate than they charge local advertisers.) Several types of criteria can be used to determine the amount of the allowance, from a flat dollar amount to a percentage of gross purchases during a specified time period.

Closely related to an advertising allowance is *cooperative advertising*. This is a contractual arrangement between the manufacturer and the resellers whereby the manufacturer agrees to pay part or all of the advertising expenses incurred in advertising the product. The manufacturer usually has quite a bit of control over the content and form of the ad, specifying purchase information, whether other marketers can be in the ad, and the scheduling of the ad. Here again, manufacturers normally do not pay for the advertising until they get some verification from the medium or a copy of the ad.[12]

Another form of advertising cooperation is a *dealer listing*. As part of a regional or national campaign, the manufacturer provides space in the ad to list all the retailer stores at which the product may be purchased. A dealer listing may be used when a manufacturer is announcing a new

Promotion
in Focus

Winning Shelf Space
With Information

Perhaps now more than at any time in retailing history, retailers know what's going on. Bar codes and scanners, and the almost infinite amount of information they make available to retailers, have changed the balance of power in the retailing world. No longer can sales reps convince retailers to give their product more space with vague arguments about "Our product is bringing you more profit than product B."

So what does a company like Miles Inc., maker of Alka-Seltzer, do when it wants shelf space for a new product like Alka-Seltzer Plus Night-Time? If the manufacturer doesn't negotiate with retailers, stores are likely to take away some of the space allotted to one of the manufacturer's old products to give to the new product. But obviously Miles didn't want the introduction of Night-Time to cut into sales of its old standby, Alka-Seltzer Plus. Another option was to use the new product's marketing budget to pay retailers "slotting allowances"— to buy shelf space, in effect.

After thoroughly analyzing the available information, Miles decided to take a two-step approach. First, it tried to persuade retailers that they should give more shelf space to the whole cold-remedy category. They presented statistics to show that sales of cold remedies had doubled in the past five years, a growth unmatched by that of other product categories. They demonstrated that cold remedies provide more sales and profits per linear foot of shelf space than do such things as cough syrups and deodorants. If retailers weren't persuaded that they should expand their space for the entire cold-remedy category, Miles used information about individual products' turnover rates to convince store owners that they should drop other brands or other sizes to give space to Miles's new and potentially more profitable product.

Miles was delighted by the strategy's success. Not only did Night-Time sell better than expected, sales of Alka-Seltzer Plus increased as well; the company was not cannibalizing its own products. As other companies become aware of the success of such approaches, look for information to become marketers' primary tool in future negotiations with retailers.

Source: Scott Hume, "Miles Combats Slotting Beast with Information," *Advertising Age* (February 22, 1988): 12.

annual turnover is estimated at 150 percent and Tupperware's at 100 percent), but it is still considered a serious problem. The critical communication linkage between Mary Kay and its customers is the beauty consultant. When consultants quit, business is lost. Mary Kay estimated that the company loses three million customers each year because of consultant terminations.

Management is also apprehensive that the rate of increase in the number of consultants might not be sustainable. Management is, therefore, increasingly concerned with raising the productivity of the individual beauty consultant. Currently, 30 percent of Mary Kay consultants generate 70 percent of the business; these 30 percent hold an average of three beauty shows per month while the remainder hold at least one show per month. Management does not know the average frequency of consultant contact with a customer but estimates that half of all repurchases result from the consultant calling a customer; in 75 percent of the cases, the consultant delivers the order to the customer. Consultants are recommended to contact their customers every two months.

Case Questions

1. What recommendations would you make to increase the motivation level of the beauty consultants?

2. Given what you have learned in earlier chapters, are other possible changes likely to negatively affect the success of this type of direct selling?

Summary

This chapter dealt with sales promotion directed at the sales force and at dealers and resellers. Sales promotion is intended to increase the productivity of the salesperson by building enthusiasm for the task. The salesperson may be a full-time employee of the company or an independent sales representative. Sales promotion activities directed at the sales force are classified as being either supportive or motivational. Supportive programs include training; sales meetings; supportive materials such as sales manuals, sales portfolios, and product models; and communication materials such as house organs and special bulletins. Motivational programs, or sales incentives, entail a step-by-step program intended to spur salespeople on to greater sales efforts.

Sales promotions targeted at the trade have specific objectives: (1) to develop in-store merchandising or other trade support, (2) to control inventory, (3) to expand or improve distribution, and (4) to motivate channel members to take some action. Techniques include point-of-purchase materials, contests, trade shows, sales meetings, push money, dealer loaders, and trade deals of various types.

Discussion Questions

1. You are the marketing manager of a new snack chip intended to compete with Frito Lay and Lay's. What trade promotions would you need to offer in order to get your product into retail outlets? Comment on your chances for success.

2. How would you develop an incentive program for a company's sales force?

3. Assume you are a sales manager for a medium-sized manufacturer of electrical components used in computers. You wish to expand your market from the New England states to the entire eastern seaboard. You have a sales force of six people and will expand it to fifteen. Outline an incentive program that would motivate these new salespeople.

4. What types of sales promotion are available to a manufacturer that must develop a desirable channel of distribution?

5. Explain the problems associated with slotting allowances. How can businesses avoid paying slotting fees?

6. Which type of sales incentive is *best*? Discuss.

7. What are the objectives of trade sales promotions? How do they differ from the objectives of consumer sales promotions?

8. Discuss the factors to consider in designing and placing a point-of-purchase display.

9. "Trade shows are always a minor component of a sales promotion program." Respond to this statement.

10. What is push money, and when would it be appropriate?

Suggested Projects

1. Interview several local wholesalers or retailers about the various trade deals they employ. Have them indicate how they evaluate the benefits of these deals. Write a two- to three-page report on your findings.

2. Collect several articles on the pros and cons of trade deals. Write a three- to five-page paper on the topic, taking a supportive perspective.

References

1. Leslie Brennan, "Sales Secrets of the Incentive Stars," *Sales and Marketing Management* (April 1990): 88–100.

2. *Incentive Marketing* (November 1986): 70.

3. Leslie Brennan, 88.

4. *Incentive Marketing* (November 1985): 19.

5. Don E. Schultz and William Robinson, *Sales Promotion Management* (Chicago: Crain Books, 1982).

6. Cyndee Miller, "P-O-P Gains Followers as 'Era of Retailing Dawns,'" *Marketing News* (May 4, 1990): 2.

7. Howard M. Turner, Jr., "The People Motivators" (New York: McGraw-Hill, 1973): 88.

8. Edward Chapman, "Plan Your Exhibit Around the Motives of Attendees," *Marketing News* (July 11, 1990): 10.

9. "Trade Shows Still Fighting a Rodney Dangerfield Image," *Marketing News* (May 14, 1990): 9.

10. H. Ted Olson, "Trade Show Techniques," *Direct Marketing* (March 1989): 82–83.

11. Judann Dagnoli and Lauri Freeman, "Marketers Seek Slotting-Fee Truce," *Advertising Age* (February 22, 1988): 12.

12. Robert D. Wilcox, "Is It 'Co-op' or 'Stick-up' for Suppliers?" *Advertising Age* (October 6, 1986): 76.

12 *Public Relations*

Consider This:

Disposable Diaper Makers on the Defensive

It's easy to see why disposable diapers have become the most visible target of the debate about the nationwide garbage problem. You don't have to be a garbage expert to know that disposables take up a lot of space—sometimes an entire supermarket aisle, and that's when they're new and compressed. Because only about 9 percent of U.S. households have a baby in diapers at any one time, banning disposable diapers is an easy way for the majority to feel as though it is doing something for the environment without making any sacrifices.

For these and other reasons, at least twenty states have begun considering taxes or outright bans on disposable diapers, and leading disposable makers like Procter & Gamble and Kimberly-Clark have begun fighting back. The two companies have a lot to lose; the $3.5 billion U.S. disposable diaper market accounts for a considerable portion of their sales. Both have mounted a campaign to stop legislative restrictions on disposable diapers and to inform the public about their side of the issue. Working alone and with the American Paper Institute and the Diaper Manufacturers Group, they have publicized information in a variety of ways and used direct mail appeals and lobbyists to get their message across.

It seems only logical that the little bundles of paper and plastic would be more environmentally harmful than old-fashioned cotton diapers that are used over and over, but as a study of Arthur D. Little Inc. pointed out, there are a lot of different ways of looking at environmental harm. Disposables do take up as much as two percent of landfill space and consume about seven times as much raw material as reusable diapers. But reusables generate 50 percent more solid waste, use six times more water, and release almost ten times more water pollutants, according to the study. A separate study found that washing diapers at home uses 9,620 gallons of water per year per child.

Naturally, the National Association of Diaper Services disputes these findings. For the Association, too, the stakes are high. Since the controversy began, households have been signing up for reusable diaper services at a record rate, and sales have been growing at a 35 to 40 percent clip.

Allen Hershkowitz, a senior scientist for a leading environmental advocacy group, may have summed the diaper situation best by saying, "The diaper debate is unresolvable." But if both sides can use information rather than invective to make their cases, perhaps the debate will lead to a more widespread understanding of the complexities of the environment.

Sources: Jaclyn Fierman, "The Big Muddle in Green Marketing," *Fortune* (June 3, 1991): 91–101. Laurie Freeman, "Diaper Image Damaged: Poll," *Advertising Age* (June 11, 1990): 1, 57. Laurie Freeman, "P&G Seeks to Defend Its Diapers," *Advertising Age* (June 11, 1990): 1, 57.

Most companies are unwilling to leave the future of their reputation and goodwill to chance. Instead, they aim to control and direct their image through public relations, or PR. Sometimes, as our opening vignette described, companies must try to remake a negative image through public relations. But wise managers understand that public relations has a broader role to play. As Walter W. Seifert, former president of the Public Relations Society of America, noted, "The public relations expert is as necessary as any other firefighter. But long before the fire begins, he is needed to build a backlog of goodwill that minimizes misadventures."[1]

In short, public relations has become a vital element of the total marketing program. The critical issue is whether or not it is done well. We begin by taking a closer look at just what public relations is and how it has developed; then we examine how managers can use the many tools of public relations as part of an effective marketing program.

An Overview of Public Relations

Basic to all public relations is communication. Public relations tells an organization's "story" to various publics. **Publics** are the various constituencies targeted to receive public relations messages. Public relations practitioners also help shape their organizations. They determine the concerns and expectations of the organization's publics and explain them to management. Thus the First Assembly of Public Relations Associations in 1978 defined public relations as "the art and social science of analyzing trends, predicting their consequences, counselling organization leaders, and implementing planned programs of action which serve both the organization's and the public interest."[2] A much simpler definition is that **public relations** is the use of information and the communication of that information through a variety of media to influence public opinion. The public relations challenges facing Perrier were severe in 1990, when its product was recalled globally after traces of benzene, a carcinogen, were discovered. "We recalled, we recycled, we publicly acknowledged we made a mistake," said Ronald Davis, Perrier Group president-CEO.[3] To make matters worse, just before the relaunch, the Food and Drug Administration required Perrier to drop the words "naturally sparkling" from its label.

During the recall, it was revealed that Perrier carbonates its water—albeit with natural carbon dioxide—after taking it out of the ground.

A Brief History

Experimentation with various forms of communication, including PR, can be traced back to antiquity. Caesar and Alexander had their publicists. Kings and emperors staged special events to enhance their images. Counselors, heralds, bards, and even court artists sometimes assumed the functions later ascribed to public relations.

Thus PR is a very old art. Early forms were crude, but the sophistication and effectiveness of PR eventually improved tremendously. The first serious outflow of printed public relations was in the field of religion, which concerned literate people in the fifteenth and sixteenth centuries. Since these books and pamphlets were widely distributed and eagerly read, their ideas proved inflammatory and Europe was soon split by religious wars. Not all printed persuasion, however, was about religion. Many of these books and pamphlets dealt with geographical, scientific, or economic matters. Also, there were books on the new worlds in North and South America, arguments over the ownership of Brazil and the East Indies, travel journals, and trade reports. In due time, political arguments culminated in the writings of Voltaire, Rousseau, and Thomas Paine. During the American Revolution, colonial leaders captured attention with such protests as the Boston Tea Party. Later, a member of Andrew Jackson's so-called kitchen cabinet, Amos Kendall, wrote the President's speeches, composed state papers, and made certain that Jackson's views were transmitted to the press in a positive way. During the Civil War, Abraham Lincoln was able to present the Northern cause in words and pictures through a collaboration with Mathew Brady. Through timely release and placement, Lincoln was able to present an image of hope or hopelessness, depending on his needs. P. T. Barnum (1810–91) was the premier press agent, a showman who invented wild and exciting language to describe his circus performers.

Historians, however, are likely to date the real beginnings of public relations from the first decade of this century, when Hamilton Wright, George Parker, and Ivy Lee were engaged in work for various clients. Ivy Lee, in particular, embraced new means of creating favorable climates for his industrial accounts. Some say he turned a cold financier, John D. Rockefeller, into a virtual saint by programming Rockefeller's charitable acts, from giving pennies to children to donating large gifts to organizations (see Figure 12.1).

Edward L. Bernays, considered the father of public relations, was the first to call himself a public relations counsel. In 1923, he wrote the first book on the subject, *Crystallizing Public Opinion,* and he taught the first

Figure 12.1

John D. Rockefeller changed his image as cold financier with the help of PR man Ivy Lee.
Bettmann.

college course on PR at New York University. It was Bernays who advised Procter & Gamble to respond to a boycott of its products by black Americans by eliminating racist advertising, hiring blacks for white-collar jobs, and inviting blacks to open-house gatherings.

The Role of Public Relations Today

The growth of public relations during the last five decades has been tremendous. Among the top three hundred companies in the United States in 1936, only one out of fifty had a full-fledged public relations department; today, the ratio is three out of four. The number of people in PR work has been estimated at as high as 145,000. The number of PR jobs at all levels is thought to be increasing faster than jobs for any other management function.[4] The U.S. Department of Commerce forecast a growth rate of 18 percent to 20 percent for the PR industry from 1988 to 1990, compared with 7 percent for advertising.

However, public relations is one of the most misunderstood and mistrusted elements in marketing. This is largely due to the poor job the public relations industry has done explaining itself to the business community and to the public at large. It seems that many companies know they must have a public relations department; they just do not know why. Consequently, management often fails to establish a role for it. Public relations may be brought into the marketing process only belatedly as a peripheral element with no real purpose.

At least one reason for this diminished role of PR may be certain misconceptions about its nature. PR involves more than promoting a favorable relationship with the public; four core characteristics of PR are often overlooked. First, the ultimate objective of PR is to *retain* as well as to create goodwill. Second, successful PR involves first doing good and then taking credit for it. As Seifert noted, "Negative news tells itself. The 'good' men do, as Shakespeare noted, 'is oft interred with their bones.' It is the job of public relations people to see that this does not happen. They are the ones who ferret out 'good' news and get it ink and air."[5] Third, PR practitioners must research and describe their target audiences completely and precisely. PR programs are usually aimed at multiple publics that have varying points of view and needs. Finally, public relations is a planned activity that begins with thinking out public relations programs, weighing them, executing them, and evaluating them. It is an organized system of events.[6]

In different organizations, public relations may take many forms, including public information, investor relations, corporate communications, employee relations, marketing publicity, and consumer services. Most important to the success of PR is how well it is integrated with the other three promotional mix elements. For the most part, companies have failed at this task. Historically, PR has been physically separated from the rest of the organization.

This historical isolation has been partly due to the nature of the work performed by PR and partly due to the people working in PR. PR has often been viewed as a luxury that received little respect from the rest of the organization. Since PR is not considered a profit generator and has difficulty verifying its accomplishments, individuals working in advertising and personal selling are reluctant to incorporate PR into their planning. Conversely, individuals working in PR are unwilling to work with others outside their field. PR people are typically trained as writers, with little background in business or marketing.[7] William Novelli, an expert in public relations, feels that this situation must change: "All communications can and should stem from common strategies, and the total program should speak with one voice."[8] Another PR expert, Yustin Wallrapp, suggests:

"There must be a real commitment to the legitimacy of PR as a part of the communication mix."[9] PR is unlikely to produce optimum results unless (1) PR is incorporated into the overall promotion plan and resulting strategies and (2) PR is placed under the leadership of the promotion manager or product manager. As long as PR is viewed as having a staff or advisory function and is called in only when there is a crisis or a needed special event, it is unlikely that public relations will ever be a legitimate part of the promotional strategy.

Managing Public Relations

Like any business endeavor, successful public relations requires a plan. However, research is a prerequisite for formal planning. Without the appropriate research, planning becomes a subjective, rather arbitrary process. Therefore, before discussing the specific steps in a public relations plan, let us examine the goals and techniques of supportive research.

Public Relations Research

In approaching a public relations issue, any organization might ask itself some fundamental questions: Who are we and why do we exist? What do other people think of us? Who are these other people? Before an organization can communicate an image to others, it should correctly identify that image. Public relations research enables an organization to make this identification.

Public relations research is nothing more than planned, carefully organized, sophisticated fact-finding and listening to the opinions of others. Talking to another person or to a small group, a speaker can get some idea of the image he or she is conveying simply by watching and listening to others. But public relations practitioners usually address large audiences at a distance. As a result, in order to know what impression they are making, they must have some planned mechanism for listening and some ways in which two-way communication can be achieved. Otherwise their efforts to communicate are likely to be misdirected and ineffective.[10]

A great deal of information could prove helpful in developing the PR strategy. The general objectives of research include probing basic attitudes, measuring actual opinions, identifying opinion leaders, identifying target markets, testing themes and media, selecting appropriate timing, and revealing potential trouble before it develops. For most organizations, basic background information includes the following:

■ Legal status of the company;

■ Functions performed or products produced by each division;

- Market penetration and relative profitability of each product;
- Complete description of each product; competition, company goals, and market trends for each product;
- New product introductions;
- Reputation of the company among competitors, vendors, customers, and shareholders;
- Plants, branches, research, and manufacturing facilities;
- Significant achievements of the company and its executives;
- Important customers;
- Existing patents;
- Membership in associations; and
- Areas of possible crisis.

Obtaining information, however, is only a first step in a PR manager's use of research. Figure 12.2, for example, shows the results of a formal survey that examined the public's impression of business. The results of

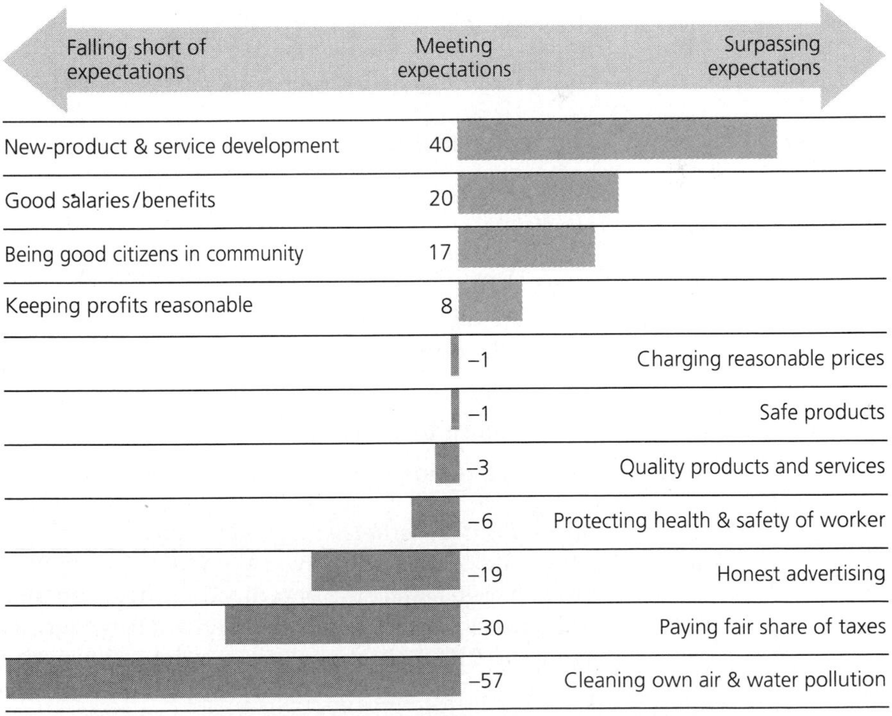

Figure 12.2

Survey of the public's impression of business.

Used with the permission of The Roper Group.

Falling short of expectations	Meeting expectations	Surpassing expectations

New-product & service development	40	
Good salaries/benefits	20	
Being good citizens in community	17	
Keeping profits reasonable	8	
	−1	Charging reasonable prices
	−1	Safe products
	−3	Quality products and services
	−6	Protecting health & safety of worker
	−19	Honest advertising
	−30	Paying fair share of taxes
	−57	Cleaning own air & water pollution

Note: Values are the point difference between perceptions of responsibility and fulfillment.

this national consumer survey provide some important insights for the PR manager. They indicate, for example, that consumers generally approve of what business is doing in respect to developing new products, paying fairly, charging fairly, and being good citizens in the community. A great many consumers also appear to hold strong opinions that are just the opposite. Business, they believe, is making poor-quality products, charging too much, paying too little, and polluting the environment as well. Such contradictory results point to the diversity of opinions held by the public. They also point to a serious problem faced by PR managers. National research results provided by companies such as The Roper Organization and A. C. Nielsen reflect a wide spectrum of attitudes and beliefs that, on average, cancel one another out. In addition, many of the "hot" issues faced by PR tend to be regional or local. It is possible that people living in Honolulu are remote from a lay-off of thirty-eight hundred employees at a company in the Detroit area. Therefore, the role of the PR manager is to intelligently assess national findings for possible relevance to his or her situation and supplement this research with local information that accurately reflects the opinions and concerns of people in that market. For example, Hill & Knowlton, a public relations firm that advises major oil companies, has discovered that the publics' attitudes and image of oil companies varies dramatically in different parts of the United States. States that border on the oceans or other waterways tend to have a far more negative image and require a different public relations strategy.[11]

Planning Public Relations

Although the steps may vary, most PR plans should contain the following six steps:

1.   Assessment of the current situation,

2.   Statement of objectives,

3.   Selection of target audiences,

4.   Selection of methods of implementation,

5.   Determination of costs, and

6.   Evaluation of results.

Assessing the Situation   A key benefit of the research process is that it keeps the organization aware of what is happening in its environment and how changes affect the organization. In some instances, the need for public relations is minimal or nonexistent. However, a crash has immediate and dramatic PR implications for an airline. Also, an immediate and expensive public relations response was required to quell the rumors and negative word of mouth surrounding the possibility that the Procter & Gamble logo had its origin in satanic cults. Therefore, an organization must constantly monitor and assess its environment, noticing when a public relations response is called for. Table 12.1 lists several situations that would call for a public relations program.

Setting Objectives   Once the current situation has been described, program objectives can be presented. Often it is best to subdivide objectives into immediate and long-range categories. This subdivision forces management to look at PR as a process rather than as a quick fix to an urgent problem. While the long-term objective for RJR Nabisco, Inc.'s tobacco division may be to create a "positive, prohealth" image, for example, several immediate objectives must be accomplished first. Immediate objectives attempt to deal with the problem at hand while still keeping the long-term issue in mind.

For example, one immediate objective for RJR was to convince the public, especially parents, that the company was making a sincere effort to keep the temptation of cigarettes away from children. Since parents are

Table 12.1   **Conditions Prompting Public Relations**

Situation	Example
Promotional opportunity	A new organization is formed to sell a new product—Toyota's Infiniti, for example.
Competitive challenge	A discount house moves into an area where competition has not been intense and existing businesses must become community oriented.
Controversy	An old private school for girls decides to go coeducational, against the wishes of the alumni and the hometown community.
Adverse publicity	A local charity staff is discovered by a reporter to be employing paroled criminals.
New image	An elderly, quiet, scholarly president of a university is replaced by a youthful, gregarious person noted for fund raising.
Catastrophe	An airline's plane crashes and all passengers are killed.
Ineffective communication	Survey results show that 21% believe Lee Iacocca is telling the truth.
Conflict of interest	The site chosen for a new Xerox Corp. plant is a forest preserve bordered by a suburban community of expensive homes.
Causes	A drug company takes on the AIDS epidemic as a personal challenge.
Public service	PPG provides booklets and safety stickers on the dangers of glass in the home.

one of the most vocal antitobacco groups, dealing with this public appeared most urgent. How could RJR immediately change the attitude of parents toward RJR from strongly negative to at least neutral? The company attempted to accomplish this objective by sponsoring a number of events for children; by not using the brand name on products for children such as candy, video games, and toys; by donating medical equipment to hospitals, and by running a full-page ad in newspapers throughout the country stating "We Don't Advertise to Children."

Because the results produced by PR are often difficult to gauge and may take a long time to appear, establishing meaningful objectives for PR is especially difficult. For the most part, PR attempts to change some component of public opinion. But public opinion is elusive, difficult to measure, and constantly changing. Although PR managers would like to take credit for changes in behavior or sales, this is seldom appropriate. (One exception occurs when the company sponsors an event or an open house, where attendance is the result of a PR effort.) Most PR objectives relate to measures of attitudes, opinions, information, and feelings, although managers recognize that these indicators can be very misleading. People tend to express their feelings and attitudes as being positive or negative, not acknowledging in-between levels. Thus, forcing someone to pick a position either for or against a controversial issue such as abortion may result in behavior that does not necessarily correspond with the person's own classifications.

Selecting the Target Audiences   Who are the people, institutions, or organizations that must be reached by the PR effort? Where are they located, and what is the most effective and efficient way to reach them? When is the best time to make contact? Careful planners list all possible target audiences, perhaps breaking them into primary and secondary publics. No relevant group should be omitted. The audiences should be researched just as carefully as the target audiences for an advertising campaign. The more the PR practitioner knows about each group, the better the message he or she can design.

In 1991, the Maytag Corporation had to engage in this kind of research for the first time in its history. Few U.S. companies have enjoyed as solid a reputation for quality as the one whose address is literally One Dependability Square. Yet things changed for Maytag after acquiring Magic Chef, Inc., maker of Magic Chef, Admiral, and Norge appliances. Maytag was hearing complaints from its dealers and customers, mostly about shoddy workmanship. *Consumer Reports* magazine rated some appliances sold by the company as among the worst around. The problem was that all appliances that now carried the Maytag name were not made in Maytag plants with Maytag pride. Maytag's response to complaints by repeat Maytag customers was first to improve the product and then to tell the consumer about the changes. *Consumer Reports* later stated: "A bit of the Maytag charm seems to have rubbed off on the brands new to the Maytag family."[12]

Implementing   Once planners have decided what they want to do and with which audiences, they must wrestle with how to do it. Implementation includes the choice of specific public relation techniques, the method of delivery, and the time of delivery. This topic will be discussed in greater detail later in this chapter.

Determining Costs   When examining the accepted plan for weaknesses, it is important to consider the budget requirements. Perhaps the most effective way to communicate with a specific audience is via prime-time television—but can the budget afford it? While dollar amounts may be important in themselves, even more important is the effectiveness of those dollars. Television, for example, may be the best solution, even though it is costly, because it reaches more people at a lower per-unit cost than the alternatives. Planners must know—not guess—what things cost. They must also be realistic and not let their desire for a solution cloud their reason. Determining an appropriate dollar allocation for public relations is difficult because of the intangibility of public relations. For example, **publicity** is the placing of news stories in the media without a charged media fee, but it is hardly free. A great many resources are used in getting "free" publicity, but determining the exact cost is virtually impossible. Similarly, how can the promotion manager accurately gauge the cost of volunteer activities, such as an executive giving a speech to a college class? Ultimately, the cost of PR must be gauged in respect to the value of the news space and the goodwill generated by the program. Matching the budget to the need, the promotion manager needs to ask: What will it take to do the job properly? The pros and cons of the various media alternatives are discussed further in Chapters 13 and 14.

Evaluating Results   The measurement of public relations' results is an elusive business. In many instances, a PR program is attempting to change attitudes and perceptions rather than behavior. PR is evaluated through both formal research techniques and informal methods.

Formal techniques include focus groups, content analysis, and monitoring. Public opinion researchers often use videotaped focus groups to measure the qualitative effects of material or messages on members of a target audience before the material is used. **Content analysis** is a technique that treats radio, television, newspaper, and magazine stories as if the media were people responding to a public opinion survey. A questionnaire covering the issues is developed, and a computer analysis (simulation) shows what is being reported, where, to how many people, over what period of time, in which media, and how the coverage changes over time. **Monitoring** is an ongoing system for keeping track of all major PR activities. It might include weekly opinion polls (as is the case for politicians) or a count of the number of press releases that appear in print during a given time. In Chapter 17, we look more closely at these and other formal measurements of the effectiveness of a PR campaign.

Informal techniques for evaluating PR are much more varied. Noting the number of people attending an event, holding informal conversations with people, or recording the number of requests for speakers may all provide informal measures of the effectiveness of a PR program.

Concept Review

1. Public relations is the use of information and the communication of that information through a variety of media to influence public opinion.
    a. PR has had a long and interesting history, with individuals such as Edward Bernap and Ivy Lee leading the way.
    b. PR continues to be a very misunderstood discipline.
    c. It goes by many titles and is often separated organizationally.
2. A public relations plan is based on research and includes the following:
    a. Assessment of the situation,
    b. Statement of objectives,
    c. Selection of target audiences,
    d. Selection of methods of implementation,
    e. Determination of costs, and
    f. Evaluation of results.

Understanding Public Relations' Publics

A public exists whenever a group of people is drawn together by definite interests in certain areas and has definite opinions on matters within those areas. Individuals are frequently members of several publics, which sometimes have conflicting interests. For example, a voter who is deciding whether to approve a school bond might be torn between feelings as a parent and as a member of a conservative group opposed to higher taxes. Americans tend to feel more comfortable than most people about belonging to numerous publics at one time.[13] In Japan, however, the *wa* (we) spirit dominates. The Japanese feel that they are all part of one public.[14]

Public relations must be sensitive to two types of publics: internal and external. **Internal publics** are the people with whom an organization normally communicates in the ordinary routine of work. The question is not "Shall we communicate with them?" but rather "How shall we communicate, and to what extent?" **External publics** are the people with whom an organization communicates but with whom it does not have regular or close ties.

Internal Publics

Typical internal publics in an industry are the employees, stockholders, suppliers, dealers, customers, and plant neighbors. The two internal publics that are perhaps most meaningful to the PR director are employees and customers.

Employees are usually divided into many subsections that differ greatly from one another and that must be approached in the ways best suited to their interests and reaction patterns. For example, among employees there are hourly paid workers, salaried workers, and managerial staff; each group has its own special characteristics, outlook, and interests.

What do employees want most from their companies? Here are some of the things that all employees usually want:

1. Security. How secure is the company and my job within it?
2. Respect. Am I recognized as a person who knows something worth knowing?
3. Participation. Do I know more about the process of which I am a part than just what happens to me?
4. Consideration. Is there an opportunity for me to express my ideas?
5. Recognition. What rewards are given for good and faithful service?
6. Opportunity. Is there a chance to advance?[15]

No company can satisfy all these needs, and conflict and dissatisfaction are inevitable. However, good PR organization and communication can modify much of this dissension and direct natural energies into greater development. Both downward and upward communications are required. Downward communication from management to employees occurs through employee magazines and newspapers, newsletters, bulletin boards, posters, films, reading racks, letters, and ceremonies. Downward communication helps employees to stay informed about factors and decisions that affect their lives. Downward communication is often well developed, although it is not always well conceived. In spite of attempts to communicate clearly to a wide spectrum of employees of varying educations, backgrounds, and interests, messages are inevitably misunderstood or distorted. Newsletters intended to praise workers may turn out to be a source of resentment. Upward communication from employees to management is much more feeble, consisting usually of surveys, suggestions programs, group meetings, and a vague open-door policy. Because of management's neglect, much of the upward communication in a company often becomes a union prerogative.

The consumer public is also a significant internal public. The consumer public is largely a responsibility of the sales and advertising departments. Sometimes, especially when consumers are numerous, public relations methods of communication beyond direct sales or conventional advertising may become important. Cause-related marketing, for example, is a popular public relations strategy that appeals to certain consumers. By contributing fifty cents to the Special Olympics for each box purchased, Kellogg's Cereal has cultivated many consumers.

Companies must answer many questions about consumers. What creates the prevailing public attitude toward a company? If public feeling is favorable, how do people acquire their impressions? How much does the public know about the company? The answers to questions like these describe public opinion, which is the starting point for any public relations messages targeted at consumers. For companies such as Procter & Gamble and Kimberly-Clark, understanding the feelings of the public about the negative effects of disposable diapers is vital. The public has been inundated with a myriad of information about this topic, much of it contradictory, and is therefore confused. Both companies want to resolve these contradictions in their own favor. Unfortunately, people who conduct research on the issue of disposable diapers also seem confused. According to one recently released survey, Americans believe that environmental protection is more important than economic growth, and they are willing both to sacrifice jobs in their communities, by virtue of shutting down ecologically unscrupulous firms, and to pay more for environmentally friendly products. According to Alan Caruba, tracker of American attitudes and actions on the environment, "This is nonsense. There is no truth to this." He notes that the Environmental Protection Agency can show that do-it-yourself auto mechanics who change their own oil disposed of 120 million gallons in 1990—more than the amount spilled in the Exxon *Valdez* accident. In addition, Caruba notes, every single environmentally friendly proposition on state ballots in the November 1990 election was defeated.[16]

Institutional advertising and publicity are the two primary types of public relations used to deliver messages to consumers. Public relations **institutional advertising** does not try to sell a particular brand but aims instead to enhance the image of the sponsoring organization. Figure 12.3 gives an example of an attempt by a new foreign manufacturer to combat possible biases against a Japanese competitor. These ads are paid for by the sponsor. Publicity means placing information in a news medium at no billed cost to the sponsor.

External Publics

External publics are composed of people and organizations that do not have an ongoing direct connection with a particular organization. For ex-

Figure 12.3

An attempt to counteract possible biases against the Japanese company Komatsu. Courtesy of Komatsu.

ample, members of the press, educators, or government officials may or may not have an interest in an industry. To some extent, an organization may choose whether to communicate with these groups. Although the list of external publics is extensive, four are most relevant.

The first is the *press;* it includes newspapers, television and radio stations, general magazines, and trade papers. All of these media serve as gatekeepers, opening the door to wider contact with a broad public. The press generally exercises a tremendous influence over public opinion, and a newswriter's words can affect the life of a project or an organization. As a group, newspeople appreciate direct, clear-cut explanations since they themselves are experts in concise exposition and are usually hard pressed for time. The PR person usually finds newspeople extremely helpful not only in getting stories into the media but, more importantly, in interpreting public feeling.

The second external public is the *government.* This public has concrete and direct effects on many businesses and other organizations. As governmental functions in the United States have expanded over the decades, the power of those associated with the government has increased tremendously. The person responsible for PR directed at the government is usually called a **public affairs officer.** The primary public relations activity employed to reach the government public is **lobbying,** which is the broad term for activities that aim to influence the policy decisions of government officials.

The *financial world* represents a third external public. Public relations people who specialize in communicating with the financial community are said to be engaging in **financial relations.** Individuals engaged in financial relations must have a basic understanding of business law, economics, and corporate finance. They deal with a wide variety of financial information, such as company acquisitions, changes in company policies and how those changes may affect stock prices, changes in the company's bond rating, and the annual report. Financial public relations is a highly skilled field and one in which amateurs may get both themselves and their companies into serious trouble quickly. Financial relations writers must meet strict standards of accuracy and timing.

The fourth external public is the *trade association.* Every business or occupation has trade or professional associations. An association's goals often include self-regulation, lobbying, public relations, or selling. Carpet manufacturers, for example, not only compete with each other but also with manufacturers that produce other floor coverings, such as plastic tile, wood, or linoleum. When all the members of the carpet manufacturers' association cooperate, they can make a concerted effort to encourage the use of carpeting instead of a substitute. By helping to increase carpeting's total share of the floor-covering market, each carpet manufacturer can acquire more business.

There is, of course, interaction between internal and external publics. Yet the same factors that create goodwill with internal publics do not necessarily create goodwill with external publics. With employees and other internal publics, there is a fair chance that all interests will coincide because all are connected with the same organization; with an external audience, the chance of such accidental coincidence of interest is slight.

Concept Review

Public relations directs its messages at internal publics and external publics.

1. Internal publics have communication with the organization in the ordinary routine of work (for example, employers, stockholders, suppliers, dealers, customers, and plant neighbors).

2.   External publics do not have close ties with a particular organization (for example, the press, the government, the financial world, and trade associations).

Tools of Public Relations

It is apparent by now that the public relations process is quite complex. In this section, the primary tools employed in PR will be examined.

Publicity

Publicists are writers who depend on experience, guile, and a great deal of talent to convince editors and reporters to carry their stories. The result of the publicist's efforts is called publicity. The credibility of publicity is much higher than that of advertising since the medium has the choice to run or not run the story and to change it as desired. Publicity can be a massive effort, such as a twelve-page lead story in *Fortune* magazine on the success of Sam Walton and the Wal-Mart chain, or a one-sentence mention of a company by Dan Rather on the evening news. Sometimes publicity verges on being illegal. For example, in 1991, when billionaire Donald Trump was still publicly involved with Marla Maples, New Retail Concepts hired Ms. Maples to be the spokesperson for No Excuses Jeans. In the initial ad, Ms. Maples was shown dumping copies of supermarket tabloids into a trash can. As expected, the Big Three television networks rejected the ad, and the media followed this story (constantly mentioning No Excuses) for over three weeks. The resulting publicity did far more for No Excuses Jeans than its ad budget could ever have done, thus illustrating the trend to purposely create ads that are more valuable as attention-getting public relations tools than as traditional advertising. "My job is to make $1 million look like $10 million or $20 million, and I'll do it any way I please as long as it's not underhanded or dishonest," says George Lois, chairman, CEO and creative director of No Excuses' current agency, Lois/GGK.[17]

The relationship between the news media and the public relations director may dictate the success or failure of any publicity effort. In many cases, it is both a cooperative as well as an adversarial relationship. The reporter is motivated by the public's right to know, and the PR person's loyalty is attached to the client or company. Also, media people expect PR people to be experts in the news business and are unlikely to pay much attention to those who are not. Successful public relations is built on reputation; once this reputation is lost, the PR person cannot function. Thus the road to media respect is via honesty, accuracy, and professionalism. The practitioner must know the requirements of each medium and make every effort to follow them.

One powerful form of publicity is a *plug*, which occurs when celebrities agree to mention a particular product, usually for some sort of compensation. This technique is discussed in the Promotion in Focus section. More conventional forms of publicity include news releases and press conferences.

The News Release   Most publicity is delivered in the form of a news release, or press release. A *news release* commits a story to paper in the style acceptable to the media for which it is intended. Some general news stories are written one way for newspapers and another for the electronic media. The release might be a single copy for a particular news outlet, or it might be reproduced by the hundreds for broad distribution. A single copy would be sent to the news editor, section editor, or a specific reporter. Multiple copies might be mailed to hundreds of editors or put on a news wire such as the Associated Press (AP) so that subscribers can pull off stories they are interested in running. Even though news releases are often targeted to a large audience, they should be written as carefully as if they were produced directly for each particular medium. Although a release may be rewritten, the better the job the PR person does, the better the chance of the release's being accepted. If a release is riddled with errors and obvious puffery, it will not even get a rewrite; it will simply be discarded.

There are certain general guidelines for submitting a news release:

1. Learn as much as possible about the particular medium being used. Especially, understand what a medium considers to be news.

2. Make sure the story is totally accurate.

3. Make sure the story is timely. If a speech or report was provided ahead of time, check to be sure it was actually delivered as scheduled.

4. Keep the story as succinct as possible, given the nature of the medium, the importance of the story, and mechanical limitations.

5. Since newspaper readers are skimmers, present the main facts in the first few sentences when submitting to this medium.

The Press Conference   On various occasions, an organization may invite the press to send representatives to hear an important announcement or to interview an important person. The Polaroid Corporation has used the press conference technique successfully to announce new inventions.

A good rule for a news conference is never to hold one if the news can be handled some other way or unless something will really be added. If the news given at a press conference could just as well have been obtained from a prepared release, then the press conference probably should not have been held.

Promotion
in Focus

Television's Free Plugs

Parents who don't want their kids to get hooked on brand-name merchandise can just turn down the television's sound or switch channels when the commercials come on, right? According to a survey conducted by *Advertising Age* and the Medill School of Journalism at Northwestern University, it's not that easy. It turns out that the only way to avoid being swamped by plugs for brand names on television is to turn the TV off altogether.

News, comedy, and even drama thrive on specifics. You don't want to hear just that an airplane crashed while taking off; you want to know what airline and what flight. Similarly, a comedian gets laughs more easily by poking fun at McDonald's or Burger King than by mentioning a nameless fast food restaurant. And perhaps the fastest way that a television drama can show that a particular character is rich is by zeroing in on the character's Rolex watch or on the Mercedes insignia on the character's car.

For these and other reasons, brand-name items pop up constantly in regular television programs, about once every five minutes, according to the study. While watching the three networks for a 24-hour period, the researchers saw Nike and Adidas logos during the sports segment of a news show; they noticed that soap opera characters were eating Drumsticks ice cream and reading *Elle* magazine; they counted more than a dozen brands in Jay Leno's routine. News programs accounted for 44 percent of the brand-name mentions, leading all other kinds of programming.

Most of the time, companies are delighted to have their products appear or be mentioned on television. Noting that a character is wearing a particular brand of jeans may influence a viewer's buying decision more than watching countless commercials. The decision by movie producers to display certain products has created controversy in Hollywood and raised the specter of feature films becoming 90-minute commercials.

In fact, companies aren't always happy when their names pop up in the news or on variety shows. Exxon no doubt wished that it could change its name when the Exxon Valdez ran aground and polluted Alaska's coastline, and a newscaster's mentioning that a particular company is under investigation or close to bankruptcy can send the value of that company's stock plummeting. Some advertisers worry that the sheer volume of brand names on television dilutes the value of their commercials.

But in general, when a McDonald's executive hears someone like Gene Siskel mention "Little Mermaid Happy Meals," that executive is going to be pleased. Occasionally you *can* get something for nothing.

Source: Scott Hume, "Free 'Plugs' Supply Ad Power," *Advertising Age* (January 29, 1990): 6.

This is an important question to ask in considering the desirability of a press conference: Is the organization really willing to answer all questions that might be asked at such a meeting? There is always the risk that a reporter will ask an embarrassing question that has little to do with the topic of the press conference. People who hold a press conference are offering to tell the whole truth. If they have anything to hide, the conference could turn out to be harmful.

Handling Bad News   In almost every corporation's life there will be some event that is perceived negatively by the public. Airlines, utility companies, chemical plants, and oil refineries, for example, have long worried about a negative image created by an accident or a calamity.

One of the most dramatic crises faced by a business was the disaster created by the wreck of the Exxon tanker *Valdez,* considered the largest commercial oil spill in history. Exxon may never be forgiven for destroying the environment and wildlife off the coast of Alaska. To make matters worse, Exxon CEO Lawrence Rawl was widely criticized for the way he and his staff handled the crisis. At first, Exxon denied the extent of the catastrophe as well as its responsibility for the cleanup. Later, admitting errors in judgment, Exxon provided a great deal of misinformation about the costs of the cleanup. The public response to Exxon was immediate and dramatic. Over forty thousand Exxon credit cards were cut up by consumers and mailed back to Exxon headquarters. One wonders whether Exxon will ever gain back the goodwill of consumers.

A public relations staff should anticipate the possibility of disaster and establish a mechanism for dealing with negative news. In the case of a power blackout from a natural disaster, for example, a utility company must have the basic facts ready to give out to reporters. It must also designate spokespeople to describe accurately the damage, dangers, time needed for repair, and other details. The company must provide telephones, space in which reporters can work, transportation, and perhaps even food. These emergency arrangements must be mapped out well in advance since there is no time to improvise coverage once a disaster strikes. More and more companies (especially those that have a high probability of crises) are formalizing emergency arrangements by forming crisis management teams. These teams assign specific tasks to individuals when a crisis does occur and define the role of public relations.

Foresight and helpfulness to the press will give the company a chance to get across its side of the story—that is, to emphasize the smallness of the loss, the continued solvency of the company, the brief interruption of service, or to give expressions of thanks. Those who help the press to cover the news during a crisis are likely to receive somewhat more consideration from the press at some other time.

In some instances, the bad news may be a disgrace. If the company president absconds with the payroll or the personnel director makes sexual advances to employees, public relations may not want to make the press aware of the news. Nevertheless, such bad news may be passed on to the press for two reasons. First, law officials or someone else may make the information public, and it may be better if the company reports it first. Second, complete honesty with the press is highly respected by news-people.

In any event, there is no use trying to deny the facts or to cover up bad news. In effect, public relations people work for the press as well as for the organization that employs them. They cannot expect to lie to the press and still preserve their usefulness as a source of news.

Publicity Photographs   The public pays attention to newspaper pictures and remembers them, but photographs can be difficult to get into a news-paper. The competition for space is great. Although a major paper may have room for as many as forty story-related photographs, there is little room available for publicity pictures. Photos may be easier to get into a newspaper than stories, however, because many news pictures are so routine that anything unusual or interesting in itself is appreciated.

Photographic prints for newspaper use should have good, but not extreme, black-and-white contrast and clear object outlines since printing quality is only fair and the pictures may be reduced in size. Complex backgrounds and wasted space should be avoided in planning the composition of the picture. Most large newspapers want 8″ × 10″ or 5″ × 7″ photos on glossy paper so that retouching, if necessary, may be done more easily. Good pictures, supplied in the form in which the paper needs them, are often most helpful in enhancing a story.

All public relations people need to be able to judge news and feature photographs and perhaps to take adequate photographs themselves. Taking personal portraits, however, is a specialty outside the province of the amateur public relations photographer. Fashions, food, architecture, and large groups of people are other subjects that need special photographic methods, and the amateur should not attempt to photograph them.

Institutional Advertising

As noted earlier, institutional advertising is communication by an organization about its work, views, and problems that aims to gain public goodwill and support.[18] The emphasis is on the image of the company rather than on the sale of a specific product. It is sometimes called **corporate advertising** or **public relations advertising.** Unlike publicity, institutional advertising is paid for by the sponsor and enables the sponsor to tell its story when it chooses and to the audience it selects. The artwork, headline, and message are exactly the way the advertiser wants them to appear, in print or on the air. On the minus side, the audience recognizes that an institutional ad is a paid pleading, so audience resistance may be raised. Publicity does not carry the handicap of being paid for by the sponsor. Nor does it incur the heavy costs associated with using mass media.

Besides high cost and low credibility, many critics claim that institutional advertising has a third weakness: ineffectiveness. Retailers in particular argue that institutional advertising is a nice luxury but has little effect on attitudes or awareness. However, a study conducted by Opinion Research Corp. revealed that an overwhelming majority (89 percent) of consumers are influenced by the reputations of companies that compete for their dollars. Furthermore, the impact of the corporate image on consumer decisions increased from 1986 through 1989. The study found that consumers believe that companies that demonstrate a concern for society in general are likely to have a sincere concern about their customers' needs. Four out of five agree with this statement: "Companies that contribute to their communities or other charities are more likely to be concerned with satisfying their customers than are companies that don't make charitable contributions."[19]

In traditional product advertising, the objective tends to be fairly clear. In institutional advertising, objectives are not so clear-cut and often are quite subtle. Ordinarily, however, the objectives fall into one of three categories.

First, a company may want the advertising to create confidence in the company that will help sell its products and make its stock appealing to investors. Second, a company may use institutional advertising to explain management's stand about matters such as a labor dispute, a bad product, or a drastic price rise. Such ads have a public relations flavor and very often are tied in with simultaneous news releases. Sometimes the ads are signed by top officials of the company. In one of its ads, Burger King addresses its initiative to deal with package pollution before McDonald's Corp. did. This bit of sarcasm intends to place Burger King and McDonald's in their proper perspective. A final objective is to express the company's philosophy about government, politics, or other aspects of society. Some executives feel keenly the need to speak out on pressing issues of the day. Texaco Inc. does just that with its Q and A ad shown in Figure 12.4.

Sponsorship

The popularity of corporate sponsorship has grown dramatically during the last decade (see Figure 12.5). Companies such as Procter & Gamble Co., AT&T, American Express Company, Coca-Cola Enterprises Inc., and Gillette Co. sponsor events in the United States, Europe, and the Far East. Virtually every major sporting event now has a corporate sponsor.

Why has event sponsorship grown so rapidly as a superior PR alterna-

Figure 12.4

Texaco shows its concern for saving energy in this institutional ad.
© 1991 Texaco Inc.

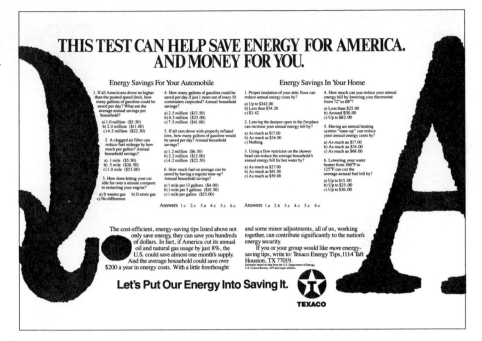

tive? First, secondary media coverage is extremely high. Volvo International states that its three-million-dollar investment in tennis is equivalent to twenty-five million dollars in advertising because of the extra media value derived. U.S. Tobacco, Kendall Oil, and Chevrolet sponsor regional tractor pulls at a cost ranging from fifty thousand dollars to one hundred fifty thousand dollars each. Nearly three million avid fans attend these events each year. The growth in event sponsorship also has a second cause: recognition of its ability to improve employee morale. The First Interstate Bank says it has contributed close to two hundred fifty thousand dollars in cash and support services to the Orange County Performing Arts Center triathlon to pump up employee morale by association with a dynamic event.[20]

Company Publications

Although no one has taken an official count, it is estimated that there are about eight thousand U.S. organizational magazines and newspapers with a readership of perhaps twenty million people. These publications cost companies about one hundred fifty million dollars. They are the most common form of company communication. Company publications range in size from a single-page mimeographed sheet to a large, elaborate, four-color magazine.

Figure 12.5

Corporate sponsorship has been increasing in popularity largely because secondary media exposure makes the sponsor's investment well worth it.
Courtesy of Fuji. Photo Film Co., Ltd.

Most of these publications are called *internals* because their audiences tend to be closely connected with the organization—employees, stockholders, dealers, and suppliers; on the outer fringes, perhaps community leaders and friends. These publications were also referred to as *house organs* in the previous chapter. *Externals* go to customers, potential customers, or general opinion leaders such as educators and legislators. Their objectives include selling company products, informing readers of product uses, and creating general prestige, goodwill, and understanding.

There is no single right way to design a company publication. Appearance, content, and objectives differ greatly. The really important thing is not how a publication looks but what it says.

Where does the news for an internal publication come from? Certain sources can be organized for regular coverage. The records of employee promotions, transfers, retirements, illnesses, hirings, and vacations are available through the personnel office. Other news items can sometimes be obtained through department heads, who will know about new production equipment, sales plans, and advertising programs; or through a network of departmental or plant correspondents whose work can be rewarded with recognition at an annual dinner and perhaps with gifts around holiday time. All news items must be carefully checked for accuracy and taste.

A really successful internal company publication is read not only by employees but also by their families and friends. It should be friendly, reliable, and frank in its purpose. It should be edited from the viewpoint of those who read it.

Motion Pictures

Although motion pictures are one of the most complex and expensive means of communication, they offer an opportunity to influence viewers in a way that no other medium can match. Motion pictures differ from sales films because motion pictures do not attempt to sell a product. Instead, they try to tell the company's story to a particular public. Motion pictures can convey ideas quickly and lastingly, with subtle emotional overtones. In today's television era, people are accustomed to receiving their information through this medium.

In fact, people are so accustomed to films that PR managers may lose sight of their weaknesses. Motion pictures are primarily limited to showing the external aspects of a subject and often seem insincere when trying to portray ideas. Not everything makes a good visual story or spectacle. In addition, motion pictures proceed at a set pace, allowing the viewer little opportunity for reflection or questioning while watching a film. The viewer often wants a clarifying two-way conversation at the end of a film, but this desire is usually not satisfied.

Furthermore, the public relations motion picture is an expensive medium for the small organization. The average production cost ranges from perhaps one thousand dollars to two thousand dollars per minute of running time, or about thirty thousand dollars to fifty thousand dollars for the average twenty-six-minute noncommercial film. Also, it is wise to budget as much for extra prints and distribution costs as the original cost of the film. Since the life of a film must be at least five years to amortize this cost, the subject matter is usually limited to activities that will not become dated. Many companies use videocassettes instead of films because of lower costs and easier production and distribution.

After a film is made, who is going to see it? Distribution may be handled by the organization itself, but most companies use the services of commercial film distributors. For a fee, these companies publicize the films, receive orders for showings, mail the films, and report on the audiences each month.

The most important point to remember about public relations films is that they must be well made. Since few public relations people are expert film producers, it is part of good planning to obtain the aid of someone who is. Instead of an entire company-produced motion picture, it is possible to have a product or company featured in a commercial motion picture. Company publicists as well as motion picture company publicists are constantly looking for opportunities to share the spotlight. The classic story relates how M&M's refused to be featured in the film *E.T.*, so George Lucas contacted Reese's about using Reese's Pieces instead. Sales for the candy increased over 170 percent after the introduction of the movie. Having learned from this incident, companies are very interested in being in the movies. The key is to make sure that the product is featured in a positive way. For example, in *Die Hard II*, Bruce Willis is shown using a Pacific Bell pay phone. However, he was supposed to be in Washington, D.C., at the time. Pacific Bell became part of a funny movie mistake.

Other Methods of PR

Several other types of PR activities have met with increasing success. Contests, award programs, and visits to plants or laboratories may bring customers. Programs and contests for students may awaken interest. Employees can often influence sales through their own PR activities. In addition, careful listening to consumers through surveys, panels, and less formal methods is the joint concern of the sales, advertising, and public relations departments. In the following sections, we describe several other important tools of public relations.

Open Houses and Tours   The value of a plant tour can be endless. Knowing something about where people work and what they produce leads to a personal interest in the work environment and an intelligent comprehension of it. Among the most common tour groups are employees and their families; townspeople; and groups of students, scientists, salespeople, dealers, and suppliers. In one company, a new public relations person discovered that salespeople coming into headquarters for training were never given a plant tour to see the manufacture of the product they were supposed to sell. In fact, many veteran salespeople had never been inside the plant.

Setting up a good plant or office visit is not simple. Some factories are too noisy, too dirty, or too dangerous to be suitable visiting locations. Other places offer little to see because the machinery is hidden or because the work is largely mental and clerical. It may sometimes be necessary to set up exhibits and pictures to show what cannot be seen.

Since people give their time and attention to a plant tour, their visit should be perfect. Guides must be courteous and well prepared, routes should be carefully laid out, explanatory signs should be posted as needed, and rest and refreshments should be provided.

Exhibits Exhibits such as those at fairs and professional meetings present special problems for the public relations planner. What should be exhibited? Will adequate traffic justify the investment? How can viewers be stopped? What makes an exhibit memorable? In many instances, the cost of an exhibit per viewer is extremely high, even though exhibit space is often sold on a charitable basis. Competition for attention is intense, and the costs of constructing and running an exhibit are high, often far beyond the probable benefits. The ideal exhibit is colorful, pictorial, and unusual. If possible, it includes participation by viewers. If they can push buttons, see pictures, and answer questions, all the better.

Other types of displays include parade floats, museum exhibits, historical exhibits, and signs at construction sites. Parade floats should be attractive and confined to a single idea. The value of floats is sometimes questionable, however, because financial competition among participants can get out of hand. Information signs at construction sites are another matter. They usually attract keen public interest. Signs, plans, and preview photos can capitalize on this interest. At the very least, signs and drawings should tell passersby what is going on and when completion is expected.

Meetings Getting a group of people together to talk things over is one of the oldest communication techniques, yet one that is often neglected today because it seems so simple. Because it is a personal experience rather than a secondhand sensation, a meeting has great power for good or ill.

One approach is a lecture meeting, perhaps supplemented by slides. An annual report meeting for stockholders, a mass meeting of employees to announce a new policy, or a semipublic lecture by a visiting scientist at a chemical plant are all examples. The audience's interest cannot be assumed unless attendance is entirely voluntary. The key weakness of a lecture is that it is one-way communication. Achieving two-way communication in a large meeting is not easy because questions are likely to be long, trivial, and digressive; yet denial of questions is not a good policy either. A possible alternative is to hold several group meetings that are small enough to allow for two-way communication. An informal social hour may also be combined with some lecture meetings.

Organized Social Activities Company picnics, holiday parties, bowling leagues, and golf tournaments are all types of public relations. How much togetherness is desirable depends on the size of the organization, where it is located, and the expectations of those involved. Generally, in larger cities, the separation between job and social life is virtually complete. If this is the case, a few well-produced formal events with a pleasant atmosphere convey the impression that the management is thoughtful and interested. In smaller communities, work and private life tend to run into each other more, and an organization may be expected to provide a greater amount of planned social activity. Management must be careful not to seem to play favorites or to be too paternalistic. Social arrangements are often better left to the employees themselves, with only cash and moral support provided by management.

Lobbying   Lobbying is an area of great sensitivity. It requires a low-pressure strategy, personal contact, and thorough knowledge of the industry. Many lobbyists are not public relations specialists but former government officials. Other public relations practitioners get into lobbying activities through their jobs with corporations or utilities. Some PR practitioners become professional lobbyists, generally representing a particular industry such as oil and gas or special interests such as senior citizens or health care organizations. Lobbyists work closely with the staffs of federal and/or state representatives and senators, who depend on them to explain the intricacies and implications of proposed legislation. Lobbyists draw on important information to influence and persuade.

Perhaps the largest lobbying group today is the tobacco industry. Faced with the possibility that cigarettes may be banned altogether, tobacco manufacturers contribute millions of dollars each year to support their issues at the federal, state, and local level. Similarly, Procter & Gamble Co. maintains a constant lobbying effort with legislators about proposed bills dealing with the environment.

Action Programs   Action programs can communicate strong messages about an organization. Giving awards for town betterment or work-related accomplishments conveys the message that the donor is interested and concerned. Giving scholarships or helping schools to develop their curricula communicates an attitude toward education. And holding seminars in which scientists can discuss their problems is an act of leadership.

Concept Review

1. Using publicity as a public relations tool requires the ability to handle media relations, news releases, press conferences, bad news, and publicity photographs.
2. Institutional ads make no attempt to sell a product but aim to enhance the image of the business.

3. Corporate sponsorships may involve a variety of events, including sporting events, parades, and entertainment. Sponsorship provides high secondary media coverage and improves employee morale.

4. Company magazines and newspapers can be internals or externals. Internals go to employees, stockholders, dealers, or suppliers, informing them of company-related events. Externals go to customers, potential customers, or opinion leaders, informing readers of product uses and creating general prestige, goodwill, and understanding.

5. Motion pictures are made available to a variety of audiences and present a positive pictorial portrayal of the organization.

6. Other methods used in public relations include open houses and tours, exhibits, meetings, organized social activities, lobbying, and action programs.

The Future of Public Relations

PR experts Newsom, Scott, and Turk summarize the future of public relations in three words—credibility, accountability, and responsibility. That is, public relations will gain the respect of its peers, be held accountable for everything it does, and deliver something worthwhile for the dollars spent. Moreover, PR will become a more important part of the marketing armory, joining advertising and sales promotion as a genuine partner rather than as a poor relation.[21] If that is the future of public relations, it holds important challenges for PR planners and practitioners. To be successful, they will have to begin with clearly stated objectives and must include means for measuring how well these objectives have been achieved. Finally, PR must be honest in everything it does. The negative reputation historically associated with PR must be replaced with one of integrity and reliability. Meanwhile, companies are likely to place increased importance on PR. With economic shortages facing manufacturers and consumers demanding better products and information and becoming more conservative, companies will have to be aware of the images they portray to all their publics and learn to modify them whenever possible.[22]

Case 12 *Trying to Change a State's Image*

Hiring a public relations firm to try to improve a state's image is hardly a new concept. Alaska wants the world to know about its great fishing and sightseeing, Washington lures visitors with its apples, and New Hampshire wants to spread the word about its skiing and tax structure. Every state is eager to lure tourists or new industries or both, and it seems natural to hire professionals to get out the word. But when the Arizona Economic Council hired Hill & Knowlton in 1990, it gave the company an unusually difficult task: to reverse the growing image of Arizona as a racist state and to stop the national isolation which that image was creating.

The Governor

Arizona's problems stem from its internal battle over creating a state holiday honoring Martin Luther King. Arizona is not the only state to resist declaring such a holiday, but it has drawn the most media attention, largely because of former Governor Evan Mecham.

Mecham, a staunch conservative, was openly derogatory of the Reverend King, and in 1986 he rescinded the state holiday that had been created to honor King. Many observers considered his attitude, actions, and remarks to be racist. Around the nation and the world, people condemned Mecham, and often their hostility extended to the citizens of Arizona, many of whom spoke out in favor of Mecham and against the holiday. What might have been a legitimate debate about the value of another state holiday soon came to be viewed as an argument about whether the state should show respect for African-Americans.

The Business Response

Mecham was impeached in 1987. The impeachment charges were not directly related to the holiday debate, but the controversy certainly provided energy for the impeachment drive. With Mecham gone, the Arizona business community began working to reinstate the King holiday. Business leaders said they supported the holiday because they wanted to honor King, but they were also clearly fearful that the state's racist image would scare away conventions and companies planning to relocate, costing millions of dollars in lost revenues. Phoenix and other cities began celebrating the King holiday, and Arizona corporations worked to save the state's image. The MLK Better America Committee raised $750,000 to promote a ballot initiative to create a King holiday. But voters defeated the proposition, and the state's businesses turned to Hill & Knowlton for help.

The NFL Issue

The biggest threat hanging over Arizona was that it would lose the 1993 Super Bowl, scheduled to be played in Phoenix, if it didn't approve the holiday. According to polls, some 60,000 Arizona citizens changed their votes from yes to no after hearing about the NFL's threat. Since the measure lost by only 17,000 votes, that response to what people saw as the NFL's intimidation may have been crucial.

Clearly, Hill & Knowlton has a difficult job to do. Should it focus on Mecham, claiming that he never represented the people of Arizona? Or play up the citizens' tough-minded individualism? Should it work to get another initiative passed or to lure businesses to Arizona despite the lack of a King holiday? Arizona's economic future may hang in the balance.

Case Questions

1. Who are the internal and external publics for the Arizona Economic Council?

2. Employing the planning framework provided in this chapter, outline a PR plan for the Arizona Economic Council.

Case Source: Melanie Johnston, "Arizona Hires PR Agency," *Advertising Age* (November 19, 1990): 6.

Summary

In this chapter, an attempt was made to put public relations in its proper perspective as a professional activity that exists as an important part of a promotional strategy. We viewed public relations' two publics, internal and external. Internal publics are the people who are already connected with an organization and with whom the organization normally communicates in the ordinary routine of work, such as employees, stockholders, suppliers, dealers, customers, and plant neighbors. External publics are composed of people who are not necessarily connected closely with a particular organization; for example, members of the press, educators, government officials, the financial world, and trade associations.

Public relations must employ the same planning format used for other promotional elements. This planning process begins with sound research. It continues with the following six steps: (1) assessment of the current situation, (2) statement of objectives, (3) selection of target audiences, (4) selection of methods of implementation, (5) determination of costs, and (6) evaluation of results.

The last part of the chapter dealt with the tools available to the PR manager. They include publicity-related tools, institutional ads, corporate sponsorships, company publications, motion pictures, and a variety of other tools.

Discussion Questions

1. There is a great deal of confusion between the terms *public relations* and *publicity.* Distinguish between the two concepts.

2. St. Ignatius Hospital in northern California has experienced a sharp decline in the number of patients admitted. It suspects one reason might be its policy of accepting patients with AIDS. What kind of research would you gather to assess the image of St. Ignatius?

3. Define a public. Describe internal and external publics. Name several publics that are of interest to the PR person.

4. With respect to the disposable diaper problem faced by Procter & Gamble Co. and other manufacturers, what else can be done to handle the negative publicity?

5. Assume that you are the PR director for the athletic program at your college or university. The NCAA just announced that they are investigating your football (or basketball) program. Outline a public relations strategy that will respond effectively to this bad news.

6. What steps might a public relations person take to prevent a firm from acquiring a negative public image?

7. What are the pros and cons of using institutional advertising? Under what conditions would it be appropriate?

8. Are there any guidelines for facilitating a healthy relationship between the news media and the firm's PR department?

9. Assume that you are the public relations director for a bank. Suppose that two people were robbed while withdrawing money from an automatic twenty-four-hour teller machine. What would your response be?

10. Assume that you are the public relations director for an airline. One of your airline's jets crashes. How would you respond?

Suggested Projects

1. Locate library material on two organizational crises, one whose outcome was positive and the other negative. Evaluate why these outcomes resulted.

2. Go through several newspapers and magazines and copy five articles that you feel are news releases. Determine the perceived objectives of these releases. How well were these objectives accomplished?

References

1. Walter W. Seifert, "The Outlook for Public Relations: Brighter Than Ever," *Public Relations Quarterly* (Summer 1973): 18–30.

2. Robert L. Dilenschneider and Dan J. Forrestal, *The Dartnell Public Relations Handbook* (Chicago: The Dartnell Corp., 1987): 78.

3. Patricia Winters, "Perrier's Back," *Advertising Age* (August 23, 1990): 1, 84.

4. "Careers in Public Relations," *Public Relations Society of America* (New York, 1989): 2.

5. Seifert, 19.

6. Dan J. Forrestal, "Placing Public Relations in Perspective," *Public Relations Journal* (March 1974): 41–46.

7. John Hebert, "Strong Ad, PR Programs Don't Happen Overnight," *Marketing News* (July 22, 1991): 18.

8. William D. Novelli, "Stir Some PR into Your Communications Mix," *Marketing News* (December 5, 1988): 19.

9. Yustin Wallrapp, "How Advertising-PR Partnership Can Succeed," *Advertising Age* (September 18, 1989): 40.

10. James J. Mullen and Michael E. Bishop, "Clinical Interviewing in Public Relations Research," *Public Relations Quarterly* (Spring 1975): 7–12.

11. Amanda Bennett, "Oil Firms Fret as Tempers Boil, Prices Jump," *Wall Street Journal* (August 8, 1990): B1.

12. Robert L. Rose, "Maytag's Acquisitions Don't Wear as Well as Washers and Dryers," *Wall Street Journal* (January 31, 1991): A1.

13. George Hammond, "Public Opinion: Do We Understand Its Function?" *Public Relations Journal* (July 1976): 8–13.

14. "'Foreign Companies' Global Awareness Cited in Study," *Marketing News* (August 1, 1988): 14.

15. Robert T. Reilly, *Public Relations in Action* (Englewood Cliffs, NJ: Prentice-Hall, Inc., 1981): 114.

16. Howard Schlossberg, "Americans Passionate About the Environment? Critic Says That's 'Nonsense,'" *Marketing News* (September 16, 1991): 8.

17. Barry Levin, "PR Gives New Life to Rejected TV Ads," *Advertising Age* (October 8, 1991): 76.

18. J. Thomas Russell and W. Ronald Lane, *Kleppner's Advertising Procedure*, 11th ed. (Englewood Cliffs, NJ: Prentice-Hall, Inc., 1990): 596.

19. "Study Shows Importance of Corporate Image," *Quirk's Marketing Research Review* (May 1989): 14–15, 39.

20. Monica de Hellerman, "What's the Bottom Line?" *Adweek Special Report* (September 19, 1988): S.E. 31.

21. Doug Newsom, Alan Scott, and Judy Van Slyke Turk, *This Is PR: The Realities of Public Relations,* 4th ed. (Belmont, CA: Wadsworth Publishing Co., 1989): 61.

22. Newsom, Scott, and Turk, 7.

13 *Promotional Media*

The Growth of Mass Media

Newspapers
The Industry and Its Audience
Buying Newspaper Space
Newspapers: Strengths and Limitations

Magazines
Magazines and Their Audiences
Buying Magazine Space
Magazines: Strengths and Limitations

Television
A Changing Industry
Understanding Television Audiences
Buying Television Time
Television: Strengths and Limitations

Radio
Stations and Networks
Buying Radio Time
Radio Research
Radio: Strengths and Limitations

Out-of-Home Promotions
Outdoor Promotion
Transit Promotion

Miscellaneous Media

Consider This:

Fragrant Appeals

How do you sell men's fragrances? Selling women's perfumes is one thing; you can use movie stars or romantic pictures or get just the right combination of name and high price to provoke people at least to sniff. But men's fragrances are different, not as socially accepted (unless, perhaps, disguised as "aftershave"), and not something to be sold with a traditional macho cowboys-and-tough guys approach.

A first step, at least according to Aramis Inc, the men's fragrances division of Estee Lauder, is to hire someone like the target market, in this case Josef Schreick. Schreick says his target is "the grey suit, pink collar man of the nineties who is not afraid to cry or bond with his family."

To prepare for a campaign, Schreick does a lot of people-watching, in malls, subways, and restaurants. He notes what people are reading, wearing, and buying. He wants to know what the trends are before they really get started.

With the kind of information he gathers from such research, Schreick uses Aramis's ad budget in some unusual ways. To promote a six-year-old fragrance, the company put 9 million scent strips in *Esquire, GQ, Vanity Fair,* and even *Vogue.* Spending the ad budget for a men's fragrance on a women's magazine is not a mistake; women buy some two-thirds of men's fragrances.

To sell the company's New West line, Schreick chose smaller, trendier magazines that he hopes are being read by people whom others watch—*Details, Egg, Interview,* and avant garde Los Angeles magazines such as *Buzz, Beach Culture,* and *Exposure.* New West also was featured in commercials on cable channels like MTV and ESPN and planned to sponsor a volleyball tournament.

Coming full circle, New West's latest offering is "Skinscent for Her" promoted with 3-D billboards and shopping bag inserts which appeared in a Sunday *Los Angeles Times* and could be redeemed for a free sample. Perhaps next will be a unisex uniscent.

Source: Michael Garry, "Tapping the Other Pink-Collar Crowd," *Marketing and Media Decisions* (September 1990): 12–13.

R egardless of how well designed and targeted an ad, sales promotion, or public relations message is, its success ultimately depends on
whether it is transmitted through the most appropriate medium. Success
requires that the message is delivered through a medium that complements the presentation, that is used consistently by members of the target
audience, and that is likely to present the message when the target audience is most receptive to it. Aramis, for example, is promoted in media
that are read or watched by a large percentage of consumers who, research
says, use an upscale male fragrance. That same research indicates that men
are not avid shoppers; therefore, the fragrance must be brought to them
directly, in the form of scented strip inserts.

Selecting and combining the appropriate media effectively is an extremely complex process. It requires the development of a comprehensive
media plan that creates a media mix appropriate for the promotion and for
the target consumer. If the mix does not suit the promotion and the consumer, the chance that the creative effort will work is very small.

Media planning remains a rather complex part of promotion. Few students begin their college careers with media planning in mind. The job
requires a penchant for numbers, detail, and organization as well as the
ability to see the big picture and generate creative solutions. Media planning also requires two kinds of knowledge. First, media planners (those
who develop and implement media plans) must have a thorough understanding of the media—of their capabilities, limitations, trends, and technology. Second, media planners must understand the components of a
media plan such as selecting media objectives, evaluating media in terms
of target markets, and scheduling.

The media plan is the topic of Chapter 14. The purpose of this chapter
is to provide information about the media.

The Growth of Mass Media

We call a medium a *mass medium* if it meets two requirements: (1) it can
reach many people simultaneously, and (2) it requires the use of some technological device to connect the promoter with the audience. Promotional
strategists are interested in mass media that are effective in delivering marketing messages. Virtually all mass media carry promotional messages.

Table 13.1   **Total National Ad Spending by Media**

| Category | 100 Leading National Advertisers | | | | |
| | Advertising Expenditures | | | Percentage of Total | |
	1990	1989	% chg	1990	1989
Magazine	$2,882.1	$2,887.7	(0.2)	8.1	8.6
Sunday magazine	247.3	235.5	5.0	0.7	0.7
Newspaper	2,009.5	1,975.2	1.7	5.6	5.9
Outdoor	267.0	242.7	10.0	0.7	0.7
Network TV	7,846.8	7,286.0	7.7	22.0	21.6
Spot TV	3,938.7	3,575.2	10.2	11.1	10.6
Syndicated TV	1,258.5	973.5	29.3	3.5	2.9
Cable TV networks	633.9	527.1	20.3	1.8	1.6
Network radio	417.4	422.1	(1.1)	1.2	1.3
Spot radio	391.5	687.3	(43.0)	1.1	2.0
Subtotal measured media	19,892.8	18,812.3	5.7	55.9	55.8
All other advertising	15,720.9	14,907.7	5.5	44.1	44.2
Total U.S. ad spending	35,613.7	33,720.0	5.6	100.0	100.0

Source: *Advertising Age* (September 25, 1991): 69. Used with permission. Copyright, Crain Communications Inc., 1991.

Traditionally, mass media are divided into four categories: print, broadcast, out-of-home, and miscellaneous. The miscellaneous category includes specialty media, the Yellow Pages, telemarketing, and direct mail, a medium that has grown rapidly during the last decade and is discussed separately in Chapter 18.

Table 13.1 shows the amount of money spent on mass media during 1989 and 1990. Note that the table contains three different sets of estimates. On the far left are the media figures for the one hundred leading national advertisers; in the middle are the total figures, as estimated by LNA/Arbitron and Radio Expenditure Reports; on the far right are estimates made by media forecaster Robert J. Coen of McCann-Erickson Advertising. Thus there are some differences in the numbers reported. For example, Coen's estimates for newspapers are far higher than the other estimates for that same medium. Obviously, these figures should only be used as general guidelines.

Another difficulty with these figures is that they are not broken down by promotion type (that is, advertising, sales promotion, public relations), and they do not include all the media-related costs incurred in carrying promotional messages. We do not know how much of the increase in expenditures on magazines can be attributed to the popularity of sales pro-

Table 13.1   **Total National Ad Spending by Media (*cont.*)**

	All U.S. Advertising Expenditures						
	Advertising Expenditures			Percentage of Total		Coen's U.S. Estimates*	
Category	1990	1989	% chg	1990	1989	1990	1989
Magazine	$6,737.7	$6,595.0	2.2	16.4	16.8	$6,803.0	$6,716.0
Sunday magazine	777.1	737.0	5.4	1.9	1.9	NA	NA
Newspaper	8,901.9	8,777.4	1.4	21.6	22.4	32,281.0	32,368.0
Outdoor	688.8	705.8	(2.4)	1.7	1.8	1,084.0	1,111.0
Network TV	10,132.3	9,559.0	6.0	24.6	24.4	9,383.0	9,110.0
Spot TV	9,293.3	9,029.4	2.9	22.6	23.0	15,644.0	14,966.0
Syndicated TV	1,587.6	1,286.7	23.4	3.9	3.3	1,589.0	1,288.0
Cable TV networks	1,110.2	952.5	16.6	2.7	2.4	1,393.0	1,197.0
Network radio	766.4	696.2	10.1	1.9	1.8	482.0	476.0
Spot radio	1,143.3	898.7	27.2	2.8	2.3	8,244.0	7,847.0
Subtotal measured media	41,138.6	39,237.7	4.8	32.0	31.7	76,903.0	75,079.0
All other advertising	87,501.4	84,692.3	3.3	68.0	68.3	51,737.0	48,851.0
Total U.S. ad spending	128,640.0	123,930.0	4.8	100.0	100.0	128,640.0	123,930.0

*Total U.S. advertising volume as estimated by Robert J. Coen, McCann-Erickson (*Advertising Age,* May 6, 1991). Used with permission. Copyright, Crain Communication Inc., 1991.

motion, the delivery of coupons and samples through this medium, or the use of magazines to deliver institutional messages, a public relations strategy. Furthermore, we do not know how much money is spent on specific media found under the "all other" category. It is unfortunate that media figures are all associated with advertising, when, in fact, sales promotion and public relations messages account for a large percentage of this total.

We do know, however, that the cost of mass media combined with the tremendous waste associated with traditional mass media has pushed many promoters toward media that are less expensive, better targeted, and easier to track. Moreover, promoters are trying to take a greater initiative when dealing with media by dictating rates, demanding greater service, and asking for guaranteed results. Media that cannot comply with such results-based guarantees either do not get the client or return to the client part or all of the money paid. The result has been turmoil in the world of mass media. Network television is making deals with cable television. For example, ABC has an 80-percent interest in ESPN. Specialty magazines targeted at small, homogeneous markets are being born and die daily. Examples of recent failures are *Emerge,* aimed at liberal blacks, and *Hippocrates,* a health magazine. And globalization means that the job of media planning and buying will become even more complex.

Concept Review

1. The success of a promotional strategy is contingent upon the effectiveness of the media plan. Media planning requires two types of information:
   A. An understanding of the strengths and limitations of the media.
   B. An understanding of all the components of a media plan.
2. A medium is considered a mass medium if it meets two requirements:
   A. It reaches many people at the same time.
   B. It requires the use of some technological device to connect the promoter with the audience.

Newspapers

Table 13.2 compares the capabilities of the major media. Mike Walsh, media director at Ketchum Advertising, succinctly noted the primary advantage that newspapers offer to promoters. "Readers actually use newspaper advertising to find goods and services. They even know where to look for the ad by section. I don't think you can say that about advertising in any other media, where ads are usually more of an intrusion." While promoters who produce thirty-minute infomercials on skin care and those who produce the various shopping programs might disagree with Walsh's assessment, newspapers do offer some special advantages to the promotion manager. Newspapers are also the oldest mass medium.

Media historians suggest that the first significant newspaper in the United States was the *New England Courant,* started by James and Benjamin Franklin in 1721. From that time until the introduction of television, newspapers were the primary source of news for Americans. Today, the role and appearance of newspapers have changed. Legions of newspapers are taking their cue from *USA Today,* which uses four-color presses and produces beautiful charts and weather maps. Newspapers are also emphasizing "soft news" such as entertainment, sports, and travel over the traditional "hard news" (that is, politics, social issues, and world events). With declining revenues and increasing costs, newspapers have also changed the way they gather the news. Large national newspapers such as the *Los Angeles Times,* the *Washington Post,* and *The New York Times* as well as newspaper chains such as Gannett and Knight-Ridder operate their own news services. But rather than support a crew of reporters, many local newspapers rely on the two major wire services, United Press and Associated Press, for international, national, and even local news. This change in the way newspapers gather news may be a major reason why both the credibility and popularity of newspapers have fallen. According to a 1990 survey, 44 percent of Americans feel that press reports are inaccurate, compared with 34 percent who felt this way in 1985. Three decades ago, many homes were receiving more than one paper, creating a penetration rate of

Table 13.2   Strategic Capabilities of Mass Media

Types of Media	Market Coverage	Cost	Cost per Thousand	Flexibility	Emotional Impact	Targetability	Reputation	Clutter	Message Length	Frequency	Immediacy	Creativity	Resellers Support	Production Quality
National newspapers	–	–	+	–	0	+	+	–	+	+	+	+	–	+
Local newspapers	+	+	+	+	0	+	+	–	+	+	+	–	+	–
Magazines	–	0	–	–	+	+	+	–	+	0	+	+	+	+
Network television	+	–	+	–	+	0	+	+	0	0	+	+	+	+
Cable television	0	+	+	+	0	+	0	+	+	+	+	+	+	+
Network radio	0	–	+	0	–	–	+	+	–	+	+	0	+	+
Local radio	+	+	+	+	0	+	0	–	–	+	+	0	+	0
Outdoor	–	+	+	–	–	–	–	–	–	0	–	0	–	0
Yellow pages	0	+	+	–	–	+	+	–	–	–	–	0	–	0

– weak capability
0 moderate capability
+ strong capability

more than 100 percent; today, the household penetration rate has dropped to 70 percent.[1]

Despite this bleak picture, newspapers still remain an important source for local news and the number one shopping medium. In this section, we take a closer look at American newspapers and what they have to offer media planners.

The Industry and Its Audience

For American newspapers, how media planners view their promotional potential is critical. Most newspapers get about 75 percent to 80 percent of their income from advertising. In fact, production of the day's newspaper begins in the advertising department. The ads are placed first, and the news must fit around them in the remaining space. In the past decade, however, national advertising as a percentage of total newspaper advertising revenue has steadily declined. (Much of the loss is tied to a loss in tobacco advertising.) Local retail advertising is newspaper's bread and butter, accounting for an average 50 percent of revenue. This is made evident in Table 13.3, which gives the listing of the top twenty-five newspaper advertisers, more than half of whom are retailers.

More than nine thousand newspapers are published in the United States today. These publications may be classified in several ways: by their physical size (standard or tabloid), intended audience (for example, financial, Spanish-speaking), and type of circulation (for example, paid or controlled). Most newspapers are "paid," that is, subscribers pay for them. A shopper such as *Thrifty Nickel* or *Real Estate Guide* is usually distributed free to certain homes in certain neighborhoods. The primary way of classifying newspapers, however, is based on their frequency of publication, either daily or weekly.

According to the magazine *Editor & Publisher*, more than 1,650 daily newspapers and more than 8,000 weeklies are published in the United States today. Most Sunday papers are published by dailies; few papers publish Sunday editions only. While the number of afternoon papers has declined by 279, to 1,150, since 1946 (due to the popularity of television evening news), the number of morning papers has increased by 191, to 525. Moreover, the number of newspapers publishing Sunday editions has more than doubled, reaching 847.[2]

The Sunday paper is considered the success story of the 1980s. Fat with news, features, and ads, the Sunday paper offers the biggest package of the week on the day that people have the most time. The average reader spends sixty-two minutes on the Sunday paper, seventeen minutes more than on the weekday edition.

Who is this reader? A key source for information about newspaper audiences is the Audit Bureau of Circulations (ABC). It was organized in 1914

Table 13.3 The Top 25 Newspaper Advertisers

		Newspaper Spending		
Rank	Advertiser	1990	1989	% chg
1	May Department Stores Co.	$218.2	$208.2	4.8
2	R. H. Macy & Co.	160.1	183.6	(12.8)
3	Sears, Roebuck & Co.	136.8	154.9	(11.7)
4	Federated Department Stores	134.5	144.0	(6.6)
5	Dayton Hudson Corp.	106.2	107.5	(1.2)
6	Montgomery Ward & Co.	82.1	67.2	22.1
7	K Mart Corp.	80.1	58.6	36.7
8	Carter Hawley Hale Stores	72.8	66.9	8.9
9	J. C. Penney Co.	70.6	81.4	(13.2)
10	American Stores Co.	69.6	81.9	(15.1)
11	AMR Corp.	60.7	41.0	48.1
12	Highland Superstores	49.0	36.2	35.3
13	General Motors Corp.	46.6	55.7	(16.3)
14	Time Warner	46.2	43.1	7.2
15	AT&T Co.	43.8	39.7	10.2
16	Tengleman Group	42.8	20.9	104.3
17	Circuit City Stores	41.3	37.6	9.7
18	Tandy Corp.	40.5	37.6	7.7
19	Woodward & Lothrop	38.1	39.8	(4.2)
20	Walt Disney Co.	36.7	24.6	49.1
21	Sony Corp.	36.1	30.3	19.3
22	Matsushita Electric Industrial Co.	33.0	28.9	14.2
23	Delta Air Lines	32.9	28.5	15.5
24	Dillard Department Stores	32.9	30.3	8.6
25	Ahold International	31.0	27.6	12.2

Note: Dollars are in millions.

Source: *Advertising Age* (September 25, 1991): 72. Used with permission.

by advertisers, their agencies, and the publishers of newspapers and magazines. Its objective is to establish standard and acceptable methods of measuring circulations of member publications. Auditors employed by ABC regularly check circulation figures. In addition, detailed analyses of the circulation of a paper by states, towns, and counties are also provided by ABC.

Some newspapers do not submit information or allow auditing of circulation information by a firm such as ABC. Because potential advertisers might be suspicious of newspapers that do not give out circulation figures, these papers do have the option of providing a publisher's statement supported by a sworn affidavit or a post office statement, a newspaper's claimed circulation figures given once each year to the post office. These statements are viewed as equivalent to ABC figures.

While organizations such as ABC provide basic information on the demographics of subscribers to a particular newspaper, additional information is provided through trade organizations such as the Newspaper Advertising Bureau (NAB). NAB reports that newspapers serve three basic functions. The first is "surveillance"; readers use papers to find information that helps them "orient themselves" to the surrounding world. Second, newspapers provide "tools for daily living," ranging from service features, television logs, and event listings to school lunch menus. And third, papers include a mix of features that divert, amuse, and entertain, whether they are news stories or personal ads.[3] Such information is quite useful to the promotion strategist, who can then determine whether a product would fit the newspaper.

In the coming years, the profile of the newspaper audience may well change. Faced with competition from other media and declining credibility, American newspapers have been looking for market niches. The Socio-Economic Research Institute of America predicts that during the next decade, the audience for newspapers will consist of better-educated people. "They want high-quality information about current events. . . . Newspapers that provide this will have the greatest chance of growth."[4] Meanwhile, desktop publishing techniques will produce great economies of scale and make targeting of specialized audiences possible for papers big and small.

Buying Newspaper Space

Table 13.4 illustrates some of the important ways in which newspapers vary. The size of their audience, the demographic characteristics of their readers, and the rates they charge for advertising space are among the characteristics media planners must consider.

Most daily newspapers offer classified advertising, including regular and display, and display advertising. **Classified ads** include all types of messages arranged by classification of interest, such as Help Wanted, Cars for Sale, and so on. Classified display ads allow more flexibility than regular classifieds because borders, larger type, white space, photos, and occasionally color may be used.

Display ads are found throughout the newspaper and generally use illustrations, headlines, white space, and other visual devices in addition to the copy text; they can be of any size. For display ads, the infrequent advertiser usually pays a standard rate per column per inch. An advertiser

Table 13.4 **Summary of Newspaper Characteristics**

Paper	Circulation	Demographics	Ad Rates	Major Advertisers
USA Today	1,750,000	35% female, avg. age 41, income $40K, 56% college educ.	Page rate $65,916	Miller Brewing Co., AT&T, Lincoln-Mercury
New York Post	507,000	50.4% male, avg. age 42, income $39.5K, 45% college educ.	Page rate $20,230	Wouldn't reveal
Chicago Sun-Times	535,844	49.6% female, avg. age 40.5, income $32.3K, 38% college educ.	Page rate $11,000	Firestone Tire & Rubber Co., Honda Dealer Assn., K Mart Corp., World Wrestling Foundation
San Francisco Chronicle/ Examiner	698,609	52% male, avg. age 40, income $42.3K, 60% college educ	Page rate $30,057	Herman's Sporting Goods, Inc., Goodyear, Sears, Roebuck and Co., Montgomery Ward

Source: *Adweek* (April 3, 1990): 5. Reprinted with permission of *Adweek*.

who uses significant amounts of space pays a discounted bulk or contract rate based on the total volume of space or number of insertions used by the advertiser at a given time. Advertisers and newspapers frequently sign annual contracts for a given space commitment. If the advertiser uses less space or makes fewer insertions than the contract calls for during the contract period, he or she pays a "short rate" on the linage used. If more space is used than called for by the contract in this period, the advertiser receives a rebate that adjusts the total expenditure to the applicable (lower) rate level.

Determining Costs　A newspaper's rate card, the *Editor and Publisher Yearbook,* and the *Standard Rate and Data Service Newspaper* list the newspapers' line rates. The rates vary depending on circulation, costs of operation, labor costs, qualitative factors, and type of newspaper.

Media buyers use the milline rate to compare the cost of promoting through different newspapers. A **milline rate** is the cost per line to reach a newspaper circulation of one million. The formula is

$$\text{Milline rate} = \frac{1,000,000 \times \text{line rate}}{\text{Actual circulation}}$$

If newspaper A has a line rate of $.90 and a circulation of 180,000, and newspaper B has a line rate of $.37 and a circulation of 75,000, the comparison figures would be as follows:

$$\text{MR (A)} = \frac{1,000,000 \times .90}{180,000} = \$5.00$$

$$\text{MR (B)} = \frac{1,000,000 \times .37}{75,000} = \$4.92$$

Most newspapers offer a lower rate to local advertisers than to national advertisers. The national rate ranges from 30 percent to 40 percent higher than the local rate. Newspaper publishers claim that this rate difference is justifiable because retailers, particularly a few leading retailers, use far more space than national advertisers in local papers; local retail advertising is news that has inherent interest. Another reason for the differential is that local retail advertising is usually prepared and placed directly by the retailer, without the intercession of an advertising agency. In order to combat their higher rate, national advertisers have developed cooperative advertising plans: national advertisers cooperate with local dealers in financing advertising that is actually placed by the local dealer at the local rate. Some large advertisers such as Continental Airlines have taken advantage of "hybrid" rates (that is, rates customized for certain customers) created by newspapers to attract advertising by airlines, car rental companies, hotels, and resorts.

Promotional Options   Advertisers can usually order specific pages or positions for an extra charge. For example, if an advertiser using the *Chicago Sun-Times* wants to ensure ad placement at the very top of the page and next to reading matter along one of its vertical sides (called full position), the advertiser may have to pay as much as 33.3 percent more. However, certain advertisers may be able to negotiate for the same position without paying extra.

Newspapers may also offer special production capabilities for additional charges. For instance, run-of-paper color (black plus one color) costs more than black and white. Color surcharges may vary from 17 percent to 35 percent extra for a full-page ad if black and one color are used. If full color (black plus three colors) is used, surcharges average from 29 percent to 62 percent extra.[5]

Color preprint is a service offered by about 96 percent of all daily newspapers. In this process, color ads are preprinted on a roll of paper that is fed into the presses. Color preprints provide the national and local advertiser with many of the "quality" advantages of magazine color while allowing each retailer to place imprinted copy next to the national advertiser's four-color ad on the same page.

A final option offered by newspapers is the supplement. Each of the syndicated supplements is compiled, edited, and printed by a central organization that then sells it to the newspapers at a fixed cost per thousand. *Parade*, for example, is distributed by Sunday newspapers all over the United States; it offers group-rate advertising charges. Printed on paper that is heavier and better finished than newsprint, supplements offer surprisingly low rates.

Newspapers: Strengths and Limitations

As noted earlier, a primary strength of newspapers is that they serve as a trusted source of information for many consumers. Sales promotion information (such as price discounts and coupons) as well as public relations information (such as open house announcements and special events) can all be delivered through newspapers. More importantly, consumers seek out this information.

Market flexibility is another advantage of newspapers. Gone are the days when one general newspaper served a particular market. Today, newspapers have the capability of reaching special interest groups, unique ethnic or racial groups, or even people living in isolated parts of the world (for example, *The Stars and Stripes* is mailed to all U.S. military personnel). Miami's *Diaria Las Americas* is a Spanish-language newspaper with circulation of over seventy thousand.

Lead time flexibility is a third advantage of newspapers. Lead time is the amount of time between when an ad must be delivered to the medium and when it is actually run. For example, the lead time for a newspaper ad is quite short, often forty-eight to seventy-two hours. Ads can therefore be changed at the last minute, or new ads can be inserted to meet an unforeseen circumstance, such as a dramatic change in the weather.

Newspapers also provide the advantage of a large pass-along audience. Not only do members of a family share the same newspaper, but newspapers are also read by people at fast-food chains, diners, railroad stations, and professional offices.

Furthermore, newspapers facilitate the effective combination of local ads or sales promotions with national promotions. A local retailer can easily tie in with a national campaign by utilizing a similar ad. For example, Computerland stores tend to employ ads that appear similar to those produced by IBM and Compaq. Newspapers also allow preprinted ads and freestanding inserts in order to accommodate national promotions.

The most serious limitation associated with newspapers is clutter. With 59 percent or more of a typical newspaper filled with ads, it is difficult to create awareness. Clutter is also a problem with the free-standing inserts that now deliver more than 50 percent of consumer coupons. FSIs are now so thick and bulky that getting through them all is a task that many readers reject, choosing instead to remove the entire packet and put it aside.

Other limitations of newspapers are also significant. Although a strength of newspapers is their currency, the one-day life of a paper means that a promotion has a very short time in which to work. The technical quality of newspapers is another problem. Porous paper and poor reproduction of print and photography often mean that an ad is unreadable. A final limitation of newspapers is the differential rate structure discussed earlier. Until this difference is reduced, newspapers will remain an unattractive alternative for national advertisers.

Concept Review

1. The Audit Bureau of Circulation is the primary source of information on newspaper circulation and rates.
2. Classified and display advertising in newspapers are sold on the basis of either a line rate or a bulk or contract rate. Newspapers charge a higher rate to national than to local advertisers.
3. . The primary strength of newspapers is that they are a trusted source of information: people look for and read newspaper ads.
4. The primary weakness of newspapers is their clutter.

Magazines

Magazines form a wild and unpredictable collection of publications—colorful, competitive, exciting. From 1900 to 1950, the number of households subscribing to one or more periodicals rose from two hundred thousand to more than thirty-two million. This magazine boon came in spite of the introduction of film, radio, television, and the paperback book. During the 1970s, more emphasis was placed on reaching special audiences not served adequately by other mass media. Thus a magazine like *Psychology Today* achieved a circulation in excess of one million within a few years. Unfortunately, *Psychology Today* went out of business and is now making a comeback.

Today, magazines are the most specialized of the mass media, dramatically demonstrating the fact that the mass audience is becoming increasingly segmented. For example, *Writer's Market* lists more than a hundred magazines that deal with farming, soil management, poultry, dairy farming, and rural life. Farming magazines are one example of **special-interest** publications, which account for more than 90 percent of the total number of magazines published today.

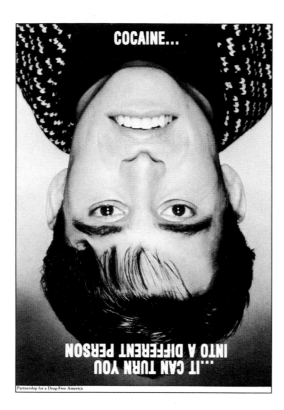

COCAINE...

...IT CAN TURN YOU INTO A DIFFERENT PERSON

The anti-drug campaign has built an effective ad series using stark black-and-white photography and cut-to-the-quick headlines. (Rotate ad for full effect.)

Courtesy of Partnership for a Drug-Free America.

NEW GRAPE FLAVOR

FREE FOR THE PICKING.

Gatorade
It's all you're thirsting for.

MANUFACTURER COUPON | EXPIRES MAY 31, 1992

BUY 1 GET 1 FREE!
BUY: Any ONE 32oz. or larger Gatorade
GET: ONE 32oz. Grape Flavor Gatorade FREE!

Quaker Oats' premium offer "Buy One, Get One Free" is not the only incentive for consumers to try Gatorade's new flavor—the luscious purple makes it ripe for picking off the page.

Reprinted with permission of The Quaker Oats Company.

The humor of the Eveready Battery Company's Energizer Bunny™—so successful as a television ad series—is captured in this clever print ad.

Courtesy of Eveready Battery Company, Inc.

Unlike most car ads, this witty and creative ad does not feature a close-up of a gleaming automobile mounted across a two-page spread.

Courtesy of American Honda Motor Co., Inc.

The Regina® Dirt Magnet.™
Be careful where you point it.

The Regina Dirt Magnet comes with a 2.75 amp motor and a complete set of attachments. All of which makes it an incredibly powerful, versatile hand vac. For information, call Ken Drescher at (201) 381-1000, ext. 14. He'll point you in the right direction. **Regina**

Although television is usually the ideal medium in which to demonstrate a product, the Regina Dirt Magnet seems to make its point successfully in this humorous print ad.

Used with permission of The Regina Company.

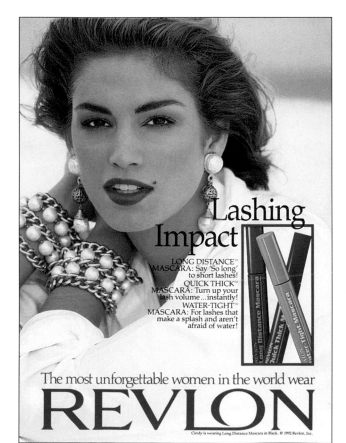

Lashing Impact

LONG DISTANCE™ MASCARA: Say 'So long' to short lashes!

QUICK THICK™ MASCARA: Turn up your lash volume...instantly!

WATER-TIGHT™ MASCARA: For lashes that make a splash and aren't afraid of water!

The most unforgettable women in the world wear
REVLON

Cindy is wearing Long Distance Mascara in Black. © 1992 Revlon, Inc.

One of the strongest ad campaigns of the nineties is Revlon's "The Most Unforgettable Women in the World" ad series: Featuring a unique theme and stunning—but varied— models, this cosmetics firm encourages the consumer to enhance her individuality.

Courtesy of Revlon, Inc.

Give-aways, such as the pack of flower seeds on this ad for Absolut, are an attractive promotion tool.

©V & S. Carillon Importers LTD.

Evidence indicates that the purchase of products such as candy are frequently unplanned; point-of-purchase displays are very likely to prompt such purchases.

Courtesy of Hershey Foods Corporation. HERSHEY'S is a registered trademark of Hershey Foods Corporation and is used with permission. Photo: Rick Rappaport.

Magazines and Their Audiences

Special-interest magazines have flourished partly as a result of the high advertising rates charged by mass-circulation, **general-interest** magazines such as *Reader's Digest, TV Guide,* and *People.* This division into special- and general-interest magazines is just one of several ways of classifying magazines.

The Standard Rate and Data Service categorizes magazines by frequency of publication and the audience to which they are directed. Monthly magazines are the largest category, followed by weeklies, semimonthlies, bimonthlies, and quarterlies. On the basis of the audience served, there are three types of magazines:

1. Consumer magazines, which are edited for people who buy products for their own consumption, generated $7.3 billion of advertising revenue in 1990. Standard Rate and Data Service divides this group into fifty-seven subclassifications as well as categorizing them on the basis of their distribution, that is, circulation-distributed (distributed to subscribers at their homes) and store-distributed (sold through retail outlets).

2. Farm magazines, which are circulated to farmers and their families, had 1990 ad revenues of $800 million. These magazines can be general (for example, *Successful Farming*) or specialized (for example, *Beef*).

3. Business magazines, which are directed at business readers, are further divided into trade papers (read by retailers, wholesalers, and other distributors), industrial magazines (read by manufacturers), and professional magazines (read by such groups as physicians and lawyers). They generated ad revenues of $3.1 billion in 1990. Business publications are often characterized as either vertical or horizontal. A *vertical* publication covers all aspects of an industry. A *horizontal* publication covers one job that cuts across several industries. *Computerworld* is an example of the former, while *Engineer Digest* is an example of the latter.

The magazine industry applies three other possible classifications to each of the three just discussed. Consumer, farm, and business magazines can also be classified by geographic, demographic, and editorial content.

1. Geographic editions. Sectional or regional editions of national publications (for example, *Time* and *Southern Living*) may be circulated in an area as large as several states or as limited as one city.

2. Demographic editions. Many magazines offer special editions for subscribers of a certain age, income, occupation, and so forth (for example, *Time* and *Newsweek* have special student editions).

Table 13.5   **Magazines Ranked by Circulation**

		Total Circulation 1989
1.	*Modern Maturity**	20,326,933
2.	*NRTA/AARP News Bulletin**	20,001,538
3.	*Reader's Digest*	16,434,254
4.	*TV Guide*	16,330,051
5.	*National Geographic*	10,829,328
6.	*Better Homes and Gardens*	8,027,010
7.	*Family Circle*	5,212,555
8.	*McCall's*	5,150,814
9.	*Ladies' Home Journal*	5,117,712
10.	*Good Housekeeping*	5,140,774
11.	*Woman's Day*	4,401,746
12.	*Time*	4,393,237
13.	*Guideposts*	4,239,396
14.	*National Enquirer*	4,222,755
15.	*Redbook*	3,906,453

*Association magazine

Source: Audit Bureau of Circulations 1990. Used with permission. Copyright © 1989 Audit Bureau of Circulations. All rights reserved.

3. Editorial content. Magazines are defined by interest category such as general editorial, women's services, and business.

As Table 13.5 illustrates, the magazines with the largest circulations reach a broad spectrum of society. *Modern Maturity*, for example, is the official magazine of the American Association of Retired Persons (AARP) and reaches all its members, which include people fifty-five years of age and older. It should be noted, however, that the first two magazines listed are mailed to all group members and therefore differ from the magazines that follow.

Information like that in Figure 13.1 comes from the Audit Bureau of Circulation, which collects and evaluates data about magazines as well as about newspapers, as discussed earlier. The total circulation of a magazine is just one of the significant pieces of data. For example, some media buyers regard newsstand sales as a good criterion of the quality of a magazine's circulation, because purchases at a newsstand are completely voluntary. By paying more per copy and taking the initiative, newsstand buyers are viewed as more serious readers. Many media analysts also carefully watch the trends in subscription sales of various magazines, especially the rate at which subscribers renew their subscriptions.

Figure 13.1

A sample audit report assembled by the Audit Bureau of Circulations.
Audit Bureau of Circulations. Used with permission.

AUDIT REPORT: Magazine

Audit Bureau of Circulations

PROTOTYPE
Anytown, USA

CLASS, INDUSTRY OR FIELD SERVED: Edited for the home-owner and providing guidance, repair maintenance and improvements of his house and property. All articles presented in "Do-It-Yourself" step-by-step format and profusely illustrated.

1. AVERAGE PAID CIRCULATION FOR 12 MONTHS ENDED JUNE 30, (YEAR):

Subscriptions:	1,039,644	
Single Copy Sales:	44,062	
AVERAGE TOTAL PAID CIRCULATION..................................		1,083,706
Advertising Rate Base during Audit Period .... to 2-1-YR	1,050,000	
since 2-1-YR	1,100,000	
Average Total Non-Paid Distribution	48,168	

1a. AVERAGE PAID CIRCULATION of Regional, Metro and Demographic Editions:

None of record

2. PAID CIRCULATION BY ISSUES:

ISSUE YEAR		ISSUE YEAR	
July/Aug.	1,088,661	Jan./Feb.	1,049,058
Sept.	1,091,200	Mar.	1,090,974
Oct.	1,081,861	Apr.	1,116,976
Nov.	1,067,123	May	1,087,705
Dec.	1,073,876	June	1,089,625

AVERAGE PAID CIRCULATION BY QUARTERS for the previous three years and period covered by this report:

Calendar Quarter Ended	YEAR	YEAR	YEAR	YEAR	YEAR
March 31		877,049	1,088,249	1,019,802	1,085,669
June 30		944,113	1,078,221	1,035,606	1,088,665
September 30	891,806	966,265	1,022,494	1,809,931	
December 31	868,607	936,603	1,000,614	1,074,287	

AUDIT STATEMENT

The difference shown in average total paid circulation in comparing this report with the Publisher's Statements for the period audited, amounting to an average of 2,635 copies per issue is accounted for by deductions made for additional newsdealer returns, publisher having underestimated returns in filing statements to the Bureau, 2,000 copies per issue; less an addition made for publisher's overestimation of duplications on the mail lists, 365 copies per issue.

To Members of the Audit Bureau of Circulations:

We have examined the circulation records and other data presented by this publication for the period covered by this report. Our examinations were made in accordance with the Bureau's Bylaws and Rules, and included such tests and other audit procedures as we considered necessary under the circumstances.

In our opinion, the total average paid circulation for the period shown is fairly stated in this report, and the other data contained in this report are fairly stated in all respects material to average paid circulation.

November, Year   **Audit Bureau of Circulations**

(04-0000-0 - #000000 - 11 - XX)

To help provide this information, the Audit Bureau of Circulation collects and evaluates the data about magazines. Briefly, the bureau checks how many copies were printed, sold at newsstands, or returned; checks how many were sold by subscription; and determines how the subscriptions were obtained, measured in terms of cut-rate sales and delinquent subscribers (ordered but not paid for). The bureau also determines the rate of renewal.

Audience profiles are also invaluable to media buyers. In general, magazine readers are better educated, better read, and better paid than other members of the population.[6] For example, *Capell's Circulation Report,* an independent research company reporting on magazine circulation) indicates that the target of *Now* magazine is women twenty-eight to thirty-eight years old with average household incomes of from thirty-four thousand dollars to forty thousand dollars. More than half are married and more than three-quarters attended college or graduate school and work outside the home. Many magazines provide reader profiles to their advertisers to influence them to buy space. A media buyer may find that the audience profile for a magazine is attractive enough to override the fact that its circulation is smaller than that of a competitor.

In summary, although total circulation is an important piece of information, evaluating a magazine usually requires a fuller portrait of its audience. Among the characteristics media buyers consider are the following:

- The percentage of the publication read completely,
- Reader loyalty,
- Reader demographics,
- The magazine's past ability to generate high response in mail-order ads,
- Special sections, and
- Number of pass-along readers.

Buying Magazine Space

Besides considering the characteristics of readers, media buyers must also consider the cost of magazine space. Only a handful of marketers can afford to pay thirty thousand dollars to eighty-five thousand dollars for a full-page pull-out in a mass circulation magazine. As a result, many smaller companies have turned to less expensive special-interest magazines, where their messages will be seen by fewer but more receptive readers.

Advertising Rates   Magazine space is sold primarily on the basis of pages or some increment of a page. For example, the rate card for *Time* Demographic Editions is shown in Figure 13.2.

TIME BUSINESS

Offers the largest all-business circulation of any magazine in the United States. All TIME Business subscriber households are qualified by job title, verified by the ABC. Provides in-depth reach to top, middle and technical management and professionals in all 50 states. Available every other week.

Rates are based on subscription circulation only.

Rate Base: 1,635,000	Black & White	Black & 1 Color	4 Color
Page	$ 56,900	$ 71,100	$ 84,100
2 Columns	42,700	53,300	67,300
1/2 Page Horizontal Spread*	79,700	99,500	117,700
1 Column	22,800	28,400	37,800
1/2 Column	20,700	24,900	NA

*Subject to limited availability

See page 17 for TIME Business Bonus Plan Discount.

TIME TOP MANAGEMENT

Circulation exclusively to owners, partners, directors, board chairpersons, company presidents, other titled officers and department heads. Subscriber households are 100% qualified by job title, verified by the ABC. Provides highly refined reach targeted to top management nationwide. Available every other week.

Rates are based on subscription circulation only.

Rate Base: 600,000	Black & White	Black & 1 Color	4 Color
Page	$ 31,300	$ 38,700	$ 46,200
2 Columns	23,500	29,000	37,000
1 Column	12,500	15,500	20,900
1/2 Column	7,800	9,700	NA

TIME CAMPUS

Circulates to America's future thought leaders and educators. Offers coast-to-coast coverage of the college market ($2 billion discretionary income) with the magazine most read by students. Available seven times in 1992.

Rates are based on subscription circulation only.

Rate Base: 400,000	Black & White	Black & 1 Color	4 Color
Page	$ 15,300	$ 19,100	$ 22,600

TIME INTERNATIONAL EDITIONS

Other editions are available. For complete details on all international editions including rates, discount structure, space availabilities and production information, refer to TIME International 1992 rate card or contact your local TIME Sales Representative.

All rates are quoted in U.S. dollars, except where noted.

	Rate Base (000)	Page B & W	Page 4C
Atlantic	645	*Ecu 26,000	Ecu 40,000
Europe	560	Ecu 24,375	Ecu 37,500
Continent	460	Ecu 23,360	Ecu 34,400
Common Market 12	434	Ecu 22,100	Ecu 34,000
Canada	350	$13,700	$17,500
Asia	270	22,463	35,380
Southeast Asia	135	11,603	18,275
South Pacific	150	5,510	8,540
Latin America	95	12,585	18,790
TIME International	**1,509**	**$ 85,641**	**$128,493**
TIME U.S.	**4,000**	**91,000**	**134,400**
TIME World	**5,509**	**176,641**	**262,893**

*European Currency Unit.

See page 19 for International Discounts.

Figure 13.2
A rate card for Time *Demographic Editions.*
Reprinted with the permission of Time *Demographic Editions.*

The rates for black-and-white ads are listed under number five in the rate card. The column labelled 1ti lists the one-time rates. The card also gives the rates for insertions of six times, twelve times, and so forth, as well as the corresponding rates for color.

Whereas newspaper rates are primarily compared by millines, magazine rates (and other media) are compared by cost per page per thousand circulation, or CPM:

$$\text{CPM} = \frac{\text{Cost per page}}{\text{Circulation (in thousands)}}$$

Even with this index, however, magazine rates can be adjusted in so many ways that making comparisons is difficult.

Magazines offer frequency discounts that result in a lower cost per unit for advertisers who run ads regularly within the contract year. For example:

13 pages or more	7%
26 pages or more	12%
39 pages or more	16%
52 pages or more	20%

Although publishers offer discounts to advertisers who contract for a certain number of insertions per year, there are times when the advertiser cannot maintain this schedule. Then the advertiser must pay the *short rate*. Thus if the twelve-time rate is twenty-five hundred dollars per page, but the advertiser can only manage six insertions (twenty-eight hundred dollars per page), the magazine will bill the advertiser for the difference at the end of the insertion year:

$$\$2800 - \$2500 = \$300 \times 6 = \$1800$$

A number of publishers, especially those with geographic or demographic editions, sometimes find themselves with extra space in some editions when they are ready to go to press. Rather than run an empty space, the publisher often offers this *remnant space* to advertisers at a big discount. Of course, material for the ad must be ready for insertion.

Promotional Options   In most cases, the double-page spread is the largest unit of space sold by magazines. The two pages normally face one another. Magazines allow one-page or double-page ads to be broken into a variety of units called *fractional page space*: vertical half-page, horizontal half-page, double horizontal half-page, island position (surrounded by editorial matter), half-page double spread, and checkerboard.

Sometimes a magazine cover or an inside page opens to reveal an extra page that folds out and gives the ad a big spread. Advertisers use these *gatefolds* on special occasions to make the most spectacular presentation in the magazine, usually to introduce a colorful product like a new model car or beautiful flooring. They are an additional expense that requires advanced planning.

The physical format of magazines also varies somewhat. The page size of a magazine is its type area, not the size of the actual page. The size of most magazines is characterized as either *standard* (8 inches × 10 inches; for example, *Newsweek*) or *small size* (4 3/8 inches by 6 1/2 inches; for example, *Reader's Digest*). These measurements are approximations; when ordering plates, advertisers must get the exact page size from the publisher. The front cover of a magazine is called the *first cover page.* The inside of the front cover is called the *second cover page,* the inside of the back cover the *third cover page,* and the back cover the *fourth cover page.* Advertisers using the latter three positions pay a premium and may even have to be put on a waiting list. A premium position is an especially favorable place in the magazine—for example, the middle of the magazine or pages following the inside front cover or facing a specific story or section of the magazine. Premium positions cost 10 percent to 25 percent more, and cover positions cost even more.

Advertisers who wish to reduce the cost of their magazine advertising may purchase *run-of-book* (ROB) space, which means that the ad can be placed anywhere in the magazine. Because these ads permit the media owners the most scheduling flexibility, they are generally the cheapest available spots.

When an ad runs all the way to the edge of the page, leaving no margin, it is called a *bleed ad.* This ad is designed to get extra attention and also gives creative directors more room to express their ideas. The option may cost an extra 15 percent to 20 percent.

Many magazines also have a provision for inserts. Examples are return cards, coupons, receipt booklets, and other kinds of outside material bound into magazines in connection with an adjoining ad. Inserts are never sold separately. Negotiating and creating such inserts is the job of the sales promotion manager. Some advertisers print their ads on foil, acetate, or heavy paper. This kind of *heavyweight insert* makes it hard for a reader to miss the ad. Readers' complaints have curtailed the use of heavyweight inserts, although their effectiveness has never been questioned. A final special type of insert consists of placing consecutive pages of advertising one right after another in order to create an impression. Sears, Roebuck and Co. commonly places eight to twelve pages together in order to advertise a particular product such as sheets and towels.

Other options are offered by mass-circulation magazines in an effort to meet the competition from special-interest magazines. For example, magazines such as *Time* offer local companies reduced rates for regional *breakouts,* messages that will appear only in copies sent to a specific geographic region. Reduced regional rates give smaller companies a chance to appear in a national magazine at a rate they can afford. *Time* also offers advertisers the opportunity to reach subscribers who are doctors, members of top management, students, educators, or even those who live in special high-income zip code areas; editions that are sent to these subscribers are known as *demo editions*.

Purchasing Procedures   Magazine advertisers are ruled by three dates. The *closing date* is the last date on which a magazine will accept advertising materials for publication in a particular issue. The *cover date* appears on the cover. The *on-sale date* is when the issue goes on sale. Thus a magazine with a January cover date could go on sale December 15. The on-sale date is important because it tells when most issues reach the reader.

Desktop publishing and satellite transmission have shortened the lead time for promotions in magazines. Desktop publishing is now mainline technology; even some of the most sophisticated publishers now produce editorial pages on personal computers. Satellites are the next step in computerization. Satellites allow computer-processed magazine pages to be sent directly to the printing operation via satellite, thus shortening the time it takes to produce the magazine. The news weeklies pioneered satellite transmission of electronic pages to tighten editorial deadlines. Now this benefit accrues to advertisers as well. *Vanity Fair* closes some pages just hours before press time, using totally electronic page composition and satellite transmission to its printer. Lead time for advertising has been cut dramatically.

Magazines: Strengths and Limitations

The ability to reach highly segmented target audiences is clearly the primary advantage of magazines. As a result, the absolute cost and the cost per thousand for magazine promotions are fairly low, but not as low as broadcast costs. Increasing audience specialization seems a certainty. Personalized editions are the next logical step. Through **selective binding** (a computerized process that allows for the creation of hundreds of editions of a magazine in one continuous sequence and personalization of advertising through inkjet imaging), consumer magazine publishers will be able to offer ultranarrow targeting previously available only through trade magazines. **Inkjet imaging** is a special computer-controlled printing process that allows parts of the message to be changed by the program. Inkjet imaging also enables the advertiser to address readers personally. You can tell a reader, "If you're interested, Mr. Jones, you can buy this product at Leroy's Hardware at 39th and Elm." Sophisticated database management allows even greater segmentation. Publishers can match subscriber lists against various public and private lists—census, auto registration, catalog lists, and so forth—and transfer that information to subscriber lists.

Another advantage of magazines is visual quality. It tends to be quite high because magazines are printed on good paper and provide superior photo reproduction in either black and white or color.

The willingness to provide value-added services reflects yet another strength. Magazines will distribute coupons, provide special editions, and print ads of various sizes. They will do most anything to please the customer. This attitude begins with rate concessions. Industry sources now estimate that more than 50 percent of publishers are offering rate concessions. Other value-added programs are tailored to the specific marketing needs of each client. Examples are tie-ins with other media outlets such as direct mail and cable. *Sports Illustrated* and ESPN have joined together to entice promoters such as Gatorade and Budweiser.

Another advantage offered by magazines is the positive attitude and involvement expressed by magazine readers. Although research shows that the average magazine reader spends only thirty minutes at most reading, it is thirty minutes of active involvement. Furthermore, readers do not consider the ads carried by magazines to be as intrusive as other ads in other media.

The key weakness of magazines is the difficulty of reaching a mass audience. Attempts to do so through magazines such as *Time* or *Reader's Digest* suggest three other limitations of magazines: high costs, wasted circulation, and limited prime positions. For example, a magazine such as *Newsweek* contracts covers and center pages to advertisers for a minimum number of issues, typically eighteen and often for one year. Long lead time is still a drawback of magazines that do not have the advanced technology described earlier.

Concept Review

1. Magazines are the most specialized of the mass media and reflects the fact that the mass audience is becoming more segmented.
2. Although special-interest magazines have grown dramatically, general-interest magazines have attempted to compete through selective binding and demo editions.
3. There are three types of magazines: consumer, farm, and business. These types can be further classified by geography, demographics, or editorial content.
4. A great deal of valuable information about the readers of magazines is available through the Audit Bureau of Circulation.
5. Buying magazine space requires a familiarity with advertising notes, promotional options, and purchasing procedures.
6. The primary benefits of magazines are their ability to target the audience and high reproduction quality.
7. On the negative side, magazines cannot reach a mass audience and are costly.

Television

The growth of television has been nothing less than phenomenal. In 1923, Vladimir Zworykin became the head of a group of forty engineers at the RCA laboratory in Camden, New Jersey. The group had resulted from a merger of television research programs at Westinghouse, General Electric, and RCA. By 1939, the Camden engineers had convinced RCA that they were ready, and modern television got its first public demonstration at the World's Fair in New York City. Within two years, the FCC adopted standards for television broadcasting suggested by a committee that represented all the major electronic companies. By 1948, the FCC was deluged with license applications; it froze the granting of licenses in order to study how it could allocate frequencies so that the broadcasts of one station would not interfere with those of other stations. When the freeze was lifted in 1952, one-third of all American families had bought a television set and were happily involved with Ed Sullivan, Milton Berle, and Lucy and Desi. By the mid-1960s, more than six hundred stations were on the air. By 1988, there were almost thirteen hundred. Along with this growth came important changes in the television industry and its audience.

A Changing Industry

For most of its brief history, the structure of the American television industry was straightforward. There were three big commercial networks and hundreds of local stations. In the past decade, however, the industry has been shaken up by the emergence of new networks, by the growth and changes in the public television system, and, most of all, by the popularity of cable television and VCRs.

Local Stations and Networks   Local stations can be either independent or affiliated with a network. Today there are four major television networks: Columbia Broadcasting System (CBS), National Broadcasting Company (NBC), American Broadcasting Company (ABC), and Fox. There are also several smaller networks—such as ESPN, CBN, and Metromedia—that operate on a regional or selective program basis. Selective program basis refers to a smaller network offering programming only during certain times of the day. Contrary to popular belief, networks produce very few of their own programs. They rely instead on individual production companies such as Tandem and Lorimar to produce the shows they need for prime time. The networks buy a product (program), provide the means to distribute that product (local affiliates), and make their money by selling commercial time to national advertisers. If the networks pay too much for a product, or if ratings are low, they cannot make a profit. The networks pay a fee (called *compensation*) to local stations to carry their programming. The networks pay this compensation at a rate of approximately 20 percent to 30 percent of the advertising revenue, while the remaining 70 percent to 80 percent is kept by the network to pay for the program and for the costs involved in getting the program to the affiliates. In turn, the affiliates sell their own advertising time. Approximately 30 percent of this revenue is sent to the network for the programming supplied. In general, affiliates make most of their income by selling local advertising. In fact, network compensation has become less important to the local stations since the 1970s and the increased popularity of cable television. Still, network affiliation is much more important than the money received from the networks. It not only allows stations to fill up air time with diverse, high-quality programming, it also generates strong lead-ins for local news and syndicated programs. Stations can also piggyback on the considerable promotion and public relations value of the networks and their leading stars. Each of the major networks has approximately 220 affiliates (Fox has approximately 110 stations that come together as a network on a regular, but limited, basis). When a station carries a network program, this is called *clearance*, because the local station clears the time for the network show. It is extremely important for a network to have as high a clearance as possible (that is, from 95 percent to 100 percent) so it can offer advertisers total market coverage. Affiliates are not required to show specific network programs, but they may lose network affiliation if they do not carry sufficient broadcasts.

Cable Television   Cable television systems were developed because obstacles such as tall buildings, forests, and mountains prevent normal television signals from reaching some viewers. Initially, the cable service built a community antenna on a hill or tall structure in order to pick up signals from conventional television stations. The cable company did not pay for the pickup but simply delivered the signals by means of a wire or cable to subscribers. By 1989, cable reached 57.1 percent of American households and generated ad revenues of nearly two billion dollars (see Figure 13.3). Experts project that by 1995, 70 percent of the homes in America will subscribe to a cable service. If the telephone companies are allowed to enter the business, providing instant cable access to areas that now have only phone service, up to 90 percent of U.S. homes could receive cable.[7]

Public Television   A few years ago, it would have been inappropriate to discuss the public television system in a book like this, because public television contained no advertising. But this is no longer the case, because of two changes that occurred during the 1980s. First, due to federal funding

Figure 13.3

Revenues generated by cable television over a ten-year span. Advertising Age (February 19, 1990): 16. Used with permission.

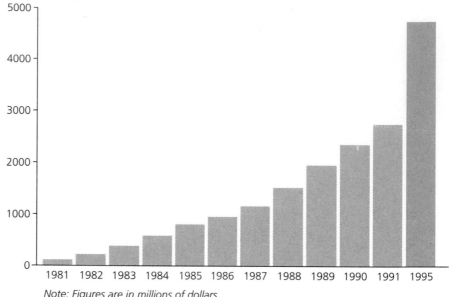

Note: Figures are in millions of dollars.

cuts, public television officials looked for new sources of funding, including advertising. Second, the FCC changed the guidelines for promotional messages on public television.

According to current FCC guidelines, messages on public television can include corporate and product logos if they are nonpromotional; business locations and telephone numbers if not used for direct response selling; and brand names, service marks, and logos. Products or services may be described in a way that is "value neutral" when shown in use. FCC (and station) guidelines prohibit the corporate message from including product promotion, price, calls to action, inducements to buy, comparative statements, competitive claims, or a program host selling program-related merchandise. The messages can be shown only during the 2 1/2-minute program breaks, preceded by a station-produced announcement that identifies a company's support but does not specify that the support is applied toward any one program.[8]

However, what the FCC will allow and what public stations will accept is not always the same. Each station maintains its own guidelines, and some are looser than others. In fact, some public stations run the same spots run by commercial stations. Public television is well suited for image campaigns that do not make comparative claims, and even campaigns that do so in a subtle manner are occasionally accepted. To announce its underwriting of the MacNeil/Lehrer Newshour, for instance, AT&T notes that it is "the right choice," a message that clearly implies AT&T's superiority over other companies.

Understanding Television Audiences

The numbers describing television's hold on Americans boggle the mind. According to figures released in 1984 by the A. C. Nielsen Company, America's television fixation reached an all-time high in 1983, when average daily television viewing per household surpassed the seven-hour mark for the first time. Over the twenty-four-hour broadcast day, on the average, about 30 percent of all households had at least one set turned on at any given moment. By the time most American children enter kindergarten, they have already spent more hours watching television than they will spend in college classrooms getting a degree.

For the media planner, however, the overall size of the television audience is not the key issue. More important are the size and characteristics of audiences for specific slots of time on specific outlets. During the 1980s, these audiences changed significantly. In 1980, cable was something households hooked up to for better reception, a VCR was a toy for the upscale market, and the Big Three networks held 90 percent of the prime-time audience. Today, cable claims nearly 40 percent of this audience, and more in some markets.

Methods of Measuring Audiences   Different methods of measuring audiences can yield different results. Four basic techniques are used to measure broadcast audiences.

The first technique uses an electronic recorder commonly called an *audimeter*, which is used for national (network) ratings. This device, developed by the A. C. Nielsen Company, is attached to the television set and makes a recording every minute the set is on. Since 1986, several rating companies have measured not only which show is being watched but also who is doing the watching. For example, the Nielsen electronic "people meter" is a small box with eight buttons—six for the family and two for visitors—that is placed on top of the television. Each member has his or her own button, and a remote control makes it possible to make entries from anywhere in the room. A sonar device sends out an alert to log in or out.

A second technique uses *telephone coincidence*. An interviewer calls households chosen at random and asks which program is being watched. Up-to-date data can be collected quickly, but the coverage in terms of time of day or day of the week is not always complete.

The *diary method* is the third technique. Preselected homes are mailed diaries in which each viewer writes down the stations and programs watched. A separate diary is provided for each television in the home and a cash award is given for cooperating. The Arbitron Ratings Company, for example, uses the diary method to record station and program ratings for both radio and television. The method provides inexpensive and fairly complete data for local markets, but the response level is often a problem.

A. C. Nielsen has about twenty-six hundred households keeping diaries of their viewing once every three weeks. Of the approximately eight hundred fifty diaries that are handed in each week, only about six hundred are usable because of sloppy record keeping. The diaries are supplemented by research from seventeen hundred household viewing meters Nielsen has installed in homes. Nielsen uses the information from these two sources to compile the Nielsen Television Index (NTI) reports. These reports are then used by national advertisers to determine their CPM, or cost per thousand. Thus CPM indicates what advertisers paid for what they received. The formula is stated as follows:

$$CPM = \frac{ad\ cost \times 1000}{circulation\ (audience\ size)}$$

If "Cheers" has an audience size of twenty-one million and a thirty-second spot costs $316,000, then the cost per thousand would be:

$$CPM = \frac{\$316,000 \times 1000}{21,000,000} = \$14.83$$

The fourth method, called *roster recall,* uses door-to-door interviews. The interviewer carries a roster of programs that were broadcast the day before and lets the person look at the roster while answering questions. Several demographic questions are also asked.

Measures of Television Audiences   The four methods of measuring audiences provide a wealth of information about the television audience. Perhaps their most significant application comes in weekly ratings provided by Arbitron and Nielsen. The ratings include two measures of the television audience: program rating and share.

A program rating is the percentage of television households in an area that are tuned to a specific program during a specific time period. Thus, if 21 million people watched "Cheers" and there are 106,300,000 total television households, the rating for "Cheers" would be

$$\frac{21,000,000}{106,300,000} = 19.7$$

A final term to understand is *share.* The percentage of television sets actually on at a particular time are referred to as "households using television" (HUTs). If 70 percent of television sets were on during "Cheers," then 74,320,000 sets were actually on, of which 21 million were watching "Cheers." The program's share would be 28.2 (21,000,000/74,320,000). Typically, the rating services report the two numbers: "Cheers" 19.7, 28.2.

Research on the local audience is used to define television markets. A **television market** is a rigidly defined geographic area in which stations generally located in the core of the area attract most of the viewing. Each county is placed in only one television market to avoid overlap although there may be several counties in a market. There are approximately two hundred television markets, accounting for more than three thousand counties. Both the Arbitron Ratings Co. and A. C. Nielsen Company measure television markets this way, Arbitron under the term *Area of Dominant Influence* (ADI) and Nielsen under the name *Designated Market Area* (DMA). The television ratings for the ADI or the DMA are very useful because those areas contain the bulk of the viewers for any city's stations.

Who Is Watching?   As a result of television's visibility and pervasiveness, there is a tremendous amount of information available about television watchers. Demographic data indicates that television continues to reach a large percentage of the people most of the time. An update of the family viewing time suggests that the seven hours and two minutes of daily viewing time reported in 1983 was seven hours and one minute in 1989.[9] Thus television appears to have remained a stable source of entertainment in U.S. homes. The segmentation of television, however, has changed the composition of television audiences. Cable programming now offers thirty or more choices that appeal to specific target audiences. For example, ESPN attracts primarily males with an above-average interest in sports and SIN attracts Spanish speakers. New types of television viewers, such as out-of-home viewers, have emerged. More than 14 percent of television-owning households now have portable six-inch-and-under sets. Nearly a quarter are used every day, while 40 percent are used weekly. Who's toting them around? Manufacturers say the most frequent users are avid sports fans who tune in at the ballpark to get play-by-play coverage or to watch conflicting games.[10] More traditional data are still available on the heavy television watcher. The heavy television viewer is female, married, has children at home, has a low level of education, is not employed outside the home, is a Southerner or a Midwesterner, has a low income, has cable television, purchases records and tapes, and is price sensitive. Conversely, individuals who have pay cable service tend to be employed outside the home, have high incomes, and have national credit cards.[11]

Buying Television Time

Television is not only an omnipresent medium but also an extremely costly one. With an average prime-time cost of $170,000 for a thirty-second commercial, the range can run from a low of $60,000 for a new show scheduled opposite a top-rated show to a high of $262,000 for "Cheers." These rates are directly related to the rating and share scores discussed earlier. There is also a match-up factor. Some shows, such as "The Cosby Show," are a perfect match with companies that have targeted the family audience.

Consequently, Cosby (NBC) can demand a higher rate even though the scores do not necessarily support this price. There are also alternatives to prime-time network commercials.

Key Purchasing Options   If media buyers decide to use television, they then face many decisions about how to use it well. Among the key choices are whether to buy time on a network or from a local station, what the level of commitment should be, and what time periods and programs should be selected.

Network and Cable Time   For mass coverage, a network buy is the best option. Placing an ad with ABC, for instance, means that all the ABC affiliates will show the commercial, thus reaching several million people simultaneously. The networks still tend to offer the most popular programs, and purchasing time on a network is relatively simple. However, the absolute cost of network advertising is very high, as is the waste. Also, a large portion of prime time is sold during the **up-front market,** a buying period (usually in May) when the networks sell a large part of their commercial time for the upcoming season.

For promoters with limited funds or limited market coverage, two alternatives to network buys may be attractive. First, the major networks offer **regional networks;** that is, promoters can select a region of the country for their promotion and pay the network a proportional rate plus a nominal fee for the splitting of the network feed. Second, promoters may turn to the smaller networks and cable television networks. These outlets charge less and can provide more targeted coverage than the major networks.

Currently, time on cable television can be purchased by negotiating rates with independent cable system operators in each market or by buying time from broadcast stations that make their signals available to cable operators via satellite. Special-interest networks like ESPN or MTV may be purchased separately from the cable system, without having to buy the other programs or networks carried by the cable system. An advertiser can also purchase time through interconnects. The interconnect technology allows the cable system to carry different programming on different ads on separate parts of their system. Thus local advertisers can show their ads on the part of the system that reaches their target market.

Spot and Local Advertising   Television advertising is divided into three categories: network, national spot, and local spot. We have already discussed the advantage of network advertising—simultaneous coverage of a mass market. However, the other two options offer certain advantages as well. When time is bought directly from local television stations, it is called **spot advertising.** Because local stations cannot usually sell time in the middle of network programs, most spot ads occur adjacent to network programs, but local stations also show them during their own programs. When a national company buys local time, it is called *national spot advertising*. In contrast, spot advertising by local firms is called *local advertising*. As a result, local advertising is virtually a synonym for retail advertising. The major spenders on local advertising include department and discount stores, financial institutions, automobile dealers, restaurants, and supermarkets. Thus a national car manufacturer such as General Motors Corp. buys network television advertising to reach the entire U.S. market; Chrysler Corp. buys national spot advertising for the Jeep Cherokee campaign because it only wants to reach markets where off-road vehicles are popular; and McDermott Chevrolet buys local spot advertising because the Gainesville, Florida, market is the primary target audience.

For the promoter, buying time from local stations rather than national networks provides flexibility. An advertiser can select particular markets at particular times on particular programs. National promoters might use spot ads in order to supplement a regional network campaign; to test new products, a media mix, or a creative strategy; or to obtain a cost-effective alternative in markets with high sales.

Still, using spot promotions has three key drawbacks. First, the likelihood of clutter is increased, because unless network advertisers have bought all of the commercial time on a program, local stations can sell time on network-originated shows only during station breaks between programs. Second, spot promotion is cumbersome for the national promoter. The promoter must communicate with stations in many markets in order to select a station, determine air time, negotiate the price, and check the promotion's appearance. And finally, if the cost-per-thousand is calculated, local television turns out to be much more expensive than national television. Hence, national companies prefer to purchase network time; when necessary, they supplement those purchases with promotions on local television.

Sponsorship, Participation, Spot Announcements, and Barter When buying television time, promoters must also determine their level of commitment. In the early days of television, it was very common for a single advertiser to sponsor an entire program, paying for production, salaries, and air time. The "Bell Telephone Hour," "Kraft Music Hall," and "Hallmark Hall of Fame" are a few examples of programs that showed only the ads of the sponsor and had a very pronounced impact on the viewing audience. Today, *sponsorships* are too expensive for most advertisers, who are unwilling to devote the majority of their budget to one thirty- or sixty-minute slot. Nevertheless, for highly seasonal products (for example, holiday toys and greeting cards), using sponsorships is still a viable strategy.

Since most advertisers cannot afford sponsorships, they opt for *participation*. In fact, almost 90 percent of all network time is sold under this format. It means that several advertisers buy spots on a particular program. An advertiser can participate in a particular program once or several times on a regular or an irregular basis. Advertisers often split major sporting events, leading to an announcement that "this part of the U.S. Open is brought to you by. . . ."

We discussed a third option earlier. National *spot announcements* are purchased from local television stations and appear during the adjacent time periods of network programs.

The final and least amount of contact a promoter can have with the television station is called *barter*. Barter is the exchange of goods without money, and it takes two forms. In the first and simpler form, a promoter exchanges goods for time. This exchange typically occurs at the local level and could entail a local furniture store exchanging office furniture for ten thirty-second spots. The second and more formal form of barter is *barter by syndication*. In this case, the promoter supplies a syndicated show to the television station at no cost. A syndicated program was originally a network program that ran its course; when the ratings got low enough, it was relegated to the minor leagues of afternoon reruns. Since the FCC passed the "Prime Time Access Rule" in 1970, syndication has become a big and complex industry. Although the rule is very involved, in brief, it forced the affiliates to look for other sources of off–prime-time programming. Syndicated programs (also called *strips*, because they appear every day, much like comic strips) are either former network shows that may still be running ("The Cosby Show"), former network shows that are still produced for syndication only ("Jeopardy"), or original programs produced for syndication ("Oprah Winfrey"). Incidentally, Viacom, the syndicator for "The Cosby Show," sold the show to 174 stations for approximately six hundred million dollars for four years. The syndicated show usually includes two minutes of commercial time for the promoter who provided the show and three minutes so that the station can sell to national or local promoters. Thus the supplying promoter has control of the messages, supplies the station with programming, and provides another source of profit for the station.

Times and Programs   For promoters buying television time, the time of day and the program being broadcast are obvious concerns. Times and programs affect the likely audience and, as a result, the rate charged for the television time. The standard time periods in television are the following:

Early morning: 6 A.M.–9 A.M.
Daytime: 9 A.M.–5 P.M.
Early fringe: 5 P.M.–7:30 P.M.

Prime access:	7:30 P.M.–8 P.M.
Prime:	8 P.M.–11 P.M.
Late news:	11 P.M.–11:30 P.M.
Late night:	11:30 P.M.–1 A.M.

These designations change somewhat as we move across the four time zones. For example, in the central time zone, everything is pushed back one hour; that is, prime time is 7 P.M. to 10 P.M. Each time period reflects different audience size and characteristics. For example, early morning audiences are fairly small and represent upscale men and women getting ready to leave for work, children, and specialty audiences, for example, viewers of exercise shows. Prime time has the largest audience and represents the family more than any other time.

To schedule purchases of television time, media buyers look at *gross rating points*, or *GRPs*, which are a measure of the viewing audience of specific programs. The ratings by Arbitron and Nielsen provide the basis for GRPs. Essentially, GRPs reflect the total rating points delivered by a set of programs. Therefore, a Monday night buy on October 4, 1991, which includes "Monday Night Football" (18.4), "Major Dad" (20.1), "MacGyver" (11.9), and "Hunter" (13.7), would deliver 64.1 GRPs. We take a closer look at GRPs in Chapter 14.

Purchasing Procedures The buying of television time is divided into several categories, depending on the nature of the buy: prime-time network buys, national spot buys, and local buys. Prime-time network buys involve the real heavyweights of the television industry—corporate advertising directors, agency media executives, and network salespeople. The major buying period for network buying is in the early spring. It entails three stages:

1. *Up-front market.* Advertisers make full-season commitments shortly after the announcement in the early spring of the fall prime-time schedules. This usually involves a commitment of five million dollars. Up-front buying is usually conducted for prime-time shows, some sports programming, and popular daytime shows. The buy is for two or more quarters of the year.

2. *Scatter market.* After the up-front market advertisers make short-term quarterly purchases, the scatter market is considered. As the name implies, the promoters do not buy spots on one show but rather negotiate for spots scattered throughout several shows, often in a number of day parts. Invariably, fewer good time slots are available, and the promoter is at a pricing disadvantage because of the smaller number of spots purchased. However, deals can sometimes be made because of poor

initial ratings or other unknowns, especially at the end of the year when promotion budgets get tight and stations become desperate to sell remaining time.

3. *Opportunistic markets.* This is essentially the remnant segment, composed of week-to-week purchases of unsold time. Remnant space may be space that was never sold because of its low desirability or space that was sold and then canceled.

To purchase local advertising, each station must be contacted in order to obtain proposals. The formal request for rates and commercial positions is called the *avail* request. Avails usually include available times and dates, prices, program ratings, total households, and GRPs. The station draws up several proposals based on the avail request.

Both network and local television time may be bought on a fixed, preemptible, or immediately preemptible basis. A fixed spot is the costliest, because it cannot be displaced by another advertiser's commercial. Preemptible spots are bought with the understanding that if another advertiser will pay more, the original advertiser will be preempted. When this happens, the station gives the original advertiser enough notice so that another arrangement can be worked out. Cheapest of all spots are the immediately preemptible spots, which the station can move as it sees fit. This situation brings up the possibility that advertisers will not want to pay for commercials that are delayed.

Discount plans can be negotiated between the promoter and the station. Networks prefer advertisers who contract for year-round package plans, since this arrangement provides guaranteed income to the network long before the promotion airs.

Television: Strengths and Limitations

No medium has a greater potential to create an impression on the minds of the consumer than television. Combining moving pictures, speaking voices, music, and convincing acting, television has the capability to run the entire gamut of human emotions (see Figure 13.4). Television allows the audience member to learn more about the product, the spokesperson, and the message because the consumer is more personally involved.

Television also offers wide flexibility in respect to market coverage. Network television allows the promoter to reach the entire country. Cable, public television, and interconnects bring a message to highly focused markets. This flexibility has reduced several of the criticisms directed at television a decade ago. Television need not be wasteful, overly expensive, or cluttered.

A third advantage of television is the important role it plays in our culture. For many people, television is their primary, most reliable source of

Figure 13.4

Television is an effective medium for the individualistic style of Anne Klein's ad series for its new line, A line. © 1991 A LINE ANNE KLEIN.

"Wedding" :30
Music: Rock guitar solo throughout.
(Open on white screen with black vertical bar.
Dissolve to close-up of bride's face. Titles appear at right side of screen)
Anncr. (VO): Uncertain about her future, Pam wore a velour scoop neck top.
(Camera pans as woman walks closer)
Anncr. (VO): And black rubberized leggings under her wedding dress.
(Camera continues pan as woman looks frightened and absorbed)
Anncr. (VO): She also hid a long black motorcycle jacket...
(Woman, in extreme close-up, turns her face and looks directly at viewer)
Anncr. (VO): ...in the choir room.
(Screen goes white, with black bar at right)
Anncr. (VO): A Line. Anne Klein.

entertainment, news, and sports. People count on television and hold a favorable attitude toward it. The Promotion in Focus section describes a study that investigates the attributes of likable television commercials.

Another advantage of television stems from its ability to deliver well-defined audiences. Research shows that there are remarkable similarities in the characteristics of viewers. Cosby delivers the family audience to advertisers such as Kraft Foods, Procter & Gamble Co., and Coca-Cola week after week. MTV delivers an audience of young people.

Although television is usually thought of as a medium for delivering advertising messages, it can also deliver sales promotion, public relations, and personal selling-related messages. For example, television has the capability of making sweepstakes exciting, of enhancing the significance of a premium, or of making a temporary price reduction even more urgent. Many public relations methods have emotional undertones that benefit from advertising. The "Just say no" antidrug campaign is much more powerful on television than in print. Finally, because of the emotional impact of television, it does an excellent job of preselling a product, thus simplifying the job of the sales rep.

The limitations of television are important and do eliminate some promoters. Television's absolute cost is still high. "Roseanne" costs $247,000 for one thirty-second spot. With production costs of $150,000 to $1,000,000, it is apparent that few promoters can afford national television. Clutter, especially on network television, does exist. As many as twenty-five separate spots can be shown during thirty minutes of prime-time programming. Finally, television does not work with products that are unattractive (for example, industrial fluids), that cannot be demonstrated (for example, Preparation H), or that do not have inherent emotional characteristics or emotional associations (such as table salt).

Concept Review

1. Television comes in four forms: network, local, cable, and public.
2. When advertising on television, promoters can buy network, spot advertising, or local, or can also opt for sponsorship, participation, or spot announcements.
3. Television market size is assessed through four techniques: audimeter, telephone coincidence, diary method, and roster recall.
4. The size of the audience for a program is assessed through rating points and share. The weight of the schedule is determined by the total number of gross rating points (GRPs) delivered.
5. Market coverage and emotional involvement are the primary strengths of television.
6. High absolute costs and clutter are the major weaknesses of television.

Radio

Several nineteenth-century inventors paved the way for the invention of radio, but credit is generally given to Lee de Forest. In 1906, he invented a special grid that enabled a vacuum tube to function as an amplifier. This formed the basis for the amplification needed to make voice transmission possible via "wireless." In 1920, Westinghouse obtained a license to broadcast, and its KDKA went on the air in Pittsburgh, Pennsylvania.

The golden age of radio is considered the period from 1926 to 1948. In 1926, RCA formed the National Broadcasting Company (NBC). A year later, NBC formed a second network to accommodate increasing demand. Radio was the magic medium, and everybody loved it. Listeners from coast to coast could hear symphonic music from the great concert halls in Boston, or they could be transported to the Grand Ballroom at the Waldorf-Astoria Hotel in New York City, where the big bands performed. For those who lived in rural isolation, radio provided a link with the outside world.

When television arrived, radio took a nose dive. By the mid-1950s, television was using many radio programs and radio stars. During the same period, the invention of the transistor reduced the size and price of the portable radio, making it truly a medium that "goes where you go." What's more, Americans were on the go, and most new cars were equipped with radios. "Drive time"—from 6 A.M. to 9 A.M. and from 3 P.M. to 6 P.M.—became radio's prime time and gave the medium a much-needed financial boost.

Today, there are more than five hundred million radios in America. Radio ad revenues in 1990 were over nine billion dollars; experts predict that they will reach twenty-two billion dollars by the year 2000.[12]

Stations and Networks

More than ten thousand radio stations are now operating in the United States. In terms of method of transmission, there are two types of stations: amplitude modulation (AM) and frequency modulation (FM). The primary difference is the distance covered by the signal.

AM signals can travel along the earth's surface up to several hundred miles. The coverage of an AM station is influenced by its power, by the height of its transmitter, and by its frequency. The estimated daytime range of a 250-watt station is approximately fifteen miles, compared with more than one hundred miles for a 50,000-watt station. A high transmitter adds to the area and quality of reception. Lower frequencies offer greater coverage than the higher frequencies.

FM signals do not follow the curvature of the earth and therefore travel only as far as the horizon, about forty to fifty miles. However, the clarity of the signal across this distance is better for FM stations than it is for AM. By 1989, FM stations accounted for 75 percent of all radio listeners and 60 percent of all radio advertising. The growth of FM stations began after many of the technological and administrative problems were resolved.

Currently, AM stations are classified as being either clear, secondary clear, regional, or local. Clear channels normally operate on the maximum power assigned AM stations (50,000 watts), and many of them (for example, WLS-Chicago, WJR-Detroit) can be heard for several hundred miles at night. Secondary clear channels are designed to serve a population center and the surrounding rural area (250 watts to 50,000 watts). A regional station operates on a maximum of 5,000 watts and shares a channel with several other stations located far enough away to eliminate signal interference. Local stations operate on a maximum of 1,000 watts and often air only

Promotion
in Focus

What Makes a Commercial Effective?

What about a television commercial makes people remember a particular product and perhaps decide to buy it? A number of research studies have focused on this question, breaking it down into smaller parts and analyzing the reactions of hundreds of television viewers. The results send some fairly clear messages to advertisers.

For starters, if you want people to feel good about your product, use some small, cuddly, friendly animals in the commercial. In one study of some 80 commercials, the four that viewers liked most were all advertising pet food. Although researcheres caution that it is difficult to fit animals legitimately into commercials for most things other than pet food, the strength of the results seems to indicate that it would be worth advertisers' time to try to get a kitten in somewhere.

Research also provides a reasonably clear answer to the question of whether viewers need to like a commercial. One school of thought has long held that the viewer's emotional response is irrelevant; a commercial just needs to get its information across. But studies show that people are twice as likely to be persuaded by a commercial that they like "a lot" than by one they feel neutral about. Experts think that people choose brands based on two general factors: the brand's utility or useful-ness, which may be based on rational or objective knowledge about the brand, and more emotional, subjective impressions of the brand. It is these subjective impressions that are most influenced by likable commercials.

So what makes a commercial likable? In all types of commercials meaningfulness is most important. Viewers want commercials to be relevant and worth remembering, true-to-life, and informative. The second most important attribute for food and beverage commercials is energy—liveliness and fast pace. For other types of commercials, the second most important factor is a negative one—the avoidance of tired, worn-out situations or ideas that rub people the wrong way.

One conclusion that marketers might draw from these studies is that television viewers are less passive and view commercials with more perception and intelligence than they are sometimes given credit for. They want meaningful commercials, not ones that are full of fast cars, glitz, and sexy bodies. But if you really want people to feel good about your product, see if you can link it with a kitten.

Source: Alexander L. Bill and Carol A. Bridgewater, "Attributes of Likable Commercials," *Journal of Advertising Research* (June/July 1990): 38–44.

during daylight hours. FM stations have three different classifications. Class A is low power, with a maximum of 3 kilowatts; Class B has a maximum of 50 kilowatts, and Class C has up to 100 kilowatts.

The term *network radio* applies only to the traditional line networks interconnected (wired) by AT&T circuits, for example, ABC and CBS. A major trend in network radio is consolidation. Experts suggest there are now only four major radio networks: Westwood One (the parent company of NBC Radio and Mutual Broadcasting System), CBS Spectrum, ABC, and Unistar. ABC has the largest number of affiliates (1,565).

Radio networks operate differently from television networks, most noticeably in the small amount of programming supplied for local stations. Since network programming is limited in time, stations may belong to more than one network, each providing specialized programming to complete a station's schedule. Thus a local station may be an affiliate of NBC and Mutual, taking sports programming and news from NBC and classical programming from Mutual. There are also special networks, such as National Black Network (NBN), whose ninety affiliates are targeted toward the African-American population. Finally, radio programming has changed dramatically during the last decade. Whereas radio was originally viewed as a true theater of the mind, it became a passive or background medium with the emergence of television. Today, radio is once again being listened to, as the result of talk shows (such as that hosted by Larry King), call-ins, advice shows, and the creation of local radio celebrities. In turn, these DJs and local radio celebrities play an important role in sales promotion activities such as grand openings and special events.

Buying Radio Time

Years ago, nearly all radio programming was live. As radio has become a more local medium, there has been a greater use of recorded shows, with little live programming except the news and on-the-spot broadcasts. This change has reduced the costs of commercials while improving the quality.

Advertising Rates   Radio cards are usually broken down into six time periods:

Morning drive time	6 A.M.–10 A.M.
Midday	10 A.M.–3 P.M.
Afternoon drive time	3 P.M.–7 P.M.
Daytime	10 A.M.–3 P.M.
Evening	7 P.M.–midnight
Late night	midnight–6 A.M.

The cost of radio time depends primarily on three classifications:

1. Drive time. Drive time refers to the periods in which the population is moving around, in transition between sleep and the activities of the day or in transition from daytime activities to the events of the evening. These are the periods in which radio listening is at its highest levels and during which the adult population is least likely to be attending to television.

2. Run-of-station (ROS). This means that the radio station can move a commercial at will within the time period, wherever it is most convenient; preemptible ROS has the lowest rates.

3. Special features. This time slot is adjacent to weather signals, news reports, time signals, traffic reports, or stock reports.

As is true in other media, advertisers pay less per commercial when they purchase spots in larger volume. Radio stations refer to volume purchases in several ways: six- and thirteen-week flights, package plans (the station puts together an assortment of times), and scatter plans (a collection of spots in drive time, daytime, evening time, and weekend time).

Promotional Options   Radio commercials may be ten, thirty, or sixty seconds long. Radio time may be bought on a network, a group of stations, or an individual station.

Network radio is available in virtually every market. It is efficient and relatively inexpensive. One buy can distribute an advertising message to several hundred affiliates. For example, Dr Pepper can buy five sixty-second spots on "Dick Clark's National Music Survey" (Mutual Broadcasting System) and reach its 950 affiliates. Prices vary by day part and are dependent on the number of affiliates, the competitive situation, the size of the network's inventory of available time, and the audience size and demographic characteristics.

There are several groups of unconnected local stations that offer a group discount on the advertising rate for purchasing time from the stations separately. These groups include McGavern Internet, Forbett Supernet, Katz Radio Group, Blair Radio Network, and Keystone Network.

Spot radio is available through all ten thousand-plus stations. This means buying individual spot ads (usually sixty or thirty seconds) on a station-by-station basis. Spot radio is an excellent means to supplement nationally a campaign that is running locally in other media. However, buying spot radio, like spot television, means dealing with nonstandardized rate structures and bookkeeping problems.

Who Listens to Radio?   Arbitron, the chief measurement service for radio audiences, reports that nearly everyone (96 percent of all persons aged twelve and older) tunes in a radio at least once a week. People listen to the radio while cooking, reading, jogging, eating, driving, and working.[13] This unusual participation makes radio a powerful means of reaching lifestyle segments and demographic groups. Age and sex are still the basic demographic measures, and radio stations divide the population by these characteristics. Young men under age twenty-five are most likely to listen to classic rock tunes played on album rock stations. Teenagers and women under age thirty commonly choose contemporary hit stations. As with the album rock stations, these are always FM stations. The music is constant and flowing; the disc jockeys seldom intrude with more than a funny line, the time of day, and the name of the song. This kind of radio programming was called Top 40 when it was on AM stations.

Young people and older people seldom listen to the same kind of radio stations. While most young people like rock, the stereotypical radio format for older people is "beautiful music"—instrumental versions of favorite songs. But not all mature adults prefer this kind of so-called elevator music. Men and women aged fifty-five and older are the primary listeners of news and talk stations. In markets where separate news and talk stations exist, men aged fifty-five and older prefer talk, while both men and women listen to all-news stations.

In general, radio remains a local medium. Characteristics of radio listeners in individual markets tend to remain stable. Therefore, the promotion manager must assess the ability of radio to reach the target audience on a market-by-market basis.

Radio Research

For radio, an Arbitron "book" is the equivalent of the Nielsen ratings of television programs. Although several smaller companies such as Media Statistics Inc., Mediastat, Burch, and RAM Research compete with Arbitron, Arbitron ratings generally determine how a radio station is doing. An Arbitron book can run up to three hundred pages or more, filled with thousands of numbers estimating how many and what kind of listeners are tuned in to a given station at a specific time of day. Major markets are served up to four Arbitron books each year; smaller markets might be served only once a year. Arbitron Radio uses the diary method of gathering data, which enables the company to report not only listening levels but also the demographics of the audience.

The Arbitron book delivers data in two broad categories, quarter-hour estimates and cumulative (cume) estimates. Quarter-hour figures indicate how many people are listening at any given moment (for example, between 10 A.M. and 11 A.M. Saturday morning); cume estimates indicate the total number of people tuned in during a specific period (for example, on Saturdays and Sundays from 6 A.M. to midnight).

Radio: Strengths and Limitations

One of the main advantages of radio is that it can deliver a highly selective audience at a very low cost. Therefore, it is one of the few media that can allow market penetration and high repetition. KQEO-KMGA Albuquerque, for example, can deliver 15 percent of the Albuquerque market with ten daily repetitions of a message for less than four hundred dollars per day. Radio is also a very agreeable medium. A radio station is tolerant of last-minute changes, unusual formats, mobile hookups, and so forth. This adaptability makes radio appealing to a wide variety of companies and businesses. A small manufacturer, a local insurance agent, and a Kroger supermarket can all use radio. Radio provides an immediacy because it is constantly delivering the latest news, time, and weather. Listeners actually listen to the radio, which means that an ad sandwiched between news announcements is listened to as well. Finally, if the promotion encourages imagination and imagery, radio can do an excellent job of creating high interest and involvement. When using radio, a humorous tactic tends to work best.

Because radio provides only sound and people tend to have the radio on while they are doing other things (driving, eating, studying, for example), radio is viewed as a passive medium. Compared to television messages, people have low recall of radio messages. Recall, however, increases when messages of high interest are on the radio (for example, news, weather, a favorite song, or a popular DJ). Finally, radio is not appropriate with certain products that are difficult to visualize or that are used infrequently (for example, medical products, clothing) or to reach a national audience simultaneously.

Concept Review

1. There are AM and FM radio stations and four major radio networks.
2. Radio stations sell their time as drive time, run-of-station, and special features.
3. Radio markets are measured through the Arbitron "book."
4. Radio offers excellent local coverage at a low cost.
5. Radio is a passive medium that does not work well with some products.

Out-of-Home Promotions

The term *out-of-home media* is a relatively new label that includes outdoor (outdoor boards and billboards) and transit media. It refers to all media that carry messages where the message or the consumer is on the move or mobile. It is a relatively minor medium that serves primarily to supplement print or broadcast. The breakdown for all the categories is shown in Figure 13.5.

Outdoor Promotion

In a sense, outdoor advertising represents the oldest medium, since it is a distant cousin of the sign. It is virtually impossible to go anywhere in this country without being exposed to outdoor advertising. Perhaps because of this constant overt exposure, outdoor advertising remains the medium most criticized by the public for desecrating the natural beauty of our country. In 1990, outdoor advertising spending declined 15 percent, compared to an 8 percent annual increase during the previous five years. This decrease was the result of controversial inner-city whitewashing campaigns protesting tobacco and alcohol outdoor boards, legislative threats, and budget-conscious advertisers.

Types of Outdoor Vehicles   There are three primary types of outdoor advertising: posters, painted bulletins, and electric spectaculars.

On posters (highway billboards), the advertising message is usually lithographed on sheets of paper and then posted on some structure. The standard-size posters in the United States are the twenty-four sheet (8 feet 8 inches high by 19 feet 6 inches long), the thirty sheet (9 feet 7 inches high by 21 feet 7 inches long), and the bleed poster (10 feet 5 inches high by 22 feet 8 inches long). The bleed poster extends the artwork right to the frame

Figure 13.5

Gross billings for out-of-home promotion. Advertising Age (October 9, 1989): 2. Used with permission.

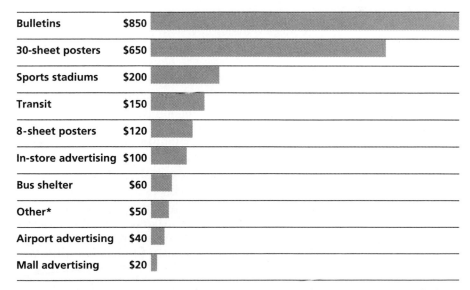

Bulletins	$850
30-sheet posters	$650
Sports stadiums	$200
Transit	$150
8-sheet posters	$120
In-store advertising	$100
Bus shelter	$60
Other*	$50
Airport advertising	$40
Mall advertising	$20

*Includes painted walls, trucks, air banners, movie theaters, golf course signage and so forth.

of the panel and is about 40 percent larger than the twenty-four sheet poster. Each poster is mounted on a standard poster structure that is 12 feet by 25 feet long. Most posters are printed on ten to fifteen individual sheets, not on twenty-four or thirty separate sheets. There is no difference in promotion costs for the three sizes, although production costs are greater for the larger types. In some markets, two smaller posters are available. These are the *junior panel*, or eight-sheet poster, which has a copy area 5 feet by 11 feet, and the three-sheet poster, which measures 46 inches high by 30 inches wide. These posters are generally used for pedestrian traffic and are often placed in shopping center parking lots or on the sides of buildings.

Painted bulletins usually measure 14 feet by 48 feet. The message is changed two or three times a year. Painted bulletins can also be painted on walls as opposed to structures such as billboards. Wall bulletins cannot be standardized in size because the shape and area on the side of a building are unpredictable. Some bulletins have cutouts that provide a three-dimensional effect. Most bulletins are illuminated.

Spectaculars are large, illuminated, and often animated signs in special high-traffic locations. Examples include the spectaculars located on Broadway in New York City or on Chicago's Michigan Avenue and even the scoreboards at athletic stadiums. Spectaculars are custom designed and are sold for time periods of one year or more.

Since outdoor promotion is such a visual medium, everything must be kept simple. People should be able to grasp the message clearly and completely in a maximum of five seconds. There should be one dominant design; five or so words of copy; bright, warm colors; and crisp lettering. Physical factors are also important. For example, the longer the poster or painted bulletin is visible to passing travelers, the better. Slower traffic is also beneficial. Obviously, it is preferable if the outdoor ad stands alone.

Buying Outdoor Promotion   During the last decade, an attempt to make the outdoor industry more professional and thereby more competitive with other media led to the adoption of the gross rating points (GRPs) system, the gathering of more data on audience segments, and the emergence of organizations such as Out-of-Home Media Services (OHMS). OHMS conducts research on the industry and provides a national buying service for outdoor and transit advertising.

If an advertiser purchases a hundred GRPs daily, the basic standardized unit is the number of poster panels required in each market to produce a daily effective circulation equal to 100 percent of the population of the market. As used by the outdoor industry, a rating point is 1 percent of the population one time. GRPs are based on the daily duplicated audience as a percentage of a market. If three posters in a community of one hundred thousand people achieve a daily exposure to seventy-five thousand people, the result is 75 GRPs.

Advertisers can purchase any number of units, although seventy-five, fifty, or twenty-five GRPs daily are most common. The number of panels required for a hundred GRPs varies from city to city. Package deals are quite common. It would cost more than $600,000 a month for a 100-GRP package in the top ten markets and $1,800,000 a month for the top one hundred markets. Outdoor is one of the few media for which no Standard Rate and Data volume is available. Advertising rates appear in the *Buyers Guide to Outdoor Advertising,* published twice a year by the Leading National Advertisers.

Posters are rented for thirty-day periods. Painted bulletins and spectaculars are bought on an individual basis, usually for one-, two-, or three-year periods. On an illuminated bulletin, the original design is painted, and twice during the year it can be repainted with entirely new copy. On unilluminated locations, one extra painting is usually provided without extra cost. In many cities, cutout displays can be rotated every thirty, sixty, or ninety days among certain choice locations.

Outdoor Promotion: Advantages and Limitations   For certain marketers, such as restaurants, motels, and gas stations, outdoor promotion can provide some real benefits.

1. By combining color, art, and short copy, outdoor ads can quickly create an association with a particular brand.

2. This medium provides repetition. If a product or service is advertised at a busy crossroads, audiences see the ad again and again. The more often the idea is repeated, the more likely it is to be retained.

3. Billboards also have immediacy and can be located in the neighborhoods that are most relevant to the promoter. A local bank can be quite sure that the majority of consumers who pass its billboard are potential customers.

4. The cost is reasonable. The cost per billboard in a major metropolitan area is about one hundred dollars a month.

5. Outdoor advertising gains attention through sheer size.

Outdoor advertising also has certain limitations:

1. Outdoor copy must be brief since it is perceived while the audience is on the move. For certain types of products, it is impossible to effectively deliver the message or demonstrate the product.

2. A great many uncontrollable factors may lessen the effectiveness of outdoor ads. Signs, trees, structures, traffic signals, or a hazardous part of the highway may distract the consumer. Or an ad placed next to others that are controversial or in poor taste could damage the image of the company.

3.   Good locations may be limited. In some communities, there may be just one spot that has a high traffic count.

4.   Many people view outdoor ads as an ecological nuisance.

Transit Promotion

Transit promotion can be considered a minor medium compared to those already discussed. Still, total annual expenditures amount to approximately twenty-five million dollars. Transit advertising is carried by more than seventy thousand vehicles, including buses, subways, rapid transit, and commuter vehicles. The consumer has a relatively long time to look at transit promotion, unlike outdoor advertising, and the promoter can get a more complete story across.

There are three primary types of transit advertising:

1.   Car cards. Typically, a car card is 11 inches by 28 inches, although widths of 42 inches by 56 inches are usually available. These cards are placed inside the vehicle along each side above the windows. In some vehicles, larger, different-shaped cards are placed at the middle or end of the vehicle. Inside displays are purchased on the basis of full-, half-, or quarter-fleet showings. A full showing in the top ten markets costs approximately $163,000 a month. These displays are sold on a rate structure based on a monthly basis with discounts granted for three-, six-, or twelve-month contracts. Since transit riders average twenty-four rides a month for sixty-one minutes per day, car cards can achieve a high level of repetition and in-depth retention.

2.   Outside displays. Exterior traveling displays are located on buses and taxis. Again, these ads are bought on the basis of showings—a hundred, seventy-five, fifty, twenty-five. Typically, a hundred showing provides enough signs to reach 85 percent of the population an average of fifteen times in a thirty-day period. Within the top ten markets, the advertiser needs to supply 3,175 vehicles with posters at a monthly cost of more than two hundred-fifty thousand dollars.

3.   Station posters. These minibillboards are located at bus, railroad, subway, and air terminals. The most common units are the two-sheet poster (46 inches by 60 inches) and the one-sheet poster (46 inches by 30 inches).

Transit promotion offers several advantages:

1.   Most notably, transit posters offer a relatively inexpensive medium for reaching a variety of people, repeatedly, in a variety of locations (for example, sidewalks and shopping centers) close to the point of sale.

2. Several techniques make the medium flexible and attractive, including backlighted displays, curved frames, optical effects, and the take-one poster.

3. Transit promotion can serve as a type of reminder ad in conjunction with other media.

The limitations of transit promotion are like those of outdoor promotion:

1. Transit cards must carry relatively short and concise messages.

2. Viewers' attention may be hard to attract and retain because of the many distractions (for example, crowded cars, traffic, noise, marked and torn signs).

3. Transit space is not available in all markets.

Concept Review

1. There are three types of outdoor advertising: posters, painted bulletins, and electric spectaculars.
2. Transit promotion can be car cards, outside displays, or station posters.
3. Outdoor and transit promotions can reach the market with a reminder message at a low cost.
4. Both outdoor and transit promotions have a short time to deliver their message and must contend with many uncontrollable factors.

Miscellaneous Media

A potpourri of miscellaneous media have emerged during the last two decades. In some instances, these media are fads that may no longer exist. In other cases, these media may provide affordable, effective, targeted message-delivery mechanisms for certain marketers. Because the list is quite long, our discussion is limited to the more viable options.

Specialty advertising includes useful articles of merchandise imprinted with a promoter's name, message, or logo. These items are used for a variety of marketing purposes: thanking customers for patronage, reinforcing established products or services, or generating sales leads. Research showed that 39 percent of the people receiving specialties could recall the name of the promoter as long as six months after they received the item, and 31 percent were still using the specialty item twelve months later.[14] Specialty advertising generates over three billion dollars in advertising billing each year.

In-store media are now estimated to represent a twelve-billion-dollar industry that is expected to grow 16 percent annually. Two examples illustrate the creativity of the industry. Information Resources Inc. is the developer of VideOcart, a monitor mounted on a shopping cart. A commercial is beamed via satellite to a store's personal computer and then transmitted by radio waves to the cart. As the cart passes an electronic trigger on the store shelf, the monitor shows the ad for the product, with a two-ad limit per aisle. Actmedia owns Checkout Channel, a national television network that delivers live programming (commercials, news, weather, and sports) while the consumer stands at the supermarket checkout counter.

We are all familiar with advertising in movie theaters and on videos. Screenvision Cinema Network, a company that distributes commercials to more than five thousand movie theaters, lists several major advertisers as clients, including Michelob, Mattel, Inc., and Chevrolet. And although the audience may be annoyed, a movie theater can add as much as fifty thousand dollars a year to its bottom line by showing commercials.

Interactive advertising represents the newest medium. Thanks to the personal computer, interactivity offers the ultimate in niche marketing: the personalized ad. The computer accepts the viewer's screen and keyboard responses and gauges how fast the person reads, what colors will encourage buying, and what product configurations will fulfill the consumer's fantasies. The viewer talks; the PC talks back. In one example, *Forbes* magazine distributed floppy disks advertising Nexus News Plus bound into 210,000 of its copies.

Finally, more than 5,500 directories are published in the United States. Directories can be industry or product specific, or they can carry a large variety of ads, as in the case of the Yellow Pages. The messages often tie in with advertising on television or in the newspaper.

The Yellow Pages is by far the largest directory outlet. Advertising expenditures paid to Yellow Pages were $7.7 billion in 1989. Many advertising agencies have specialists who work on their clients' Yellow Pages advertising. The primary purpose is to establish the trademark as the reference point and then list all the local dealers under that trademark. The dealers may then run their own ads separately. Often the manufacturer pays for the retailers' ads through a manufacturers' coop program. For example, Ford may pay for a Yellow Pages ad that lists all the Ford dealers in the metro San Diego area, as well as individual ads for each dealer.

Concept Review

Several miscellaneous media have special capabilities:

1. Specialty advertising: Imprinting a promoter's logo or name on useful articles can be used to thank customers for patronage, to reinforce the product or service, and to generate sales leads.
2. In-store media: Customers can watch commercials while they shop or wait at the checkout counter.

3. Interactive advertising: In this medium one can receive and respond to advertising through a personal computer.
4. Directories: The ads in directories often tie in with advertising on television or in the newspaper.

Case 13 *Advertising on the Media of the Future*

For the past decade, each innovation in home information and entertainment has meant another machine to clutter up the home of the up-to-date American family: a personal computer, a compact disc player, a VCR, a cordless phone. But as the machines become increasingly sophisticated, they promise a new world in some ways simpler than the past. In the not-too-distant future, American families may have just one reasonably small screen/keyboard/printer/disc reader that will integrate all the functions of today's electronic gadgets. Such radical changes will require advertisers to take a new approach to reaching customers.

The marriage of the personal computer and the telephone has already changed the way millions of people live and work. While voice traffic on phone lines has been increasing by only about 6 percent each year, data traffic increases at three times that rate. Of the 25 million American households with personal computers, about six million have modems connecting the computers to phone lines, and that number is certain to grow.

Videotex

To serve these people whose computers are linked to the world's telephone networks, a number of companies have sprung up to supply what is generically known as videotex services. Videotex companies offer such things as on-line data bases, information sources, news updates, and travel and ticketing information. With services such as Prodigy, a joint project of IBM and Sears, users have access to an electronic "mall" of some 180 advertisers. The bottom fifth of the user's screen is filled automatically with ads, and the browsing user can call up more ads at any time.

The power that this new medium gives consumers worries some advertisers. Marketers may find it more difficult to catch the eye of someone electronically "strolling" past vendors. Other advertisers, however, see this kind of change as a benefit to both parties. A consumer who searches out information about a product through videotex is almost certain to have a real interest in the product and is therefore much more likely to make a purchase than is a casual window-shopper. Providing such people with the information they want will be a new challenge for promotion managers, but it will certainly not make their jobs obsolete.

Interactive Media

In some ways, marketers' jobs may become easier, because both videotex and interactive television, another of the new media, send information in both directions. Subscribers to services like Prodigy and interactive television networks provide the networks with demographic information. Knowing who their customers are allows advertisers to fine-tune the information they send a particular customer, based on such factors as the customer's age, gender, income, and interests.

Interactive television, still in its infancy, will take this process one step further. While a commercial is showing, the screen may ask viewers to indicate whether they like the commercial, how often they use the type of product advertised, and whether they would like to get a coupon for it. Viewers would respond with a hand-held device, giving advertisers almost instantaneous information on how new campaigns will be accepted. Experts predict that in the future, advertisers will know so much about who is on the other end of the line or watching the screen that they will be able to tailor ads not just for particular demographic groups but for individuals. That may be a scary thought for people who fear Big Brother entering their living room, but for advertisers it opens up a whole new world.

Case Sources: Blayne Cutler, "The Fifth Medium," *American Demographics* (June 1990): 25–29, 60–61. Maureen O'Donnell, "New Media," *Adweek* (September 11, 1989): 202–203.

Case Questions

1. What are some of the promotional strategy implications of the interactive media discussed?
2. What are potential problems with these media?

Summary

This chapter examined the various media used in promotion. Each medium was described in terms of its general characteristics and its advantages and disadvantages. Newspapers remain the number one medium in terms of advertising dollars and are still the best way to reach the local market. Magazines have become very specialized and are excellent for reaching a targeted audience. Television represents the best way to communicate an emotion-laden message to a mass audience. Thanks to cable, television now has the capability of being more focused. Radio is a good support vehicle targeted at a local audience. The same is true for out-of-home media.

Discussion Questions

1. Under what circumstances would spot television advertising be more appealing than national television advertising?

2. Why would a manufacturer of high-quality running shoes probably select magazines as the primary medium?

3. What are the implications of cable interconnect systems?

4. Prepare an argument in favor of the use of radio instead of television as the primary medium for a promotion.

5. Would specialty media be appropriate in introducing a new automobile? Why? Why not? What about the Yellow Pages?

6. What techniques are used by rating services to gather and provide data concerning television viewership?

7. What are the primary advantages and disadvantages of cable television?

References

1. Gary Hoenig, "Newspapers," *Adweek* Supplement (September 1, 1989): 175.

2. "Newspapers 1990," *Adweek* (April 23, 1990): 5.

3. Jon Berry, "These Are the Good Old Days," *Adweek* (April 23, 1990): 8.

4. Hoenig, 176.

5. *Advertising Age Yearbook 1982:* 173.

6. "Study of Media Involvement," *Audits & Surveys* (March 1988): 14.

7. Stephen Battaglio, "Television Business," *Adweek* (September 10, 1990): 54.

8. Joe Mandese, "Going Public: A Proposal to Ease Advertiser Access to Public TV Stations Could Open the Medium to More Messages," *Marketing and Media Decisions* (September 1990): 34–35.

9. "Time Spent Viewing TV," *Adweek* (November 12, 1990): 19.

10. Hanna Rubin, "Out-of-Home Viewers Worth Pitching," *Adweek* (January 19, 1989): B.T. 32.

11. "Television Viewing Habits," *Direct Marketing* (December 1987): 30.

12. Wayne Walley, "Radio Rebuilds Its Ad Base," *Advertising Age* (August 13, 1990): 26.

13. Michael Hedges, "Radio's Lifestyles," *American Demographics* (February 1986): 32–34.

14. Kevin T. Higgins, "Specialty Advertising Thrives—Even in Tough Times," *Marketing News* (October 11, 1989): 18–20.

14 *Developing the Media Plan*

Marketing and Media

Creating a Strategy

Assess the Situation
Set Media Objectives
Design the Media Strategy

Choosing Tactics

Evaluate Media
Select Media
Determine the Media Budget

Management Science and Media Planning

Retrieval and Estimation Models
Optimization Models
Simulation Models
Media Buying Models

Consider This:

Attack or Attract?

Two of the world's largest credit card companies, Visa and American Express, vie for customers' and merchants' loyalty. Visa spends a considerable portion of its advertising budget attacking American Express, pointing out that merchants can make a lot more money off of purchases made with Visa because Visa charges merchants less—about two percent, compared to the 3.5 percent that American Express charges. American Express has not taken such attacks lying down; it has responded with ads informing merchants that its card users charge on average 140 percent more per year than do Visa card holders.

But the bulk of American Express's attention is aimed at attracting customers and merchants with cooperative promotions. One such campaign was its Weekend Privileges promotion, begun in 1990 with print, television, and direct-mail advertising. The company had found through focus groups that its cardholders wanted to do more on the weekends but didn't have many imaginative ideas. Cardholders already do about one-third of their shopping on the weekend, and 72 percent of them take short weekend trips. American Express also knew that hotels, airlines, and rental car companies tend to be less busy on the weekends. So it devised its campaign to be attractive both to merchants and to cardholders.

Led by Disney World, Hertz, American Airlines, and Hilton Hotels, a growing list of merchants offered customers discounts on weekend purchases made with American Express cards. The company planned to run cooperative advertisements with individual merchants.

American Express spent some $25 million in the first three months of the campaign. Some of that money went to make ads that were a dramatic departure from its "Portraits" campaign, which featured famous people and their American Express cards. Instead of focusing on people, the new ads concentrate on what anyone can do with the cards, suggesting, for instance, what parents can do with the kids this weekend. The company's radio ads didn't focus on people at all; one began with a phone ringing and being answered by an answering machine declaring that the homeowners were off at the mall, shopping.

The Weekend Privileges campaign seemed sure to win some good will from merchants and cardholders. If it also won over some Visa cardholders, it might signal a shift in the way credit card companies compete.

Source: Kim Foltz, "Weekends: A Time for Credit Cards," *The New York Times* (September 10, 1990): 12.

*I*n order to be effective, a promotional message must reach a particular audience. It must attain *aperture*—that optimum point in place and time when the audience is most likely to utilize the message. American Express was able to attain aperture for two diverse audiences because the company did the necessary research. It realized that the card holder audience needed time to plan a trip, and that the media schedule should deliver ads seven days a week. Even ads seen on the weekend would remind the card holder of what was available through American Express charges. This same sort of coverage was not needed for the merchant target since these individuals could be reached more easily and with a far more focused message.

Finding aperture is becoming more and more difficult for the promotion manager. The average consumer has 22 television channels to choose from. Some 11,500 magazines are in print. Boston alone has 14 AM and 16 FM radio stations. Catalogs, direct-mail advertising, and out-of-home media bombard consumers at their homes, offices, and all points in between. While the number of media choices is expanding, the time consumers have to spend with media is not.

The task facing the media strategist was recently expressed by Keith Reinhard, chairman and CEO of DDB Needham Worldwide: "In the future, the most important part of the promotion strategy will be to identify which media vehicles attract which consumers, and what media patterns those consumers follow through a day or week or month, and then to intelligently program messages on the consumer's own personal 'media networks.'"[1] Media strategists have a tremendous amount of factual information about media, including information about circulation, audience characteristics, buying patterns, rates, and competition. But because of the great difficulty in comparing media and the virtually unlimited number of media combinations possible in each situation, selecting the appropriate media plan is still quite arbitrary and somewhat subjective. This chapter discusses the primary components of the complicated process of developing a media plan.

Marketing and Media

An effective media plan must take into account all the marketing components. Several marketing factors constantly interact with media decisions, and vice versa. We first look at the parts of marketing that have an impact on media decisions.

To begin with, the media plan should be contingent on the firm's overall marketing objectives. Until these objectives are delineated clearly, media considerations must wait. The marketing objectives should be comprehensive enough to suggest media directions clearly. For the media planner, marketing objectives should affect the kinds of media selected and how they are used. In a sense, marketing objectives serve as controls for media planning.

Most marketing objectives relate directly to market share; others relate to communication objectives. For example, a market-share objective for Keebler Cookies might be to increase market share of the fancy cookie market to 12 percent by attracting the Mexican-American consumer in the Southwest region. A marketing-communication objective might be to increase the overall awareness of the Keebler brand name in regions that account for two-thirds of sales. Both objectives provide insights into the type of media plan to employ. The market-share objective indicates the use of media that appeal to Mexican-Americans; for example, Spanish-speaking radio and television and Spanish-language newspapers that are released only in the southwestern United States. The marketing-communication objective suggests a much broader media strategy that would reach target areas where sales are high. It would be a far more expensive strategy than the first.

The product also influences the media effort. The price of the product, its newness, stage in the life cycle, and means of distribution suggest the type of consumer who purchases the product. This information also suggests what media mix will present the product to the appropriate audience. A product such as an expensive fishing boat clearly implies a unique group of media as well as a particular schedule. A high-priced product that appeals to a prestige-conscious market segment would not be promoted in *Reader's Digest* or the *Enquirer*.

Closely related to the influence of the product on media is the profitability of the product. It is difficult to justify expensive network television for a product that has a very small profit margin. A small margin may also affect the amount of retailer support that can be expected. If there will be little local retail advertising support, this fact must be taken into account when developing the media strategy. A company such as Jimmy Dean Sausage, for example, has concentrated on regional television since retailers do not feature this product and because a small profit margin dictates little waste in the media strategy.

The channels of distribution influence the media plan in several ways. First, it is wasteful to buy media in markets where the product is not available. Second, certain kinds of resellers are better able to utilize particular media. For example, wholesalers tend to be good at using direct mail and catalogs. Third, particular resellers may be impressed by manufacturers who use certain media. National television, for example, impresses most retailers. Fourth, consumers who buy the product at particular kinds of outlets may expect to locate product information in certain media. Consumers who purchase groceries at supermarkets expect to find product information as well as coupons in print media and direct mail.

The media plan should also take into account the other elements of the promotional strategy. In particular, the amount of effort devoted to advertising, personal selling, and sales promotion can dictate much about the media strategy. For example, if personal selling is emphasized, then trade publications might be the only medium used. But if the promotional strategy relies on mass advertising, then a comprehensive media mix is needed. If the strategy calls for the use of coupons, then the media plan must include use of a medium such as newspapers to distribute the coupons. The Promotion in Focus section details how DDB Needham Worldwide has approached the problem of coordinating promotional strategy and media planning.

A great many other marketing factors can also affect media decisions. Financial constraints have altered many a media plan. For example, in an earlier chapter we discussed how top management at Apple nearly stopped the showing of the "1984" commercial because of financial concerns. It is very important to consider all aspects of marketing before designing the media plan.

There are two stages in developing a media plan: the **media strategy,** which provides a series of basic decisions that must be made in relation to the target market and the means for reaching these decisions, and the tactical part of the media plan, which involves detailed plans for implementing the media strategy. The primary components of the media planning process are shown in Figure 14.1.

Figure 14.1

The primary components of the media planning process.

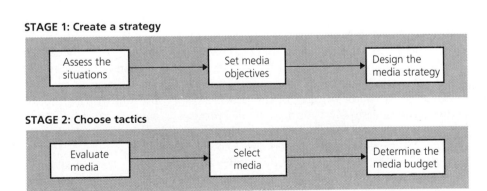

STAGE 1: Create a strategy

Assess the situations → Set media objectives → Design the media strategy

STAGE 2: Choose tactics

Evaluate media → Select media → Determine the media budget

Promotion
in Focus

The Media Make the Message

Suppose you lived in suburban Philadelphia and had to drive to New York twice a week on business. You might be very susceptible to an Amtrak ad about how cheap and easy it would be to hop a train in Philadelphia and be in New York before you'd finished reading the Sunday *Times*. But if the commercials ran on the morning and evening news, when you're generally stuck in traffic, Amtrak would never get through to you and would lose a potential customer.

In other words, to be effective, a commercial or promotion of any kind must use the right media to get through to its target audience as well as convey the appropriate message for that audience. Yet too often in the world of advertising, the "creative" people—those responsible for coming up with the ideas, images, and copy—are separated from the media planners who determine what combination of print, television, radio, and so forth, to use.

DDB Needham has set about to reverse this process by using what it calls "personal media mapping." At the beginning of the process of constructing a campaign for a particular product, the agency carefully determines what media the product's intended users are likely to pay attention to, and when. They might catch the tired Philadelphia-to-New York commuter,

for instance, by posting a billboard near the highway where the commuter is likely to be stuck in traffic. In fact, in the process of creating a campaign for Amtrak, the company sent people to drive Interstate 95 to Florida, determining where drivers would be most tired and most open to Amtrak's message.

Similar assessments led to the positioning of commercials for the New York State Lottery Long around game shows like Wheel of Fortune and on the radio at times when the agency imagined that commuters would be thinking about ways to make easy money. And they led a yogurt maker to concentrate its ads in special-interest magazines that readers are likely to read cover-to-cover rather than in more general women's magazines that readers might just leaf through.

Other ad executives say that DDB Needham is not offering anything new and that "creative" and "media" people work side-by-side in many good agencies. In any case, the company's approach has a lot to teach anyone in the field of promotion. Creating a great message is only half the battle. The other half is getting it to the right people at the right time.

Source: David Kalish, "Media First," *Marketing and Media Decisions* (September 1990): 24–25.

Concept Review

A media plan must take into account all the marketing components:

■ Marketing objectives,

■ Product,

■ Profitability,

■ Channels of distribution, and

■ Promotional strategy.

Creating a Strategy

The process of media planning begins with a situation analysis and proceeds to the establishment of media objectives. Once these objectives are set, planners can outline a strategy that suggests specific activities in order to achieve objectives. In this section, we examine these first steps in developing the media plan.

Assess the Situation

It is vital that a thorough analysis of the situation be conducted before engaging in the actual media planning. The situation analysis requires gathering all the information relevant to the situation. Next comes an assessment of which situational factors are most important. For example, for fast-food retailers such as Burger King and Wendy's, the aging of the population and the trend toward healthier diets are two of the most important situational factors influencing the media plan. A great deal of this information may already be available through the marketing department; in other cases, research must be conducted. Types of information that would prove useful to the media planner include the following:

■ Company and brand history,

■ Company and marketing objectives,

■ Proposed target markets,

■ Product characteristics (strengths and weaknesses),

■ Distribution network,

■ Competitive situation,

■ Promotional history,

■ Economic situation,

■ Regulatory situation,

■ Cultural and social factors, and

■ Resource situation.

Once the media planner feels that all pertinent information has been gathered, the next step is to identify which factors will have the greatest bearing on the media plan. Some companies, for instance, are inclined to follow the lead of their competitors. In this case, a great deal of effort will be devoted to gathering additional information about their competitors' media plans, including a spending analysis across media categories. Planning for media in foreign countries presents other problems. A media strategist entering the Hong Kong market quickly realizes that cultural mores and regulations prohibit a host of media alternatives. Billboards cannot be used, for instance, and radio will not carry contest or sweepstakes messages.

Horror stories abound of media strategists who did not do their homework. For example, when Honda introduced the Acura Legend, the company assumed the car would appeal to white male executives making over seventy-five thousand dollars. The initial media plan emphasized business magazines, direct mail, and early morning television. In fact, the product appealed to a much broader target audience, and Honda had to expand its media plan accordingly. This cost Honda millions of dollars in wasted media placement as well as time.

Set Media Objectives

As in any aspect of business, a media plan must begin with specific objectives. Without objectives, the media strategy lacks direction and control. Media objectives are usually stated in terms of four dimensions: reach, frequency, continuity, and costs. The first two are often combined in one statement of desired monthly or quarterly effective reach.

Reach and Frequency   **Reach** is the number of people or households exposed to a particular media vehicle or schedule at least once during a specified time period (usually weekly or monthly). If program X is seen at least once in a four-week period by six out of ten homes, the reach is 60 percent. Although determining reach is complicated when dealing with several media vehicles, a variety of guide manuals and mathematical techniques exist to make the necessary calculations.

High-reach goals are appropriate when the communication goals are very broad or cognitive—for example, if the goal is to achieve consumer attention, awareness, or knowledge. When reach goals are high, a wide range of media vehicles are needed with low duplication between vehicles and media categories.

Frequency is the number of times within a given period that a consumer is exposed to a message (usually figured on a weekly and/or monthly basis). If a promotional message is given a total of twenty-one exposures during a one-week period, the total frequency is 21 and the average frequency is 3 (21/7 days = 3 exposures per day). These measures indicate the intensity of a particular media buy.

High-frequency goals make sense when the promoter aims to change attitudes and behavior. When frequency goals are high, the media plan should provide a great deal of duplication within and between media vehicles and categories. Thus the media strategy should focus on the continuous use of a fixed group of media categories, subcategories, and vehicles. For example, Healthy Choice frozen dinners are advertised in all the traditional women's magazines, on daytime television, and through cooperative ads with local supermarkets.

Calculating GRPs   The two measures, reach and frequency, can be combined to reflect the total weight of a media effort. This combined measure is called **gross rating point** (GRP) and is derived by multiplying reach times frequency. Recall from Chapter 13 that a rating point is equal to a certain number of viewers and is therefore equivalent to reach. All the viewers together are also called *gross impressions*. Thus if program A has an audience of 250,000 viewers, then each time the promoter uses that program the value in impressions is 250,000. If the promoter showed an ad four times during the program, the number of gross impressions would be 1,000,000. The term *gross* is used because the planner has made no attempt to calculate how many *different* people view the show. Since rating points are equal to gross impressions, it is easier to use GRPs. For example, if three thirty-second spots were shown on "Wheel of Fortune" every day for seven days and the rating for "Wheel of Fortune" was 29.3, then the GRP would be as follows:

$$GRP = 29.3 \times (3 \times 7) = 615.3$$

This number is not necessarily good or bad. The experience and judgment of the media planner play a big part in assessing whether 615 GRPs is adequate. Of course, GRPs would be calculated for the total media schedule. Although gross rating points originated with broadcast audience measurement, GRP is now used to represent print and out-of-home audiences as well. Table 14.1 gives additional examples. Again, the GRP of 859 is subject to the judgment of the media planner that this figure would accomplish particular media objectives.

Effective Frequency and Reach   Suppose a media buy has a GRP of 1,100. Does this media buy have more total weight than the example given in Table 14.1 of a GRP of 859? Yes is the tentative answer, but the specific reach and frequency levels must be appraised. Gross rating points do not account for the varying impact of ensuing exposures on a promotion. This is a serious limitation. Two measures—effective frequency and effective reach—are used in order to adjust for this limitation.

Table 14.1   **Calculating GRPs**

	Ratings (Reach)	×	Number of Announcements or Insertions (Frequency)	=	GRPs
Television					
"Roseanne"	21		4		84
"L.A. Law"	12		2		24
"General Hospital"	2		1		2
"Bill Cosby Show"	18		5		80
"Matlock"	19		4		76
"Today Show"	10		8		80
"Evening News"	14		12		164
Magazines					
Field and Stream	11		4		44
Time	19		10		190
Playboy	23		3		69
Fortune	28		2		56
Total GRPs					859

Effective frequency is the number of promotional messages needed for a message to have its desired effect on individuals. That is, effective frequency reflects an assumption about the effect of the first, second, third, and all other exposures to a promotion. What is the minimum number of times the prospect should come in contact with the message? And what is the maximum number of times necessary for message effectiveness? The answers are, as planners call it, a judgment call. Although no one knows exactly what the optimum number of exposures is, there are three general approaches to the problem: linear, decreasing return, and learning curve. The *linear approach* suggests that each exposure adds as much purchase probability as the one preceding it. If each exposure produces a purchase probability of 2 percent, then 4 exposures produce an 8 percent probability and 10 exposures produce a 20 percent probability. The linear approach supports greater frequency as being better. The *decreasing return approach* assumes that the first exposure is the most powerful, and each ensuing exposure is less effective. Advocates of this approach opt for low frequency. The *learning curve approach* suggests that the effectiveness of each exposure increases more than an equal amount up to a certain point and that subsequent exposures add little. Exposure 1 produces a 2 percent probability, exposure 2 increases the probability to 5 percent, exposure 3 produces 9 percent, and so forth, up to 7 exposures. This approach searches for the optimum number of exposures and does not advocate frequency for its own sake.

When measuring effective frequency, impact should also be taken into account. **Impact** is the intrusiveness of the message. That is, was the message actually perceived by the audience? Being in the room with the television on does not mean that the viewer actually sees every ad that flashes across his or her eyes. Research uses a variety of techniques to tell the promotional manager whether impact has actually taken place.

Effective reach builds on the concept of effective frequency. However, whereas effective frequency seeks to determine the average number of times a person must be exposed to a message before communication occurs, **effective reach** measures the number of prospects who are aware of the message. Reach simply counts the percentage of people who are exposed to the message at least once, and perhaps only once. However, it is not enough to expose a market to a message once; people must also be aware of it. For each promotional message, there are two reach components: empty reach (that is, those in the audience exposed to a message who still have no awareness of it) and effective reach (that is, those exposed enough times to be aware of the message).

Continuity   The objective regarding the timing of media insertions is called **continuity.** How should media dollars and messages be allocated throughout the promotion campaign? Should the message be delivered continuously and uniformly, or should there be times when no media is purchased and other periods when a large part of the media budget is allocated? Product characteristics, market size, budget, and a number of other considerations determine the answers to these questions. For example, Mattel, Inc. might allocate 10 percent of its budget in September, 20 percent in October, 20 percent in November, 40 percent in December, and 10 percent during the rest of the year. These allocations correspond to their products being seasonal.

Typically, three continuity options are considered: continuous, pulsing, and flighting. Briefly, continuous is scheduling media at the same level throughout the year, pulsing is scheduling media erratically to coincide with some factor (for example, a seasonal product), and flighting is scheduling media within a flight, that is, a thirteen-week period of time. These terms will be discussed later in this chapter when we consider scheduling.

Cost   Cost considerations represent a final media objective. Media planners usually receive a specific budget and must plan accordingly. They must be aware of factors such as unit costs (for example, the cost of a thirty-second television ad on a prime-time network), production costs, available discounts, and the various trade-offs between cost, production quality, size, and location. As a bottom-line cost figure, media planners normally use the cost per thousand (CPM). The CPM analysis allows the planner to compare vehicles within a medium (for example, one magazine with another or one program with another) or to compare vehicles across media (for instance, the CPM of radio compared with that of newspapers). Although the analysis can be done for the total audience, it is more valuable to base it only on the portion that has the target characteristics. To calculate the CPM, two figures are needed: the cost of the unit (for example, the page or thirty seconds) divided by the estimated reach. Some planners prefer to compare on the basis of rating points instead of reach. This is called cost per rating point (CPRP) and the calculation is parallel, except that rating points become the divisor. These cost considerations will be discussed further in the section on the media mix. This is calculated by dividing the cost of placing a promotion message by the medium's circulation or rating (that is, cost per rating point). These cost considerations will be discussed further in the section on the media mix.

In conclusion, the media planner can use reach, frequency, GRPs, continuity, and cost as a basis for expressing goals. For example, a local Ford dealership wants to develop a media plan to support an end-of-the-model-year short-term campaign to rid itself of inventory. The media objectives are to reach a relatively small number of prime prospects as many times as possible, on a daily basis, with a low CPM. Local television and radio would probably achieve these objectives. On the other hand, if a manufacturer were introducing a new nondurable consumer product, and the advertising objective was to create a 75 percent level of brand awareness in the target market, the related media goal might be to achieve a high level of reach, with moderate frequency levels.

Design the Media Strategy

Once the determination of the media objectives has been completed, the promotional planner must next develop a comprehensive strategy that details how these objectives will be reached. This is a very detailed document and addresses several questions. Whom should the message be targeted at? Are there multiple targets? When should they receive the message? Are there unique characteristics or requirements needed from the media selected? Several elements are part of a comprehensive media strategy.

Describe the Target Audience   Although the overall marketing plan describes the target market, this information must be translated into a format that can be the basis for the media plan. Media strategists need information that will allow them to pinpoint the most effective means for delivering the message to the appropriate consumer. Whereas creative strategists attempt to understand those for whom they will create promotional messages, media strategists make sure that a particular media audience matches the intended target audience. Media strategists want to select those media that are most efficient in delivering messages to people who are in the target market and to avoid media that deliver a high proportion of messages to nonprospects.

In short, media strategists are primarily interested in information that will help them relate certain consumer characteristics to particular media. They are most concerned about media audience characteristics. Information about the various characteristics must be available for all media so that valid comparisons can be made. In most instances, demographic data are available for all media. Mediamark Research Incorporated (MRI) is a single-source continuing survey that provides the advertising industry with detailed demographic and market segmentation information about media audiences. Reports are issued each spring and fall. Figure 14.2 reports the life cycle patterns for all adults across a number of magazines; note that there are four life cycle patterns and four numbers within each pattern. For example, if we look at the magazine *Discover* for respondents eighteen to thirty-four and married, youngest child under 6, we find from column A that there were 458,000 adults in this audience. Column B says that the 458,000 adults represent 2.6 percent of the total population in that life cycle, thus showing that 2.6 percent of adults in that life cycle are reached by *Discover*. Column C indicates that the 458,000 adults represent 8.9 percent of the total adult audience of *Discover*, and Column D is an index used to compare the composition among various magazines within the given life cycle classification. Composition represents the average demographic characteristics of the United States on those dimensions, with an index of 100 indicating an exact match; more than 100 represents a percentage greater than the average; and less than 100 represents a percentage less than the average. The 93 index means that *Discover* is 7 percent lower than the national average (100) for composition of those in that life cycle.

On rare occasions, psychographic data may also be collected, or data related to purchasing behavior may be available. Thus *Better Homes and Gardens* reports that 65 percent of its subscribers are full-time homemakers, have children at home, and cook most meals from scratch from psychographic data collected. What is important is that media strategists have useful and comparable data.

As an example, suppose a media planner promotes a hot cereal that has two primary target markets—children and senior citizens. The manufacturer decides to deliver the advertising message to senior citizens. The media planner would want to know the characteristics of senior citizens. People in this age category tend to have lower incomes, have no children at home, live a more sedentary lifestyle, and have poorer health. Thus the media planner might identify characteristics related to lifestyle, health, and age as well as to the product being advertised.

This task completed, the media planner must consider which of the

BASE: ADULTS	TOTAL U.S. '000	RESPONDENT 18-34 1-PERSON HOUSEHOLD				RESPONDENT 18-34 AND MARRIED, NO CHILDREN				RESPONDENT 18-34 AND MARRIED, YOUNGEST CHILD <6				RESPONDENT 18-34 AND MARRIED, YOUNGEST CHILD 6+			
		A '000	B % DOWN	C % ACROSS	D INDEX	A '000	B % DOWN	C % ACROSS	D INDEX	A '000	B % DOWN	C % ACROSS	D INDEX	A '000	B % DOWN	C % ACROSS	D INDEX
ALL ADULTS	180974	5733	100.0	3.2	100	7320	100.0	4.0	100	17331	100.0	9.6	100	5310	100.0	2.9	100
AIR GROUP ONE (GR)	1883	*70	1.2	3.7	117	*144	2.0	7.6	189	*37	.2	2.0	21	*29	.5	1.5	52
AMERICAN BABY	3557	*58	1.0	1.6	51	*133	1.8	3.7	92	1631	9.4	45.9	479	*137	2.6	3.9	131
AMERICAN HEALTH	3851	*119	2.1	3.1	98	*107	1.5	2.8	69	*335	1.9	8.7	91	*108	2.0	2.8	96
AMERICAN LEGION	3312	*38	.7	1.1	36	*18	.2	.5	13	*75	.4	2.3	24	*54	1.0	1.6	56
AMERICAN WAY	1061	*12	.2	1.1	36	*49	.7	4.6	114	*50	.3	4.7	49	*8	.2	.8	26
ARCHITECTURAL DIGEST	3148	*114	2.0	3.6	114	*147	2.0	4.7	115	*256	1.5	8.1	85	*61	1.1	1.9	66
AUDUBON	1581	*87	1.5	5.5	174	*77	1.1	4.9	120	*95	.5	6.0	63	*18	.3	1.1	39
BABY TALK	2258	*25	.4	1.1	35	*141	1.9	6.2	154	889	5.1	39.4	411	*17	.3	.8	26
BASSMASTER	3202	*75	1.3	2.3	74	*181	2.5	5.7	140	492	2.8	15.4	160	*203	3.8	6.3	216
BETTER HOMES & GARDENS	31366	528	9.2	1.7	53	1399	19.1	4.5	110	3577	20.6	11.4	119	1287	24.2	4.1	140
BHG/LHJ COMBO (GR)	49749	818	14.3	1.6	52	2181	29.8	4.4	108	5584	32.2	11.2	117	1989	37.5	4.0	136
BLACK ENTERPRISE	1904	*33	.6	1.7	55	*23	.3	1.2	30	*239	1.4	12.6	131	*30	.6	1.6	54
BON APPETIT	4631	*139	2.4	3.0	95	*306	4.2	6.6	163	*311	1.8	6.7	70	*158	3.0	3.4	116
BRIDE'S MAGAZINE	3957	*198	3.5	5.0	158	*313	4.3	7.9	196	*220	1.3	5.6	58	*84	1.6	2.1	72
BUSINESS WEEK	6136	*249	4.3	4.1	128	344	4.7	5.6	139	505	2.9	8.2	86	*148	2.8	2.4	82
THE CABLE GUIDE	14853	391	6.8	2.6	83	704	9.6	4.7	117	1488	8.6	10.0	105	*398	7.5	2.7	91
CAR & DRIVER	5327	*250	4.4	4.7	148	*135	1.8	2.5	63	562	3.2	10.6	110	*165	3.1	3.1	106
CAR CRAFT	2505	*66	1.2	2.6	83	*110	1.5	4.4	109	*388	2.2	15.5	162	*140	2.6	5.6	190
CHANGING TIMES	3426	*67	1.2	2.0	62	*103	1.4	3.0	74	*139	.8	4.1	42	*123	2.3	3.6	122
CHICAGO TRIBUNE MAGAZINE	2336	*97	1.7	4.2	131	*89	1.2	3.8	94	*173	1.0	7.4	77	*54	1.0	2.3	79
COLONIAL HOMES	2293	*57	1.0	2.5	78	*101	1.4	4.4	109	*224	1.3	9.8	102	*116	2.2	5.1	172
CONDE NAST LIMITED (GR)	21230	1047	18.3	4.9	156	1248	17.0	5.9	145	1840	10.6	8.7	91	550	10.4	2.6	88
CONDE NAST WOMEN (GR)	28258	1724	30.1	6.1	193	2378	32.5	8.4	208	2693	15.5	9.5	100	798	15.0	2.8	96
CONSUMERS DIGEST	4676	*138	2.4	3.0	93	*252	3.4	5.4	133	*375	2.2	8.0	84	*111	2.1	2.4	81
COSMOPOLITAN	12118	640	11.2	5.3	167	790	10.8	6.5	161	1596	9.2	13.2	138	*362	6.8	3.0	102
COUNTRY HOME	5761	*146	2.5	2.5	80	*207	2.8	3.6	89	717	4.1	12.4	130	*388	7.3	6.7	230
COUNTRY LIVING	10372	*183	3.2	1.8	56	735	10.0	7.1	175	1343	7.7	12.9	135	*600	11.3	5.8	197
CREATIVE IDEAS FOR LIVING	2310	*51	.9	2.2	70	*50	.7	2.2	54	*319	1.8	13.8	144	*44	.8	1.9	65
DELTA SKY	1255	*44	.8	3.5	111	*87	1.2	6.9	171	*22	.1	1.8	18	*4	.1	.3	11
DIAMANDIS MAGAZINE NTWK (GR)	22747	1195	20.8	5.3	166	1067	14.6	4.7	116	2208	12.7	9.7	101	656	12.4	2.9	98
DISCOVER	5132	*269	4.7	5.2	165	*228	3.1	4.4	110	458	2.6	8.9	93	*125	2.4	2.4	83
DISNEY CHANNEL MAGAZINE	5709	*84	1.5	1.5	46	*218	3.0	3.8	94	929	5.4	16.3	170	*341	6.4	6.0	204
EAST/WEST NETWORK (GR)	3848	*169	2.9	4.4	139	*301	4.1	7.8	193	*231	1.3	6.0	63	*39	.7	1.0	35
EBONY	9519	398	6.9	4.2	132	*227	3.1	2.4	59	704	4.1	7.4	77	*253	4.8	2.7	91
ELLE	2298	*154	2.7	6.7	212	*327	4.5	14.2	352	*82	.5	3.6	37	*75	1.4	3.3	111
ESQUIRE	3673	*184	3.2	5.0	158	*134	1.8	3.6	90	*239	1.4	6.5	68	*73	1.4	2.0	68
ESSENCE	3485	*183	3.2	5.3	166	*77	1.1	2.2	55	*296	1.7	8.5	89	*108	2.0	3.1	106
FAMILY CIRCLE	24570	300	5.2	1.2	39	944	12.9	3.8	95	2845	16.4	11.6	121	1107	20.8	4.5	154
FAMILY CIRCLE/MCCALLS (GR)	41859	640	11.2	1.5	48	1600	21.9	3.8	95	4801	27.7	11.5	120	1893	35.6	4.5	154
FAMILY HANDYMAN	4022	*17	.3	.4	13	*122	1.7	3.0	75	*399	2.3	9.9	104	*166	3.1	4.1	141
FIELD & STREAM	13794	291	5.1	2.1	67	630	8.6	4.6	113	1790	10.3	13.0	136	*538	10.1	3.9	133
FLOWER & GARDEN	3620	*53	.9	1.5	46	*164	2.2	4.5	112	*285	1.6	7.9	82	*132	2.5	3.6	124

Figure 14.2

The four life cycle patterns for adults across a number of magazines.
"Mediamark Research Magazine Total Audiences Report: Spring 1990," M-1, (Media-mark Research, Inc. 1990): 44. Used with permission.

many ways of describing consumers is most appropriate to the particular product. A general guideline will help: The number of dimensions to be considered should be limited to no more than three or four. For example, media planners for Clairol hair products might be most interested in demographics such as gender, occupation, income, and age. If more dimensions are considered, comparing media across these characteristics becomes almost impossible. The more criteria included in a definition of a consuming group, the fewer the people who will meet all the criteria.

Note that the media strategist can set audience objectives only in terms of those audience characteristics that have been measured. Although it would be desirable to collect demographic, psychographic, and product usage data from media sources, typically only demographics are available.

Determine Dispersion Requirements Many people believe that the primary objective of a media plan is to deliver a message to as many consumers as possible. *Dispersion* refers to a media policy that places the message in as many different programs and spots as possible to avoid duplicating the audience. The request for *maximum dispersion* means that reach has priority over frequency. In this case, the media buyer should avoid duplicating programs as much as possible. Using different shows increases the opportunity for different or unduplicated audiences. Thus a media planner might describe comparable strategies as follows:

- Plan I: ten nighttime television appearances in a three-month period. This plan guarantees that 60 percent of the national television audience will see the message at least once during the three-month period.

- Plan II: eight daytime television announcements during a three-month period. This plan guarantees that 50 percent of the television market will see the message at least once.

Since both plans cost the same amount, it appears obvious that Plan I is superior to Plan II, but several other considerations should be examined before making this decision.

First, the coverage should be compared not only in gross impressions but in terms of the specific target audience as well. For example, although Plan II appears inferior, if the target audience is women between the ages of twenty-five and forty-four, they are the primary recipients of the message in Plan II. Dispersion of messages means dispersion of messages among prospects, as defined by the advertiser.

A second consideration is to specify more clearly what the phrase *at least once* really means in a given situation. Although a certain percentage of the audience will see the message at least once, a percentage of that group will also see it more than once. For example, an advertiser follows Plan I and purchases a nighttime television scatter plan, which means that twenty-four messages appear in a variety of programs to achieve maximum dispersion.

The promotional message appears in six television programs during the three-month period, and the total audience for these six programs is 51.5 million (program or PGM 1 = 6.3 million, PGM 2 = 9 million, PGM 3 = 4.7 million, PGM 4 = 11.2 million, PGM 5 = 9.4 million, and PGM 6 = 10.9 million). This total figure of 51.5 million is often referred to as gross impressions. However, since some of these audience members receive the message more than once, an adjustment must be made to determine how many new viewers are actually added by each additional program. That is, even though the first program delivers 6.3 million and the second 9 million, 3.1 million are the same people. After removing this redundancy from all six programs, the actual number of people exposed to the message is 12.8 million. This number is referred to as the **net coverage.** Dividing the total number of homes reached by a media plan by the net coverage of that plan produces the **average frequency of contact.** Average frequency of contact provides media planners with another basis for comparing plans:

Plan I: Average frequency of contact = 51,500,000/12,800,000 = 4.2
Plan II: Average frequency of contact = 43,600,000/16,500,000 = 2.6

The smaller the number, the better the coverage of the plan. Therefore, Plan II is the better plan.

A third consideration is the distribution of frequency of exposures. Research results indicate that the most effective media plan tends to concentrate message delivery at the middle of the frequency range rather than at the extremes. (See Figure 14.3.) Rather than achieving one exposure to many people and many exposures to a few people, it would be best for the majority of households to receive two or three advertising exposures, with the balance receiving only one or two. Media planners may wish to make such frequency distribution goals explicit in their media strategy statements so that these goals are included in the criteria established to evaluate alternative plans.

Determine Concentration Requirements   Promoters of products like toys, turkeys, snow skis, and cold remedies face some special problems related to the continuity objective. Promoters must concentrate their messages at a particular time of the year or in a particular part of the country. Under these conditions, the media planner must deal with a series of decisions.

Figure 14.3

Ideally, the majority of households should be subjected to three or more exposures.

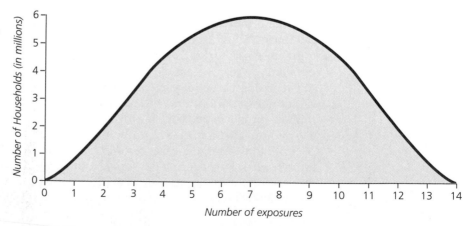

When should the campaign start? When should it peak? How should the budget be distributed? Can the same campaign be run in various geographic areas? The answers reflect not only traditional spending patterns but also pressures from retailers and the direct sales organization.

Identify Inherent Qualities Required of Media   Many media exert qualitative effects on the messages they carry. The *qualitative media effect* is what the medium does to enhance or depreciate a message after the medium has delivered the message. Vehicles that exist oblivious to their surroundings and that deliver the message in an environment that is bereft of value may create a negative effect. Similarly, some companies avoided advertising during the evening news during the Gulf War because of the negative association with "bad news." In contrast, the *Washington Post* might enhance the quality of a message because of the high-quality reputation of its editorials.

A promoter may exist anywhere on this qualitative continuum. For example, a promoter might not be concerned with minimizing cost and may have little concern with the quality of the medium. For example, consider the products advertised in supermarket tabloids. These are often questionable, low-quality products to begin with. Consequently, the promoter could place a message on the sides of abandoned buildings, taxicabs, and matchbook covers. At the other extreme, promoters of high-fashion women's clothing may feel it is critical that their messages appear in fashion magazines such as *Glamour* and *Vogue*. The perceived quality of these publications by the large target audience should enhance the message.

The important factor is that the interaction between the medium and the message should be complementary. Although the Franco-American Corporation may wish to sponsor opera and ballet programs, the consumer might have trouble associating the San Francisco Ballet Company with Spaghettios. If promoters cannot derive significant qualitative value by placing a message in a particular medium, they probably should not do so. Perhaps the qualitative goal can be met through some other means than the media strategy.

Analyze Implications of Message Content   A final consideration for the media planner is to match the medium with the message. Creative directors produce specific messages with a variety of factors in mind. We have previously discussed the influence of the product on message content. In turn, the resulting message content has a bearing on the medium selected to deliver it. Messages that carry a great deal of detailed information suggest print over broadcast. Messages with a strong emotional appeal suggest broadcast over print.

The possibility also exists that the medium will be selected first, and the message will be created with television or magazines in mind. By law, cigarette marketers can only use print. Media strategists plan knowing the essence of the message that their media plan will deliver and adjust the plan accordingly.

Concept Review

1. The process of media planning begins with a situation analysis. Gathering primary and secondary information and determining which information is pertinent to the media plan are first steps.
2. Media objectives determine direction and control for the media plan and are stated in the following dimensions:
   a. Reach: Number of people or households exposed to a media vehicle at least once during a specified time period.
   b. Frequency: Number of times within a given period that a consumer is exposed to a message.
   c. Gross Rating Points: Calculated by multiplying reach times frequency or adding the rating points delivered by a media schedule.
   d. Effective Frequency: Number of exposures needed to produce optimum results.
   e. Effective Reach: Number of prospects aware of the message.
   f. Continuity: The timing of media insertions.
   g. Cost Considerations: Several cost factors must be considered; media is normally budgeted according to its cost per thousand.
3. The design of the actual media strategy includes the following factors:
   a. Describe the target audience,
   b. Determine dispersion requirements,
   c. Determine concentration requirements,
   d. Identify inherent qualities required of media, and
   e. Analyze implications of message content.

Choosing Tactics

Once a media strategy is in place, what does a media planner do in order to implement it? Most of the tactics are carried out by the time and space buyers in the media department of advertising agencies. The process of selecting tactics usually consists of three stages:

1. Evaluate media.
2. Select media.
3. Determine media budget.[2]

Evaluate Media

A thorough evaluation of all the media relevant to a particular strategy is an important aspect of any media plan. Chapter 13 describes the strengths and weaknesses of the various media. There are several objective and subjective factors to consider. Some of the important objective considerations are the following:

■ Matching media type with target market characteristics,

■ Matching media type with media objectives,

■ Determining the relative cost of reaching a particular prospect with a particular message through a particular medium, and

■ Determining the effect of competition on the media choice.

Subjective factors include these:

■ Judging the consumers' perceptions of various media,

■ Matching the creative approach and the capabilities of various media to implement that approach, and

■ Evaluating the media's environment in respect to editorial policy, entertainment value, and so on.

Collecting the necessary information to appraise these factors may require extensive primary research by the sponsoring firm or its agency. This research is both expensive and time consuming. As a result, many promoters rely heavily on research findings provided by the medium, on experience, and on subjective appraisal.

Every media planner should follow two guiding principles when evaluating media. The first is to realize that the medium simply carries the message; it is not the instrument that accomplishes the final effect. The medium should be evaluated not in terms of whether it will sell the product but in terms of how much it will facilitate the delivery of the message.

The second principle is to appreciate the fact that the total audience attracted to a particular medium may be much larger than the target audience embedded within this total. That is, fewer prople see the promotional messages within the newspaper than see some part of the newspaper, and still fewer see a particular promotion. Media planners must understand the difference between exposure opportunity and actual exposure. Not everyone who passes an outdoor board, a car card, or a poster actually looks at the ad at that location. Media planners must do the best they can to develop information or estimates of the relation between exposure opportunity and actual exposure. Effective reach is one measure of this process.[3]

Select Media

Once media planners have considered the media objectives and the qualitative and quantitative characteristics of various media, they must make several important decisions. These decisions can be divided into two general categories: mix decisions and timing decisions.

Before beginning this discussion, it is important to note that these decisions are always restricted by the size of the budget. Budgets are never large enough to accomplish all that the media planner has in mind. The media planner must work within the budget provided, even though the media plan turns out to be a compromise that may not totally satisfy the established objectives. Every media decision must relate back to the budget.

The Media Mix   The media planner faces a series of decisions when selecting a medium or combination of media—the *media mix*. These decisions do not necessarily occur before the timing decisions but in conjunction with them. That is, the scheduling possibilities of a medium such as network television may dictate the need for an additional medium in order to meet reach and frequency objectives.

In this section we examine some of the key questions a media strategist should consider when drawing up the media mix.

Number of Insertions   One key question for the media strategist is how effective various media are. Media planners need to determine the ideal number of insertions they should use in a particular medium within a given period of time. Armed with this information, media planners should be able to set up minimum usage criteria for different media, relate the criteria to the dollar cost of such minimum usage, and build an estimate of the cost of implementing various plans.

There is little agreement and no well-developed general knowledge about how many insertions in a particular medium are ideal. One might conclude that the required concentration of units in a particular medium depends on the objective of the program. For example, if the objective is to reach a large number of people and to have them recall the message in the short run, then it would probably be best to concentrate the messages during a thirteen- to fifteen-week period, to spread these exposures across a large group of consumers, and to reduce exposure frequency as time progresses.

Planners may find that either rules of thumb or research-based evidence is available for a particular situation, even though there are no general agreed-upon usage rules for individual media that cover all situations. Many sophisticated practitioners have developed their own rules for particular situations through continuous testing in the marketplace, through continuous analysis of sales patterns, or both.

Relative Efficiency   Even if media planners have some research knowledge or arbitrary rules for determining patterns of media usage, it is likely that they will also want to know about the relative efficiency between media and within media. In other words, can one vehicle reach the same objective for a lower cost than other vehicles?

The standard measure of relative efficiency within media is the *cost per thousand* (CPM) computation. The formula was explained earlier. Suppose that a media planner wishes to reach bank executives twenty-four to thirty-four years old and is considering three magazines: *Bankers Magazine, Bank News,* and *Bank Systems & Technology.* The media planner would start by learning the one-page cost (black-and-white or four-color) and enter it into the numerator of the equation. For the sake of illustration, let us assume that the insertion costs for a black-and-white, full-page ad in the three publications are as follows:

Bankers Magazine	$1,420
Bank News	930
Bank Systems & Technology	3,670

Calculating the denominator of the equation is more difficult. One approach is to use the circulation of each magazine. This information is available and reliable. However, this figure does not reflect actual people, since it includes businesses, libraries, and other institutional subscribers. So the media planner may use some measure of the people reached by the particular vehicle as the denominator. The audience measure employed is contingent on the target audience characteristics specified in the media objectives. This type of information may be available through the medium itself or through private research companies such as Simmons Media Studies. In our example, the relevant audience is males, twenty-four to thirty-four years of age. Suppose the total audience fitting this description for each magazine is as follows:

Bankers Magazine	49,511
Bank News	9,279
Bank Systems & Technology	25,692

The cost-per-thousand computations for a black-and-white, full-page ad for each magazine are as follows:

$$Bankers\ Magazine = \frac{\$1,420}{49,511} = \$28.68$$

$$Bank\ News = \frac{\$930}{9,279} = \$100.22$$

$$Bank\ Systems\ \&\ Technology = \frac{\$3,670}{25,692} = \$142.85$$

These values are referred to as the *cost per thousand–target market* (CPM-TM) since it includes an audience adjustment. A comparison of three daytime soap operas in terms of CPM-TM is shown in Figure 14.5. Note that the information in Figure 14.4 is sufficient to calculate the *cost per rating point* (CPRP), another indicator used to evaluate media alternatives. With this

Figure 14.4

A comparison of three daytime soap operas. Advertising Age *(May 28, 1990): 36. Used with permission.*

No.1 daytime show "The Young and the Restless" (CBS)	No.2 daytime show "General Hospital" (ABC)	No.3 daytime show "All My Children" (ABC)
Rating — 8.0	Rating — 7.4	Rating — 6.5
Cost per 30-second spot — $17,200	Cost per 30-second spot — $19,200	Cost per 30-second spot — $17,800
CPM women, 18 to 49 — $6.51	CPM women, 18 to 49 — $6.22	CPM women, 18 to 49 — $5.70

technique, many vehicles can be compared. The only limiting factor is whether the necessary audience information is available.

Comparing the efficiency of different types of media is quite different. The key question is whether audience data are truly comparable from medium to medium. The answer is usually no, for three reasons. First, the audiences of different media are measured in different ways. For example, A. C. Nielsen measures audiences based on television viewer reports of the programs watched; outdoor audience exposure estimates are based on counts of the number of automotive vehicles that pass particular poster locations. Second, each of these measurements deals with different aspects of consumer involvement. In measuring the audience for an outdoor poster, it is assumed that every passing automobile contains an attentive passenger. In electronic measurements of national television audiences, there is assurance that the set is on and the person is probably in the room, but it is not certain that he or she is watching the program. Third, comparisons based on audience exposure do not reflect the potential value of the medium, which depends on how well the promoter exploits the medium's ability to attract consumers. The ability to attract cannot be reflected in cost-per-thousand computations.

Despite these limitations, many media planners still resort to the cost-per-thousand computation. Table 14.2 displays other criteria a media planner can employ in comparing media categories.

Effects of Multiple Media   Finally, to select the appropriate media mix, media planners should appraise the implications of using multiple media. Above all, they should consider the possible benefits of placing a message once in two media versus twice in the same medium. Some people see no media at all, and others concentrate on one medium to the exclusion of others; both these factors lead to a greater cumulative coverage from a media mix program than from the use of a single medium.

A second implication is that a media mix program tends to even out the frequency of exposure within the total audience. When twelve messages

Table 14.2 **Some Criteria for Comparing Media**

	Television			Radio		Newspapers			Magazines				
	Network	Spot	Cable	Network	Spot	National	Local	Supplements	Consumer	Business	Farm	Outdoor	Direct Mail
Audience Factors/ Data													
Typical adult rating (%)	16	16	2	2	2	14	40	25	20	20	20	60	2+
Reach (H,M,L)	H	M	L	L	L	L	H	H	H	L	L	H	M
Frequency (H,M,L)	M	H	H	H	H	M	M	L	L	L	L	H	L
Selectivity		X	X	X	X		X		X	X	X		X
Seasonal usage				X	X						X		
Controlled circ.										X	X		X
Geographic flexibility		X	X		X		X		X	X	X	X	X
Local coverage		X	X		X		X		X			X	X
Ethnic appeal			X		X		X		X			X	X

	Television			Radio		Newspapers			Magazines				
	Network	Spot	Cable	Network	Spot	National	Local	Supplements	Consumer	Business	Farm	Outdoor	Direct Mail
Message Factors/ Data													
Vehicle audience weight	80.0	72.5	62.5	40.0	37.5	35.0	35.0	35.0	52.5	52.5	52.5	47.5	65.0
Long message life							X	X	X	X	X	X	
Simple message	X	X		X	X							X	
Emotional appeal	X	X	X	X	X			X	X				X
Immediacy				X	X	X	X						
Control ad placement	X	X	X	X	X							X	X
Editorial association	X		X	X		X	X	X	X	X	X		
Supporting medium		X	X	X	X	X	X	X		X	X	X	X
Good response measures						X	X	X	X	X	X		X
Good ad reproduction								X	X	X	X	X	X

Table 14.2   Some Criteria for Comparing Media (*cont.*)

	Television			*Radio*		*Newspapers*			*Magazines*				
	Net-work	Spot	Cable	Net-work	Spot	Na-tional	Local	Supple-ments	Con-sumer	Busi-ness	Farm	Out-door	Direct Mail
Efficiency Factors/ Data													
Typical unit cost ($000)	90	50	2	3	8	48		200	75	10+	5+	500	
CPM (Adults, nearest $1)	6	9	3	3	4	17	11	11	10	20+	20+	2	500+
Production cost (H,M,L)	H	M	L	M	L	H	L	M	M	M	M	H	H
Production-flexible			X		X		X					X	X
Discounts	X	X	X	X	X	X	X		X	X	X	X	

H = High   L = Low
M = Medium   X = possess that characteristic

Source: Kent M. Lancaster and Helen E. Katz, *Strategic Media Planning,* (Lincolnwood, IL: NTC Business Books, 1989): 98–99. Used with permission.

are played on two different media (for example, radio and television), the heavy users of each medium receive a lower, more even dose of the message than they receive when all twelve are played on radio. Finally, the use of a media mix permits messages to be delivered in different ways to those audience segments that are exposed to several media. An individual listening to the radio version of a message, for example, will pick up on different cues than those noted in the television version of the message. The person perceives two unique messages even though a large percentage of both messages are identical.

The Timing of Media   The timing of media refers to the actual placement of promotions. Timing decisions are dictated by the media objectives. If the media objectives indicate that the target audience receives the message at a particular time or with a certain level of impact, timing decisions are at issue. Timing includes not only the scheduling of promotions but also their size and position.

Scheduling   The effectiveness of a media schedule depends in large part on four considerations.[4]

1. *Exposure.* How many exposures are created by the media schedule? As discussed earlier, evaluating this aspect of a media schedule entails counting the number of exposures that can be obtained. In the case of magazines, the number of exposures is the circulation figure converted

into a CPM number; for television, the basic unit of counting is the GRP. In addition, this figure should be adjusted for exposure to actual advertising rather than vehicle exposure. If there is any reason to believe that readership for some vehicles is higher than for others, the basic CPM figures should be adjusted accordingly.

2. *Segmentation.* Who is exposed and what percentage represents members of the target audience? Delivering people who are not in a target segment has little value. Data to consider in evaluating this aspect of a schedule might include demographics, lifestyle profiles, and product usage. Describing segments in terms of factors such as these allows further adjustment in the CPM and GRP figures.

3. *Media-option source effect.* Does exposure in one vehicle have more impact than exposure in another? The media-option source effect provides three qualitative measures of media alternatives. The first is the *media class source effect,* which compares different types of media (for example, television ads versus magazine ads). The second qualitative measure, *media option characteristics,* examines the effect of variations in size (full page or half page), length (thirty seconds or sixty seconds), color (black and white or color), and location. Finally, the *vehicle source effect* compares the impact of a single exposure in one vehicle with a single exposure in another vehicle. A Pioneer Stereo ad in *Esquire* might make a greater impact than the same ad in *Time,* even if the audience were the same.

4. *Repetition effect.* What is the relative impact of successive exposures to the same person? Although it may take a minimum number of successive exposures to penetrate the consumer's mind, beyond this point the value of successive exposures will eventually diminish. The key is to make the correct assumptions about the value of successive exposures. Such assumptions must consider the timing of the exposures (that is, people forget between exposures), differences in appeals, interest level, month, product characteristics, and so on. Some campaigns make a strong impact quickly; others take a long time to create awareness.

Some people conclude that three exposures within a purchase cycle are all that are needed to induce attitudinal or behavioral change.[5] Herbert Krugman, advertising theorist, suggests that each of the first three exposures has a different purpose. The first exposure elicits a "what is it?" response. The second exposure continues the evaluation and information-gathering process. The third exposure provides a reminder that the audience member has not acted on the message. Exposures beyond the third simply repeat the process and serve no real benefits.[6] Of course, this is a rather simplistic explanation and does not account for many other considerations. Detailing the schedule takes place after assessing these four considerations. The schedule shows specific vehicles carrying messages on particular dates or at particular times. It should be based on the continuity objectives discussed earlier.

Recall that one of three continuity patterns may be followed, as Figure 14.5 illustrates. The first is **continuous.** This pattern is called for if the audience needs to be exposed to the message constantly because of the nature of the product (that is, it is purchased frequently and regularly) and excessive competition. A continuous pattern also assumes that the media budget is very large.

A second pattern, **flighting,** calls for heavy scheduling during shorter time periods in order to increase reach and frequency in the hopes that these effects will carry over into longer time periods. A media planner may therefore concentrate media buys in a thirteen-week period rather than over fifty-two weeks. This strategy allows the media planner to buy media at better rates. Compared with a more diluted schedule, flighting also may create a much better impact on the consumer. This advantage is still debatable since a short-run impact may not carry over through the rest of the

Figure 14.5

The three scheduling alternatives.

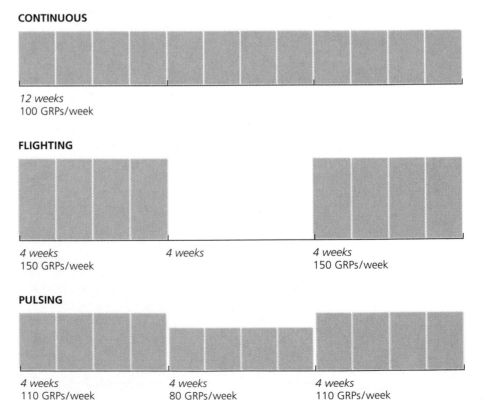

CONTINUOUS

12 weeks
100 GRPs/week

FLIGHTING

4 weeks   *4 weeks*   *4 weeks*
150 GRPs/week   150 GRPs/week

PULSING

4 weeks   *4 weeks*   *4 weeks*
110 GRPs/week   80 GRPs/week   110 GRPs/week

year. If impact does not carry over, the entire effort could be wasted. On the other hand, if the company has limited promotional funds, this strategy could be the most effective. Flighting might also prove appropriate for seasonal products whose season fits the thirteen-week time frame.

A variation of flighting is **pulsing,** which is a combination of continuous advertising and flighting, with continuous advertising "emphasized" during the best sale months. Because this approach tends to minimize waste, (that is, delivering messages when the consumer is not in the market), it represents the best of both of these techniques. Not all promoters should use pulsing, however. It best fits products that are sold year-round but that have heavy sales at intermittent periods such as stationery products, hot dogs, beer, and linens and towels (often featured as white sales).

Size and Position   Timing of the media effort also involves determining the size and position of a particular promotion within a medium. Although a great deal of research has been conducted in this area, the results are not conclusive.

We do know that simply doubling the size of an ad does not double its effectiveness. Although a larger promotion creates a higher level of attraction and greater opportunity for creative impact, the extent is still undetermined. Equivocal results have been reported for print media of various sizes and for television and radio commercials of various lengths. Depending on what advertisers have to say and how well they can say it, a thirty-second commercial may do the job much better than a sixty-second commercial. Bigger or longer may not always be better. Still, the media planner must consider the possible positive effects. The size or length chosen should also be related to the objectives.

Guidelines regarding positioning are only slightly more enlightening. In general, there is some evidence to suggest that within a print medium (1) the inside cover and first few pages get a slightly better readership, (2) placement of compatible stories adjacent to an ad may enhance its effect, and (3) having many competing ads on the same page detracts from effectiveness. Findings related to broadcast media are almost nonexistent.

Determine the Media Budget

How much to spend on promotion and media is a strategic decision. It depends on sales potential, objectives, and affordability. The promotion budget must be viewed as a function of the marketing of the brand or company. It is not possible to reconcile ambitious marketing goals with a modest promotional budget. Conversely, it makes no financial sense to have an ambitious budget if the marketing goals are modest. A comprehensive discussion of promotion budgeting is given in Chapter 16. In most instances, since media represent 80 percent of that budget, they are carefully considered.

The media planner's role in this decision making can vary greatly. In respect to the total dollar amount given to the media planner by top management, the media planner's control tends to be limited. The media planner is often given a dollar figure, which may or may not be sufficient to implement the media strategy. Ideally, the media planner is allowed to gather and present to management media cost information, which is considered as part of the budget determination process. This information includes promotion expenditures by the competition, the cost of media, and the audience delivery affordable at given budget levels. Figure 14.6 shows an example of a media budget.

Brand Report No.170
Luxury-Car Expenditures
January–December 1989

	Media total	BAR network television	BAR spot television	BAR cable television	BAR syndicated television	RGR spot radio	LNA magazines	MR newspapers	LNA Sunday magazines	LNA outdoor	BAR network radio
Cadillac DeVille/Fleetwood	$14,780.9	$10,371.5	$259.6	$330.6	—	$54.2	$3,384.3	$334.5	$48.2	—	—
Lincoln Town Car	13,592.8	6,303.6	2,484.7	246.3	$9.4	154.5	4,322.5	—	—	$69.5	—
Buick Electra	6,666.2	1,935.9	144.8	86.5	—	42.2	—	188.0	—	—	$714.4
Acura Legend	47,916.7	23,647.5	7,409.5	1,306.8	—	1,921.9	12,978.7	652.3	—	—	—
Lincoln Continental	6,131.4	1,128.1	754.5	—	576.4	—	2,907.5	706.5	—	—	—
Volvo 740	5,853.6	—	186.4	202.5	—	—	5,096.6	366.1	—	—	—
Cadillac Brougham	2,697.8	912.5	73.5	4.7	—	—	1,472.7	234.4	—	—	—
BMW 3 Series	14,944.5	2,909.9	4,345.3	458.9	—	—	5,552.5	2,725.6	62.7	—	—
Cadillac Eldorado	1,562.8	1,100.2	141.5	46.2	—	—	292.0	52.2	—	—	—

Note: Figures are in millions of dollars.

BAR Arbitron's Broadcast Advertiser's Report
LNA Leading National Advertisers
RER Radio Expenditure Reports
MR   Media Records

Figure 14.6

A media budget for luxury automobiles.
Marketing & Media Decisions *(May 1990): 87. Used with permission.*

Media planners must cope with several timing problems related to the budget. They cannot always abide by the budgetary schedule used by the rest of the business. The budgetary calendar does not coincide with the typical calendar year, which may begin on January 1 or July 1. Due to product seasonality, media availability, and several other factors, media budgets can start or end on any date.

Another timing issue has to do with lead time. Media planners often have to move quickly in order to make media buys. Corporate executives may take weeks or months to evaluate and approve budgets.

A final issue related to timing is rooted in the dynamic nature of media planning. Media buying has often been compared to buying and selling stocks. Every day media buyers negotiate with hundreds of media about such factors as rates and special discounts. Media representatives are constantly putting together media packages and desperately trying to sell unsold space or time in minute-by-minute contact with media planners. Media buyers without adequate budgets or contingency funds are unable to engage in this negotiation process and may wind up spending millions of extra dollars on media.

Concept Review

There are three tactical decision areas associated with the media plan:
1. Media must be evaluated in respect to two guiding principles: how it will facilitate the delivery of the message and what the actual exposure provided by a particular medium is.
2. The specific media are selected and two important decisions are made:
    a. The media mix: determining which media work best together.
    b. The timing of media: entailing scheduling and selecting size and position.
3. The media budget is determined.

Management Science and Media Planning

With the advent of the computer, the application of management science to media planning has become widespread. In fact, media planning problems seem ideal for management science techniques because of the massive amounts of available data and the possibility of employing several alternatives.[7] Nevertheless, those trying to apply computer technology to media planning face numerous problems.

First, despite the vast amount of available data, data still tend to be medium specific. There is still no satisfactory way to compare several media simultaneously.

A second problem is the constantly changing values of comparable media elements. For instance, media space and time are discounted in terms of quantity, but these discounts are not necessarily equivalent. Similarly, the value a particular medium can deliver varies with the time and place. For example, the value of network television is much greater when programs are being shown for the first time (as compared to the rerun period or the summer, when television viewing goes way down). Finally, the value delivered by a particular medium also varies depending on the media objectives. A software manufacturer specializing in banking might have a high-reach objective and value a magazine such as *Bank Systems & Technology* over *Bankers Magazine*.

A third problem is that creating the best media schedule requires some idea about how to combine all the elements—including message form, placement in time, and media vehicles—to produce the greatest effect.

Because of these problems and others, advertising practitioners have not paid a great deal of attention to management scientists. Steve Farella, executive vice president and director of corporate media services at Wells Rich Greene advertising, explains: "There are some departments that see [the computer] as a very integral part of the media planning process. We don't do that. . . . We still think that media thinking can be done independent of the machine."[8] In fact, many practitioners have developed a good deal of specific knowledge about how media work for their products, services, or institutions on the basis of market testing. Other practitioners have reached conclusions about how best to use media based on their own extensive experience. Many practitioners readily accept the results of their own experience over the results produced by management scientists.

Figure 14.7 indicates the level of adoption of computer technology for some specific applications. There have been four main lines of development: retrieval and estimation models, optimization models, simulation models, and media buying models.

Retrieval and Estimation Models

The computer allows vast amounts of data to be stored and retrieved in a meaningful format. Companies collect a great deal of information about their customers. They can also purchase data about consumer characteristics, behaviors, and lifestyles. Some computer programs can combine this data, along with media usage data, to create alternative media schedules or campaigns and compute the relevant cost per thousands. These computer models can also estimate the potential reach for individual media as well as various media combinations.

Optimization Models

Optimization models attempt to modify data on audience characteristics, measures of reach and frequency (in order to eliminate problems on irrelevant relationships), and so forth. The modified data can then be com-

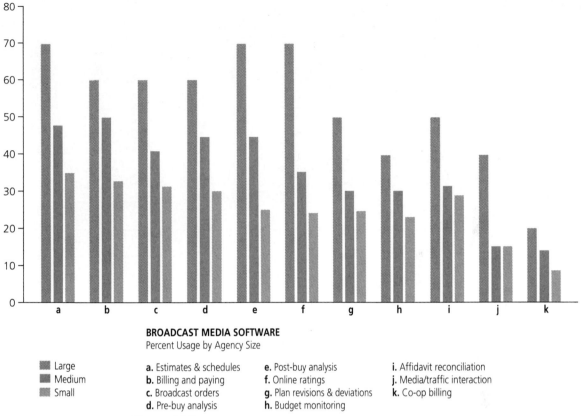

BROADCAST MEDIA SOFTWARE
Percent Usage by Agency Size

Large
Medium
Small

a. Estimates & schedules
b. Billing and paying
c. Broadcast orders
d. Pre-buy analysis

e. Post-buy analysis
f. Online ratings
g. Plan revisions & deviations
h. Budget monitoring

i. Affidavit reconciliation
j. Media/traffic interaction
k. Co-op billing

Figure 14.7

Agency use of media technology.
Marketing & Media Decisions *(October 1989): 54. Used with permission.*

pared and the optimal plan selected. One such model is shown in Figure 14.8. Note that it is impossible for research to produce "perfect" information; its purpose is to produce better information than was previously available.

Simulation Models

These models compare media plans by simulating their effects on typical consumer behavior such as purchase, store visits, coupon redemption, and information requests. The models allow media planners to compare many plans without committing to an actual plan. The models can even specify particular market segments and make comparisons for each.

Simulation models cannot eliminate the difficulty of comparing media. Selecting the appropriate consumer characteristics is not easy. Nor does

Figure 14.8

The process for selecting an optimum advertising research model.
Anthony F. McGann and J. Thomas Russell, Advertising Media, *2nd edition (Homewood, IL: Richard D. Irwin, 1988): 44. Used with permission.*

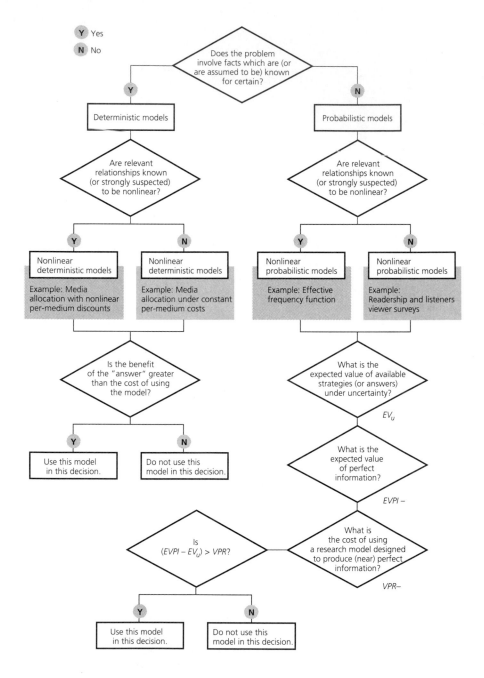

this technique account for the impact of multiple combinations of media or the deterioration of media effect.

Media Buying Models

The actual processing of media buys, along with invoicing, remains one of the most archaic dimensions of media planning. However, the barriers to efficient media buying are not technological; they are human. Media sales reps want to keep their jobs, users are reluctant to give up a paper trail of transactions, and companies do not want to foot the bill for developing the standards necessary for interchanging data electronically. There are a few breakthroughs, however.

With Media Management Plus, for example, agencies can explore what-if scenarios with narrow audience segments, giving them as much if not more information than their reps have. Agencies can also do postbuy analyses and line-by-line comparisons or orders and affidavits. With this system, Pizza Hut monitors its 26 regional agencies buying in 160 television markets.

Another product that links buyer and seller is Hot-Net, a system sold by Info-Edge. Hot-Net lists avails and last-minute inventory; it also makes electronic mail possible through CompuServe, a public bulletin board and data exchange service.[9]

Concept Review

With the advent of the computer, media planning has adopted several types of management science.
1. Retrieval and estimation models collect vast amounts of audience and media data, combine them into alternative media schedules, and estimate the effectiveness and cost of each.
2. Optimization models provide a systematic way of selecting and modifying media-related information.
3. Simulation models allow the testing of various media strategies without committing actual resources.
4. Media buying models actually make the specific media purchases, accounting for all the contingencies possible in this process.

Case 14 *Crayola on the Comeback Trail*

Background

What do you do when your chief product seems to be at the end of its product life cycle, when your customers have turned to newer, more modern substitutes, and when your brand name seems destined to evoke feelings of nostalgia rather than excitement? Some companies let the product die and try to succeed with new and different ones. Others rethink their approach and try to broaden their appeal.

That's what Binney & Smith, makers of Crayola crayons, decided to do in 1990. The company had done well for years by selling its products to parents. Parents bought crayons because they viewed them (and the company promoted them) as an educational tool and because the parents remembered what fun crayons were when they were kids. But our culture changes so fast that today's kids often have no use for toys that delighted their parents. And while parents still make most of the buying decisions for their kids' toys, children today have both more spending power and more influence over their parents' spending than did previous generations.

Targeting Different Markets

So now Crayola is marketing its product to both children and parents. Its first ad aimed directly at kids was called "Crayola Rock 'n' Rolls." Borrowing its approach from MTV, the commercial uses rock music, eye-catching colors, and hip kids, and airs at times when young kids are most likely to be watching TV.

At the same time, the company began a new campaign aimed at parents. The slogan emphasizes nostalgia, trying to elicit fond memories of the parents' own early years: "Crayola. Childhood isn't childhood without it." But the copy, running in parents' and women's magazines, focuses on the parents' role as *parents,* stressing how little effort crayons require from parents.

With the two ends of the age spectrum covered, Crayola is also reaching for the middle. It now makes ColorWorks, colored pens, pencils, and erasable crayon sticks, all aimed at a teenage audience. Traditionally, kids have given up crayons at about the age of 7, but Crayola is hoping that teens will decide that coloring can be cool and will make posters with their ColorWorks pens.

Color Change Controversy

The company's most controversial move was to change colors for the first time in 32 years. A survey showed that kids, no doubt influenced by the popularity of loud, artificial colors in the culture at large, wanted brighter colors. So Crayola replaced eight of the older, subtler colors with more brilliant, eye-opening shades. The response was similar to that which greeted the introduction of New Coke. Many parents were outraged at the loss of their favorite colors, even though their kids preferred the new ones.

So Crayola, taking its cue from Coca-Cola, reintroduced its classic colors, pleasing everyone and basking in the free publicity.

It's too soon to tell how well crayons can survive in a world of video games and Ninja Turtles. But by rethinking its product and audience and developing a varied media campaign, Binney & Smith has given its most important product a fighting chance.

Case Questions

1. Given the information provided in this case, outline the strategic and tactical considerations to evaluate in developing this media plan.

2. What other media alternatives might have worked for Crayola?

Case Source: Cara Appelbaum, "Bright Ideas for Crayola Ads," *Adweek* (September 10, 1990): 64.

Summary

The importance of a well-developed media plan cannot be underestimated. It begins with a situation analysis that assesses environmental factors that have an important bearing on media planning. Determining the media objectives comes next. Media objectives are usually stated in terms of reach, frequency, continuity, and costs. Media objectives lead to the media strategy, which in turn provides direction for media tactics. The media strategy encompasses several different activities, including describing the target audience, determining the message dispersion requirements, determining concentration requirements, identifying inherent qualities required of the media, and analyzing implications of message content. Media tactics deal with three decisions. First, evaluating media alternatives based on qualitative and quantitative factors. Second, selecting specific media. Third, determining the media budget.

The chapter concludes with a discussion of how the computer has become an integral part of media planning. Four computer-assisted media planning techniques were discussed: retrieval and estimation models, optimization models, simulation models, and media buying models.

Discussion Questions

1. Explain why so much importance is placed on developing an exceptional media plan. Describe the two stages in media planning.

2. Assume that you are on a committee to choose the best media plan from several alternatives. The other members favor Plan A because it reaches more people at least once at approximately the same cost as the other plans. What might you say to convince them that a judgment based on that criterion alone is erroneous?

3. How would you evaluate the distribution of exposure frequency that a given media plan delivers?

4. What is meant by the terms *reach, frequency,* and *continuity*? Why are these elements critically important to the media planner? Explain the concept of gross rating point and demonstrate how it is derived.

5. Define what is meant by *effective reach* and *effective frequency*. How do these terms differ from *reach* and *frequency*?

6. What are the problems encountered when executing the media strategy?

7. Explain the difference in determining the relative efficiency between media as opposed to within media.

8. Why is budget determination the last stage rather than the first stage in executing media strategy?

9. Many practitioners rely on media-supplied information, experience, and their own subjective appraisal to evaluate media. Can you explain why more objective considerations are not used?

10. How many repetitions are enough? Explain.

Suggested Projects

1. Contact a local business and devise a one-year media schedule for the business.

2. Survey the media department of five advertising agencies. Ask them about their use of computers in media planning. Write a report on your findings.

References

1. Bickley Townsend, "The Media Jungle," *American Demographics* (December 1988): 8.

2. Anthony F. McGann and J. Thomas Russell, *Advertising Media*, 2nd ed. (Homewood, IL: Irwin, 1988).

3. J. M. Agostine, "How to Estimate Unduplicated Audiences," *Journal of Advertising Research* (March 1961): 11–14.

4. David A. Aaker and John G. Myers, *Advertising Management,* 4th ed. (Englewood Cliffs, NJ: Prentice-Hall, Inc. 1990).

5. Michael J. Naples, *Effective Frequency: The Relationship Between Frequency and Advertising Effectiveness* (New York: Association of National Advertisers, 1979): 79.

6. Herbert E. Krugman, "What Makes Advertising Effective?" *Harvard Business Review* (March/April 1975): 96–103.

7. Dennis H. Gensch, "Computer Models in Advertising Media Selection," *Journal of Marketing Research,* 5 (November 1968): 423–4.

8. Joe Mandese, "The Merge/Purge Program," *Marketing and Media Decisions* (October 1989): 48–50.

9. Cathy Madison, "Media Buyers Plug into Electronic Deal-Making," *Adweek* (April 30, 1990): 27.

Additional Readings

1. Arnold Barban, Donald W. Jugenheimer, and Peter B. Turk, *Media Research Sourcebook and Workbook* (Lincolnwood, IL: NTC Business Books, 1989).

2. Robert W. Wall, *Media Math: Basic Techniques of Media Evaluation* (Lincolnwood, IL: NTC Business Books, 1987).

3. Rachel Kaplan, "What Can Media Planners Expect in the 1990s?" *Inside Print* (January 1989): 51.

4. Jack Sissors and Lincoln Bumba, *Advertising Media Planning* (Lincolnwood, IL: NTC Business Books, 1988).

5. Bradley Johnson, "Nestlé U.S. Units Join for Media Clout," *Advertising Age* (January 14, 1991): 3,46.

6. John Masterton, "The New Negotiators," *Media Week* (July 22, 1991): 16–19.

7. Greg Clarkin, "Buying by Bytes," *Marketing and Media Decisions* (May 1990): 44–45.

8. Joe Mandese, "The Biggest Game in Town," *Marketing and Media Decisions* (May 1990): 35–43.

9. Stanley E. Cohen, "The Dangers of Today's Media Revolution," *Advertising Age* (September 30, 1991): 18.

10. Gary Levin, "Meddling in Creative More Welcome," *Advertising Age* (April 9, 1990): S1.

15 *Personal Selling*

Understanding Personal Selling

Types of Selling
The Process of Personal Selling
Style of Communication in Personal Selling
A Model of Personal Selling

Managing a Sales Force

Setting Sales Objectives
Motivating the Sales Force

Personal Selling and the Promotional Mix

Pros and Cons of Personal Selling
Determining the Role of Personal Selling
Integrating Personal Selling

The Sales Force of the Future

Consider This:

Kimberly-Clark Counts on Its Sales Force

Kimberly-Clark, once a bulk-paper producer, has had uneven success breaking into the consumer products branch of the paper business. In the 1970s, it almost gave up on disposable diapers entirely because its Kimbies brand wasn't selling well, but then it came out with Huggies, now the market leader. It removed itself almost entirely from the bathroom tissue market in 1984 when it stopped making Kleenex Boutique bathroom tissue. At the time, the company said it wanted to devote its manufacturing capacity to making paper towels and facial tissues, dominated by its Kleenex brand.

So Kimberly-Clark's decision in 1990 to reenter the bathroom tissue market seemed both surprising and risky. The overall market is growing only as fast as the population, so sales for the new entry could grow only if it attracted buyers away from other premium brands or convinced economy-brand buyers to start paying more. The competition in the high-quality bathroom tissue market is fierce. Procter & Gamble commands 30 percent of the market with its White Cloud and Charmin brands, and industry giants Scott Paper and James River also offer strong products.

Kimberly-Clark made the move counting on two main strengths. One is its new manufacturing process. The company says it blow-dries the tissues, which it claims makes them softer than using industry-standard roll driers.

More importantly, the company is counting on its sales force, known for its excellent training, aggressiveness, and creativity. As a market analyst put it, "They'll get their product on the shelves."

Kimberly-Clark's use of its sales force is unusual. Unlike some of its competitors, Kimberly-Clark involves its salespeople in many facets of marketing, especially promotion. Its sales force was instrumental in choosing the name, shape, and filling for Huggies diapers. It influences the company's decisions about deals given to resellers, coupons, and the discounts offered with the new tissue. Sometimes salespeople even have some say about advertising copy.

So far, the company's confidence seems well-founded. In a difficult, competitive market, the new product gained a market share of nine percent in the first year.

Source: Marj Chaslier, "Kimberly-Clark Enlivens Market for Toilet Paper," *The Wall Street Journal* (July 23, 1990): B1.

K imberly-Clark's selling efforts illustrate a key point of this textbook: the promotional effort should be developed into a total strategy. If personal selling and other promotional activities are blended into an effective strategy, advertising and sales promotions make the job of the salespeople much easier, and communication between the salespeople and the rest of the promotional process ensures that promotional efforts complement each other.

Few companies achieve the coordination illustrated in our opening vignette. Individuals working in personal selling are separated from people in promotion not only by organizational charts but also by inherent differences. Most salespeople view other aspects of promotion as activities that may help presell a product or company but that accomplish little else. Advertising agencies rarely consider the needs and suggestions of salespeople, and salespeople rarely pay attention to information about an advertising campaign.

The only way that personal selling will be integrated with other aspects of promotion is through the concerted efforts of top management. Much of the integration problem may stem from a failure to understand what salespeople do. Before considering how selling efforts should be managed and combined with other promotional tools, we begin with a description of the job of personal selling.

Understanding Personal Selling

Personal selling is the primary promotional method used to increase sales. While the other promotional mix elements contribute to sales, their impact is often indirect. This is not the case with personal selling, where the individual's livelihood is contingent on closing sales. This fact is emphasized by the massive size of personal selling. The number of people employed in advertising is in the thousands. In personal selling, the number is in the millions.

There are many definitions of personal selling. A rather straightforward definition holds that **personal selling** is the face-to-face presentation of a product or an idea to a potential customer by a representative of the company or organization.

This definition highlights a key difference between personal selling and other promotional tools: personal selling involves a type of communication that is very different from the mass communication that characterizes advertising, sales promotion, and public relations. In personal selling, information is presented personally; there is immediate feedback; and adjustments can be immediate as well.

Personal selling differs from other elements of promotion in two other key ways. First, the task and the problems of selling primarily involve interpersonal relations. In advertising, for example, the creative output forms the heart of the task. In selling, this place is held by relations—between salespeople and their customers, between salespeople and their supervisors, and between salespeople and others in the organization. Second, historically, the selling function has been separated organizationally from the other areas of a business, including advertising.

Behind these generalizations about personal selling lie many variations in tasks, style, and measures of success. In the rest of this section, we examine the varied types of selling, the different tasks of salespeople, and the many factors that can influence their success.

Types of Selling

No two sales jobs are exactly alike. Even when two sales jobs have identical titles and job descriptions, the ways each job is performed may differ. Nevertheless, one can use a variety of bases to categorize types of sales jobs. The following typology offers some important differences:[1]

1. *Responsive selling.* The salesperson reacts to the buyer's demands. The two major types here are route driving and much of retailing. Drivers who deliver soft drinks or fuel oil and clerks in appliance or clothing stores are examples.

2. *Trade selling.* As in responsive selling, the salesperson is primarily an order taker, but there is more emphasis on service. Trade selling involves calling on dealers, taking orders, expediting deliveries, setting up displays, and rotating stock. This type of selling predominates in the food, textile, apparel, and household products industries. Recall from Chapter 11 that special tasks, such as the assembly of point-of-purchase displays, are performed by this type of salesperson. Often these salespeople are an integral part in supporting trade deals.

3. *Missionary selling.* Although missionary salespeople normally do not take orders, there are instances where they do. Their primary responsibility, however, is to explain a new product (religion) to the market before the total product is available (the institutional church). The classic example of a missionary salesperson who often takes the order in addition to explaining the product is the pharmaceutical detail person who calls on physicians in order to explain about new drugs offered

by the drug company. The missionary salesperson gives physicians free samples of the drug and encourages them to give the samples to patients and note the results. The salesperson hopes that physicians will specify that particular drug when prescribing to future patients.

4. *Technical selling.* The salesperson solves customers' problems through expertise and experience. Technical selling is common for industrial goods such as chemicals, machinery, and heavy equipment. The salesperson's ability to identify, analyze, and solve customers' problems is essential. Typically, technical salespeople call on prospects who have identified a problem and assume the salesperson's company offers possible solutions.

5. *Creative selling.* The salesperson "order getter" emphasizes and stimulates demand for products. This type of selling is usually related to new products or to an existing product that is being introduced into a new market. The salesperson must convince prospects that they have a problem, that the problem is serious, and that the salesperson's product or service is the best solution. Salespeople working for Procter & Gamble Co., Compaq Computers, and Arthur Anderson Consulting all engage in creative selling. For example, a sales rep working in the health and beauty aids division of P&G makes several sales presentations to supermarket purchasing managers in order to sell Head and Shoulders 2 in 1.

The Process of Personal Selling

The particular activities associated with personal selling vary somewhat from company to company, but in general selling involves the following steps:

1. Attaining knowledge,
2. Prospecting,
3. Preparing for the sale: the preapproach,
4. Approaching the sales presentation,
5. Giving the sales presentation, and
6. Follow-up with postsale activities.

Attaining Knowledge　Modern salespeople must be equipped with facts and figures. They need a thorough knowledge of the buyer's motives, characteristics, and behavior as well as factual information about their own company, its products, and the competition.[2] The amount and kind of information required depend on the type of product, product line, characteristics of the customer, organizational structure, and type of selling. If a company has a very simple product line and few competitors, the level of working knowledge might remain quite basic. In contrast, salespeople for companies like Dow Chemical, which has extensive product lines and many competitors, need extensive technical training in order to understand their products, how customers use their products, and the strengths and limitations of their competitors' products.

Prospecting   Locating new prospects and then obtaining permission to present a sales presentation are key activities for a salesperson. Prospecting is a continuous task because existing customers are always lost through transfers, retirement, and the aggressiveness of competitors; meanwhile, new buyers are constantly entering the marketplace. Surveys estimate that the typical salesperson spends at least thirty minutes each day prospecting, and that 20 percent to 25 percent of the calls made are on new customers.[3]

Prospecting methods and sources vary for different types of selling. However, the most common methods of prospecting are as follows:

1. Inquiries. Most companies receive a steady supply of sales leads from their advertising, telephone calls, and catalogs.

2. Endless-chain method. The salesperson obtains at least one prospect lead from each person interviewed.

3. Center-of-influence method. This is a modification of the endless-chain method in which the salesperson cultivates people in the territory who are willing to supply prospecting information.

4. Public exhibitions, demonstrations, and trade shows. People attending these events are often already interested in the product.

5. List. Individual sales representatives may develop prospect lists of their own by referring to such sources as public records, classified telephone directories, and club memberships.

6. Friends and acquaintances. These people are often a source of prospects for new sales representatives.

7. Cold-canvass method. The salesperson makes calls on every individual or company belonging to a particular group.

A key part of the prospecting task is qualifying the person in order to determine whether he or she is a prospect. Answers to the following five questions will help determine who the good prospects are:

1. Does the prospect have a want or need that can be satisfied by the purchase of my product or service?

2. Does he or she have the ability to pay?

3. Does he or she have the authority to buy?

4. Can the prospect be approached favorably?

5. Is the prospect eligible to buy?

Preparing for the Sale: The Preapproach   Following the prospecting stage, it is necessary to discover more about the prospect and to add flesh and bones to the bare skeleton of an idea. This task is known as the preapproach.

During this stage, salespeople gather additional personal and business information about prospects in order to qualify them further—that is, to determine whether a prospect has any unique conditions, personal information, history with the firm, and so forth. Some of this information can be gleaned from the prospect directly, the rest may require discussions with knowledgeable people in the industry. The information gathered during preapproach helps salespeople determine the best approach to prospects, identify problem areas, and avoid mistakes.

Approaching the Sales Presentation   Following the preapproach, the salesperson begins the approach, the lead-in to the sales presentation. An approach may have several objectives, but essentially it is the strategy employed to gain the attention of the prospect and make him or her receptive to the sales presentation. It should also provide the salesperson with an easy transition to the heart of the sales presentation. Some salespeople use phone calls or personal letters to approach prospects. Phone contacts save time for the salesperson because they reduce waiting time. Letters allow salespeople to include other information—drawings and product specifications, for instance—about the products that cannot be easily communicated by phone. Both of these methods of approaching prospects have the disadvantage that buyers find it fairly easy to say no over the phone or throw away letters as just more junk mail.

Regardless of the approach method used, the salesperson must immediately establish a rapport upon entering the buyer's office. Establishing a rapport can assume a number of directions. In some cases, comments about unfinished business from previous sales calls will get the buyer's interest. Another approach is for the salesperson to inform the buyer of the benefit that can be derived from the product being sold.

Giving the Sales Presentation   A successful sales approach is very important in making the transition to the **sales presentation,** the major part of the sales process. The purpose of the sales presentation is to explain in full detail how the product meets customer requirements. The salesperson must inform the prospect of the characteristics and benefits of the product as well as be persuasive that the product will satisfy the prospect's needs.

Talking about the weather, the Super Bowl, or business conditions are easy means of getting a sales call started. For some salespeople, a more effective opener and one that conveys understanding is to begin the conversation by talking about the organization or the person being called on.

Ultimately, every presentation gets to the reason for the salesperson's being there—the product. If the sales presentation is to be effective, it is extremely important that the sales representative's claims about the product are believable. The salesperson's background knowledge of the account should help establish the most effective presentation. If the call is on a new prospect, knowledge of similar organizations will provide clues about how to develop the benefit story that has the greatest chance of being effective.

Structure of Sales Presentations   Sales presentations may be grouped into five different categories.[4] The "fully automated" sales presentation is the most highly structured. Salespeople have very little to do when using this approach. Movies, slides, or filmstrips dominate the presentation. The salesperson's role is to set up the film, answer questions, and write up the order. Telemarketers also use this technique. Once a person is qualified, a prerecorded sales presentation is played. In the "semiautomated" approach, the salesperson reads from prepared aids such as flip charts or brochures. If necessary, the salesperson can also add comments. A third technique is the "memorized" or "canned" sales presentation. In this approach, the salesperson presents a standard company sales presentation and makes very few changes. "Organized" sales presentations are characterized by the complete flexibility the salesperson has regarding the wording of the sales presentation. A company-prepared outline is followed, but the salesperson can present the elements in that outline in any sequence. Organized sales presentations allow for more participation on the part of the customer, better enabling the salesperson to understand the buyer's needs and requirements. Finally, "unstructured" sales presentations are designed so that the salesperson and buyer together can more fully explore the product and how it fits the needs of the buying firm. This type of presentation is most effective when the salesperson and buyer stay on the problem of interest.

Handling Objections   An integral part of the sales presentation is meeting the objections brought up by the prospect. Some customers may raise only irrational or nebulous objections that have nothing to do with the product, the company, or the seller. There is also the unspoken objection, which is considered but not expressed. In handling objections, there are two basic questions to consider: Why do people object? What techniques are available to meet these objections? Table 15.1 depicts some of the more common objections and how they should be handled. Such techniques are not specific, and salespeople often learn how to handle objections through trial and error.

The Close   The good salesperson is always closing. Closing the sale refers to the salesperson asking the buyer for the order. The salesperson must

Table 15.1   **Methods of Handling Objections**

Techniques	Description	Example
Direct Denial	Defend your company against the criticism.	"Mr. Jones, you simply are wrong about that point."
Indirect Denial	Refer to a third party who had a similar objection and state how it was resolved.	"Mr. Smith expressed a similar concern. We called headquarters and had our answer in ten minutes."
Boomerang	The objection is turned back on the user.	"I'm glad you brought that up. That's exactly why I'm here."
Compensation	Admit the validity of the objection and offer a compensation.	"While it's true that we can't promise seventy-two-hour delivery, the quality of our product is twice as good as Brand X."
Pass Up	Ignore the objection as invalid.	"Let's go back and talk about some key features."
Question	Ask and listen.	"How much did you plan to spend?"

ask for the sale, otherwise the time has been wasted. The close is the ultimate test of sales ability, and a salesperson's income is highly correlated to a successful close.

There are several difficulties associated with closing a sale. Many potentially successful salespeople fail because they are afraid to close. If they never have to ask for the sale, they are never rejected. More often, the close is unsuccessful because the presentation is unsuccessful. Prospects cannot be expected to buy if they do not understand the presentation or if they cannot see the benefits that will accrue as a result of the purchase. Finally, a salesperson may not have good closing skills. Some salespeople become so fascinated by the sound of their own voices that they talk themselves out of sales that have already been made.

A nod of the head, a twinkle of the eye, and a smile all may be interpreted as signals of a buyer's readiness to buy. When one of these signals occurs, the salesperson should not hesitate to attempt to close the sale. The basic idea is to incorporate a few trial closes in the sales presentation. A *trial close* should be in the form of a question and should ask for an opinion on the part of the buyer: "Do you have any other questions?" or "Where should we go from here?"

Follow-up with Postsale Activities   An effective selling job does not end when the order is written up. Postsale services can build customer goodwill and lay the groundwork for many years of profitable business relations. These services can ensure repeat business and generate leads to other prospects. If mechanical installation of the product is necessary, the sales representatives should make certain the job is done properly. It is necessary to make sure that the buyer understands all points in the sales contract and the guarantee. In addition, salespeople should reassure customers that they have made the right decision by summarizing the product benefits, repeating why it is better than the discarded alternative choices, and pointing out how satisfied they will be with the product's performance. In general, all these activities by salespeople serve to reduce customers' postdecision anxiety.

Style of Communication in Personal Selling

It is not sufficient for the salesperson to simply present the right information to buyers. There is a right and a wrong way to sell in person. We refer to this set of principles as a style of personal selling. It incorporates five considerations:[5]

1. **Pace** is the speed at which the salesperson moves to close a sale. It is important for the salesperson to understand the customers so that the pace does not lose or alienate them.

2. **Scope** refers to the variety of benefits, features, and sales terms discussed. Some sales presentations are designed to appeal to all customers and employ a broad scope. For high-priced, customized products, the presentation tends to have a narrower scope, focusing on the most important benefit to the buyer.

3. **Depth of inquiry** is the extent of the salesperson's effort to learn the details of the buyer's decision process. The appropriate depth is affected by (1) the salesperson's previous experience with the prospect, (2) the extent to which several people are involved in the purchase decision, and (3) the prospect's disposition toward the product before the presentation.[6]

4. The opportunity for two-way communication between the buyer and the salesperson reflects a simple rule of thumb in personal selling: two-way communication must be initiated and maintained. Salespeople must really listen in order to match the product with customer needs.

5. The variety of sensory appeals. Because it is very difficult for buyers to visualize intangibles or complex products, flip charts, slides, product demonstrations, written proposals, and the like all help customers visualize product benefits.

    The Promotion in Focus section describes a very elaborate type of sensory appeal—scale models. These models are effective both in demonstrating the product and in offering the product as a premium to reward the prospect for listening to the presentation.

A Model of Personal Selling

Understanding how the salesperson does his or her job helps the marketing manager to employ personal selling as part of the marketing strategy. However, the relationship between the buyer and seller is just a part of the environment that shapes the effectiveness of personal selling. Coupling their marketing knowledge with research findings, Enis and Chonko developed a model of personal selling that attempts to identify the factors that influence the process.[7]

Figure 15.1 outlines the Enis-Chonko model. It involves five elements, three types of personal relationships, and four types of process relationships.

The *elements* in personal selling, according to this model, are the following:

- The *salesperson*, the most important element,
- The *market*, which consists of the buyers whom the salesperson aims to please,
- The *organization* that supplies the product that is being sold,

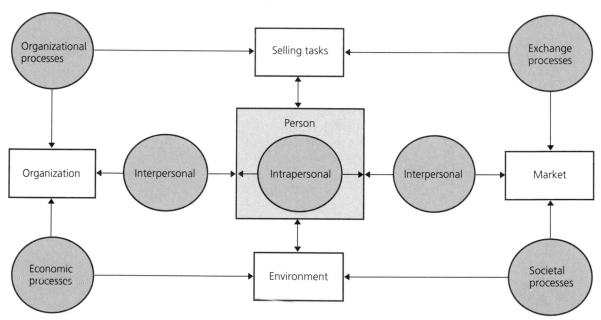

Figure 15.1

A model of personal selling.
Ben M. Enis and Lawrence B. Chonko, "A Review of Personal Selling: Implications for Managers and Researchers," from G. Zaltman, ed., Annual Review of Marketing *(Chicago: American Marketing Association, 1978), p. 277. Reproduced by permission of the American Marketing Association.*

- The *selling environment*, which includes physical features (such as buildings, streets, and climate) and institutional features (businesses, schools, and hospitals, for example), and
- The *selling task*—in other words, the responsibilities of the salesperson.

Three types of *personal relationships* occur among these elements, as Figure 15.1 illustrates:

- *Intrapersonal relationships* are the individual characteristics of salespeople (such as their traits, attitudes, and capabilities) that influence their success or failure. Research suggests that empathy, ego drive, and efficiency are significant traits among successful salespeople. The more similar the characteristics of customer and salesperson, the more likely a sale will result.[8]
- *Interpersonal relationships* occur between the salesperson and the buyers in the market and between the salesperson and other members of the organization. Research suggests two characteristics of a relationship established by successful salespeople: (1) the salespeople see buyers as active participants, not passive targets to be acted upon, and (2) the salespeople make prospective buyers view themselves favorably and view the salesperson as believable and trustworthy.[9]
- *Extrapersonal relationships* are the relationships between the salesperson and the groups (church, clubs, teams) of which he or she is a part. Every salesperson has certain roles within the organization and within the larger social environment.

In addition, four types of *process relationships* occur among the elements in the selling process:

- *Organizational processes* include the production process, the financial process, and the marketing process.
- *Exchange processes* include the exchange of the product and legal title for payment and the exchange of information about product operation, warranty provisions, and suggestions for product improvements. In most transactions, the salesperson acts as the catalyst for exchange processes.
- *Economic processes* refer to competition and regulation. Because customers can satisfy their desires in ways other than consuming the products of the salesperson's organization, it is important for the salesperson to view competition from the customer's perspective.
- *Societal processes*. Three basic processes operate in any society: (1) demographic processes, by which a society's population grows and changes, (2) structural processes, by which societies organize for growth and change, and (3) normative processes, which include the formation and change of values.

The importance of the Enis-Chonko model is not only that it attempts to categorize all the factors involved in the personal selling process but also that it provides a yardstick against which all types of personal selling can be measured.[10]

Concept Review

1. Personal selling is the face-to-face presentation of a product or an idea to a potential customer by a representative of the company.
2. There are five types of selling: responsive, trade, missionary, technical, and creative.
3. The most common tasks in the personal selling process are the following:
    a. Attaining knowledge,
    b. Prospecting,
    c. Preapproach,
    d. Approach,
    e. Sales presentation, and
    f. Follow-up.
4. According to the Enis-Chonko model, the personal selling process includes the following:
    a. Five primary elements: the salesperson, market, organization, selling environment, and selling task
    b. Three types of personal relationships: intrapersonal, interpersonal, and extrapersonal
    c. Four types of process relationships: organizational, exchange, economic, and societal

Managing a Sales Force

Most sales executives agree that strong sales supervision is a key ingredient in building an excellent sales force. A typical sales force is composed of men and women with diverse backgrounds and experience levels, often separated from headquarters by thousands of miles. By necessity, many salespeople become the primary connection between the customer and the company. Consequently, there is a strong tendency for salespeople to be independent and hold the attitude that they are running their own business. In the recent past, sales managers made overt attempts to decrease this independence by requiring salespeople to report for weekly meetings. Because of the high cost of travel combined with the communication capabilities of laptop computers, this pattern has changed. Today, salespeople find themselves walking a thin line, splitting loyalties between customers whom they see on a regular basis and the company, which they see infrequently but which pays their salary. The sales manager may be the

Promotion in Focus

Miniature Mammoths

If you're a salesperson for Caterpillar, how do you visit a potential customer and show off your product, when that product is as big as a house and weighs 40 tons? Pictures and blueprints just aren't very convincing; people want to know how the machine moves. And when you make your exit, what do you leave behind for the customer that's more memorable and appropriate than a pen or a baseball cap?

Sales Guides of Mequon, Wisconsin, has the answers. The company does make standard promotional items like pens and hats, but its specialty is articulated (meaning that the parts move) die-cast scale models of heavy equipment—backhoes, bulldozers, trucks, forklifts. The company's founder, Norm Stern, and his son Scott are quick to point out that they do not sell toys. They make the models from actual blueprints, on a 1:25 to 1:50 scale, and the blades, booms, and bodies tilt, extend, and dump exactly as they do on the real machines.

The models are not cheap. Making the die for a model can cost $15,000 to $40,000, and individual miniatures sell for up to $40. But if a model can help secure a sale of a big piece of equipment, it is easily worth the price.

Some sales reps use the models to demonstrate the abilities of a new machine. Caterpillar's manager of conventions and exhibits says, "They are more than just giveaways. They are quality products with significant points on each of them so that certain sales features can be demonstrated." Others use them as a free sample, a handout not unlike the freebies offered in supermarkets. Hyster, a forklift manufacturer, finds that its direct-mail campaigns that offer models turn up many more qualified potential buyers than do campaigns without the models.

Sales reps say they could live without the models, and few sales actually depend on them. But the Sterns' creativity in finding a new approach to promotion means they sell 75,000 to 100,000 models a year. Definitely not kids' stuff.

Source: Bill Kelly, "Toys Aren't Us," *Sales and Marketing Management Magazine* (August 1986): 56.

only contact the salesperson has with the organization. In turn, the sales manager becomes the boundary spanner between the company and the sales force. The sales manager defines and interprets policy, directs the daily efforts of the sales force, coaches the sales force, and helps salespeople resolve problems.

The sales manager's task is far more complex than it was twenty years ago. Products and services are more diverse and sophisticated. Buyers are more knowledgeable. Consequently, sales managers have had to become proficient at four sets of business activities:

1. Planning. Planning involves the formulation of objectives and strategies for personal selling. Taking into account both internal and external factors, sales managers should organize and plan a firm's personal selling effort so that it is consistent with other aspects of a firm's marketing program.

2. Staffing. The staffing function is concerned with the activities sales managers undertake to build a quality sales force. These activities include recruiting, selection, and training.

3. Implementing. This set of activities involves carrying out the firm's sales plans. Implementing includes the design of programs to direct the efforts of the sales force toward the achievement of the firm's sales objectives.

4. Controlling. This set of activities is concerned with the performance of salespeople. Performance must be monitored and evaluated so that any necessary adjustments in the sales program can be made.

Although all these tasks are important to the success of the sales management effort, a few are more important to the overall promotion effort. These will be discussed next.

Setting Sales Objectives

Company and marketing objectives for sales growth, profits, market share, and cash flow must be translated into more specific objectives for the sales department and the sales force (see Figure 15.2). Targets and quotas provide concrete statements of these objectives. A **sales target** is simply the desired level of sales for a given product or product line in a specified period of time. A **sales quota** is a fair share of the overall sales target allocated to a salesperson, territory, or some other segment of the operation.

Targets and quotas differ depending on the circumstances and the purposes considered. Variations between companies are considerable, but most targets and quotas are based on the following:

- Sales volume. A desired level of sales is established as a basic objective.

- Activities. A target or quota is attached to activities considered benefi-

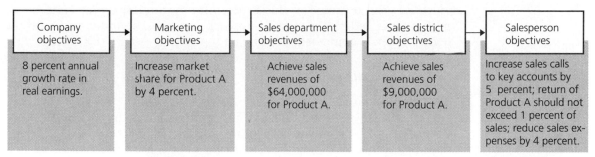

Figure 15.2

Company objectives for sales growth translated into specific objectives for the sales force.

cial in reaching desired performance; for example, the number of calls made, new accounts, and displays secured.

- Budgets. A target or quota is based on cost savings or profit margins.
- Combinations. Targets or quotas are based on two or more of the preceding.

Developing targets and quotas can be viewed as a three-step decision: (1) select the types of targets or quotas to be used, (2) determine the relative importance of each type, and (3) set the level of each type. Table 15.2

Table 15.2 Operation of a Sales Quota Plan

Salesperson	Types	Quota Level	Actual	Percentage Attained	Weight	Weighted Attainment Percentage
Jim Wills	Sales volume	$300,000	$270,000	90	2	180
	New accounts	10	11	110	1	110
	Calls	80	60	75	1	75
					Total: 4	365

Performance index = 365/4 = 91.25

Salesperson	Types	Quota Level	Actual	Percentage Attained	Weight	Weighted Attainment Percentage
Jill Howell	Sales volume	$250,000	$250,000	100	2	200
	New accounts	8	6	75	1	75
	Calls	75	75	100	1	100
					Total: 4	375

Performance index = 375/4 = 93.75

illustrates the outcome of this process for two salespeople. Note that a performance index is calculated for each person. The individual with the higher index is doing better on the job.

Motivating the Sales Force

One might assume that because a salesperson is an adult who is experiencing some level of personal and monetary success that providing motivation and discipline would be unnecessary. In fact, these two tasks are the most time-consuming aspects of the sales manager's job. Motivation provides positive incentives; discipline involves the use of negative incentives.

Sales managers use several types of motivators. Among the most common are financial and extra incentives, security, opportunity for advancement, a meaningful job, status, personal power, self-determination, and pleasant working conditions.[11]

Financial and Extra Incentives   There is sufficient evidence that monetary rewards are still the primary motivator of the average worker. There is little reason to believe that this conclusion is not true for salespeople as well. Financial incentives can be divided into two categories: *base compensation* and *extra compensation,* which includes incentives such as bonuses, optional programs (for example, stock purchase and profit sharing), prizes, and awards. During economic downtimes, cash appears to be the most effective financial incentive.

To attract and hold good salespeople, a compensation plan must meet the employees' requirements. And to make sure the salespeople's efforts are profitable and consistent with the company's overall marketing program, the compensation plan must also meet the requirements of the company. Balancing these two sets of requirements is not always easy.

There are three basic types of compensation for salespeople. An old, familiar form of compensation involves paying a fixed amount each pay period. *Straight salary* compensates people for time spent on the job. This approach appeals to a salesperson who is concerned about security and the ability to plan personal finances. It is not effective in motivating exceptional performance since no reward is made available. From the company's point of view, straight salary represents a fixed sales cost. Such a cost is controlled, and as long as sales are satisfactory, the burden is not serious. If sales slip, however, a fixed sales cost can become a problem. An additional advantage of the straight salary approach is that it permits the sales manager to require salespeople to perform nonselling activities, such as paperwork or inventory audits, which they tend to avoid when paid on a commission basis. Salary programs are most appropriate when it is difficult to relate the efforts of individual salespeople to the size or timing of a sale.

Thus salary programs are more common in industrial than in consumer product selling, as is the case when several specialists on a team sell complex aerospace products to airlines and the government. Salary is also appropriate in situations where products are presold through advertising or sales promotion and the salesperson primarily takes orders.

The second compensation approach is *straight commission.* Under a commission plan, salespeople are paid a fixed or sliding rate of earnings based on their sales volume or profit contribution. The commission rewards people for getting orders. It also motivates them to exceed established standards of productivity. Since salary is tied directly to sales productivity, this compensation plan virtually pays for itself. On the other hand, it is difficult for salespeople to make a living on a straight commission program if they hit a slow period or take a little longer to get started. However, for experienced, successful salespeople who wish to have no ceiling on their income, the straight commission is a powerful incentive.

Straight commission works best when maximum incentive is needed and when a minimum of aftersales service and missionary work is required. This situation exists for most organizations that sell housewares and cosmetics door-to-door. Mary Kay Cosmetics, Tupperware, Avon, and Amway all use straight commission programs. Commissions are also popular in the retail sale of automobiles and trucks. Other types of businesses that use straight commission plans include life insurance, real estate, stock brokerage, wholesale clothing, and printing.

The *combination plan* attempts to eliminate the limitations of the straight salary and straight commission programs and assume their advantages. The salesperson's base salary is usually high enough to provide the financial security that the employee desires; it is also low enough so that its fixed-cost character does not seriously affect the firm in periods of declining sales. In addition to the base salary, an incentive is paid in the form of a commission—usually on sales greater than a set quota.

The primary benefit of combination plans is that they allow the compensation program to be tailored to the needs of a particular firm. For example, if a firm wanted a modest amount of incentive, 80 percent of the compensation could be in the form of salary and 20 percent in commissions. Firms that needed more push to move their products could raise the commission portion of the package to 30 percent or 40 percent of the total wages. Combination plans are widely used in industrial firms that sell building materials, machinery, electrical supplies, and paper products. This plan is less popular in consumer product companies.

Virtually all organizations also offer extra incentives to their salespeople. Discussed earlier in Chapter 11, *extra incentives* (sales promotions) include a variety of awards given to salespeople for achieving specific goals. The awards fall under three categories: cash, merchandise, and travel. A recent survey by *Incentive* magazine reports that travel remains the award of choice (36 percent); merchandise was second (33 percent), and cash was preferred by 31 percent. Companies spent $5.7 billion on extra incentives in 1990.[12]

Other Motivators   Security is important to many people. To provide a more secure environment, companies may offer better salaries, better fringe benefits, and an atmosphere that assures salespeople that the company respects them and considers them to be valuable.

Opportunity for advancement is another motivator. In most companies, salespeople tend to follow one of two career paths. Either they are not interested in being promoted to management, or they are using their current job as a steppingstone toward a sales management job. For both career paths, the sales manager must develop a clear and fair set of criteria that a person must meet in order to be promoted.

Managers also motivate salespeople by making them feel that their job is important. Sales managers must learn to raise the status of selling within the firm on the basis of its absolute contribution to the firm and to the economy. In companies where this has been done, morale in the sales department is seldom a problem. Sometimes, as discussed in the Promotion in Focus section on Chuch Piola, the individual raises the image of the sales profession.

Closely related to the status of the sales job is status for the individual. In many companies, status may mean little more than conferring titles and labels that generate personal prestige. Being called a sales representative or a client representative, for example, may seem more impressive than being called a salesperson. Receiving the label *CLU* (Chartered Life Underwriter) or "member of the million-dollar round table" means a great deal to a life insurance salesperson. Status can also be conveyed through the quality of the company car provided, a handsome company-provided briefcase, or the size of an expense account.

Opportunities to increase their authority may also motivate salespeople, even if the authority is somewhat contrived and superficial. In other instances, the power can be very real and might involve giving salespeople the right to make decisions that they were not allowed to make before.

Similarly, sales managers can motivate salespeople by giving them authority over their own actions. Individuals tend to enter the sales field because of the independence it provides. They resent being told what they should do and how they should do it. Although total autonomy is impossible, considerable self-determination can be established by delegating as much authority and responsibility as possible to lower levels in the organization.

Finally, good working conditions also tend to improve productivity. Many aspects of the sales job (for example, long hours and extensive travel) are unattractive. Intelligent sales managers try to allow their salespeople to live well by providing a nice car and allowing them to eat at good restaurants and stay at pleasant hotels. It is better to economize in other areas than to limit the work environment of the salesperson.

Concept Review

1. Sales managers must become proficient at four sets of business activities:
   a. Planning,
   b. Staffing,
   c. Implementing, and
   d. Controlling.
2. The sales manager must also be responsible for setting sales targets and sales quotas.
   a. Targets are the desired level of sales for a given product in a specified period of time.
   b. Quotas are a fair share of the overall sales target allocated to a salesperson, territory, or some other segment of the operation.
3. Sales managers motivate salespeople through the following:
   a. Financial and extra incentives,
   b. Security,
   c. Opportunity for advancement,
   d. A meaningful job,
   e. Status,
   f. Personal power,
   g. Self-determination, and
   h. Pleasant working conditions.

Personal Selling and the Promotional Mix

So far, we have described what salespeople do and how sales managers can ensure that they do their job effectively. Also noted were the many difficulties associated with the task of integrating personal selling with the other three elements of the promotion mix. With this information as background, we return to the more complicated task described at the outset of the chapter: how to create a strategy for personal selling that will complement the other three promotional elements and produce a synergy that will help achieve promotional objectives.

Pros and Cons of Personal Selling

Personal selling has several important advantages over other elements of the marketing mix. Most notably, it is more flexible than other promotional tools. Salespeople can tailor their presentations to fit the needs, motives,

Promotion in Focus

Don't Give Up on Cold Calls

Most companies trying to scare up new business these days don't use much shoe leather. Machines do the work. Computers churn out thousands of letters a day, while automatic-dialing machines reach hundreds of households with minimal attention from the person who tends them. Calling on someone face-to-face, especially without a prior introduction or a good reason to think that the person is a prospective customer, seems like a foolish waste of resources.

But is it? Think of how you respond to people who want your money. Most of the direct mail you get probably goes directly to the trash. As phone solicitations become ever more common, many people have even more negative responses to them, hanging up as soon as they realize what the caller's mission is. But for most people, sending the salesperson at the door on his or her way is a different matter. If the salesperson has a relaxed attitude, a winning smile, and perhaps a bit of humor about the sales pitch, you might not slam the door.

That's the difference between face-to-face cold calls and other approaches to drumming up new business—the human element. So says Chuck Piola, who has made some 15,000 cold calls in his sales career. His most recent, and most successful, enterprise is NCO Financial Systems, a collection agency that had 64 clients in 1986, when Piola started working for it, and now has 1,700.

Piola tries to make sure that he's a "breath of fresh air" for anyone he talks to. He treats everyone in a company as though he or she has something to offer, usually approaching them with the line, "I wonder if you can help me out?" His friendly but assertive manner helps him get past secretaries to make an initial contact, and then he uses that person's name to work through a company's bureaucracy until he has found the right person, the one who could actually offer him some work. Piola has to deal with rejection and be just as friendly at the end of a bad week as he is at the beginning. But his success indicates that in an era when impersonal machines handle so many things in the business world, a human face can provide the edge a company needs.

Source: Jay Ginegan, "King of the Cold Calls," *Inc.* (June 1991): 101–107.

and behavior of individual customers. As salespeople see the customer's reaction to an approach, they can also make the necessary adjustments immediately.

Personal selling also minimizes wasted effort. In advertising, much of the cost is devoted to sending the message to people who are not real prospects. In personal selling, a company can pinpoint its target market far more effectively than can be done with any other promotional device.

An important managerial advantage of personal selling is that the result is usually an actual sale. Consequently, measuring effectiveness and determining the return on investment are far more straightforward for personal selling than for other promotional tools, where recall or attitude change is often the only measurable effect. Of course, this situation is changing and direct action is now an expected result from advertising, sales promotion, and public relations.

Another advantage of personal selling is that a salesperson is in an excellent position to encourage the customer to take action. The one-on-one interaction of personal selling means that the salesperson can effectively respond to objections and ask for the sale as many times as necessary. Being able to attempt a close repeatedly is a unique element of personal selling. An ad may tell a viewer to take action immediately, but it cannot offer the varied reasons to buy that a salesperson can.

A final advantage of personal selling is the performance of managerial and communication tasks by the field sales force. A salesperson can collect payment, make financial adjustments, service or repair products, return products, and collect information that might prove useful to engineering, production, or marketing departments.

High cost is the primary disadvantage of personal selling. With increased competition, higher travel and lodging costs, and higher salaries, the cost per contact will continue to increase. Many companies have attempted to control costs by shifting to commission compensation, thereby guaranteeing that the salespeople pay their own way. This shift has created another problem: commission-only salespeople may become risk aversive and only go after clients who have the highest potential return. This problem is partially reduced through the use of techniques such as telemarketing and toll-free numbers to qualify prospects. Telemarketing can further reduce costs by serving as an actual selling vehicle. Hard-to-reach prospects and prospects with a low likelihood of success can be pitched at a fraction of the cost of sending out a salesperson.

Another disadvantage associated with personal selling is the problem of finding and retaining high-quality people. Experienced salespeople sometimes realize that the only way they can keep their income ahead of the cost of living is to change jobs. Conversely, because of the push for profitability, businesses try to hire experienced salespeople away from competitors rather than hiring college graduates, who take three to five years to reach the level of productivity of more experienced salespeople. This difficulty in attracting college students has thrown the personal selling vocation into an unbalanced situation.

Determining the Role of Personal Selling

In view of the strengths and limitations of personal selling, how should the promotion manager use this promotional tool? Each promotional tool has a unique responsibility, and each has a part to play in reaching promotional objectives. Essentially, advertising builds awareness of the product, informs the customer about product features, and persuades the customer that the advertised brand is the best choice. Sales promotion prompts more immediate action by adding value to the product. Finally, personal selling helps answer customer questions and provides an opportunity to persuade buyers to sign purchase orders—to close the sale.

For many companies, personal selling is the most important element in the promotional mix. However, as we discussed in Chapter 3, the appropriate combination of promotional tools depends on several factors, including the market. In general, personal selling is emphasized in industrial markets or in selling to resellers but plays a small role in promoting in consumer markets.

As an example, consider the effect of the product on the appropriate mix. The whole notion of self-service is based on the assumption that products such as cereals and canned vegetables require little personal selling. Mass advertising provides brand awareness, basic product information, and retail-related information. Sales promotion provides an extra incentive to buy. Personal selling is not really necessary if the product is in the store. In contrast, a technical product such as an automobile or an appliance that requires explanation or demonstration or both usually requires a salesperson to sell it.

The distribution channel also has an important influence on the role of personal selling. Although K Mart does not need a salesperson to stand at its candy counter, personal selling is important when Hershey Foods Corp. is trying to compete against Nestlé Enterprises, Inc. for the K Mart business. Personal selling may be important at one level of the channel of distribution and not at another. To the purchasing agent at K Mart, the Hershey salesperson *is* Hershey. The relationship is between the two people, not the two companies. Promises are made between the two and a bond of trust is established. Companies often lose customers after the transfer or promotion of the sales representative. In fact, the success of a business may depend on how well salespeople are recruited, trained, compensated, and cared for.

Are there instances when personal selling should be the dominant or only promotional element? Yes. Chuck Piola's company, NCO Financial Systems, is an example of a company using personal selling only. Can personal selling be severely reduced or even eliminated? Again, the answer is yes. Catalog companies such as L. L. Bean and Land's End have virtually no sales force. These extremes are rare, however, and a promotional mix that includes both mass selling and personal selling is typical.

We have already alluded to the advantages of personal selling and the conditions that prompt its use. In general, when a personal confrontation between buyer and seller is important, personal selling dominates. It is unlikely, for instance, that we would buy a big ticket item such as a luxury automobile without a salesperson. Personal selling includes the need to share information, the adjustments to various types of relationships, and the motivation to cause the customer to decide. Likewise, personal selling is necessary when the nature of the product necessitates personal involvement, when the company is following a push strategy, or when the product is in the maturity stage of its life cycle.

Ultimately, the vice president of marketing or the promotion manager employs four criteria in determining the role to be played by personal selling in the promotional strategy:

1. The nature of the information that would have to be exchanged in order to promote the product or service.

2. The promotional objectives.

3. The promotional mix alternatives available to the organization, with special concern for the firm's capabilities to implement each one.

4. The relative cost of personal selling compared to the other promotional mix elements.

An example of a company that clearly emphasizes personal selling over the other three mix elements is Artesia Waters, bottler of Artesia water. The company was started in 1979 by Rick Scoville, who was selling glue to bottling accounts for H. B. Fuller. Artesia bottled water is drilled from the huge Edwards Aquifer, 520 feet below the municipality of San Antonio, Texas. It differs from competitors such as Perrier in that it does not come up to the surface like spring water, nor does it touch any contaminants in the ground. Initially, Scoville was president, director of manufacturing, and sales force. Today, one-on-one is still the way Artesia is promoted. Heavy competition from companies such as Perrier, the need to convince store managers that Artesia is a superior product, and a limited budget have all pushed personal selling to the forefront in Scoville's promotional plan.[13]

Integrating Personal Selling

Bringing personal selling and three mass selling components together remains a major frustration in most businesses. Because of the organizational, cultural, and logistical factors already discussed, it is very difficult to integrate and coordinate personal selling with the other three components. Nevertheless, there is value in pointing out those occasions when personal selling (and the promotional mix elements) would benefit by being combined directly.

Personal Selling and Advertising   Under what conditions is the personal selling–advertising combination optimal? Advertising can reach large audiences simultaneously with a vivid message. The message must be quite general and the copy relatively short; opportunity for feedback and adjustment is virtually nil. Because personal selling offers the exact opposite set of strengths and weaknesses, advertising and personal selling tend to be complements of one another. When audience coverage, vivid presentation, explanation, feedback, and adjustment are all important to the success of the marketing program, combining advertising and personal selling is appropriate. This tends to be the case with the introduction of new products, especially when the cooperation of resellers is critical. When Pillsbury introduced its new low-fat cake mixes, the company ran a great deal of consumer advertising in order to make the consumer aware of this new product. However, it was just as important for the sales force to call on every supermarket manager and explain the product's benefits, show market research results, and offer trade incentives. As noted earlier, advertising can also provide sales leads when introducing a new product or promoting an existing one. Including a toll-free number or a mail-in coupon in an ad can provide a salesperson with a list of hundreds of prospective customers. Marketers of business-to-business products are particularly effective at this tactic.

In summary, when advertising is needed to create awareness and provide basic information, but personal selling is necessary to complete the exchange process, the advertising–personal selling tandem makes the most sense.

Personal Selling and Sales Promotion   Whereas personal selling and advertising are viewed as equivalent complementary techniques, sales promotion is both an important tool used by sales reps and a complement. As you might recall, a great deal of trade sales promotion is delivered by the sales rep as part of the sales presentation. Price deals, premiums, contests, and other incentives represent part of the repertoire that can make the sales process much more successful. These sales promotions are often coordinated with an equivalent consumer sales promotion to give both more impact. For example, Dole pineapple might run a "Trip to Polynesia" sweepstakes with consumers and with resellers.

Sales promotion can also complement personal selling. An IBM salesperson knows that the customer has already been presold because of the direct mail discount coupon that the buyer received and the opportunity to sample the product. Conversely, salespeople can explain sales promotions more fully or even deliver premiums or prizes to lucky customers. Sales promotions add to the value of the product or service. In turn, that extra value makes the product or service easier to sell. Therefore the personal selling–sales promotion combination is particularly effective in very competitive situations where products are similar and the salesperson needs something extra to create a competitive advantage.

Personal Selling and Public Relations   Some people would argue that the salesperson is the most important public relations strategy in many organizations. If we look at public relations as the shaping and maintenance of goodwill, this is clearly the case. In some instances, the use of the salesperson as a public relations provider is informal and revolves around the salesperson's day-to-day activities. The salesperson would probably view activities such as taking a customer out to lunch, remembering the names of his children, responding to questions or complaints promptly, and treating people with empathy as part of getting the sale rather than as public relations. However, the salesperson can also be involved in more formal public relations activities that help both the salesperson and the public relations manager. For example, salespeople are encouraged to get involved in community activities, head the United Way campaign, join the Lions, or coach Little League. Salespeople are also excellent at explaining the company's products to people or organizations that request such information. Leading plant tours or hosting open houses are two other PR activities that salespeople do well. Finally, salespeople are usually an integral part of trade shows, meetings with customers, and any other event where customers and the company are together in an informal setting. Top salespeople often man the booths at trade shows, for example.

Concept Review

1. Compared with other promotional techniques, personal selling has the advantage of being more flexible, involving less wasted effort, producing sales, prompting customers to take action, and leading the salesperson to perform managerial tasks.
2. Personal selling also has several disadvantages: it is very costly, and it is difficult to find and retain high-quality people.
3. Personal selling complements and supplements the other promotional techniques.

The Sales Force of the Future

What will the salespeople of the year 2000 look like? Will they be replaced by computers and electric-order entry? Will they still operate as independent operators who are assigned a territory and a quota? Will the high costs of trade deals and competing in a global marketplace change the traditional salesperson? Although we can speculate about dramatic changes in the nature of personal selling, the traditional salesperson will likely remain intact for several decades. Why? Simply because many products will still need to be sold personally by a knowledgeable, trustworthy person who is willing to resolve problems twenty-four hours each day.

Still, there will be major changes in personal selling. Computer technology will play a role. Increasing efficiency in selling has become a critical concern for many U.S. companies. The cost of a sales call has increased dramatically, the growing complexity of business has resulted in more sales calls required per order, and the decentralization of business has resulted in more small or mid-sized accounts to service. Currently, companies such as Hewlett-Packard and Fina Oil and Chemical provide laptop computers to all salespeople. Computer-based sales tracking and follow-up systems allow salespeople to track customers.[14] This means that salespeople can assess customers in respect to their buying patterns, profitability, and changing needs. Pulling this information up on the computer screen saves the salesperson time and allows customization of the sales presentation.

Sales teams began in the 1980s and will continue to gain in popularity because customers are looking to buy more than a product. A sales team includes several individuals who possess a unique expertise and coordinate their efforts relative to a particular prospect. They are looking for sophisticated design, sales, education, and service support. The salesperson must act as the quarterback, ensuring that the account relationship is managed properly and that the proper support personnel is available to the customer. Procter & Gamble is one company that has adopted the team approach. P&G has twenty-two sales executives who coordinate the sales efforts of various P&G divisions in their assigned market areas. Each manager coordinates key account teams composed of sales executives from P&G's grocery division. As many as three key account teams may be in each market. The market manager supervises a logistics team composed primarily of computer systems and distribution executives. The team works closely with retailers to develop mutually compatible electronic data and distribution systems. P&G hopes the team approach will reduce the pressure for trade promotions by providing greater service.[15]

The salesperson of the future will have to adjust to new forms and new sources of competition. With the increased capabilities and acceptance of direct marketing, for example, salespeople will have to realize that some customers will purchase a product without contact with a salesperson. Complete product catalogs, featuring computers, electronics, and classic automobiles, are mailed directly to customers, providing all the information about the product the customer needs to know. Questions can be answered through a toll-free number. Salespeople of the twenty-first century will either have to integrate direct marketing as part of their own presentation or they will have to offer the customer benefits not available through direct marketing. More will be said about direct marketing in Chapter 18.

This has become a very small planet. Salespeople today are already facing foreign competition. Companies in Japan, Taiwan, and South Korea are introducing the United States to thousands of new products every year. The salesperson of the future must know how to respond to foreign competitors and enter their markets as well. Chapter 19 discusses international promotion.

Case 15 *Slow Changes at Fuller Brush*

The Fuller Brush Company is an American institution. The name and the stereotypical "Fuller Brush Man" are so well known that they are often referred to in comedy routines and cartoons and even became the subject of a 1948 movie, *The Fuller Brush Man.* Yet the image of an enthusiastic, upbeat older man going door to door with a case full of brushes seems outdated in this age of guard dogs and phone sales. Fuller's ability to survive in the 1990s is a tribute both to the strength of its original concept and to its ability to change with the times.

Alfred C. Fuller was born in Nova Scotia in 1885 and headed to Boston at the age of 18. After short stints in a variety of jobs, Fuller went to work for the Somerville Brush and Mop Company and discovered both that he had a knack for selling and that people needed good brushes for a variety of purposes. On New Year's Day, 1906, he set up a workbench in his sister's basement, and with a wire-twisting machine and a supply of horsehair, hog bristles, and fiber, he began to make Fuller brushes.

Since that inauspicious beginning, the essential aspects of the Fuller approach have remained largely unchanged. The brushes are high quality, still made from natural bristles and real wood. An old Fuller slogan, "45 brushes—69 uses—head to foot—cellar to attic," still sums up pretty well the company's offerings. But what has always made Fuller stand out is its approach to direct sales.

Traditional Sales Approach

The salesman knocks on the door, steps away as the door is opened, smiles, and says "I'm your Fuller Brush Man, and I have a gift for you."

Before the homeowner is really aware of having invited him in, the Fuller Brush Man is sitting on the living room couch with his case open, demonstrating some of the dozens of brushes he has along, filling the room with cheerful, friendly chatter. Two-thirds of the time, he has an order before he makes his exit, leaving behind the free Handy Brush. A few days later, he reappears with the merchandise and leaves with the payment, about half of which goes into his own pocket.

This scenario has been repeated millions of times since 1906, and it is still being reenacted today, with some modern variations. The core of the approach is the attitude and the sales pitch. Successful Fuller Brush representatives are experts at getting a foot in the door, winning a few minutes of the homeowner's time for the complete demonstration. Experienced salespeople know their repeat customers and treat them as friends, leaving gifts for birthdays and special occasions, providing advice and recommendations consistent with their customers' tastes.

Fuller's sales reached a peak in 1965 of $110 million, but dropped to $50 million in 1982. The problem? The times had changed more quickly than the company. With more and more women entering the workforce, Fuller representatives find fewer people at home, and rising crime rates and general distrust of strangers mean that fewer salespeople are allowed in to give their demonstrations. Even though Fuller watched as rival Avon grew with a largely female salesforce, Fuller was slow to hire women and discouraged part-time salespeople.

Successful Changes

But all that has changed. Four out of five Fuller representatives are female now, and some ninety percent work part-time. The company has raised its commission rate, from 35 to 50 percent, and sales have now topped the $150 million mark. At the same time, Fuller has recognized that it can't survive on direct sales, although they still account for over half of its revenues. In 1987 it began nationwide distribution of a catalogue that so attractively conveyed the company's attitude, history, and products that it won a Gold Award from *Catalog Age* magazine. In its biggest break with tradition, Fuller opened two retail stores in 1987 and began making plans for kiosks in shopping centers around the country. And it has expanded its product line to include cutlery, door locks, and air fresheners, and about half of its profits come from Mexico, where it sells a successful line of cosmetics.

Even the work of the sales reps has changed somewhat. Most representatives have given up personal "cold calls." They slip a catalogue under the door or make a phone appointment first, although they're careful not to try to make sales over the phone. With increased sales incentives and company training, it seems likely that Fuller brushes will be sold door-to-door well into the next century.

Case Questions

1. What are some of the other ways Fuller could use advertising, sales promotion, and public relations to solve existing problems?

2. Based on our discussion of the trends in personal selling, do you feel that companies such as Fuller will exist in twenty years? Will they have to change the personal selling function? How?

Case Sources: "Brushing Up at Fuller," *Newsweek* (September 7, 1987): 44. Gerald Carson, "The Fuller Brush Man," *American Heritage* (August-September 1986): 26–31. "Fuller Brush Man Uses Soft Sell, Humor to Boost Sales," *Marketing News* (January 18, 1988): 3. "Gold Award: Fuller Brush Has an Old-Fashioned Flair for Salesmanship," *Catalog Age* (September 1989): 87, 89. Kerry Hannon, "A Foot in the Door," *Forbes* (October 20, 1986): 134–36. Harvey Shore, "Brush Strokes: The Life and Thought of Alfred C. Fuller (1885–1973)," *Business Quarterly* (Spring 1986): 16–17.

Summary

This chapter introduces the final component of the promotion mix—personal selling. Personal selling is defined as the face-to-face presentation of a product to a potential customer by a company representative. The salesperson usually follows seven main steps: attaining knowledge, prospecting, a preapproach, an approach, the presentation, closing, and follow-up. The model developed by Enis and Chonko, however, indicates that many factors beyond the salesperson's actions influence the effectiveness of personal selling. Their model provides a general framework for understanding the elements, relationships, and processes that affect personal selling.

The chapter also touches on the tasks assigned to the sales manager. The process begins with setting objectives, either sales target objectives or sales quota objectives. Motivating the sales force can be accomplished through a variety of means. Financial and extra incentives, security, and opportunity for advancement still seem to work best.

The chapter concludes with a discussion of how personal selling and the other promotional elements fit together. Acknowledging the specific pros and cons of personal selling is the starting point in assessing the role of personal selling. Certain conditions suggest that personal selling should dominate. There are also occasions when personal selling is unnecessary.

Finally, combining personal selling with each of the other mix elements offers specific benefits.

Discussion Questions

1.   What contributions can personal selling make to a firm that advertising or sales promotion cannot provide?

2.   Discuss the pros and cons of personal selling.

3.   How can you motivate salespeople? Discuss the major problems.

4.   "Personal selling should be a separate part of the organization. We create the sales, not those fools in advertising." Evaluate this statement by explaining the problems that result in an organization that professes this opinion.

5.   The relative importance of personal selling is a function of several factors. What are they?

6.   How can the findings of the Enis–Chonko personal selling model be used by promotion managers?

7.   What is meant by a style of communication in personal selling? Explain the key ideas behind each of the components.

8.   What are the implications of the rapid advances of technology and the high cost of selling on the future of personal selling?

9.   Suggest five guidelines for successful personal selling.

10.   What are the problems faced in motivating sales personnel? Identify three types of sales jobs. What type of motivation would work best with each?

Suggested Projects

1.   Contact two salespeople (one who sells industrial products and one who sells consumer products). Interview them about the steps they follow in selling their products. How do they differ? How are they alike?

2.   Write a two-page essay on how personal selling and the other promotional techniques could complement one another.

References

1. Ben M. Enis, *Personal Selling: Foundations, Process and Management* (Santa Monica, CA: Goodyear, 1979): 1.

2. G. D. Bruce and B. M. Bonjean, "Self-Actualization Among Retail Sales Personnel," *Journal of Retailing* 44 (Summer 1969): 73–83.

3. J. W. Thompson and W. W. Evans, "Behavioral Approach to Industrial Selling," *Harvard Business Review* 47 (March–April 1969): 69–83.

4. Marvin A. Jolson, "Should the Sales Presentation be 'Fresh or Canned'?" *Business Horizons,* 16 (October 1973): 83, 85.

5. John I. Coppett and William A. Staples, "A Sales Mix Model for Industrial Selling," *Industrial Marketing Management* (1980): 32.

6. *Ibid.*

7. Ben M. Enis and Lawrence B. Chonko, "A Review of Personal Selling: Implications for Managers and Researchers," in G. Zaltman, ed., *Annual Review of Marketing* (Chicago: American Marketing Association Publications, 1978): 276–304.

8. *Ibid.,* 279.

9. J. O'Shaughnessy, "Selling as an Interpersonal Process," *Journal of Retailing,* 47 (Winter 1971–72): 32–51.

10. Enis and Chonko, 297.

11. Stan Kossen, *Creative Selling Today,* 2nd ed. (New York: Harper and Row, 1982): 423–24.

12. "Sales Incentives," *Incentives* (September 1990): 55–58.

13. "Rick Scoville Tests the Waters," *Sales and Marketing Management* (July 1990): 30–31.

14. Shawn Clark, "Sales Force Automation Pays Off," *Marketing News* (August 6, 1990): 9.

15. Laurie Freeman, "P&G Rolls Out Retailer Sales Teams," *Advertising Age* (May 21, 1990): 18.

16 *Developing the Promotion Appropriation*

The Planning Framework

Preliminary Considerations
Assessing the Situation
Sales and Cost Forecasts
Strategic Decisions

Determining Appropriations for Advertising

Predetermined Budgetary Methods
Strategy-Determined Budgeting Approaches

Determining Appropriations for Other Forms of Promotion

Sales Promotion Budgeting
Public Relations Budgeting
Personal Selling Budgeting

Marginal Analysis: The Budgetary Ideal

Consider This:

The Best Laid Plans

Bill Kleine is disgusted. Kleine is the vice president of marketing for Mountain West Airlines, a small commuter airline serving Wyoming, Montana, Colorado, and Utah. He just received the evaluation of his proposed promotion budget for fiscal 1991. For the first time, he felt that he had done all his homework. Research provided him with detailed information on his primary target market, the frequent business flyer. Based on that information, he and promotion manager Ralph Crum devised an innovative strategy. It emphasized quality service and convenient scheduling. Print ads would be developed for five regional magazines and the zone editions of *Business Week* and *Time*. Combined with a three-week telemarketing program, a direct mail campaign was to be sent to fifty thousand business travelers. Finally, special promotions were to include a discount coupon applied to future flights for customers whose flights are more than fifteen minutes late and a free flight if a connection is missed.

Kleine spent two weeks gathering all the necessary cost data associated with the proposed campaign. He even developed three versions of the budget: Version A = $745,000, Version B = $680,000, Version C = $610,000. Well, he now knows what management thinks of his efforts; the promotion budget is just $500,000, the same as last year. Bill is told that his research is interesting and his strategy appears on target, but business is down and $500,000 is all Mountain West can afford. At least this year Bill and Ralph will have a set of guidelines for allocating the money, even if it is not enough.

*B*ill Kleine's situation is not unusual. Many promotional managers realize that the only way to get the desired appropriation is to ask for 50 percent more than is needed. The executives of many companies still search for assurance that promotional expenditures are necessary to the well-being of the firm. Even the most experienced and sophisticated managers are never sure whether they have allocated the right amount to promotion.

At the outset of our discussion, a terminology problem needs to be cleared up. The words *appropriation* and *budget* are often used as if they meant the same thing. However, **appropriation** actually means the maximum amount of dollars allocated for a specific purpose; **budget** means the nuts-and-bolts details of *how* this sum of money will be used. The promotion appropriation is the topic of this chapter. The promotion budget is really determined by the overall promotion strategy. Only one technique discussed in this chapter, the objective-task method, is driven by strategy. In most cases, an appropriation is determined first, then the allocation of these monies is considered. That is why the budgeting decision was included separately for each of the promotional elements.

Let us begin our discussion by presenting a planning framework employed for promotional appropriation and budgeting.

The Planning Framework

It should be apparent by now that the basic planning framework in strategic management remains the same regardless of the area of application. The planning framework used for promotional appropriation and budgeting determination is shown in Figure 16.1. Note that "sales/cost forecasting" is a new element. Its inclusion is predicated on the need to base an appropriation decision on accurate sales and cost estimates. Note also that the appropriation and budget decisions are kept separate, in keeping with our earlier discussion. It is possible that the order could be reversed.

Preliminary Considerations

Because managers have been engaged in the appropriation and budgeting process for many years, there is an assumption that the process is settled.

Figure 16.1

*The planning frame-
work used for promo-
tional appropriation
and budgeting deter-
mination.*

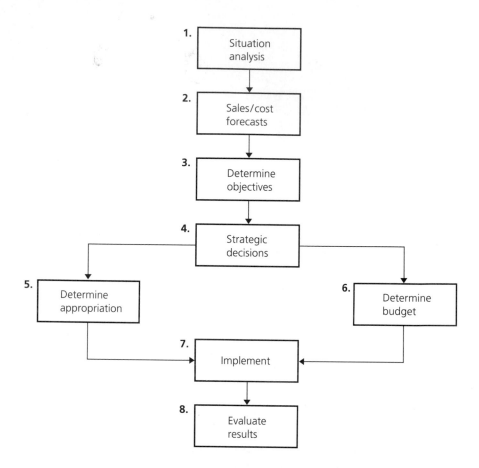

Nothing could be further from the truth. Although there have been attempts to make the process objective and scientific, more often it is an art,
based primarily on educated guesses, tradition, or the financial condition
of the company. One industry expert observed: "Of all the decisions marketing managers must make, questions concerning promotional allocations
are thought to be the most difficult."[1] Therefore several preliminary considerations need to be mentioned before one can truly understand how
appropriation and budgeting decisions are made. A primary consideration
is to identify the general approach the organization has toward the appropriation process, including identifying its attitude, identifying the primary
decision makers, and assessing how marketing allocates promotional
costs. In a typical American business, the method for determining the appropriation for promotion fails to reflect ideas about the importance of promotion. Most businesspeople recognize that promotion is important to corporate growth and health. Indeed, the level of investment appropriated
for promotion has increased during the last fifteen years. Still, many bus-

inesspeople act as if promotion were a current expense of selling rather than an investment in building an enduring consumer relationship. They often estimate sales for some ensuing period and then set their promotion budget after manufacturing, administration, direct selling costs, and acceptable profit levels have been established.

A company's promotion appropriation budget is often based on what is traditional for a company of its size in its industry. The general level of promotional expenditures within an industry tends to settle into a competitive equilibrium that remains more or less undisturbed until one firm finds a more successful or efficient manner of spending promotional dollars or settles on a marketing mix that is distinctly different from the industry pattern. Many managers do not feel that they can safely depart from the existing scale of promotion for similar products. They fear that if they reduce the percentage, they will lose their part of the market; if they increase it, they will invite an equal and harmful response from competitors. Instead of thinking about how promotion works to produce sales, executives often set promotional appropriations by routinely applying a set of decision rules year after year. Like any business decision, the promotion appropriation is shaped by the process used to determine it. Whether the appropriation is wise and effective depends in part on who has a role in deciding the appropriation, how the appropriation is defined, and how the decision is applied.

A wide range of individuals can participate in determining the promotional appropriation. If a product manager system is employed, the project manager probably exerts the greatest influence. In consumer goods companies, the advertising manager plays a large role. If the expertise of an advertising agency is relied on heavily, it has a strong impact. If a company manufactures nonconsumer goods or if it is small, then the decision might be made solely by a top manager or even the company president. In retail stores, the advertising manager and general manager usually determine the appropriation. In general, the more people who are involved in making a decision and the less directly involved they are in implementing the promotional strategy, the more likely a conservative appropriation becomes.

A final preliminary consideration is assessing how a company allocates expenses, especially promotional expenses. It is important to determine ahead of time which expenses will be charged to each department. In the past, marketing has often been a catchall department, and any expense item that appeared to relate to the consumer or the product was automatically charged to the marketing or advertising appropriation. This situation became so bad that in 1960 *Printer's Ink* magazine published budgetary guidelines to help managers determine which expenses belong to advertising. Table 16.1 shows which cost items belong to advertising, which do not, and which are borderline. It is not difficult to decide about 80 percent of the cost items, but the borderline items present serious questions. For

Table 16.1 Proper, Improper, and Borderline Charges for the Advertising Account

Items That Belong in the Advertising Account	Items That Are Borderline as to Where They Belong	Items That Do Not Belong in the Advertising Account
Space and time costs in regular media	Catalogs for consumers	Premium handling charges
Advertising consultants	Classified telephone directories	House-to-house sample distribution
Ad-pretesting services	Space in irregular publications	Packaging charges for premium promotions
Institutional advertising	Advertising aids for salespeople	Cost of merchandise for tie-in promotions
Industry directory listings	Financial advertising	Product tags
Readership or audience research	Dealer help literature	Showrooms
Media costs for consumer contests, premium and sampling promotions	Contributions to industry ad funds	Testing new labels and packages
Ad department travel and entertainment expenses	Direct mail to dealers and jobbers	Package design and artwork
Ad department salaries	Office supplies	Cost of non-self-liquidating premiums
Advertising association dues	Point-of-sale materials	Consumer education programs
Local cooperative advertising	Window display installation costs	Product publicity
	Charges for services performed by other departments	Factory signs
	Catalogs for dealers	House organs for salespeople
	Test-marketing programs	Signs on company-owned vehicles
	Sample requests generated by advertising	Instruction enclosures
	Costs of exhibits except personnel	Press clipping services
	Ad department share of overhead	Market research (produced outside)
	House organs for customers and dealers	Samples of middlemen
	Cost of cash value or sampling coupons	Recruitment advertising
	Cost of contest entry blanks	Price sheets
	Cross-advertising enclosures	Public relations consultants
	Contest judging and handling fees	Coupon redemption costs
	Depreciation of ad department equipment	Corporate publicity
		Market research (company produced)
		Exhibit personnel
		Gifts of company products
		Cost of deal merchandise
		Share of corporate salaries
		Cost of guarantee refunds
		Share of legal expenses
		Cost of detail or missionary people
		Sponsoring recreational activities

Table 16.1 **Proper, Improper, and Borderline Charges for the Advertising Account (*cont.*)**

Items That Belong in the Advertising Account	Items That Are Borderline as to Where They Belong	Items That Do Not Belong in the Advertising Account
Direct mail to consumers	Mobile exhibits	Product research
Subscriptions to periodicals and services for ad department	Employee fringe benefits	House organs for employees
	Catalogs for salespeople	Entertaining customers and prospects
Storage of advertising materials	Packaging consultants	Scholarships
	Consumer contest awards	Plant tours
		Annual reports
		Outright charity donations

Printer's Ink (December 16, 1960): 27.

example, if advertising writes the copy and arranges for the printing of a contest entry blank, should the copy and printing be advertising or sales promotion expenses? In addition, since these guidelines are over thirty years old, they do not reflect the new promotional elements that have emerged, nor do they reflect the increased complexity of the allocation process. Public relations is particularly difficult. Because many business executives feel that entertaining a client or business acquaintance falls under the heading of public relations, the costs are charged to the promotion budget.

Assessing the Situation

In deciding the amount of money to allocate to promotion, the astute decision maker should evaluate the relevant situational factors. Which factors are influential depends on whether the promoter is a manufacturer or a retailer.

Situational Factors Influencing the Manufacturer For manufacturers, key factors to consider when determining the promotion appropriation include the following:

- The product, including its type, stage in the life cycle, and strategic components,
- The market,
- The competition,
- The financial condition of the company,
- Research guidelines, and
- The distribution system.[2]

The Product   Certain elements of the product have a tremendous impact on the promotional appropriation. We examined these elements in Chapter 3 when we discussed how the type of product, the stage in its life cycle, and its strategic components affect the need for promotion and the effectiveness of particular types of promotion. For instance, it takes substantially more promotion dollars to launch a new product than to keep an old one going. The same is true for convenience products compared to durable products. Products such as milk, cigarettes, and soft drinks require mass selling techniques that presell the product. Consumer durables such as furniture and appliances require an emphasis on personal selling. If a product cannot be clearly differentiated in the mind of the prospect, then the product is best sold through a sales representative. Marketers are reluctant to spend money on promotion if price is used to create brand preference. Emotion-based products such as cosmetics, perfumes, and cars profit more from advertising than do products bought for primarily rational reasons, such as industrial machinery.

The Market   Both the size and nature of the market influence the promotional appropriation. Manufacturers who expect to cover a national market rather than a regional one will obviously spend more money. Maxwell House Coffee directs all its promotional efforts at coffee drinkers, while Gallo Winery is trying to turn nonwine drinkers into wine drinkers. These opposite strategies require different promotional tactics and different dollar requirements to support them. Characteristics of the market, including demographics and psychographics, the attitudes and perceptions of the consumer toward the manufacturer, the amount of brand loyalty toward the firm and its competitors, and the usage level of the product should all be considered.

The Competition   Many companies monitor the expenditure of their competition and match these amounts either directly or proportionately. Expenditure information is available through observation or industry statistics. As we discuss later in this chapter, matching is in many ways an ineffective strategy. There are instances, however, when a major competitor dramatically increases the budget for a particular brand, and the only recourse is to match this increase.

The Company's Financial Condition   When a company faces falling profits or when there is a general economic downturn, one of the first budgets to be cut is promotion, especially advertising and public relations. Promotion is viewed as a cost item that does not contribute directly to profitability. When business booms, promotion is usually reinstated. Realistically, then, the promotional allocation is limited by what a company can afford. As a practical matter, a ceiling on the allocation always exists. The promotion manager should be aware of this approximate dollar limit before beginning the planning process.

Research Guidelines   Small companies use little research to guide their decisions; they rely instead on experience and tradition. For the more sophisticated organization, marketing surveys, media data, census material, forecasts, and many other types of research are available.

The Distribution System   A channel of distribution can be quite long and include many intermediaries (that is, wholesalers and retailers). Or it can be quite short and direct, as it is for a manufacturer who uses a catalog and the mail to distribute products. A long, complex channel may require a large promotion appropriation to support the product because of the divided efforts of the intermediaries. For example, Coca-Cola Enterprises Inc. follows an intensive distribution policy because its products must be available in every possible outlet. Since these outlets usually carry competing brands of soft drinks as well, Coca-Cola cannot expect the intermediaries to carry much of the promotional effort. A retailer may engage in some cooperative advertising, but little more. Consequently, Coca-Cola must engage in extensive mass promotion, especially advertising and couponing, that will pull the product through the channel.

On the other hand, clothing manufacturer Hart, Schaffner, and Marx distributes its suits through an exclusive dealership arrangement. Since the retailers are guaranteed the sole right to sell the brand, they in turn provide certain promotional efforts for the manufacturer. The retailer will engage in extensive personal selling as well as local advertising. Much of the promotional effort and cost will be taken off the shoulders of the manufacturer.

Situational Factors Influencing the Retailer   Many of the factors just discussed have a direct bearing on the promotional budget for retailers as well as for manufacturers. However, retailers who engage in promotional budgeting must also consider a variety of factors that are unique to retailing. Specifically, these factors include the following:

1.   Age of store. New stores require more advertising.
2.   Location of store. Bad locations may require more promotion.
3.   Merchandising policies. Discount stores usually need a greater amount of mass selling in order to create product turnover.
4.   Competition. The greater the level of competition, the more promotion is needed.
5.   Media availability. The size of the community often dictates the type and extensiveness of the media that can be employed.

6. Size of the trading area. Promotion tends to increase with market size.

7. Support from the manufacturer. Manufacturers may provide retailers with advertising support, point-of-purchase displays, sales training, and other promotional support that will reduce the expenditures required of the retailer.

Sales and Cost Forecasts

Regardless of the company's objectives, a sales and cost forecast is necessary. Sales for the coming year can never be known exactly and therefore require a managerial estimate or forecast. This may be total management judgment (for a completely new product) to judgment supplemented by previous experience with similar situations. A variety of techniques are used to produce this forecast. *Executive judgment* bases the sales estimate on the intuition of one or more executives. It is also possible to survey customers, the sales force, or experts in the field. Two techniques that are far more complicated are time series analysis and market tests. *Time series analysis* uses the company's historical data and tries to discover a pattern or patterns in the firm's sales over time. The method assumes that past sales patterns will continue. *Market tests* involve making a product available to buyers in one or more test areas and then measuring purchases and consumer responses to marketing tactics. These results are then projected onto the entire marketplace.

Sales forecasts are used in determining the appropriation in at least two ways. First, the general trend in sales (that is, up, stable, down) provides a general guideline for the direction the appropriation should take. Second, many companies set their appropriation as a percentage of projected sales. (This method will be discussed in more detail later.)

Forecasting costs also has a more direct bearing on the appropriation and budget decisions. Costs *must* be forecasted in order to serve as justification for a particular request. Agency-related costs, media costs, production costs, special events costs, entertainment costs, and coupon distribution costs must all be estimated and totaled. Most of this information about costs is available either through secondary sources or through the provider of the service or product. References such as the *Standard Rate and Data Service* tell what media costs will be for a specified period of time. Production houses readily provide cost estimates. Several calls may be necessary before all the cost information is gathered, but it can be done. There are also computer databases that provide a great deal of cost information. Cost information is usually guaranteed for a given period of time; rate increases or decreases are noted, and dates for revised cost information are provided. Buying broadcast media during the up-front market, for instance, is one way of controlling ever-changing media costs.

Setting Objectives   A strong relationship exists among the promotional objectives, the appropriation/budget objectives, and the expenditure of funds required to meet the promotional objectives. Assuming that an organization has specific promotional objectives, it should be a fairly straightforward matter to estimate the promotional expenditure necessary to reach these objectives. However, the appropriation and budgeting process is also affected by its own objectives. Thus these objectives provide an important linkage between the promotional objectives and the resulting appropriation.

Essentially, appropriation/budgeting objectives tend to be either quantitative and/or qualitative.

Quantitative objectives are concerned with the ability of the appropriation to maximize profit, sales, or market share. (The theoretical foundation for these quantitative objectives is marginal analysis, which is discussed later in the chapter.) At this point, we present these quantitative goals in a simpler context. Maximization of profits suggests that the emphasis would be on promotion contributing to profitability. The amount of profit depends on the costs associated with each promotional element. Complying with such an objective would emphasize keeping costs low or making sure that high-cost items have very high payoffs. For example, media would be chosen that had a low CPM, or markets would be targeted that produced high profit margins.

Sales-based objectives attempt to maximize expected sales. A special concern is to avoid overspending. *Overspending* means that continued spending would produce sales at a decreasing rate. The saturation point has been reached and further spending is wasteful. *Underspending* is also a concern. If expected sales are below their expected maximum, promotional spending is too low. Forecasting and tracking sales are mandatory if sales-based objectives are to be achieved.[3] Since constant monitoring of the market and parts of the market is part of this process, budget flexibility is important. That is, money should be available at a moment's notice to take advantage of sales trends.

Reaching market share objectives is similar to maximizing sales in that the company has to estimate a sales curve. However, the company also has to estimate competitors' sales curves, which together with the firm's, comprise the market. Estimating a competitor's sales curve is difficult because it also requires estimating how the competitor's sales will respond to a particular level of expenditure. This difficulty in making estimates is possibly why so many false budgets are leaked to promotional trade publications; either a high appropriation intimidates competitors altogether or a low appropriation induces competitors to underspend. Maintaining market share means matching competitors' spending, and gaining market share means outspending the leading competitors.[4]

Qualitative objectives address the subjective issues achieved through the appropriation rather than the quantitative issues of profit, sales, and market share. In this context, the goal is to assess the extent to which the dollars spent achieve the qualitative objectives associated with the promotion plan discussed in earlier chapters. In the case of media selection, for instance, qualitative objectives dealt with whether the medium selected matched the image of the company, or if the tone of the medium was appropriate, or whether the right people were understanding the message in the manner intended. Qualitative appropriation/budget objectives indicate the extent to which the dollars allocated will achieve these promotional objectives at an optimum level. Is a compromise appropriation the norm? Or will the appropriation attempt to maximize? In other words, to what extent is the company willing to support its strategy?

Strategic Decisions

Few areas of promotion exhibit such a wide range of strategic sophistication as the appropriation and budgeting decision. Despite the fact that billions of dollars are spent on promotion every year, the majority of the companies spending these dollars use decision processes that are based on little if any strategic thinking.[5] Although this pattern has not proven detrimental to many of these companies, there is growing evidence that marketing managers are using more sophisticated techniques in setting promotional appropriations and budgets. Traditional subjective methods are gradually being replaced by data-driven approaches.[6] These approaches may provide an additional competitive advantage to those willing to commit. First, however, we will discuss the subjective methods of appropriation.

Concept Review

1. Distinction should be made between appropriation and budget.
2. The planning framework for promotional appropriation and budgeting determination include the following:
   a. Preliminary considerations,
   b. Assessing the situation,
   c. Sales and cash forecasts,
   d. Setting objectives, and
   e. Strategic decisions.

Determining Appropriations for Advertising

The budgetary approach used by a particular advertiser varies with the product, the size of the appropriation, and tradition. Table 16.2 lists some of the key techniques for determining the size of the appropriation and indicates their popularity among consumer and industrial advertisers. In

Table 16.2 **Methods Used to Set Advertising Budgets**

Allocation Method	*Percentage of Respondents Using Each Method[a]*	
	Consumer (1981)[b]	Industrial (1984)[c]
Quantitative models	51	3
Percent anticipated sales	53	16
Competitive parity	24	21
Per unit of sales	21	2
Percent past year's sales	20	23
Arbitrary	4	13
Objective task	63	74
All-you-can-afford	20	33

[a]Figures exceed 100% due to multiple responses
[b]Patti/Blasko, $n = 54$
[c]Blasko/Patti, $n = 64$

Vincent J. Blasko and Charles H. Patti, "The Advertising Budgeting Practices of Industrial Marketers," *Journal of Marketing* 48 (Fall, 1984): 104–110. Permission granted by the American Marketing Association.

the following sections, we describe the advantages and disadvantages of some of these methods.

Predetermined Budgetary Methods

Earlier, we alluded to the fact that promotion budgets are often handed down to the promotion manager by management fiat. That is, with little or no input from the promotion manager, a top manager predetermines that a specific dollar figure should be allocated to promotion. The following discussion describes the budgetary techniques used under these conditions.

Percentage of Sales Of all the methods developed over the years, the percentage of sales technique has probably been the most popular. In its simplest form, this approach is based on a fixed percentage of sales of the previous year, of an anticipated year, or of an average of several years. One advantage of this method is that expenditures are directly related to funds available—the more the company sold last year, the more it presumably has available for promotion this year. Another advantage is its simplicity. If businesspeople know last year's sales and have decided what percentage they wish to spend on promotion, the calculation is easy. As noted in Table 16.3, percentage of sales figures available for industries provide a general guideline for budgeting.

Table 16.3   Advertising Expenditures as a Percentage of Net Sales

Industry	Ad/Sales Ratio 1989	Industry	Ad/Sales Ratio 1989
Food Products		**Instruments and Related Products**	
Food and Kindred Products	7.8%	Optical Instruments and Lenses	0.6%
Meat Products	1.2	Photographic Equipment	3.6
Dairy Products	4.7	Watches, Clocks, and Parts	3.0
Canned Foods	6.9	**Misc. Manufacturing Industries**	
Flour and Other Grain Products	9.4	Jewelry and Precious Metals	1.8
Bakery Products	1.7	Musical Instruments	3.4
Malt Beverages	8.4	Toys and Games	14.2
Apparel		Sporting and Athletic Goods	5.5
Apparel and Other Finished Products	2.9	Pens and Other Writing Instruments	5.4
Furniture and Fixtures		**Communications**	
Household Furniture	4.8	Radio Broadcasting	8.6
Office Furniture	1.2	Television Broadcasting	2.5
Printing and Publishing		Cable and Pay TV	2.2
Newspapers	3.6	**Wholesaling**	
Periodicals	3.7	Autos and Other Vehicles	2.8
Books	3.3	Computers and Software	0.2
Chemicals and Allied Products	2.7	Drugs	0.1
Industrial Inorganic Chemicals	16.5	Food	1.5
Plastic Materials and Synthetic Resins	1.2	**Retailing**	
Soap and Other Detergents	7.7	Lumber and Other Building Materials	1.8
Paints, Varnishes, and Lacquers	3.7	Department Stores	2.9
Machinery and Equipment		Variety Stores	1.9
Farm and Garden Machinery and Equip.	1.4	Grocery Stores	1.3
Metalworking Equipment	5.5	Automotive Dealers and Gas Suppliers	0.7
Computing and Office Equipment	1.2	Apparel and Accessories	2.4
Refrigeration Equipment	2.3	Women's Ready-to-Wear	2.7
Electric and Electronic Equipment		Furniture and Home Furnishings	5.0
Household Appliances	4.2	Eating and Drinking Places	9.3
Household Audio and Video Equip.	2.8	Eating Places	3.3
Transportation Equipment		Mail-order Houses	5.7
Motor Vehicles and Car Bodies	1.7		
Motor Homes	1.7		

Table 16.3   **Advertising Expenditures as a Percentage of Net Sales (*cont.*)**

Industry	Ad/Sales Ratio 1989	Industry	Ad/Sales Ratio 1989
Misc. Service Industries		Motion Picture Production	9.8
Hotels and Motels	3.4	Educational Services	5.0
Personal Services	5.7		

Notes: The Ad/Sales Ratio shows the advertising and promotional budget for each selected industry as a percentage of net sales.

This table is based on *Advertising Ratios & Budgets,* an annual study of advertising and promotional expenditures of major U.S. corporations published by Schonfeld & Associates, Inc. The study contains 1988 historical and current-year forecasts of advertising budgets for more than 5,700 publicly owned companies in over 390 different industries. Figures are compiled from 10-K reports filed with the Securities and Exchange Commission. Cautious interpretation is advised, however, since companies may vary on their interpretation of what constitutes advertising and/or promotional expenditures. Also, large companies operating in several different fields may be listed only in their primary industry sector, and figures for privately owned companies do not appear. Copies of *Advertising Ratios & Budgets* are available at a cost of $295 from Schonfeld & Associates, Inc., 1 Sherwood Drive, Lincolnshire, IL 60069.
Schonfeld & Associates, Inc. This report cannot be reproduced or distributed without the expressed written consent of Schonfeld & Associates, Inc.

Copyright © 1989 by Schonfeld & Associates, Inc.

The percentage of sales method also suffers from several serious limitations. Most notably, it assumes that promotion is a result of sales rather than a cause. It does not take into account the possibility that sales may decline because of too little promotion or that sales do not take advantage of a rising potential. Another related factor is the possibility that a point may be reached when additional promotional dollars generate a lower and lower result. Using the percentage of past sales may mean underspending when the potential is great and overspending when the potential is low.

A way of dealing with this tendency to overspend or underspend is to relate the promotional appropriation to forecasted sales rather than past sales. This is possible for businesses that are able to employ a reliable forecasting technique. Many businesses, however, do not have this capability. Nevertheless, using future sales acknowledges the facts that promotion precedes sales and is an important factor in producing sales.

Perhaps the most effective manner in which to use the percentage of sales technique is to examine both past sales and forecasted sales. This examination not only provides more stability but also assures that market potential is accounted for. Regardless of its limitations, the percentage of sales method will no doubt remain popular.

Unit of Sales   The unit of sales method is very much like the percentage of sales technique. Instead of dollar sales, the base is the physical volume of either past or future sales. This unit value is then multiplied by a fixed amount of money in order to derive the total appropriation. For example, General Motors Corp. might allocate $340 per unit for advertising.

This method exhibits the same strengths and weaknesses as the percentage of sales method, and the same solutions apply. It is commonly used for high-ticket items such as automobiles and appliances. Its use is prompted more by tradition than by logic.

Competitive Parity   Many promoters base their allocations on competitors' expenditures. Information on expenditures is available readily through sources such as *Advertising Age* magazine, A. C. Nielsen, and government reports. This technique is rarely the sole determinant of the appropriation but is normally used in conjunction with other criteria.

The competitive parity technique has the advantage of recognizing the importance of competition in promotion, and it often helps minimize market warfare. It is also simple to use since the only information required is the dollar amount expended by competitors.

The fact that this technique is based on a simple dollar amount also suggests a limitation. Important competitors may reflect a wide variety of budgetary sizes and directions. It is impossible for a company to adjust to greatly varying competitors. Another drawback is that competitive parity assumes that a company's objectives are the same as its competitors, and this can be a treacherous assumption. It also assumes that competitors' allocations are correct. Finally, information on competitive advertising expenditures is available only after the money has been spent.

All-You-Can-Afford   With the all-you-can-afford method, the amount left over after all the other relevant company expenditures are made is allocated to advertising. Companies of all types and sizes use this method. It is particularly popular when introducing a new product. As unsophisticated as the approach appears, it often produces effective results. If a company is doing a good job allocating to the other elements of its business, it may not be surprising that the amount left over for advertising fits the needs of the company.

Strategy-Determined Budgeting Approaches

In contrast to the techniques just discussed whose uses are motivated by simple rules of thumb and industry traditions, there are several budgeting techniques that are based on the promotional strategy itself. These bottom-up approaches begin with the input of people implementing the promotional strategy, continue on to the promotion manager, and ultimately reach top management, accompanied with documentation supporting the budget amount requested. Admittedly, these techniques are more difficult to use, and some organizations may lack the necessary expertise or resources. Nevertheless, they coincide with the formal planning process recommended throughout this book.

Objective-Task   The most popular technique is the objective-task method. The promotion manager starts with a thorough study of the market and product in order to set logical promotional objectives. The next step is to define objectives in such terms as awareness, attitude change, and coupon redemption to be achieved during a particular time period. After the objectives are set, the promoter must determine how much money will be necessary to achieve them. If the associated costs are greater than the money available, then either the objectives are adjusted or more funds are found.

The primary advantage of this method is that it develops the budget from the ground up. This is proper managerial procedure and it works. It does not rely on past sales, future sales, what the competition does, or any other factors beyond those that are under the control of the decision maker.

The task method is especially well adapted to new product introduction when advertising must be developed more or less from scratch. It is also well adapted to situations in which major changes are undertaken in the advertising or marketing program for established products.

One drawback of the objective-task method still casts doubt on its superiority to other methods. The results of this method are only as good as the stated objectives and the preciseness in assigning dollar amounts to these objectives. Stating objectives and assigning accurate dollar amounts are difficult tasks to do well. In some instances, objectives are vague or even contradict one another.

Mathematical Models   During the last three decades, a significant growth in the use of quantitative techniques in promotional budgeting has occurred. Sometimes these quantitative formulations involve the application of mathematical models developed in other fields, such as physics or psychology. Other times they reflect original thought about the ways in which advertising might interact with other marketing forces and with the consumer. One such model that has achieved recent popularity is shown in Figure 16.2. This sales-response computer simulation model is known as Prod II. It requires estimates of various media and marketing inputs (usually derived from past experiences) and then simulates a number of possible outcomes. The budget derived is based on the optimal set of inputs. The sequence of the model is as follows:

1.   Inputs are mathematically simulated for different amounts. Inputs are gross rating points (GRPs) delivered and marketing variables such as price and distribution.

Figure 16.2

Microcomputer simulation framework: Prod II.
Fred S. Zufryden, "How Much Should Be Spent for Advertising a Brand?" Journal of Advertising Research *(April/May 1989): 26. Used with permission.*

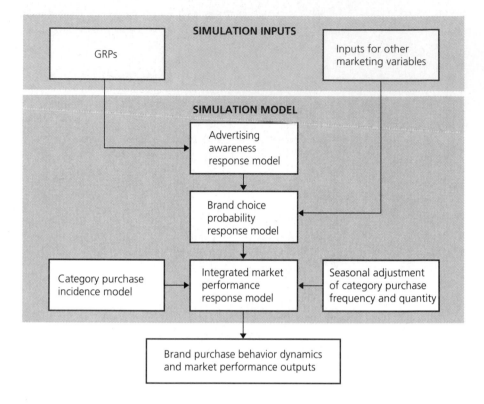

2. The ability of each level of GRPs to deliver a specific level of awareness is simulated.

3. The various awareness levels and marketing variables are simulated as an input to brand choice probability.

4. The variable of brand choice probability, along with the category purchase incidence model (that is, when people buy products in this category) and seasonal adjustment of category purchase (that is, how often and how much), is inputted to integrated performance response model (that is, the likelihood that purchase will occur).

5. Finally, the various performance response models are assessed in terms of the financial benefits of each model. This assessment indicates an optimum program that will produce an optimum budget.

Mathematical models have not found wide acceptance in the industry for a variety of reasons. First, they require types of experimentation and formal analysis that may be beyond the capabilities of many companies. Second, the process is time consuming and expensive. Third, the models have not been successfully modified so that a model developed in psychology is not valid in marketing. Although we are likely to see a great many more quantitative budgeting models proposed by theorists in the years ahead, their extensive use in actual practice will be much slower in coming.

The Experimental Approach   The experimental approach is an alternative to modeling. Rather than using past history to validate a budget, the promotion manager uses tests and experiments in one or more market areas to determine the results of variations that might be tried. The experimental approach relies on test feedback for input. A typical example is a budget based on test market data. A product might be tested simultaneously in several markets with a similar population, brand usage level, and brand share. Varying advertising and budget levels would be determined for each market. Before, during, and after the expenditure, sales and awareness would be measured in each market. By comparing the results, estimates can be made on how the varying budget levels might perform nationwide. The budget that produced the best results would then be used.

To a great extent, this technique eliminates the problems associated with the other budgetary approaches. The major drawbacks in this approach are the time and expense (in the low six figures annually) involved in getting the data and the difficulty of controlling the environment. Anheuser-Busch is one company that has been using the experimentation approach for many years; the company has increased total sales and profits while decreasing advertising costs per barrel.

Payout Planning   The payout plan is used in conjunction with budget-setting methods to assess the investment value of the promotions. It projects future revenues generated and costs incurred, usually for a two- or three-year period. Its purpose is to show what level of expenditures needs to be made, what level of return might be expected, and what time period is necessary before the return will occur. Payout planning is a useful budgetary technique when a new product is introduced with a commitment to invest heavily in promotion in order to stimulate awareness and product acceptance. It acknowledges the likelihood that this situation will diminish company profits for the first year or two. Management naturally wants estimates of both the length of time that promotional dollars must be invested before sales occur and the expected profit flow once the brand has become established.

The key to the payout plan is the accuracy of the forecasting. Forecasts must be made of sales over time, factors affecting the market, and costs. A successful brand typically grows in its early years and then levels off at a stable market share. Investment in promotions is high in the beginning and low later on.

The payout plan is a useful planning tool, but it does have limitations. Most notably, it cannot account for all the uncontrollable factors that may affect the plan. New competitors, legislation, natural disasters, and new technologies are just a few of the contingencies influencing the plan. Also, the assumptions underlying the plan tend to be optimistic. What happens if the product has no competitive advantage or the promotion is not effective? Clearly, top management would react badly to a payout plan that is two or three years behind the projected break-even point.

Concept Review

The following methods are used for determining appropriations for advertising:

A. Predetermined budgetary methods
1. Percentage of sales: fixed percentage of last year's or forecasted sales
2. Unit of sales: fixed dollar amount of each unit sold
3. Competitive parity: proportionate match of the amount spent by competitors
4. All you can afford: amount left over after all other relevant expenditures are made
B. Strategy-determined budgetary methods
1. Objective-task: totaled costs to achieve objectives
2. Mathematical models: application of mathematical models to budgetary decisions
3. Experimental approach: tests of various budget allocations in various markets
4. Payout planning: projects future revenues generated and costs incurred

Determining Appropriations for Other Forms of Promotion

The methods we have described for determining the appropriations for advertising are also used to set appropriations for other elements of the promotion mix. Most companies use more than one of these methods. In fact, the method used may vary from division to division or even between functional areas. For example, a company might use competitive parity to set its personal selling budget, percentage of sales to establish the advertising budget, and all-you-can-afford for the other promotional activities. Or a company might use mathematical modeling for new products and percentage of sales for mature products. In the following sections, we examine appropriation techniques used with the other promotional elements. Many of these techniques overlap with those used in advertising.

Sales Promotion Budgeting

One serious difficulty associated with sales promotion is the vast number of activities that fall under this label. As a result, there is ongoing uncertainty about which activities should be the financial responsibility of sales promotion. The most recent *Sales Promotion Handbook* offers the following list of activities that should be covered by the sales promotion budget:

1. Research
2. Travel
3. Sales education
   a. Training literature
   b. Films and visuals
   c. Housing and administration
4. Promotional literature
5. Dealer services
6. Sales tools and equipment
7. Fairs and exhibits
8. Educational material for schools
9. Sales contests and campaigns
10. Dealer and other meetings
11. Community relations
12. Speakers' bureau
13. Publicity
14. Trade associations[7]

When these activities overlap with the other promotional elements, the costs should be shared. For the most part, the extent to which sales promotion is allowed to share its financial burden depends on who is in charge of sales promotion. Most large companies use a brand management system, and the brand manager is responsible for determining the total amount to be invested in sales promotion. Since this individual usually has the responsibility for the total marketing budget, it is likely that sales promotion will be kept in perspective and treated fairly.

When the brand management system is not used, the promotion manager usually develops a total sales promotion budget for the department that includes all expected expenses. Salaries, sales promotion activities, department expenses, ongoing costs, and similar charges are individually budgeted. Either approach benefits from an internal accounting system capable of providing budgetary control.

Most of the budgetary methods discussed in determining advertising appropriations are used with sales promotion as well. Five primary techniques are used to allocate funds to sales promotion:

1. Predetermined ratios. These involve rules of thumb based on company policy or historical precedent, possibly modified by the strategic position of the brand.

2. Objective-task method. Objectives for sales promotion are stated and plans are developed to accomplish these objectives at minimum cost.

3. The build-up approach. The budget begins with the necessary promotion expenses and successively adds the less necessary programs.

4. Competitive parity. The budget mirrors that of a close competitor, scaled up or down accordingly.

5. Theoretically optimal expenditures. A sales response model is used to find the budget that will maximize profits. The model is either solved analytically or by using a simulation approach. The "optimal" budget may not be taken literally but stated as a guideline or starting point for other budgets.[8]

While senior managers often specify predetermined ratio guidelines, historical precedent (that is, last year's allocation) is the most commonly used method of allocation.[9] This use of historical precedent is discouraging since the objective-task and theoretically optimal expenditures methods have much more intuitive appeal. Part of the problem may be the recency of sales promotion as part of the promotional strategy and the difficulty of implementing the more complicated budgetary techniques. Sales promotion people may simply not be up to the challenge. The Promotion in Focus section suggests several guidelines that may facilitate the use of these more sophisticated budgetary techniques.

Public Relations Budgeting

Compared to the other three areas of promotion, public relations uses the least sophisticated budgeting techniques. Essentially, public relations managers follow one of four strategies in setting budgets. The first is equivalent to the all-you-can-afford technique. Because public relations is often at the end of the line when funds are allocated, the amount given to public relations is typically much lower than that given to advertising and sales promotion.

Competitive parity is the second technique. However, since the amount that competitors spend on public relations is very difficult to gauge, the amount chosen is often an approximation based on what public relations activities competitors are observed doing. Because many public relations costs cannot be observed, this technique suffers from serious miscalculation problems.

A version of the objective-task method is a third budgeting technique used in public relations. This budgeting technique is usually contingent on the objectives established for the other promotional elements. For example, a sales promotion program such as a special event is also the responsibility of public relations. The objective established for the special event

Promotion in Focus

Integrating Sales Promotion Efforts

*I*n many companies, sales promotions take a back seat to advertising. While a business may hire an advertising agency to create a powerful message and get it across in the most efficient way, it is likely to be much less organized about its sales promotions. Companies that view sales promotions as something extra to be handled when someone has time undercut the strategic marketing value of the promotion and spend their sales promotion budget foolishly.

Many companies don't even know what that budget is, since money for sales promotions tends to get handed out piecemeal to copywriters, art studios, printers, and other agencies. These various functions need to be integrated and brought under centralized control. A company that regularly uses a media advertising agency should seriously consider hiring a sales promotion agency to handle all of the sales promotion chores and work with the media agency.

Before planning any sales promotion activities, the company needs to know what the goals of the promotion are. Often companies run the same promotions year after year without analyzing their effectiveness or value. A sales promotion agency can help take a hard look at what has been done in the past and recommend changes. How does sales promotion fit in with the rest of the company's marketing mix? Even a well-conceived sales promotion will be ineffective if its goals are not consistent with an overall marketing strategy.

A sales promotion agency can be most helpful in creating fresh new promotions, once it has been given clear goals and budget limitations. New approaches are not necessarily more expensive, and in the process of integrating all activities connected to a sales promotion, the agency may find that some activities are redundant or ineffective. A company now spending money on dealer incentives, price reductions, special packaging, and consumer education may find that a creative new approach to just one of these areas will be more effective and save a good deal of money. If you're going to use sales promotions at all, experts say, take them seriously and make sure they're all working together.

Source: Peter Adler, "Get Top Mileage from Sales Promotion Budget," *Marketing News* (February 29, 1988): 9.

by sales promotion dictates the public relations objective, which in turn can be assigned a cost figure.

The final budgeting technique follows a cost accounting approach. Simply stated, the public relations manager develops a list of activities and events that he or she would like to implement in the upcoming year. An itemized list of costs is developed and compared with a budget ceiling or submitted to top management for approval. Adjustments then follow.

Although there is no evidence supporting the benefit of one of these techniques over another, one would assume the same logic expressed earlier applies.

Personal Selling Budgeting

In most institutions, the dollar figure allocated to personal selling is calculated independently from that of the other promotional functions. That is, the personal selling budget is determined by the marketing director and the sales manager with little concern for what the other three mix elements are spending. This tendency toward having a separate budget is a major reason why coordinating personal selling with advertising, sales promotion, and public relations has been so difficult.

There are two cost categories associated with personal selling. The first cost category is labeled direct selling expenses or *field selling expenses*. The second category is labeled indirect selling expenses and includes moving expenses, special entertainment expenses, and special promotional expenses. Many companies have drastically reduced this cost area in recent years. The cost of physically moving a salesperson and purchasing and financing a new home has simply become prohibitive. The popularity of the four-martini expense account lunch has also fallen on hard times because of governmental pressure as well as excessive costs. Therefore this discussion will concentrate on direct selling expenses.

Figure 16.3 shows a suggested process for developing a personal selling budget. The fifteen step process begins with a list of the location of each sales territory, followed by a sales forecast for each metro area. Steps 3 through 9 indicate all the direct cost items associated with each metro area. These cost items are totaled under step 10. Step 11 totals the specific cost items for all metro areas. Step 12 projects sales of the territory. Step 13 calculates the percent of the territory's sales that will be accounted for by total sales of the metro area listed. Step 14 enters the budgeted salaries. Step 15 enters total forecasted expenses for the metro areas from column 10. Step 16 adds 14 and 15 for a total budget figure. The derivation of the dollar amounts placed in each of the cost categories can be percentage of sales, objective-task, all-you-can-afford, or some combination of these methods. Here again, the simpler methods prevail.

Preparing a Sales-Costs Budget

1. Metro areas	2. Projected sales	3. Lodging costs	4. Meal costs	5. Auto rental	6. Misc. expenses	7. Entertainment	8. Transportation	9. Promotional	10. Total metro expenses
11. Metro totals									
12. Projected total territory									
13. Percent of total	____%	____%	____%	____%	____%	____%	____%	____%	____%

14. Budgeted salaries _____

15. All-metro total _____

16. Actual expenses _____

Figure 16.3

Components considered in preparing a personal selling budget.
Sales & Marketing Management *(February 26, 1990): 12. Reprinted with the permission of Bills Communications.*

Concept Review

1. Sales promotion and public relations use many of the same budgeting techniques as advertisers.
2. Budgeting for personal selling considers the following categories:
   a. Direct selling expenses
   b. Indirect selling expenses

Marginal Analysis: The Budgetary Ideal

Hundreds of approaches are used to determine how much to spend on promotion. However, the theoretical basis for determining the size of the promotion budget is **marginal analysis.** In theory, it means that a business adds to the budget as long as the incremental expenditures are exceeded by the marginal revenue that they generate, and that this process continues until the marginal revenue and marginal costs are equal.

Figure 16.4

Illustration of marginal analysis.

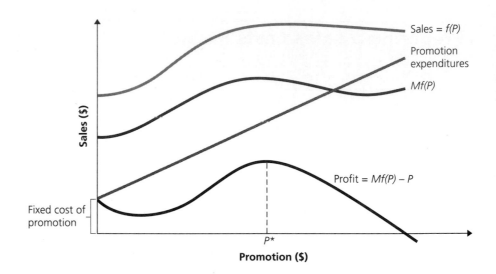

This model is illustrated in Figure 16.4. Assume that the only determinant of dollar sales *(S)* was the amount spent on promotion *(P)*:

$$S = f(P)$$

Also, assume that *f(P)* has the general shape drawn in Figure 16.5. Thus, if *M* is the gross margin on sales, then *Mf(P)*, the gross margin curve, would simply be a scaled version of *f(P)*. The difference between *Mf(P)* and *P* then represents a profit function:

$$\text{Profit} = Mf(P) - P$$

The optimal level of promotion expenditure is that level that will maximize profit. In our example, the optimal level is *P**, in which the marginal revenue obtained from the last dollar invested is $1 (the slope of the profit curve at *P** = 0). A dollar invested in promotion above the level *P** will yield less than $1 profit.

Although the *f(P)* curve is portrayed as being *S*-shaped (see Figure 16.4), the shape and parameters determining the curve can vary tremendously. However, at least in the case of advertising, there are several reasons why an *S*-shaped curve seems justified: (1) there is always some sales return for additional advertising investment, but the rate of return declines as more money is spent, (2) no amount of advertising investment can push sales above some limit imposed by the culture and the competitive environment, (3) there are threshold levels of advertising such that expenditures below the treshold have no effect on sales, and (4) some sales will be made even with no advertising investment. These propositions are depicted in Figure 16.5.

Figure 16.5

An illustration of the four propositions that justify the f(P) curve.
Figure from Advertising by Kenneth A. Longman, copyright © 1971 by Harcourt Brace Jovanovich, Inc., reproduced by permission of the publisher.

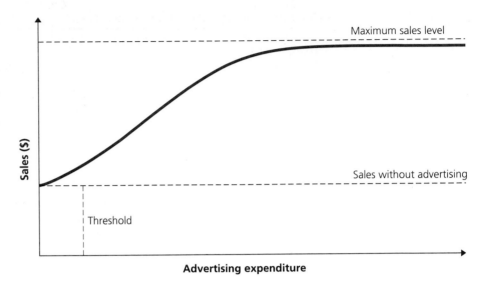

Marginal analysis has also been applied to budgets for personal selling. Although the primary benefit of marginal analysis in this context is to determine the optimum size of the total sales organization, it has a secondary advantage of providing a basis for making adjustments in the sales force throughout the year. Both decisions have a direct impact on the personal selling budget. The application of marginal analysis is straightforward. If an additional salesperson is hired, total sales should increase as should total selling costs. If a person is let go, sales will decline and so will expenses. In general, the manager will hire another person if the gross margin on the additional sales rises more than the selling cost increases—that is, if the extra salesperson will contribute more in gross margin than in cost. When replacing salespeople, the opposite reasoning applies. That is, salespeople will be replaced if they don't contribute marginally.

This decision-making process is illustrated in the following example. Suppose that a company currently has fifty salespeople at a total cost of $800,000 and a total profit of $1,060,000 (see Table 16.4). One of the salespeople has announced the intention to quit and the personnel manager has reported that three qualified people are available as replacements. The information found in Table 16.4 can be used to evaluate the following alternatives:

1. Do not replace the salesperson.
2. Replace the salesperson.
3. Expand the force by one or more.

Table 16.4   **Marginal Analysis of Sales Force**

Number of Salespeople	Profit Contribution		Selling Cost	
	Total	Marginal	Total	Marginal
49	$ 900,000		$780,000	
50	1,060,000	70,000	800,000	20,000
51	1,120,000	60,000	820,000	20,000
52	1,170,000	50,000	840,000	20,000
53	1,210,000	40,000	860,000	20,000

If the salesperson is not replaced, gross margin will drop by $70,000 while $20,000 will be saved. Hiring one person to replace the departing salesperson will generate a $40,000 differential, hiring two people will increase net profit by $30,000, and hiring three people will generate another $20,000 and a larger market share. Thus, fifty-two salespeople represent the optimum sales force size, since the marginal profit is still greater than the marginal cost.

Although there are no examples of marginal analysis applied to sales promotion or public relations, there is no reason why this rationale would not work. In sales promotion, the applicable units relate to levels of couponing, sampling, or price discounting. For public relations, the units of input are information releases, special events, or participation in open houses. The marginal unit sales from any given increase in these inputs can be calculated, producing a similar curve to that in Figure 16.6. With the exception of the threshold level, most of these propositions have been widely accepted in the advertising industry.[10]

Although marginal analysis reflects an important ideal, applying it in practice has been difficult, if not impossible. The first problem relates to the assumption that sales are a direct result of promotional expenditures. This assumption may be valid in the case of direct-mail promotion, but it is questionable in most other types of promotion. The assumption that sales are determined solely by promotion expenditures is obviously faulty in practically all situations. Even if a researcher could isolate and control all the relevant variables for one time, there is no guarantee that the derived response curve would be valid in the future.

Second, marginal analysis ignores how the sales-response relationships change if copy strategy, media strategy, or other elements of the marketing mix are changed. Some changes can cause the response relationship to become more or less efficient by making dollars work harder or easier.

Third, marginal analysis does not account for the cumulative effect of past promotional effort on future sales. A consumer who buys a microwave oven in February could be affected by advertising seen in December in addition to an encounter with a salesperson six months earlier. There is also the possibility that advertising might attract buyers who become loyal customers for many years. To date, marginal analysis is not able to accommodate the *lag effect* of promotion.

There are continuing efforts to adjust the marginal analysis technique in order to reduce these limitations. Some researchers have developed sophisticated experiments in which the various budget variables affecting sales are manipulated and the results are compared. Elaborate statistical regression models are added to these experiments to provide even greater predictability. However, the high level of expertise required to implement these techniques has discouraged their use. Instead, promotional managers have opted for simpler budgetary methods.

Concept Review

1. Marginal analysis is a theoretical basis for setting a promotion budget.
   a. A business continues to supplement the promotion budget as long as the incremental expenditures are exceeded by the marginal revenue that they generate.
   b. The optimal level of promotion expenditure is the level that will maximize profit.
2. Marginal analysis is difficult to implement because of the following:
   a. It is impossible to judge whether sales are the direct result of promotion.
   b. It does not consider changes in different elements of promotional strategy.
   c. It does not account for the cumulative effect of past promotions.

Case 16 *United Way Changes Its Ways*

Few business organizations have gone through more changes than the United Way. The organization began in Denver in 1887 when the first United Community Campaign was organized. Community Chest was the name employed from the 1920s through the 1940s. The organization then became known as the United Fund or the United Givers. It was not until the 1970s that the name United Way became prevalent.

The intent of the United Way remains consistent—to raise money simultaneously for several worthwhile causes, thus cutting down on duplication of fund-raising drives and saving time and frustration for donors. Individual charities within local United Ways receive on the average one-fourth of their funding from the annual United Way campaigns. The remainder of funding comes from grants and bequests, from government agencies in fees for contracted services, and from supplemental fund-raising drives. These supplemental drives are approved or condoned by the United Way.

As one would expect, the marketing program for United Way to date has been very simple. The national office was responsible for coordination, long-range planning, and providing some services to the approximately 2,100 local United Ways in the United States and Canada. Headquarters furnished the local organizations with technical support for local campaigns and tried to build and maintain good relations with large corporations. More specific activities had to do with the development and production of films and other materials for use by voluntary solicitors and the media, development and production of planning and budgeting manuals, review of national agency programs, publication of various newsletter series, training of locals in management techniques and fund raising, maintenance of a lending library of pertinent reports, and the execution of public opinion and market research. For example, one research effort found a direct correlation between contributor knowledge of United Way and support.

All the advertising for the United Way has been through the support of the Advertising Council, a social marketing organization formed for the purpose of supporting selected nonprofit causes with the creation and placement of donated professional advertising. An advertising agency, Bozell & Jacobs, International, volunteered to create the advertising and the National Football League agreed to support the United Way on its televised games. Later, the National Hockey League and National Basketball Association agreed to similar arrangements. The entire cost to United Way for the NFL series was $200,000, the cost of production.

Promotion efforts at the United Way have changed, however. The United Way is planning to develop a series of print, television, and radio ads that will be targeted at the general public. These ads will run the entire year, not just during campaigns. United Way faces one other unusual problem. Since the money spent on promotion has been donated and should go to the various charities, the public is very critical about spending on other programs.

Since top management at United Way has never had to develop a promotional budget before, there is a great deal of confusion as to where to begin and what the process should look like. There appear to be two camps thus far. One group simply wants to come up with a total appropriation based on the experiences of for-profit businesses with comparable revenue and cost figures. This group has identified six such businesses and has estimated that eleven million dollars would be necessary to support a one-year advertising program. The allocation of this money to the various components of the advertising strategy would be based on cost figures submitted by the people responsible for each component.

The second group, headed by staff economist John Blair, wishes to employ a marginal analysis approach in deriving the appropriation. The group argues that having detailed support for such a large financial decision is particularly important when an organization is spending donated money. Admittedly, there will be some problems making all the necessary forecasts that are part of the marginal analysis approach. In the worst case scenario, intelligent assumptions can substitute for hard data.

Case Questions

1. Given the situation faced by United Way, assess the appropriateness of the two appropriation techniques suggested.

2. Are there other techniques United Way should consider? Which ones? What advantages are offered by these alternative techniques?

Summary

Many factors influence the promotion budget—for example, the product and where it is in the life cycle, objectives, the financial condition of the company, research guidelines, the distribution system, market scope, and competition. The effectiveness of the budgetary process depends in part on who makes the decisions, what is included in the budgets, and the establishment of a reserve fund and regular review process.

Although the ideal technique for making the promotion appropriation is marginal analysis, it is not a realistic option for most companies. The more popular techniques range from the simple (percentage of sales) to the complex (mathematical models).

Discussion Questions

1. What are the first two budget decisions that a promotional manager must make? How is the manager influenced by competition when making these decisions?

2. Differentiate between the terms *appropriation* and *budget*. What is the role of each?

3. Discuss the factors that influence the absolute size of the appropriation.

4. Describe both the marginal analysis and the objective-task methods of determining the appropriation. How are the two methods comparable?

5. What is the problem with using the competitive parity approach when developing the appropriation for a new product? Suggest an alternative approach.

6. In addition to selecting the method of budgeting and subsequently determining the size and allocation of the budget, what other factors should the manager consider?

7. What factors influence the promotion allocation of the retailer?

8. Describe the experimental approach to budgeting. What are the drawbacks associated with this method?

9. There are several difficulties in appropriating a budget for sales promotion. Discuss them.

10. What is the procedure for developing a payout plan for new products?

Suggested Projects

1. Interview two local businesspeople (one retailer and one manufacturer) and ask them to discuss the method they use to establish their promotion budget. Compare your findings from the two interviews.

2. Write a two-page essay defending the use of predetermined budgeting methods.

References

1. Donald C. Marschner, "Theory Versus Practice in Allocating Advertising Money," *Journal of Business,* 40 (July 1967): 286–302.

2. Gary L. Lilien et al., "Industrial Advertising Effects and Budgeting Practices," *Journal of Marketing* 40 (January 1976): 16–24.

3. Leonard M. Lodish, *The Advertising and Promotion Challenge* (New York: Oxford University Press, 1986): 92–94.

4. John Philip Jones, "Ad Spending: Maintaining Market Share," *Harvard Business Review* (January–February 1990): 38–42.

5. Nigel F. Piercy, "The Marketing Budgeting Process: Marketing Management Implications," *Journal of Marketing* 51 (October 1987): 45–59.

6. James E. Lynch and Graham J. Hooley, "Increasing Sophistication in Advertising Budget Setting," *Journal of Advertising Research* 30 (February/March 1990): 67–75.

7. Ovid Rio, *The Dartnell Sales Promotion Handbook*, 7th ed. (Chicago: The Dartnell Corp., 1987): 91–92.

8. Paul W. Farris and John A. Quelch, *Advertising and Promotion Management: A Manager's Guide to Theory and Practice* (Radner, PA: Chilton, 1983).

9. Roger A. Strang, *The Promotional Planning Process* (New York: Praeger, 1980).

10. Julian L. Simon, "Are There Economies of Scale in Advertising?" *Journal of Advertising Research* (June 1965): 15–20.

17 Measuring Promotional Performance

Promotion in Perspective

What Should Be Tested?
Should We Test?
When Should We Test?
How Should We Test?

Measuring Advertising Performance

Pretesting: Communication and Behavior
Concurrent Testing: Communication and Behavior
Posttesting: Communication
Posttesting: Behavior

Measuring the Performance of Sales Promotion

Pretesting Sales Promotion
Concurrent Testing of Sales Promotion
Posttesting Sales Promotion

Measuring the Performance of Public Relations

Exposures
Change in Awareness, Comprehension, or Attitude
Sales and Profit Contributions

Measuring the Performance of Personal Selling

Evaluating the Salesperson
Evaluating Personal Selling as a Part of Promotion

Consider This:

Tying Agency Pay to Performance

A major change is taking place in the relationship between advertising agencies and some of their clients. For the first time, clients are tying the compensation they pay agencies to the measured performance of the ads created by the agency. For example, General Foods is no longer paying the traditional 15 percent commission on media and production billings. Instead, its basic commission rate is now 13 percent, but it pays up to a three percent bonus to agencies that produce ads that General Foods rates highly.

RJR Nabisco, Inc., Campbell Soup Company, Hershey Foods Corp., and Nestlé Enterprises, Inc. have all adopted incentive-based plans. Often the plans include punishments as well as bonuses. A General Foods agency that receives an average rating doesn't get a bonus, and one that gets a below-average rating is likely to lose General Foods' business. Before the start of a campaign, General Foods works with its agencies to establish performance criteria. Then General Foods rates the agency's performance on each criterion, using a ten-point scale. At the top of the criteria list are sales volume and market share; the company wants to make sure the ads are having the desired effects. But because a product's sales are dependent on many factors that have nothing to do with advertising, General Foods makes sure that it includes other criteria in its agency evaluations.

How to measure an agency's performance is the thorniest question in performance-based pay systems. RJR Nabisco relies on advertising research rather than sales numbers. The research tells the company whether consumers remember an ad and what kind of emotional response they have to it. Making a consumer remember a product and feel good about it is about as much as a company can ask an ad to do.

In part because of the lack of a standardized measure of performance, some agencies are wary of the new system. They feel they may be penalized because of a product's inherent weaknesses, not because of the quality of their ads. But at least some of RJR Nabisco's agencies seemed happy with the switch. Under the commission-plus-incentive plan, a number of RJR's agencies received a 20 percent bonus, and for one company, that meant one million dollars.

Sources: Marcy Magiera, "Carnation Links Pay, Research," *Advertising Age* (March 6, 1989): 1. Walecia Konrad, "A Word from the Sponsor: Get Results or Else," *Business Week* (July 4, 1988): 66. David W. Stewart, "Measures, Methods, and Models in Advertising Research," *Journal of Advertising Research* (June/July 1989): 54–60.

A s noted in the opening vignette, one of the most difficult problems faced by the promotion manager is determining whether objectives have been achieved. This problem is primarily a result of the uncertainty surrounding the correct measures to use in making the assessment. Even major corporations such as General Foods disagree about what constitutes promotional performance. Is performance best measured through awareness, recall, attitude change, coupon redemption, sales, or some other indicator? Part of this confusion can be blamed on advertising agencies and research companies that convinced promotion managers that awareness and attitude measures are surrogates for more definite indicators, such as market share. The vignette indicates that the agencies and research companies are beginning to pay the price for their decisions. Some research professionals have reacted defensively; others have responded by addressing the concerns of the promotion manager. Simply stated, promotion managers want to be guaranteed that the measurement of promotional performance is done accurately and responds directly to the promotional objectives.

Complying with this request has been neither easy nor universal. There are serious and unresolved questions regarding what to measure, how to measure, and what the measurements mean. Two equivalent companies can take entirely different paths in measuring performance and yet derive equivalent findings. There are also pragmatic issues. Gearing up to do state-of-the-art research is quite expensive. It requires new technology, training, and time. Nevertheless, this research should be the goal of any promotion manager who wishes to engage in formal planning and strategic implementation. The intent of this chapter is to address the philosophical and pragmatic issues related to the evaluation of promotional performance.

Promotion in Perspective

Before we can sensibly address the problem of measuring performance, it would be helpful to reconsider what promotion is and what it is supposed to do. In Chapter 1, we defined promotion as persuasively communicating to target audiences the various components of the marketing program in order to facilitate exchange between the marketer and the consumer and to help satisfy the objectives of both. Implied in this definition is the understanding that all promotion is driven by one or more stated objectives. Established standards, however, are meaningless unless there is a valid mechanism for measuring to what extent they have been reached. The objectives of marketers range from the very subtle (for example, a slight repositioning of a brand) to the very direct (for example, market share). Overall, the task of promotion can be reasonably construed as disposing people to change attitudes and/or behavior as requested by the marketer.

This chapter is concerned with evaluative research, which measures the effectiveness of the promotional planning process. It differs from the research conducted to analyze target markets or to select media, which we discussed in earlier chapters. While evaluative research may take place at various times throughout the promotional process, it is carried out with the specific purpose of assessing the effects of various strategies. Thus evaluative research allows the promotion manager to evaluate the performance of specific program elements and provides input into subsequent situation analyses. It is a necessary ingredient of a continuing planning process.

In order to conduct evaluative research, the promotion manager should ask four related questions: What should be tested? Should we test? If so, when? And how?

What Should Be Tested?

The basic problem in assessing promotion is to relate a specific effort to specific results. Did the new Tylenol ad cause ad viewers to increase their understanding of the drug's benefits? Did the twenty-five-cent coupon for Chef Boyardee Chicken and Spirals increase its sales? Both the effort and the results are difficult to isolate. In addition, controversy surrounds the question of what measured results would qualify as effective promotion. The problem of assessing the short-term versus the long-term effects of promotion also remains unresolved. Top management often argues that unless the dollars spent on promotion generate sales, then they have been wasted. (The recent preference for sales promotion over advertising reflects this line of thinking.) Others argue that too many uncontrollable factors affect sales and market share for promotion to be held accountable for them.

As we discussed in Chapter 8, hierarchy of effects models provide one way of resolving this debate. In one version, consumers go through seven steps to arrive at the point of purchase: unawareness, awareness, knowledge, liking, preference, conviction, and purchase. Promotion should move consumers through these steps toward purchase. Thus each step

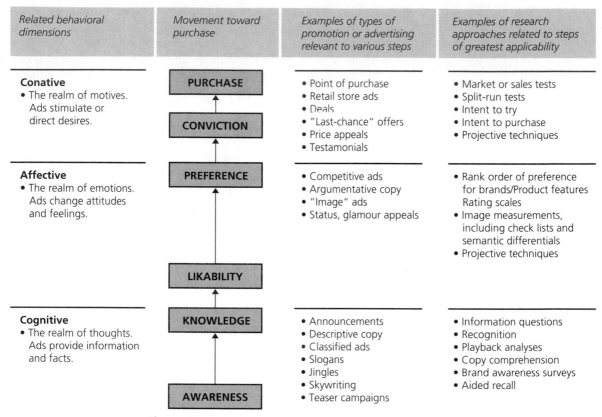

Related behavioral dimensions	Movement toward purchase	Examples of types of promotion or advertising relevant to various steps	Examples of research approaches related to steps of greatest applicability
Conative • The realm of motives. Ads stimulate or direct desires.	**PURCHASE** ↑ **CONVICTION**	• Point of purchase • Retail store ads • Deals • "Last-chance" offers • Price appeals • Testamonials	• Market or sales tests • Split-run tests • Intent to try • Intent to purchase • Projective techniques
Affective • The realm of emotions. Ads change attitudes and feelings.	**PREFERENCE** ↑ **LIKABILITY**	• Competitive ads • Argumentative copy • "Image" ads • Status, glamour appeals	• Rank order of preference for brands/Product features Rating scales • Image measurements, including check lists and semantic differentials • Projective techniques
Cognitive • The realm of thoughts. Ads provide information and facts.	**KNOWLEDGE** ↑ **AWARENESS**	• Announcements • Descriptive copy • Classified ads • Slogans • Jingles • Skywriting • Teaser campaigns	• Information questions • Recognition • Playback analyses • Copy comprehension • Brand awareness surveys • Aided recall

Figure 17.1

Forms of promotion as related to the hierarchy of effects model.
Adapted from Robert J. Lavidge and Gary A. Steiner, "A Model for Predictive Measurements of Advertising Effectiveness," Journal of Marketing *25 (October 25, 1961): 59–62. Permission granted by the American Marketing Association.*

suggests a legitimate objective for a promotional campaign. For each step, Figure 17.1 illustrates some appropriate forms of promotion and corresponding ways of measuring effectiveness.

In this text, we categorize all results as well as efforts into just two components: communication and behavior. That is, we assume that the effectiveness of promotion equals the extent to which the communication worked and, if appropriate, changed behavior.[1]

To fill in the details of the equation, managers should consider the objectives of the promotion. If a manager is evaluating the effectiveness of a 20-percent discount in a line of children's play clothes, for example, then measuring attitude change would not give the most useful information. There are many less expensive ways of evaluating effectiveness. Assume that the discount was offered in order to move 70 percent of the company's out-of-season merchandise. In measuring the effects of the discount, counting inventory before the discount was initiated and after would provide reliable sales results. Although sales-related objectives are appropriate for sales promotion and personal selling, this is not the case for advertising and public relations, which are somewhat removed from the creation of sales. Referring back to the hierarchy model in Chapter 8,[2] this basic difference in the appropriateness of sales-related objectives is reflected in the fact that the four middle elements (awareness, knowledge, liking, and preference) are all concerned with communication tasks via-à-vis advertising and public relations. That is, the primary strength of advertising and public relations is to communicate with a mass audience, providing enough salient information so that the product being advertised is now known, understood, and preferred by the consumer. Sales promotion and personal selling provide the impetus to take action. The impetus entails the necessary motivation (conviction) to get up and dial a toll-free number, visit a store, sign on the dotted line, pay cash, or hand over a Visa card (purchase).

Communication Factors   Recall from Chapter 7 that persuasive communication depends on the proper manipulation of the message, the source, the means of delivery, and the control of noise. Given the importance of these communication factors to effective promotion, it is necessary to determine the measurable elements in each as well as the techniques used to make these measurements. Determining the measurable elements will be addressed now; the discussion of techniques will be covered in the section detailing the specific promotional mix functions.

Message Variables   There are numerous elements in a typical promotional message. Words, music, color, visuals, layout, headlines, and the logo can all affect the outcome of a promotional message. All these message elements are more or less important to the various individuals involved in its creation. For example, the marketing manager or product manager who initiates the communication and provides the primary direction for its design is most concerned that the focal concept is delivered clearly through the message. A **focal concept** is the key idea(s) that the message contains. Sometimes the focal concept is very specific, such as product safety in the case of Volvo. In other cases, the focal concept is a general mood or attitude that the message is supposed to deliver. Coke ads suggest that drinking Coke and fun go together. The copywriter or commercial director may have an entirely different set of message variables to test. The copywriter is concerned with whether the headline attracts attention. Is it understood as intended? Are funny words perceived as funny? Is the long technical copy interesting to the reader? Is "25% off" easier to understand than "now $1.99"? The art director wants to know if the photograph works better than the line drawing. Is the red background more soothing than the yellow? The television commercial director is concerned with whether the 1950's rock 'n'roll background music turns some people off. Does the fast pace of the commercial distract the viewer from understanding the message? There are literally hundreds of questions such as these that are asked during and after the creative process. Because of testing and retesting every important element of a promotional message, it often takes weeks or months to produce positive results.

Source Variables   The source could be a celebrity, an animated character, a background voice, an actor, or someone singing a jingle. Key questions include whether the source that delivers the message creates the desired result. Factors to evaluate might include the following: the attitude change produced through the source, the trust or credibility associated with the source, the likability of the source, and the possibility that the source will dominate the message (that is, the consumer will not remember the name of the sponsor). This last concern becomes quite real with high-profile celebrities such as Bill Cosby, Bo Jackson, and Jay Leno. Should actors be used or real people? Although actors do a much better job delivering the message, they lose their credibility when we see them pretending to be a real person for four different advertisers during a particular evening. Some sources have a real saturation problem. The use of corporate CEOs as spokespeople has grown since the success of Lee Iacocca. Some top executives, however, do more harm than good. Once these source-related variables have been identified, there are a number of techniques available to measure attitude, likability, credibility, wearout, and so forth.

Delivery Variables   Promotion messages can be delivered in a variety of ways. Messages carried through advertising are normally delivered through the mass media, the topic of Chapter 14. A tremendous amount of research is available to support mass media decisions. The promotion manager can compare the effectiveness of one medium class with another (for example, newspaper versus television), specific vehicles within a class (station WTBS versus WGN, for example), size or length of the ad, and position in the vehicle. The promotion manager can specify very precise media objectives and be fairly sure that the measures are available to assess these goals.

Sales promotion messages can be delivered through conventional mass media as well as nonconventional media. For example, Campbell Soup Company can deliver a coupon for its new soup through print advertising, a free-standing insert, or a direct mail coupon drop. The company can also offer samples of the product at the point of sale by setting up a soup kettle at the end of a supermarket aisle and having a person pass out cups of soup. How is this variable evaluated? Campbell's promotional objective is to get the new product into 50 percent of U.S. kitchens within thirty days of market entry. Speed of coupon delivery, coupon redemption, and product trial are the responsibility of sales promotion. Measuring these factors is quite complicated, and sales figures are often considered surrogates of these other variables since sales creation is considered the strength of sales promotion.

The process becomes even more confusing when we consider public relations. In the case of publicity, counting the number of lines and/or stories appearing in the popular media is often considered an indicator of success or failure. But how does one compare the relative goodwill produced through a story in *Time* with a plant tour or the sponsorship of a 10K run? Goodwill is a very vague phenomenon; public relations still finds it difficult to develop objectives and measures that facilitate the selection of delivery mechanisms. More will be said about measuring public relations later in the chapter.

Even personal selling has the capability to compare delivery mechanisms. Issues such as the timing of message delivery, who should deliver the message, and the size of the message are all considerations. Typically, the measure of performance is sales. However, other intermediary measures might also be considered. Examples include the number of sales calls made, the percentage sold, the type of products sold, the cost per sale, and the profit per sale. A good sales manager is constantly taking measures such as these and making adjustments as needed. Paine Webber Investments, for example, discovered that it is very important that high-dollar accounts be serviced by older, successful investment advisors.

Behavioral Factors   The behavioral factors associated with promotion include intent to buy, purchase, and brand loyalty. In the hierarchy model, these factors lead up to conviction and purchase. We have already alluded to the difficulties in associating advertising with sales. Nevertheless, advertisers are faced with increasing pressure to produce sales. In some cases, advertisers are willing to opt for action measures that suggest an intent to buy but fall short of actual purchase. Among these action measures are brand choice, store visits, and contact (such as calls or written responses). These action measures are appropriate early in the product life cycle, when creating awareness or educating the consumer is a prerequisite to commitment. There may also be historical evidence showing a strong correlation between intention to buy and actual purchase, as is the case with high involvement products, such as automobiles and fashion.

Where these action measures prove unsatisfactory, advertisers have turned to sales tracking companies such as Nielsen Marketing Research, Information Resources, Inc., SAMI Market Segmentation Service, and

D. H. Macey & Associates. Companies such as these use three primary methods of obtaining sales data: monitoring warehouse shipments to resellers, cash register scanning at the stores, and conducting household diary panels. The ultimate sales test is to set up specific controls so that the advertiser can manipulate the ad as well as who receives it and then determine the sales results. Experiments can be done by the advertiser: test cities with comparable characteristics receive or do not receive the ad, and sales are measured. Experiments can also be done by research firms such as Behavior Scan, which has the capability of combining split-cable television (that is, different people on the cable system receive different versions of the ad or no ad) with checkout scanning equipment that is also tied to the specific cable subscribers.

Market share has also been a behavioral objective assigned to advertising. However, the connection is usually obscure, and advertising is considered only one of several variables that contribute to the increase or decrease in market share.

Sales promotion and personal selling consider all the behavioral variables just discussed. Moreover, since the connection is more obvious, sales promotion and personal selling have refined these measures. For example, sales promotion often considers incremental sales rather than sales. **Incremental sales** are the additional sales produced by the sales promotion. It eliminates people who would have purchased the product anyhow, regardless of the availability of a coupon, rebate, or price reduction. Personal selling often considers sales figures relative to profitability. In other words, the costs associated with producing one dollar in sales are just as important as the sales themselves. Likewise, the cost of gaining 1 percent of market share may be greater than the benefits.

Should We Test?

Several benefits come from testing promotional efforts. First, testing increases the efficiency of promotions by helping managers eliminate unproductive alternatives. The Nissan Motor Corp. USA found this to be the case when it introduced the Infiniti through a series of ads entitled "the rocks and trees approach" by critics. Initial tests showed that an automobile ad that does not show the car raises curiosity but does not give reasons to buy. The campaign was changed. Second, information from testing can help managers avoid disasters that can destroy the campaign or even the organization. A controversial Pepsi ad featuring Madonna was dropped after pretest results indicated that viewers perceived it as overly provocative and disgusting. In addition, testing gives a basis for future planning. Finally, tests provide feedback to those who create and implement the promotional campaign.

There are also problems that may preclude testing. First, testing costs a great deal of money. A complete testing program for one year ranges from one hundred thousand dollars to five hundred thousand dollars. Second, windows of opportunity for promotions can be very short and may not allow enough time for testing. Third, the adequacy of the testing instruments and the meaning of the results are often questionable. High recall scores may be more a reflection of an unusual appeal than effective communication. Fourth, testing can create internal tensions and squabbles. People may disagree about what to test, especially since management is reluctant to support tests that are not related to sales. Creative people, especially copywriters, resent having research dictate the words they must use. Finally, testing encourages people to engage in activities that increase ratings but have little to do with objectives.

To decide whether to test, managers should weigh the costs and benefits of testing. Unfortunately, most marketers tend either to ignore this step or to concentrate on just one or two key factors. The decision to test is often based on the testing capabilities offered by the marketer's agency or by the rationale, "If it ain't broke, don't fix it."

When Should We Test?

If testing is worthwhile, the next question addresses the timing of the testing process. The possible answers may be classified as pretesting, concurrent testing, and posttesting.

Pretesting (also known as evaluative research) is research conducted before the audience is exposed to the promotion. Pretests are useful when managers need to examine possible problems before resources are spent on the actual message. For example, a manager may want to know whether a potential spokesperson is credible. A survey might satisfactorily answer the question before the commercial is actually produced and distributed.

Concurrent testing evaluates the promotional effort while it is running in the marketplace. This form of testing may be the most difficult to implement and maintain, but it has several advantages. It allows the researcher to quickly determine to what extent the message is reaching the desired target market. Concurrent testing may also indicate whether the message is being interpreted properly and may measure the effects of the message. Most importantly, this technique allows adjustments to be made immediately.

Posttesting is research conducted after the audience has been exposed to the message, medium, or spokesperson. It is designed to determine to what extent the promotional objectives have been attained. It allows researchers to evaluate how well they did and then to make appropriate changes.

How Should We Test?

There are literally hundreds of specific tests used to evaluate promotion. However, all these measurement devices can be placed into three categories: experiments, surveys, and mechanical techniques.

Experiments give individuals a controlled exposure to the message, and the change in their opinion, attitude, or some measurable action is then evaluated. Experiments may take place in the laboratory or in the field. For example, an advertising agency designs three print ads in which the copy, illustrations, size, and other factors are all kept the same. The only element that is changed in the three ads is the spokesperson; one is African-American, one is Caucasian, and one is Asian. The objective of the experiment is to measure the effect of these manipulations on attitude toward the product. One thousand names are randomly selected from a master list. (In randomization, everyone has an equal chance of being selected or assigned.) Then these people are randomly assigned to view only one of the ads. All the people fill out the attitude questionnaire. Finally, statistical tests are conducted to determine the difference in attitude among the three groups.

An experimental design is valuable because it provides results that can be evaluated through the most advanced statistical tests in order to determine their validity and reliability. **Validity** means the concept is confirmed to be what it claims to be. **Reliability** means that the same results are repeated time after time. Companies balk at using experimental designs because of their high costs.

In a survey, interviews or questionnaires are used to obtain information about people's exposure to a particular message, medium, or person, and the resulting changes in their attitudes or actions. People are simply asked what they think, feel, or do. Statistical analysis of the responses yields a measure of correlations between the reports of exposure and the changes in attitude or action.

Like the experimental approach, the survey method requires that the researcher deal with conceptual and technical matters. If a survey is to have any use at all, the researcher must take care that the design of the sample, the questionnaire construction, and the interviewing methods do not bias the results. Surveys are much easier and faster to conduct than experiments. However, the fact that surveys do not meet the criteria of an experiment means that alternative factors could be producing the measured results.[3]

Mechanical measurement techniques collect information through a device. Physiological devices, the most common type of mechanical techniques, will be discussed later. These devices usually measure involuntary responses of the autonomic nervous system; thus these techniques offer objectivity. The use of these techniques tends to vary by agency size and commitment to this type of research technology.

Concept Review

1. Evaluative research helps determine whether promotion has reached its objectives and suggests ways to improve promotional efforts.
2. The evaluative process requires answers to four questions:
   a. What should be measured?
      (1) Communication factors, which include message variables, source variables, and delivery variables.
      (2) Behavioral factors, which include intention to buy, purchase, and brand loyalty.
   b. Should we test?
   c. When should we test?
      (1) Pretesting.
      (2) Concurrent testing.
      (3) Posttesting.
   d. How should we test?
      (1) Experimental approach.
      (2) Survey design.
      (3) Mechanical measurement.

Measuring Advertising Performance

Until the 1920s, copy and media testing were practically unknown in advertising. Today, they are a common part of the research efforts of most medium- and large-sized agencies. In addition, syndicated researchers conduct independent research. Since most of the performance research techniques were developed in the advertising industry, it is not surprising that most of the discussion will be in an advertising context. Essentially, managers in sales promotion and public relations have adapted these techniques for their respective fields.

Syndicated media research may be purchased directly by the advertiser, or it may be sold to agencies and provided to the clients. Usually done on a regular basis, it is designed to meet the needs of current as well as potential clients. As noted in Table 17.1, syndicated research is big business. The television rating services of A. C. Nielsen and the television and radio rating services of Arbitron Ratings Co. are well-known examples. Publication and audience research are done by companies such as the Simmons Market Research Bureau (SMRB) and Mediamark (MRI). Media trade associations such as the Newspaper Advertising Bureau (NAB), Audit Bureau of Circulations (ABC), and the Advertising Research Foundation (ARF) conduct syndicated research as well.

Tables 17.2 and 17.3 summarize studies of current practices in advertising research. Table 17.2 reports on a survey of ninety-four of the top ad agencies. The respondents were asked to indicate their usage patterns in areas of advertising research: (1) media factors, (2) sources of audience

Table 17.1   **The Top Twenty Research Companies**

Rank		Company, Headquarters	Gross U.S. Research Revenues	
1990	1989		1990	1989
1	1	A. C. Nielsen Co., Northbrook, Ill.*	$468.6	$426.0
2	2	Arbitron Co., New York	230.6	253.5
3	3	IMS International, Zug, Switzerland*	199.1	181.0
4	4	Information Resources Inc., Chicago	136.3	113.8
5	5	Westat, Rockville, Md.	74.8	65.9
6	6	M/A/R/C, Las Colinas, Texas	56.9	47.9
7	7	Maritz Marketing Research, Fenton, Mo.	53.2	46.1
8	8	MRB Group, Ealing, England	45.8	44.6
9	9	NFO Research, Greenwich, Conn.	45.5	42.0
10	11	Abt Associates, Cambridge, Mass.	43.4	37.9
11	12	Gallup Organization, Princeton, N.J.	40.5	37.0
12	10	Market Facts, Chicago	40.2	39.0
13	13	NPD Group, Port Washington, N.Y.	31.0	30.0
14	15	Walker Research, Indianapolis	28.8	26.5
15	14	Burke Marketing Research, Cincinnati	25.2	27.1
16	17	Intersearch, Horsham, Pa.	25.1	21.9
17	16	Starch INRA Hooper, Mamaroneck, N.Y.	22.7	22.4
18	18	Chilton Research, Radnor, Pa.	22.6	21.8
19	19	Research International, London	19.9	19.8
20	21	National Research Group, Los Angeles	18.0	14.0

Note: Dollars are in millions.

Reprinted with permission from *Advertising Age,* Vol. 62, No. 23 (June 3, 1991): 32. Copyright, Crain Communications, Inc., 1991.

data, and (3) methods for evaluating communication effects. The percentage reported reflects the number of people using each technique or measure. The results indicate that these top agencies measure media performance in terms of reach, gross rating points, CPM to target, average frequency, effective reach, and frequency distribution. The top three sources used when assessing audience data were Arbitron, A. C. Nielsen Company, and Simmons Market Research. Finally, communication effectiveness is measured primarily through recall, advertising exposure, awareness, and attentiveness.

In contrast to the general research-related findings shown in Table 17.2, the information in Table 17.3 reports on the specific type of television copy research used by a survey sample of 112 advertising agencies. The first column shows the number of agencies; the second translates this number into a percentage. The top three reported tests were evaluate finished ads (93.8 percent), undertake preliminary background or strategic research in preparation for advertising commercials (92.9 percent), and evaluate rough commercial execution of other formats prior to finished commercial (91.1

Table 17.2 Report on Media, Audience and Communication Measures Used in Advertising Research

Factors Evaluated in Media	Percent
Reach	90.4
Gross rating points	89.4
CPM to target	88.3
Average frequency	87.2
Effective reach	86.2
Frequency distribution	75.5
Quintile distribution	43.6
Others	30.8

Sources of Audience Data	Percent
Arbitron	92.6
A. C. Nielsen Company	78.7
Simmons Market Research	76.6
Mediamark Research, Inc.	63.8
RADAR	52.1
Media Records	45.7
The Birch Report	22.3
Monroe Mendelson	10.6
Others	40.5

Communication Effects Evaluated	Percent
Recall	58.5
Advertising exposure	52.1
Awareness	47.9
Attentiveness	43.6
Purchase	31.9
Recognition	24.5
Preference	18.1
Attitude toward brand	18.1
Prepurchase behavior	17.0
Comprehension	16.0
Interest	16.0
Knowledge	14.9
Intentions	12.8
Attitude toward ad	11.7
Conviction	8.5
Others	9.6

Source: P. J. Kreshel, K. M. Lancaster, and M. A. Toomey, "How Leading Advertising Agencies Perceive Effective Reach and Frequency," *Journal of Advertising* 14, no. 3 (1985): 32–38. Used with permission.

Table 17.3   **General Findings Regarding Copy Research**

Type of Copy Research	Number of Agencies	Percentage
Undertake preliminary, background, or strategic research in preparation for advertising campaigns.	104	92.9
Evaluate copy ideas, storyboards, other formats prior to rough commercial.	85	75.9
Evaluate tough commercial execution of other formats prior to finished commercial.	102	91.1
Evaluate finished commercials.	105	93.8
Evaluate television campaigns.	98	87.5
Test competitive commercials.	73	65.2
Test commercials for wearout.	29	25.9

Total number of respondents: 112

B. Lipstein *et al.* "Television Advertising Copy Research: A Critical View of the State of the Art," *Journal of Advertising Research* 24, no. 2 (April/May 1984): 21–25. Used with permission.

percent). It is interesting to note that two of the three techniques were pretests, and the top-rated test was a posttest. This fact suggests a strategic orientation in at least this facet of advertising. Correctly, advertising copy should be evaluated before being implemented.

The sophistication of tests of advertising performance has grown dramatically over the years, especially since the advent of the computer. Figure 17.2 shows the framework that will organize our discussion of these tests. Two warnings are worth noting. First, many of the techniques discussed can be employed in more than one of the six cells in the figure. Second, several of these techniques are used to assess performance of sales promotion and public relations as well.

Pretesting: Communication and Behavior

The appeal of testing an ad before running it in the media is obvious. The test might give some assurance of success before the money is spent. Although there is no sure-fire way of predicting success, certain methods of pretesting can give helpful information if used intelligently.[4] These methods include tests of consumer opinion or awareness, physiological measurements, readability tests, and test marketing.

Tests of Opinion or Awareness   *Opinion methods* is a catchall classification for the simplest method of evaluating ads. People readily give their opinions. When shown a proposed ad, they will state whether they think it

	Communication: Source, message media		**Behavior:** Psuedo-purchase, purchase
Pretests	• Focus groups • Checklists • Split-run • Readability	• Physiological • Direct mail • Theater • On-the-air	• Test marketing • Single-source
Concurrent	• Recall • Attitude • Tracking • Coincidental		• Single-source • Diaries • Pantry checks
Posttests	• Readership • Recall • Awareness	• Attitude • Association • Audience assessment	• Single-source • Split-cable • Inquiry • Sales counts

Figure 17.2

A matrix of evaluation measures used in promotion.

would get their attention, how interesting they think it is, which advertising claims they believe, and how likely they believe it is to cause them to buy the product or service. They will also compare ads on the basis of all of these functions and give opinions at any stage of an ad's development. Most opinion methods are simple, fast, and inexpensive.

Opinions may be solicited from any member of the general public—from the prospective consumer, to the creative person, to the advertising expert. However, researchers must watch out for pitfalls associated with each of these sources. People associated with the advertising business are usually prejudiced. This prejudice may be unconscious, based on allegiance to client brands or on conviction regarding the superiority of particular techniques. Conversely, when consumers give their reactions to ads, it is assumed that they try to report the influence of the advertising on themselves. In fact, however, consumers frequently try to give "expert" opinions on ads. This may be due to the assumption that the researcher expects them to be experts or the self-imposed idea that everyone is an expert on advertising because it is so pervasive and simple. In either case, it is common for individuals to want to report what they think other people like or dislike rather than to speak directly for themselves.

Opinions about behavior entail a special problem: they are likely to be speculative. When respondents are shown ads and asked such behavioral questions as whether the ads would catch their attention or motivate them to send in the coupon, the respondents can only guess.

Opinion ratings are usually made by interviewing respondents individually. When a sufficient sample has been obtained, the total is called a *consumer jury.* In a variation, respondents are brought together in a group in order to get the benefits of group discussions and judgments. Specific procedures used to obtain ratings include focus groups, program analysis, and on-the-air testing.

Focus Groups   A typical focus group consists of eight to ten people who are potential users of the product. A moderator usually supervises the group, providing direction and control. The format depends on what is being evaluated. For example, when Kellogg Co. wanted to test the concept "Corn Flakes are a high-fiber alternative," it conducted nearly a hundred focus groups of people from forty to fifty-five years old living throughout the United States. Some groups were all male; some, all female; and some, mixed. Groups were videotaped; then management evaluated the tapes.

Usually focus groups serve as a pretest device, but they are also useful for concurrent and posttesting. They may be used to evaluate copy, a concept, a product name, or a campaign. To compare ads for the same product, two or more ads are presented, and members of the group are asked: "Which of these ads do you like least?"

The rating given by focus groups appears to have a high positive correlation with the success of the ad. Therefore, there is general agreement that focus groups do reflect the consumer's point of view. Focus groups are also relatively inexpensive, and they can be organized and completed quickly.

Still, some problems in using focus groups do exist. Foremost is the inability to draw concrete conclusions from focus groups. These groups often view only parts of a promotion. Some are asked to make value judgments that are beyond their capabilities. For example, it would be impossible for members of a focus group to determine whether a particular ad would prompt them to buy the product without a great deal of additional information. It is therefore important not to have expectations of a focus group that are beyond its capabilities. Also, focus groups are small and may not be representative of the target market. Careful selection and evaluation of focus group participants is necessary to avoid this problem. Finally, since members are being paid they tend to say what they think the researcher wants to hear.[5] The group moderator must always be sensitive to this problem.

Program Analysis   Paul F. Lazarsfeld and Frank Stanton designed a technique specifically for broadcast media, called the *program analyzer;* it allows members of an audience to indicate likes and dislikes continuously throughout a program, including the commercials. Each seat in a room or auditorium is equipped with right-hand and left-hand switches for signal-

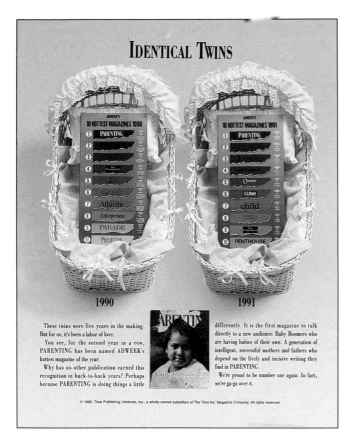

In this ad *Parenting* magazine relies on product comparison, a basic promotion tactic.

Comedy Central makes an appeal to potential advertisers with humor from a popular television skit and movie.

▶**Bulldozing**

If it's out there, it's in here. **NYNEX** Yellow Pages

These billboards—the first posted as a teaser, the second as a reveal—feature one of the clever puns made on listings in Nynex Yellow Pages.

The Bud Bowl, run during the Super Bowl, is a spectacular, multi-million-dollar ad series recognized for its uniqueness and creativity.

Courtesy of Anheuser-Busch International, Inc.

General Mills received a printing award for this design of its sample package for Golden Grahams.

Courtesy of Bemis Company, Inc. Used with the permission of General Mills, Inc.

An opportunity too small to miss.

Micromarketing works. And we can prove it.

The medium is VideOcart — an interactive computer screen on a supermarket cart, manufactured in alliance with IBM. Shoppers find it helpful, friendly and fun.

The strategy is radical localization — a message customtailored to the shoppers in a particular store, on a particular week, delivered precisely at the moment of maximum leverage. In the supermarket aisle, as the customer approaches your product.

It's a burst of national mar-

keting energy at the personal point-of-sale. In about a hundred major market stores by the end of '91. In over 2000 stores by the end of '93.

The result is unprecedented behavior change. Measured by actual scanner data — a 33% *average* sales increase. That's without price promotion. All for less than half the cost-perviewer of a TV spot delivered to a mass market sometime during the week before they shop.

The brands on board are some of the biggest names in marketing. P & G, Pepsico, Wal-Mart, Kraft/General Foods, Kroger,

Nabisco, Hershey and more. They know micromarketing is the future. They know VideOcart is the most powerful micromarketing medium available today. Do they know something you don't know?

To find out more...to explore the possibility of being the only VideOcart advertiser in your product category...call for our free VHS video. Or ask for a personal presentation. Call Jill Brusso at (312) 987-5000.

VideOcart
POWER AT THE POINT OF SALE.

Transit/pop media such as VideOcart are growing because of their ability to reach consumers during aperture.

Courtesy of VideOcart, Inc.

SPAM developed its "Gang '90" ad campaign and mountain bike offer to appeal to British teenagers—a large and important international market.

Photo of SPAM® luncheon meat provided courtesy of Geo. A. Hormel & Company and New Forge Foods Ltd.

An example of *Time* magazine's international marketing strategy.

Courtesy of Time, Inc.

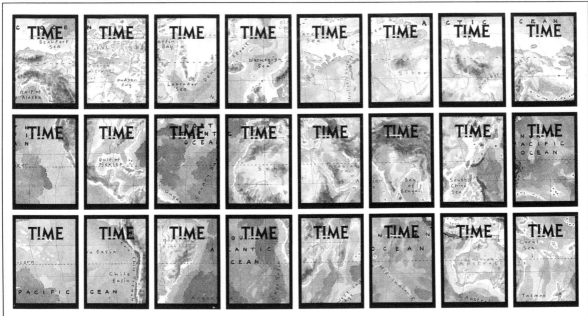

TIME Covers the World

And the world uncovers TIME: more people get their global news from TIME each week than from any other newsmagazine. More relevant articles. More diverse features. More authoritative interviews and profiles. More stunning photography. **Ask for TIME at your newsstand. To subscribe, please write to:**

TIME International, Ottho Heldringstraat 5, 1066 AZ Amsterdam, The Netherlands or FAX: (31 20) 61 72 068.

ing likes and dislikes as the presentation proceeds. When neither control is operated, it is assumed that the person is indifferent.

Other types of mechanical voting equipment have been developed, but some investigators find paper ballots satisfactory. Schwerin Research Corporation, for example, uses a procedure in which people mark their reactions on a ballot when numbers are flashed on a screen. Each critical point in the script has a number assigned to it, and the ballot has corresponding places in which to indicate favorable or unfavorable reactions.

Like many other procedures, program analysis permits researchers to apply a variety of approaches. Investigators usually go beyond collecting ballots. In order to test a group's memory of commercials, they may ask the members to write down all the sales points they can remember. Then the group is likely to be invited to discuss what they did and why they reacted to the program and commercials in a particular way at any selected point.

On-the-Air Tests   Another method of pretesting opinions, called *on-the-air testing*, analyzes a new commercial by comparing it with an existing commercial. The test commercial is aired in one or more cities, either in place of the regular commercial or in a new time period. Viewers who saw the new commercial are interviewed by telephone to determine their brand attitudes, their ability to play back the commercial message, and their brand knowledge. This information is compared with the responses of people who saw only the existing commercial.

Other Methods   Another popular way of pretesting opinions is the *ante-room trailer* method. A mobile home or recreation vehicle is parked near a shopping center. People are invited into the trailer and may be offered some incentive for participating. They enter a comfortable room that contains easy chairs, magazines, and a television set showing a prerecorded program. Test commercials are interspersed throughout the program. After the commercials have been shown, the subjects are interviewed and the effectiveness of each commercial is ascertained.

Tests of opinion with standardized format are readily available to any advertiser who has the necessary resources. However, agencies and advertisers have designed many opinion pretests in order to meet special needs. For example, the McCann-Erickson agency originated the *sales conviction test*. In this test, the agency asks heavy users of a particular product which of two ads would be most likely to convince them to buy the product. Then the interviewer asks them how they came to their decision and whether they disliked any part of the ad. Each test involves at least eighteen hundred interviewees in New York, Chicago, Los Angeles and in a distant suburb of each city. The final score, however, comes from an analysis of the respondents' comments rather than a straight counting of the votes for each ad.

Physiological Measures   Over the years, advertisers have been intrigued by the possibility of hooking people up to an intricate apparatus that will magically show which ad is best. Of the many techniques tried, five are worthy of special note:

1. *Eye movement tracking.* Participants are asked to look at a print ad or television commercial while a sensor aims a beam of infrared light at their eyes. A portion of the light reflected by the cornea is detected by the same sensor, which electronically measures the angle between the beam reflected by the cornea and the center of the eye's pupil. This information can be processed to show the exact spot in the ad or on the television screen where the eye is focused.

2. *The pupillometer.* This device measures pupil size when a person is exposed to a visual stimulus such as an ad or a package. The assumption is that pupil size increases with interest.

3. *The psychogalvanometer.* This device is a part of the lie detector apparatus. Two zinc electrodes are attached to the subject, one on the palm of the hand and the other on the forearm. When the subject is exposed to an ad, emitted perspiration on the palm results in lower electrical resistance, which is recorded on a revolving drum.

4. *The tachistoscope.* This device controls exposure to a print message in order that different parts of the ad can be shown without revealing the other parts, so that the tester can tell at what point each part is perceived. Advertisers can thus find out how long it takes respondents to get the intended point of an illustration or headline.

5. *Brain waves.* Through the use of the electroencephalograph (EEG), data can be collected from several locations on the skull, for several electrical frequencies at each location and up to one thousand times per second for each of these. By measuring the electrical activity in various parts of the brain, this technique can tell the researcher when the subject is resting or when there is attention to a stimulus.[6]

These mechanical tests suffer from several limitations. First, because respondents may feel threatened by these devices, the validity of the results is questionable. Second, there is a great deal of uncertainty as to what this machinery actually measures. Increased perspiration may provide a measure of emotional arousal, but is it a meaningful reflection of advertising effectiveness?

Readability Tests   An ad must be readable before it is set in final form. The length of the words and sentences and the impersonality of the writing are some of the elements that influence readability. Short words and short sentences make for easier reading.

The Flesch formula, developed by Dr. Rudolph Flesch, is a widely accepted technique for measuring readability. The formula uses four elements as they appear in 100-word writing samples:

Average sentence length

Average number of syllables

Percentage of personal words

Percentage of personal sentences

For example, Flesch contends that "fairly easy" sentences average 14 words in length and have 139 syllables per 100 words. The Flesch formula cannot be used for radio and television writing because a good announcer can make difficult copy sound very simple.[7]

Test Marketing   A *test market* might be used to test some element of an ad or a media mix in two or more potential markets. The test markets should be representative of the target market. Some cities, such as Buffalo, Indianapolis, and San Antonio, are considered excellent test markets because their demographic and socioeconomic profiles are very broad. That is, they have virtually all income, race, ethnic, and education categories represented within the city. In a typical test market, one or more of the test cities serve as controls while the others are the test. In the control markets, the researcher can either (a) run no advertising or (b) continue to run the old ad. The new ad is used in the test cities. Before, during, and after the advertising is run, sales results in the test cities are compared by checking inventories in selected stores. In addition, test markets can measure communication variables such as recall, awareness, and correct message interpretation. A rather sophisticated test market was recently conducted by Kraft Foods. Two versions of a cross-promotion print ad were tested. One version contained the headline, "1990 Super Choices Sweepstake" and the other, "The More Super Choices Coupons You Redeem, the More Chances You Have of Winning." Coupon redemption was used as the performance measure.[8] The second headline won.

Materials for Pretesting   Even if an ad has been completed, it may still be pretested before being distributed in case some elements have the potential for causing problems. To preview print ads, advertisers use several types of special material. In folio (short for *portfolio*) testing, a cross section of consumers examines a portfolio of ads, usually at home. A dummy publication is material especially prepared by a magazine or newspaper for testing purposes. It includes editorial material and fifteen to twenty ads. Copies of the dummy publication are distributed to a sample of consumers who are told to read the publication in a normal fashion. A tip-in is a page that is glued to the binding of a real magazine in such a way that a reader cannot tell it from the regular pages. Some copies will have the tip-in ad, some will have the regular ad. Later, people who have read the publication with the tip-in page are questioned.

For broadcast commercials, it is often too expensive to produce several completed commercials for testing. In such cases, animatic or live-action roughs fill in. An artist draws key frames of the commercial in sequence, then the drawings are photographed and a sound track recorded. Finally, a film is made of the drawings. Admittedly, a live-action rough does not contain all the elements of the finished commercial, but the essence is there. This technique is best suited for researching brand awareness and recall.

Concurrent Testing: Communication and Behavior

As mentioned earlier, concurrent testing takes place while the advertising is actually being run. There are three primary techniques: coincidental surveys and attitude tests assess communication effects; tracking studies evaluate behavioral results.

Coincidental Surveys   This technique is most often used with broadcast media. Random calls are made to individuals in the target market. By discovering what stations or shows are being seen or heard, the advertiser can determine whether the target audience is hearing the message and, if so, what information or meaning is being received. Although the surveys employed tend to ask basic information, this technique can be useful in identifying obvious problems.

Attitude Tests   In Chapter 5, we discussed the relationship between an attitude—an enduring favorable or unfavorable disposition toward a person, thing, idea, or situation—and consumer behavior. Researchers measure consumers' attitudes toward elements of an ad or toward a brand being advertised either concurrently or as a posttest. The measurement techniques for print and broadcast are virtually identical. Researchers survey individuals who were exposed to the ad, asking questions about the spokesperson, the tone of the ad, its wording, and so forth. Results that show strong negative attitude scores may prompt the advertiser to pull an ad immediately.

There are five techniques to measure attitudes in this context:

1. Direct questions. Respondents express how they feel toward a particular brand, ad, or element of the ad through an open-ended format.
2. Rating scales. Respondents indicate their feelings on a progressive scale (for example, from strongly agree to strongly disagree or from easy to use to very hard to use).
3. Checklists. Respondents check characteristics or feelings considered appropriate. For example, "Which is the primary benefit of Gold Medal Flour?": price, quality, convenience.
4. Semantic differential. Characteristics of concern are displayed as bipolar opposites on a seven-point scale. For example, "Would you say the Ford Escort is economical to drive? expensive to drive? How does it compare to the following competitors?
5. Partially structured interviews. General questions are asked in order to allow respondents to discuss the general topic area and reveal attitudes.[9] Elements of the ad are not addressed directly.

Attitudinal tests are viewed as testing an important element in promotional evaluation and are one step higher on the hierarchy. Similar to tests of opinions, attitude tests tend to reflect a more directed emotional reaction. That is, people have opinions about a great many things but hold strong attitudes about relatively few. There is also the assumption, right or wrong, that a favorable attitude is an indication that the person is more likely to purchase a brand than if he or she has an unfavorable attitude. There is little solid evidence that this correlation is always accurate. In addition, the ability to accurately measure attitudes about any subject is challenged by many experts in the field.

Tracking Studies   *Market tracking* studies follow the purchase activity of a specific consumer or group of consumers over a specified period of time. These studies combine conventional marketing research data with information on promotional spending. Compared with other tests, tracking studies provide fuller integration of data and a more complete view of the market.

Researchers use market tracking for both concurrent testing and post-testing. It may serve two basic objectives: (1) to show where the marketer stands in terms of sales or market share in respect to the competition, at a point in time after implementing some promotion; and (2) for reassessment, that is, to help the marketer understand how the market responds to changes he or she made in the promotion strategy.

Tracking studies evaluate both copy and media, and they influence a wide range of decisions. The primary criterion, however, remains purchase. Higher sales for one creative or media strategy, compared to those produced by an alternative strategy, implies that the former strategy is better. Tracking studies have had an impact on decisions to abandon as well as to continue advertising. They have guided promoters to change copy and to alter a campaign strategy. Because spending information is integrated into the analysis, much of the impact of tracking studies deals with decisions about media. Tracking studies have influenced definitions of the target market, the selection of vehicles, the schedule, and the mix between advertising and sales promotion, as well as the media mix.

Several methods are used to collect tracking data: wave analysis, consumer diaries, pantry checks, and single source.[10]

Wave Analysis   This technique assumes that the effects of advertising build over time and that multiple measures provide a clearer picture of this phenomenon. Wave analysis involves a series of interviews during a campaign. The process begins with a set of questions asked of a random sample of consumers on a predetermined date. The first question usually qualifies the person as someone who remembers hearing or seeing the ad. Once the person is qualified, a series of follow-up questions is asked. The answers serve as a benchmark and allow adjustments in the message content, media choice, and timing. Perhaps two months later, another series of random calls is made and the same questions are asked. The second wave is compared with the first. The process may continue until management is satisfied with the market penetration.

Consumer Diaries   Sometimes advertisers ask a group of representative consumers to keep a diary while a campaign is being run. The consumers may be asked to record activities such as brand purchased, brands used for various activities, brand switches, media usage, exposure to competitive promotions, and use of coupons. The advertiser can then review these diaries and determine factors such as whether the message is reaching the right target audience and if this audience is responding to the message as intended. Although the technique is limited in terms of the amount and accuracy of the information obtained, it has served well as an early warning system. One common finding from consumer diaries is the indication that no attitude or behavioral change has occurred because of exposure to the campaign. Frito-Lay is a major user of this technique.

Pantry Checks   The pantry check provides much of the same information as the diary method but requires little from the consumer. A researcher goes to homes in the target market and asks what brands or products have been purchased or used recently. In one variation of this procedure, the researcher counts the products or brands currently stocked by the consumer. The consumer may also be asked to keep empty packages, which the researcher then collects and tallies. The purpose is to correlate product usage with the introduction and completion of the campaign.

Single-Source Tracking   Thanks to scanners, combined with computer technology and data on the use of electronic media, researchers are very close to showing a causal relationship between advertising and sales. To set up a *single-source tracking system,* researchers first recruit people living in a particular market to join a consumer panel. The system has four elements:

1. Participants receive a card (with an identification number) that they give to the checkout clerk each time they make a purchase in a super-market. Scanners identify the person and record his or her purchases so researchers know who they are and what they buy.

2. The panel members (who are all cable subscribers) are split into matched groups, with each group receiving a different version of a television ad. Electronic test market services transmit the appropriate commercial to the appropriate home so the advertiser knows which household sees which commercial.

3. Meters record the television viewing by panel members. Thus researchers know whether they saw the commercial, when they saw it, and how many times they saw it.

4. Print advertising, coupon distribution, and other promotional activity are all controlled. Researchers therefore know what else influences a household's decision to buy or not to buy.

The possibilities for isolating single variables in electronic test markets are almost limitless. Researchers can increase the frequency of advertising or try a different media schedule. They can see whether an ad emphasizing product convenience will stimulate sales to two-career families. They can try an ad that plays up the product's fiber or vitamin content or compare the effectiveness of a two-for-one promotion and a cents-off coupon.

There are only three electronically based single-source services: Arbitron's Scan America, Nielsen's Scan Track, and Information Resource's Info-Scan. In early tests, Arbitron reported that Scan America improved the efficiency of advertising (in terms of reaching the client's target audience) by an average of 43 percent.[11]

Critics contend that current single-source data systems are just fancy versions of the old paper-and-pencil diary and provide little insight into which elements in the promotion are making a difference and why the consumer reacts in a particular manner to particular cues. New techniques,

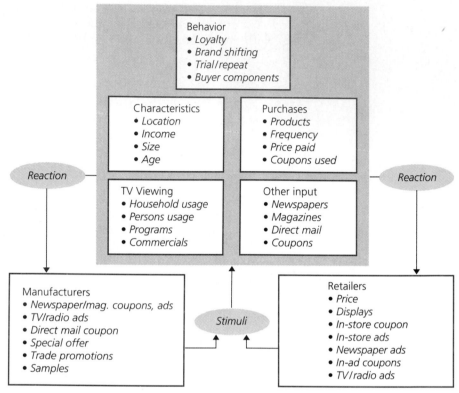

Figure 17.3

The Nielsen Scantrack system.
Laurence N. Gold, "The Evolution of Television Advertising–Sales Measurement,"
Journal of Advertising Research *(June/July 1988): 24. Used with permission.*

such as the Nielsen Scantrack household panel, address these limitations. Figure 17.3 outlines the Scantrack system. Using multiple regression techniques combined with current scanning data, researchers can control specific elements and calculate estimates of errors.

Posttesting: Communication

More testing occurs after the advertising has run than before, even though resources have already been spent on the ad. The popularity of posttests is explained in part by the limitations of pretesting. In addition, posttests indicate who listened to the message and can thereby provide a basis for planning future messages. The most widely used methods of posttesting fall into three categories: readership, recall, and attitude change.

Readership (Recognition) Daniel Starch is credited with being the primary developer of readership (recognition) tests. Readership tests provide a mechanism for breaking a print ad into its more important components (that is, headline, visuals, body copy, logo) and then how these elements are remembered by a sample of readers. The intent of the test is to show advertisers that the mere presence of an ad does not mean that readers notice it. The test goes as follows:

1. The Starch organization sends copies of a recent issue of a magazine or newspaper to a certain number of interviewers.

2. The interviewers find a certain number of people who saw the publication (within ten days after the date of publication for weeklies).

3. The interviewer goes through an unmarked copy of the publication with respondents and asks them to indicate the ads they read. When the ads are a half page or larger, the interviewer asks respondents which components they saw.

To assure high-quality results, no respondent is asked to view more than one hundred ads, and each respondent starts at a different point in the publication.

Starch regularly covers most of the major magazines. The expense of the readership tests is borne partly by the publishers, which use the results to bolster sales, and partly by ad agencies, which use the results to indicate the impact of an ad. The agencies receive copies of the magazine with a set of stickers on each ad showing what percentage of men and women observed each part; Figure 17.4 shows an example. Each ad is evaluated in terms of several criteria: (1) *noted* includes the percentage of people who remembered seeing the ad, (2) *associated* includes those who not only noted the ad but also saw or read some part of it that clearly indicated the brand or advertiser, and (3) *read most* includes the percentage who read half or more of the written material.

Readership tests allow the advertiser to compare ads across several dimensions, such as color, size, and copy. This technique also suggests which elements are most successful in gaining attention. Against these strengths, three weaknesses should be weighed. Probably the most important is the fact that the Starch test measures readership, but readership does not necessarily translate into sales or penetration of an idea. Another limitation is the danger that readership scores will lead advertisers to use trick means of getting high readership. Finally, results can be misleading, because readers are frequently confused. They are often unsure whether they saw a particular ad in one magazine or another, or if they really saw it at all.

Recall Tests Like the readership test, the recall test depends on the memory of the respondent. In readership tests, researchers show specific ads

Figure 17.4

An example of the Starch readership test results.
Courtesy of Shell Oil Company. Reprinted with permission from Starch/INRA/Hooper.

to respondents. In contrast, *recall tests* give little or no aid to respondents because the object is to measure the penetration of the ad.

Perhaps the most famous recall test is the Impact service offered by Gallup and Robinson, a prominent research firm. Before respondents are interviewed, they must answer questions to prove that they have read the magazine. After being accepted, they receive cards showing the names of all the products advertised in full or double pages in the issue. After respondents have listed each ad they think they have seen, they are asked to tell what the ad looks like. They are next asked to tell all they can about what the advertiser said—what the sales points were, what message the advertiser tried to get across, and the like. Respondents are also asked to tell the interviewer what they got out of the ad. Next they are asked whether the ad made them want to buy the product or find out more about it. And finally, the interviewer asks questions to find out whether the respondent is a prospect for the product advertised.

The Impact method is designed to measure the depth of impression an ad leaves on the reader's mind. Three dimensions of an ad's impression are reported: proven name registration (the percentage of qualified readers who can recall the ad and describe it with the magazine closed), idea penetration (the respondent can describe the contents of the ad), and conviction (the respondent wants to see, try, or buy the product).

To evaluate television commercials, Burke Research Corporation has developed a *day-after recall* test. The day after a commercial is aired, interviewers conduct telephone interviews with a sample of television viewers to determine the extent of brand name recognition as well as recall of various selling points communicated by the commercial. Typical scores range from 15 percent to 30 percent recall.

Recall tests do a good job of providing information on the penetration of copy. They also help gauge the extent to which a message provides the correct impression. On the negative side, there is not necessarily a relationship with sales. Recall tests are also quite expensive, and not all companies can afford them. There is also the problem that some people have better memories than others. Recall tests cannot account for these differences. Also, various elements that are part of general communication (for example, stories adjoining the ad, poor reproduction quality) can become confused with the advertising message.

Attitude Change Measures When used for posttesting, attitude measurement tests generally try to assess the effectiveness of advertising or other promotion in changing the evaluation of the company and/or its brands. As noted earlier, it is assumed that a favorable change in attitude predisposes people to buy a product. Recall and attitude tests are often combined in an attempt to determine if there are major differences between consumers who remember the advertising messages and those who do not. Attitude tests at this stage in the process are also used to measure changes in consumer perceptions of a brand or measure degrees of acceptance of various claims made in the advertising.

Because attitude change is perceived to have more bearing on purchase than recall, attitude measures are highly regarded and heavily used by many promotion managers. In addition, testing attitudes can be done with ease and minimum expense. Nevertheless, there are serious problems associated with attitudes and their measurement. Although a promotion manager assumes that he or she is measuring attitude toward the brand, attitudes toward ad execution and a host of other factors are often being tapped instead.

Posttesting: Behavior

Although most marketers feel the ultimate payoff from advertising should be a change in behavior—phone response, store visit, or direct sales—measuring advertising's contribution to sales has proven extremely difficult and expensive. Nevertheless, techniques are available for getting at the sales effectiveness of advertising, and researchers continue to experiment with new and better testing methods. Inquiry tests and sales tests are discussed in this section.

Inquiry Tests   The idea of checking the effectiveness of ads through inquiries is an old and obvious one. The thinking behind the test is simple enough. The advertiser runs a certain number of ads and offers some inducement to reply to them. The offer may be a booklet, a sample of the product, a toll-free number, or something else of value. This approach then divides the cost of the ad by the number of inquiries to find the cost per inquiry.

Inquiry testing may be used to check media, individual ads, or campaigns. To check the effectiveness of two ads, a promoter might run ad A one day and ad B the next in the local paper. The ad that produces the most inquiries per dollar is best.[12]

Another version of the inquiry test is the split-run test. Split-run refers to the practice of testing ads by running two or more different versions of the same ad on the same issue date but in different editions of a newspaper or magazine. The different ads appear on the same day in identical positions. Any element of the ad may be checked—copy, illustration, headline, coupon redemption, or readership. In some instances, the advertiser tests four entirely different ads.

Split-run is also available on cable television. The cable system is able to show different commercials for the same product in different households simultaneously. Later, viewers' opinions are surveyed by phone, mail, or personal interview.

Split-run testing can be used as a pretest or posttest. Sometimes a split-run test is conducted on alternative versions of a completed ad. If a company has produced different versions of an ad for different market segments and wants to find out whether a standardized ad would suffice, posttesting with a split-run may provide the answer.

There are several advantages associated with inquiry testing. The results indicate that the person not only read or saw the ad but also took some action. Action is a much stronger indicator than recall or awareness. Moreover, there is fairly good control of the variables that influence action, especially if split-run is used. However, one can question the sincerity of a person who expresses an interest in the product or service being offered. Also, unless one element is being modified, one is never sure why one ad is better than another. Finally, inquiry tests are time consuming; it may take three to four months before replies are measured.

Sales Tests   In previous sections, we have discussed attempts to evaluate the relationship between advertising and sales. There are several posttests that presumably reflect a relationship between a particular ad and a particular sale.

Comparing past sales with current sales is a common approach, particularly with the big catalog houses like Sears, Roebuck and Co. and Montgomery Ward. These businesses assume that a particular ad placed in a catalog is responsible for the sales generated. If sales increase from year to year, the credit is given to the ad. This is a type of direct marketing, the subject of the next chapter.

Field tests are also used to examine the impact of ads on sales. For example, various ads may be run in several comparable markets; then the difference in sales is analyzed. Matched groups of consumers can also be exposed to different ads.

<table>
<tr><td>Concept
Review</td><td>1.</td><td>Consumer opinion or awareness tests, the most common type of pretest, query consumers about different facets of an ad. This information can be gathered through consumer juries, focus groups, program analysis, and on-the-air testing.</td></tr>
<tr><td></td><td>2.</td><td>Mechanical devices measure physiological responses to advertising.</td></tr>
<tr><td></td><td>3.</td><td>Readability tests examine the various components of the ad that make it more or less readable.</td></tr>
<tr><td></td><td>4.</td><td>Test marketing allows the researcher to test various elements of the ad by showing different versions in different test markets.</td></tr>
<tr><td></td><td>5.</td><td>Live-action roughs allow the researcher to test a very rough version of a television commercial.</td></tr>
<tr><td></td><td>6.</td><td>Coincidental surveys randomly contact consumers and ask about ads seen.</td></tr>
<tr><td></td><td>7.</td><td>Attitude tests assess strong positive or negative consumer attitudes after exposure to an ad.</td></tr>
<tr><td></td><td>8.</td><td>Tracking studies attempt to match the ad with related behaviors. Methods include the following:</td></tr>
</table>

a. Wave analysis, which compares the results of interviews at various points in time;

b. Consumer diaries, consumer records of purchases and ads seen or heard;

c. Pantry checks, inventories by a researcher of products purchased by the consumer; and

    d. Single-source tracking, in which consumers' purchases are recorded through scanners and correlated with their television viewing.
9. Posttesting to evaluate communication may use the following:
    a. Readership (recognition) tests, which attempt to gauge who is seeing an ad and to what extent.
    b. Unaided recall tests, which assess how much of an ad the respondent can remember.
    c. Attitude change measures, which compare attitude scores before and after exposure to the ad.
10. Posttesting to evaluate behavioral effects of advertising may use the following:
    a. Inquiry tests, which record various responses consumers make to some element of the ad.
    b. Sales tests, which compare the differences in sales before and after exposure to the ad.

Measuring the Performance of Sales Promotion

Measuring the effectiveness of sales promotion can be just as complicated as measuring the effectiveness of advertising. Part of this complexity is a result of the nature and diversity of sales promotion objectives. Recall from Chapter 10 that four proactive objectives were noted: (1) to create additional revenue or market share, (2) to enlarge the target market, (3) to create a positive experience with the product, and (4) to enhance product value and brand equity. Reactive objectives were also delineated: (1) to match competition, (2) to move inventory, (3) to generate cash, and (4) to go out of business. Several of these objectives are directly related to sales, and many of the same sales-based measurement techniques discussed earlier are also used with sales promotion. Intermediate objectives, such as trial purchase, trading up, and multiple purchases, are more difficult to measure and require customized measures developed by sales promotion managers. Sales promotion also attempts to reach communication objectives, such as awareness and attitude change, through an increase in perceived value. Although awareness and attitude are legitimate objectives, coming up with valid ways to measure these responses and separating the effect of the media have proven very difficult.

    A second reason for the complexity in measuring sales promotion performance revolves around the organizational structure supporting sales promotion. Two dimensions of the structure are particularly relevant. First, sales promotions are often delivered to the end user through one or more resellers. The effectiveness of a sales promotion is therefore dependent on the abilities of the reseller as well as on the promotional strategy. Wholesalers and retailers who actively support a marketer's sales promotion can greatly enhance its performance. The opposite is also true. A second organizational problem stems from the fact that sales promotion services are as diverse as the many activities that fall under the umbrella of sales promotion. Some service companies build trade show booths or supply audiovisual equipment for sales promotion events. Others plan or implement promotion strategies. No matter how broad or narrow their scope of operations, all these suppliers have assumed the categorical title of sales promotion agency. The use of this title complicates the design of meaningful data collection measures since many agencies deal only with a very small part of sales promotion and the cost of doing research is prohibitive.

Despite these limitations, a great deal of effort has been devoted to improving the quality of sales promotion performance measures. Simple measures, such as counting the number of coupons redeemed, are still used and provide valuable information. Advanced mathematical models have recently found their way into sales promotion testing. For example, elaborate regression models are able to determine the contribution of various sales promotion tactics on sales. Sales promotion has borrowed heavily from advertising as well. There are definite similarities, and the use of advertising performance measures in sales promotion along with the pretest, concurrent test, and posttest framework appears appropriate. There is one major difference, however, between the evaluation of advertising and the evaluation of sales promotion. Evaluations of advertising tend to emphasize communication measures. For sales promotion, evaluation tends to focus on behavioral measures. As the field of sales promotion grows in sophistication, the evaluation of communication variables will increase.[13]

Pretesting Sales Promotion

In general, sales promotion managers are reluctant to pretest. Short lead time and concern for alerting competitors are two reasons for this hesitation. Instead, managers tend to rely heavily on experience ("What worked before will work again") and determine that sales promotion is best evaluated through sales, its ultimate goal. Although experience and sales are important, there are benefits in pretesting before spending the money or committing unresolvable strategic mistakes. Pretests consider communication and behavioral variables. Since many of these measurement techniques were discussed earlier, only brief mention will be made in the discussion that follows.

Pretesting Communication   There is a wide variety of measures used to pretest the communication elements of sales promotions. In addition to the typical communication elements found in advertising (that is, headline, copy, and visuals), an overriding communication element contained in most sales promotions is perceived value. **Perceived value** is the calculation the consumer makes in his or her mind whereby the extra value contained in the sales promotion is compared to the risks in accepting the offer. For example, a consumer determines whether 40 percent off on an unknown brand of shoes is worth the risk of buying an unfamiliar product. Some promotions—price-offs, bonus packs, rebates and refunds, and trade coupons—provide an immediate value. Others, such as premiums and continuity programs, give gifts to enhance value. A third group—samples, demonstrations, warranties, contests, and sweepstakes—provides a promised or implied value. Measuring perceived value is complicated. Consumers might be asked to evaluate the trade-off through a survey questionnaire. Or, the researchers can vary the level of value through discounts and rebates and assess how consumers respond to each level.

This assessment can be done through several different devices. Focus groups and consumer panels are common. Other techniques include the ballot method, portfolio tests, the jury method, and mall intercepts. The *ballot method* consists of mailing a printed ballot to a list of consumers. The sales promotions to be evaluated are illustrated and some additional information is given about each one. Consumers are asked to vote for the one they like best and return the ballot to the research firm. *Portfolio tests* are similar to the ballot method except a portfolio of sales promotions is developed and shown to consumers in person. While portfolio tests are more expensive than the ballot method, the information obtained is considered more accurate. The *jury method* is a combination of the previous two techniques except the jurors are paid for their evaluation and may be knowledgeable about sales promotions. The *mall intercept* technique involves stopping people at random in a mall and showing them the various promotions for evaluation. Although print and television can be tested, it is the most expensive device.

Pretesting Behavior   The most common device used to pretest the behavioral response to sales promotion is the market test. Depending on the specific sales promotion technique, the behavioral response considered could be trial purchase, purchase, repeat purchase, incremental purchase, and so forth. We have already discussed the process of market testing. In sales promotion pretesting, market tests usually consist either of testing two separate markets against each other or matching several stores in the same market against one another. In either case, the sales promotion device or program being tested is the only variable manipulated. All else is kept constant.

Pretesting Sales Promotion with Resellers   If resellers are unhappy with the sales promotion effort, they will either reject it outright or give it only partial support. It is therefore important to get the evaluation of resellers before implementation. It is possible to pretest with resellers some aspects of sales promotion programs—particularly materials that are used in-store or that rely on the reseller's cooperation to make them work. The easiest way to pretest a sales promotion program is simply to go to several key retailers or wholesalers and discuss the plan with them. It is occasionally more efficient to contact a third party, such as a marketing organization, that has strong ties with resellers.

Concurrent Testing of Sales Promotion

Concurrent testing is evaluating the performance of sales promotion while it is still running. As noted in the advertising section, this allows the promotional strategists to modify the sales promotion in order to increase performance or eliminate it to reduce negative consequences. For sales promotion, essentially all concurrent testing is done in terms of sales or some variation of sales. Historically, sales data were collected daily or weekly and various comparisons were made. For example, matched markets were compared, results were compared with forecasts, and sales among competing stores were compared. Thanks to advances in scanner research capability, sales information can be combined with a great deal of consumer information to provide a very elaborate analysis of a specific sales promotion device or program. For marketers who do not have access to such technology, traditional sales comparisons are still employed.

Posttesting Sales Promotion

Since the stated objective of sales promotion is to create sales, it is not surprising that most of the efforts to develop valid and reliable measures of performance are found at the posttest stage. Although sales and market share remain the predominant areas of interest, communication and behavioral factors are also considered.

Communication Posttest Measures   Usually, the information sought to measure the effectiveness of communication elements relates to consumer awareness and attitudes. The information-gathering devices, however, are much simpler than the techniques used in advertising research. For example, the most common methods for measuring consumer awareness and attitudes are telephone calls, mailed questionnaires, and personal interviews. Direct mail is the least expensive method and personal interviews by far the most expensive. The information sought is usually related to changes in consumer awareness, attitude, or actions in reference to a specific sales promotion event. As noted in the Promotion in Focus section, measuring the effectiveness of sales promotion events is not easy.

Posttesting is also done through in-store observations and interviews and follow-up survey interviews with responders and nonresponders to a promotion. In-store observations and intercept interviews with shoppers at the point of purchase are particularly relevant for store-distributed promotions such as samples and premiums.

Promotion in Focus

Sponsoring the Event, Not the Broadcast

Sporting events are gold for advertisers. If viewers come to associate a product with something they feel passionately about—their favorite NFL football team, for instance—they may wind up feeling passionate about that product, much to its manufacturer's delight.

The television networks understand how valuable such association can be for marketers. They have been paying more each year for sports broadcasting rights and demanding more from advertisers for each 30-second spot. In 1991, for instance, the three big television networks paid over $1 billion for broadcast rights to sporting events, 85 percent more than they paid in 1989, which meant they needed to collect $3.3 billion in ad revenue to keep their profit margins. The resulting high costs of commercials during sports events broadcasts is one of the factors leading many companies to consider sponsoring the events themselves, using on-site marketing instead of commercials.

One concern of many companies considering sponsorships is the difficulty of knowing what effect the sponsorship has on the public. Advertisers are used to measuring viewers' responses to commercials, but how do you measure the effect of a billboard in deep center field or the logo on the side of a race car? Some consultants tackle this challenge by using surveys of event participants and by auditing the sales of a sponsor's products in the event area. Others are trying to equate a sponsor's name exposure with minutes of television commercials. Joyce Julius & Associates watches broadcasts of sports events and adds up the seconds that TV viewers can clearly see a sponsor's brand or logo.

To find out how cost-effective the sponsorship is, Joyce Julius calculates what the exposure time would cost if it were bought as television commercial time. The consultants then compare this figure to the sponsor's investment. Because event sponsoring tends to require a good deal of preparation by the sponsor, Joyce Julius feels that a sponsor should get exposure worth four times its investment.

Being able to measure a return on investment has attracted a number of companies to event sponsorship. These companies have also found that people watching sporting events tend to notice who's sponsoring it, and a majority come away with favorable impressions of the sponsors. So as the price of air time continues to rise, advertisers may increasingly find alternatives to standard commercials.

Source: Scott Hume, "Sports Sponsorship Value Measured," *Advertising Age* (August 6, 1990): 22.

Behavioral Posttest Measures   Techniques are available that assess the extent to which sales promotion affects the behavior of resellers and consumers. Monitoring sales is the most common technique. Data-gathering techniques include market testing and tracking studies. The interpretation of these figures varies. For example, traditional break-even analysis can be employed. First, fixed costs and variable costs of the promotion are determined; second, the variable contribution margin of the brand is determined; and, finally, break-even sales volume for the promotion is calculated. Multiple regression analysis is also applicable. This statistical technique estimates the contribution of several variables acting jointly on a single dependent variable—sales. By its basic nature, the analysis of sales promotions tends to fit this technique well. Finally, there are statistical models built into the scanner systems that can provide a very detailed analysis.

Measuring the Performance of Public Relations

Ascertaining the results of a public relations effort is, for several reasons, the most neglected branch of the art. Such evaluation deals with that most difficult thing to measure—changes in human opinion. Public relations contribution is difficult to measure because it is used along with other promotional tools. If PR is used before the other tools come into action, its contribution is easier to evaluate.[14] Because evaluation of the results of public relations is difficult, it is also expensive. However, once an organization feels that a public relations effort is reasonably successful, it is usually inclined to spend a lot of money to estimate the degree of success.

This evaluation process may be informal or scientific. It may involve a few people seated around a table or a massive survey. It can take a few hours or a few weeks. Basically the process seeks to answer the question, "How did we do?" As is the case with all promotional elements, public relations needs to understand to what extent its programs achieved objectives.

In Chapter 12, we described some of the primary methods used to evaluate a public relations effort: focus groups, content analysis, monitoring, and informal observations. These methods can be used to measure exposure, psychological change, or behavioral change.

Exposures

The easiest measure of PR effectiveness is the number of exposures created in the media. Publicists supply the client with a clipping book showing all the media that carried news about the product and a summary statement such as the following:

Media coverage included 3,500 column inches of news and photographs in 350 publications with a combined circulation of 79.4 million; 2,500 minutes of air time on 290 radio stations and an estimated audience of 65 million; and 660 minutes of air time on 160 television stations with an estimated audience of 91 million. If this time and space had been purchased at advertising rates, the cost would have amounted to $1,047,000.

This exposure measure is not very satisfying. There is no indication of how many people actually read, heard, or recalled the message nor what they thought afterward. There is no information on the net audience reached since publications overlap in readership. Because publicity's goal is reach, not frequency, it would be useful to know the number of unduplicated exposures. Nor does this exposure measure indicate whether these figures reflect positive or negative coverage. However, there is evidence that better exposure measures are on the horizon.

Change in Awareness, Comprehension, or Attitude

A better measure is the change in product awareness, comprehension, or attitude resulting from the PR campaign (after allowing for the impact of other promotional tools). For example, how many people recall hearing the news item? How many told others about it (a measure of word of mouth)? How many changed their minds after hearing the news item? The Potato Board learned, for example, that the number of people who agreed with the statement "Potatoes are rich in vitamins and minerals" went from 36 percent before the campaign to 67 percent after the campaign, a significant improvement in product comprehension.

Sales and Profit Contributions

Sales and profit impact, if obtainable, are often the most satisfactory measure of the results of public relations. For example, sales of 9-Lives increased 43 percent at the end of the "Morris the Cat" PR campaign. However, advertising and sales promotion had also been stepped up, and their contribution must be allowed for. Suppose total sales increased $1,500,000; based on experience, management estimates that PR contributed 15 percent of the total sales increase. Then the return on PR investment is calculated as follows:

Total sales increase	$1,500,000
Estimated sales increase due to PR (15%)	225,000
Contribution margin on product sales (10%)	22,500
Total direct cost of PR program	− 10,000
Contribution margin added by PR investment	$ 12,500
Return on PR investment ($12,500/$10,000)	125%

Measuring the Performance of Personal Selling

Because of the typical organizational separation, the performance measures developed in personal selling are quite different from those found in other areas of promotion. To begin with, the personal selling function is evaluated by the sales manager and the marketing manager. Their task is twofold: (1) to evaluate the sales production of various sales territories and (2) to evaluate the performance of the salesperson responsible for that territory. Performance standards are compared with actual performance, and adjustments are made. It is unlikely that the performance of personal selling as part of the total promotional strategy would be of interest to or the responsibility of the sales manager. Therefore promotion managers need to evaluate the relative performance of personal selling. That is, the promotion manager would be primarily concerned with whether personal selling cooperated in implementing personal selling's part of the promotion strategy rather than in sales performance. Each level of evaluation will be discussed.

Evaluating the Salesperson

The goal of this evaluation is to determine appropriate corrective action by separating the causes of performance measurements into two categories: those that are controllable by the individual salesperson and those that are not. In terms of importance and long-term implications, the three most controllable determinants are volume, activities, and quality.[15]

Volume Analysis　Sales volume is the simplest type of sales performance measurement and probably the most often used. Volume analysis can be appraised in terms of both effectiveness and efficiency. In terms of effectiveness, actual sales performance of a particular salesperson can be compared with the previous year's sales, the present year's budget, the sales performance of other salespeople, the number of sales closed, the number of accounts in his or her territory that are inactive, and his or her concentration on sales of special merchandise.

As with effectiveness, sales efficiency can be measured in many ways. Experience suggests four measures: gross margin on sales, contribution to profit, expense to sales ratio, and market share. The employment of basic accounting procedures quickly provides the appropriate data to run these tests for an individual salesperson, across salespeople, or across territories.

Activity Analysis　A manager's understanding of salespeople's performance has often been increased by examining their activities as well as their sales volume. Again, the possibilities are numerous.

The effectiveness of the sales force can be evaluated with respect to the number of sales calls, new accounts opened, and complaints received. The precision of these analyses might be improved by looking at efficiency as well as effectiveness. For example, calls per day and costs per call might provide more useful information than just the raw number of calls. It might also be interesting to look not just at the number of new accounts opened but at the size of each account. Perhaps the number of complaints should be balanced by the number of sales. Finally, sales representatives may be putting in long hours, but they may not be selling hours; a look at the ratio of selling time to total time may also provide useful insights.

Evaluating Personal Selling as a Part of Promotion

Poor cooperation between sales management and promotion management has meant that this type of evaluation is rarely performed. Personal selling is often reluctant to provide the information requested by the promotion manager because of distrust and the feeling of separateness mentioned earlier. Consequently, the quality of the information tends to be poor. However, a more inherent problem is that there is little evidence that companies actually have objectives that specify how personal selling should contribute to the overall promotional effort. The nature of the evaluation therefore relies heavily on subjective criteria developed by the promotion manager. For example, a promotion manager may be very concerned with whether the salesperson uses the sales promotion materials provided, including point-of-purchase displays, catalogs, brochures, pamphlets, and cooperative advertising programs. It might also be important whether these materials were used correctly. How is this information gathered? Surveys of the sales reps is one possibility, although the reps are reluctant to answer such surveys. Another possibility is to check up on them. The problems this could cause are fairly obvious. Consequently, the validity and reliability of this information are suspect. The other area in which salespeople might be evaluated is communication. Do salespeople provide feedback from customers about programs, competition, market information, or program effectiveness? This information is difficult to quantify, and the results may produce simple yes or no categories. This facet of evaluation remains the weakest in promotion. It is unlikely the situation will improve until the organizational and perceptual boundaries separating personal selling from the other three promotional elements are removed.

Concept Review

1. Sales promotion performance is evaluated using many of the same tests used in advertising. In addition, there are the following:
    a. Pretesting sales promotion (for example, communication, behavior, resellers).
    b. Concurrent testing.
    c. Posttesting (for example, communication, behavior).

2. Public relations performance is difficult to evaluate. It is usually assessed by analyzing the following:
   a. Exposures.
   b. Awareness, comprehension, or attitude change.
   c. Sales and profit margin.
3. Personal selling performance is normally evaluated by the sales manager. Methods include the following:
   a. Volume analysis.
   b. Activity analysis.
   c. Analysis of selling qualities.

Case 17 *Advertisements That Are Good For Your Health*

People who work for advertising agencies have to get used to negative public perceptions about the work they do. Consumer advocates charge agencies with subliminally coaxing people to buy products they can't afford or don't want or need. Public service ads have a reputation for being unrealistic and preachy, and even the anti-drug ad campaigns get criticized for using inaccurate information and ignoring deadly but legal drugs.

A Healthy Victory for Ads

But ad agencies around the country have been feeling a little better about public acceptance of their work as a result of the state of California's anti-smoking campaign. The campaign's ads have won the respect of viewers and media critics and have apparently done their job—getting people to quit smoking.

The anti-smoking campaign is the result of a taxpayer referendum in 1988; voters approved a 25 cents-per-pack tax on cigarettes, with the money to be used to warn citizens, particularly those in high-risk groups, of the perils of smoking. The state wanted at least half of its 30.5 million residents to be aware of the ads, a goal that was quickly reached.

Targeting Minority Groups

Part of the success of the ads is attributed to their specific targeting of young people, pregnant women, Spanish speakers, Asians, and African-

Americans. A Los Angeles advertising agency, Keye/Donna/Pearlstein, was the lead agency, but Muse Cordero/L.A. and The Hispanic Group/ Santa Monica, two minority-owned ad shops, get credit for the effectiveness of ads directed at ethnic markets. Early studies showed that 78 percent of California's African-Americans, 85 percent of its Spanish-speaking population, and 62 percent of its Asian population had seen or heard at least one of the campaign's television or radio spots.

The Results

Within six months, three out of four California residents indicated that they were aware of the ads. Almost half of the adult smokers who had seen the ads said they intended to quit, as compared to 39 percent of those who hadn't seen the ads. The ads have led to more positive attitudes towards good health among both adults and students, and early surveys showed a slight drop in smoking by students.

The ads break the stereotype of bland, unrealistic public-service messages. Rosemary Romano, director of public information for the federal Office on Smoking and Health, says they "are hard-hitting, the quality is excellent, and they cover a range of issues."

Although the tobacco industry fought hard against the original referendum, it had no plans to organize a counterattack. The industry trade group, the Tobacco Institute, disputes claims of success by the anti-smoking campaign, pointing out that tobacco sales had fallen 14 percent statewide in 1989, before the campaign began. Some people may, in fact, be quitting more because of the extra cost of smoking than because the ads are having the desired effect. But judging from the requests from around the nation and around the world to borrow or buy the ads, the particular agencies involved, and the entire industry, should view the California anti-smoking campaign as a major sign that ad agencies can do effective work for the public good.

Case Questions

1. What are the problems associated with the effectiveness measures mentioned in this case?

2. Suggest a measurement process that would better meet the assessment objectives cited.

Case Source: Pat Hinsberg, "Anti-Smoking Ads Capture an Audience," *Adweek* (November 5, 1990): 18.

Summary

Measuring promotional performance is one of the most important yet unsettled areas of promotion. In this chapter, four important questions are considered: (1) what to measure, (2) whether or not to test, (3) when to test, and (4) which test is best.

In respect to the first question, it is critical to determine exactly what effects are expected from a promotional effort. What should be measured depends on circumstances. Measurements of sales, market share, recall, and attitude change may all be appropriate in certain situations. Whether or not to test is a function of whether the cost of obtaining this information exceeds the benefits derived. Many types of tests are available. There are specific tests for each promotional area.

Discussion Questions

1. The marketing manager for a large cereal manufacturer wishes to increase sales by 10 percent through a massive promotional effort including television, print, coupons, a sweepstakes, and event sponsorship. Evaluate whether the sales objective is an appropriate way to evaluate performance of this promotional strategy.

2. What prominent decisions should the promotion manager consider when measuring promotional performance? Elaborate.

3. What are the major limitations in measuring the effectiveness of the promotional program?

4. What are the most common measures of advertising effectiveness?

5. Select an advertising objective and create several rough ideas for ads that relate to the objective. Finally, devise an experiment that can measure the relative effectiveness of those ads.

6. Explain the utility of the model for measuring advertising effectiveness. What are the stages involved in the model?

7. Assume that a severely limited budget has motivated the promotion managers to re-evaluate the methods that are used to test advertising. In the past, pretests, concurrent tests, and posttests were used. In light of the budget constraints, your associates feel that only post-testing should be considered. Do you agree?

8. Why were inquiry tests developed? In what ways can they be utilized?

9.   What information would you require to empirically audit the public relations performance?

10.   What mistakes are made by sales managers who use sales volume alone to measure sales performance?

Suggested Projects

1.   Outline a performance evaluation program for a fast-food retailer such as McDonald's, Burger King, or Kentucky Fried Chicken.

2.   Visit an advertising agency and discuss its techniques for measuring effectiveness with an account executive or top-level manager. How does the agency's approach compare with the techniques discussed in this chapter?

3.   Go to your campus library and identify five or six secondary research sources that provide companies with assistance in measuring performance. Describe the type of information they provide.

References

1.   Charles Ramond, *Advertising Research: The State of the Art* (New York: Association of National Advertisers, 1976).

2.   Robert J. Lavidge and Gary A. Steiner, "A Model for Predictive Measurements of Advertising Effectiveness," *Journal of Marketing* 25 (October 1961): 59–62.

3.   Johan Arndt, "What's Wrong with Advertising Research?" *Journal of Marketing Research* 16 (June 1976): 9.

4.   H. D. Wolfe, J. K. Brown, S. H. Greenberg, and G. C. Thompson, *Pretesting Advertising Studies in Business Policy,* no. 109 (New York: National Industrial Conference Board, 1963).

5.   David W. Stewart, "Measures, Methods, and Models in Advertising Research," *Journal of Advertising Research* (June/July 1989): 54–60.

6.   Michael L. Rothschild, Ester Thorson, Judith E. Hirsch, Robert Goldstein, and Byron B. Reeves, "EEG Activity and the Processing of Television Commercials," *Communication Research* (April 1986).

7.   Rudolph Flesch, *The Art of Readable Writing* (New York: Harper & Row, 1974).

8.   Julie Liesse, "KGF Taps Data to Target Consumers," *Advertising Age* (October 8, 1990): 3, 88.

9.   Don E. Schultz, *Strategic Advertising Campaigns*, 3rd ed. (Lincoln, IL: NTC Business Books, 1990): 550.

10.   James F. Donius, "Market Tracking: A Strategic Reassessment and Planning Tool," *Journal of Advertising Research* (February/March 1985): 15–19.

11. Wally Wood, "Update: Single Source," *Marketing and Media Decisions* (September 1989): 116–117; Laurence N. Gold, "TV Ad Testing Enters New Generation," *Marketing News* (October 23, 1989): 2.

12. Simon Broadbent, *Spending Advertising Money* (London: Business Books, 1975).

13. Robert C. Blattberg and Scott A. Neslin, *Sales Promotion: Concepts, Methods and Strategies* (Englewood Cliffs, NJ: Prentice-Hall, Inc., 1990): Chapter 39.

14. Robert L. Dilenschneider and Dan J. Forrestal, *The Dartnell Public Relations Handbook* (Chicago: The Dartnell Corporation, 1987): Chapter 6.

15. Richard R. Still, Edward W. Cundiff, and Norman A. P. Govoni, *Sales Management*, 3rd ed. (Englewood Cliffs, NJ: Prentice-Hall, Inc., 1976): 377.

Additional Readings

1. Robert J. Schreiber and Valentine Appel, "Advertising Evaluation Using Surrogate Measures for Sales," *Journal of Advertising Research* (December 1990/January 1991): 27–31.

2. Howard Schlossberg, "Jane and the Gang Track Trends with 'Public Domain Research,'" *Marketing News* (June 10, 1991): 1–21.

3. Kim Foltz, "New Research Tool: The Video Conference," *The New York Times* (April 18, 1991): C15.

4. Scott Hume, "Power of Persuasion: Nielsen, Research System Join for New Service," *Advertising Age* (March 11, 1991): 24.

5. Chris Whittle, "Measuring the Landings," *Adweek* (May 27, 1991): 12.

6. Cyndee Miller, "Research Aids Retailers Before They Pop Up Their P-O-P Displays," *Marketing News* (January 7, 1991): 19.

7. Gerald Lukeman, "Analysis Shows New Way to Think About TV Recall Scores," *Marketing News* (April 15, 1991): 24.

8. Mary L. Nicastro, "Break-Even Analysis Determines Success of Sales Promotions," *Marketing News* (March 5, 1990): 11.

9. Betsy Spethmann, "PSA Effectiveness Study Unveiled," *Advertising Age* (April 8, 1991): 46.

PART

V

SPECIAL APPLICATIONS

18

Promoting Through Direct Marketing

Consider This:

Teaming Up to Target Families

What do CBS and Quaker Oats Company have in common? On first glance, not much. CBS produces television shows, Quaker Oats oatmeal and toys. But in 1990, the two companies teamed up in an unusual direct-mail campaign that may be a wave of the future.

CBS had always shied away from direct-mail. After all, the company doesn't actually sell a product. Its goal is to get television viewers to flip the channel to CBS, a tall order for a direct-mail campaign. Besides, the potential target audience for an American television network is 90 million households, and mailing to even a fraction of them would be prohibitively expensive.

But Quaker's idea was too good for CBS to pass up. Quaker was not trying to reach every American household, just 18 million or so, concentrating on families with incomes above $25,000. It timed the first mailing in early October, when fall TV shows premier and the rating wars heat up. And it had done its homework on its target audience so that it knew demographic information about the households it was mailing to and could make at least an educated guess about whether they would be more likely to buy Cap'n Crunch or Quaker Natural.

So all CBS had to do was create fliers for its fall TV shows and send them out with the Quaker coupons. It could assume that people would be interested enough in the coupons at least to glance through the CBS mailings. And if the demographic targeting worked right, a coupon for a kids' cereal and an ad for a Saturday morning cartoon show would get to tired parents just when they were trying to figure out how to win a moment's peace on the weekend. Because of the highly targeted nature of the mailing, local CBS affiliates could add their own promotions to the package. For its part, Quaker hoped that the CBS fliers would add some excitement to its coupon package, making it stand out from competitors' offerings. And it hoped that CBS's ads for its own family-oriented shows would complement Quaker's family image.

Advertisers in related industries—like hotels and airlines—have long known that joint promotions can benefit both parties. But if this "Quaker Direct" campaign proves to have been profitable, it may lead the way for more joint ventures linking apparently unrelated companies.

Source: "Quaker and CBS Combine in Direct Mail Campaign," *Marketing News* (September 17, 1990): 5.

*F*ew areas of marketing have gone through more dramatic change and turmoil than direct marketing. Until recently, most consumers viewed direct marketing as junk mail and junk products. Today, marketing planners have eagerly accepted direct marketing as a way of more effectively reaching target audiences, and consumers see it as a vehicle for selecting and receiving products with a minimum of effort. Even companies in areas as diverse as CBS and Quaker have found it advantageous to join forces through direct marketing. This recent acceptance of direct marketing was instigated by a handful of visionaries who saw that the benefits of mail order were applicable to many types of product/service delivery systems. Virtually all media have the capability of incorporating the strategic elements of direct marketing.

Direct marketing is another vehicle for distributing the promotional effort. Simultaneously, because of its value-added benefits, direct marketing is also a special type of sales promotion. In this chapter, we explain the basic components of direct marketing, describe the decisions it requires of managers, discuss direct marketing media, and illustrate how direct marketing and the rest of promotion interact.

An Overview of Direct Marketing

According to the Direct Marketing Association, direct marketing "is an interactive system of marketing which uses one or more advertising media to effect a measurable response and/or transaction at any location."[1] Pete Hoke, Jr., publisher of *Direct Marketing* magazine, adds one element to this definition: "In direct marketing, a database—a customer file—must exist."[2] Embedded in this definition are five components.

First, direct marketing is an *interactive system,* that is, the prospective customer and the marketer engage in two-way communication. As a result, direct marketing allows for precise feedback rather than the surrogate measures of effectiveness used in the rest of marketing.

A second trait of direct marketing is that the system always provides a *mechanism for the prospect to respond.* Because response is possible, the size of the nonresponse as well as the characteristics of nonresponders have considerable impact on planning.

Third, direct marketing can occur at *any location;* it does not require a retail store or a salesperson. Instead, the order can be made at any time of the day or night and can be delivered without the consumer leaving home.

The fourth and key element in the definition is *measurable response.* That is, direct marketing allows the marketer to calculate precisely the costs of producing the marketing strategy and the resulting income. Its measurable response represents the primary benefit of direct marketing and is undoubtedly a reason for its recent popularity.

The final element is the necessity for a *database of consumer information.* Through the information in databases, the direct marketer can target communications to an individual consumer or a specific business customer who has been identified as a viable prospect. To marketers, direct marketing offers the ability to reach appropriate target audiences with the right benefits. There are three benefits to consumers: convenience, efficiency, and compression of decision-making time. For example, when a consumer buys shirts by mail from Land's End, every step of the process is smoothly executed, from the toll-free conversation with the order-taker to prompt delivery of well-made, fully guaranteed shirts, billed to a Visa card at a cost far lower than many retail stores charge. The customer even receives a little packet of spare buttons and a note of thanks. Many retail stores pay less attention to customer satisfaction.

A Definitional Quagmire

Despite the apparent simplicity of the definition and elements of direct marketing, some confusion still exists as to the complete meaning of direct marketing. Dick Damrow, an expert on direct marketing, suggests a need to better define the concept. "The fact that it takes a two-page spread in every issue of *Direct Marketing* magazine for three of the best in the business to define it is a tragic reflection of our ability as communicators."[3] A look at three questions should help clarify the definition.

First, what makes direct marketing a distinct type of marketing? Most of the material in this course has dealt with indirect marketing. Companies such as Kraft General Foods, Ford Motor Co., and Best Foods represent indirect marketers. They distribute their products through a network of resellers (that is, wholesalers and retailers) who then make their product available to the customers. Direct marketers tend to skip resellers and contact the customer directly. Some direct marketers, such as L. L. Bean, have retail stores, but retail sales represent a very small part of their business. Table 18.1 lists other differences between direct and indirect marketing.

Second, is the promotion associated with direct marketing distinctive? Ads for Coca-Cola, Levi's 501 jeans, and Pert shampoo are not intended to cause an immediate change in behavior. Known as **awareness advertising,** its primary purpose is to create and maintain brand awareness. Through creating the proper image, repetition, and correct media placement, aware-

Table 18.1 **Key Differences Between Direct Marketing and Indirect Marketing**

Indirect Marketing	Direct Marketing
Reaches a mass audience through mass media.	Communicates directly with the customer or prospect through more targeted media
Communications are impersonal.	Can personalize communications By name/title Variable messages
Promotional programs are highly visible to competition, since mass media is used.	Promotional programs (especially pretests) are relatively invisible to competition
Amount of promotion controlled by size of budget.	Size of budget can be determined by success of promotion
Desired action either unclear or delayed.	Specific action always requested Inquiry Purchase
Incomplete/sample data for decision-making purposes Sales call reports Marketing research	Comprehensive database drives marketing programs
Analysis conducted at segment level.	Analysis conducted at individual/firm level through personalization
Use surrogate variables to measure effectiveness Advertising awareness Intention to buy	Measurable, and therefore highly controllable

Source: Mary Lou Roberts and Paul D. Berger, *Direct Marketing Management* (Englewood Cliffs, N.J.: Prentice-Hall, 1989): 4. Reprinted by permission of Prentice-Hall, Inc.

ness ads reinforce the positive elements of the brand in the mind of consumers. They also can deliver extra value through coupons, rebates, and sweepstakes.

In contrast, promotion associated with direct marketing usually takes the form of **direct-response advertising.** It is designed to motivate customers to make some sort of response, either an order or an inquiry. Direct-response advertising is directed to prospects through vehicles such as direct mail, telemarketing, print, broadcast, and point-of-purchase displays. Figures 18.1 and 18.2 show two ads that demonstrate the differences between awareness and direct-response advertising.

Third, is the selling effort employed differently with direct marketing? With indirect marketing, the role of the salesperson is usually quite important. Marketers use a sales force to sell to resellers and/or end users. Direct marketing has less reliance on personal selling. Instead, it engages direct-order marketing or direct-response selling.

Figure 18.1
This ad is an example of awareness advertising, the primary purpose of which is to create and maintain brand awareness.
Used with permission of © Campbell Soup Company.

Direct-order marketing uses nonpersonal media to sell a product or service without salespeople's help. Print, broadcast, and direct mail carry the primary responsibility for initiating and closing the transaction, whether through an order blank contained as part of the ad or a toll-free telephone number. It is critical, therefore, that the direct order piece contain all the necessary information for the consumer to make the purchase.

Although salespeople are required to complete the sale, **direct-response selling** uses nonpersonal media in a way that makes a measurable contri-

Figure 18.2

Here is an example of direct-response advertising, which is designed to motivate consumers to make some type of response—either an order or an inquiry.
Courtesy of Lilliput Motor Co., Ltd.

bution to selling. For example, the advertising for AT&T's Pro Watts service contains a toll-free number to call for further information or to make a sales appointment. This type of direct marketing has become the primary lead-generating device for many sales forces.

The State of the Industry

The origin of direct marketing goes back many years. Orvis issued its first catalog, offering fishing equipment, in 1844, and the Tiffany catalog made its debut a year later. Montgomery Ward launched its mail-order business in 1872, and Sears entered the field in 1886. In the early 1900s, L. L. Bean and the Book-of-the-Month Club came on the scene. It was after World War II, however, that the national magazines turned to the mails as the battleground for their mass circulation wars, and direct mail entered a period of rapid growth and development.

Today, the successors of these direct-mail pioneers are employing high technology, including computers and database management. With these tools, marketers gather a sophisticated mailing list of customers and prospects and enhance it with relevant data to help predict buying behaviors. The object is quite simple: to identify the most likely buyers before incurring the substantial costs associated with direct marketing.

Direct marketing is indeed a big business. Table 18.2 lists the top twenty direct-marketing agencies in 1990 and 1989. Ogilvy & Mather Direct was the top agency, followed by Wunderman Worldwide. A survey of the top two hundred direct-marketing agencies showed billings of $4.1 billion in 1990 compared with $3.4 billion in 1988. Direct mail accounted for $1.4 billion of $2.1 billion in direct-response media billing by the two hundred agencies.

Types of Direct Marketing

Direct marketing can take three forms: the one-step process, the two-step process, and the negative option.

1. *One-step process.* The consumer responds to an ad in a media vehicle and receives the product by mail. A *bounce-back* brochure promoting related merchandise may be included with the product.

2. *Two-step process.* The potential customer must first be qualified before ordering the product. Insurance companies use the two-step process when they require a physical exam before enforcing the policy. Similarly, a company selling high-ticket items, such as land or furniture, may require a preliminary credit check. Or a company may charge a fee for a catalog of direct-mail merchandise; the fee can be used as a credit toward purchases.

3. *Negative option.* The customer joins a plan such as those offered by record or book clubs to automatically receive unrequested merchandise at regular intervals. The initial merchandise is often offered with a free gift or at a discount price.

Concept Review

1. Direct marketing is an interactive system of marketing that uses advertising media to effect a measurable response or transaction at any location. Every direct-marketing system must have a database.

Table 18.2   **The Top Twenty Direct-Response Agencies**

Rank '90	Rank '89	Agency, Headquarters	Direct-response Volume 1990	Direct-response Volume 1989	Media Billed as % of 1990 Volume TV	Radio	Print	Direct Mail
1	1	**Ogilvy & Mather Direct,** New York	$354,180	$304,980	25.5%	0.2%	3.2%	68.3%
2	2	**Wunderman Worldwide,** New York	254,374	232,776	28.7%	0.5%	22.1%	48.7%
3	3	**Rapp Collins Marcoa,** Chicago	243,160	226,000	8.8%	0.7%	13.4%	31.1%
4	4	**Direct Marketing Group,** New York	146,200	149,600	NA	NA	NA	NA
5	6	**Kobs & Draft Advertising,** Chicago	134,300	116,900	15.2%	2.5%	13.1%	10.5%
6	11	**Bronner Slosberg Humphrey,** Boston	127,226	79,789	NA	NA	NA	NA
7	5	**Grey Direct,** New York	120,000	119,000	12.5%	NA	25.8%	51.7%
8	14	**DMCA Direct,** Bridgeton, Mo.	107,768	61,345	NA	NA	NA	100.0%
9	8	**Saugatuck Group,** Westport, Conn.	102,399	100,690	NA	NA	0.5%	NA
10	7	**Barry Blau & Partners,** Fairfield, Conn.	100,916	101,175	NA	NA	NA	NA
11	16	**Chapman Direct,** New York	100,097	48,198	14.0%	1.0%	16.0%	60.0%
12	9	**Bowest Dentsu & Partners,** Los Angeles	97,119	92,401	NA	NA	NA	NA
13	13	**Cohn & Wells/ Eurocom,** San Francisco	96,027	64,393	NA	NA	4.9%	95.1%
14	10	**Devon Direct Marketing & Advertising,** Berwyn, Pa.	94,200	82,000	NA	NA	3.4%	57.0%
15	12	**Customer Development Corp.,** Peoria, Ill.	68,527	68,873	NA	NA	NA	100.0%
16	18	**Saatchi & Saatchi Direct,** New York	61,936	43,542	NA	NA	NA	NA
17	19	**GSP Marketing Services,** Chicago	55,236	43,315	NA	NA	NA	NA
18	15	**Lowe Direct,** New York	52,500	55,000	NA	NA	NA	NA
19	17	**Ayer Direct,** New York	50,000	48,000	NA	NA	NA	NA
20	23	**Perkins/Butler Direct Marketing,** New York	49,000	35,000	NA	NA	NA	NA

Note: Dollars are in thousands.

Advertising Age (May 20, 1991): 32.

2. Three perspectives clarify direct marketing:
   a. Indirect marketing versus direct marketing.
   b. Awareness advertising versus direct-response advertising.
   c. Direct-order selling versus direct-response selling.
3. Direct marketing is a $4.1-billion industry.
4. There are three types of direct marketing:
   a. One-step,
   b. Two-step, and
   c. Negative option.

Managing Direct Marketing

Direct marketing employs the same planning framework suggested throughout this text. It is unique, however, in respect to the elements considered important to the success of direct marketing. For example, direct marketing is dependent on the quality of its database. It also uses special media to deliver messages. The primary components of direct marketing are shown in Figure 18.3. Many of these components are familiar through discussions in earlier chapters. The material addressed here is applicable to direct marketing only.

Managing the Database

The database is the very essence of direct marketing. Simply stated, a **database** contains information about customers and prospects that has been collected over a considerable time.[4] According to the Direct Marketing Association, a marketing database has four primary objectives:[5]

1. To record names of customers, expires (names no longer valid), and prospects;

2. To provide a vehicle for storing and then measuring results of advertising (usually direct-response advertising);

3. To provide a vehicle for storing and then measuring purchasing performance; and

4. To provide a vehicle for continuing direct communication by mail or phone.

Most databases are not designed exclusively for marketing, but have applications for several functions within an organization. Although a computer is not required, practically speaking, it is impossible to effectively maintain a database of useful size without one.

Obtaining a mailing list is the first step toward establishing a database. Overall, using a database system involves five steps:

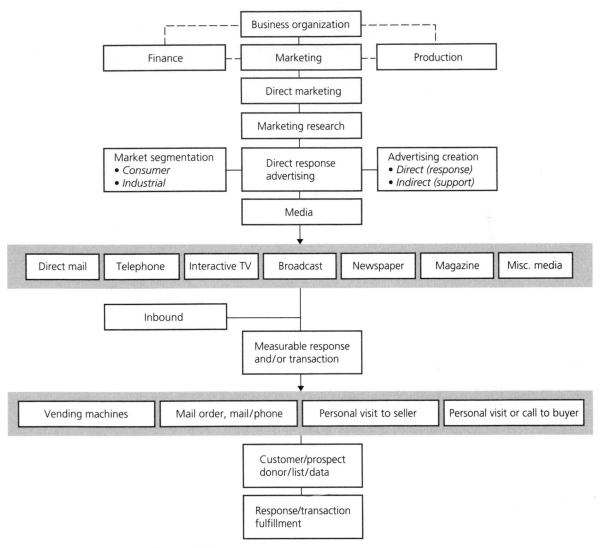

Figure 18.3

The primary components of direct marketing.
Direct Marketing *(September 1990): 2. Used with permission.*

1. Capture, organize, and maintain existing marketing data;
2. Convert the data into useful information that has possible application to company strategies;
3. Apply the database to specific strategies;
4. Test results; and
5. Capture new data and integrate them into the existing database.

Companies may develop their database internally or externally or use a combination of internal and external means. Internal, or in-house, databases are derived from customer receipts, credit card information, or personal information cards completed by customers. The internal approach is cost-effective as long as the company has the expertise and resources.

Many companies have neither the resources nor the expertise to develop in-house database systems. These companies can obtain commercial databases from firms whose sole purpose is to collect, analyze, categorize, and market an enormous variety of detail about the American consumer.[6] Companies such as National Decision Systems, Persoft, and Donnelly Marketing Information Systems are only a few of these firms. From such information as income, education, occupation, and census data, their databases can describe life in individual neighborhoods across the country with amazing accuracy. The ad for Epsilon suggests the capabilities of one such company (see Figure 18.4).

Designing a Direct-Marketing Strategy

The direct-marketing strategy details the events and methods needed to complete an objective. It includes decisions in five areas: (1) the offer, (2) the medium, (3) the message, (4) timing and sequencing, and (5) customer service.

The Offer   The proposition made to customers is often referred to as the offer. It is the key to success or failure, and the manner in which it is presented can have an equally dramatic effect. The selection and design of the offer should be supported by comprehensive research. When creating an offer, managers must consider numerous factors.

To begin with, there is a *price*. The correct price must not only include a sufficient markup but also reflect what competitors are charging and what consumers expect to pay. Odd-pricing (for example, $7.95), multiple unit pricing (such as two for $29.95), and giveaways (for example, $49.95 plus free steak knives) are common pricing strategies in direct marketing. The components of the price should be stated clearly and concisely.

The cost of *shipping and handling* can be an important part of the offer. Who should pay these costs? Can they be added to the base price of the product without adversely affecting sales? Recent increases in postal rates have shifted this cost burden to consumers in several instances.

Optional features are part of the basic offer. Special colors and sizes, personalization, or large-type editions are a few examples. Certain options can dramatically increase sales, while others prove unappealing. This is an area in which research is very important.

Many offers contain a *future obligation*. Book clubs and record clubs are two industries that normally ask for a one- or two-year commitment. The

If you understand her needs, you can win her business.

You can assume that she's upwardly mobile, possibly juggling the demands of family and career. But beyond that, what do you really know about her? What does she buy? What are her interests? Her needs?

If you want to compete in the 90's, you'll need all the answers. Because to get her attention and her business, you'll have to communicate on a personal, one-to-one basis. This is true for all – from airlines to banks, packaged goods manufacturers to retailers.

Epsilon can help you open direct dialogue, establish long-lasting relationships, and sell more business. We offer a powerful combination of database technology and marketing expertise that gets clients closer to their customers.

For more than 20 years, we've provided a full range of database marketing solutions and services – including strategic consulting, research and analysis, information management, and creative communications techniques – to help companies sell products and services to millions of individual customers. We can do the same for you.

Call Bob Drummond at 617–273–0250 and find out how Epsilon's database marketing solutions can help you get closer to your customers.

epsilon
A subsidiary of American Express

Figure 18.4

This ad for Epsilon suggests the capabilities of database marketing.
© 1992 Epsilon Data Management, Inc. All rights reserved.

system of sending products at regular intervals and billing automatically allows the marketer to charge a very low price for the first order, knowing there will be a long-term payout.

The availability of *credit* may be the most important element of an offer. Research indicates that if either commercial credit (such as Visa or MasterCard) or house credit (for example, an installment plan or Discover) is available, the average order size increases 15 percent.

Extra *incentives*, such as free gifts, discounts, sweepstakes, and toll-free ordering privileges, can all increase the attractiveness of an offer. Yet there

Table 18.3 **Offers Frequently Used in Direct Marketing**

Offer	Description
Free Trial	Gives the customer the chance to experience product for a short period of time before final commitment.
Get-a-friend	Rewards current purchaser for bringing in new customers.
Sample	Provides the potential customer with a limited amount of product at no cost.
Conditional Sale	Prearranges the possibility of long-term acceptance based on short-term experience.
Free Information	Makes information available upon request prior to purchase.
Contest	Offers possible give-aways with either purchase or no purchase required.
Discount	Reduction from the base price for cash, an introductory offer, or a volume purchase.
Till Forbid	Products will be shipped continually till customer sends a forbid future shipments notice.
Lifetime Membership	Initial fee guarantees reduced prices for life of member.
Load-up	Offers the customer a chance to buy a part of the total product (e.g., set of books) with an opportunity to buy rest of product.
Gift (Free, Secret, Cash-up)	Provides the customer with a gift for a specified compliance.
Multiproduct	Separate order sheets for individual products.
Bounce-Back	Include product offers with the delivered product for future purchase.

is also the risk that the customer will have little interest in the incentive or, more importantly, that the cost of the incentive will inflate the price.

Time and quantity limits create urgency in the mind of the customer. Suggesting that an offer will end on a certain date or that a product is a limited edition moves the prospect to action. It is important that the time or quantity limits are legitimate. Limits that are repeatedly extended quickly lose their impact.

The *guarantee* is an automatic part of any direct-marketing offer. Whenever people order products by phone or mail, they perceive risk. They must be assured that they can back out of a mistake. Sometimes there is a "guaranteed buy-back" offer. Some guarantees even pay "double your money back." The free issue wording says simply: I may cancel my reservation after looking at the premier issue.

Table 18.3 lists the offers most often used in direct marketing. Depending on the marketer's objectives, the offers may be used separately or in combination. Many of the same pretest techniques of communication described in Chapter 17 can be used in pretesting the offer.

The Medium and the Message   Selecting the medium to deliver the direct-marketing message and selecting the message itself are related decisions.

Table 18.4 **Leading U.S. Companies Ranked in Worldwide Sales Through Mail Order**

1989 Rank	Company Name	Sales Segment	Mail Order Sales ($ MMs)
1	J.C. Penney	General merchandise, insurance	3,170.8
2	United States Services Automobile Association	Insurance	2,738.5
3	Time Warner	Books, magazine subscriptions, cable TV	2,636.5
4	Reader's Digest	Books, collectibles, general merchandise, magazine subscriptions	1,584.0
5	Associated Communications	Cable TV	1,545.7
6	Sears, Roebuck & Company	General merchandise, insurance, auto clubs	1,519.8
7	GEICO	Insurance	1,516.6
8	Newhouse	Magazine subscriptions, cable TV	1,195.0
9	Otto Versand (Spiegel)	General merchandise, sporting goods, apparel	1,149.9
10	Primerica (Fingerhut)	Audio-video, food, general merchandise, insurance	1,124.4
11	AT&T	Business services, consumer electronics	1,123.2
12	MCI	Business services	1,050.0
13	American Automobile Association	Auto clubs, insurance	1,030.8
14	QVC Network	General merchandise, industrial	936.5
15	Comcast Cable	Cable TV	842.7
16	FPL Group	Insurance	824.8
17	Home Shopping Network	Apparel, health, general merchandise	774.0
18	Campeau	Apparel, general merchandise	749.9
19	United Telecom	Business services	720.0
20	UA Cablesystems	Cable TV	696.0
21	Continental Cablevision	Cable TV	691.5
22	U.S. Government	Business services, collectibles, health, educational services	666.9
23	American Express	General merchandise, insurance, magazines	640.1
24	20th Century Industries	Insurance	596.0
25	May Department Stores	General merchandise	562.3

Source: *Direct Marketing* (July 1990): 28. Used with permission.

The message strategies discussed in earlier chapters are equally applicable to direct marketing. The media used in direct marketing have been specially developed to accommodate the unique advantages of direct marketing. More will be said about direct-marketing media later in this chapter.

Timing and Sequencing   There is a great deal of similarity between the timing and sequencing of direct marketing and of advertising. The direct marketer must consider questions about repetition, seasonality, flighting versus pulsing, and one-shot programs versus campaigns. One difference, however, is the greater emphasis placed on this strategic element in direct marketing. In advertising, creative execution receives most of the attention; the key to the success of direct marketing, however, is reaching the right person at the right time. Direct marketing experts estimate that 70 percent of the success of direct marketing is contingent on making the correct timing and sequencing decisions.[7] Much of this success is dependent on the quality of the database. Still, there are general rules of thumb that are widely known in the industry. For example, the direct-mail industry realizes that two follow-up mailings are necessary in order to produce minimal response. Another given is that Christmas catalogs must be received no later than six weeks before Christmas Day.

Customer Service   Direct marketing owes its rise from junk-mail status to credibility to the introduction of customer service. The importance of service cannot be overstated. The types of customer services offered—toll-free telephone numbers, free limited-time trial, and acceptance of several credit cards, for example—are important techniques for overcoming customer resistance to buying via direct-response media. The level of service is equally important. Speed and accuracy in filling orders, careful handling of customer complaints, and guaranteed return policies have been critical to the success of direct marketers such as L. L. Bean, J. Crew, and Spiegel.

Evaluating Direct Marketing

Throughout this chapter, there are frequent references to the fact that direct marketing is the most measurable element in the promotional mix. The basic philosophy of direct marketing is quite simple: there is no reason to invest a large amount of resources in a direct-marketing program unless it has a high probability of success. Because direct marketers have control over both outbound communication to their customers and prospects and inbound communication from customers and prospects (responses), they are able to estimate the probability of success with a fairly high degree of accuracy. In general, direct marketers evaluate profitability and customer characteristics and response.

Profitability Analysis The bottom line for direct marketing is profitability. It is not surprising, therefore, that every decision in direct marketing (for example, to rent or buy a list) is viewed as a separate profit center, with the equivalent of a profit/loss statement being generated. In turn, this profit estimate determines whether to expand or reduce an activity or, more generally, what the optimal choice of level or decision should be.

A great deal of this emphasis on profitability in direct marketing is the result of a mathematical framework developed by Robert Kestanbaum and his organization, Kestanbaum & Company, in 1967. Kestanbaum lists four basic growth strategies to generate higher revenue/profits in the long run:[8]

1. Invest in new customer acquisition.
2. Invest in new media for presenting offers.
3. Add products or service to your line.
4. Expand the number of times customers and prospects are contacted.

Each of these strategies can be utilized to achieve specific financial goals:

1. Maximize sales.
2. Maximize profits.
3. Maximize profit as a percent of sales.
4. Maximize return on investment (ROI).

Kestanbaum goes on to say that maximizing return on investment is the most meaningful goal in the long run. One key to achieving this goal is to make sure that no components of revenue, contribution, or profit are overlooked in the process of evaluating this return.

From this perspective, profitability analysis is a matter of considering the appropriate revenues and costs and determining the resulting contribution or profit. This analysis can be performed on a promotion-by-promotion basis or by grouping elements together. For example, we might evaluate three rented mailing lists as a group. For catalogs, it is often considered more strategically useful to group items by merchandise category and construct an aggregate profit and loss statement.

Customer Characteristics and Response Direct marketers are also interested in their customers. Specifically, they want to know if their messages are reaching the right people and if the people are reacting in the manner suggested. Three techniques are used in direct marketing to make this type of assessment: responder/nonresponder survey, tracking studies, and geo-demography.[9]

Responder/Nonresponder Surveys As the term suggests, **responder/nonresponder surveys** attempt to identify differences between people who did and did not respond to the direct-marketing program. The goal is to improve the next direct-marketing effort. Since the marketer has a list of both responders and nonresponders, this technique entails a follow-up survey by telephone or mail in order to identify the demographic and psychographic characteristics of both groups and the reasons why they did or did not respond. This information serves as a guide for offering products in the future, for modifying the language in a direct-mail piece, or for selecting a different mailing list.

Tracking Studies   In this context, tracking studies are usually surveys that gather a limited amount of information from a large number of people by simply counting responses over time. Syndicated national surveys are ideal for tracking studies because the marketer shares costs with the research firm's other participating clients and can purchase as few as one question in the interview. Some syndicated systems conduct personal in-home or telephone interviews once a month or quarter. Other systems maintain ongoing mail panels that can be sent self-administered questionnaires as needed. The cardinal rule in conducting tracking studies is to change the questionnaire as little as possible over time to maintain the comparability of results.

Geodemography   This technique has evolved during the last decade and appears to be tailor-made for direct marketing. **Geodemography** analyzes an existing database on the principle that birds of a feather flock together. That is, people who live together in small geographic areas such as blocks and ZIP code units tend to have more similar demographic characteristics than people who live elsewhere. One system, PRIZM, has given its clusters colorful names such as "Blueblood Estates," "Bunker's Neighborhood," and, at the low end, "Hardscrabble." Geodemographic systems can be used to track the demographic quality of responders or to do automatic responder/nonresponder studies, using only addresses as resources.

Concept Review

1. A direct-marketing strategy contains five components:
   a. The offer, which contains a price, the cost of shipping and handling, optional features, future obligation, credit, incentives, time and quantity limits, and a guarantee.
   b. The medium. Direct marketing uses direct mail, catalogs, mass media, and telemarketing.
   c. The message.
   d. Timing and sequencing.
   e. Customer service.
2. There are a number of techniques used to evaluate direct marketing:
   a. Profitability analysis.
   b. Customer characteristics and response.

Using Direct-Marketing Media

Direct marketing is possible only because a special set of media have evolved. The four most common direct media are (1) direct mail, (2) catalogs, (3) mass media direct marketing, and (4) telemarketing.

Direct Mail

Direct mail delivers the message and the product through the U.S. Postal Service or a private delivery organization. Direct mail has been used to generate orders, presell activities prior to the field salesperson's visit, qualify prospects for a product, follow up a sale, announce special sales in local areas, and raise funds for nonprofit groups.

Figure 18.5 shows the recent growth in direct-mail sales. It was a $183

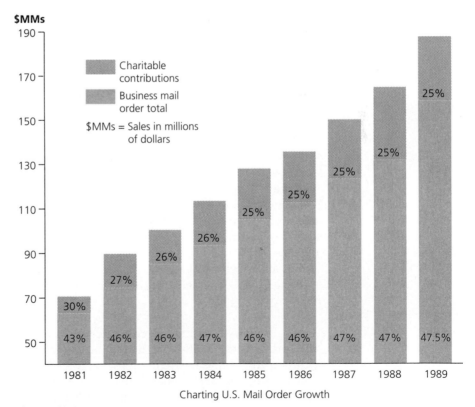

Charting U.S. Mail Order Growth

Figure 18.5

Recent growth in direct-mail sales.
Direct Marketing *(July 1990): 27. Used with permission.*

billion industry in 1989. Table 18.4 lists the top users, headed by J. C. Penney Company, Inc., with direct-mail sales of $3.1 billion.

There are a number of advantages associated with direct mail as compared to traditional mass media. First, the medium offers a variety of formats and provides enough space to tell a complete sales story. Second, since direct mail has little competition when received, it can actively engage the reader's attention. Third, it is now possible to personalize direct mail across a number of characteristics, such as name, product usage, and income. Fourth, direct mail is particularly conducive to marketing research and can be modified until the package matches the desired target audience. Fifth, although this is hard for some people to imagine, there are individuals who like to receive direct mail. Finally, direct mail allows the marketer to reach audiences who are inaccessible by other media.

The primary drawback of using direct mail is the widespread perception that it is junk mail. Many people throw away direct-mail pieces before opening them—despite the energy spent on designing envelope copy that will entice the receiver into opening the package.

A second disadvantage of direct mail is the high cost per prospect reached. However, a direct-mail campaign may still be less expensive than trying to reach a particular target group through other media. Furthermore, marketers are working to improve direct mail. The Direct Marketing Association (DMA), for example, is testing ride-alongs (or piggybacking) in which direct-response pieces are inserted into bags for delivery with magazines.[10] The DMA is also working with the U.S. Postal Service on a bar-coding program designed to help automate mail processing.

A final disadvantage is the new competition facing direct mail—fax machines, which now do many of the same things accomplished by direct mail. An interesting possible replacement for direct mail is the disposable videocassette, which wears out after about ten viewings. Philmax is the primary developer. The idea behind the inexpensive disposables "is basically to replace direct mail. We think it's going to bring direct mail into the video age," says Philip Brecher, a Philmax co-owner.[11] He envisions video catalogs and magazines and video versions of product instructions.

The effectiveness of a direct-mail piece is contingent on the quality of the mailing list, the elements of the package, and the copy.

Lists   To successfully solicit customer orders, managers need accurate and up-to-date lists; ideally, the lists should include only those who are in a position to purchase. There are two types of lists. *Internal* (house) lists are collected by the business and include customers, former customers, prospects, and inquiries. *External* lists include names that are collected and sold by sources outside the company.

The internal list is usually more meaningful since most of those on the list will be familiar with and interested in the product. The internal list should be part of the company's database and should include as much information as possible about the customers. To identify important behavioral data, Robert Kestanbaum, an authority on direct marketing, coined the acronym FRAT, which stands for frequency, recent, amount (monetary), and type of purchase. Other relevant information is how customers paid, where they live, what they purchased, how long they have been customers, and when they bought last. Each company must consider its own needs when developing its list.

External lists are purchased from list brokers, whose names can be found in trade directories or in the local Yellow Pages. The list broker works for both the list renter and the list owner, and it is the list owner who pays the broker's fees. List prices range from thirty dollars to one hundred dollars or more per thousand names, plus the broker's commission. The list broker must be aware of most available lists. Generally, list owners make their lists available to any reputable broker who has a potential renter. Some renters use only one list broker; others use many list brokers. The broker guarantees a level of accuracy or maximum undeliverable rate, usually no more than 7 percent to 10 percent. A good list broker gives helpful advice on testing procedures, develops suggestions for better results in future mailings, and ensures that the mailing complies with the list owner's standards.

In renting an external list, a marketer may select one of two general types. *Compiled* lists identify people who share some common interest, such as snow skiing, retirement housing, or gourmet cooking. Lists of *inquiries or customers from other companies* are provided by both competing and noncompeting companies. Lists from noncompeting companies identify individuals who either bought a related product or purchased through direct mail.

A marketer who used either a compiled list or an inquiry/customer list would be able to select business lists or consumer lists as well. Each of these categories can be further refined until the marketer specifies just one characteristic, for example, income or telephone exchange.

The sophistication of the mailing-list industry is phenomenal. Millions of names can be compiled, segmented in thousands of ways, and merged or "overlayed" with other data sets. However, mailing lists have one major problem—perishability, or churning. People on the lists move, marry, divorce, die, retire, and change attitudes. Between 15 percent and 25 percent of the names and addresses on a typical list change each year. Consequently, the accuracy of lists must be checked periodically; four times per year is best.

A list can be checked in three ways. "Nixie" removal is the first. Mail that is returned by the U.S. Postal Service is nixed from future mailings. Change of address forms can also be included in all mailings. Finally, status can be checked for internal data such as purchase status or change of address.[12]

Direct-Mail Packages   Everything in a direct-mail package must be designed to work in harmony. The package must stand out from other mail in the mailbox and encourage the receiver to open it. The components of the package should reflect a total design concept. The classic direct-mail package consists of a mailing envelope, letter, circular, response device, and return device.

- Mailing envelope. The direct-mail selling process begins with the mailing envelope. Teaser copy or a "flash" (for example, "important, don't delay!") is often used to rouse interest and lead the reader to open the envelope. Teaser copy is especially valuable when advertisers are mailing third class to a new or unknown list.
- The letter. The letter should be personalized, speak to the self-interest of the reader, and elicit interest.
- The circular. The circular gives the details of the product—the specifications, color, pricing, photographs, guarantees, and endorsements. It presents the primary selling message and can take the form of a booklet, broadsheet (an oversized enclosure or jumbo folder), brochure, flier, or single sheet.
- Response device. The response device is the order form, often including a toll-free phone number. It should summarize the primary selling points and be simple to read and fill out. Any available information (for example, the customer's existing account number or name and address) should be printed on the device. Finally, since the order form becomes a legal document, it is important to clear all wording with the firm's legal department.
- Return device. The return device is any mechanism that allows the customer to return the necessary information. It can be an information request form, an order form, or a payment. Typically, a response envelope is generally provided unless a card is used as a response device. The envelope serves as an incentive and is convenient, especially if the postage is prepaid.[13]

Writing Direct-Mail Copy   To write good copy, the direct-mail copywriter needs good information about the producer, the customer, and competitors. The direct-mail copywriter must know why people buy. Customers may be hesitant about characteristics of the product, such as whether it will fit, its actual color, or its level of performance. Good copy clearly translates selling points into benefits and emphasizes the buyer's self-gratification.

The recipient's reluctance to buy strongly influences direct-mail copywriting. A successful story must be told again and again to the target audience. It is useful to track the purchase history of each prospect. Follow-up mailings should be more directed and less general than the first contact. The offer must be stated immediately and emphatically. Moreover, the writer must convince the customer that what is promised will be delivered. Finally, good copy makes it easy to take the desired action. Requested action should be simple, specific, and immediate.

The large amount of copy space available in direct mail as compared with mass print media presents a temptation as well as an opportunity. There is a tendency to include excess material and use ultracreative formats. But the objective of direct mail is to sell, not to impress. Each word and picture must support that objective.[14]

Catalogs

Catalogs have changed dramatically over the last century. Born out of the need to provide products to people living in isolated locations, the catalog has become a shopping and purchase vehicle used by virtually all consumers, employed women in particular. Strapped for time, the modern consumer now accepts catalogs as a reliable and trustworthy alternative for the purchase of all types of products, from doormats to computers to trips around the world. The Christmas season has become the real boom time for catalogs.[15] In a Gallup poll that asked consumers how they planned to use catalogs during the 1990 Christmas season, of the majority planning to purchase from a select group of catalogs, 53 percent indicated they would spend over two hundred dollars.

Catalog developers now use sophisticated marketing tools. Catalogs have become more and more specialized, both in terms of products carried and consumers targeted. Even the old reliable Sears, Roebuck and Co. catalog offers several product-specific versions. Catalog companies have also contributed to the development of mailing lists by selling and purchasing massive lists. Finally, the production quality of catalogs has improved, so that most copy and layout strategies are as good as those in the best print ads.

There are four general types of catalogs. *Retail catalogs* contain merchandise equivalent to that found in the sponsors' stores. Their intent is to build store traffic inside the trading area and mail-order sales outside it. Service Merchandise is an example. *Full-line merchandise catalogs* contain all the merchandise found in a complete department store, plus other products such as appliances and home-related remodeling and installation materials. Sears is an example. *Business-to-business catalogs* contain products that are sold from one business to another in order to reduce the costs associated with personal selling. Amway catalogs are an example. And finally, *consumer specialty catalogs,* such as those sent out by L. L. Bean, contain a line of related products, such as camping equipment, that are sent only to those consumers considered potential customers.

Dick Hodgson, catalog expert, notes four criteria that must be met for a catalog to achieve success.[16] First, the consumer must be convinced that the product is special and only available through the catalog. Second, the catalog sponsor must be perceived as an authority or expert in that field. L. L. Bean, for example, is considered a true authority on outdoor apparel. Third, consumers must feel that they are receiving a legitimate deal. Products available at an equivalent price at a local retailer are no bargain. Finally, consumers must be satisfied with their purchases. Since consumers have an inherent fear of products ordered through catalogs, proper fit, correct colors, promised performance, and money-back guarantees are all factors to be considered when selecting products to sell through a catalog.

Environmental factors also influence the success of mail-order catalogs, as highlighted in Table 18.5.

Everything in a catalog must make a harmonious contribution to the whole. The cover must immediately attract the prospect's attention. The photography must generate interest. The copy should be easy to read, highly descriptive, and concise yet comprehensive. The merchandise selected for sale must create an optimum mix in terms of quality and depth. The order form should be easy to follow and fill out. Finally, the shipping charges should be congruent with the value of the product; for example, shipping charges of $3.75 on a $5.00 item are out of line.

Table 18.5   **Factors Contributing to the Success of Mail-Order Catalogs**

Socioeconomic Factors	External Factors	Competitive Factors
More women joining the work force	Rising cost of gasoline	Inconvenient store hours
Population growing older	Availability of WATS, toll-free lines	Unsatisfactory service in stores
Rising discretionary income	Expanded use of credit cards	Difficulty of parking, especially near downtown stores
More single-parent households	Low-cost data processing	"If you can't beat 'em, join 'em" approach of traditional retailers
Growth of the "me" generation	Wide accessibility of mailing lists	

Source: An exhibit from John A. Quelch and Hirotake Takeuchi, "Nonstore Marketing: Fast Track or Slow?" *Harvard Business Review* (July/August 1981): 77. Reprinted by permission of the *Harvard Business Review*. Copyright © 1987 by the President and the Fellows of the Harvard College. All rights reserved.

Mass Media Direct Marketing

Television, radio, magazines, and newspapers offer another form of direct-response marketing. The fact that mass media are already classified by demographic and geographic characteristics means that direct-marketing messages can be targeted at certain geographic areas, market segments, or market areas with a history of higher response rates. Direct marketers must weigh the benefit of specific targeting against several disadvantages of using mass media. Unlike direct mail and catalogs, mass media impose time and space limitations on the advertiser. Appeals carried in mass media must compete with the editorial or program content and other ads. And there are extremely high costs associated with mass media.

Since earlier discussions considered these media and the guidelines for effectively creating ads in each, only considerations unique to direct marketing will be discussed here.

Using Print   Print ads can carry a direct-marketing appeal by simply providing information about the product and an order form or a toll-free number for ordering it directly from the manufacturer. The copy tends to be direct and concise with little emotionalism and few claims. There must be a "call to action"; if the reader is not asked to order the product, then the copy should cite other actions—filling out a coupon or calling a number, for example. The copy should be benefit oriented, and the design should lead the reader through the ad in logical order. Sufficient space for address information and signature should be provided in the order blank. The terms of the offer, including price, must also be clearly stated. The order form should be keyed or coded so marketers can determine the origin of incoming customer orders or inquiries. The key or code is the most important part of the order card because it indicates the source of sales.

In addition to the standard full-page or partial-page formats, other print ad formats are available. A *magazine insert*, for example, can be a multipage piece or a reply card bound next to a full-page ad. *Bingo cards* appear in the back of magazines and give consumers an easy way to request information on products and services. The publisher prints designated numbers for specified literature, and the consumer circles the number of the desired information. *Newspaper inserts* include single-page pieces, multipage booklets, perforated coupons, or gummed reply envelopes. *Sunday supplements,* such as *Parade* and *Family Weekly,* are edited nationally but appear in the local Sunday editions of many newspapers.

Using Television and Radio   Television is well suited to demonstration of a direct marketer's product. Television is used in three major ways: to sell a product or service, to generate leads for a product or service, and to support direct-response advertising in other media (for example, Publishers' Clearing House or Time-Life Books). Immediate response can be obtained by providing viewers with a toll-free number. Direct-marketing television commercials are usually two minutes long. At least one-fourth of this time is devoted to ordering information.

Air and production costs are far lower for direct radio response than for television. Direct radio can be scheduled quickly and, if live, can be revised at the last minute. Radio is also more efficient than television in attracting particular types of listeners.

Few direct-response advertisers use television because of its high cost and the short duration of the commercials. Radio has its own limitations, however, including the lack of visualization and the fact that many listeners are otherwise engaged when hearing the ad. Because listeners often do not have pencil and paper handy, the response must be easy to remember, such as a telephone number that spells a word. Repeating the information helps as well. However, both television and radio may be too broad for some marketers.

Cable television has become the primary broadcast medium for many direct marketers. It is less expensive, more targeted, and allows longer messages than television. Cable has produced two special forms of direct-message delivery systems. The first is the various types of *home shopping channels.* The Home Shopping Network (HSN) began this direct-message delivery system with an all-day program format that presented item after item, gave the price, and indicated an order mechanism. Companies such as J. C. Penney have developed similar home shopping systems. Their success has been limited and some feel their future is in doubt. Infomercials are the second type of direct-marketing cable delivery system. An **infomercial** is a thirty- or sixty-minute ad. Also called an **advertorial,** this format has been criticized because the ads are often written in a manner that makes them sound like regular programming. As indicated in the Promotion in Focus box, infomercials are declining in popularity.

Using Teletext and Videotext   Teletext and videotext (or viewdata) represent the two newest additions to direct-marketing mass media. Both offer text and graphic presentations on demand, but the similarity stops there.

Teletext is a system of transmitting frames of information via a regular television broadcast signal. It is a one-way transmission via the vertical blanking interval—the interval in which the television signal leaves the bottom of the screen and jumps back to the top to start scanning again. Given the short transmission time between frames, only a limited amount of information can be transmitted per frame. A viewer can pluck these frames off the air and make them appear on the screen by pressing the correct buttons on a teletext-modified television set. The frames appear superimposed over an existing program or on a separate channel reserved for teletext.

To date, teletext has had limited commercial application. This slow evolution is partly due to the expense of implementing this technology over a broad range of users. In addition, the limited volume of data (or number of frames) available and the requirement that ordering be accomplished via mail or telephone dampen the appeal of teletext. Nevertheless, teletext holds enormous potential as a direct-marketing strategy.

In contrast, *videotext* suffers from none of these limitations. It ties an individual television set to a remote host computer via telephone line or coaxial cable. Videotext has unlimited capacity to store and deliver information. It is also totally interactive through the same telephone line or cable over which the data are received. By activating a keyboard or keypad, the user can make a request, which then appears on the television screen. The user can obtain product information, order, and pay for the merchandise right at the television set. This technology is gaining in popularity.

Telemarketing

The newest marketing medium is *telemarketing,* which combines telecommunications technology, marketing strategies, and information systems. It can be used alone or in conjunction with advertising, direct mail, sales promotions, personal selling, and other marketing functions.

There are two types of telemarketing: inbound and outbound. An inbound or incoming telemarketing call originates with the customer. Calls originating with the firm are outgoing or outbound.

Inbound calls are customer responses to a marketer's stimulus, whether a direct-mail piece, a direct-marketing broadcast, a catalog, or a published toll-free number. Since it is almost impossible to schedule customer calls, every effort must be made to ensure that the lines are not blocked. Having many lines is very costly, however.

In 1987, a national survey comparing users and nonusers of toll-free numbers found that users are equally likely to place orders in the morning, afternoon, or evening.[17] Late evening or night is the least desirable time to order. Retired people and people not employed outside the home prefer placing toll-free orders on weekdays. College graduates, multiple wage earners, people employed outside the home, and people with high incomes are more likely to place orders on Saturday.

Although most inbound telemarketing occurs via toll-free 800 numbers, the 1-900 number has also grown in popularity, from twenty-seven million dollars of business in 1985 to five hundred fifteen million dollars in 1990. Its increased popularity is a direct result of the 1989 introduction of interactive 1-900 numbers, which enable callers to respond to questions and leave information via touch-tone phones. Interactivity has allowed direct-marketing programs to become much more sophisticated. Media and entertainment companies have been in the forefront of promoting via 1-900 numbers. For example, Phone Programs created a 900 program to promote HBO's "Tales from the Crypt" horror show. For two dollars a call, viewers hear elaborate sound effects and answer horror trivia questions for a chance to win prizes.[18]

Outbound telemarketing is used by direct marketers whenever they take the initiative for a call—for opening new accounts, qualifying, selling, scheduling, servicing, or profiling customers. Wide Area Telephone Service (WATS) is often used as an economic long-distance vehicle. Outbound telemarketing is generally most efficient if the call is directed to a prospect who has been prequalified in some way, since the cost per telephone call is quite high.

Telemarketing has four primary applications: order taking, customer service, sales support, and account management. Order taking is the traditional use and also an excellent means of possible cross-selling. Olan Mills Studios uses more than nine thousand local telemarketers to sell photograph packages, frames, and related items, with a response rate of 3 percent. Customer service usually means handling complaints or initiating cross-selling opportunities by informing customers of new features, models, or accessories. To provide sales support for the field sales force, telemarketers schedule sales calls, confirm appointments, maintain supplies, make credit checks, and sell marginal accounts. Account management replaces the personal contact with customers. If well planned, an ongoing relationship can be maintained between certain customers and telemarketing sales specialists.

Telemarketing is definitely a viable promotional alternative. It raises hundreds of technical and cost-related questions that are beyond the scope of this book. It must be carefully planned and guided by experts. Although the supposed benefit of telemarketing is cost saving because of its ability to segment the market, it is not cheap. Telephone calls range from three dollars to five dollars for consumer market calls and from six dollars to ten dollars for business market calls. Cost-efficient results will be attained only if the prospect list is targeted and the telephone is not used for random attempts.[19]

Concept Review

There are several types of media used in direct marketing:
1. Direct mail delivers the message and product through the U.S. Postal Service or a private delivery organization. Its success is based on the quality of the lists, the package, and the copy.

2. Catalogs fall into four categories: retail, full-line merchandise, business-to-business, and consumer specialty.
3. Mass media used by direct marketing include magazines, newspapers, radio, television, teletext, and videotext.
4. Telemarketing includes inbound and outbound calls.

The Trouble with Direct Marketing

Tremendous growth and poor early management have created some serious problems in the direct-marketing industry. Many of the troubles are symptoms of managerial nearsightedness, a failure to consider long-term goals and the organization as a whole.

Short-Term Tactics Versus Long-Term Strategies

In 1981, Ed Ney, then CEO of Young & Rubicam, was asked whether direct marketing in the future was "an oasis or a mirage." "The difference between general [indirect] marketers and direct marketers," Ney said, "is the difference between the cost of goods sold and the price of success."[20] Ney was referring to brand personality built over the years versus the "one shots" that frequently characterize direct marketing. Examples of the short-term approach crop up daily in consumer mailboxes: mailings that look like telegrams, air-express packages, legal communications, or government documents. Short-term direct marketing does get a response—for a while, until customers become wary. But at what price? This kind of direct marketing creates short-term, disloyal customers who were really fooled into responding.

In contrast, American Express spends hundreds of thousands of dollars a year sending "love letters," communications that might typically congratulate customers on their tenth anniversary as card members. The objective of the communication is to reinforce a customer's relationship with American Express over the long term.

Connected to the short-term emphasis of direct marketers is their tendency to be more interested in tactics than in underlying strategy. This is true for two reasons. First, direct marketing entails technical intensity. The complex, demanding, and problem-prone manufacturing of databases tends to focus direct-marketing practitioners narrowly on tactics. The personalization of direct marketing through sophisticated databases is a case in point. People pay attention when marketers call them by name, and they are flattered if marketers know a little bit about their needs, tastes, and preferences. However, people get very upset if they think marketers know too much about them or if marketers seem to be misusing this

Promotion in Focus

Infomercials—The Ultimate Hybrid

How much can you say about a product in 30 seconds or a minute? Back in the days when most vendors sold their wares in markets or door-to-door, a convincing salesperson could probably create a spiel that would last all day, demonstrating the product, answering questions and objections, talking about its history and competitors, really giving the product a chance. The 30-second commercial is to a product what the sound bite is to a political campaign—a tantalizing peek at the whole.

Because of the frustration some advertisers feel about the limitations of the average commercial, many must have welcomed the birth in the 1980s of the "infomercial." You may never have heard the name, but you've probably seen part of one. When you flipped the channel, you probably thought at first that you had turned to a new game show—there was so much excitement, energy, and good feeling. Finally, if you stuck with it, you noticed that everyone was talking about a product or service, the same one, time after time. And if you stayed until the end of the half hour, you got your hunch confirmed: you were watching a paid commercial announcement.

Infomercials developed into a $500 million-a-year business in just six years. At their heyday, one dollar spent on media was generating two dollars in sales. Infomercials sold skincare products, motivational programs, get-rich-quick schemes, products that promised one thousand household uses. Even huge companies like AT&T began getting interested in them. They seemed capable of providing the perfect blend of information, demonstration, and sales pitch.

But from the beginning, many people were suspicious of infomercials. Many viewers felt conned when they realized they were watching a giant commercial, and anyone who remembered Dan Ackroyd's old Saturday Night Live commercial routines was likely to get too strong a sense of deja vu. Some infomercials pitched products that sounded too good to be true—a diet patch, cures for impotence and baldness.

But it may be too early to declare the infomercial dead. The recession has made air time less expensive, which works in favor of infomercials, and infomercial producers have formed a trade group to police their own products. There may yet be a viable forum for advertisers who feel shortchanged by the standard commercial.

Source: Steven W. Colford, "Infomercials Fade," *Advertising Age* (March 4, 1991): 3, 50.

personal information. Direct marketers seem unconcerned with how this potentially dangerous tactic fits into the overall strategy of the firm.

A second source of the tactical emphasis of direct marketing is organizational. Direct marketing is controlled and managed by people at relatively low levels in many firms. These people might not be privy to the strategic goals of their companies or might not understand the strategic thinking. The result of this deficiency is tactical executions floating free of any strategic context.

Nonintegrated Versus Integrated Approaches

All too often, direct marketing does not mesh with a company's operations, its distribution systems, communications, research, overall strategy, or even its culture. For example, direct marketers have been part of programs that have failed because they are so successful: catalog companies run out of inventories, costing them not only short-term sales but long-term goodwill, or financial firms generate too many leads for their salespeople to follow up.

Another common failure in integration involves direct marketing and advertising. Direct-marketing messages and advertising messages seldom reinforce each other because the people who do direct-response advertising are not usually integrated with the people who do advertising. Nor is the advertising agency integrated.

Integrating Direct Marketing with Promotion

Direct marketing is just one of several tools available to the promotion manager. It has distinct advantages over indirect marketing, and many companies use it as their primary promotional technique. However, direct marketing requires the manager to learn a new jargon and a new technology. Strategically, the promotion manager must assess when the move to direct marketing is advantageous. Combined with other promotional techniques, direct marketing can have a powerful effect. Clearly, direct marketing is going to grow in acceptance.

Concept Review

Several disadvantages of direct marketing are as follows:

- It is not effective as a long-term strategy.
- Direct marketing messages are seldom integrated with a company's advertising messages.
- Integrating direct marketing with promotion requires the promotion manager to learn new jargon and technology.

Case 18   Am Ex Does It Direct

Background

In the late 1980s, American Express was faced with a serious dilemma. The card division was highly decentralized. There were about eight product groups, including the green card, the gold card, supplemental cards, card-members services, and insurance, and each had its own managers. At the time, the company was spending nearly two hundred million dollars in television and print image/awareness advertising. However, direct mail, because it was not perceived as advertising, was not covered by the ad budget. Direct mail was procured separately by each individual product group using its own promotion budget.

There was a lot of stress in the company because of direct mail. The various groups fought among themselves to get access to the house list of card members. Since the direct-mail pieces were designed, written, and managed by many sources, the quality varied, and the coherence of the overall communication was extremely difficult to control. In particular, the company's outside computer service bureau seemed to be in constant trouble. The Am Ex director of advertising decided the time had come to hire a few direct-marketing professionals to set things right in the card division.

Assessing the Problem

Stephen Johns was the field research director assigned to evaluate direct marketing at Am Ex. He had worked for Direct Marketing Research, Inc., for seven years and had thirteen years of previous experience with direct mail. During the first few months, Johns informally conducted the first "census" for Am Ex direct mail. He realized that although the company's focus was on the two hundred million dollars of general advertising, hidden in all those separate product groups was a total of nearly another two hundred million dollars being spent in direct mail. On the average, Am Ex was sending out more than one million pieces per day, all targeted at about 10 percent of the nation's pickiest consumers. The profitability was usually excellent, but one million pieces every day was clearly excessive. The response from top management was immediate and the challenge was straightforward: find effective ways of reducing the volume of direct mail.

After careful consideration of various alternatives, Johns determined there were two underlying problems. First, there was a need to target the right people. Research indicated that less than 1 percent of the prospective customers who received Am Ex pieces responded either by requesting additional information or by joining the Am Ex program. Since the response rate for the credit card industry is approximately 2 percent to 3 percent, the Am Ex program was far less successful than those conducted by competitors such as Visa and MasterCard. Analysis of current mailing lists indicated that the socioeconomic characteristics employed by Am Ex as a basis for its lists were very general and applied to a wide range of people. Men and women age forty and over with annual incomes of thirty-five thousand dollars were typical criteria used. The second problem was a result of the first. Am Ex was receiving numerous complaints from customers and noncustomers about the deluge of junk mail from Am Ex. These complaints were a major source of ill will toward the company and conflicted with the upscale reputation Am Ex wanted.

One tentative solution suggested by Johns was a list exclusion procedure. Am Ex management would offer all card members an opportunity to remove themselves from the company's promotional mailing lists. Management was leery of the idea since all communication with card members depended on direct mail.

Case Questions

1. Suggest changes Am Ex could make in order to provide better control over its direct-mail operation.
2. What other direct-marketing techniques could Am Ex consider?

Summary

This chapter introduces a special category of marketing, direct marketing. It differs from conventional marketing in two important ways. First, the only way to receive the product is through direct contact with the provider. Second, this direct contact between provider and customer requires some unique adjustments in the marketing strategy, particularly promotion. The promotional effort employed in conjunction with direct marketing is called direct-response advertising.

There are three types of direct marketing: the one-step process (the consumer can respond immediately), the two-step process (the prospect must qualify before purchase), and the negative option (the customer joins a plan with an ongoing commitment).

The bulk of the chapter details the components of the direct-marketing strategy: the offer, the medium, and the message. The offer includes a host of factors—price, shipping and handling, options, future obligation, credit, incentives, time and quantity limits, and guarantees or warranties. The medium represents the heart of direct marketing. It is the vehicle used by the marketer to deliver the message, receive the order, and deliver the product. Four such vehicles are (1) direct mail, (2) catalogs, (3) mass media, and (4) telemarketing. While the creative principles remain the same for this category of marketing, the objectives and media used require creative adjustments.

Discussion Questions

1. Discuss the primary differences between direct-marketing advertising and general advertising.

2. Select two print ads you consider to be direct marketing, one directed at ultimate consumers and one at a business. Critique each in respect to how well it makes the offer, includes sufficient information, and provides a mechanism for responding.

3. "Direct marketing still sends junk mail and sells junk products. Its popularity is just a fad." Comment on this statement.

4. Discuss the various types of databases available to direct marketers. What are the characteristics of a good database?

5. What are the advantages and the disadvantages of direct mail? How has the evolution of the mailing list affected direct mail?

6. As vice president of marketing for a seed company, you are in the process of designing a direct-mail package aimed at experienced gardeners living throughout the United States. Describe the contents of the package and give an example of the copy you might use.

7. Discuss the four requirements of a successful catalog.

8. Contrast broadcast and print media in terms of their effectiveness for direct marketing.

9. Discuss the differences between inbound and outbound telemarketing.

10. What risks does the consumer often associate with direct marketing? How can the marketer counteract these fears?

Suggested Projects

1. Select a consumer product that is not normally sold through direct marketing (for example, over-the-counter drugs, automobiles, pets).

Create a direct-marketing campaign for this project. Be sure to specify your objectives and indicate the parts of the offer as well as the medium and the message.

2. Contact three mailing-list houses. Compile several consumer profiles and ask for a cost estimate for one hundred thousand names containing these traits. Also have the houses indicate the guarantees that go with the list. Write a report on your findings.

References

1. *Direct Marketing* (October 1990): 22.

2. William B. Beggs, Jr., "Direct Marketing: Heading in Many Different Directions," *Link* (May/June 1990): 29.

3. M. E. Ziegenhagen, "Let's Stop Diluting Direct Marketing," *Business Marketing* (February 1986): 88.

4. Fred R. McFadden and Jeffrey A. Hoffer, *Data Base Management* (Menlo Park, CA: Benjamin/Cummings, 1985): 3.

5. *Ibid.*

6. Rich Roscitt and I. Robert Parket, "Direct Marketing to Consumers," *Journal of Consumer Marketing* Vol. 5, No. 1 (Winter 1988): 5–14.

7. "DM Marketplace," *Direct Marketing* (August 1986): 88.

8. Robert Kestanbaum, "Growth Strategies for Direct Marketers," *Direct Marketing Association, Release 110.2,* January 1984.

9. Robert Stone, *Successful Direct Marketing Methods,* 3d ed. (Lincolnwood, IL: National Textbook Company, 1986): 451–52.

10. "Harried Pace in Race: Cost Spiral Fuels Direct-Mail Alternatives to Postal Service," *Advertising Age* (September 25, 1989): S-1.

11. Joanne Lipman, "Direct Mailers Study Disposable Videos," *The Wall Street Journal* (May 30, 1990): B3.

12. "Sroge Lists Leading Mail Order Firms," *Marketing News* (12 June 1981): 3. Bodo Von Der Wense, "Planning, List Selection, Copy, Layout, Timing, Testing Can Make or Break Direct Mail Pieces," *Marketing News* (November 14, 1986): 7.

13. Robert Stone, p. 2.

14. *Ibid.*

15. Alison Fahey, "Catalogs High on Yule Lists," *Advertising Age* (September 24, 1990): S-1.

16. "Tailoring Catalogs to Fit Corporate Personality, *Advertising Age* (October 27, 1986): 5–21.

17.   Anita Brown, "Pay to Play," *Marketing and Media Decisions* (September 1990): 16–17.

18.   "Behavior and Attitudes of Telephone Shoppers," *Direct Marketing* (September 1987): 50–51.

19.   Herbert D. Hennessey, "Matters to Consider Before Plunging into Telemarketing," *Marketing News* (July 8, 1983): 2.

20.   Herbert Katzenstein and William S. Sachs, *Direct Marketing* (Columbus, Ohio: Charles E. Merrill Publishing Company, 1986): 4.

19 *International Marketing and Promotion*

Strategies for International Marketing and Promotion

Going International
Market Entry Strategies
Standardization Versus Customization
Assessing the Environment

The Major Players in International Marketing and Promotion

Europe 1992
The Pacific Rim
The Eastern Bloc
The Americas
Africa

Designing an International Promotional Strategy

Advertising
Personal Selling
Sales Promotion
Public Relations

Consider This:

Procter & Gamble Takes On Europe

As one of the world's leading packaged goods companies, Procter & Gamble (P&G) has long sold its products around the world. But its recent moves in Europe provide a sense of how important the broadening European market is and of how American-based companies must learn to adjust as they move into different markets.

P&G's 1989 introduction of Vidal Sassoon Wash & Go to Germany was a fairly straightforward exporting of a successful American product. Wash & Go is sold in the United States as Pert Plus, the leading shampoo-conditioner in the American market. Leo Burnett International, which handles the product worldwide, spent $5 million introducing Wash & Go to Germany, compared to about $15 million spent on Pert Plus promotion in the United States. Within ten months, Wash & Go had become the number three shampoo in Germany, with a market share of over 7 percent.

P&G has had a somewhat more difficult job introducing its Always sanitary protection products to Europe, especially Great Britain. The market is fragmented and highly competitive, with some comparable products selling for considerably less than Always. British sanitary practices, however, pose a potentially greater problem. Always napkins tend to clog pipes when flushed, which is not a problem in most of Europe. But in Great Britain, where some 70 percent of sanitary napkins are flushed down the toilet, a reputation of gumming up the pipes could create a major marketing nightmare.

A different set of problems faces P&G as it races to bring its brands to newly opened markets in Eastern Europe. The markets in such countries as Hungary, Poland, and Czechoslovakia are new and largely unknown, and initial market research has revealed some surprises. For instance, after showing Hungarians several versions of a toothpaste ad, P&G found that viewers preferred a less authoritarian version of the spokesman. Even language can be a problem. In Czechoslovakia, P&G found that consumers preferred copy written in German rather than Czech or English.

For clever marketers, such discoveries are opportunities rather than problems. Companies that understand their new markets and address them well will succeed, even if it does take a little more work than is required to introduce a new product to the United States.

Sources: Dagmar Mussey, "P&G Cleans Up in Europe with 2 in 1 Shampoo," *Advertising Age* (October 8, 1990): 54. Dagmar Mussey and Elena Bowes, "P&G Eyes Europe for Always," *Advertising Age* (June 24, 1991): 6. Jennifer Lawrence, "P&G Marches into Europe," *Advertising Age* (September 30, 1991): 10.

*T*he marketing of Wash & Go in Europe by Procter & Gamble Co. is one example of international marketing and promotion. In the words of Jeannett and Hennessey, **international marketing** is "the performance of marketing activities across two or more countries."[1] The willingness of Procter & Gamble to engage in international marketing is not unusual. The Boeing Co. sells many of its airplanes outside the United States. Airbus, a European conglomerate, sells a great many of its planes in the United States. Banks have been international marketers for nearly a century. In the last two decades, however, more and more companies have turned to international marketing.

By 1990, the scope of international marketing had broadened to include many nonmanufacturing activities. Retailers such as K Mart, Bloomingdale's, and Wal-Mart import 20 percent to 40 percent of the merchandise found on their shelves. Service industries such as hotels, restaurants, and health care are constantly looking for opportunities in other countries.

The decision to become an international marketer has enormous ramifications. For example, new manufacturing plants may have to be built, products may have to be redesigned, new sources of raw material may have to be found, and new distributors may have to be found. Promotion managers generally need to make adjustments too, since communication in an unfamiliar culture presents a wide range of problems.

The objectives of this chapter are twofold. First, this chapter will provide an overview of strategic issues and environmental factors in international marketing. Second, the adjustments required to promote in an international setting will be discussed.

Strategies for International Marketing and Promotion

For many U.S. marketers, opportunities to gain market share or increase revenues domestically are virtually nonexistent. Perhaps market saturation has occurred, and all the people who need the product now have it. Or the product is faced with a competitive disadvantage, and consumers no longer consider it an acceptable alternative. Or excessive competition exists, and none of the marketers is able to generate needed profits. Regardless of the reasons, marketers throughout the world are faced with the difficult decision to move outside their borders and compete in another land. Before making this decision, however, the marketer must carefully examine the pros and cons inherent in international marketing. Employing the formal planning process offered throughout this book is a necessary first step. However, this planning process is complicated by the fact that international marketing requires strategies at two levels: the strategy for entering international markets and the strategy for reaching the consumers within each market. These issues will be discussed next.

Going International

There are three primary reasons why companies decide to market in countries other than their own. The first and most notable reason is **market saturation,** which means that the domestic market has reached maturity and stopped growing. Profits have also slowed or even declined. Foreign markets hold out a chance for new growth. In the case of the U.S. pet food industry, for example, introducing U.S. products into Europe increased not only sales volume but also the profit margin, because certain economies of scale were achieved. Greater profits can also be generated in certain foreign countries because of lower labor costs, looser regulations, land available for manufacturing plants, and so forth.

Sometimes companies enter other markets because their customers move there first. U.S. advertising agencies have opened offices in other countries in order to serve their multinational clients. Parts suppliers serving Japanese car makers have moved to the United States for the same reason.

Companies also enter the international arena for purely defensive purposes. Certain U.S. companies have launched businesses in Japan to check the advance of Japanese competitors. Likewise, Siemens has entered the U.S. market in response to AT&T entering Europe. This defensive expansion has proven to be a risky strategy since many of these companies have no competitive advantages in the new markets.

Strategic planning for international marketing requires essentially the same process as the one we outlined in Chapter 1. However, three considerations must be addressed before designing a marketing strategy for an international operation: (1) market entry strategies, (2) standardization versus customization, and (3) environmental adjustments.

Market Entry Strategies

Moving into another country is neither simple nor automatic. There are right and wrong ways to gain entry, both from the perspective of the marketer and of the foreign country. Figure 19.1 depicts the primary entry strategies. Each will be discussed briefly.

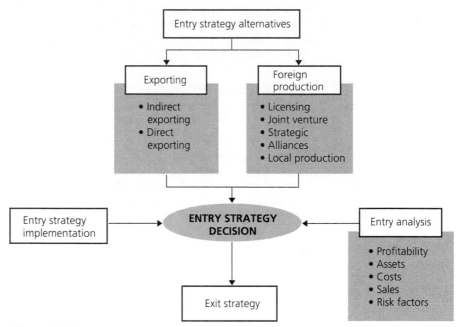

Figure 19.1

Primary market entry strategies.
Jean-Pierre Jeannet and Hubert D. Hennessey, Global Marketing Strategies, *2nd edition, © 1992. (Boston: Houghton Mifflin Company, 1992): 292.*

To **export** is to sell a product in another country without making a commitment to local production. Because of the limited size of the foreign market, the exporting company manufactures its products at a central location, thereby gaining certain economies of scale. Either indirect exporting or direct exporting is possible. **Indirect exporting** employs a marketing intermediary in the exporter's country of operation who specializes in selling products in foreign countries. This is the arrangement that Kao, a Japanese maker of soap, cosmetics, and other household products, employs in several European countries. **Direct exporting** uses intermediaries located in the foreign markets. Thus the exporter must make a contact for each country, but that contact may have greater expertise and access than the indirect marketing intermediary. Procter & Gamble Co. uses this market entry strategy in most of South and Central America.

Instead of exporting, a marketer might enter a foreign market by creating a physical presence in that country. Licensing is the most passive option. Under **licensing,** a company assigns the right to a patent or a trademark to another company for a fee or royalty. The foreign company then has the right to sell the product or process, and the domestic marketer does not have to make an equity investment. Licensing has proven to be very successful for Federal Express, whose small satellite hubs are more practical in geographically isolated countries.

In a **joint venture,** a foreign company invites an outside partner to share stock ownership in the new unit; both companies share the risk of the new venture, but the partners may not contribute resources equally. Often, the foreign partner simply facilitates entry into the country since governments look more favorably on joint ventures that include a local business. Such was the arrangement between French aluminum producer Pechiney and American National Can.

Strategic alliances are the most recent entry strategy. They go beyond a joint venture in that all the participating companies pool their resources on a somewhat equal basis. AT&T has found strategic alliances to offer important competitive advantages. Its partnership with Italtel, Italy's state-owned telephone equipment maker, is an example.

Finally, a company may create a presence in another country by establishing local manufacturing. For example, Japanese auto makers such as Honda and Toyota have found it advantageous to manufacture in the United States because of cost factors, tariffs, and laws. Similarly, Ford Motor Co. operates large manufacturing plants in several countries and sells most of its output in the country where it is manufactured.

The method used to enter a foreign market has a direct bearing on promotion. Most notably, the amount of control retained by the marketer varies by strategy. In the case of indirect exporting, for example, little control is kept by the sponsoring organization. The chances of the marketing intermediary accepting the promotion strategy or implementing it correctly tend to be low. Conversely, establishing a clear presence in a foreign country through a manufacturing plant and a marketing team helps ensure that the promotion strategy will be implemented completely and correctly. In many countries, the use of certain promotional techniques can be employed only if the foreign marketer has a relationship with a host partner. In the Middle East, for example, joint ventures are virtually mandatory.

Standardization Versus Customization

Before entering a foreign market, a company must decide to what extent it is willing to customize its marketing effort to accommodate each foreign market. Naturally, the more the company standardizes its effort, the less trouble it incurs and the greater the assumed profitability. But is some customization inevitable?

Theodore Levitt, a Harvard professor, has argued against customization. In 1983, in "The Globalization of Markets," he suggested that world markets are being driven "toward a converging commonality" in which people everywhere are motivated by two common needs: high quality and reasonable price. Therefore, the "global corporation sells the same thing in the same way everywhere."[2] He uses McDonald's as one example. Furthermore, segmenting markets by political boundaries and customizing marketing strategies on the basis of national or regional preferences is not cost-effective. Levitt urges companies to adopt a "global orientation" by which they view the world as one market and sell a global product. Companies that do not become true global marketers will perish, says Levitt.[3]

Critics argue that Levitt's assumptions are not realistic. Products and strategies must be adapted to the cultural needs of each country. Philip Kotler, a professor of marketing at Northwestern University, champions the tried and true method of selling: tailoring to the local culture. Each national market is different, hence products and promotional strategies must be designed to fit the local culture. He cites several examples to support his position, including the classic Coca-Cola "Mean Joe" Greene commercial that was adapted for each of the fourteen countries in which it was shown.[4] M&M/Mars attempted to enter the European market by creating versions of its candy bars with a better grade of chocolate in order to compete with Swiss Nestlé and Cadbury-Schweppes.

Are there global markets? The answer is yes. Many countries have market segments with similar demands for the same product. Eastman Kodak Co., Gillette Co., and Timex have been selling standard products in similar fashion worldwide for decades. Does the world represent a global market? Hardly. There will always be obstacles to standardization, including cultural, political, economic, and other environmental factors. McDonald's restaurants in Hawaii and Japan offer sushi; those in Germany serve beer. Levitt's assumptions are not realities yet, and perhaps they never will be.

One study indicates that consumer goods companies are taking globalization seriously. Sixty-one percent of nonfood companies said they were working toward a global strategy on existing brands. When asked their opinion of global new product development for the future, about two-thirds of the executives believed that more and more companies would eventually adopt the global approach touted by Levitt.[5]

Whether a company assumes a standardized or a customized posture toward foreign markets has a direct bearing on the promotional effort. Standardization means taking the existing promotional strategy, making sure that everything is translated properly, and otherwise using it unchanged in the foreign country. Customization has far greater implications and makes promotion very complex. Extensive research is conducted on a country-by-country basis. Separate agencies may be hired for each market, and separate strategies are developed.

Assessing the Environment

The most difficult part of operating in a foreign market is identifying and then adjusting to factors of the local culture. Language is an obvious difference between countries, but many economic, political, legal, and cultural factors may make marketing and promotion difficult.

The Economic Environment   Two economic factors indicate the relative attractiveness of an export market. The first is the *size of the market*. If a firm already sells abroad, the international marketers must determine market size not only for present markets but also for potential markets. Market size for any given product is best described by two general indicators: (1) population: growth rates and distribution; and (2) income: distribution, income per capita, and gross national product (GNP). For example, projections of the increase in population from 1990 to the year 2000 are 0.7 percent for North America and 3.0 percent for Africa. Several countries such as Belgium and Hungary are expected to lose population. Projections of the increase in income for that same period for the United States are 7.3 percent, and income for Africa is expected to decline.

The *nature of the economy* is the second factor of importance. This factor is divided into four categories:[6]

1. The nation's physical endowment. This includes a country's natural resources such as minerals and waterpower, its topography (for example, rivers, lakes, forests, deserts, and mountains), and its climate, including temperature range, wind, rain, snow, and humidity.

2. The nature of economic activity. This means the stage of economic growth with respect to a country's agriculture, manufacturing, and service industries.

3. Infrastructure. This includes the external facilities and services available in a country, such as transportation, energy, communication, financial institutions, advertising agencies, and research firms.

4. Urbanization. This means the extent to which a country is urbanized.

The more favorable these factors are, the more attractive the foreign market. Deficiencies in one or more of these four indicators could require major adjustments in the marketing strategy.

Political and Legal Environment   Studies have shown that international marketers consider nationalism and dealing with governments to be major problems facing their companies. At least three political/legal factors should be considered in deciding whether to do business in a country.

The first is the role of the government in the economy. In the United States, Canada, and most European nations, the role of the government is mostly regulatory. But in much of the world, governments take a participatory role by owning businesses outright, being in partnership with local businesses, or being the exclusive or primary customer within the country.

The international marketer must understand these policies and laws and know how to accommodate them.

A second factor is the ideology of the country toward business in general and marketing in particular. A firm can usually market effectively in a socialist society, if private enterprise is allowed. Democratic societies are the most receptive to business.

A third factor is the stability of the country's political environment. Frequent changes of regime, violent disruptions, demonstrations, and cultural divisions suggest a high level of instability. But gradual and nonviolent change does not place the international marketer at risk.

Closely connected to a country's economic stability is the stability and nature of the exchange rate for its currency. When the U.S. dollar's value is high compared to most foreign currencies, U.S. goods are expensive for foreign buyers, which gives a price advantage to foreign countries. When U.S. economic conditions result in a low-valued dollar relative to foreign currencies, U.S. products are bargains for foreign customers.

Legal environments are even more complex. The international marketer must keep track of United States laws, international laws, and domestic laws in each of the firm's foreign markets. The task of maintaining current knowledge of export controls, antitrust laws, boycott activities, treaties, patents, and so on is staggering and requires expert input that is truly a full-time job.

Cultural Environment   Adjusting to cultural differences is perhaps the most difficult task facing international marketers. Culture is the sum total of learned behavioral traits that are manifested and shared by members of a society. Table 19.1 gives some specific examples. Culture is human-made and learned rather than acquired genetically. Unless special efforts are made to determine local cultural meanings for every market, the marketer is likely to proceed with plans that result in unwanted responses.

A number of cultural elements affect marketing and promotion. The following have particular relevance:

- Material culture. The availability of electricity, metric system of measurement, automobile transportation, appliances, mass media, highway systems, mass retail outlets, telephones, efficient mail systems, and so forth.

- Language. The extent of literacy, richness of vocabulary, number of dialects, bi- or trilingual citizens, linguistic unity, and definitional differences.

- Aesthetics. Differences in music, art, drama, dance, color, and form.

- Education. Differences in the process of transmitting skills, ideas, and attitudes as well as training in particular disciplines.

Table 19.1   **A Sampling of Cultural Variations**

Country/ Region	Body Motions	Greetings	Colors	Numbers	Shapes, Sizes, Symbols
Japan	Pointing to one's own chest with a forefinger indicates one wants a bath. Pointing a forefinger to the nose indicates "me."	Bowing is the traditional form of greeting.	Positive colors are in muted shades. Combinations of black, dark gray, and white have negative overtones.	Positive numbers are 1, 3, 5, 8. Negative numbers are 4, 9.	Pine, bamboo, or plum patterns are positive. Cultural shapes such as Buddha-shaped jars should be avoided.
India	Kissing is considered offensive and not seen on television, in movies, or in public places.	The palms of the hands are placed together and the head is nodded for greeting. It is considered rude to touch a woman or shake hands.	Positive colors are bold colors such as green, red, yellow, or orange. Negative colors are black and white if they appear in relation to weddings.	To create brand awareness, numbers are often used as a brand name.	Animals such as parrots, elephants, tigers, or cheetahs are often used as brand names or on packaging. Sexually explicit symbols are avoided.
Europe	Raising only the index finger signifies a person wants two items. When counting on the fingers, "one" is often indicated by thumb, "two" by thumb and forefinger.	It is acceptable to send flowers in thanks for a dinner invitation, but not roses (associated with sweethearts) or chrysanthemums (associated with funerals).	Generally, white and blue are considered positive. Black often has negative overtones.	The numbers 3 or 7 are usually positive. 13 is a negative number.	Circles are symbols of perfection. Hearts are considered favorably at Christmas.
Latin America	General arm gestures are used for emphasis.	The traditional form of greeting is a hearty embrace followed by a friendly slap on the back.	Popular colors are generally bright or bold yellow, red, blue, or green.	Generally, 7 is a positive number. Negative numbers are 13, 14.	Religious symbols should be respected. Avoid national symbols such as flag colors.
Middle East	The raised eyebrow facial expression indicates "yes."	The word "no" must be mentioned three times before it is accepted.	Positive colors are brown, black, dark blues, and reds. Pink, violets, and yellows are not favored.	Positive numbers are 3, 7, 5, 9, while 13, 15 are negative.	Round or square shapes are acceptable. Symbols of six-pointed star, raised thumb, or Koranic sayings are avoided.

James C. Simmons, "A Matter of Interpretation," *American Way* (April 1983): 106–111; and "Adapting Export Packaging to Cultural Differences," *Business America* (December 3, 1979): 3–7.

- Religion. The existence and importance of various religions.
- Attitudes and values. Basic beliefs about wealth, material gain, acquisition, change, risk taking, and marketing (especially selling, advertising, unnecessary products, and profits).
- Social organization. The importance of the various institutions that define how people relate to others (for example, kinship networks, social classes, castes, and special interest groups).[7]

The manner in which all of these factors combine to create a cultural profile is shown in Table 19.2 for the Islamic culture.

Concept Review

1. Marketers move into foreign markets for three reasons:
   a. Domestic market saturation.
   b. The needs of customers.
   c. The actions of competitors.
2. There are several strategies for entering foreign markets:
   a. Exporting (direct and indirect).
   b. Licensing.
   c. Joint venture.
   d. Strategic alliances.
   e. Local manufacturing.
3. Marketers must decide whether to standardize or customize their marketing effort when entering foreign markets.
4. Adjustments must be made to the following factors:
   a. The economic environment (the size of the market and the nature of the economy).
   b. The political/legal environment (the role of government, the country's ideology toward marketing, the stability of the government).
   c. The cultural environment (material, language, aesthetics, education, religion, attitudes/values, social organization).

The Major Players in International Marketing and Promotion

There are a great many foreign markets that are important to U.S. businesses. The world market is extremely dynamic; new market opportunities emerge daily, while others close. Consider the opening and closing of the China market in 1990. Several markets, however, have remained stable and offer a substantial and reliable source of revenue for a large number of U.S. businesses.

Table 19.2 **Marketing in an Islamic Framework**

Elements	Implications for Marketing
I. Fundamental Islamic Concepts	
A. *Unity*: Concept of centrality, oneness of God, harmony in life.	Product standardization, mass media techniques, central balance, unity in advertising copy and layout, strong brand loyalties, a smaller evoked size set, loyalty to company, opportunities for brand-extension strategies.
B. *Legitimacy*: Fair dealings, reasonable level of profits.	Less formal product warranties, need for institutional advertising and/or advocacy advertising, especially by foreign firms, and a switch from profit maximizing to a profit satisfying strategy.
C. *Zakaat*: 2.5 percent per annum compulsory tax binding on all classified as "not poor."	Use of "excessive" profits, if any, for charitable acts; corporate donations for charity, institutional advertising.
D. *Usury*: Cannot charge interest on loans. A general interpretation of this law defines "excessive interest" charged on loans as not permissible.	Avoid direct use of credit as a marketing tool; establish a consumer policy of paying cash for low value products; for high value products, offer discounts for cash payments and raise prices of products on an installment basis; sometimes possible to conduct interest transactions between local/foreign firm in other non-Islamic countries; banks in some Islamic countries take equity in financing ventures, sharing resultant profits (and losses).
E. *Supremacy of human life*: Compared to other forms of life, objects, human life is of supreme importance.	Pet food and/or products less important; avoid use of statues, busts—interpreted as forms of idolatry; symbols in advertising and/or promotion should reflect high human values; use floral designs and artwork in advertising as representation of aesthetic values.
F. *Community*: All Muslims should strive to achieve universal brotherhood—with allegiance to the "one God." One way of expressing community is the required pilgrimage to Mecca for all Muslims at least once in their lifetime, if able to do so.	Formation of an Islamic Economic Community—development of an "Islamic consumer" served with Islamic-oriented products and services, for example, "kosher" meat packages, gifts exchanged at Muslim festivals, and so forth; development of community services—need for marketing or nonprofit organizations and skills.
G. *Equality of peoples*	Participative communication systems; roles and authority structures may be rigidly defined but accessibility at any level relatively easy.
H. *Abstinence*: During the month of Ramadan, Muslims are required to fast without food or drink from the first streak of dawn to sunset—a reminder to those who are more fortunate to be kind to the less fortunate and as an exercise in self-control.	Products that are nutritious, cool, and digested easily can be formulated for Sehr and Iftar (beginning and end of the fast).
Consumption of alcohol and pork is forbidden; so is gambling.	Opportunities for developing nonalcoholic items and beverages (for example, soft drinks, ice cream, milk shakes, fruit juices) and nonchance social games, such as Scrabble; food products should use vegetable or beef shortening.

Table 19.2 **Marketing in an Islamic Framework (cont.)**

Elements	Implications for Marketing
I. *Environmentalism*: The universe created by God was pure. Consequently, the land, air, and water should be held as sacred elements.	Anticipate environmental, antipollution acts; opportunities for companies involved in maintaining a clean environment; easier acceptance of pollution-control devices in the community (for example, recent efforts in Turkey have been well received by the local communities).
J. *Worship*: Five times a day; timing of prayers varies.	Need to take into account the variability and shift in prayer timings in planning sales calls, work schedules, business hours, customer traffic, and so forth.
II. Islamic Culture	
A. Obligation to family and tribal traditions	Importance of respected members in the family or tribe as opinion leaders; word-of-mouth communication, customer referrals may be critical; social or clan allegiances, affiliations, and associations may be possible surrogates for reference groups; advertising home-oriented products stressing family roles may be highly effective, for example, electronic games.
B. Obligations toward parents are sacred	The image of functional products could be enhanced with advertisements that stress parental advice or approval; even with children's products, there should be less emphasis on children as decision makers.
C. Obligation to extend hospitality to both insiders and outsiders	Product designs that are symbols of hospitality, outwardly open in expression; rate of new product acceptance may be accelerated and eased by appeals based on community.
D. Obligation to conform to codes of sexual conduct and social interaction. These may include the following:	
1. Modest dress for women in public	More colorful clothing and accessories are worn by women at home; so promotion of products for use in private homes could be more intimate—such audiences could be reached effectively through women's magazines; avoid use of immodest exposure and sexual implications in public settings.
2. Separation of male and female audiences in some cases	Access to female consumers can often be gained only through women as selling agents, salespersons, catalogs, home demonstrations, and women's specialty shops.
E. Obligations to religious occasions; for example, there are two major religious observances that are celebrated—Eid-ul-Fitr, Eid-ul-Adha	Tied to purchase of new shoes, clothing, sweets, and preparation of food items for family reunions, Muslim gatherings. There has been a practice of giving money in place of gifts. Increasingly, however, a shift is taking place to more gift giving; due to lunar calendar, dates are not fixed.

Mushtaq Luqmani, Zahir A. Quraeshi, and Linda Delene, "Marketing in Islamic Countries: A Viewpoint," *MSU Business Topics*, Summer 1980, pp. 20–21. Reprinted by permission.

Europe 1992

By the time this book is published, Europe 1992 will be a reality. Virtually free trade will exist among Germany, France, Italy, the United Kingdom, Spain, the Netherlands, Belgium, Denmark, Greece, Portugal, Ireland, and Luxembourg. Although these nations will retain their status as independent countries, they will merge into the largest single market in the world, with more than 320 million consumers and buying power 25 percent larger than that of the United States. This unification will allow marketers to develop one standardized product for all twelve nations instead of customizing products to satisfy the regulations and restrictions of each country. Currency will be standardized, as will the banking system and the laws governing product delivery and business operations.

Although many legal borders have come down in Europe in 1992, assuming that cultural borders will also end would be a mistake. Table 19.3 lists differences in marketing restrictions that still persist in Europe. Judie Lammon, research director for J. Walter Thompson Co., London, predicted, "The Europe of the year 2000 will be characterized by just as much diversity as it is now, indeed more so, but the difference is that diversity

Table 19.3 **Differences in Marketing Restrictions**

Country	Cigarettes	Condoms	Feminine-Hygiene Products
England	No TV ads. No people or animals in ads.	No TV ads before 9 P.M. Can't show product outside packet. Sold via vending machines.	No TV ads during family viewing hours or religious programming. Can't show product outside package. Can't mention product's physical qualities. Can't use the words *menstruation, period,* or *flow.*
France	No ads on TV. Ad content restricted to copy and elements appearing on pack or carton. No point-of-purchase displays.	Partial nudity in TV ads. Can promote only as prophylactic. Free sampling with print ads.	TV ads at all times of day; can show product. TV ads can't use models under age 16, but print can.
Italy	No TV, outdoor, or point-of-purchase displays. Sponsorships of sporting and cultural events permitted.	No ads on state-run TV; can run at all times on privately owned stations. Promoted only as contraceptive.	No TV ads during mealtimes.
Greece	No restrictions. No health warning required on ads or packaging.	No TV or radio ads.	Information not available.

Saatchi & Saatchi International, Ansell/London, London International, DDB Needham/Paris, Philip Morris. Reprinted from *Adweek* (August 21, 1989): 41.

and fragmentation will be in lifestyle, values, and individualistic choices that cross boundaries."[8]

The Pacific Rim

The Pacific Rim countries include Japan, China, South Korea, Taiwan, Singapore, Hong Kong, the Philippines, Malaysia, Indonesia, Australia, and Indochina. Together, these countries represent 1.5 billion people.[9]

The Pacific Rim abounds with opportunities. Asia is the world's hottest market for cars, telecommunications equipment, airline seats, paint, and a host of other products. It is also crowded with competitors, including not only Japanese companies but also growing conglomerates from other countries in the region (see Table 19.4). By 1990, Asian producers outside Japan had already gained 25 percent of the global market for personal computers.[10]

Japan, however, is the leader in the Pacific Rim. The Japanese have made tremendous inroads into world consumer markets for automobiles, motorcycles, watches, cameras, audio and video equipment, and real estate.

Table 19.4 **Rising Companies in Asia**

	Sales in millions	Profits in millions	Business Activities
Samsung (*South Korea*)	$35,189	$515	Electronics, shipbuilding, insurance, trading
Daewoo (*South Korea*)	$19,981	$115	Electronics, construction, autos, heavy machinery
Lucky-Goldstar (*South Korea*)	$19,964	$285	Electronics, chemicals, trading, construction
Ssangyong Group (*South Korea*)	$7,422	$172	Cement, trading, oil refining, construction
Formosa Plastics (*Taiwan*)	$6,613	$425	Plastics, chemicals, textiles, plywood
Li Ka-Shing Group (*Hong Kong*)	$3,481	$1,644	Real estate, telecommunications, energy, trading
Singapore Airlines (*Singapore*)	$2,653	$625	International airline
Charoen Pokphand (*Thailand*)	$2,600*	N/A	Poultry breeding and processing, feed mills
Sime Darby (*Malaysia*)	$1,569	$101	Rubber and other plantations, trading, tires
Siam Cement (*Thailand*)	$1,235	$155	Cement, machinery, construction

*Estimate

Fortune (Pacific Rim 1990): 26, © 1990 Time Inc. All rights reserved.

Long criticized by Westerners because of its reluctance to accept imports, Japan appears to be opening its domestic market to foreign competitors. Younger Japanese are clamoring to buy more Western products. Because the costs and difficulties of entering Japan remain formidable, the rest of Asia may offer richer rewards for international marketers. For example, Singapore is very receptive to outside investments and is eager to establish relationships with foreigners (see Figure 19.2).

Figure 19.2

Asian countries are becoming an increasingly resourceful market for U.S. businesses.

Courtesy of Singapore E D B.

The Eastern Bloc

Thanks to the policy of *perestroika* initiated by former Soviet leader Mikhail Gorbachev, the Soviet Union, Poland, Hungary, Yugoslavia, Czechoslovakia, Rumania, and Bulgaria were opened to international marketing in 1990 and 1991. Businesses throughout the world are lining up to enter. General Motors Corp. has established joint ventures in Hungary and Rumania. Siemens, Federal Express, Coca-Cola, Procter & Gamble Co., and Occidental Petroleum Corp. are just a few of the U.S. companies seeking partnerships and customers. More recently, of course, the Soviet Union has been dismantled, replaced by the Confederation of Independent States. As a result, doing business with Confederation countries may be very risky for several years.

The economic and political situation in Eastern Europe will remain volatile for many years. Foreign marketers must carefully monitor events and proceed cautiously. A case in point is the experiences of companies trying to enter the former Soviet Union. McDonald's negotiated with the Soviet bureaucracy for twelve years before it signed an agreement in 1988 to open twenty restaurants and a food distribution center in Moscow. The operation of a Moscow McDonald's is very different from that of an equivalent McDonald's in the United States. Employees (of whom there are 650) cheer, whistle, and clap as the first customers arrive at 10 A.M. Atypical of restaurants in the former Soviet Union, customers are served in sixty seconds or less. The store is staffed by twenty-seven teams of three—a cashier, a server, and a helper—plus assistants and managers. Around mealtimes and on weekends, customers can wait up to two hours. About forty of the original employees have been promoted to crew managers, and their salaries have risen from $2.00 to $3.20 or $4.00 an hour.[11] It took sixteen years of business with the Soviets before Pepsi-Cola International, with twenty bottling plants on Soviet soil, aired the first-ever paid commercial on Soviet television.

The Americas

The Americas refer to all the countries in North America, Central America, and South America. The attractiveness of these countries to United States businesses varies greatly. In 1989, the United States and Canada signed the Free Trade Agreement (FTA), which essentially merged American and Canadian markets to form the largest free-trade zone in the world. The agreement calls for the elimination over a ten-year period of most tariffs and other restrictions so that goods and services can flow more easily across the U.S.-Canadian border. Although trade relations between the United States and Mexico are not as formalized as those with Canada, the relationship has been flourishing in recent years. In 1990, a

Mexico–United States free-trade agreement similar to the Canadian FTA was proposed. Several countries in Central and South America have formed a Latin America alliance. There are four major market agreements in Latin America: the Andean Common Market, the Central American Common Market, the Caribbean Community and Common Market, and the Latin American Integration Association. Latin America continues to face a number of problems that make it difficult to achieve significant economic integration and cooperation between countries. The low level of economic activity, political turmoil, and extreme differences in economic development from country to country are stumbling blocks to the success of these market agreements.

Africa

A recent study by the World Bank predicts that poverty is likely to decline in the 1990s everywhere in the world except in the forty-seven nations that make up sub-Saharan Africa. There, the number of impoverished people is expected to rise by eighty-five million. With its political and economic situations in disarray, this region still offers great potential.[12] If individual nations manage to get their political houses in order, they could become huge markets. Angola, for example, has large mineral resources and ample land, although wars and financial mismanagement have prevented the country from realizing its potential. South Africa has the most successful economy in the region, and once apartheid is dismantled, U.S. consumer-product companies will be there in a hurry.

Concept Review

Several markets offer both a substantial and reliable source of revenue for many U.S. businesses:

- Europe 1992,
- The Pacific Rim,
- The Eastern Bloc,
- The Americas, and
- Africa.

Designing an International Promotional Strategy

Promotion in international marketing plays the same role as it does in domestic operations—communication with the firm's audiences to achieve certain goals. For many foreign markets, however, the promotional emphasis tends to be on personal selling over the other mix elements. Three main functions for international promotion are suggested: (1) to support overseas agents, (2) to open new markets, and (3) to develop sales in the foreign market.[13] This list suggests the supportive role played by advertising, sales promotion, and public relations in many foreign markets. For many of these markets, a promotional mix like that used in the United States is appropriate. However, the mix must still be evaluated on a country-by-country basis because the availability and the appropriate use of the promotional elements vary from market to market. In this section, we examine each element of the mix and how the special problems of international marketing affect its use.

Advertising

Improved broadcasting technology, including satellite transmission, has stimulated the growth of mass communication and, concurrently, mass advertising in virtually every corner of the world. As noted in Table 19.5, worldwide spending on advertising is led by Unilever NV with $1.9 billion in 1990. In some instances, advertising precedes the product and creates a market for it, as was the case for Polaroid's SX-70 camera. The same print and television ads used in the United States were used in Great Britain because many of the ads were already familiar to a large number of the English since they travel frequently to the United States. To create effective international advertising, promotion managers should carefully consider the opportunities offered by the environment, the message, and the media mix.

Analyzing the Promotional Opportunity   One factor influencing effectiveness is the role advertising plays in a country. Some countries, such as the Netherlands, are very receptive to a sophisticated multimedia campaign. Others, such as Ethiopia and Italy, are not as interested in advertising because of economic conditions or culture.

The availability of media is a second consideration. Media may be restricted by the government or by the communication infrastructure. In Africa and the Mideast, for example, there is a low rate of television ownership.

Government regulations represent a third factor that influences effectiveness. Red tape and restrictive laws and policies often overwhelm marketers. Cigarette advertising, for example, is banned in some or all media in Canada, England, Ireland, France, Italy, Denmark, Norway, Sweden, and several other countries.

The competitive situation is another variable affecting international advertising. The intensity of competition varies tremendously. Depending on

Table 19.5 **Leading Advertisers Worldwide in 1990**

Rank	Advertiser	Primary Business	Countries in Which Spending Was Reported for 1990	U.S. Spending 1990	W'wide Spending 1990	Non-U.S. as % of W'wide
1	Unilever NV Rotterdam/London	Food	Argentina, Australia, Austria, Brazil, Britain, Canada, Chile, Denmark, Finland, France, Germany, Greece, India, Italy, Japan, Malaysia, Mexico, Netherlands, Pan Arabia, Puerto Rico, South Africa, Spain, Switzerland, Taiwan, Turkey	$ 568.9	$1,933.9	70.6
2	Procter & Gamble Co. Cincinnati	Personal care	Austria, Britain, Canada, Chile, Denmark, France, Germany, Greece, India, Italy, Japan, Lebanon, Mexico, Netherlands, Pan Arabia, Philippines, Puerto Rico, Spain, Taiwan, Thailand	2,284.5	3,420.1	33.2
3	Nestlé SA Vevey, Switzerland	Food	Argentina, Austria, Brazil, Britain, Canada, Chile, France, Germany, Greece, India, Italy, Japan, Malaysia, Netherlands, Pan Arabia, Philippines, Puerto Rico, Spain, Switzerland, Taiwan, Thailand	635.9	1,239.4	48.7
4	PSA Peugeot-Citroen SA Paris	Automotive	Argentina, Britain, France, Germany, Italy, Netherlands, Norway, Pan Arabia, Spain, Switzerland	9.1*	606.3	98.5
5	Philip Morris Cos. New York	Food	Argentina, Austria, Britain, Canada, Denmark, France, Germany, Hong Kong, Indonesia, Italy, Japan, Lebanon, Malaysia, Netherlands, Pan Arabia, Spain, Taiwan	2,210.2	2,721.4	18.8
6	Toyota Motor Corp. Toyota City, Japan	Automotive	Australia, Britain, Canada, Germany, Indonesia, Japan, Norway, Pan Arabia, Switzerland, Thailand	580.7	1,039.2	44.1
7	Renault SA Paris	Automotive	Austria, Britain, France, Germany, Italy, Netherlands, Pan Arabia, Spain, Turkey	0.0	442.0	100.0
8	Fiat SpA Turin, Italy	Automotive	Britain, France, Germany, Italy, Netherlands, Spain, Switzerland	0.7*	441.6	99.8
9	Canon Inc. Tokyo	Electronics	Canada, France, Germany, Japan, Netherlands	119.5	530.5	77.5
10	General Motors Corp. Detroit	Automotive	Austria, Britain, Canada, Finland, France, Germany, Italy, Netherlands, Norway, Pan Arabia, Spain, Switzerland	1,502.8	1,911.8	21.4

*Indicates that U.S. spending figures include measured media only as reported by LNA/Arbitron Multi-Media reports.

Reprinted with permission from *Advertising Age* (October 28, 1991): 5-6–7. Copyright, Crain Communications Inc., 1991.

the market, international businesses might compete solely against other international companies or also against national ones.

A final practical consideration is the availability of effective advertising agencies. There is normally a high correlation between the number and quality of advertising agencies and the economic environment in a country. A scarcity of agencies is not always a serious problem, however. Based on its needs, an American company might use an international or a global agency, a local foreign agency, an export agency, its usual domestic agency, or its house agency. Table 19.6 lists the top advertising agencies in the world. WPP London leads the group with 1990 gross income of almost three billion dollars.

Selecting the Message   Any book or article on international marketing offers numerous examples of how some marketer (usually American) made a horrible advertising blunder by using a word that translated negatively, a color that connoted evil, or a song that was perceived as too sensual. Every facet of a message—words, tone, pictures, context, spokesperson, and appeal—must be carefully screened. Obviously the advertising must use the language of the country, but the words must be more than just technically accurate and perfectly translated. They must reflect the tone, emotion, and inherent heart of the language. A key to successful communication in a foreign market is to intimately understand the nuances of the culture, especially the language, values, and attitudes of its consumers. The process of designing the message must therefore begin with the cultural context, not the individual consumer.

The market itself offers several areas to consider with respect to message design, as the following questions show:

Is the product used for the same purpose in all countries? Campbell Soup Company learned that its soups are used very differently in the United States and in Eastern and Western Europe. Consumers in France, for example, would never consider using canned soup as the base for a sauce.

What is the motivation for purchasing the product? The same product may be purchased for a mixture of functional, convenience, and status reasons, with a different combination of motivations in each country. In underdeveloped countries, for example, McDonald's provides more status than it does convenience.

Who is the key decision maker? In patriarchal cultures, the father makes most purchase decisions. In the case of certain products (for example, cereal, toys, fast food), children take a very active role. However, the influence of children on product purchase varies a great deal from country to country, and marketers must examine this purchase pattern closely before making any generalizations.

Table 19.6 **Leading Advertising Agencies Worldwide**

Rank '90	Rank '89	Advertising Organization, Headquarters	Worldwide Gross Income 1990	Worldwide Gross Income 1989	Worldwide Capitalized Billings 1990	Worldwide Capitalized Billings 1989
1	1	WPP Group, London	$2,715.0	$2,404.0	$18,095.0	$16,052.0
2	2	Saatchi & Saatchi Co., London	1,729.3	1,575.8	11,861.7	10,802.4
3	3	Interpublic Group of Cos., New York	1,649.8	1,493.7	11,025.3	9,984.6
4	5	Omnicom Group, New York	1,335.5	1,177.9	9,699.6	8,405.3
5	4	Dentsu Inc., Tokyo	1,254.8	1,262.7	9,671.6	9,695.5
6	6	Young & Rubicam, New York	1,073.6	925.6	8,000.7	6,652.0
7	11	Eurocom Group, Paris	748.5	472.3	5,065.7	3,195.5
8	7	Hakuhodo Inc., Tokyo	586.3	585.5	4,529.4	4,449.2
9	9	Grey Advertising, New York	583.3	489.9	3,910.4	3,267.4
10	8	Foote, Cone & Belding Communications, Chicago	536.2	506.5	3,554.8	3,371.8
11	12	D'Arcy Masius Benton & Bowles, New York	532.5	471.5	4,406.7	3,803.1
12	10	Leo Burnett Co., Chicago	531.8	483.8	3,585.4	3,245.5
13	13	Publicis-FCB Communications, Paris	430.0	358.8	2,910.7	2,405.4
14	14	Roux, Seguela Cayzac & Goudard, Issy les Moulineaux, France	346.2	224.4	2,354.5	1,713.1
15	19	BDDP Worldwide, Boulogne, France	236.0	151.3	1,487.4	1,061.2
16	16	Bozell, Jacobs, Kenyon & Eckhardt, New York	214.0	201.0	1,570.0	1,475.0
17	15	N W Ayer, New York	185.9	210.5	1,469.2	1,398.2
18	17	Tokyu Agency, Tokyo	170.3	165.7	1,387.0	1,322.7

Table 19.6 **Leading Advertising Agencies Worldwide (cont.)**

Rank		Advertising Organization, Headquarters	Worldwide Gross Income		Worldwide Capitalized Billings	
'90	'89		1990	1989	1990	1989
19	18	Daiko Advertising, Osaka, Japan	159.5	152.1	1,246.9	1,214.1
20	22	Alliance International Advertising Group, London	141.8	124.9	945.0	837.9

Note: Dollars are in millions.

Reprinted with permission from *Advertising Age* (March 25, 1991): S-8–9. Copyright, Crain Communications Inc., 1991.

Cultural mores represent a key factor impinging on message design. For example, in Germany and France, many women do not shave their legs or underarms. Thus razor blades are positioned as a special occasion purchase. The Japanese view deodorant differently so Feel Free deodorant described its product as youthful, chic, and convenient rather than as a solution to odor problems. As noted in Chapter 5, these cultural mores express human values. As pointed out in the Promotion in Focus section, values even determine how people want to receive product information. Eastern Europeans, for example, do not trust advertising and want to know just the facts about the product.

The presence or absence of market segments also dictates message appeal in foreign countries and represents one of the more successful ways of standardizing promotional strategies. For example, a market segment such as college students is very similar from country to country. Levi's uses the same basic appeal to the worldwide youth market for its 501 jeans. International jet setters respond similarly to appeals for fine jewelry, luxury cars, and expensive cosmetics. Similarly, when countries join together in order to share economic resources, transportation networks, or technologies, they create common interests that can also serve as the bases for promotional appeals. A decision must also be made whether to run a promotion in one or several local languages. For example, some citizens of Switzerland speak mostly German, others speak mostly French, and most speak English.

Figure 19.3 illustrates how one U.S. company customized its ads to fit a particular country.

Selecting Effective Media   Only print consistently reaches a worldwide market. In fact, media limitations represent the area of greatest frustration for the international promotion manager. Although media standardization

Figure 19.3

How one U.S. company designed its ad campaign to suit a foreign country.
Courtesy of AT&T.

is growing, there is still lack of uniformity. Television stations in Brazil, for example, use a different frequency than the United States, so television ads produced in the United States must be electronically converted before they can be aired. Conventional media such as print, radio, and television are bound either by legal restrictions or technical limitations. Commercial radio is still not available in Norway, Denmark, Sweden, Finland, Switzerland, and Saudi Arabia. In Norway, Denmark, Sweden, and Saudi Arabia, commercial television is not available for advertisers. Even when some media are available, access may be partially restricted. In Germany, for example, advertisers have access to commercial television only during a few blocks of several minutes each at several time slots.

Accessibility limitations are even more severe. In underdeveloped countries, few people have a television or radio and few are literate. Therefore, advertising in broadcast and print media tends to reach a very limited

Promotion in Focus

Just the Facts

Thousands of Western companies are doing everything they can to try to sell their products to the newly opened markets in Eastern Europe and what used to be the Soviet Union. But many of them are finding that they can't sell to East Germans the same way they have long sold to West Germans. It may take years before Western attitudes towards advertising completely replace those built up over years of communist rule.

A 1990 conference on marketing organized by *Advertising Age* magazine in Moscow highlighted some of the perceptions that Western marketers will have to overcome and the kind of information that newly formed Russian ad agencies will need to gather. The Russian and Eastern European audiences have been used to factual ads, with little smiling and little appeal. Often the government-controlled media ran ads for products that no one really wanted. That fact, and the prevalence of government propaganda on television, has made many viewers suspicious of all ads.

The Russian advertising executives were particularly interested in learning about the subtler aspects of advertising. They knew little about how theoretical strategies relate to actual campaigns or about how to use psychology to their benefit. They thought of advertising as a creative activity but knew little about advertis-

ing as a science governed by generally accepted laws.

These attitudes explain the Eastern European rejection of a number of Western ads. Eastern European viewers will have to be weaned slowly from their diet of straight facts. Some need information just to figure out how to use unfamiliar Western products. Others simply don't like the lifestyle-oriented Western ad approach and the aggressive, silly, or incomprehensible commercials. Many viewers objected to a commercial for Adidas in which tennis star Steffi Graff charges the net while a lion roars. They prefer "Direct Information," a 4-minute block of information into which any marketer's product can be plugged.

If that's the way they want it, that's the way smart Western advertisers will give it to them, at least for now. No doubt Eastern European viewers will gradually come to accept the ads that their Western counterparts take for granted. But it's worth asking if we could learn something from them, too. Is "just the facts" such a bad idea?

Sources: Elena Bowes, "Lifestyle Ads Irk East Europeans," *Advertising Age* (October 8, 1990): 56; Joel Ostrow, "Ad Perestroika: Soviets Soak Up U.S. Know-how," *Advertising Age* (October 29, 1990): 50.

market, primarily the wealthy and better educated. Pepsi-Cola and Coca-Cola have been very successful in reaching the masses through radio ads that people on the street hear played in bars and hotels.

The quality of transmission and reproduction equipment supporting foreign media is a serious deterrent as well. Poor-quality printing and the lack of high-grade paper are examples. Television stations in many countries lack professional expertise and are unable to correctly show or schedule commercials.

International media technology is emerging. In 1985, Sky Channel, a satellite television channel then owned by Rupert Murdoch, was available to 12.5 million viewers. In Norway and Sweden, where the government prohibits advertising on native television broadcasts, 98 percent of the viewers with access to Sky watched it at least once during a three-month period.[14] There has also been a growth in global syndication of U.S. television network programs, thus opening up many new markets to promoters.

Developments in direct mail offer important media inroads into foreign markets. In Southeast Asian markets where print media is scarce, direct mail is considered one of the most effective ways to reach those responsible for purchasing industrial goods.[15]

Concept Review	Several considerations are necessary when designing advertising for other nations.

1. Overall factors to consider:
   a. Role of advertising
   b. Availability of media
   c. Government regulations
   d. Competitive situation
   e. Quality/availability of advertising agencies
2. In selecting the message, the promotion manager must:
   a. Accurately reflect language, values, and attitudes
   b. Understand how the product is used and what motivates purchases
   c. Identify appropriate decision makers
   d. Understand cultural mores
   e. Attempt to identify market segments
3. Considerations in selecting the medium:
   a. Assess the availability and standardization
   b. Assess technical limitations

Personal Selling

Personal selling is the most common promotional tool used in foreign markets. It may be the dominant mix element under at least two conditions:

(1) when the use of advertising or media is restricted, and (2) when the wage scale is so low as to allow the employment of a large local sales force.

The international marketer must first determine the role personal selling should play in each market compared with the other mix elements. Once this decision is made, the day-to-day administration of the sales force begins. Administration entails many of the same basic tasks associated with managing the domestic sales force: recruitment, selection, training, motivation, compensation, and evaluation.

Recruitment and Selection   Salespeople are usually recruited and selected within the local market by individuals who know the market best. Two other sources of salespeople are also available: *expatriates,* people who are not natives of the local country but who take a two- or three-year assignment in a particular foreign market; and *cosmopolitan personnel,* people who are familiar with numerous foreign markets and work in several countries simultaneously. It is becoming increasingly difficult to find high-caliber expatriates who are willing to live abroad for extended periods, and it is very expensive to hire cosmopolitan personnel.[16]

There are some restrictions on recruiting and selecting salespeople in foreign countries. Most notable is the negative view in many countries of sales as a career. This attitude may cause the best candidates to shy away from sales. The number of people with the desired characteristics and educational background may also be limited. Furthermore, many countries impose sanctions on the hiring of expatriates and cosmopolitans. In Argentina, for instance, foreign companies must make every effort to hire a local salesperson before they are allowed to bring in an outsider. Even then, a limit is imposed.

Dealing with these restrictions has forced many international marketers to design sales positions to fit the strengths and weaknesses of specific countries. Thus the responsibilities of the job vary from market to market. In Spain, for example, IBM has a Spanish salesperson who deals with the technical selling issues.

Training   Training location and content depend on the nature of the job and the previous preparation of the sales force. For local salespeople, training usually occurs in the host country and concentrates on information about the company and product. For expatriates, training is done initially at home with a focus on the customs and special problems in the host country. For both types of personnel, sales training must cope with problems that may be caused by long-established behaviors and attitudes. Americans, in particular, often think there is little to be learned from a foreign culture or a different way of doing things. This attitude is a mistake.

Since there is often a physical separation between the international mar-keter and the local sales force, continuing training is very important. Home office personnel should frequently check on the effectiveness of the train-ing effort and assess the level of retention.

Motivating and Compensating   Techniques of motivation and compensa-tion must be designed to meet local needs. In many foreign countries, sell-ing is a low-status job, and the proper cultural behavior is not to talk to strangers. In countries where selling has low status, superior training, titles, and financial rewards are all helpful. In the end, each method used to motivate a foreign salesperson should be examined for cultural compatibility.[17]

Controlling and Evaluating the Sales Force   The control and evaluation techniques used in the United States are also applicable to foreign markets. However, the manager must learn about the local market in order to ap-praise its potential and assign territories and sales quotas. Comparison of markets is an additional task; it gives the manager a better idea of the pos-sible range of performance.

Dealing with multiple markets that have very different sales potential makes evaluation a trying task. Should salespeople be evaluated on indi-vidual performance, or should they be compared to salespeople in other markets? Evidence supports comparison.[18]

Sales Promotion

The decision to use sales promotion internationally is normally the third choice after due consideration is given to personal selling and advertising. Nevertheless, sales promotions are often more attractive than other pro-motional elements. Consumers in less wealthy countries tend to be espe-cially interested in saving money through price discounts, product sam-pling, premiums, or contests. Furthermore, sales promotion may provide a strategy for bypassing restrictions on advertising. It is also a way of reaching people who live in rural and less accessible parts of the market.[19] Both Coca-Cola and PepsiCo set aside part of their Latin American ad-vertising budget for carnival trucks that make frequent trips to isolated villages to promote their products. These trucks provide free entertain-ment, including movies, and distribute free products along with coupons for additional products. Product samples may also be left with local stores, as well as premiums such as clock signs, clothing, and temperature gauges.

Restrictions against sales promotion are often more severe in foreign countries than they are in the United States (see Figure 19.4). For example, laws may not permit promoters to give premiums or gifts. Even when they

	U.K.	Ireland	Spain	Portugal	Greece	France	Italy	Netherlands	Denmark	Belgium	Luxembourg
In-pack premiums	■	■	■	■	■	●	■	●	●	●	▲
Multiple-purchase offers	■	■	■	■	■	■	■	■	●	●	▲
Extra product	■	■	■	■	■	■	■	●	■	●	■
Free product	■	■	■	■	■	■	■	■	■	●	■
Free mail-ins	■	■	■	■	■	■	■	■	●	●	●
With-purchase premiums	■	■	■	■	■	■	■	●	●	●	▲
Cross-product premiums	■	■	■	■	■	■	■	●	●	▲	▲
Collector devices	■	■	■	■	■	●	■	●	●	●	▲
Competitions	■	■	■	■	■	●	■	●	●	■	●
Free drawings	■	■	■	■	■	■	■	▲	▲	▲	▲
Share-outs	■	■	■	■	■	●	●	▲	▲	▲	▲
Sweepstakes/lottery	●	●	●	●	●	●	●	●	▲	●	▲
Money-off vouchers	■	■	■	■	■	■	●	■	●	■	●
Money-off next purchase	■	■	■	■	■	■	●	■	▲	■	▲
Cash backs	■	■	■	■	■	■	▲	■	■	■	▲

■ Permitted   ● May be permitted   ▲ Not permitted

Figure 19.4

Restrictions against sales promotion in foreign countries.
Reprinted with permission from Advertising Age *(April 30, 1990): S-11. Copyright, Crain Communications Inc., 1991.*

are permitted, the value of the premium may be limited to a percentage of the value of the product purchased, or the premium may have to be directly related to the product purchased (for example, a decanter given with a salad dressing mix). In France, promoters are required to keep records of their sales promotion expenditures and the dollar amounts are limited. In many Spanish-speaking countries, the typical inexpensive toys and games found in children's cereals have been banned because of lack of value. Yet Procter & Gamble Co. successfully included a free nativity scene in each box of one of its detergents. Again, the influence of culture is evident.

Coupons, the most frequently used tool in the United States, are prohibited in many countries and tend to play a minor role in countries such as Sweden or the United Kingdom where they are used. In most overseas markets, price reductions in the store are the most important sales promotion tool, followed by reductions to wholesalers and retailers. Also of importance in some countries are product samples, double-packs, and in-store displays. Distrust of foreign marketers makes warranties mandatory in some countries.

Problems in gaining the involvement and cooperation of resellers represent a very serious barrier to sales promotion in foreign markets. Wholesalers and retailers often lack the appropriate facilities to properly process or merchandise promotional materials. They may not understand the sales promotion or be able to explain how it works to their customers.

If the promotion manager can overcome such constraints, the opportunities for sales promotion in foreign markets are impressive. This is particularly true when the company has a competitive edge in a particular market. Since sales promotion tends to enhance the basic value of a product, products that are highly regarded will benefit most from sales promotions, regardless of the country.

Public Relations

To a large extent, public relations is the international marketer's attempt to create a positive image of itself in the host country. PR is a vital part of any international marketing program.

Public relations plays both a proactive and a reactive role for most international marketers. It is proactive in the sense that an international company develops a PR strategy specifying a promotional mix, including scheduling and budget allocations. The strategy might include press releases, news conferences, plant tours, and sponsored events. Reactive public relations refers to how the international marketer plans to respond to unplanned events such as product failures, catastrophes, and personnel misbehaviors. Since host countries are very sensitive to the indiscretions of foreign visitors, reactive public relations must be particularly responsive.

Effective international public relations begins with primary research. This research should (1) identify the relevant publics in each market, (2) assess how various public relations events or issues will affect the various publics, and (3) determine the most effective public relations strategy to use in presenting or responding to these events or issues. Too often, public relations practitioners fail to conduct this research.

Armed with this information, however, public relations practitioners can anticipate potential problems and react appropriately. Many international marketers have come to the realization that they cannot always give in to government or public demands. To illustrate an exception, however, Anheuser-Busch agreed to sponsor an educational program about drunk driving in conjunction with its entry into Taiwan.

Two final pieces of advice are in order. First, the best public relations strategy in foreign markets is to take a proactive rather than a reactive position. This means doing things that the host country will truly appreciate. PepsiCo has done this by sponsoring the Pepsi Sports Games in Mexico since 1988. Second, it is important that executives in charge of public relations have prestige and influence.

Concept Review

Promotional mix elements have applications in addition to advertising in foreign markets.

1. Personal selling is especially attractive in foreign markets when advertising is restricted or wages are low. The sales force may include locals, expatriates, and cosmopolitans.
2. Sales promotion is an attractive substitute for advertising or personal selling in underdeveloped countries. But it is heavily restricted in foreign markets.
3. Public relations is used to create a corporate image in foreign markets. Public relations strategies should be based on extensive research.

Case 19 *Advertising in Japan*

Many Americans stereotype Japanese business methods as being deliberate and plodding, weighed down by tradition. But recent developments in the Japanese advertising world have shown how wrong this image is and have underscored how important it is for Western businesses to keep abreast of the developments in Japanese markets and among Japanese marketers.

One major development in Japanese advertising is the creative use of alternative media. Search Vision, for instance, projects images on aircraft or balloons. Del-Vision creates 3-D displays that don't require special glasses because of its use of curved mirrors. Magic Vision mixes images of actual objects and reflections using a film industry technique called glasswork.

The approaches of two major American razor manufacturers show how different Western attitudes can be towards advertising in Japan. Gillette is the world's leader in wet-shave razors, but it has been battling to gain above 10 percent of the Japanese market. It has long relied on the appeal of Western products and images. When the Japanese market opened to foreign razor manufaturers in 1962, Gillette decided to use its own sales force rather than contract with a Japanese distributor. And although it has occasionally used Japanese actors in its commercials, Gillette has generally promoted its products in Japan with the same commercials used in the

West. To sell its popular new Sensor razor, for instance, Gillette used almost exactly the same commercial and packaging as it was using in the United States. Its Sensor campaign helped raise its share of the Japanese razor market to 25 percent.

But that doesn't seem to worry Warner-Lambert, whose Schick brand has over 60 percent of the wet-shaver market. From the beginning, Schick has tried to do things the Japanese way. In 1962, while Gillette was trying to crack the Japanese market on its own, Schick contracted with Seiko corporation to handle its distribution, a strategy that quickly gave it a big lead over its main rival. Schick proudly points out that it hasn't used a non-Japanese actor in its commercials for years. It even changed the name of its answer to the Sensor from "Tracer" to "FX" because, the company says, the Japanese find the name easier to pronouce.

Both companies recognize that the largest barrier to Japanese sales growth may be the popularity of electric razors. To appeal to young people before they have developed the electric-razor habit, Schick offers free razors to teenagers and uses Japanese pop stars, sexy ads, and promotions in popular comic books. Gillette has a lot of catching up to do.

Case Questions

1. How would you evaluate the recent success of Gillette relative to that of Schick?

2. What factors should Gillette consider in order to be successful in Japan?

Case Sources: Yukimo Ono, "Gillette Tries to Nick Schick in Japan," *The Wall Street Journal* (February 4, 1991): B1. David Kelburn and Julie Skur Hill, "Creatively Cracking Through Ad Clutter," *Advertising Age* (December 10, 1990): 41. Julie Skur Hill, "Patiently Racing Around the World," *Advertising Age* (December 10, 1990): 35.

Summary

Business firms enter foreign markets because of market saturation at home, locations of customers, and actions of competitors. This chapter deals with some of the primary factors to consider before entering a foreign market. It also examines how promotion must change in order to be successful in foreign markets.

The chapter begins with a discussion of the various strategies for entering foreign markets: exporting, licensing, joint ventures, and strategic alliances. Levitt's concept of globalization is also discussed. The issue of whether companies should standardize their marketing efforts across markets and countries is still being debated.

Next, the chapter considers the various environmental factors that influence the decision to go international. These factors include (1) the economic environment, (2) the political and legal environment, and (3) the cultural environment.

Foreign markets that provide a stable and substantial source of revenue and/or products for businesses in the United States include Europe 1992, the Pacific Rim, the Eastern Bloc, the Americas, and Africa.

The chapter concludes with an appraisal of the factors to be considered before implementing a promotional strategy in a foreign country. Advertising, for example, is affected by the attitude toward advertising, language differences, the role of advertising, the availability of media, government regulations, and the competitive situation. Personal selling is limited by many of these same considerations, plus the difficulty of finding, training, and retaining competent salespeople. Sales promotion faces the most severe restrictions. To maintain the goodwill of the host country, public relations practitioners should take an active, assertive posture toward the task, and PR executives should be prestigious enough to deal with foreign officials.

Discussion Questions

1. Discuss the reasons why a company would be prompted to move into foreign markets.

2. What must marketers consider before deciding whether or not to become involved in international marketing?

3. Cummins Engine has determined that the U.S. market for its primary products is saturated. It would like to enter Mexico. Describe the entry strategies available.

4. Many countries have a low literacy rate. In what ways might a company adjust its marketing program to overcome this problem?

5. A U.S. luggage manufacturing company with annual sales of more than one hundred million dollars has decided to market its products in South America. Evaluate the factors the company should consider.

6. Why are television and radio not available as advertising media in certain countries? Cite some ways an advertiser can get around this limitation.

7. To what extent is the advertising system of a country affected by the political system?

8. Discuss the primary factors to consider before engaging in sales promotion activities in a foreign country.

9. What alternatives do advertisers have in selecting an agency for advertising in a foreign country?

10. Describe the difficulties associated with selecting and training a sales force in a foreign country.

Suggested Projects

1. Interview two foreign students on your campus to determine if their buying habits differ from those of students in the United States. Consider factors such as product availability, who makes the buying decision, when products are purchased and how often.

2. Go to the library and examine the foreign ads highlighted in *Advertising Age.* How do these ads differ from U.S. ads selling comparable products? What are the similarities?

References

1. Jean-Pierre Jeannett and Hubert D. Hennessey, *International Marketing Management* (Boston: Houghton Mifflin Co., 1988): 5.

2. Theodore Levitt, "The Globalization of Markets," *Harvard Business Review* (May–June 1983): 92.

3. Levitt, p. 94.

4. Philip Kotler and Gary Armstrong, *Marketing: An Introduction* (Englewood Cliffs, NJ: Prentice-Hall, Inc., 1990): 477.

5. Dean van Nest, "Global Marketing Strategy: A Study of U.S. Consumer Goods Companies," unpublished dissertation, Pace University, 1985.

6. Vern Terpstra, *International Marketing* (Chicago: Dryden Press, 1987): 63–74.

7. Erik Wiklund, *International Marketing* (New York: McGraw-Hill, 1986): 18.

8. Janette Martin, "Beyond 1992: Lifestyle Is Key," *Advertising Age* (July 11, 1988): 59.

9. Betsy Sharkey, "Getting to Know You," *Adweek Special Report* (June 6, 1988): 34.

10. "The Rising Power of the Pacific," *Fortune* (Fall 1990): 9.

11. Rosemarie Boyle, "McDonald's Gives Soviets Something Worth Waiting For," *Advertising Age* (March 19, 1990): 51.

12. Wiklund, p. 194.

13. *Ibid.*

14. "Profile of Sky Watchers," *International Advertiser* (June 1986): 22.

15. Terpstra, p. 381.

16. Burton W. Teague, *Compensating Foreign Service Personnel*, Report no. 818 (New York: The Conference Board, 1982): 2.

17. Teague, p. 4.

18. "American Abroad: IVECO's Man in Yugoslavia," *Sales and Marketing Management* (June 1987): 77.

19. "International Direct Mail—The Most Misunderstood International Medium," *International Marketing* (January 1982): 88–92.

Glossary

A

advertising: Any paid form of nonpersonal communication and promotion of ideas, goods, or services by an identified sponsor. *(Chapter 1)*

advertising allowance: Money paid by the manufacturer to the reseller for advertising the manufacturer's product. *(Chapter 11)*

advertising campaign: A campaign that includes a series of ads, placed in various media, that are designed to meet objectives and are based on an analysis of marketing and communication situations. *(Chapter 9)*

advertorial: A thirty- or sixty-second ad; also called an infomercial. *(Chapter 18)*

application: Combined with retrieval, the final stage in information processing; the use of relevant information to solve a problem or meet a need. *(Chapter 5)*

appropriation: The maximum amount of dollars allocated for a specific purpose. *(Chapter 16)*

attention: The second step of the information-processing sequence in which the consumer must devote mental resources to stimuli in order to process them. *(Chapter 5)*

attitude: An enduring disposition, favorable or unfavorable, toward some object. *(Chapter 5)*

average frequency of contact: The product obtained by dividing the total number of homes reached by a media plan by the net coverage. *(Chapter 14)*

awareness advertising: Advertising whose primary purpose is to create and maintain brand awareness. *(Chapter 18)*

B

baby boomers: People born in the United States between 1946 and 1964. *(Chapter 4)*

bait advertising: An alluring but insincere offer to sell a product or service that the advertiser does not really intend or want to sell. *(Chapter 6)*

bait price: A price intended to hook customers so that they may be switched to another, more expensive or more profitable item. *(Chapter 3)*

banded pack: An offer in which two or more units of a product are sold at a reduced price compared to the regular single-unit price. *(Chapter 10)*

BBB: See Better Business Bureau.

behavioral learning: A form of learning that does not require awareness or conscious effort but depends instead on an association between events. *(Chapter 5)*

belief: A proposition that reflects a person's particular knowledge and assessment of something. *(Chapter 4)*

Better Business Bureau (BBB): An agency for

monitoring and publicizing unfair and deceptive practices. *(Chapter 6)*

bonus pack: A price deal that includes an additional quantity of the product free when a standard size of the product is purchased at the regular price. *(Chapter 10)*

boutique agency: A specialty shop that deals in a few services. *(Chapter 8)*

brand: The name, term, design, symbol, or any other feature that identifies the good, service, institution, or idea sold by a marketer. *(Chapter 3)*

branding strategy: The process of developing and selecting brand names and brand marks. *(Chapter 3)*

brand loyalty: Loyalty that is the result of the consumer's involvement with the product decision. *(Chapter 5)*

brand mark: That part of the brand that cannot be spoken, such as a symbol, picture, design, distinctive lettering, or color combination. *(Chapter 3)*

brand name: That part of a brand that can be spoken, such as words, letters, or numbers. *(Chapter 3)*

budget: The details of how the appropriation will be used. *(Chapter 16)*

buying allowance: A payment by a manufacturer to a reseller if a certain amount of product is purchased during a certain time. *(Chapter 11)*

C

campaign: A planning tool that coordinates the delivery of the message to various audiences. *(Chapter 1)*

cease and desist order: An order that requires the advertiser to stop the specified advertising practice within thirty days and that prohibits the advertiser from engaging in the practice until after the hearing. *(Chapter 6)*

centrality: A characteristic of an attitude that depends on the degree to which an attitude is tied to values. *(Chapter 5)*

central processing: Also called elaborate processing; information processing that involves active manipulation of information. *(Chapter 5)*

cents-off deal: A price reduction; also called price discount. *(Chapter 10)*

channel of distribution: The marketing mechanism used to present, deliver, and service the product for customers. *(Chapter 3)*

classified ads: All types of messages arranged by classification of interest. *(Chapter 13)*

classical conditioning: A type of behavioral learning in which a response is learned as a result of the pairing of two stimuli. *(Chapter 5)*

Clayton Act: Federal legislation that declared illegal those activities that have the probable effect of substantially lessening competition or of creating a monopoly. *(Chapter 6)*

cognitive dissonance: A theory that dissonance exists when there are inconsistencies among a person's cognitions. *(Chapter 5)*

cognitive learning: A form of learning that involves thought and conscious awareness. *(Chapter 5)*

commercial bribery: The act of influencing or attempting to influence the actions of an employee by giving the employee a gift without the knowledge of the employer. *(Chapter 6)*

communicators: A component of every communication system consisting of source and receiver. *(Chapter 7)*

comparison advertising: Advertising that involves the comparison of two or more specifically named or recognizably presented brands of the same generic product or service class in terms of one or more specific product or service attributes. *(Chapter 6)*

complex decision making: A decision-making process that requires a search for information and an evaluation of alternatives. *(Chapter 5)*

concurrent testing: Research that evaluates the promotional effort while it is running in the marketplace. *(Chapter 17)*

consumer market: Consumers who buy and

use goods for their own personal or house-hold use. *(Chapter 2)*

consumer products: Products purchased for personal or family consumption with no intention of resale. *(Chapter 3)*

consumer sales promotions: Promotions directed at the ultimate users of the product. *(Chapter 10)*

consumer sampling: Giving a product to a consumer either free or for a small fee. *(Chapter 10)*

content analysis: A PR technique that treats radio, television, newspaper, and magazine stories as if the media were people responding to a public opinion survey. *(Chapter 12)*

contest: An activity that requires some act of skill that necessitates a judge or judges to make a relative comparison. *(Chapter 6)*

continuity: The timing of media insertions. *(Chapter 14)*

continuous pattern: Constant message exposure. *(Chapter 14)*

continuity program: A sales promotion technique designed to hold a brand user for a long time by offering ongoing incentives. *(Chapter 10)*

copy platform: A document that outlines the creative strategy. *(Chapter 9)*

core values: Dominant cultural values. *(Chapter 4)*

corporate advertising: Also called institutional or public relations advertising. *(Chapter 12)*

cost-based pricing: A strategy whereby the company competes by having lower prices than competitors. *(Chapter 3)*

coupons: Legal certificates offered by manufacturers and retailers that grant specified savings on selected products when presented for redemption at the point of purchase. *(Chapter 10)*

creative mix: The manner in which visual and verbal elements are combined in an ad. *(Chapter 9)*

creative strategy: A strategy outlining the message that needs to be conveyed to the

audience. It flows from the advertising objectives. *(Chapter 9)*

creative tactics: The means for carrying out the creative strategy. *(Chapter 9)*

credibility: The extent to which the receiver perceives the source to be truthful or believable. *(Chapter 7)*

culture: The sum of learned beliefs, values, and custom that regulate the behavior of members of a particular society. *(Chapter 4)*

customs: Overt modes of behavior that constitute culturally approved ways of behaving in specific situations. *(Chapter 4)*

D

database: A system that contains information about customers and prospects that has been collected over a considerable time. *(Chapter 18)*

dealer loader: A premium that is given by a manufacturer to a retailer for buying a certain amount of product. *(Chapter 11)*

defamation: Anything that tends to damage a reputation; often divided into slander, or oral defamation, and libel, or written defamation. *(Chapter 6)*

demand-based pricing: A strategy whereby the company competes by focusing on the needs and wants of consumers. *(Chapter 3)*

depth of inquiry: The extent of the salesperson's effort to learn the details of the buyer's decision process. *(Chapter 15)*

direct-action advertising: Advertising that is intended to produce a quick response. *(Chapter 8)*

direct exporting: Exporting that uses intermediaries located in the foreign markets. *(Chapter 19)*

direct-order marketing: Marketing that uses nonpersonal media to sell a product or service without salespeople's help. *(Chapter 18)*

direct premium: An incentive given free with the purchase at the time of the purchase. *(Chapter 10)*

direct-response advertising: Advertising designed to motivate customers to make some sort of response. *(Chapter 18)*

direct-response selling: Selling that uses non-personal media as well as salespeople to complete a sale. *(Chapter 18)*

display ads: Ads that include illustrations, headlines, white space, and other visual devices in addition to the copy text. *(Chapter 13)*

display allowance: Payment to the retailer by the manufacturer so that the retailer will select the manufacturer's display. *(Chapter 11)*

E

effective frequency: The number of promotional messages needed for a message to have its desired effect on individuals. *(Chapter 14)*

effective reach: The number of prospects who are aware of the message. *(Chapter 14)*

elaboration likelihood model (ELM): A way of understanding why variations in elaboration occur and how they influence communication. *(Chapter 5)*

ELM: See elaboration likelihood model. *(Chapter 5)*

elaborate processing: Also called central processing; information processing that involves active manipulation of information. *(Chapter 5)*

embedding: The process of burying a message, word, or picture within an ad yet leaving it visible to the naked eye. *(Chapter 7)*

emotional appeal: One of two categories into which messages can be divided. *(Chapter 7)*

emotional motive: A motive characterized by feelings that may emerge without careful thought or consideration of social consequences. *(Chapter 5)*

endorsement: Any advertising message that consumers perceive as reflecting the opinions, beliefs, or experiences of an individual, group, or institution; also called testimonial. *(Chapter 6)*

export: To sell a product in another country without making a commitment to local production. *(Chapter 19)*

exposure: The beginning of the information-processing sequence when the consumer is exposed to some source of stimulation. *(Chapter 5)*

external publics: The people with whom an organization communicates but with whom it does not have regular or close ties. *(Chapter 12)*

F

fair use: The term that seeks to define conditions under which material may be reproduced or included in other works. *(Chapter 6)*

FCC: See Federal Communications Commission. *(Chapter 6)*

Federal Communications Commission (FCC): A federal regulatory agency that has jurisdiction over radio and television stations and networks in matters of advertising messages that are deceptive or in poor taste. *(Chapter 6)*

Federal Trade Commission (FTC): An investigative and regulatory federal agency established to monitor and take legal action against unfair business practices. *(Chapter 6)*

feedback: Explicit or implicit response to a message. *(Chapter 7)*

financial relations: A branch of PR that specializes in communicating with the financial community. *(Chapter 12)*

flighting pattern: Heavy scheduling of the message during shorter time periods. *(Chapter 14)*

focal concept: The key idea a promotional message contains. *(Chapter 17)*

focus group: A controlled interview situation in which eight to ten people are brought together to share ideas and answer questions about a concept or product. *(Chapter 2)*

forward buying: Buying more merchandise

than is needed during a deal period. *(Chapter 11)*

frequency: The number of times within a given period that a consumer is exposed to a message. *(Chapter 14)*

FTC: See Federal Trade Commission. *(Chapter 6)*

full-service agency: An advertising agency that includes five functional areas: creative, media, financial, support services, and account management. *(Chapter 8)*

G

general-interest magazines: One way of classifying magazines. *(Chapter 13)*

geodemography: A technique that analyzes a database in terms of geography. *(Chapter 18)*

gross rating point (GRP): The total weight of the media effort, derived by multiplying reach times frequency. *(Chapter 14)*

group: Two or more people who interact to accomplish either individual or mutual goals. *(Chapter 4)*

H

habit: A means of making a decision without the use of additional information or the evaluation of alternative choices. *(Chapter 5)*

hierarchy of effects model: A model that proposes that ads can move consumers closer to buying a product step by step—from being unaware of a product to buying it. *(Chapter 8)*

high-involvement decision: A decision that is important to the consumer. *(Chapter 5)*

household: An individual or a group of people who share a common dwelling. *(Chapter 4)*

I

impact: The intrusiveness of the message. *(Chapter 14)*

incremental sales: Additional sales produced by the sales promotion. *(Chapter 17)*

inertia: A type of brand loyalty that develops when a consumer is not highly involved in the initial decision to buy a product and makes no commitment to the product but simply responds to the positive reinforcement it provides. *(Chapter 5)*

indirect-action advertising: Advertising that stimulates demand over a longer time. *(Chapter 8)*

indirect exporting: Exporting that employs a marketing intermediary in the exporter's country of operation who specializes in selling products in foreign countries. *(Chapter 19)*

industrial products: Products purchased by an organization or an individual that will be modified for or distributed to an ultimate consumer in order to make a profit or meet some other business objective. *(Chapter 3)*

industrial users: Business institutions that buy products or services to use in their own businesses or to make other products. *(Chapter 2)*

initiator: One of the two communicators in the traditional communication model; also called source or encoder. *(Chapter 7)*

infomercial: A thirty- or sixty-second ad; also called an advertorial. *(Chapter 18)*

inkjet imaging: A computer-controlled printing process that allows parts of the message to be changed by the program. *(Chapter 13)*

institutional advertising: Advertising that creates a positive attitude toward the seller. *(Chapter 8)*

instrumental conditioning: A type of behavioral learning in which a response is learned or strengthened because it has been associated with certain consequences. *(Chapter 5)*

intensity: A characteristic of an attitude that depends on the affective component of an attitude; the strength of feeling toward the object of an attitude constitutes the intensity of the attitude. *(Chapter 5)*

interference: Distortion of the communication process. *(Chapter 7)*

internal publics: The people with whom an organization normally communicates in the ordinary routine of work. *(Chapter 12)*

J

joint venture: A strategy for entering a foreign market in which a foreign company invites an outside partner to share stock ownership in the new unit. *(Chapter 19)*

L

licensing: A strategy for entering a foreign market in which a company assigns the right to a patent or a trademark to another company for a fee or royalty. *(Chapter 19)*

lifestyle: An orientation of an individual or a group toward consumption, work, and play. *(Chapter 2)*

lobbying: Activities that aim to influence the policy decisions of government officials. *(Chapter 12)*

logo: Another term for brand mark. *(Chapter 3)*

loss leader: A dramatically low price offered in order to attract customers. *(Chapter 3)*

lottery: An activity that involves a payment or other legal consideration in exchange for a chance to win a prize. *(Chapter 6)*

low-involvement decision: A decision that is not important to the consumer. *(Chapter 5)*

M

mail premium: An incentive that requires the customer to take some action in order to receive the premium through the mail. *(Chapter 10)*

marginal analysis: The theoretical basis for determining the size of the promotion budget. *(Chapter 16)*

market: An aggregate of people who, as individuals or organizations, have needs for products or services and have the ability, willingness, and authority to purchase such products or services. *(Chapter 2)*

market aggregation strategy: A strategy that calls for creating a single product supported by a single marketing program designed to reach as many customers as possible. *(Chapter 2)*

marketing intelligence: Any information, derived from either internal or external sources, that is useful in developing a marketing strategy. *(Chapter 1)*

marketing mix: The set of marketing tools—price, channel of distribution, product, and promotion—that a firm uses to pursue its marketing objectives in the target market. *(Chapter 1)*

marketing objectives: State specific marketing standards to be reached under certain operating procedures by a certain date. *(Chapter 1)*

marketing opportunity: A need or want that is not being adequately satisfied. *(Chapter 1)*

marketing plan: The central instrument for directing and coordinating the marketing effort; part of the strategic plan. *(Chapter 1)*

market saturation: The situation in which the domestic market has reached maturity and stopped growing. *(Chapter 19)*

market segment: A group of consumers who have one or more similar characteristics. *(Chapter 1)*

market segmentation strategy: A strategy that divides the market into several segments, each of which tends to be homogeneous in all significant aspects, and from these segments identifies, evaluates, and selects target markets. *(Chapter 2)*

marketing strategy: The most important part of the marketing plan, which links the strategic plan with specific marketing programs. *(Chapter 1)*

message variables: The specific elements used to communicate an idea and the way these elements are organized. *(Chapter 7)*

milline rate: The cost per line to reach a newspaper circulation of one million. *(Chapter 13)*

model: Also called initiator or encoder. *(Chapter 7)*

monitoring: An ongoing system for keeping track of all major PR activities. *(Chapter 12)*

motive: An inner drive or pressure to take action in order to eliminate tension, to satisfy a need or solve a problem, or to restore a sense of equilibrium. *(Chapter 5)*

multiattribute attitude model: A method used to measure a person's overall attitude toward a brand by determining the consumer's evaluation of individual attributes of the brand, the consumer's idea for those attributes, and the importance the consumer assigns to those attributes. *(Chapter 5)*

N

NAB: See National Association of Broadcasters.

NAD: See National Advertising Division.

NARB: See National Advertising Review Board.

NARC: See National Advertising Review Council.

National Advertising Division (NAD): The investigative staff of the National Advertising Review Council. *(Chapter 6)*

National Advertising Review Board (NARB): A regulatory group whose members represent national advertisers, advertising agencies, and nonindustry fields whose purpose is to monitor false and misleading advertising and resolve issues referred by the National Advertising Division. *(Chapter 6)*

National Advertising Review Council (NARC): A self-regulatory association that maintains high standards of honesty and accuracy in national advertising. *(Chapter 6)*

National Association of Broadcasters (NAB): An organization that has codes of conduct for radio and television that specify products that cannot be advertised and that give guidelines to follow when presenting ads. *(Chapter 6)*

net coverage: The actual number of people exposed to the message. *(Chapter 14)*

nonelaborate processing: Also called peripheral processing; information processing that does not involve active manipulation of information. *(Chapter 5)*

norms: Expectations about what behavior is appropriate. *(Chapter 4)*

nuclear family: Consists of two adults of opposite sex, living in a socially approved sexual relationship with their natural or adopted children. *(Chapter 4)*

O

overlay: A combination of sales promotion tools delivered through the same vehicle. *(Chapter 10)*

P

pace: The speed at which the salesperson moves to close a sale. *(Chapter 15)*

packaging: The container that holds the product. *(Chapter 3)*

perceived value: The calculation the consumer makes in his or her mind whereby the extra value contained in the sales promotion is compared to the risks in accepting the offer. *(Chapter 17)*

perception: Step three in the information-processing sequence in which meaning is assigned to stimuli received through the senses. *(Chapter 5)*

perceptual mapping: A process that creates a "map" of consumers' perceptions of the similarities and differences among products or brands by applying a family of mathematical programs known as clustering and classification techniques. *(Chapter 2)*

peripheral processing: Also called nonelaborate processing; information processing that does not involve active manipulation of information. *(Chapter 5)*

personal selling: Interpersonal communication with one or more perspective purchasers for the sake of making sales. *(Chapter 1)*

point-of-purchase (POP) display: A special display provided free to the retailer by the manufacturer in order to promote a particular brand or group of products. *(Chapter 11)*

position: The image that the product projects in relation to images projected by competitive products and by other products marketed by the company. *(Chapter 2)*

posttesting: Research conducted after the audience has been exposed to the message, medium, or spokesperson. *(Chapter 17)*

power: An element of source attractiveness that depends on the receiver's perception that the source has the ability to administer rewards or punishments. *(Chapter 7)*

premium: A tangible reward received for performing a particular act, usually purchasing a product. *(Chapter 10)*

pretesting: Research conducted before the audience is exposed to the promotion. *(Chapter 17)*

price: The amount the customer pays for a good or a service. *(Chapter 3)*

price bundling: A special price (usually lower) charged when certain products are bundled together. *(Chapter 3)*

price copy: Message content that is devoted principally to the subject of pricing. *(Chapter 3)*

price deal: A special, lower price that saves the customer money on purchase of a product. *(Chapter 10)*

price discount: A price reduction; also called cents-off deal. *(Chapter 10)*

price fixing: The illegal act of setting prices in concert with competitors. *(Chapter 6)*

product: A bundle of attributes, either tangible or intangible, offered by the firm. *(Chapter 3)*

product advertising: Advertising that informs or stimulates the market. *(Chapter 8)*

product differentiation: A series of strategic decisions that results in a state or marketplace position in which the product offering is perceived by the consumer to differ from the competition on any physical or nonphysical product characteristic. *(Chapter 2)*

product life cycle: A predictable pattern of development. *(Chapter 3)*

product positioning: A process that attempts to identify the salient perceptions, attitudes, and product-use habits of the consumer, assess how the marketer's product is perceived relative to these factors, and then place the product in its most advantageous light. *(Chapter 2)*

promotion: The marketing function concerned with persuasively communicating to target audiences the components of the marketing program in order to facilitate exchange between the marketer and the consumer and to help satisfy the objectives of both. *(Chapter 1)*

promotional mix: The utilization of the four tools of promotion—advertising, personal selling, public relations, and sales promotion—in a manner that helps achieve promotional objectives. *(Chapter 1)*

promotional strategy: A plan that details how the organization expects to achieve its promotional objectives. *(Chapter 1)*

psychographics: Relating psychological variables to buyer behavior. *(Chapter 2)*

public affairs officer: The person responsible for PR directed at the government. *(Chapter 12)*

publicists: Writers who depend on experience, guile, and a great deal of talent to convince editors and reporters to carry their stories. *(Chapter 12)*

publicity: The placing of information in a news medium at no billed cost to the sponsor. *(Chapter 12)*

public relations (PR): The use of information

and the communication of that information through a variety of media to influence public opinion. *(Chapter 12)*

public relations advertising: Also called institutional or corporate advertising. *(Chapter 12)*

publics: The various constituencies targeted to receive public relations messages. *(Chapter 12)*

puffery: Advertising or other sales representations which praise the item to be sold with subjective opinions, superlatives, or exaggerations, vaguely and generally, stating no specific facts. *(Chapter 6)*

pull strategy: A strategy that directs marketing efforts at the ultimate consumer and emphasizes large advertising expenditures. *(Chapter 3)*

pulsing pattern: A combination of continuous and flighting patterns, with the continuous pattern emphasized during the best sales months. *(Chapter 14)*

push money: An extra payment given to salespeople for a specified meeting. *(Chapter 11)*

push strategy: A strategy that directs marketing efforts at resellers and thus depends greatly on their personal selling abilities. *(Chapter 3)*

R

rational appeal: One of two categories into which messages can be divided. *(Chapter 7)*

rational motive: A motive supported by a systematic reasoning process that people perceive as being acceptable to their peers. *(Chapter 5)*

reach: The number of people or households exposed to a particular medium vehicle or schedule at least once during a specified time period. *(Chapter 14)*

rebate: Also called refund. *(Chapter 10)*

receiver: One of the two communicators in the traditional communication. *(Chapter 7)*

reference group: Any person or group that serves as a point of comparison (or reference) for an individual in the formation of general or specific values, attitudes, or behavior. *(Chapter 4)*

refund: A certain amount of money given back by the marketer when a customer buys a product alone or in combination with other products; also called rebate. *(Chapter 10)*

regional networks: A region of the country that is selected for a promotion and for which promoters pay the network a proportional rate plus a nominal fee. *(Chapter 13)*

reliability: The fact that the same results are repeated time after time. *(Chapter 17)*

resellers: Wholesalers and retailers collectively. *(Chapter 3)*

responder/nonresponder survey: A survey that attempts to identify differences between people who did and did not respond to a direct-marketing program. *(Chapter 18)*

retention: Step four in the information-processing sequence in which information is stored for later reference. *(Chapter 5)*

retrieval: Combined with application, the final stage in information processing; the process by which information is recovered from the memory storehouse. *(Chapter 5)*

Robinson-Patman Act: Federal legislation that amended the Clayton Act and restricted discriminatory practices between sellers and large-scale buyers. *(Chapter 6)*

role: A prescribed way of behaving based on the situation and a person's position in the situation. *(Chapter 4)*

S

sales incentive: Also called spiffs or PM. *(Chapter 11)*

sales presentation: The major part of the sales process that explains in full detail how the product meets customer requirements. *(Chapter 15)*

sales promotion: Marketing activities that add

to the basic value of the product or service for a limited time and directly stimulate consumer purchasing, stimulate the channel members to carry the product and/or promote the product or service, or stimulate the effort of the sales force. *(Chapter 1)*

sales quota: A fair share of the overall sales target allocated to a salesperson, territory, or some other segment of the operation. *(Chapter 15)*

sales target: The desired level of sales for a given product or product line in a specified period of time. *(Chapter 15)*

scope: The variety of benefits, features, and sales terms discussed. *(Chapter 15)*

secondary values: Less permanent values than core values; can be influenced by promotion; serve as the basis for subcultures. *(Chapter 4)*

selective binding: A computerized process that allows for the creation of hundreds of editions of a magazine in one continuous sequence and personalization of advertising. *(Chapter 13)*

Sherman Antitrust Act: Federal legislation dealing with restraint of trade that makes all such activities, including monopolies, illegal. *(Chapter 6)*

simple decision making: A decision-making process that does not require an information search or alternative evaluation. *(Chapter 5)*

situation analysis: An attempt to identify and appraise all the environmental factors that affect the marketing plan. *(Chapter 1)*

social class: Refers to the position on a social scale based on the criteria such as occupation, education, and income. *(Chapter 4)*

socialization: The process by which people acquire the skills, knowledge, and attitudes necessary to function in society. *(Chapter 4)*

sociocultural environment: A combination of the sociological and cultural variables that influence a person's life. *(Chapter 4)*

source: One of the two communicators in the traditional communication. *(Chapter 7)*

special-interest magazines: One way of classifying magazines. *(Chapter 13)*

spot advertising: Time bought directly from local television stations. *(Chapter 13)*

strategic alliance: A strategy for entering a foreign market in which the participating companies pool their resources on a somewhat equal basis. *(Chapter 19)*

strategic plan: The broadest planning tool, which provides direction for the entire organization. *(Chapter 1)*

sweepstakes: An activity in which a prize may be awarded by chance without any charge or obligation. *(Chapter 6)*

stereotyping: The process of forming and applying overall impressions of categories of people, events, or things. *(Chapter 2)*

T

target market: A selected market segment that can be best served from a competitive point of view. *(Chapter 1)*

television market: A rigidly defined geographic area in which stations generally located in the core of the area attract most of the viewing. *(Chapter 13)*

testimonial: Any advertising message that consumers perceive as reflecting the opinions, beliefs, or experiences of an individual, group, or institution; also called endorsement. *(Chapter 6)*

theory of reasoned action: A theory that the best predictor of behavior is intention to act. *(Chapter 5)*

tie-in: A sales promotion tool that is combined with a product of another noncompeting marketer. *(Chapter 10)*

trade: Wholesalers and retailers who handle or distribute the marketer's product; also called resellers or dealers. *(Chapter 11)*

trade coupons: Coupons offered to the local

retailer as a tie-in to be carried in the retailer's ads; the manufacturer pays for the advertising and gives the retailer an allowance up front. *(Chapter 11)*

trademark: A brand name or brand mark that is legally protected through registration with the Patent and Trademark Office of the Department of Commerce. *(Chapter 3)*

trade sales promotion: Sales promotion directed at resellers who distribute products to ultimate consumers. *(Chapter 11)*

trade shows: Regularly scheduled events at which manufacturers display their products and take orders. *(Chapter 11)*

U

up-front market: A buying period when networks sell a large part of their commercial time for the upcoming season. *(Chapter 13)*

V

validity: The fact that the concept is confirmed to be what it claims to be. *(Chapter 17)*

value-added advertising: Advertising that has the capacity to endow a brand with a symbolic meaning that makes it more valuable in the consumer's eyes. *(Chapter 8)*

values: A general statement that guides behavior and influences beliefs and attitudes. *(Chapter 4)*

W

Wheeler-Lea Amendment: Federal legislation that further established the role of the Federal Trade Commission to protect businesses and consumers from unfair, deceptive, or anticompetitive business activities; enabled the FTC to provide true consumer protection. *(Chapter 6)*

word of mouth: Messages that are exchanged between individuals and are not under the control of the sponsor. *(Chapter 7)*

Name Index

Subject Index